Walk in the Light Series

The Final Shofar

Understanding the Signs and the Mysteries of the End of the Age

Todd D. Bennett

Shema Yisrael Publications

The Final Shofar
Understanding the Signs and the Mysteries of the End of the
Age

First printing 2014

ISBN 10: 0985000422
ISBN 13: 9780985000424
Library of Congress Number: 2013922301

Printed in the United States of America.

Please visit our website for other titles:
www.shemayisrael.net

For information write:
Shema Yisrael Publications
123 Court Street
Herkimer, New York 13350

For information regarding publicity for author interviews call
(866) 866-2211

The Final Shofar

Understanding the Signs and the Mysteries of the End of the Age

"Blow the shofar in Zion,
and sound an alarm in My set apart mountain!
Let all the inhabitants of the land tremble;
For the day of YHWH is coming,
for it is at hand."
Joel 2:1

Table of Contents

Acknowledgments

I must first and foremost acknowledge my Creator, Redeemer and Savior who opened my eyes and showed me the Light. He never gave up on me even when, at times, it seemed that I gave up on Him. He is ever patient and truly awesome. His blessings, mercies and love endure forever and my gratitude and thanksgiving cannot be fully expressed in words.

Were it not for the patience, prayers, love and support of my beautiful wife Janet, and my extraordinary children Morgan and Shemuel, I would never have been able to accomplish this work. They gave me the freedom to pursue the vision and dreams that my Heavenly Father placed within me, and for that I am so very grateful. I love them all more than they will ever know.

Loving thanks to my father for his faithfulness along with his helpful comments and editing. He tirelessly watched and held things together at the office while I was away traveling, researching, speaking and writing.

Introduction

This book is the final book in a larger body of educational work called the *Walk in the Light* series. It is the culmination of the series, and it is the product of my lifetime search for truth. That quest never ends, but it is time for this series to come to an end. It is my hope that this book, and the entire series, will help those seeking the truth to focus on and walk the straight path of truth prescribed by the Creator.

Having grown up in a major protestant denomination since I was a small child, I had been steeped in doctrine that often seemed to contradict the very words contained within the Scriptures. I always considered myself to be a Christian although I never took the time to research the origins of Christianity or to understand exactly what the term Christian meant. I simply grew up believing that Christianity was right and every other religion was wrong or deficient.

Now my beliefs were founded on more than simply blind faith. I had experienced a "living God," my life had been transformed by a loving Redeemer and I had been filled with a powerful Spirit. I experienced His guiding Hand and His unmerited favor throughout my life.

I knew that I was on the right track, but I always felt something was lacking. I was certain that there was something more to this religion called Christianity; not in terms of a different God, but what composed this belief system that I subscribed to, and this label that I wore like a

badge.

Throughout my Christian walk I experienced many highs and some lows, but along the way I never felt like I fully understood what my faith was all about. Sure, I knew that "Jesus died on the cross for my sins" and that I needed to believe in my heart and confess with my mouth in order to "be saved." I "asked Jesus into my heart" when I was a child and sincerely believed in what I had done. In fact, I know that that was a very significant moment in my relationship with my Creator. The problem was that the relationship seemed distant to me. It was not as close as I envisioned or desired.

As I grew older, I continued in my faith and my desire for a deeper more intimate relationship with my Creator. Along the way, I found myself progressing through different denominations, each time learning and growing, always adding some pieces to the puzzle, but never seeing the entire picture.

College ministry brought me into contact with the baptism of the Holy Spirit and more charismatic assemblies. While these people seemed to practice a more "complete" faith than those in my previous denominations, many of my original questions remained unanswered and even more questions arose. It seemed that at each new step in my faith I added a new adjective to the already ambiguous label "Christian." I went from being a mere Christian to a Full Gospel, New Testament, Charismatic, Spirit Filled, Born Again Christian. Despite these added elements, I could never get away from the lingering uneasiness that something was still missing.

For instance, when I read Matthew 7:21-23 I always felt uneasy. In that Scripture most English Bibles indicate that Jesus says: *"Not everyone who says to Me, Lord, Lord, will*

enter the kingdom of heaven, but he who does the will of My Father Who is in heaven. Many will say to Me on that day, Lord, Lord, have we not prophesied in Your name and driven out demons in Your name and done many mighty works in Your name? And then I will say to them openly (publicly), I never knew you; depart from Me, you who act wickedly [disregarding My commands]." The Amplified Bible.

This passage of Scripture always bothered me because it sounded an awful lot like the modern day Christian Church, in particular, the charismatic churches which I had been attending where the gifts of the Spirit were operating. According to the Scripture passage it was not the people who *believed* in the spiritual manifestations that were being rejected, it was those who were *actually doing* them. I would think that this would give every Christian pause for concern.

First of all "in that day" there are *many* people who will be calling Him "Lord." They will also be performing incredible spiritual acts in His Name. Ultimately though, the Messiah will openly and publicly tell them to depart from Him. He will tell them that He never "knew" them. He specifically defines them by their actions, which is the reason for their rejection; they acted wickedly or lawlessly. In short, they disobeyed His commandments. Also, it seems very possible that while they thought they were doing these things in His Name, they were not, because they may have never known His Name. In essence, they did not know Him and He did not know them.

I think that many Christians are haunted by this Scripture, because they do not understand who it applies to or what it means. If they are truly honest they must admit that there is no other group on the face of the planet that it can refer to except for the "Christian Church." This series

provides the answer to that question and should provide resolution for any who have suffered anxiety over this verse.

Ultimately, my search for answers brought me right back to the starting point of my faith. I was left with the question: "What is the origin and substance of this religion called Christianity?" I was forced to examine the very foundations of my faith, and to examine many of the beliefs that I had inherited. I was determined to test them against the truth of the Scriptures.

What I found out was nothing short of earth shattering. I experienced a parapettio, which is a moment in Greek tragedies where the hero realizes that everything he knew was wrong. I discovered that many of the foundations of my faith were not rocks of truth, but rather the sands of lies, deception, corruption and paganism.

I saw the Scripture in Jeremiah fulfilled right before my eyes. In many translations, this passage reads: "*O LORD, my strength and my fortress, My refuge in the day of affliction, The Gentiles shall come to You from the ends of the earth and say, 'Surely our fathers have inherited lies, worthlessness and unprofitable things. Will a man make gods for himself, which are not gods?'*" Jeremiah 16:19-20 NKJV

I realized that I had inherited lies and false doctrines from the fathers of my faith. I found that the faith I had been steeped in had made gods which were not gods. I then saw very clearly how many could say "Lord, Lord" and not really know the Messiah. I discovered that these lies were not just minor discrepancies, but critical errors that could possibly have the effect of keeping me out of the New Jerusalem if I continued to practice them. (Revelation 21:27; 22:15).

While part of the problem stemmed from false

doctrines that have crept into the Christian religion, it also had to do with anti-Semitism imbedded throughout the centuries and even translation errors in the very Scriptures that I was basing may beliefs upon.

A good example could be found in the verse following the one quoted above from the Prophet Jeremiah (Yirmeyahu) where most translations provide: "*Therefore behold, I will this once cause them to know, I will cause them to know My hand and My might; and they shall know that My Name is the LORD.*" Yirmeyahu 16:21 NKJV.

Could our Heavenly Father really be telling us that His Name is "The LORD"? This is a title, not a name and by the way, won't many people be crying out "Lord, Lord" and be told that He never knew them? It is obvious that you should know someone's name in order to have a relationship with them. How could you possibly say that you know someone if you do not even know their name?

I realized that this was one of the missing pieces in my relationship with my Creator. This led me to ask the question: "What is the Name of our Heavenly Father?" The answer to this seeming mystery lies just beneath the surface of the translated text. In fact, if most people took the time to read the translators notes in the front of their "Bible" they would easily discover the problem.

You see the Name of our Creator is found in the Hebrew Scriptures almost 7,000 times. Long ago a false doctrine was perpetrated regarding speaking the Name. It was determined that the Name either could not, or should not, be pronounced and therefore it was replaced.

Thus, over the centuries the Name of the Creator which was given to us so that we could know Him and be, not only His children, but also His friends, was suppressed and altered. You will now find people using descriptions,

titles and variations to replace the Name. Some examples are: God, Lord, Adonai, Jehovah and Ha Shem ("The Name"). These titles, particularly The LORD, are inserted in place of the actual Name that was provided in the Hebrew text. What a tragedy and what a mistake!

One of the Ten Commandments, also known as the Ten Words, specifically instructs us not to take the Name of the Creator "in vain" and "*He will not hold him guiltless who takes His Name in vain.*" (Exodus 20:7). Most Christians have been taught that this simply warns of using the Name lightly or in the context of swearing or in some other disrespectful manner. This certainly is one aspect of the commandment, but if we look further into the Hebrew word for vain - שׁוא (pronounced shaw) we find that it has a deeper meaning in the sense of "desolating, uselessness or naught."

Therefore, we have been warned not only to avoid using the Name lightly or disrespectfully, but also not to bring it to naught, which is exactly what has been done over the centuries. The Name of our Creator, which we have the privilege of calling on and praising, has been suppressed to the point where most people do not even know the Name, let alone use it.

This sounds like a conspiracy of cosmic proportions, and it is. Anyone who believes the Scriptures must understand that there is a battle between good and evil. There is an enemy, ha shatan (the adversary), who understands very well the battle that has been raging since the beginning. He will do anything to distract or destroy those searching for the truth, and he is very good at what he does. As you read this book I hope that you will see the evidence of this battle as satan works to complete his kingdom on earth.

My hope is that every reader has an eye opening experience and is forever changed. I sincerely believe that the truths contained in this book, and the *Walk in the Light* series, are essential to avoid the great deception that is being perpetrated upon those who profess to believe in, and follow the Holy One of Yisrael.

This book, and the entire series, is intended to be read by anyone who is searching for the truth. Depending upon your particular religion, customs and traditions, you may find some of the information offensive, difficult to believe or contrary to the doctrines and teachings that you have read or heard throughout your life. This is to be expected, and is perfectly understandable. Please realize that none of the information is meant to disparage anyone or any faith, but merely to reveal truth.

The information contained in this book had better stir up some things or else there would be no reason to write it in the first place. The ultimate question is whether the contents align with the Scriptures and the will of the Creator. My goal is to strip away the layers of tradition that many of us have inherited, and get to the core of the faith that is described in the Scriptures.

This book should challenge your thinking and your beliefs and hopefully aid you on your search for truth. May you be blessed in your journey of faith as you endeavor to Walk in the Light.

I

In the Beginning

How this grand physical and spiritual universe came into existence is a much pondered and debated subject. Most of the realm of science is trying desperately to explain away a Creator, turning rather to speculations involving pure chance or even extraterrestrials. Science cannot cope with spiritual matters, and therefore it attempts to segregate the physical and the spiritual, opting for purely physical explanations for the beginning of our present existence.

Beginnings are important because they provide a context for everything that follows. If we are simply the product of random and chance mutations over vast periods of time, then our existence has no particular purpose other than to do what ever suits us until we die. If we have been planted here by some alien race then that presumes that there is life beyond the planet earth, although that has never been proven.

Further, the idea of another race similar to our own evolving on a planet like earth, then surreptitiously visiting our planet and later abandoning us is beyond the realm of possibility.[1] Nevertheless, many in science, and even religion, are leaning toward this view as purely evolutionary explanations fade into oblivion. Astrobiology now seeks to find the answer on another planet either in the Milky Way or some other distant galaxy.

Incredibly, while much of the world searches for an

answer excluding intelligent design by a Creator, it is really the most plausible explanation for existence, but only if we honestly assess the facts. The problem is that so many have been programmed to believe that science is an unbiased quest for truth, that they have been swayed by the wild imaginations and false teachings of what has actually become anti-god religion.

It is important to understand that truth does not require our belief, acceptance or agreement to exist. Truth is not subject to the parameters and instruments designed by modern science. Truth derives from the very Creator of the universe, yet science seems to believe if truth can be redefined, then so can the Creator.

Now to be fair, not all scientists are "anti-god" and certainly not all of them are intentionally deceiving mankind. There can be no doubt that modern science, as an institution, has become squarely opposed to God. Incredibly, the more sophisticated that science and scientific equipment become, the complexity and design of life becomes all the more apparent. This has resounding implications because if man was, in fact, created in the image of a Creator and specifically placed in a universe created for him, then everything has a purpose.

Scientific advances actually point to complexity and design, rather than randomness and chance. The 4 bit digital 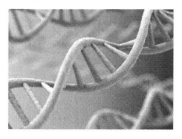 coding found in DNA is currently beyond mankind's comprehension. As we learn more about our design it appears that there are unique harmonics emitting from the sun, the planets. The earth actual resonates at 7.83 MHz, known as the Schumann resonance. Even out DNA emits a signature resonance. Experiments have revealed that "living chromosomes function just like solitonic/holographic computers using the endogenous DNA laser radiation." So DNA reacts to language, modulated laser rays and even to radio waves. DNA can actually be damaged, repaired and transformed or recoded through sound.[2]

We can therefore see the connection between all of creation and sound. We now know that the universe is finite, and this present existence is essentially a digital simulation. There was clearly a Grand Designer Who wrote this "software code" and transmitted it into the DNA. That mysterious code operates in man, and controls the physical universe that mankind inhabits.

Anyone familiar with computer programming understands that when you write a program it requires logic, design and purpose. You cannot create a functional program by interspersing random code, and when you mutate the code of a functioning program it crashes. It must be written and then debugged in order to fulfill its purpose.

Random and chance mutations do not make the design better, they turn it into junk code. The program becomes non-functional. This simple example reveals how woefully deficient evolution is. It relies upon countless mutations to supposedly lead to order and functionality. Evolution, from its inception, was grounded in ignorance and flawed data, incorrectly believing that cells are simple, rather than the mind boggling complex systems that they really are.[3]

It presently takes more faith to believe that this world and all we know was a chance event than it does to believe in a Creator. Therefore, those scientists opposed to a Creator are required to exercise increasingly more "blind faith" as they ignore the evidence clearly before them.

What many fail to realize is that evolutionary theories are merely a means to end. If you can sell evolution to society, or should I say "indoctrinate" society through public

education and a mandatory curriculum, you can essentially discard the Creator. Once you take God out of the picture, then you have the ability to make yourself a god.

Of course, this is the goal of eugenics, and Charles Darwin's teaching on the Origin of Species promoted such thinking. In fact, his relative, Francis Galton, is considered by some to be the father of eugenics. Eugenics has been a justification for killing millions throughout history. Of course, to a believer in evolution and eugenics this is perfectly acceptable, and even natural, since the notion of natural selection dictates the survival of the fittest.

This thinking then opens the door to all sorts of enhancements, from mechanical implants to genetic modifications as we currently see in transhumanism. Transhumanism covers a broad spectrum involves the crossing of species barriers and the mixing of different species to create new beings. As we will soon discover, genetic manipulation is nothing new, and it ultimately stems from defiance against the Creator. We currently see mankind striving to become like gods, and the sciences have become the primary avenue to accomplish this goal. In fact, science has essentially become juxtaposed against the Creator. As people express faith in science they often lose their faith in the Creator.

So how does all of this relate to the title of the book you might be asking. Quite simply, the Scriptures[4] provide a very different story than science has been developing. Those texts describe an event when the Creator spoke our present physical reality into existence. All of Creation is the manifestation of His spoken Word into the physical realm, and the Messiah is the manifestation of the Creator within Creation.

It was the "sound" or "utterance" of the Creator that initiated our beginning, not some unexplained "big bang." It was the emitted sound, powered by the Creator, that brought order to chaos. This creation event crossed dimensions and established time as we know it. You would think that science would love the Scriptures, but because it has become a "godless" religion, it ignores and rejects the Scriptural account of Creation.

Thankfully, we do not need science as the Scriptures provide us with ample information about the beginning. We start our investigation on "the beginning" with the book commonly referred to as Genesis. That text is actually called "beresheet" in Hebrew, which literally means "in beginning." It is often helpful to examine the Hebrew origins of the texts that describe creation since that was the original language in which they were written, and it is the language spoken by the Creator.[5]

Now many are familiar with the Modern Hebrew Language brought out of Babylon by the House of Judah after their 70 year exile, but this is not the language we will be referring to.[6] Rather, we will be examining the Ancient Hebrew language that consists of pictographs, each of which tell a visual story. When combined we are able to gain incredible insight and depth into the meanings of words. A comparison chart of the Ancient and Modern Hebrew fonts can be found in Appendix A.

Now we will begin to examine those ancient texts and see what they tell us about our beginnings. In the English account of Creation we read: "*¹ In the beginning God created the heavens and the earth. ² The earth was without form, and void; and darkness was on the face of the deep. And the Spirit of God was hovering over the face of the waters.*" Beresheet 1:1-2.

There are many things that are important to point out that can only be seen in the Hebrew – too many for this discussion. So profound are the messages imbedded within the first word and sentence that volumes could be written. As we examine the Hebrew we will reveal some of those items and we will also be correcting some translation errors.

For one, the Hebrew does not describe "God" as the Creator, but rather Elohim. Elohim (𐤉𐤆𐤄𐤋𐤀) is actually the plural form of "El" (𐤋𐤀). Hebrew reads from right to left so the first character is the "aleph" (𐤀) which is the first in the Hebrew "alephbet" (alphabet). It is followed by the "lamed" (𐤋), which represents a shepherd's staff.

The original Hebrew Scriptures never refer to the Creator as "God." "God" is a word of Teutonic origin which refers to a pagan deity.[7] The title used in the Hebrew text to describe the Creator is Elohim. It is the plural form of El, which means "Mighty One" or "Power." Therefore it was Elohim Who was present during Creation, and therefore Elohim Who can provide a witness to Creation.[8] That is how we were given this account that was ultimately transcribed by Moses.

So in the beginning Elohim created and He created through the "alephbet." The Aleph represents Elohim – the first – the strength. The aleph (𐤀) is the pictograph of an ox head and means: "strength." Of course the emphasis of this pictograph and the symbol of that strength is the two horns.

The Hebrew word for horn is "qeren" (𐤍𐤓𐤒) and the first time that we read the word "qeren" in the Scriptures is in the Book of Joshua, specifically Joshua 6:5. This is a very mysterious book in many ways, including this first mention of the "horn." A literal translation describes the "Jubilee Horn."

Anyone familiar with the Scriptures knows that the "horn" blown at the Jubilee is the "shofar." The word "shofar" is commonly translated as a "ram's horn," but a shofar would not be exclusively

restricted to a ram.

With this understanding I hope that the reader can begin to understand the significance of the title of this book. The "shofar" is a horn – a horn that is used for sound. We can see that the horn will play an important part in creation, and the way that Elohim communicates with His people. Before anything could be physically seen in Creation, there were the two horns, essentially emitting sound, which created. Just as there was a beginning shofar there will be a final shofar.

As we proceed throughout this discussion we will see the shofar mentioned throughout the Scriptures, although most people unfamiliar with the Hebrew language have never heard of this word. In fact, despite the fact that the shofar is mentioned throughout the Scriptures, if you exclusively read an English translation, it is likely that you will never see this word.

Instead, you will likely read the word "trumpet." This is not an accurate translation since a trumpet is not a shofar. There are very obvious and important distinctions between these two sound emitting devices. Most obvious is the fact that a trumpet is a metallic instrument crafted by men, while a shofar is an animal horn created by Elohim.

While the trumpet may be used as a musical instrument, the shofar is used to announce, to assemble and to warn. They are different and distinct. This is the problem with translations and as we continue our examination of Scriptures these translation issues will be a constant concern.

While the "aleph" (𐤀) is the first letter in the Hebrew language, the "bet" (𐤁) is the second letter. Interestingly, the first word that we read in the Hebrew text is "beresheet." It is viewed as 𐤕𐤉𐤔𐤀𐤓𐤁 in the ancient Hebrew. Again, it is important to recognize that Hebrew reads from right to left, which is the opposite of English.

So in the Hebrew we see this first word beginning with the second letter in the "alephbet" – bet (𐤁). As a result, the first letter aleph (𐤀), representing Elohim stands outside creation. The aleph (𐤀) was before the beginning, outside of this cycle which we will later see involves created time.

Elohim actually speaks all of creation, including time, into existence, and Elohim is actually building a house. We know this because the letter bet (𐤁) actually means "house." Since it is the first letter in the Scriptures we can discern that they contain a message concerning a house. In most Hebrew scrolls the letter bet (𐤁) is enlarged, as if to point special attention to it. In fact, in the text, the "bet" (𐤁) is translated as "in." The rest of the word is "resheet" (𐤕𐤉𐤔𐤀𐤓) which actually means: "beginning." So being "in" the "house" is the primary emphasis of the text. This reveals the very purpose of creation.

When exactly was this "beginning" is a question many grapple with. While those from a western perspective generally perceive this as some point on a line in the distant past, it really means the beginning of a cycle. It is important to understand that the Hebrew language and thought are cyclical. Hebrew was, after all, the language of the Creator and it is easy to see the cyclical nature of all Creation. It is therefore the ideal language to know and understand the Creator and Creation.[9]

So Elohim is building a house within the construct of cyclical time. Through the cycles of time this work will be accomplished. It will also be accomplished through a covenant as we can see from the word "beresheet" (𐤕𐤉𐤔𐤀𐤓𐤁), which concludes with the letter "taw" (𐤕). Taw (𐤕) actually represents a "mark" – the mark of a covenant.

We can see this point very clearly when we closely

examine the word "beresheet" (X𝗓W𝗄ᐪ𝟓). The first two letters, "bet" (𝟓) and "resh" (ᐪ), when combined with the last two letters, "yud" (𝗓) and "taw" (X), form the word "brit (X𝗓ᐪ𝟓). The word "brit" (X𝗓ᐪ𝟓) actually means: "covenant."

At the center of this "brit" (X𝗓ᐪ𝟓), this covenant, we see "esh" (W𝗄) which means: "fire." Just as we saw the focus on the house, we know that it is the house for a son, which is "bar" (𝟓ᐪ). The son who will create – "bara" (𝟓ᐪ𝗄). All of these concepts give us great insight into the meaning and purpose of creation from the beginning.

This simple word study exercise is intended to reveal the amazing depth of the Hebrew language. If you only read the Scriptures in the English language, or any other translated language for that matter, you will be missing much of the message. This was by no means an exhaustive examination of the one word – "beresheet." In fact, we will continue to examine this word as we continue this discussion.

As we can see, with just a little analysis, this first word, consisting of six letters, provides an incredible amount of information only seen in the Hebrew. When we recognize that the "aleph" (𝗄) stands first before the "bet" (𝟓), outside of this cycle of time we are left with the number 7. Seven, as we shall see, is an incredibly important number, especially when examining time.

In the context of the beginning it starts with the "aleph" (𝗄) outside of time and ends with the taw (X) within time – the Aleph Taw (X𝗄). The "taw" (X) is the end of the beginning (beresheet). It is also the last letter in the Hebrew alephbet. As we continue this discussion we will see a great mystery revealed through the Aleph Taw (X𝗄).

The importance of the number seven can be seen if we look at the first seven words in the Hebrew text where we are provided with more incredible information. The first seven

words in the Hebrew text actually set forth the pattern of time. The seven days in a week represent seven millennium.

The first sentence contains seven Hebrew words, six of which are commonly translated into English as: "*In the beginning God created the heavens and the earth.*" In Modern Hebrew it appears as follows: "אֱלֹהִים אֵת הַשָּׁמַיִם וְאֵת הָאָרֶץ בְּרֵאשִׁית בָּרָא". Notice all of the dots, dashes and other markings above and below each Hebrew character. These are known as vowel points, called "neqqudot," in Hebrew. They were added by the Masorites to assist people in pronouncing the language. These markings are man-made additions, and are not found in original Hebrew texts.

In fact, it is important to understand that the so-called "Modern Hebrew" language is not the same character set as the original Hebrew language. Modern Hebrew was believed to have been brought back from Babylon after the exile of the House of Judah (Yahudah).[10] That is why they are often referred to as Chaldean flame letters. It was not the language written by the very ancient patriarchs.

Therefore, throughout our investigation for truth, we will be examining the ancient script. This was the original language spoken and written by mankind. It actually tells a story through pictographs.[11]

If we look at the first five English words quoted above, we see only three Hebrew words – "Beresheet bara Elohim." Now if this were written in Ancient Hebrew it would read from right to left as follows:[12]

ᑯᘔᗡᄼᐻ ᗋᐺᗱ ᙭ᘔᗯᙦᗋᗱ

There are many mysteries contained within the Hebrew script that cannot be readily discerned from simply reading a translation. We already examined the first word,

but let us examine it a bit more as it appears with the enlarged "bet" (𝟻).

X ꜙ w ⟨ ꜙ 𝟻

Again, the first Hebrew word in the Scriptures, translated as "in the beginning," is "beresheet." As seen above, it begins with the letter "bet" (𝟻) which means: "house." The character actually represents the floor plan for a tent or a house. This particular bet (𝟻) is quite unique, because it is the second letter in the Hebrew alphabet, and the first letter in the Scriptures. Many question why the Scriptures did not begin with the aleph (𝘬), which is the first letter in the Hebrew alphabet. This is a mystery only understood in the timing of the creation of the spiritual universe before the physical universe.[13]

Here we see that the "aleph" (𝘬) actually first appears as the third letter in the Hebrew text and completes the word "bara" (𝘬 ꜙ 𝟻) contained within beresheet (X ꜙ w ⟨ ꜙ 𝟻). "Bara" means: "create" and it was not only the first three letters in the Hebrew text, but it is also the second word in the Scriptures. So we see "create" two times in the first two words of the Hebrew text indicating that there were two creations, the creation of a spiritual universe followed by the physical universe.

After the two creations we see the third word, which begins with the aleph (𝘬). This first primary usage reveals the significance of the letter throughout the text, and that third word is Elohim (𝟅 ꜙ 𝘬 ⟨ 𝘬). Elohim literally means: "Mighty Ones" or "Powers." So the Aleph (𝘬) represents the "Powers" which interestingly is plural and signifies the Elohim transcending both the spiritual and physical existence.

So the "aleph" (𐤀) is hidden "in the beginning" as was discussed. It is essentially outside of time. Instead, the first letter in the text is the "bet" (𐤁). The first "bet" (𐤁) is also unique because it is larger than the other letters. While some might think that this is simply a decorative touch, or illuminated letter, added by a scribe, they would be missing a tremendous truth. You see, throughout the Hebrew text there are instances of these "jots and tittles" which are intended to emphasize a point or send a message.[14]

From the beginning of the Scriptures we can see that there is an emphasis on "the house." As it turns out, all of creation is intended as a House, and through the process of time, Elohim is building a "family" to fill that House. Indeed, from this "first" word we can discern many things. For instance, if we remove the House, the bet (𐤁), we are left with "resheet" (𐤀𐤔𐤉𐤓). Resheet means: "first – choicest." It is sometimes translated as "firstfruits." So then the House is for the firstfruits of Elohim.

We also see the word "brit" (𐤁𐤓𐤉𐤕) surrounding the word "esh" (𐤀𐤔). Brit means: "cutting or covenant" and esh means: fire. So we should be looking for a covenant involving fire as a means of gathering the Firstfruits into the House. We also see the "aleph" (𐤀) and the "taw" (𐤕) surrounding the mysterious word "shi" (𐤔𐤉), which means: "gift or present."[15] So we see the gift or offering couched within the Aleph Taw (𐤕𐤀), a subject of great importance that will be examined throughout this book.

So there are important messages built into the language, although this is only one way of studying the Scriptures. Another is through the study of the numerical values of the letters and words. This form of examination is commonly called Gematria. It is important to understand that each Hebrew character has a numerical value. There is no separate set of numbers in the Hebrew language, so every word has multiple dimensions of meaning as well as a numerical value. The values for each character can be seen in the Hebrew Language Study Chart in the Appendix.[16]

Throughout this text we will, at times, examine the numerical values of the words which can expand our understanding, and reinforce certain ideas. For instance, the numerical value of "beresheet" is 913. The word for house is "beit" (X Z Y), and it has a numerical value of 412. The word for head is "rosh" (W ⟨ ⟨), and it has a numerical value of 501. When combined, their values equal 913 – the same as beresheet.[17] So we can see that the beginning is all about the house.

Now each of these words, "beit" (X Z Y) and "rosh" (W ⟨ ⟨), have Hebrew characters associated with them. As we already discussed, the Hebrew character "bet" (Y), means "house." The Hebrew character "resh" (⟨) means: "head." When we combine bet (Y) and resh (⟨) we have "bar" (⟨ Y). The Hebrew word "bar" (⟨ Y) is not only the first two letters of "beresheet," but also the word for "son."[18] The possibilities and avenues of discovery are endless, and they reveal the beauty and spirituality of the Language of the Creator. Indeed, it is the very language of Creation.

Having made the point that there are great mysteries and messages found in the ancient language, let us return to the matter of time. The remainder of the first sentence has profound information about how this house will be filled. As stated previously, it even provides a framework for time. Here is the entire sentence.

ᴚ⟨⟨ᴚ X⟨Y ⁴ᴢ⁴Wᴚ X⟨ ⁴ᴢᏝⱢ⟨ ⟨⟨ᴣ XᴢWⱢ⟨ᴣ
7   6   5   4   3   2   1 ←

Now remember that Hebrew reads from right to left. That is why you see the first word Beresheet, all the way to

the right. Phonetically the sentence reads as follows:

Beresheet bara Elohim et ha'shamayim w'et ha'eretz

→ 1   2   3   4   5   6   7

If you read it out loud, you just spoke Hebrew. There are seven words, although only six are translated into English. In a basic English translation you will read "In beginning Elohim created the heavens and the earth." There is something critical that never gets translated out of the Hebrew, and it is essential to understanding how the Covenant House would be built.

Couched within this framework for time itself we see another great mystery – the Aleph Taw (X𐤊), also called the "et" because that is how it is pronounced. This verse actually contains two instances of the mysterious Aleph Taw (X𐤊).[19]

While the Aleph Taw (X𐤊) is spoken in Hebrew, pronounced "et," it goes unnoticed in the English. There are some who simply place a grammatical function to the "et" while others see it as a mystery to be interpreted from the context of the passages where it is found.[20]

The aleph (𐤊) is the first letter in the Hebrew alephbet. It symbolizes a "bull" or "ox" and means: "strength." The taw (X) is the last letter in the Hebrew alphabet. It represents a "mark" or "covenant." So this "strength of the covenant" is present 2 times in the first seven Hebrew words of the Scriptures.

In the first instance we see the Aleph Taw (X𐤊) stand alone in position 4, untranslated but spoken. In the second instance it is in position 6, attached to a "vav," or rather "waw" (Y), which represents a "peg" or a "nail." Again, in the second instance the Aleph Taw (X𐤊) is untranslated but spoken.

Some interpret this untranslated but spoken Aleph Taw (✗✗) as representing the Messiah, revealed as the Word, sometimes referred to as the Memra.[21] The reason is because the Aleph Taw (✗✗) contains within it all the characters of the Hebrew language. Therefore, it is believed that the Messiah is the manifestation of Elohim within creation, all of which was accomplished through the language – the spoken word.[22]

In fact, we can discern from the Scriptures that the Aleph Taw (✗✗) would visit with Adam in the Garden when he said: "*I heard Your ✗✗-voice in the garden, and I was afraid because I was naked; and I hid myself.*" Beresheet 3:10.

Therefore, we see two instances of the Messiah, one being hidden, and the other attached to a "nail" which literally stands between the heavens – "ha'shamayim" (ים‎שמ‎ה) and the earth – "ha'eretz" (ארץ‎ה). That fits in perfectly with the notion that Creation is all about a House for the first son, the Messiah, Who will be the head of the House filled with the firstfruits of His harvest. This will become clearer as we continue the discussion.

It is commonly believed that this verse begins a pattern of sevens that will be repeated throughout the Scriptures. Some also conclude that they reveal seven millennium as the framework for the ages of time that we currently live within. As we continue to examine the text, we read about how Elohim actually created everything in six days and rested on the seventh. So these seven words reveal the pattern of sevens.

The phrase "in the beginning" is essentially describing the beginning of the physical existence that we know and observe. It also describes the very beginning of time as we know it. It has been proven that time is a physical dimension, and as with other matters in this physical creation, it can be measured.[23] Despite the fact that we can measure time, it

appears that there are still mysteries associated with this fourth dimension that we do not fully understand.

So far, these simple examples from the first seven words of the Scriptures should demonstrate the importance of examining the text in the original language. It is through the characters of this particular language that the Creator chose to express His purpose and plan. While translations into another language are an attempt to transmit this ancient message to more modern cultures and peoples, they will always fall short. A translation will never be able to relate all of the hidden messages and nuances that are contained in the ancient text.

That having been said, let us look a bit further into the beginning, or rather "the first." We have already mentioned the mathematical impossibility of life existing on another planet like earth and that life being transplanted here. Pure evolution is equally implausible.

The notion that this incredible finite universe in which we live out our existence was the result of some random explosive event is beyond absurdity – it is sheer lunacy. The possibility of such an occurrence is beyond statistical possibility and defies reality.[24] As evolutionists and astrobiologists seek out other species on other habitable planets their quest is clearly futile, although it appears to fit a requisite for the end of days.[25]

Those who propound such a notion typically do so to support their disbelief in a Creator and their faith in the various hypotheses of men who desire to disprove the Creator – something that of course is impossible. They propound their religion, or rather anti-religion, with more faith than someone who believes in a Creator. This is so because they utterly fail to explain where the matter and energy came from that were the ingredients of the explosion. They also fail to explain how the space that the event

occurred within came into existence.

There clearly was a creation event, but instead of being chaotic, which could only result in perpetual chaos, we see incredible order coming out of chaos. That order derives, in part, from the unseen and also unexplained force that has been labeled gravity. There have been recent discoveries concerning dark matter, revealing that there is much hidden in this marvelous and complex universe.

The cosmos are actually held together and kept in order by invisible forces. This should be a constant reminder that there is a Creator keeping Creation in check. We see in this order certain predictable and constant "laws" which can actually be distilled down to mathematical equations. Indeed, at the heart of this ordered, albeit sometimes tumultuous universe, is mathematics.[26]

Like software running a universal supercomputer, math, combined with the fuel of the Creator, keeps everything running. There are "laws of physics" which are predictable, known and calculated. Due to the existence of these known constants we can be assured that this Creation was indeed, intelligently designed. Mathematics, as it turns out, is one of the ways that we know there is a Creator. Indeed, many great minds unwittingly communicate with the Creator when they search for truth through formulas and equations.

They are seeking constants and truths within the framework of our physical existence. If they were merely evolutionists, this would, of course, be an exercise in futility since life, to the evolutionist, is a result of chaos, chance and time. To seek for constants in a universe of chaos would be futile. Thus every mathematician must have, at a minimum, a spark of faith to seek truth in numbers. As we shall soon see, mathematics is actually the language of the Creator when we recognize that numbers and letters are really one and the

same.[27]

With that understanding, we can then look directly to the handiwork of the Creator to learn more about Him and His plan.

Let us now explore the creative process further. The second verse of Beresheet reads as follows: "*The earth was without form, and void; and darkness was on the face of the deep. And the Spirit of God was hovering over the face of the waters.*" Beresheet 1:2

This is actually describing the creation, or recreation, of the physical universe although it is quite a mysterious text. I find it helpful to examine the text using a more mechanical translation as follows: "*and the land had existed in confusion and was unfilled and darkness was upon the face of the deep sea and the wind of "Elohiym [Powers]" was much fluttering upon the face of the water*"[28]

An interesting part of this event is the Spirit, which is "ruach" (ᕼᎩᕴ) in the Hebrew. The head is the point of the body were we breath and "ruach" means: "breath." Interestingly, when we look at the word for "spirit" we can see the head that emits the breath which "connects" (Ꭹ) the fence (ᕼ). So we can see how the "ruach" brought order to Creation. The Creator, the unseen Aleph (ᛕ), actually emitted or exhaled all of the matter into existence through the Aleph Bet. He then bound it together through the vav (Ꭹ), and then set a fence around the cosmos, essentially placing it into a container. The universe, after all, is finite.

The first word of the text actually gives some further insight into creation. Again, if we look at the first three letters of the word beresheet, "in beginning," we see "bara" (ᛕᕴᎩ) which means "created." This word literally means: "son (ᕴᎩ) aleph (ᛕ)." So we see the "son of Aleph" creating at the beginning. This may be why the text begins with a bet (Ꭹ), instead of an aleph (ᛕ).

It appears that the mysterious Aleph Taw (**×ᛕ**) is a hint to the Son, the Word or "Memra" of Elohim in the physical creation, being instrumental in the Creation process. Once we understand that Elohim, through Aleph Taw (**×ᛕ**) created the Heavens and Earth, we are then told how everything was created – through speaking the Aleph Taw (**×ᛕ**).

The "ruach" was "hovering" or "fluttering" over the deep. The word in Hebrew is "merachefet" (**×ﬧᛘᛩ⅄**). The root of this word is "rachaf" which is likened to "shaking or vibrating." This gives an indication of how things were created. Up to this point we are not specifically told how the earth and the waters were created. After we are told of the Spirit "vibrating," we then understand that Elohim created through speech.

Speech involves sound, which is actually vibration. "Sound is a mechanical wave that is an oscillation of pressure transmitted through a solid, liquid, or gas, composed of frequencies within the range of hearing."[29]

Therefore, creation involved frequencies and while sound is often thought to be separate from light, it must be understood that the major difference from mankind's perspective of these frequencies is the result of our different and unique organs that help us detect sound and light. We have eyes to detect light and ears to detect sound, but there is evidence to suggest that our brain can actually "see sound."[30]

These frequencies that went forth from the Creator created or set straight the chaos that already existed.[31] From those frequencies emitted by the Creator we exist and we too receive and transmit frequencies. Many fail to recognize this very fundamental form of communication and the power that is contained therein.

Every aspect of Creation involves frequencies, and we all act and react according to the frequencies that surround us. A kind word or a beautiful song can uplift your mood, while an insult or noise can bring you down. These particular frequencies can result in what is known as wave phenomena, the ability of sound to organize and re-pattern matter. They essentially have power to create and power to destroy. That was what was happening when the Spirit was hovering over the waters.

So we can see that there is a power in the spoken word, and thus there is a great degree of importance which attaches to the spoken word. This brings us back to the Hebrew language, specifically the Ancient Hebrew language. No one knows for sure what the earliest script looked like, since we only have archaeological finds that were written by different individuals, there are obviously variations.

If you had ten different individuals write out Beresheet 1:1 in English in their own handwriting, you would very likely have ten different looking sets of characters. While they would all be in English, and while they would all be representing the same letters and words, they would all look a bit different. Likewise, when we look at ancient renderings of the Hebrew language, we have variations.

Thankfully, the different characters of the ancient language have known meanings, which helps us discern their likely rendering. For the purpose of this discussion, the author has developed a character set of the ancient language using examples from archaeology. This character set should aid the reader in their understanding of the language.

Interestingly, there are 22 characters in the Ancient Hebrew language. Each tells a story and has a message. The fact that there are 22 characters is by design, as we shall see. Everything was created by and through the Hebrew alphabet (alephbet), spoken well before anything was written. Since we were not there we must read what happened. The Psalms record: *"By the Word of the LORD the heavens were made, and all the host of them by the breath (ruach) of His mouth.*" Psalms 33:6.

Now we read this text in English, but it was originally spoken and written in Hebrew. Not in Modern Hebrew, but Ancient Hebrew. So this text has various levels of translation, and it is describing how the physical universe was created by The LORD. So far we have seen that Elohim created, and Elohim is a title. In this text we are actually provided the Name of Elohim in Hebrew, but the English translators have hidden the Name by using yet another title – The LORD.

If we look at the Hebrew text we see an actual Name spelled yud (𐤆) hey (𐤀) waw (𐤉) hey (𐤀) – 𐤀𐤉𐤀𐤆. The Name of the Creator is represented by 4 Ancient pictographs.[32] In more ancient levels of antiquity it was represented as 𐤉𐤀𐤉𐤆 and 𐤔𐤉𐤅𐤉. In the Modern Hebrew it would look like this: יהוה. While each character is a pictograph with meaning, for pronunciation purposes, each character is treated as a consonant.

There are no written vowels in the Hebrew language, thus the invention of the neqqudot, which were previously mentioned. The added vowel points would guide people in the vocalization of the text although the ancient texts did not contain any vowel points. Therefore, throughout this book, to aid the reader in pronouncing the Name, we will use the English equivalent of those consonants written from left to right – YHWH.[33]

Here again, we have another simple, yet powerful example, of issues that must be recognized and addressed in our quest for truth concerning Creation and the Creator. It is important to understand that the letters and characters spoken by the breath, or spirit, of YHWH and found in Modern Hebrew texts are not the same as the most Ancient Language. If we desire to truly understand the original

meaning it is best to view the original language.

While we now have a compilation of Hebrew texts known as the Torah, the Prophets and the Writings where we find accounts of the past, it is important to recognize that these texts were not available for thousands of years. The alephbet itself contained the truth of Creation and a message for all of the world. That truth can be seen in the pictographs. Each character represented a picture that cannot necessarily be recognized in the more modern scripts.

Those pictures told a story, as we have already seen. For instance the aleph (𐤀) appeared as an "ox." It had two horns which signified strength and it was the first of all the letters. It is followed by the bet (𐤁), which signifies the "house." When we combine these two letters together we have "ab" (𐤁𐤀), which represents the "strength of the house." The word "ab" (𐤁𐤀) actually means: "father." The third letter is gimel (𐤂) which represents a camel. It means to "lift up" or "transport." The gimel (𐤂) is followed by the dalet (𐤃) which means: "door." So we can see from the first 4 letters that the strength of the house, the father, will raise us up to the door of the house."

The story continues on multiple levels as we trace the alephbet in its order and examine the meanings of, not only the characters, but the relationships of the meanings. There is even deeper meaning found in the numerical values of the characters and the combination of letters. As the Aleph (𐤀) proceeds to the Taw (𐤕), the entire covenant is revealed. Indeed the Taw (𐤕) is a mark which represents a "covenant." So the entire alephbet leads us to a covenant.

The ancient alephbet contains the entire plan of Elohim for His Creation. The blueprint is essentially encrypted within the characters in their specific order seen here from right to left.

X W ⟨ ⨿ ⊡ ⌐ ⊙ ∓ ⅄ ⅄ ⅃ Υ ⟋ ⊗ ⊟ ⊐ Υ ⊣ ◁ ⌐ ⊋ ⋖

As we already saw, the Bet (⅃) was actually the first letter in the written Scriptures and the Bet (⅃) actually represented the "house" of creation. When we examine these 22 letters with the understanding that the Aleph (⋖) preceded and was outside of that created "house" we are left with 21 letters in the created "house."

This explains the patterns of seven that are so interlaced throughout creation as we can see with light and time. In fact, the characters of the alephbet are actually the building blocks of creation when empowered by the Creator.

It is the original representation of the sound frequencies emitted by the Creator. It is actually the physical, visual representation of the sound of creation. So essentially, the pictographs unify the frequencies of sound and light.[34]

When we combine those characters, especially into groupings of three, we are provided with concepts and roots that develop into words. It has been said that "the letters of the Hebrew alphabet are like stones, and each whole word is like a house. Just as a house is built of stones, so is a word built of letters."[35]

This book is written in English, which is a western language. Western languages are very different from eastern languages. These language distinctions (east v. west) are important because they determine the way people communicate, and how people think. Believe it or not, people in the East actually think differently from people in the West. Eastern thought tends to be cyclical, while Western thought is linear.

Western languages tend to be very abstract, while Eastern languages tend to be very concrete. Western languages tend to be static while Eastern languages are active. In fact, an example of how opposite they are is demonstrated by the fact that Eastern languages typically flow from right to left, while Western languages tend to flow from the left to the right.

This is significant and explains why there are often so many differences between Eastern and Western religions. Language actually influences the way we perceive the world that we live in. This is the source of many of the tensions that exist in the world today – the disconnect between Eastern and Western cultures.

As we start to understand our beginnings from a Hebraic perspective we can then better understand the end. The original alephbet actually tells a story through the pictures that they represent. At the very heart of the alephbet, we see the kaph lamed ($\mathcal{C}$ Υ). The kaph represents a "hand" (Υ), and the lamed ($\mathcal{C}$) represents a "shepherd's staff."

So amidst and centered between the aleph ($\mathcal{K}$) and the taw (X) is kaph lamed ($\mathcal{C}$ Υ). We can see then that the Aleph Taw ($\mathsf{X}\mathcal{K}$) is there to lead as a shepherd – the Great Shepherd. That is at the heart of the story, and through this discussion we will be examining that story. It has been told both through language and creation – it has been lived by mankind.

After the creation of the physical universe described in the first five days, mankind was created on day six followed by the seventh day, which was set apart. The set apart seventh day was the only day given a name. It was called the Sabbath, essentially the crescendo of creation.[36]

We are not told of an eighth day, so the assumption is that a seven day cycle continues from that time forward. Indeed, there is every reason to believe the day count that exists today constitutes an unbroken cycle of sevens that began the first week of creation.

During the creation process we see the formation of the physical universe, including time itself. The sun and the moon were actually provided to mark time, and we know that time flowed in cycles. We saw that the bet ($\mathit{5}$) was the first letter in the written Torah, and it was enlarged to draw our attention to it. While the bet ($\mathit{5}$) was the first letter in the written Scriptures, it was not the first letter of the first spoken word.

Indeed, the first word spoken by Elohim is found further on at Beresheet 1:3. In English we read: "Let there be," which is "yehi" (𐤆𐤉𐤆) in Hebrew. It comes from the root "hayah" (𐤄𐤆𐤄) which means: "be or exist." In each case the emphasis is on the "arm" (𐤆) and the "spirit" or "breath" (𐤄). We are shown to "behold" (𐤄) "the arm" (𐤆). This was none other than the Arm of the Creator bringing forth His will in the physical creation. The first creative words spoken involved two Hebrew words consisting of 6 characters - 𐤄𐤉𐤗 𐤆𐤄𐤆.

In English we read: "let there be light" or "exist light." So the first thing that was brought forth into the creation was "light" – "owr" (𐤄𐤉𐤗). The Script reveals "strength" or "first," represented by the aleph (𐤗), connected by the vav (𐤉) to a head (𐤗). So this "light" is preeminent in creation. Remembering that each Hebrew character has a numerical equivalent we can discern that the gematria for the word "light" (𐤄𐤉𐤗) is 207 (𐤗 = 1, 𐤉 = 6, 𐤄 = 200).

Interestingly, the word for "light" has the same numerical value as "adabar" (𐤄𐤅𐤃𐤗) when YHWH was talking about obeying all "the words" that He would speak.[37] It also has the same value as the word "ra'ah" (𐤉𐤗𐤄), which means: "see." In fact, that particular word actually has the same characters as light (𐤄𐤉𐤗). The concept of "seeing," and "light" are therefore very intimately connected.

So this "owr" (𐤄𐤉𐤗) is related to the spoken word of YHWH, and it is something to be seen. It is important to note that this light was not the sun or the stars, as we often think of as sources of light. The heavenly bodies that emit light were not created until the 4th day. So the light of the first day was different from the light of the 4th day.

After all of creation was spoken we read about a special place known as the Garden of Eden more accurately the Garden in Eden. "Eden" (𐤏𐤃𐤍) is often interpreted to mean "paradise" and this Garden was located within Eden. So it was actually a garden located within paradise. Interestingly, when we examine this word in Hebrew it is more revealing. It actually proclaims: "see" (𐤏) "the door" (𐤃) "to life" (𐤍). So in this special place we are to see the door to life. That door leads to the garden.

The word for "garden" is "gan" (𐤂𐤍) which means an "enclosed" or "protected" space. It implies a wall and a gate. So this would have been the place with the door. The gimel (𐤂) represents a "camel" and means to "lift up" or "transport." Once again, the "nun" (𐤍) represents "life." Amazingly, it looks like a sperm cell, which is the method that YHWH chose to plant the life of man.

So there was a special enclosed place in Paradise that was separated from the rest of creation. It was meant as a place to lift up and carry life – the life of mankind. One could say that it was like a womb. In fact, this is where 𐤀𐤕-the man (𐤀𐤕-𐤄𐤀𐤃𐤌) was placed. In the English you cannot see the Aleph Taw (𐤀𐤕), but the Hebrew plainly reveals a mystery with this man.

Out of Eden flowed a river that watered the Garden and from there it parted into 4 different rivers. The fourth river is known as Euphrates, which is actually "Perath" (𐤐𐤓𐤕) in Hebrew. This will become significant as we continue the discussion.

Clearly, we all know that a garden is a place where seeds are planted. Those seeds are cultivated to produce fruit, and ultimately more seed. It is a place where we are able to witness the true beauty and mathematics of the life emanating from YHWH.

The gematria value of Eden is 124. This is the same value as the word "moadi" (𐤓𐤃𐤏𐤉), found in Vayiqra 23:44, which means: "appointed time." Interestingly, in that passage we see 𐤗𐤕-moadi (𐤓𐤃𐤏𐤉-𐤗𐤕). So the Aleph Taw (𐤗𐤕) is connected with the Appointed Times. The Appointed Times refer to specific times when Creator decides to meet with His people at the place that He resides. In other words, He invites us to His House, and we can see from this connection that His House is Paradise. Many of those Appointed Times are announced by the blast of a shofar. (Psalm 81:3). It is there where we bring the fruits of the harvest as a witness and demonstration of His blessings.[38]

The Hebrew word for "garden" is "gan" (𐤍𐤂). The gematria value for "gan" (𐤍𐤂) is 53. This is interesting because there are some very important concepts in the Scriptures that carry the same value. For instance, the word "aben" (𐤍𐤁𐤀), which means: "stone" has the value of 53. The stone is something with much Messianic significance, particularly when we examine an event where Jacob actually "lifts up" a stone and anoints it with oil. That stone was called the et-ha'aben (𐤍𐤁𐤀𐤄-𐤗𐤕). Notice the Aleph Taw (𐤗𐤕) attached to this anointed stone. To anoint something is "moshiach" in Hebrew – the source of the word "messiah."[39]

The "aben" is also very intriguing because it constitutes the unity of two words: father – "ab" (𐤁𐤀) and son – "ben" (𐤍𐤁). The father is the "strength" (𐤀) of the house (𐤁), while the son fills the house (𐤁) with life or seed (𐤍). Both of these words are united at the bet (𐤁) - the House.

The gematria value for father (𐤁𐤀) is 3, and the value of son (𐤍𐤁) is 52. When added together we have 55, which is the same value as "the land" – ha'adamah (𐤀𐤃𐤌𐤄𐤀). This is the word used to describe the planet in Beresheet 1:25. The earth is "the house" that we saw being built from the first letter of the Hebrew Scriptures – the enlarged bet (𐤁).

Since the "father" (𐤀𐤁) and the "son" (𐤁𐤍) each have a bet (𐤁), when they are combined into one word they are connected by one house, again resulting in the gematria value for "aben" (𐤀𐤁𐤍) of 53. Another word with incredible significance that equals 53 is "ha'yobel" (𐤄𐤉𐤅𐤁𐤋), also known as "the Jubilee."

The Jubilee is a year that occurs every 50 years on the Calendar of YHWH.[40] This is an important time when Land and inheritance rights are restored. The Jubilee is all about being restored to our homes, which we have lost. We should all anticipate a future Jubilee when mankind is permitted back in the Garden. They are both related concepts. The Scriptures specifically call the Jubilee "qadosh" (𐤒𐤃𐤅). (Vayiqra 25:12). The Hebrew word "qadosh" (𐤒𐤃𐤅) means" "set apart."

The principles of life were found in the Garden. It was a special "enclosed" place where man could commune with the Creator. It was "set apart" – qadosh (𐤒𐤃𐤅). This is the condition that man must be in to dwell in the presence of Elohim. The Scriptures are clear on this point, because YHWH describes Himself as "qadosh." "*You shall be qadosh* (𐤒𐤃𐤅) *for I YHWH your Elohim am qadosh* (𐤒𐤃𐤅)." Vayiqra 19:2, 11:44, 20:7, 20:26, 21:8. It was in the Garden that we find the source of life – the Tree of Life. Only the qadosh ones can partake of the Tree of Life.

We also saw that YHWH used the seed to propagate and multiply life. In the Garden there was food to eat, only that which was seed bearing and was green.[41] Man was placed within the garden and commanded to "be fruitful and multiply." His residency came with certain conditions. It was the very House of YHWH, and this of course was where YHWH would communicate with man – face to face. So we can see through the creation process, the many levels that YHWH chose to communicate by and through His Creation.

Now let us examine the creation of man. As man was brought into existence we see something very interesting. In the Hebrew text it describes the man as "et-haAdam" (𐤌𐤃𐤀𐤄-𐤕𐤀).[42] Only in the Hebrew do we see the Aleph Taw (𐤕𐤀) attached to "haAdam" (𐤌𐤃𐤀𐤄) which literally means: "the man." Therefore, we see man made in the image of Elohim, because this was a pattern. The Image of Elohim in creation was the Aleph Taw (𐤕𐤀).

Elohim placed man in the House and gave him a job. This was the place where man was given purpose: "to work and to guard." (Beresheet 2:15). Elohim was revealing through this man the purpose of His Creation.

Adam was given authority over this creation. He named the animals. He was given power to choose and responsibility to care for things. He was essentially given charge over this newly established Kingdom – the Kingdom of YHWH on the earth.

Once man was placed in a House, represented by the Garden, it was time to fill the House. He was a prince populating the Kingdom of his Father. A mate would come from "the adam" made in the image of YHWH. This pattern revealed that YHWH would bring forth a mate for Himself, from Himself.

We read about the "birthing" process by which this was accomplished in Beresheet 2:21-22. "*[21] And YHWH Elohim caused a deep sleep to fall on Adam, and he slept; and He took one of his ribs, and closed up the flesh in its place. [22] Then the rib which YHWH Elohim had taken from man He made into a woman, and He brought her to the man.*"

Notice that Adam was placed in a "deep sleep." The word to describe this "deep sleep" in Hebrew is "tardemah" (𐤀𐤌𐤃𐤓𐤕), which is like "a trance, coma or death." So we are given a picture of Adam dying and giving birth to the woman. After the "birth" he is resurrected. This is a pattern that would be repeated again in the future.[43] Ultimately, the Messiah would come as a Son of man, and He too would give "birth" to a family to fill the House of Elohim – Beit El. He too must shed His blood, die and be resurrected in order to populate His Father's Kingdom.

This leads to a very important detail regarding the "birthing" process from Adam. In the text, we read how a "rib" was taken from the man to form the woman. Some believe that it was not actually a rib that was taken from Adam, but rather something even more profound. The word for "the rib" in the passage is: "et-hatzelah" (𐤏𐤋𐤑𐤄-𐤕𐤀). The first thing that should get your attention is the fact that there is the Aleph Taw (𐤕𐤀) actually attached to the word: "hatzelah" (𐤏𐤋𐤑𐤄).

This reveals that something special is going on in this "birthing" process. It could be that the Aleph Taw (𐤕𐤀) is actually participating in the creation of woman. The hey (𐤄) is translated as "the" but it also means: "behold." So we should really focus on the root word "tzelah" (𐤏𐤋𐤑). This word is simply translated to mean: "curve," "slope" or "side." This is what causes many to think of a rib, which is curved.

When we look at the word we see something even more incredible. The tsade (𐤑) actually represents a "hook" and means: "righteous." The lamed (𐤋) represents a staff or a goad and means: "control, instruct." The ayin (𐤏) represents an eye and means: "to see or know." Notice that all three characters are curved and when combined they mean: "righteous instruction seen."

The gematria for "tzelah" is 190, and it shares the same

value as "qetz" (**ק ץ**), which means: "end" as in "end of a cycle" or "end of an age." It also shares the same value with the Hebrew word "tzeetz" (**ץ ז צ**) which means: "flower, bloom or wings." It is the root of "tzitzit" (**ת ץ ז צ**), which are the "wings" or "tassels" that we are to wear on the four corners of our garments. The "tzitzit" contain a thread of blue, and are intended to remind us of the commandments. (Bemidbar 15:38).

So we see through this process the righteous instructions brought forth from the man that would bloom, or take flight, through the woman.

There is something in our bodies where the righteous instructions of the Creator are located, the three dimensional digital coding that drives our physical bodies – our DNA. Therefore "the curve," that is referred to could very likely be the DNA double helix. In other words, the Aleph Taw (**ת א**) took the genetic code from the man, and from that same coding He made the  woman. Of course, a rib would clearly contain DNA so that is a very plausible situation, but it is amazing how many levels of understanding can be found in the Hebrew language.

When we look at the ordinal values in the Aleph Bet we see that the "tsade" (**צ**) is number 18, the "lamed" (**ל**) is number 12 and the "ayin" (**ע**) is number 16. When these values are added together they amount to 46, which amazingly is the number of chromosomes per cell in the DNA of mankind.[44]

This gets interesting when we realize that the Aleph (**א**) is the first letter in the Aleph Bet, which has an ordinal value of 1. The Taw (**ת**) is the last letter in the alephbet, which has an ordinal value of 22. Therefore, the Aleph Taw (**ת א**) has an ordinal value of 23, the number of chromosomes in a sperm and an egg. This is also the gematria value for "live" which is rendered as ⁅ⵣ⵳ in Beresheet 1:20, and ⵣ⵳⁅ in Beresheet 6:19. In both instances their gematria value for "live" is 23.

It is intriguing when we examine the union between man and woman. The text records: "*Therefore a man shall leave his* ✗⚹-*father and* ✗⚹-*mother and be joined to his wife, and they shall become one flesh.*" Beresheet 2:24. When the text mentions father and mother there is an Aleph Taw (✗⚹) attached to each, revealing that both man and woman are made in the image of Elohim, and the Aleph Taw (✗⚹) is "imaged" in each of them.

This becomes more profound when we realize that all of mankind has 23 pairs of chromosomes - 22 pairs of autosomes and 1 pair of sex chromosomes. So men and women are the same in the 22 pairs of autosomes, and the distinction between men and women is the additional sex chromosome. So at the core of all mankind are the 22 autosomes.

Remember that there are 22 letters in the alephbet. If the Aleph Taw (✗⚹) consists of all the letters in the alephbet, then we can see that the image of the Aleph Taw (✗⚹) would look like a man. We can also discern that those letters were meant to create and procreate. There are a number of related words that all share the same gematria value as 22, such as "sacrifice," "sprinkle" and "hyssop."[45]

When the 23 chromosomes of a man are added to the 23 chromosomes of a woman, they become united as one, which is echad (⊲⵳✗) in Hebrew. This union results in a total of 46. Amazingly, the word "elohi" (ⵣ⁅ⵍ✗), equals 46, as was used to describe YHWH the Elohi of Shem, Noah's son. (Beresheet 9:26).

Each DNA molecule holds an incredible amount of information, placed there by none other than the Creator. DNA carries our genetic information, and is found within the nucleus of every living cell. Therefore, the righteous instructions from the Creator are within each of us - in every living cell of every living organism.

DNA is the familiar double helix shape connected with the four base letters - Adenine, Cytosine, Guanine, Thymine or ACGT. The 4 Base letters ACGT with each combination of 3 make Codons - the 64 Codons that, in turn, deliver specific instructions to cellular chemistry. Codons manufacture protein. It is the various sequencing of amino acids within the proteins that give rise to specific shapes and functions of the proteins.

Thus, there is a language built into this process, and scientists have even assigned alphabetical letters to amino acids. This process is empowered, instructed and controlled by DNA. It is known as "The Language of Life" and evolutionists are plagued with the question "What is the source of the biological messages encoded within the DNA?" Without DNA there is no replication, and evolution cannot explain life without the existence of DNA.

The manner in which that DNA transmits the "righteous instructions" is nothing short of a miracle. The DNA strand actually unravels during a process known as "transcription." A messenger RNA strand reads the instructions. This RNA is processed and exported from the nucleus into the cytoplasm, where it is translated by ribosomes, and then constructed into protein chains as per the transmitted instructions.

Those chains are then folded into a protein and transported to the needed location. This entire process is life. It is powered by an invisible force that no evolutionist could possibly explain by mere electro-chemical reactions. It is the very power of the word "EXIST" spoken at the beginning by the Creator.

This process played out by the DNA is the very

essence of creation. Through "the Word" Elohim created all that is in existence. It was the sound of the spoken Word that constituted the creative force. In fact, it has been said that the Hebrew language is actually the DNA of creation.[46]

As the DNA opens, transmits and closes, we see how YHWH creates. Adam was opened, his information was transmitted to the woman, and then he was closed. The man and the woman, although two separate beings, are made to be unified to become one flesh – echad. Through that union the woman is opened, the man plants his seed into the womb of the woman, and she bears fruit.

Unification is known as "echad," and it is how the Creator creates. We see this through all of creation. It is the trademark of YHWH. We even saw this with a day, as YHWH unified day and night to make a unified day on Day 1. He divided the light from the dark, and then unified. YHWH also describes Himself as Echad. So He too has been divided and unified so that He can create.[47] That is why He uses the descriptor "Elohim" which is the plural form of El.

Echad (𐤀𐤇𐤃) has a gematria value of 13, which shares the same value as love – "ahabah" (𐤀𐤄𐤁𐤄). Now anyone familiar wth the Name of YHWH should see the similarity. YHWH (𐤄𐤅𐤄𐤉) has a gematria value of 26, which is essentially "love unified." The only difference between these two words is the "ab" (𐤀𐤁) which means "father," and the "yaw" (𐤉𐤅), which means: "arm unites."

So we can see great truths hidden within the Name of YHWH, and through the DNA we can see YHWH actually communicating on a cellular level. One could say that DNA is the cellular language of life. It is the fingerprint of YHWH - it is His Image. So Adam being made in the image of YHWH involved YHWH placing His DNA within the man.

In fact, the life of the man is the blood, which pumps

through his veins.[48] His name actually refers to that blood, which is "dam" (**ﬦﬤ**) in Hebrew. The gematria value of blood is 44. Again, we can see the 22 letters of the alephbet intimately connected with the blood by a factor of 2. Remember that the Hebrew letter with the gematria value of 2 is bet (**ﬨ**), and the bet (**ﬨ**), literally represents a "house."

The blood is very interesting because YHWH chose it as the means to maintain life in "the adam." Some have speculated that blood is, in fact, congealed light.[49] This notion makes for interesting thought as we consider the speeding up of the blood into light. This would make sense as those who follow the Ways of YHWH are often referred to as Children of Light.[50]

This is particularly interesting when we consider the fact that blood, which sustains our life, contains somatids. Somatids are "ultramicrosopic subcellular living and reproducing entities, which many scientists believe are the precursor of DNA, and which may be the building block of all terrestrial life."[51]

So man and woman were created by the voice of YHWH. They were filled with His Spirit of Life – the light of life imparted into His Creation. They were literally clothed with this light. They were given instructions, and they were actually designed and built specifically to obey His instructions.

They were commanded to bear fruit by reproducing other children of this light who would populate the kingdom. We know that YHWH provided everything that they needed in the Garden, but there is a question as to what things were like outside the Garden. It was not the same, that is certain. Through their offspring, it is likely that they would expand the Kingdom of Light to encompass the entire planet that had previously undergone judgment.

While in the Garden man was commanded "*to tend*

and keep it." Beresheet 2:15. The Hebrew word for "tend" is "abad" (◁𝟋⊙) and the Hebrew word for "keep" is "shamar" (𝟈𝑦W). Both of these words are verbs and they involve action. These concepts are very important as we shall see throughout our discussion and another way of describing Adam's mission is *"to work and to watch"* or *"to do and to guard."*

After we are told what Adam was <u>to do</u> in the Garden we are then told of one specific commandment that he was given. The Scriptures record: *"[16] And YHWH Elohim commanded the man, saying, 'Of every tree of the Garden you may freely eat; [17] but of the tree of the knowledge of good and evil you shall not eat, for in the day that you eat of it you shall surely die.'"* Beresheet 2:16-17.

Now this was by no means the only command given to man, but it happened to be the first one that was transgressed - that is why we are provided the specific details of this particular command. Adam was surely given instructions concerning his duties and what was expected of him as he and his Creator walked and fellowshipped together in the Garden.

This command was specifically given to Adam and the emphasis on "die" in the Hebrew text cannot be ignored. The text actually provides "mooth h'mooth" (ㄨㄒ𝑦目 ㄨㄚ𝑦). The word "die" (ㄨㄚ𝑦) is repeated twice, separated by the "het" (目). Notice that the ancient "het" (目) looks like a ladder. The "het" (目) has the gematria value of 8, and it signifies the "connection" or "link" between YHWH and man. It is the "gate" or "ladder" that connects heaven and earth. So Hebrew text is revealing that the access that man has to the Creator will be cut off. That is true death, being separated from the source of life.

Indeed, we read that "death" did come upon man and woman. The connection was severed due to disobedience and

we will later see the important connection that the "het" (ᛘ) has with the Covenant established to renew the relationship.

We will now examine the event that severed the connection between YHWH and man. The Scriptures record an incident when the woman was deceived by a serpent that had entered the Garden.

"*¹ Now the serpent was more cunning than any beast of the field which YHWH Elohim had made. And he said to the woman, Has Elohim indeed said, You shall not eat of every tree of the garden? ² And the woman said to the serpent, We may eat the fruit of the trees of the garden; ³ but of the fruit of the tree which is in the midst of the garden, Elohim has said, You shall not eat it, nor shall you touch it, lest you die. ⁴ Then the serpent said to the woman, You will not surely die. ⁵ For Elohim knows that in the day you eat of it your eyes will be opened, and you will be like Elohim, knowing good and evil. ⁶ So when the woman saw that the tree was good for food, that it was pleasant to the eyes, and a tree desirable to make one wise, she took of its fruit and ate. She also gave to her husband with her, and he ate. ⁷ Then the eyes of both of them were opened, and they knew that they were naked; and they sewed fig leaves together and made themselves coverings.*" Beresheet 3:1-7.

Adam and the woman both transgressed a command – they partook of the fruit of the tree of knowledge of good and evil - better known as the Tree of all knowledge. Prior to the incident involving the Tree of All Knowledge, the Scriptures provide that "*they were both naked, the man and his wife, and they were not ashamed.*" Beresheet 2:25.

When Adam and the woman partook of this forbidden fruit, their eyes were suddenly opened to their "nakedness" which is "arom" (ᛘᛘᛘ⊙) in Hebrew. They were suddenly afraid and made for themselves coverings of leaves, likely leaves from the very tree from which they partook the fruit.

Most people who read this account will ask: "What

could have possibly happened to cause such a sudden change in their perception and how could eating a piece of fruit do such a thing?" While the fruit of that particular tree may have had special "powers" there is likely more to the story than meets the eye. This episode was a sensual event and we read in the text the emphasis placed upon the senses of touching, tasting and seeing.

The act of eating, drinking and tasting is at times used in the Scriptures in a metaphorical fashion to describe intimacy. For example in Song of Solomon we read *"Like an apple tree among the trees of the woods, so is my beloved among the sons. I sat down in his shade with great delight, and his fruit was sweet to my taste."* Song of Solomon 2:3 NKJV The Proverbs speak about a man drinking water from his own cisterns and not being enraptured by an immoral woman. Proverbs 5:15 We are encouraged to: *"Taste and see that YHWH is good."* Psalms 34:8

The key is that they now "knew" that they were naked. Prior to the incedent they were naked and unashamed. The word for "naked" prior to the incident was "arom" (**ﬡﬡﬡײַ**) in Hebrew. (Beresheet 2:25) After the incident the word for naked changed a bit to "eerom" (**ﬡﬡײַײַ**). It has the same meaning, but we see a "yud" (**ﬡ**) added and a "vav" (**ײַ**) removed. The "vav" (**ײַ**) is a connector and the removal of the "vav" (**ײַ**) reveals the "disconnect" between man and YHWH. The yud (**ﬡ**) represents an arm, so we can see that there will now be needed an arm - the Arm of YHWH - to reestablish the link.

Interestingly, the gematria value of "eerom" (**ﬡﬡײַײַ**) is 360, and we can see that this is the beginning of a cycle leading back to restoration. Another word that equates to 360 is "sheniy" (**ﬡײַﬡ**) which means: "second." We understand that we will need a "second" Man, the Arm of YHWH, to complete this cycle of restoration. Interestingly, we see that the word "shechem" (𐤔𐤊𐤌) also equals 360. Shechem is an important place in the Covenant process. It means "shoulders," and interestingly between the "shoulders" was where Shem and Japheth placed the garment to cover the nakedness of their father Noah. (Beresheet 9:23) We will discuss this further in the text because both of these incidents involving "nakedness" are related.

Now Adam and Hawah had been naked before the incident except many believe that the were actually clothed in light. So they lost their light through sinning and their nakedness was now exposed. Now they "knew" they were naked, which is "yada" (𐤏𐤃𐤉) in Hebrew. Interestingly, the man and the woman were not the only ones who were naked during this event. The Scriptures record that the serpent was also "arom" (𐤌𐤅𐤓𐤏), which was the same word to describe the man and woman as naked. Relative to the serpent, the word "arom" (𐤌𐤅𐤓𐤏) is usually translated as "cunning" in English translations so people miss the real meat of this encounter.

The word translated "the serpent" is "ha'nachash" (𐤔𐤄𐤍𐤄) in Hebrew. The noun "nachash" (𐤔𐤄𐤍) can mean a "snake, serpent or one who practices divination." (see Debarim 18:10). The adjective "nachash" (𐤔𐤄𐤍) means: "bright or brazen." So was it actually a snake or was it some bright, serpentine being? There is no specific name given to the serpent, and it is possible that the text is a word play that will have greater significance as we proceed with this discussion.

No matter how you describe this "serpent," something happened here which should draw our attention to the prohibitions found within Leviticus 18-20. Most commentators allude to the fact that something graphic occurred, but typically shy away from the details. While the text provides the "G-rated" account, the actual event was likely "X-rated." They had not only eaten a piece of fruit, they had participated in evil – through their disobedience they had sinned.

The man and woman were given access to life and were dwelling in paradise. They were given the incredible responsibility of building the Kingdom of YHWH on planet earth. The serpent was now calling Elohim a liar and promising them that they would "exist" (𐤀𐤆𐤀) as Elohim. The serpent told them that they would become Elohim if they ate of the fruit. So they desired to elevate from their created position. They sought more than they were given. They believed the serpent, and they ate the fruit. Their eyes were indeed opened and they were suddenly ashamed. This prompted them to cover themselves and hide.

Their reaction reveals that the event involved more than eating a piece of fruit. It was a perversion of the creative process previously described through the union of the man and the woman. It was so bad that the man and woman felt compelled to sew fig leaves together and cover their sexual organs.

When they heard the voice of YHWH in the Garden they hid themselves. Interestingly, when the Hebrew text inserts the Aleph Taw (𐤕𐤀) between "hear" (shema) and "the voice of YHWH Elohim." (Beresheet 3:8). Indeed the Aleph Taw (𐤕𐤀) is literally connected to the "voice" - 𐤋𐤅𐤒-𐤕𐤀.

So YHWH called out to the man and the woman. He communicated through speech and His voice is connected with the Aleph Taw (𐤕𐤀). They could not hide for long, they were eventually found and needed to come clean. Their conduct had repercussions. Their disobedience upset the equilibrium of creation and shook the cosmos. It infected a holy, set apart, creation and spread like a disease.

YHWH had to protect His creation and quarantine

man before he partook of the Tree of Life. He had to sever the connection between Himself and Creation. This disconnect meant the separation from the source of Life. Man was supposed to be the representative of YHWH on the planet and a conduit for His Life. By severing the relationship it meant certain death for all of Creation.

Incredibly, by quarantining man, it allowed an opportunity to salvage, or "save" him. He could not remain in the house, but YHWH revealed His plan of restoration through the punishments rendered upon the perpetrators.

When rendering judgment on the nachash (WℲⴘ), often referred to as the serpent, YHWH Elohim made the following proclamation: "*And I will put enmity between you and the woman, and between your seed and her seed; it shall bruise your head, and you shall ⴘXⴾ bruise his heel.*" Beresheet 3:15.

What is really interesting in this passage is the inclusion of the word "beyn" (ⴘⵉⴘ) four times in the Hebrew text. It cannot be seen in the English rendering above. The word "beyn" (ⴘⵉⴘ) can mean "between," but it also means "perceive or understand." Again, you will not see this in an English translation, but it would seem that the text is crying out for us to understand a mystery hidden within the passage - a mystery connected with the Aleph Taw (Xⴾ). Remember the hey (ⴘ) means "behold." So the solution to the problem seems to be provided – "*Behold the* Xⴾ *Who will be bruised.*"

Another interesting point is that the "nachash," also known as "the serpent" had seed. So this serpent had seed and the only place that it could have been planted was in Hawah. This is a highly controversial subject, but it is without question that the serpent was intent on building his own kingdom through his own offspring.

Most believe that the serpent was satan, although this is not necessarily the case. Actually, "satan" is not a name, it is an angelic position. In the Hebrew we actually read "ha'shatan" (𐤉𐤀𐤅𐤔𐤄) which means: "the adversary." So it really should be referred to as "the satan." No doubt that the satan was in Eden, but the serpent could have been acting as an agent of satan. Some believe that the satan spoke through the serpent. Interestingly, the Targums identify the angel Sammael as being present in the garden at the tree. (Targum Pseudo-Jonathan: Genesis). Other sources name the angel Satanael and Mastema. The satan was, after all, a cherub, not a serpent. (Ezekiel 28:14).

Here is a lamentation for the King of Tyre often attributed to the satan. *"12 Thus says Adonai YHWH: You were the seal of perfection, full of wisdom and perfect in beauty. 13 You were in Eden, the garden of Elohim; Every precious stone was your covering: The sardius, topaz, and diamond, beryl, onyx, and jasper, sapphire, turquoise, and emerald with gold. The workmanship of your timbrels and pipes was prepared for you on the day you were created. 14 You were the anointed cherub who covers; I established you; you were on the set mountain of Elohim; you walked back and forth in the midst of fiery stones. 15 You were perfect in your ways from the day you were created, till iniquity was found in you. 16 By the abundance of your trading you became filled with violence within, and you sinned; Therefore I cast you as a profane thing out of the mountain of Elohim; and I destroyed you, O covering cherub, from the midst of the fiery stones. 17 Your heart was lifted up because of your beauty; You corrupted your wisdom for the sake of your splendor; I cast you to the ground, I laid you before kings, that they might gaze at you."* Ezekiel 28:12-17.

This is clearly speaking of an angelic being, known as a cherub. The cherubs are very powerful four winged creatures that surround the Throne of YHWH on the mountain of Elohim. Notice that this cherub was *"the anointed cherub that covers."* In Hebrew we read "et-cherub m'moshiach ha'sawkak" (𐤊𐤊𐤅𐤎𐤄 𐤇𐤅𐤔𐤌𐤌 𐤁𐤅𐤓𐤊-𐤕𐤀).

There is something very unique about this particular cherub. He was associated with the Aleph Taw (𐤗𐤊). He covered, or rather, "defended" the Throne. He was "anointed" (moshiach) which is where we get the word "messiah."

Also notice the physical description of this being. He was not covered with eyes, like the other Cherubim. This anointed cherub was covered with precious stones - The sardius, topaz, and diamond, beryl, onyx, and jasper, sapphire, turquoise, and emerald with gold. This Cherub also had instruments built into his being – timbrels and pipes. So this was a very unique and powerful being, charged with defending the Throne.

Many have been taught his name is Lucifer, but that is not accurate. The name Lucifer derives from Jerome's translation of Isaiah 14:12 in the Latin Vulgate. The word in Hebrew is "heylel" (𐤋𐤋𐤆𐤉). It refers to "praise" and some believe that the satan was the highest Angel, a Cherub in charge of worship before the Throne of YHWH. Interestingly, he is called "ben-shakar" which literally means: "son of the dusk" or "son of dark." So "Lucifer" is a fictitious Latin name ascribed to the satan. While the satan was perfectly created, after the fall he was likened to the darkness before the sun rises. The Messiah is the morning star, (Revelation 22:16), or the day star, represented by the sun. The sun brings light to the darkness.

So the satan had a specific function in the heavens and now he has now set himself in opposition to YHWH. This once anointed (moshiach) Cherub has set himself against The Annointed - The Messiah.

It is understood that the satan led a rebellion against YHWH. He was actually "anointed" but desired to be the Messiah, with his own bride and his own kingdom. He actually can transform himself into an angel of light. (2 Corinthians 11:14). Although he has been cast down from his

position, he desires to give the appearance of light. We can even see this desire through the use of the Latin name Lucifer. Lucifer actually means: "light bearer."

While he was originally created perfect, sin entered into him. Here is the description rendered from Isaiah 12: "*12 How you are fallen from heaven, O Heylal, son of dusk! How you are cut down to the ground, you who weakened the nations! 13 For you have said in your heart: I will ascend into heaven, I will exalt my throne above the stars of Elohim; I will also sit on the mount of the congregation on the farthest sides of the north; 14 I will ascend above the heights of the clouds, I will be like the Most High. 15 Yet you shall be brought down to Sheol, to the lowest depths of the Pit.*" Isaiah 12:12-15.

In his desire to sit on the throne and be like YHWH, the satan led the rebellion against the Kingdom of YHWH. This is why he is called "satan" which means "adversary" in Hebrew. Satan is connected with the Dragon whose tail swept a third of the stars out of the sky. (see Revelation 12:4). As a result, it is believed that a third of the angels actually followed him in his rebellion. This was the beginning of a battle that would rage until the end. There is an imbalance in the heavens and the earth that will be restored through the mystery of the Messiah fulfilled through mankind, as YHWH would replace the anointed Cherub and the third of the angels – known as the "sons of Elohim." YHWH would now populate His kingdom with mankind.

The reason that the satan is so utterly opposed to mankind, is because man was made to be elevated to where he wanted to sit. Man is destined for the Throne. Through the Aleph Taw (✕✿), mankind can join with YHWH and rule and reign upon the Throne - the very Throne that the satan was supposed to defend. This would prove to be an epic battle of the ages. It was going to reap great destruction, and there would be casualties on all sides. In the end, the seed of

the woman would triumph over the seed of the serpent.

After the punishments were rendered, YHWH shed the blood of innocent animals to reveal that innocent blood would provide an atonement, or covering, for the sin of man. YHWH clothed the man and the woman in the skins of the slaughtered animals. They were like costumes or disguises, that hid their sin from the face of YHWH.

The taint of sin was still there, just covered (atoned). As a result, the inner sin began to work death in both the man and the woman. Beings that were created in the image of an eternal Elohim, intended to live forever, were now infected with sin and were dying. Death is very repulsive to the Creator as it is the antithesis of His essence, which is life.

So disobedience resulted in expulsion from the source of life in the garden, and it introduced the process of death into creation. Creation and the events surrounding the Garden communicate the truth of YHWH. We are not provided much information regarding life outside the Garden, but it was surely not paradise.

We know this from the punishments meted out to the participants of the sin in the Garden. (Beresheet 3:14-19). In the midst of the punishment, there was a promise given which gave hope to mankind, the Promise of a deliverer.[52] There were patterns built into Creation, and the cycles of time intended to reveal how this deliverer would accomplish the task.

The pattern of the first week provided a pattern for this present existence. We know from the first week of Creation that time was reckoned by the passage of days. Each day is controlled by the circuit of the sun and progresses from evening to night to morning and back to evening. A day actually begins at evening and ends the following evening.[53] There would be six days followed by the seventh day, called the Sabbath, and then the count would reset.

This seven day count is a remembrance of Creation and constitutes a week, known as a "shabua" (⊙𐤉𐤅) in Hebrew. The seven day week count has continued since the very first week. The passage of weeks was therefore marked by the sun.

Interestingly, this count began before there was a sun. Recall that the sun, the moon, the planets and the stars were not created until day four. So the sun actually marked a passage of time that could be calculated prior to its creation. Here is an account of what occurred on Day 4 of creation week:

> "[14] Then Elohim said, 'Let there be lights in the firmament of the heavens to divide the day from the night; and let them be for signs and seasons (moadim), and for days and years; [15] and let them be for lights in the firmament of the heavens to give light on the earth' and it was so. [16] Then Elohim made two great lights: the greater light to rule the day, and the lesser light to rule the night. He made the stars also. [17] Elohim set them in the firmament of the heavens to give light on the earth, [18] and to rule over the day and over the night, and to divide the light from the darkness. And Elohim saw that it was good. [19] So the evening and the morning were the fourth day." Beresheet 1:14-19.

We see that there were specific lights placed in the firmament of the heavens. These were to help divide and distinguish the day from the night. The sun is the <u>greater</u> light – "gadol" (𐤋𐤃𐤅) in Hebrew. This means it is greater in rank, power and magnitude. Indeed, the moon emanates no light from itself, but rather reflects the light of the sun.

The moon is known as the lesser light, but it still has a very specific and important purpose. It actually rules the sky by night along with the stars. Indeed, the moon is considered to be a faithful witness.[54] The moon is actually made for what are commonly translated as "seasons." "*He appointed the moon for seasons (moadim); the sun knows its going down.*" Psalm 104:19.

Up to this point we have quoted some common English translations where the moon has been associated with "seasons." That is a serious translation error, and you should have noticed the word "moadim" in parenthesis. The word often translated as "seasons" is "moadim" (𐤌𐤏𐤃𐤉𐤌) in Hebrew. It is another form of the word "moadi" (𐤌𐤏𐤃𐤉) that we already mentioned is an Appointed Time.

The reason this is a translation error is because "moadim" does not refer to seasons, but rather specific "Appointed Times." Again, these Appointed Times are special times that occur each year as patterns to reveal the plan of YHWH to His people. They are a way that YHWH communicates to His people through Creation and time. As people observe these Appointed Times, they learn about YHWH, His righteous path and His plan to redeem His people. We will be discussing the significance of the Appointed Times throughout this book. The important thing, for now, is to realize that they are not "seasons" as some believe - ie. spring, summer, fall and winter.

So from the beginning YHWH built these Appointed Times into creation and used the sun and the moon as virtual "hands on the clock" to tell time. The sun marks the passage of days, and the moon marks the passage of months. The passage of solar day cycles also marks the passage of weeks. The progression of the moon, from one new moon to another, marks the passage of months.

Now through the passage of months we obviously see the progression of the seasons, but the Appointed Times are not the seasons themselves. The seasons are actually determined by times known generally as "tequfahs" or rather "tequfot." These "tequfot" are essentially "turns," commonly known as the solstices and equinoxes.

The word for return, "shoob" ($\mathcal{Y}\Upsilon W$), also has great significance as the seasons "return" to their beginnings. Just as Creation turns and returns, we are also to remember to turn from wickedness and return to YHWH. Therefore, as we live our lives through these visual cycles of Creation we are reminded of our relationship with the Creator. This, of course, is the meaning of the Appointed Times. They are intended to draw us back to YHWH, and keep us on His path. The Appointed Times are a rehearsal revealing how we "teshubah" ($\mathfrak{Z}\mathcal{Y}\Upsilon W X$).

So aside from telling time and marking the Appointed Times, we learn from Beresheet 1:14 that the sun, the moon and the stars are also made to be "signs." Now in our modern English we usually think of a sign as something two dimensional with words written on it that provides information or direction. The sun, the moon and the stars were the first signs, and the word in Hebrew for sign is "owt" ($X\Upsilon\mathbf{K}$). Notice that the word is very similar to light – "owr" ($\mathbf{9}\Upsilon\mathbf{K}$). That is because they share the same root ($\Upsilon\mathbf{K}$), which literally means – "strength or power connects." If we view the aleph ($\mathbf{K}$) as representing Elohim we see the sign – "owt" ($X\Upsilon\mathbf{K}$) as Elohim connecting the covenant. The word for "owt" ($X\Upsilon\mathbf{K}$) also has the same numeric value as the "w'et" ($X\mathbf{K}\Upsilon$) that connected the heavens and the earth in Beresheet 1:1 – 407. We also see light – "owr" ($\mathbf{9}\Upsilon\mathbf{K}$) as Elohim connected to the Head of Creation.

Interestingly, the aleph ($\mathbf{K}$) with a value of 1, is often attributed to YHWH. The vav (Υ), with a value of 6, is often attributed to man. As YHWH "connects" to man we are left with the value of 7, and we can see why the number 7 is so predominate in Creation.

Because of this shared root with light, we discern that the sign is illuminated and something to be seen. Accordingly, those heavenly bodies designated for signs emit and/or reflect light. Very interestingly, the first time that a "sign" is mentioned in the text is Beresheet 1:14 and it is not spelled ✕𐤉𐤊, but rather ✕𐤊. You will find ✕✕𐤊 in the text but the final ✕ is to pluralize the word from sign to signs. So the "first" sign is clearly the Aleph Taw (✕𐤊), and one could conclude that all signs point and lead to the Aleph Taw (✕𐤊), which represents the Messiah.

Time, as it turns out, has limits. Particularly the time of this creation where the sun and the moon mark that time. We can see that time set within the framework of seven, and we even see the Messiah, represented by the Aleph Taw (✕𐤊), within that framework on two occasions.

It is commonly understood that there is a connection between a day and a thousand years.[55] As a result, it appears that there is a framework of seven thousand years within which the purposes of YHWH are to be completed. At first glance, this appears to be in drastic opposition to the notion promoted by science that the universe is billions of years old. It must be remembered that something happened between *"In the beginning"* (Beresheet 1:1) and *"The earth was without form, and void; and darkness was on the face of the deep."* (Beresheet 1:2).

There was an existence, and likely a great judgment, prior to Day 1 when the clock of our existence essentially "started ticking." That clock has been counting down since the beginning and functions within a seven thousand year framework. As this clock count draws us to the end of the age, we should expect to see judgment according to the patterns provided through the life of a man named Noah.

2

The Days of Noah

The disobedience of the man and the woman resulted in their expulsion from Paradise - the house that had been prepared for mankind to commune with Elohim. The gateway to Elohim had been closed, and was now guarded by cherubim. In fact, the text describing this is quite revealing.

"*So He drove out* X✗-*the man; and He placed east of the Garden of Eden* X✗-*the cherubim and* X✗ *a flaming sword which overturned every* X✗-*way, to guard (shamar) the way to the tree of life.*" Beresheet 3:24. So there were these mysterious cherubim with a blazing sword to guard the Tree of Life. Adam was supposed to guard the Garden and now we see this job given to the cherubim, directly connected with the Aleph Taw (X✗). We also see that the Aleph Taw (X✗) guards "the way" to the Tree of Life.

There was no way that man would partake of the Tree of Life, but for the way being provided by the Aleph Taw (X✗). Because the Tree of Life was inaccessible, from that point forward in time, things rapidly deteriorated for mankind, and all of Creation that had previously been intimately connected with mankind.

Eve gave birth to two sons. These two sons may have been twins with two different fathers stemming from the incident in the Garden. Again this is highly controversial, but it is certainly possible and explains how the seed of the serpent and the seed of the woman could fulfill prophecy. According to 1 John 3:12 Cain was "from (ἐκ) the wicked one." The Greek word "ek" (ἐκ) is a primary preposition denoting origin. Thus, the text seems to be confirming that Cain came from the serpent seed.

The two sons who came from Eve (Hawah)[56] became the first recorded perpetrator and victim of homicide. If indeed Cain (Qayin) was from the seed of the serpent, then we can see two kingdoms represented by two sons. Qayin killed Abel (Hebel), and mankind appeared to be doomed from the start.[57] This was the beginning of a battle that appeared to be short lived.

The seed of Adam had been cut off. In fact, if Hebel was conceived in the Garden, it is likely that he was in the image of YHWH, as was Adam. In an act of mercy, YHWH essentially replaced the murdered son Hebel with another son named Seth. Seth would continue the "righteous line" that had been "cut off" by Qayin. Interestingly, Seth was specifically born in the image of Adam - in his fallen state. (Beresheet 5:3) So we now have a seemingly insurmountable problem for mankind. How could man become regenerated back into the image of YHWH?

Part of the answer was already seen in the language regarding man being "naked." Another part was seen by the shedding of the blood at the gate of the Garden. The problem was in the blood. It had lost the light of life. Another Adam was needed, and we can trace the man through the generations contained in the Scriptures.

There was a very interesting clue provided through the genealogies of the two offspring of Hawah. Qayin received a "mark" from YHWH so that no one would kill him. (Beresheet 4:15) This would allow the line of Qayin to continue. From the line of Qayin we are only provided with seven generations that ended with the offspring of Lamech who had 2 wives, bearing 3 sons and 1 daughter. (see Beresheet 4:16-22) So while the line of Qayin likely continued, it is only recorded for seven generations. This appears to have prophetic significance.

From the line of Seth we can trace a continuous line through the ages. While the line of Qayin ends at the seventh generation, the line of Seth contains a very interesting individual named Enoch in the seventh generation. Enoch, better known as Henoch (ᕼᎩᎩᕼ), was also the name of the second son of Qayin. The first time we read this name in each geneology we read "at-Henoch" (ᕼᎩᎩᕼ-ᚷᚲ).

Here is what we read about Henoch in the lie of Seth. *"21 Henoch lived sixty-five years, and begot Methuselah. 22 After he begot Methuselah, Henoch walked with ᚷᚲ-the Elohim three hundred years, and had sons and daughters. 23 So all the days of Henoch were three hundred and sixty-five years. 24 And Henoch walked with ᚷᚲ-the Elohim; and he was not, for Elohim took him."* Beresheet 5:21-24

So while the seventh generation from Qayin seemingly ends, the seventh generation from Seth walks with Elohim and "is not." The tradition is that Enoch never died, but rather was translated to the heavens. If we examine this within the pattern of the seven day pattern of creation, we can see that after the Sabbath "millennium" those who walk with Elohim will be translated, while those who do not will come to an end. This reveals the struggle between to seed lines that will continue to the end.

We know that from the Creation of the first man there were 10 generations that led up to a man named Noah. We are specifically provided these genealogies to provide us with his bloodline. The importance of this will become evident as we proceed. The life of Noah, and the 10th generation are significant because we know a worldwide flood occurred during his life as judgment upon the planet.

While there was a line of individuals who followed the ways of YHWH, most of creation was in a state of disobedience, or rather lawlessness.

Remember that YHWH gave man certain instructions for living. These instructions are commonly referred to as "Torah" (ᐊᕿᎩX). This word is often translated as "the Law," but that does not do justice to the meaning. You see "Torah" has with it the implication of leading to a path of life and blessing. YHWH wants the best for His creation and His Torah is meant to guide Creation back to the place of blessing. It is not simply a list of do's and don'ts. It is instruction in righteousness that draws men closer to YHWH.[58]

The Torah was meant to be a blessing. Sadly, when the Torah is equated with "Law" people often perceive it as arduous and restrictive rules meant to make their lives miserable and take away their enjoyment. They then view it as bondage and rebel. Sadly, we see all too often that over time, men repeatedly forget YHWH and stray from His ways

Now when we consider mankind during that period we tend to make some very incorrect assumptions. Because of the ideas of Darwinism and evolution we think that the farther we go back into the past, the more primitive was man's condition. This is an egregious and erroneous assumption, because man was once very closely connected with the workings of the planet and the universe. Man had a very good understanding of the Creator, having been taught by the High Priest Adam, who had been directly connected with the Creator.

The farther we progress from Adam, it seems the farther mankind has drifted from those ancient understandings, save certain ones directly instructed and guided by YHWH.

We tend to confuse our materialistic inventions with evolution, which is not necessarily a proper correlation. Industrial progress does not necessarily correlate with physiological development. No doubt, through communication and shared information, man has been able to collectively develop many incredible machines, tools and buildings, but this is not necessarily the first time that man has collectively excelled.

For instance, archaeologists have discovered a very sophisticated, highly advanced mechanical computer known as the Antikythera Mechanism. It is named such because it was found in a ship wreck off the coast of the Greek Island Antikythera It is believed to have been originally designed by Archimedes in Syracuse in 3rd Century BCE.

Archimedes was killed by Roman Legionaires during the plundering of Syracuse and it is thought that General Marcellus took with him two astronomical machines built by Archemedes. The point is that the bronze Antikythera mechanism is over 2,200 years old. It is literally an ancient computer.[59]

Imagine nearly 2,000 years earlier, prior to the flood. The earth's atmosphere was much different enabling men to live incredibly longer lives. They all spoke the same language, and were able to easily share knowledge and information. They were originally connected to the Creator until being ejected from the Garden. Now imagine that men were later given wisdom, information, instruction and guidance from fallen angels. The implications are extraordinary and profound.

As it turns out, the ancients were actually very sophisticated. Our modernity consists largely of industrialization, production and consumption on a massive scale. While they may not have been modern in the way that we define modernity, they were clearly advanced. There are evidences of ancient knowledge and sophistication scattered all over the planet. The problem is that these remnants, relics and ruins do not fit within the accepted paradigm of history so they are either ignored or suppressed.[60]

We do not know precisely what things were like prior to the flood. It is evident that the planetary atmosphere and conditions were different than we observe today.[61] The occupants of the planet may have used advanced materials or they likely built with wood. Even the finest wood structures would deteriorate over time. Obviously much was wiped out, except for larger stone structures and inscriptions.

Many of the ancient structures that endured the flood and time are viewed as "mysteries" or alien in origin, because there is no recorded historical explaination for their existence or construction.[62] For  instance, the Stone of the Pregnant Woman in Baalbeck, Lebanon is considered to be the largest hewn stone in the world weighing approximately 1,000 tons. It is unknown how such a stone could be moved, even with "modern" construction equipment.

While it is often attributed to the Romans, it is more likely a product of antediluvian society, as are the countless other unexplained structures and artifacts found around and beneath the planet. Most people do not make that connection due to their evolutionary predispositions.

Again, from these unexplained structures, ancient writings, and even the Scriptures, we can discern that pre-

flood culture was likely highly advanced. Imagine the Ark built by Noah. It was an enormous structure and quite an engineering feat. While YHWH provided the design – Noah built it. So obviously men were able to build large structures, and one of the reasons may be due to the existence of giants.

Sadly, the sin of the garden, influenced by the serpent, better known as the "nachash"[63] spread like a virus throughout the world. Adam was taken from the ground, and mankind was intimately tied to the rest of creation. As the sin of man continued, it corrupted all of creation.

It appears that things spiraled when "the sons of Elohim" began mating with "the daughters of men."

"*[1] Now it came to pass, when men began to multiply on the face of the earth, and daughters were born to them, [2] that the sons of Elohim saw the ✕✗-daughters of men, that they were good (✕ ✔ ⊗); and they took women for themselves of all whom they chose. [3] And YHWH said, My Spirit shall not strive with man forever, for he is indeed flesh; yet his days shall be one hundred and twenty years. [4] There were Nephilim on the earth in those days, and also afterward, when the sons of Elohim came in to the daughters of men and they bore children to them. Those were the mighty men who were of old, men of renown. [5] Then YHWH saw that the wickedness of man was great in the earth, and that every intent of the thoughts of his heart was only evil continually. [6] And YHWH was sorry that He had made man on the earth, and He was grieved in His heart. [7] So YHWH said, 'I will destroy man whom I have created from the face of the earth, both man and beast, creeping thing and birds of the air, for I am sorry that I have made them.' [8] But Noah found grace in the eyes of YHWH.*" Beresheet

6:1-8.

There are many who speculate what exactly was happening with the "sons of Elohim." To qualify as a son of Elohim, one must be a directly related to Elohim. The "sons of Elohim" were direct creations of Elohim. They were in the Kingdom, and thus part of the "family" of Elohim. The term "sons of Elohim" is "beni ha'Elohim" (ㄅㄐㄋㄈㄥㄈㄐ-ㄥㄐㄢ) in Hebrew.

As was mentioned previously, each Hebrew character has a numerical equivalent. As a result, all Hebrew words and phrases carry numerical values. The Gematria value for "beni ha'Elohim" is 153. This will become more significant as we continue the discussion.[64]

Their rightful place was in the heavens, not on the earth. We know that the "sons of Elohim" were present during creation, when YHWH laid the "cornerstone," known as the "aben panan" (ㄋㄐㄋ ㄐㄢㄈ). The "sons of Elohim" witnessed this event and shouted for joy. (Job 38:7) The Book of Jude refered to the "sons of Elohim" in Beresheet 6:2 as *"angels which did not keep their first estate, but left their own habitation."* Jude 6

The Book of Job also describes specific days when the "sons of Elohim" came to "present" themselves before YHWH, along with the satan. This reveals that the sons of Elohim had access to YHWH. This heavenly realm was their domain. Interestingly, the text in Job reveals the rebellion going on. In the Hebrew the word translated as "present" is more accurately rendered as "take a stand." So the sons of Elohim were confronting YHWH with satan as their leader. (see Job 1:6, 2:1)

The earth was made for man, and woman was created specifically for man. She was a part of man, an extension of man and they were perfectly fit for one another to become one – echad. To cross the bounds set by the Creator was an abomination. This is especially true since mankind was in an unclean state and therefore the "sons of Elohim" were defiling themselves, thus prohibiting them from presenting themselves before the Throne of YHWH.

Most translations state that the "sons of Elohim" found the daughters of men to be "beautiful." They make it sound as if this was some romantic love story that spanned the heavens and the earth - angelic beings falling in love with beautiful women, getting married and settling down to raise families. That was definitely not the case.

The Hebrew word translated as "beautiful" is "towbote" (✗𐤠⊗), which literally means they were "good." A better translation might be "functional" or "suitable."

They did not get married. They "took" whatever women they "chose." The Hebrew word for "took" is "laqach" (𐤟𐤠𐤋) which means: "sieze, carry away." This sounds more like raping, pillaging and slavery. There is nothing to indicate that the daughters of Adam voluntarily entered into these relationships, although that may have been the case. They could have been seduced like Hawah was seduced by the serpent.

The bottom line is that they seized and carried away these daughters of Adam, and used them in order to copulate, as the serpent had done with Hawah in the Garden. This was, after all, the act that resulted in the prophetic judgment concerning the "seed" of the serpand and the "seed" of the woman. (Beresheet 3:15) Now this likely got very personal, because the text literally states that "the Adam" began to multiply and daughters were born. It then refers to the "sons of Elohim" mating with the "daughters of Adam." So it could have been specifically Adam's daughters who were being defiled, or other daughters of other men.

The sons of Elohim mating with women resulted in offspring. This was the battle between two seeds, the seed of man and the seed of the serpent. The battle began in the Garden. You see man had essentially been toppled from his throne. He was no longer a king in a castle, represented by the Garden of Eden. Adam had been deposed, and was in exile. This was an attempted coup and the sons of Elohim were building their kingdom using the daughters of Adam to produce a hybrid species.

This was genetic manipulation and cross breeding of the highest order. They were, after all, spiritual beings mixing with the image of Elohim. There is confusion as to what the offspring were actually called. This is because of the use of the term "Nephilim" (𐤟𐤆𐤋𐤉𐤟) in the above text. Most English translations translate Nephilim as "giants," while others define Nephilim as "fallen ones." So the Nephilim are either the offspring of the sons of Elohim mating with women, or they are the fallen sons of Elohim. In either case there was clearly a race of beings being promulgated upon the earth by the fallen sons of Elohim. Those lines can actually be traced throughout the Scriptures and have various names, that is why many people fail to make the connection

According to Scriptures the Nephilim were: " . . . *the mighty ones who were of old (olam), men of renown (ha'shem)."* Beresheet 6:4. The Hebrew word for "mighty ones" is "gibborim" (𐤟𐤆𐤘𐤁𐤉). The word usually implies strength – like a warrior, and often is used in reference to giants. While "adam" is the Hebrew word for "man," the word for "men" in this passage comes from the root "anash." The Hebrew word "anash" (W𐤟𐤀) actually means: "exceedingly wicked." The Hebrew word for "renown" is "ha'shem" (𐤟W𐤀) which means: "the name." Finally, the word "olam" (𐤟𐤋𐤉𐤏) means: "ages." So these beings were from the ages.

So these Nephilim and their offspring are described as wicked mighty ones. These were the mighty ones known through the ages (olam) - the gods and demi-gods of mythology and pagan religions. That is why people remembered their names (ha'shem). In fact, it is very likely that these were the ancient mythological beings that remain with us to this day.

Beyond the myths, we can see traces of these ancient beings and their architectural handiwork all throughout the earth. Recent discoveries at Göbekli Tepe in Turkey have revealed what is thought to be the oldest temple complex ever unearthed. It is a large Neolithic sanctuary located on top of a hill in southeastern Anatolia in Turkey. It is filled with large megaliths and strange animal carvings.

Of course Eastern Turkey is the source of the Euphrates River, which is extremely important when we examine our ancient beginnings. It is also the region where we see Nemrut (Nemrud), an ancient volcano named after none other than Nimrod, an individual who we will be examining further in the text. The region also contains another smaller Mount Nemrut (Nemrud), often called the Mountain of the Gods. It is an ancient site littered with large sculptures of "the mighty ones" worshipped as the gods.

It appears that many of the Nephilim offspring were actually giants, who were worshiped as gods. It is important to note that the word "Nephilim" does not necessarily have to mean "giant." In fact, throughout the Scriptures the giants are referred to as "Rephaim" (רֵפָאִים). While  the terms are sometimes used interchangeably, the Nephilim are generally considered to be the originators of the species. (Bemidbar 13:33).

The offspring, who were typically giants, are

described by a variety of names such as "the Anakim." They were the descendants of Anaq (𐤐𐤄𐤏) who came from the Nephilim. They were also the Zumim, the Emim (Debarim 2:11), the Horites (Debarim 2:12), the Zamzummim (Debarim 2:20) and the Avim (Debarim 2:23) (see also Beresheet 14:5). The Nephilim, in propagating these giant beings, were corrupting YHWH's creation. Remember that man was made in the "image" of YHWH. His genetic coding reflected that image.[65]

So when the sons of Elohim mixed with mankind, a hybrid race of beings resulted. They were an abomination. They did not procreate according to the manner prescribed by YHWH. The Scriptures record that everything is to reproduce according to its kind.[66] This was a law of creation. YHWH provides very specific rules for procreation in order to avoid genetic corruption. This is why He emphasized time and again the severe curses associated with incest and crossing species boundaries.[67]

The Nephilim and their offspring were not inserted into Creation by YHWH. Their presence was an aberration and disrupted the order of creation. They were not made in the image of Elohim, and their very presence and existence defiled creation and defied the laws of reproduction established in the beginning. Since mankind was made in the image of YHWH, the blueprint of this "image" was found in his DNA. The Nephilim offspring had corrupted DNA, therefore, they needed to be removed from creation.

This is often the reason why we read about YHWH instructing His people to completely destroy certain people groups in the Covenant Land – their DNA was corrupted. If you desire to dwell with YHWH, you must reproduce according to His express design and instruction. You must also exist in His image.

There is no doubt that prior to the flood those who dwelled upon the earth were in a fallen state. The very reason why mankind was corrupted was because of the sexual corruption in the Garden. Make no mistake about it, the incident involving "eating from the tree of the knowledge of good and evil" was a sexual event. The nachash was

attempting to defile mankind and destroy his standing and position in the Kingdom.

Once expelled from the Garden, men were no longer dwelling in the House of Elohim, and their actions reflected that fact. The hope was to get mankind reunited and restored, but men could no longer be classified with the sons of Elohim. While Adam was originally created in the image of Elohim, after the fall men were born in the image of Adam.[68]

Again, the sons of Elohim were messengers often described as angels. They were "sons of Elohim" because they were originally part of the Kingdom of Elohim. Once they defied Elohim, they were then called fallen messengers or fallen stars, because they came down from the heavens to the earth. They are referred to as "Watchers" in some texts, and they were breeding with the "daughters of men" or rather "the daughters of the man" (ᛉᐊᚴᔕ ᙭ᎩᎩᎠ-᙭ᛮ).[69]

Notice the Aleph Taw (᙭ᛮ) affixed to the word translated as "daughters" (᙭ᎩᎩᎠ) in Beresheet 6:2. There is a great mystery in this text seen only in the Hebrew. In order to be in the image of Elohim, your DNA must contain the Aleph Taw (᙭ᛮ). The Aleph Taw (᙭ᛮ) is essentially the "seal" or the "key" that unlocks the door, and provides entrance to the way back to the garden. The perfect order of creation found within the Aleph Taw (᙭ᛮ) was being polluted, down to the level of genetics.

In fact, it appears that there was corruption of the pure genetic coding within all of creation. This resulted in

not only a race of giants, but also other genetic aberrations sometimes called Chimera. (Beresheet 6:4). Archaeologists routinely discover giant remains throughout the earth, and they attempt to explain this "phenomenon" as related to some disease or defect, such as the pituitary gland.[70] Ancient relics and artifacts are commonly found depicting chimeras.

Archaeology also uncovers remains of other mythological creatures that do not necessarily fit within the modern evolutionary paradigm, although the ancients understood their origins.[71] The appearance of giants was not an isolated phenomenon, and as their numbers increased matters only got worse. The genetic tampering was not simply limited to man, but involved all species. It appears that the Watchers were bent on corrupting all of Creation, knowing full well that it would lead to annihilation.

We know that man was special over all of Creation. It is possible that there was incredible jealousy brewing amongst some of the Angelic beings that they sought to destroy man. Whatever their motive, through the nachash and the watchers, creation was corrupted to such an extent that YHWH was determined to destroy man and the corrupted creatures.

As was previously mentioned, man was likely highly advanced. Indeed there were specialties attached to certain individuals very early on after the creation account.[72] Adam, himself had been "plugged in" to the Creator while in the Garden. In fact, man was at his pinnacle in the Garden, and

has been in a state of decline ever since. That is diametrically opposed to the evolutionary model that portrays man on a path of ascension, rather than decline.

In the Book of 1 Enoch we read a description of how the corruption occurred.

"⁶:¹ And it came to pass when the children of men had multiplied that in those days were born unto them beautiful and comely daughters. ² And the angels, the children of the heaven, saw and lusted after them, and said to one another: Come, let us choose us wives from among the children of men ³ and beget us children. And Semjaza, who was their leader, said unto them: I fear ye will not ⁴ indeed agree to do this deed, and I alone shall have to pay the penalty of a great sin. And they all answered him and said: Let us all swear an oath, and all bind ourselves by mutual imprecations ⁵ not to abandon this plan but to do this thing. Then sware they all together and bound themselves ⁶ by mutual imprecations upon it. And they were in all two hundred; who descended in the days of Jared on the summit of Mount Hermon, and they called it Mount Hermon, because they had sworn ⁷ and bound themselves by mutual imprecations upon it. And these are the names of their leaders: Samlazaz, their leader, Araklba, Rameel, Kokablel, Tamlel, Ramlel, Danel, Ezeqeel, Baraqijal, ⁸ Asael, Armaros, Batarel, Ananel, Zaqıel, Samsapeel, Satarel, Turel, Jomjael, Sariel. These are their chiefs of tens. ⁷:¹ And all the others together with them took unto themselves wives, and each chose for himself one, and they began to go in unto them and to defile themselves with them, and they taught them charms [2] and enchantments, and the cutting of roots, and made them acquainted with plants. And they [3] became pregnant, and they bare great giants, whose height was three thousand ells: Who consumed [4] all the acquisitions of men. And when men could no longer sustain them, the giants turned against [5] them and devoured mankind. And they began to sin against birds, and beasts, and reptiles, and [6] fish, and to devour one another's flesh, and drink the blood. Then the earth laid accusation against the lawless ones. [8:1] And Azazel taught men to make swords, and knives, and shields, and breastplates, and made known to them the metals of the earth and the art of working them, and bracelets, and ornaments, and the use of antimony, and the beautifying of the eyelids, and all kinds of costly stones, and all [2] colouring tinctures. And there arose much godlessness, and they committed fornication, and they [3] were led astray, and became corrupt in all their ways. Semjaza taught enchantments, and root-cuttings, Armaros the resolving of enchantments, Baraqijal (taught) astrology, Kokabel the constellations, Ezeqeel the knowledge of the clouds, Araqiel the signs of the earth, Shamsiel the signs of the sun, and Sariel the course of the moon. And as men perished, they cried, and their cry went up to heaven . . ." Book of 1 Enoch, Chapters 6:1-8:3

Now 1 Enoch is one of what are considered to be 5

separate texts: 1) The Book of Watchers; 2) The Book of Luminaries; 3) The Dream Visions; 4) The Epistle of Enoch; and 5) The Parables of Enoch.

1 Enoch is considered to be the oldest of the 5 texts, although it is not considered to be "canonized" Scriptures. Nevertheless, pre-Maccabean fragments were found with the Dead Sea Scrolls. Clearly this text was considered to be a valuable resource by the ancients.[73] The New Testament Book of Jude quotes 1 Enoch 1:9, and 1 Enoch is referenced in 1 Peter 3:19-20 and 2 Peter 2:4-5. As a result, the text is valid and therefore it is helpful to examine this ancient text to enhance our understanding of the Scriptures.

In fact there is another ancient text known as the Book of Yasher that provides much detail concerning the mysterious man named Enoch. Primarily what we know from the Scriptures is that he was the father of Methuselah, he lived three hundred sixty five years *"And Enoch walked with Elohim; and he was not, for Elohim took him."* Beresheet 5:24 This is a mysterious event to many. Tradition holds that Enoch was born on the Appointed Time of Shabuot and also "taken up" on Shabuot.[74] That tradition will have more significance as we continue this discussion.

Now back to the text of 1 Enoch. Notice the mention of Azazel, considered to be one of the worst of the Watchers. This account actually provides insight into the mysterious ritual surrounding the Yom Kippur (Day of Atonement) ritual involving a goat sent into the wilderness for Azazel. (see Vayiqra 16)

Azazel was the ruler of a host of rebellious angels. He taught mankind how to make weapons and trained them in the art of war. Essentially, he taught men how to destroy themselves, and his goal was to destroy mankind. This was particularly egregious in the eyes of YHWH.

To Azazel is ascribed fault for teaching "all

wickedness on earth." He revealed the secrets of the world that were prepared in the heavens. (1 Enoch 9:6). It is believed that he and other "sons of Elohim" taught the conjuring of spells and interdimensional powers. Azazel is also found in fragments of the ancient text known as *The Book of Giants*.

As a result, Azazel was bound in chains and thrown into the Abyss along with his hosts. (1 Enoch 54:4) His fate was sealed. He would be cast into the lake of fire on the day of the great judgment, but not before he was released to wreak havoc one more time. (1 Enoch 10:4-9.) We will examine that event further on in the text.

The Book of 1 Enoch clearly describes how certain "knowledge" was transmitted to mankind that ultimately accelerated the corruption of living beings. This corruption included the mixing and likely manipulation of genes.

We know from ancient accounts, mythology and even archaeology that giants and great beasts dwelled upon the earth. These were genetic mutations, monsters and even gods to some. They wreaked havoc upon the earth. We read that "the whole earth was filled with blood and wickedness" and "the souls that died cry and lament to the gates of heaven." (1 Enoch 9:9 and 10). These gates were the entry points to heaven. These were the gates that the Nephilim used to ascend to the earth, and now the souls of those killed were crying to those gates." They were likely pleading that those gates be closed.

In the surviving fragments of the ancient historian Berossus, we read a description of the Cosmogony and Causes of the Deluge. In his account he writes of an amphibious being named Oannes. This seems to be where the Dagon traditions derived. This Oannes is described, according to the account of Apollodorus, as a creature that came out of the Erythraean sea. "The whole body of the

being was like that of a fish; and had under a fish's head another head, and also feet below, similar to those of a man, subjoined to the fish's tail."

"This Being in the day-time used to converse with men; but took no food at that season; and he gave them an insight into letters and sciences, and every kind of art. He taught them to construct houses, to found temples, to compile laws, and explained to them the principles of geometrical knowledge. He made them distinguish the seeds of the earth, and showed them how to collect fruits; in short, he instructed them in every thing which could tend to soften manners and humanize mankind. From that time, so universal were his instructions, nothing has been added material by way of improvement. When the sun set, it was the custom of this Being to plunge again into the sea, and abide all night in the deep; for he was amphibious." After Oannes, there appeared other beings like him.

Here is a description of the beings that inhabited the planet before the flood according to this Oannes.

"There was a time in which there was nothing but darkness and an abyss of waters, wherein resided most hideous beings, which were produced of a twofold principle. Men appeared with two wings, some with four and with two faces. They had one body but two heads; the one of a man, the other of a woman. They were likewise in their several organs both male and female. Other human figures were to be seen with the legs and horns of goats.

Some had horses' feet; others had the limbs of a horse behind, but before were fashioned like men, resembling hippocentaurs. Bulls likewise bred there with the heads of men; and dogs with fourfold bodies, and the tails of

fishes. Also horses with the heads of dogs: men too and other animals, with the heads and bodies of horses and the tails of fishes. In short, there were creatures with the limbs of every species of animals.

Add to these fishes, reptiles, serpents, with other wonderful animals, which assumed each other's shape and countenance. Of all these were preserved delineations in the temple of Belus at Babylon."

Obviously, we cautiously read this historical account provided by a hybrid creature, but it does confirm how corrupted things had become within creation. In fact, the Book of Yasher details the mixing of species by men. " . . . and the sons of men in those days took from the cattle of the earth, the beasts of the field and the fowls of the air, and taught the mixture of animals of one species with the other, in order therewith to provoke YHWH; and Elohim saw the whole earth and it was corrupt, for all flesh had corrupted its ways upon earth, all men and all animals." Yasher 4:18 This is also confirmed in Jubilees 5:2-3.

According to the Book of 1 Enoch, the Watchers who defiled themselves with women were bound up and imprisoned. "[11] And YHWH said unto Michael: Go, bind Semjaza and his associates who have united themselves with women so as to have defiled themselves [12] with them in all their uncleanness. And when their sons have slain one another, and they have seen the destruction of their beloved ones, bind them fast for seventy generations in the valleys of the earth, till the day of their judgment and of their consummation, till the judgment that is [13] forever and ever is consummated. In those days they shall be led off to the abyss of fire: and [14] to the torment and the prison in which they shall be confined forever. . . ." 1 Enoch 10:11-14

I Enoch and the Book of Jubilees agree with the Scriptures, which show that a portion of the fallen angels are currently restrained. The Book of Jubilees is another text, like I Enoch, which is not "canonized" because it clearly has errors, but it can provide some history, or at least an understanding of what people thought was history. Both I Enoch and Jubilees were found with the Dead Sea Scrolls.

The Scriptural text of Jude provides: "*And the angels who did not keep their own position, but left their proper dwelling, he has kept in eternal chains in deepest darkness for the judgment of the great Day.*" Jude 6. According to II Peter 2:4: "*For indeed Elohim did not spare the angels who sinned, but cast them down in chains of darkness into the low regions and delivered them to be kept for the judgment of torment.*" (*Magiera NT Peshitta translation*). The place they are kept in a spiritual prison is called "the Abyss." (see Luke 8:31)

There are still fallen angels who remain unrestrained and the Book of I Enoch explained what would happen to the offspring of the Nephilim. "[8] And now, the giants, who are produced from the spirits and flesh, shall be called evil spirits upon the earth, and on the earth shall be their dwelling. [9] Evil spirits have proceeded from their bodies; because they are born from **men**, and from the holy Watchers is their beginning and primal origin; they shall be evil spirits on earth, and evil spirits shall they be called. [10] As for the spirits of heaven, in heaven shall be their dwelling, but as for the spirits of the earth which were born upon the earth, on the earth shall be their dwelling. [11] And the spirits of the giants **afflict**, oppress, destroy, attack, do battle, and work destruction on the earth, and cause trouble: they take no food, but nevertheless hunger and thirst, and cause offences. And these spirits shall rise up against the children of men and against the women, because they have proceeded from them." I Enoch 15:8-11

The flood of Noah was a reset for creation. The corrupted beings were wiped out and the clean were protected and delivered through judgment. Tampering with the genetic coding of man, often called "transgenics" is a corruption of the blueprint of Creation. The crossing over of species barriers, and the blending of species, is an assault on the "image of YHWH." Man was made in the Image of YHWH. YHWH placed His Image in our genetic code. The image of YHWH is under attack today, just as it was in the days of Noah.

We know that in the present, there has been demonic genetic experimentation occurring throughout the world for decades. There are countless documented cases of "abductions" involving experiments of men, women and animals. These are not ETs or aliens performing these experiments. This is simply a ruse intended to deceive mankind. Entities such as the incubus and the succubus have been seducing men and women for centuries, collecting their bodily fluids like a vampire collecting blood. It may be that they actually need the DNA of man to rejuvenate their hybrid DNA that does not contain the image of Elohim.

Working in tandem with these dark forces, either wittingly or unwittingly, are numerous governmental agencies, pharmaceutical companies and private laboratories diligently working in the field of transhumanism. The goals are varied. Some governments are seeking to create a "super soldier" empowered by the genes of animals. Some companies are trying to dodge governmental regulations by experimenting on unclassified hybrid beings, instead of men, women or animals. Still others are seeking to rid the world of sickness and disease by helping "evolve" mankind into a higher species.

No matter what their expressed goal is, they are repeating the sins of the fallen sons of Elohim, and may actually be working with them. It is possible that the Nephilim offspring have been refined to the point that they look and act just like men and women. The only difference is their DNA. It is important to remember that the Scriptures specifically state that there were Nephilim before and after the flood. (Beresheet 6:4). The defilements and abominations resulting from the Nephilim before the flood are once again a reality in the laboratories of the world. The nightmarish experiments are resulting in the stuff of science fiction fantasy. These technologies are progressing at an incredible rate and the ultimate goal is the same now as it was then – to snuff out the image of Elohim from creation.

Amazingly, the serpent is using man to bring about his own destruction. The goal can clearly be seen from the logo of The Academy of Medical Sciences. While they may view their objective as bringing about healing, the ultimate result of transhumanism and human enhancement is destruction. As the DNA of man, animals and even insects and plants are being spliced and mixed, we are seeing a repeat of the Days of Noah.

While there are countless "sightings" of creatures and supposed alien beings throughout the world, it is quite evident that these phenomena are the result of the tinkering of men and angelic beings. While the Nephilim and their offspring may very well be operating with sophisticated technology on and off the planet, they are not evidence of living beings evolved on other planets in outer space. They are more from another dimension than they are from another galaxy.

Therefore, in the future, if you hear about sentient beings, posing as aliens, and appearing on Earth to enlighten mankind you can be certain that it is simply a new face on an

old deception. They are a corruption and a disruption to the order of creation. Mankind was not created by these "aliens." Rather, it is these aliens that have been trying to destroy mankind.

It is important to understand that these mutations are not "all Gods creatures" as many purport. Just because something appears or exists on this planet, does not mean that it was intended by Elohim to exist. These hybrid beings even defy the entire notion of evolution, where life improves through supposed "natural selection." There is nothing "natural" about human enhancement. It is purposeful manipulation and it is expressly forbidden by Elohim.

The Scriptures clearly affirm that man was made in the Image of YHWH – period. Yahushua[75] the Messiah affirmed that when He came in the flesh of a man. So what we are seeing with the rise in alien sightings, and a likely future alien visitation, is a resurgence of the corruption seen in the days of Noah. This was foretold by Yahushua, and it was something we were to look for as a sign of His return.

*"As it was in the **days of Noah**,*
so it will also be in the days of the Son of Man."
Luke 17:26, Matthew 24:37

One clear similarity is the fact that judgment is coming and people are not expecting it. Another similarity will be the condition of the planet. Here is a description of Creation during the days of Noah. *"So Elohim looked upon the earth, and indeed it was corrupt; for all flesh had corrupted their way on the earth."* Beresheet 6:12. The earth was corrupt, and the flesh was corrupt. The root for the word "corrupt" used twice in this passage is "shachat" (ΧᴴW) which means: "ruin" or "pit" as in Sheol.[76]

Since the message of YHWH was imbedded within

the very blood and genetic makeup of man, the cross breeding and resulting abominations were a direct affront to YHWH. It essentially involved breeding the image of YHWH out of His creation. It was an all out assault by the serpent to complete what began in the garden and beyond. These two kingdoms were in conflict and man was on the losing end. In fact, things were nearing extinction when YHWH finally intervened. YHWH actually caused an Extinction Level Event (ELE) that saved mankind and destroyed the serpent's line.

Thankfully, not everything had been corrupted, and YHWH provided a means for deliverance just in time. There was still an unblemished bloodline in Noah. While some of the pre-flood myths indicate that there was cross breeding throughout creation, including the animals, there were also pure bloodlines in certain species of animals.[77]

We previously read that Noah found "grace" in the eyes of YHWH. The Hebrew word translated as "grace" is "hen" (𐤉𐤇) which means: "favor or kindness." Interestingly, from the ancient language we see the "het" (𐤇) that looks like a fence. One cannot ignore the fact that it resembles an untwisted strand of DNA. In fact, in one of the oldest archaeological renderings of the letter "het" (𐤇), a 19th Century BCE proto-Canaanite inscription from Wadi-el-Hol, we can actually see the "het" as a three dimensional double helix.

The "nun" (𐤍), which represents "life," looks exactly like a sperm cell in the most ancient script (𐤍). We can plainly see that the ancient Hebrew language is crying out from the past, and providing us with incredible information. From the language we can discern that Noah was genetically pure. His "seed" was "protected" and untainted. In fact, Noah was

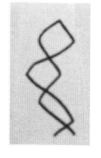

described as "*a just man, perfect in his generations. Noah walked with Elohim.*" Beresheet 6:9

Noah walked with Elohim, which means he obeyed the commandments. The word for "just" in Hebrew is "tsedeek" (ꟼ𐤆◁𐤍) which means: "righteous." The word for "perfect" in Hebrew is "tamayim" (ᱼ𐤆ᱼ𐤗) which actually means: "without spot or undefiled." This is the same word used to describe the Passover Lamb as well as other sacrifices made before YHWH.[78]

He was still a man, tarnished by the sin of the Garden, but his blood was undefiled. That is one of the reasons why we were provided with his geneology, so that we could follow his bloodline and insure that it was undefiled by the Nephilim.[79]

Because of his undefiled condition, Noah was chosen by YHWH to enter into a Covenant relationship with Him. Noah was told about the Covenant as follows. "*[17] I am going to bring floodwaters on the earth to destroy all life under the heavens, every creature that has the breath of life in it. Everything on earth will perish. [18] But I will establish ✕𐤊 My Covenant with you, and you will enter the Ark - you and your sons and your wife and your sons' wives with you. [19] You are to bring into the ark two of all living creatures, male and female, to keep them alive with you. [20] Two of every kind of bird, of every kind of animal and of every kind of creature that moves along the ground will come to you to be kept alive. [21] You are to take every kind of food that is to be eaten and store it away as food for you and for them. [22] Noah did everything just as Elohim commanded him. 7:11 Then YHWH said to Noah, Come into the ark, you and all your household, because I have seen that you are righteous before Me in this generation. [2] You shall take with you seven each of every clean animal, a male and his female; two each of animals that are unclean, a male and his female; [3] also seven each of birds of the air, male and female, to keep the species alive on the face of all the earth. [4] For after seven more*

days I will cause it to rain on the earth forty days and forty nights, and I will destroy from the face of the earth all living things that I have made. ⁵ *And Noah did according to all that YHWH commanded him.*" Beresheet 6:17-7:5

Elohim informed Noah that He was going to wipe out life on the planet, but would "establish" His Covenant with Noah. The word "establish" derives from the Hebrew word "quwm" (**ᗰ ᕀ**), which means "to stand" or "raise up." In the Hebrew text we see that the Aleph Taw (**ᐅᐊ**) is an integral element of "establishing" the Covenant that specifically belonged to YHWH. He chose Noah to enter into His Covenant relationship.

As a result, Noah would be saved along with his family and some select creatures. The rest of existence would be destroyed and certain species became extinct, as can be seen from the fossil record. Only those beings on the Ark would survive, and it is important to recognize that there was a distinction between "clean" (**ᗰᕁᖻᗰ⊗**) animals and "unclean" (**ᗰᕁᖻᗰ⊗ ᐊ𝘭**) animals.

The English translation is not very clear as to exactly how many clean animals were brought aboard. It could read 7 animals or seven pairs of animals. The Hebrew provides more clarity as we read: "seven (**ᗰ⊙𝟓ᗯ**) seven (**ᗰ⊙𝟓ᗯ**) male and female." So it would seem seven males and seven females of every clean animal.

It is important to understand that there is, and always was, a distinction between clean and unclean, righteousness and sin. We currently find those distinctions written as instructions within the Torah, but they were always present in creation. Clearly, Noah knew those distinctions, and we already discussed that he was literally described as "righteous" and "clean." The instructions of YHWH were no doubt handed down by Adam, although by this time only Noah and his family were actually following them. The

Scriptures define "unclean" and those animals are not to be confused with the Nephilim offspring, which were an "abomination."

Again, this entire flood event was about cleansing the planet of the abominations. YHWH was making a distinction between the pure line of Noah, along with the pure animals, as opposed to the abominations on the earth. In fact, when we read all the subsequent genealogies in the Scriptures, they are also there to insure the pure genetic line, undefiled from Nephilim influence.

YHWH was protecting mankind. He was still intent on building His Kingdom through His Image. He would protect the 8 who walked with Him while at the same time judging the rest of the planet. Of course, it is no coincidence that the Hebrew letter "het" (ﬣ) has the numerical equivalent of 8. Recall how the "het" (ﬣ) is connected with the DNA and the blood. These 8 "pure" individuals would be used to establish the Covenant that would be the framework for restoring the Kingdom of Elohim on earth.

After YHWH gave the promise, there came a time when He commanded Noah to actually build the Ark. So YHWH gave Noah a promise coupled with a task. Noah had to build the Ark, store all of the food for the occupants and make all of the necessary preparations for their "voyage."

If Noah did not continue to obey YHWH by building the Ark, he would have been killed along with the rest of creation. Instead, Noah believed the promise, and his actions were consistent with his belief. Because of the obedience of Noah we see the continuation of man and animals. Noah was, in essence, like Adam. He was the father of all of mankind, and because of his obedience man would continue their physical existence.

Regardless of how you perceive Noah and the flood, there is no way around the fact that it was his conduct – his obedience – that set him apart. Because of his walk, he found favor in the eyes of YHWH, and he and his family would be spared from the flood. Noah was not an arbitrary choice, he was chosen because of his walk. He was chosen to build an Ark – a vessel that would save a portion of creation. This is important to remember as we examine a future planetary judgment at the end of the age.

According to the Dead Sea Scrolls, Noah was told by a messenger that the flood would occur after a certain number of Shemitah cycles. Most people are unfamiliar with the concept of Shemitah cycles, but it is a most important pattern established on the first week of creation – the pattern of sevens. In the case of the Shemitah cycle, it is a pattern of seven years.

Every seventh year in the count is a Shemitah year which, essentially is a Sabbath year – a year of rest. These Shemitah years are then counted seven times and after the seventh Shemitah year is a Jubilee year. This is how the Creator gauges time, and it is this calculation of time that is imbedded within the Covenant relationship with YHWH.

Therefore, every Jubilee cycle contains seven Shemitah Cycles each consisting of seven years. The seven Shemitah cycles, totaling 49 years, are followed by one Jubilee Year. These 50 years form a Jubilee cycle. You might be wondering why this is important when talking about the story of the flood. The reason why it is mentioned here is because, according to the Dead Sea Scrolls 1 QapGen Col. 6, the flood was to occur in the year that followed a Shemitah cycle.[80]

This would have either been Year 1 of a new Shemitah cycle or a Jubilee Year. In fact, it is very likely that it was the eighth year in Jubilee Cycle 34. Since it is known that the flood began on Day 17 of Month 2 and the year has been determined to be 2,328 BCE.[81] The point is that YHWH had

Noah counting Shemitah cycles. The importance of the Shemitah count is extremely significant when examining time and creation.[82]

In fact, through this system of reckoning time it was actually revealed how much time man would be given on Earth. The Scriptures record that when YHWH saw the condition of things He declared: *"My Spirit shall not strive with man forever, for he is indeed flesh; yet his days shall be one hundred and twenty (120) years."* Beresheet 6:3

Many believe that YHWH was giving a limit to the number of years that individual men would be allowed to live, but that is clearly not the context nor is it true since men were recorded as living far longer than 120 years after that declaration. YHWH was speaking of mankind and indicated that He was not going to allow their existence to continue indefinitely.

Clearly men were rebellious, and YHWH was not going to contend with them forever. He was establishing a limit, and it would be within that period of time He would gather His chosen into His Kingdom through His Covenant. The 120 "years" that YHWH was referring to are actually 120 "cycles" – more specifically – Jubilee Cycles. Since a Jubilee Cycle is 50 years we can discern that YHWH was giving mankind 6,000 years. So this beginning that we read about in Beresheet was placed within a finite universe, and it was given an expiration date.

This pattern was, of course, established during the first week of creation. As a result, many understand that YHWH would allow men 6,000 years until He would establish His Sabbath reign – the millennial Kingdom. For the time being, He was going to allow them to continue, but He would start over with a righteous man and his seed.

The Scriptures record that: *"Noah did everything just as Elohim commanded him."* Beresheet 6:22 As a result, the Ark

was ready to deliver him and his family when the flood waters came. The floodwaters did indeed come and they wiped out all of the Nephilim, men, animals and mutant beings left on the planet. This raises an interesting question concerning the Nephilim because the Scriptures specifically state: "*There were Nephilim on the earth in those days, and also afterward.*" Beresheet 6:4

The question is: If the flood destroyed all of the Nephilim, how did they exist "afterward?" Indeed, the Scriptures identify the Nephilim living in the Land of Canaan after the Exodus from Egypt.

Clearly we can only speculate on this point. While some believe that a daughter-in-law of Noah carried Nephilim genes, the Ark was only for those who were pure. It is unlikely that YHWH would provide protection for the very thing He was judging and cleansing from the planet. That would make the flood a futile act.

The solution could be as simple as fallen "sons of Elohim" descending after the flood and repeating what they had done previously. There is actually another seemingly incredible possibility that could explain many other ancient mysteries. There are numerous ancient writings that indicate the existence of flying machines – spaceships if you will. These are often referred to as Vimanas and descriptions of these craft can be found in Sanskrit writings such as the Mahabharata, Ramayana and the Vedas.

Clearly mankind was given incredible knowledge by the fallen angels. Knowing there was an impending judgment for their actions, it is plausible that the Nephilim offspring developed an escape plan. This might explain how the Nephilim offspring could escape the judgment of the flood and appear afterward. It could also explain the various myths associated with gods flying through the air, habitating other planets as well as their ascending and descending to and from

the heavens.

Now this is pure speculation, but it could account for many confusing historical accounts and even provide a plausible explanation for the UFO and alien abduction phenomena. If this connection exists, we can see the stage being set for events in the future when supposed extraterrestrials appear and deceive much of mankind. Again, this is purely speculative. It is also possible that all of the Nephilim offspring were wiped out by the flood and fallen angels merely repeated their abominations after the flood.

For now it is important to remember the purpose of the planetary flood. It revolved around the fallen sons of Elohim and the corruption they wrought upon the planet earth. Currently we are seeing a resurgence of this age-old assault on mankind. Science has leapt into the arena of genetic experimentation that currently knows no bounds.

The genetic corruption spans from human cloning and "enhancement" to cross species hybridization. Modern medicine has turned into a drug mill, essentially filling people with chemical substances that only alleviate symptoms, but do not cure anything. It is "Pharmacia," not medicine. The medical profession is pumping toxic vaccines upon populations that are veritable witches brews, filled with chemicals, animal tissue and even tissue from aborted children. This is nothing short of witchcraft and it is killing the population through the blood and the DNA.

Valdamar Valerian, Ida Honoroff, Eustace Mullins, and other s have exposed the fact that vaccinations lead to the very diseases they are meant to prevent and have cost the world millions of deaths. W.B. Clark wrote in the New York Press in 1909: "Cancer was practically unknown until the cowpox vaccination began to be introduced . . . I have seen 200 cases of cancer, and I never saw a case of cancer in an unvaccinated person . . ."[83]

In fact, much of the food that people eat is poison. Major corporations are creating Genetically Modified Organisms (GMO's) through engineered seeds with "termination genes" and poison resistance. They are toxic seeds of death and with all of this tampering, much of which is unknown to the general public, we should expect to see a repeat of how things were during Noah's time as the Shemitah clock counts down to judgment.

When the floodwaters receded, it was time for a new beginning. Interestingly, YHWH protected those in the Ark, and He also replanted plants and trees. In fact, the olive tree was the first tree mentioned in this renewed creation. As a result, the Olive Tree actually represents the "firsts" or "beginnings" (resheet) of YHWH. When Noah exited the Ark, we read that he and his sons entered into a Covenant with YHWH. Blood was shed as Noah, acting as a mediator for all of mankind, made an altar and made sacrifice unto YHWH.

"*8 Then Elohim spoke to Noah and to his sons with him, saying: 9 And as for Me, behold, I establish My Covenant with you and with your descendants after you, 10 and with every living creature that is with you: the birds, the cattle, and every beast of the earth with you, of all that go out of the ark, every beast of the earth. 11 Thus I establish My Covenant with you: Never again shall all flesh be cut off by the waters of the flood; never again shall there be a flood to destroy the earth. 12 And Elohim said: This is the sign of the Covenant which I make between Me and you, and every living creature that is with you, for perpetual generations: 13 I set My rainbow in the cloud, and it shall be for the sign of the Covenant between Me and the earth. 14 It shall be, when I bring a cloud over the earth, that the rainbow shall be seen in the cloud; 15 and I will remember My Covenant which is between Me and you and every living creature of all flesh; the waters shall never again become a flood to destroy all flesh. 16 The*

*rainbow shall be in the cloud, and I will look on it to remember the
everlasting Covenant between Elohim and every living creature of
all flesh that is on the earth. ¹⁷ And Elohim said to Noah, This is
the sign of the Covenant which I have established between Me and
all flesh that is on the earth.*" Beresheet 9:8-17.

Notice that YHWH repeatedly refers to the
Covenant as "My Covenant." In other words, it belongs to
Him and no one else. This Covenant is an everlasting
Covenant. The word "everlasting" is "olam" (𐤏𐤋𐤅𐤌) in
Hebrew and actually refers to something hidden or
concealed. It is generally understood to mean "through the
ages." It went beyond the life of Noah, or his immediate
descendants for that matter. YHWH promised that He
would never again cut off all flesh by a flood, and never again
would He use a flood to destroy the whole earth.

There was no corresponding duty or obligation
required from man or the animals. The Covenant was a
promise accompanied by a sign – the bow. So the ultimate
blessing associated with this Covenant was unconditional.
There was no further obligation from mankind. Noah had
done the work to get them to the point of the Covenant. He
had paid the price, and now the rest of mankind and creation
would reap the reward – the sakar. We see the pattern of a
"clean" and "righteous" man working in collaboration with
YHWH to save mankind. Their work would benefit others
who would follow in the Covenant.

The fact that there was a sign attached to the
Covenant is significant. Remember that the Hebrew word for
sign is "owt" (𐤀𐤅𐤕). It can mean a "mark" or a "token" and
is intended to be a visible sign or reminder of the Covenant,
just like the sun, the moon and the stars were meant for
signs. We shall see that YHWH attaches these marks or
signs to His Covenants. In the case of the Covenant with
Noah and all creation, we see the bow as the sign of that

particular Covenant. It was a sign placed in the sky visible to all creation.

The word for bow in Hebrew is "qesheth" (✗ W ⴼ).

One cannot help but see the relationship between the first sliver of a renewed moon, which marks the beginning of a month, and the rainbow, which is also a sliver of light. Instead of a new month, YHWH was revealing a new age.[84]

It is interesting that the light of the qesheth consists of seven colors. These seven colors correlate to the seven ages, or days, in the weekly plan of YHWH. They also correlate to the seven Spirits described by the Prophet Isaiah (Yeshayahu)[85] which are represented in the menorah. The seven colors of the rainbow correlate to the Throne of YHWH.[86] This sign was likely a reminder that the Throne of YHWH would someday appear in the heavens and descend upon the earth after another future judgment.

While we continue to see floods on the earth, we have never seen the entire planet judged by water since the time of Noah – a promise kept. The earth is full of sin that cries out for judgment. This cry is heard in the Throne Room of YHWH that is colored by the sign of the promise as a continual reminder. As a result, YHWH remembers His Covenant and keeps His promise by not judging the earth by a flood.

There is a pattern established here. As YHWH makes Covenant with His creation, He uses a man as the mediator. In this instance, Noah represented mankind and creation. Part of this Covenant process also involved the shedding of blood.

The Scriptures record: *"20 Noah built an altar to YHWH, and took of every clean animal and of every clean bird, and offered burnt offerings on the altar.* [21] *And smelled YHWH* ✗𐤊 *a soothing aroma. Then YHWH said in His heart, 'I will never again curse* ✗𐤊 *the ground for man's sake, although the imagination of man's heart is evil from his youth; nor will I again destroy* ✗𐤊 *every living thing as I have done.'"* Beresheet 8:20-21.

Noah had already been saved, but the future promise was sealed by the shedding of the blood. So the Covenant with Noah was essentially two fold. First, Noah had to obey and act in faith in order to be in a place where he and his family, along with the animals, could be saved. Second, YHWH promised that He would never again destroy the planet by a flood.

This was an everlasting Covenant made for all of mankind as Elohim had done with Adam, except that this Covenant was unconditional. It is a unilateral Covenant made between YHWH and mankind. Only YHWH has to keep the Covenant, and He gave a continuing sign of this Covenant for all future generations to see.

Man could not save himself from judgment, and the only way to life was through obedience. Ultimately, it was YHWH Who provided the salvation. To emphasize this point, there are three instances of the un-translated Aleph Taw (✗𐤊) in Beresheet 8:21 when the burnt offerings were being made to YHWH. There are also three instances of the Aleph Taw (✗𐤊) when YHWH declares that He will make a Covenant. (Beresheet 9:9-10). So we can see that the Aleph Taw (✗𐤊) would be at the center of the salvation and restoration of Creation through a Covenant with YHWH.

The reason why we emphasized the days of Noah is because something was destined to repeat through time. Some day in the future the planet would once again become corrupted as it was in the days of Noah. That corruption would lead to judgment and it would be a sign of the coming of the Messiah – the Aleph Taw (✗𐤊). Therefore it is

important to understand the conditions of those days and how mankind later proceeded to rebel at a place known as Babylon.

3

Babylon

The Scriptures provide us with an account of the descendants of Noah as follows:

"*¹ Now this is the genealogy of the sons of Noah: Shem, Ham, and Japheth. And sons were born to them after the flood. ² The sons of Japheth were Gomer, Magog, Madai, Javan, Tubal, Meshech, and Tiras. ³ The sons of Gomer were Ashkenaz, Riphath, and Togarmah. ⁴ The sons of Javan were Elishah, Tarshish, Kittim, and Dodanim. ⁵ From these the coastland peoples of the Gentiles were separated into their lands, everyone according to his language, according to their families, into their nations. ⁶ The sons of Ham were Cush, Mizraim, Put, and Canaan. ⁷ The sons of Cush were Seba, Havilah, Sabtah, Raamah, and Sabtechah; and the sons of Raamah were Sheba and Dedan.*" Beresheet 10:1-7

Shem, Ham and Cush were all born prior to the flood and lived through the flood. They all had wives and apparently had children afterward. They saw the corruption that had previously existed and lived through the judgment. One would expect that they would teach this lesson to their children and guide them in the ways of YHWH as they began to establish homes and communities.

Although it seemed that things might return back to they way they were intended to be, the corruption of the planet continued after Noah's sons had children. There is an account of Noah becoming intoxicated, a vile act being perpetrated upn him by Canaan, the son of Ham. Some traditions describe it as a sexual act while others describe Canaan as actually castrating Noah. If we see Noah in the role of Adam, clearly the assault was on to destroy the seed of Adam by going straight to the source. Noah ended up cursing Canaan, the youngest son of Ham, for his actions. Canaan was the namesake for the land that would ultimately become filled with giants, and be promised to the descendants of a man named Abraham. (Beresheet 9:21-25)

The Scriptures do not specify where all of the descendants of Noah settled, but we can discern much simply by looking at the names of various regions. We also have extra-Scriptural information. From those sources we can discern that: "Cush lived in the 'land of Shinar,' which most scholars consider to be Sumer. There they developed the first civilization after the Flood. The sons of Shem - the Semites - were also mixed, to some extent, with the Sumerians. We suggest that Sumerian Kish, the first city established in Mesopotamia after the Flood, took its name from the man known in the Bible as Cush. The first kingdom established after the Flood was Kish, and the name 'Kish' appears often on clay tablets. The early post-Flood Sumerian king lists (not found in the Bible) say that 'kingship descended from heaven to Kish' after the Flood. (The Hebrew name 'Cush' was much later moved to present-day Ethiopia as migrations took place from Mesopotamia to other places.)"[87]

The origin of the word "shinar" is very intriguing. For instance some believe that it is a Semitic word deriving from "shene nahar" thus meaning: "two rivers." Still others believe that "shinar" must come from the Hebrew "shene," meaning "repeat," and "naar," meaning "childhood." "Shinar," therefore, must mean "land of the Regenerator."[88] Both of these make sense when we consider that it was located between the Tigris and the Euphrates River, and when we

consider what was going on there.

This would be the location where the Nephilim would attempt to "regenerate" the serpent kingdom that began in the Garden. It was even located near the original location of Eden.

So Cush, a son of Ham, settled in Sumer with his sons Seba, Havilah, Sabtah, Raamah and Sabtechah. After reading about the second generation from Noah the Scriptures provide the following:

"*⁸ Cush begot Nimrod; he began to be a mighty one on the earth. ⁹ He was a mighty hunter before YHWH; therefore it is said, 'Like Nimrod the mighty hunter before YHWH.' ¹⁰ And the beginning of his kingdom was Babel, Erech, Accad, and Calneh, in the land of Shinar. ¹¹ From that land he went to Assyria and built* ✗✦-*Nineveh,* ✗✦-*Rehoboth Ir,* ✗✦-*Calah,* ¹² *and* ✗✦-*Resen between Nineveh and Calah (that is the principal city).*" Beresheet 10:8-12

This passage should give the reader pause. Where did this Nimrod come from? We just read that "*the sons of Cush were Seba, Havilah, Sabtah, Raamah and Sabtechah.*" If Nimrod was a son of Cush, why was he not listed in the geneology above? Instead of being called a "son" like the others, we read that Cush "begot" Nimrod. We also read who Mizraim "begot" and who Canaan "begot," but nothing is mentioned regarding Ham's son Put. It is possible that Cush was not a direct son of Cush, but rather removed by various degrees.

So the line of Ham has certain mysteries associated with it. For the purposes of this discussion we will focus on Nimrod. Some speculate that this was not so much a name as it was a derogatory label that means: "we will rebel" or "he who made all the people rebellious against Elohim."[89]

There is some confusion regarding this individual because of ambiguous origins and translations. For instance, why did he "begin to be" a mighty one. The word translated as "began" is "halel" (𐤋𐤋𐤄) in Hebrew. It means: "to pierce, to bore, to wound, defile." The word translated as "be" is "hayah" (𐤄𐤉𐤄) in Hebrew, which means: "to exist or become." So Nimrod was a defiled existence, or he came into existence by piercing or wounding.

This becomes even more intriguing when we examine the Scriptures that further describe him as *"a mighty hunter before YHWH."* This is a somewhat ambiguous term more specifically described as *"a mighty hunter in the face of YHWH."* There is an element of provocation and defiance associated with this individual.

"Nimrod was mighty in hunting, and that in opposition to YHWH; not 'before YHWH' in the sense of according to the will and purpose of YHWH, still less, . . . in a simply superlative sense . . . The name itself, 'Nimrod' from *marad,* 'we will revolt,' points to some violent resistance to God . . . Nimrod as a mighty hunter founded a powerful kingdom; and the founding of this kingdom is . . . to have been the consequence or result of his strength in hunting, so that hunting was intimately connected with the establishing of the kingdom. Hence, if the expression 'a mighty hunter' relates primarily to hunting in the literal sense, we must add to the literal meaning the figurative signification of a 'hunter of men' (a trapper of men by stratagem and force); Nimrod the hunter became a tyrant, a powerful hunter of men."[90]

So there was much more to this man than his ability to kill animals. He built an enormous kingdom spanning from Babylon to Assyria. Interestingly, these are two kingdoms that would play an important role throughout history. It should be noted in the text the Aleph Taw (𐤗𐤕) associated with four cities in Assyria.

Assyria actually has a particularly special role. We already saw it mentioned at the very beginning when it referenced the Rivers Hiddekel and Euphrates coming from the one river in Eden. (Beresheet 2:4). Assyria is actually "Asshur" (𐤀𐤔𐤅𐤓) in Hebrew and means: "successful." It was the land populated by the second son of Shem and was named after him – Asshur.

The life of Nimrod is focused on rebellion – rebellion against YHWH. The kingdom that he established is often referred to as Babylon. It is both a Kingdom and a City that, we shall see, are diametrically opposed to the Kingdom of YHWH and the City of Jerusalem. The kingdom of Babylon originated with the Sumerians, and the city came to be known as Babel. We do not know if there was a different name. The conflict between these two Kingdoms will become clear as we continue to follow the history of man.

Sadly, mankind did not learn the lesson of the flood. It did not take long for corruption to infiltrate civilization, and men eventually rebelled against YHWH. Men began to worship creation and developed a form of worship in Babylon commonly called "sun worship." This was at the center of the Tower of Babel incident.

Here is the account. "*¹ Now the whole earth had one language and one speech. ² And it came to pass, as they journeyed from the east, that they found a plain in the land of Shinar, and they dwelt there. ³ Then they said to one another, Come, let us make bricks and bake them thoroughly. They had brick for stone, and they had asphalt for mortar. ⁴ And they said, Come, let us build ourselves a city, and a tower whose top is in the heavens; let us make a name for ourselves, lest we be scattered abroad over the face of the whole earth. ⁵ But YHWH came down to see the city and the tower which the sons of men had built. ⁶ And YHWH said, Indeed the people are one and they all have one language, and this is what they begin to do; now nothing that they propose to do will be*

withheld from them. [7] *Come, let Us go down and there confuse their language, that they may not understand one another's speech.* [8] *So YHWH scattered them abroad from there over the face of all the earth, and they ceased building the city.* [9] *Therefore its name is called Babel, because there YHWH confused the language of all the earth; and from there YHWH scattered them abroad over the face of all the earth.*" Beresheet 11:1-9

Many have been taught that mankind was simply building a tall structure at Babylon. While we cannot know for certain, it seems clear that there was a revival of the previous corruption that had led to the flood. In fact, some sources indicate that the tower was intended to protect men from the anticipated consequences of their actions – i.e. another flood.

The historian Josephus, in *Antiquities* 1: iv: 2, describes the following: "Now it was Nimrod who excited them to such an affront and contempt of God. He was the grandson of Ham, the son of Noah - a bold man, and of great strength of hand. He persuaded them not to ascribe it to God, as if it were through his means they were happy, but to believe that it was their own courage which procured that happiness. He also gradually changed the government into tyranny - seeing no other way of turning men from the fear of God, but to bring them into a constant dependence upon his own power. He also said he would be revenged on God, if he should have a mind to drown the world again; for that he would build a tower too high for the waters to be able to reach, and that he would avenge himself on God for destroying their forefathers."

Interestingly, "babel" can literally mean: "gate of El" or "gate of the gods."[91] It is believed that the inhabitants were attempting to ascend to the heavens using this as a sort of portal or star gate. We will later see such a gateway at a place called "Beit El" or rather "House of El." (Beresheet 28) The ancient historian Berossus in his writing *History of Babylonia* confirmed the Tower of Babel event, and indicated that the inhabitants of Babel were "glorying in their own strength and size, and despising the gods, undertook to raise a tower whose top should reach the sky." This sounds as though they were giants.

A clue to what was actually happening at Babel can be found in the repeated phrase concerning Nimrod as "mighty" which is "gibor" (ﬡﬤﬠ) in Hebrew. The word is used three times to describe Nimrod, and it is the same word used to describe the hybrid giant beings that existed prior to the flood. This is when it is important to recall the phrase: "*there were Nephilim on the earth in those days, and also afterward.*" (Beresheet 6:4). These beings existed before the flood and afterward.

So there was something unique about Nimrod, and likely the inhabitants of Babel. We already saw the strange language concerning how Nimrod came into existence. In fact there is a powerful message associated with Nimrod in the text where it describes him as the begotten of Cush. In the text we read "et-nimrod" (ﬡﬤﬥﬧ-﬩ﬨ). (Beresheet 10:8).

The Aleph Taw (﬩ﬨ) was attached to his name, so not only was Nimrod against YHWH, it appears that he tried to function in place of YHWH as a type of false messiah – an anti-christ. The Messiah was to be the Second or Last Adam - the One Who would restore mankind and lead men back to the Garden. Here we see Nimrod as an anti-messiah, leading men away from YHWH.

It is significant to note that the gematria value of "Nimrod" is 294. Another word with this value is "Melchizedek." Melchizedek is the King of Jerusalem and the Priest of the Most High Elohim.[92] So Nimrod stood in direct opposition to YHWH and His Priestly King. He could be described as an anti-messiah. He may have presented himself as a messiah to the people. He was a king and a priest, but not to the Most High Elohim.

Nimrod became a world leader who united mankind under one political, economic and religious system. While he portended to protect and save the people in his kingdom, he actually lead them away from YHWH toward death. To legitimize his position he actually took on the mantle of Adam as a high priest of mankind and his authority apparently derived from the very "coat of Adam." The covering placed upon Adam by Elohim after being expelled from the Garden.

There is tradition that: "These coats were handed down from father to son, and thus came into the possession of Noah, who took them with him into the Ark, whence they were stolen by Ham. The latter gave them to his son Cush, who in turn gave them to Nimrod, and when the animals saw the latter clad in them, they crouched before him so that he had no difficulty in catching them. The people, however, thought that these feats were due to his extraordinary strength, so that they made him their king."[93]

These coats would have actually been a symbol of the Covenant made with Adam on behalf of mankind. They were the literal covering, or rather blood atonement, that kept them alive, albeit outside of the Garden. If the legends are true, Nimrod would have used that skin as his symbol of authority. So he was cloaked with the coat of Adam, giving the illusion that he was the Messiah, the Second or Last Adam when, in fact, through his treachery, he made YHWH into the enemy of men. He was literally a wolf in sheep's clothing.[94] So here we see this Nephilim offspring assuming the role of Adam, building a kingdom in the former location of the Garden, attempting to restore the connection with the heavens.

There is scant information in the Scriptures about Nimrod, but plenty of tradition as we have already seen. Here are some more traditions concerning Nimrod included in the Jewish Encyclopedia. "In Rabbinical Literature: Nimrod is the prototype of a rebellious people, his name being interpreted as 'he who made all the people rebellious against [Elohim]' (Pes. 94b; comp. Targ. of pseudo-Jonathan and Targ. Yer. to Gen. x. 9). He is identified with Cush and with Amraphel, the name of the latter being interpreted as 'he whose words are dark' (אמר נפל; Gen. R. xlii. 5; for other explanations see below). As he was the first hunter he was consequently the first who introduced the eating of meat by man. He was also the first to make war on other peoples (Midr. Agadah to Gen. x. 9). Nimrod was not wicked in his youth. On the contrary, when a young man he used to sacrifice to [YHWH] the animals which he caught while hunting ('Sefer ha-Yashar,' section 'Noah,' pp. 9a et seq., Leghorn, 1870). His great success in hunting (comp. Gen. x. 9) was due to the fact that he wore the coats of skin which God made  for Adam and Eve (Gen. iii. 21). Nimrod is generally considered to have been the one who suggested building the Tower of Babel and who directed its construction. [Elohim] said: 'I made Nimrod great; but he built a tower in order that he might rebel against Me' (Hul. 89b). The tower is called by the Rabbis 'the house of Nimrod,' and is considered as a house of idolatry which the owners abandoned in time of

peace; consequently Jews may make use of it (Ab. Zarah 53b). After the builders of the tower were dispersed Nimrod remained in Shinar, where he reestablished his kingdom. According to the 'Sefer ha-Yashar' (*l.c.*), he at this time acquired the name 'Amraphel' in allusion to the fall of his princes (אמר נפל) during the dispersion. According to the Targum of pseudo-Jonathan (to Gen. x. 11), however, Nimrod had left Babylonia before the building of the tower, and had gone to Assyria, where he built four other cities, namely, Nineveh, Rehobot, Calah, and Resen (comp. Nahmanides *ad loc.*)."[95]

There are many scholars who believe that Nimrod was none other than Gilgamesh. In 1872 George Smith discovered what are referred to as the Gilgamesh Tablets. These were located in the Assyrian library of Asherbanipal located in the British Museum. The ancient text came to be known as the Epic of Gilgamesh. It was a sort of antithetical version of the Scriptures, a tradition woven with Sumerian mythology. Gilgamesh was described as the King of the City of Uruk. The text makes this vile treacherous man into a hero who defeats "Huwawa" – the one who sent the flood. One cannot ignore the similarity to the Name of YHWH, when pronounced as "Yahuwah."

If the connection between Gilgamesh and Nimrod is accurate, then Nimrod was likely a giant - a sort of demigod. In fact, some sources claim that Gilgamesh was two-thirds "god" and one-thirds "man."[96] This would certainly link him with the Nephilim. It also clearly reveals how Nimrod stood in defiance to YHWH.

Very interestingly, a team of archaeologists in Iraq recently claimed to have discovered the Tomb of Gilgamesh/Nimrod.[97] Imagine if the DNA of this ancient anti-christ were discovered and "revived."

According to a BBC article describing the discovery: "In the book - actually a set of inscribed clay tablets - Gilgamesh was described as having been buried under the Euphrates, in a tomb apparently constructed when the waters of the ancient river parted following his death. 'We found just outside the city an area in the middle of the former Euphrates river, the remains of such a building which  could be interpreted as a burial,' Mr. Fassbinder said. He said the amazing discovery of the ancient city under the Iraqi desert had been made possible by modern technology. 'By differences in magnetization in the soil, you can look into the ground,' Mr. Fassbinder added. 'The difference between mudbricks and sediments in the Euphrates river gives a very detailed structure.' This creates a magnetogram, which is then digitally mapped, effectively giving a town plan of Uruk. 'The most surprising thing was that we found structures already described by Gilgamesh,' Mr. Fassbinder stated. 'We covered more than 100 hectares. We have found garden structures and field structures as described in the epic, and we found Babylonian houses.' But he said the most astonishing find was an incredibly sophisticated system of canals. 'Very clearly, we can see in the canals some structures showing that flooding destroyed some houses, which means it was a highly developed system.'"[98]

This is certainly consistent with our earlier assertions that ancient civilizations were highly developed. Indeed, their understanding of astronomy was highly advanced. We see in Sumerian drawings a depiction of the sun at the center of the solar system surrounded by 10 planets. Modern astronomers did not discover Uranus until 1781, Neptune in 1846, and Pluto in 1930.

The 10th planet is believed by some to have been destroyed, and remaining as the asteroid belt between Mars and Jupiter. Others believe that this mysterious planet is Planet X, sometimes referred to as Nibiru. Notice the depiction of the hexagram representing the son. The Sumeriand worshiped the sun as a god. So the hexagram can represent the sun god.

We also know from other drawings that the Sumerians knew about the rings of Saturn. Modern astronomy did not "re-discover" the rings until 1659 by Christian Huygens.

In the sophisticated city of Uruk, a form of worship developed that was centered around this "god-man" and away from YHWH. It was directed towards the heavens and the celestial bodies from whence the "fallen stars" derived.

This was the origination of what is known as "sun worship." It involved the Nephilim beings, the fallen stars" and their progeny. This is why many confuse ancient mankind's interaction with these hybrid beings as alien contact. It is vital to distinguish so-called aliens from the Watchers who were spiritual, intra-dimensional beings, that crossed over into the physical realm and interacted with mankind.

Babylon was a system that directed worship away from YHWH toward the "fallen stars" and celestial bodies. As a result, we often see star patterns such as the hexagram and the pentagram associated with various pagan

practices The place where this all originated was called Babel, likely after the confusion of the languages to memorialize the event.

Man had gone from disobedience to outright rebellion. It was a government and political system that excluded YHWH, and was essentially in defiance to YHWH. Tradition indicates that Nimrod suggested building the Tower. That "tower" was not simply a tall building, it was a Temple of worship, often called a ziggurat. It was designed to be a path leading up to the heavens - a gate to the heavens. They were places where the heavens and the earth were connected. It was likely a pyramid shaped object, or a step pyramid, as archaeology reveals.

Deriving from this system we see the development of the trinity as the wife of Nimrod, Semiramis later became worshipped as the "Queen of Heaven."  Semiramis, also known as Ishtar and Easter, was said to have conceived a son, from the rays of the sun god during the spring fertility season. She later gave birth to a son named Tammuz on the winter solstice.[99] So you see that Easter and Christmas derived from Babylonian sun worship, and they are very important events in pagan religions that worship an antichrist.

Semiramis is often depicted with a cup and the rays of the sun emanating from her head. This should look familiar to anyone who has seen the Statue of Liberty in America, which is a replica of a pagan goddess. The sun rays emitting from the head are connected with other pagan goddesses such as Athena.

These Babylonian derived traditions continued after the division of the languages and the separation of the peoples. What originated at babel under a common language was spread across the planet in different languages using

different names. In modern society we are very much influenced by Babylon

Society continues to worship and be controlled by those same forces that flourished from Babylon. The same worship system that started there and continued through time is thriving today. Obviously the majority of the Christian religion celebrates Babylonian holy days. This occurred when the Roman Emperor Constantine, in a deft political maneuver, established the Christian religion as the official state religion of the Roman Empire.

Of course, Rome was a pagan culture so it was important not to disrupt the citizens of the Empire. Constantine established the Christian religion by merging the fresh movement involving the Yisraelite Messiah with Babylonian sun worship.

We can trace Babylonian derived sun worship all the way to our modern day societies. America stands out as one of the most extraordnary and mysterious of all. The reason why it is mysterious is because it is veiled. For instance, when you view the capital of the United States of America it was uniquely layed out as a Masonic city, and includes a variey of pagan symbols.

Among them you can actually see a pentagram inside

a pentagon, inside a pyramid. These occult symbols are set amidst and around the architecture, which is largely Greco-Roman. If you took away the cars and the technology you would think you were in an ancient pagan city. Among all of the various structures one cannot miss the

ancient pagan sexual symbols involving the phallus, and the womb.

All ancient sexual rites trace back from Babylon and ultimately to the Garden. The "nachash," also known as "the shining one" and "the serpent" rebelled against YHWH and was set to populate his own kingdom. He was described as *"the anointed cherub who covers."* (Ezekiel 28:14). He was permitted access to the Throne Room and Eden. He was perfect in wisdom and beauty until iniquity was found in him. He apparently persuaded many of the sons of Elohim and the angels to join with him. He likely instructed them on how to copulate with women since he was the first recorded being to have sexual relations with mankind.

Remember that the "daughters of Adam" suited the needs of the Nephilim. The Nephilim were "sons of Elohim," but they fell from their first estate. They left the family of Elohim and were intent on building their own family - their own race separate from mankind. The daughters of men had wombs that would incubate their seed and emit the master race of the fallen ones.

The nachash committed this act with the first woman – Hawah. He was the one that started this abominable practice that was repeated by the Nephilim. This hybrid race was meant to wipe out mankind, not simply to coexist. Indeed, if it were not for the flood, these diabolical beings would have succeeded. There were only 8 undefiled people left on the planet when Noah and his family were saved.

After the flood, the Nephilim changed their methods. A direct assault on mankind would meet with the same fate. Through Babylon, we see a system of religion incorporating mankind to accomplish the means of their own end. If mankind could be deceived into rebelling against YHWH, then YHWH would judge and destroy them. The Nephilim could then go about building their "family" and let YHWH

do the killing. Of course, this was exactly what Balaam did when he advised King Balak how to sabatoge the Yisraelites. (Bemidbar 31)

At the heart of Babylonian sun worship is sex, just as it was at the heart of the actions of the Nephilim. The ancient Babylonian myths involving Nimrod run deep. There is a tradition that Nimrod was killed by Shem, the son of Noah. His body was cut up into 14 pieces and distributed to the peoples of the region. Semaramis apparently collected all of the pieces save one – his genitals. Nimrod was thus reconstructed with all of his parts although the missing piece was replaced with what is now known as an obelisk. The obelisk represents the erect phallus of Nimrod collecting and emitting the rays of the sun. This was how Semaramis was allegedly impregnated.

Nimrod somehow "began to exist" as a mighty one. (Beresheet 10:8). If he were somehow a product of Nephilim manipulation, perhaps through his mother, that means when his body was killed, his spirit became disembodied. Of course, this was the destiny of all of the Nephilim offspring. Creation was made for man, and Sheol is a place for the souls of men. These disembodied spirits of the Nephilim offspring had no place to reside. This likely accounts for the various ghost sightings recorded through time. The Book of 1 Enoch calls them "evil spirits." (1 Enoch 15:8-11). Indeed, we shall see that the Nephilim offspring, the Rephaim, are referred to as "shadows" or "ghosts."

You see, it is important to understand that there is an order of the heavens. Just as we see governments and kingdoms on earth, there is also a "Divine Council" in the Heavens. The Scriptures do not provide a specific hierarchy, but there is much we can discern from the Scriptures and supporting texts. The peoples of the earth generally believed that the "gods" ruled from a mountain.

The Scriptures tell us that Elohim rules from a heavenly mountain – Mount Zion. He has a Throne Room guarded by Cherubim - four to be precise. There were also seraphim, and "elders" who sit upon thrones. How these beings are placed in an angelic hierarchy is subject to debate.

Popular Christian thought provides three orders of angelic beings as follows: 1) Seraphim, Cherubim, Thrones, 2) Dominations, Virtues, Powers; 3) Principalities, Archangels, Angels. This order was provided in *De Coelesti Hierarchia, the Celestial Hierarchy.* It was written in Greek around the 5th Century CE, by Pseudo-Dionysius the Areopagite.

Jewish tradition generally provides ten ranks of angelic beings as follows: 1) Chayot HaKodesh, 2) Ophanim, 3) Erelim, 4) Hashmallim, 5) Seraphim, 6) Malakim, 7) Elohim, 8) Bene Elohim, 9) Cherubim, and 10) Ishim.

Interestingly, many acknowledge a "vice-regent" slot, filled by YHWH Himself in another form known as "The Angel of YHWH" or "The Word of YHWH." While YHWH sits upon the Throne, this "vice-regent," Who many recognize as The Messiah, interacts with mankind directly.[100] The Messiah as the Son of Elohim actually reigns over the "sons of Elohim." The sons of Elohim were actually set up as "princes" over the nations after the Babel incident.

There is a text from the Scriptures that plainly indicates this as can be seen from the oldest versions of the Septuigant and the Deda Sea Scroll which states: *"⁷ Remember the days of old, consider the years of many generations. Ask your father, and he will show you; your elders, and they will tell you: ⁸ When the Most High divided their inheritance to the nations, when He separated the sons of Adam, He set the boundaries of the peoples according to the number of the sons of Elohim."* Debarim 32:7-8

This particular translation issue varies from the Masoretic Text and has been detailed in other books in the

Walk in the Light series. It has particular significance in this discussion because the Masoretic Text provides "children of Yisrael" instead of "sons of Elohim." "Sons of Elohim" is actually supported by the Book of Yasher as well as Targum Pseudo-Jonathan. If this is the case, it gives us a better understanding of how YHWH administers Creation.

These "sons of Elohim" are sometimes described as the "hosts of heaven." They are the beings that Yisrael was warned not to worship. The following passage provides the warning and appears to confirm that YHWH apportioned them among the people. "*And take heed, lest you lift your eyes to heaven, and when you see the sun, the moon, and the stars, <u>all the host of heaven, you feel driven to worship them and serve them, which YHWH your Elohim has given to all the peoples under the whole heaven as a heritage</u>.*" Debarim 4:19.

These "sons of Elohim" ended up being worshipped and we are given a glimpse of the Heavenly Court where YHWH expresses His displeasure with the "sons of Elohim" and renders judgment that they would be punished. They would die like men.

"*[1] Elohim stands in the congregation of the mighty; He judges among the elohim. [2] How long will you judge unjustly, and show partiality to the wicked? Selah [3] Defend the poor and fatherless; do justice to the afflicted and needy. [4] Deliver the poor and needy; free them from the hand of the wicked. [5] They do not know, nor do they understand; they walk about in darkness; all the foundations of the earth are unstable. [6] I said, You are gods, and all of you are sons of the Most High. [7] But you shall die like men, and fall like one of the princes. [8] Arise, O Elohim, judge the earth; for You shall inherit all nations.*" Psalm 82:1-8.

With that understanding, let us return to what happened in Babylon, because this is the reason why the "sons of Elohim" were set over the nations. The union, involving the phallus of Nimrod emitting the rays of the sun into Semaramis, resulted in the mythical Tammuz. Those "rays from the sun" were most likely from an angelic being. Now we can see this myth played out in numerous cultures throughout time, and around the world.

In fact, the symbols and monuments of this Babylonian sun worship are found throughout the entire planet. There are enormous cities and temple complexes underwater. There are cities and temple complexes that are known throughout the Americas and Asia. In fact, there are enormous pyramids in China that make the pyramids in Giza, Egypt pale in comparison.

Nevertheless, when we consider the effects of Babylonian sun worship we immediately think of Egypt. Most notably, we see the exact myths originating in Babylon being described in the Egyptian trinity of Osiris, Isis and Horus. The reason these three are mentioned is because they are the gods specifically embellished in American architecture. This was explicitly laid out in the Walk in the Light series book entitled *Restoration*.

We will examine this subject very briefly here. To begin, the so-called Washington Monument is the largest obelisk ever known to exist in the world. It measures 6,666 inches tall, and 666 inches wide at the base on each of the 4 sides. It represents the erect phallus of Osiris, and stands before the dome of the Capital building that represents the womb of Isis.

Inside the womb, the imagery is really quite astounding. The enormous painting, entitled the *Apotheosis of Washington*, was painted by Constantino Brumidi who also provided services for 3 years in the Vatican under Pope Gregory XVI. The word "apotheosis" actually means to make someone a god. So in this depiction George Washington is made a god. He is seated on a throne in the clouds, the center of a pagan Roman trinity. There is a rainbow beneath the throne, and one cannot ignore the implications relative to the Throne Room of YHWH.

Instead of being surrounded by Cherubim, this pagan throne room is filled with Roman gods such as Libertas and Victoria, seated to the right and the left of this American god. To his right is Libertas holding a Roman fasces and an open book. To his left is Victoria holding a sheaf and sounding a trumpet. The imagery takes one straight  to the Book of Revelation with the opening of the books, and the sounding of trumpets.

The problem is that this is not YHWH on the throne, but rather the President of the United States of America. His position and hand gestures are mimicking the representations of Jupiter and Zeus. In fact, below the Apotheosis there used to be a statute of George Washington appearing as the sun god. This is extremely important as we examine the connection between the Roman Empire and the United States of America. This womb of Isis within the District of Columbia is the place where the office of the  President of the United States will become a god. This is exactly what happened in Rome.

The throne room is surrounded by seven Roman gods and goddesses, namely: Minerva, Neptune, Venus, Mercury, Vulcan, Ceres and Flora. These Roman gods are represented giving guidance, direction and empowerment to the developing nation. Thus, America is represented as being formed and developed by the Roman gods. There is one goddess, uniquely American, named: Columbia.

The entire depiction, where the President becomes enthroned as a god, is surrounded by 72 pentagrams - as if this is some sort of gateway to another realm. The number 72 is incredibly significant when we consider the spirit realm and the occult. While the occult often distorts truth, we should understand that there is sometimes truth veiled behind lies. This circle of 72 pentagrams appears to act as a gate to heavens - to the very throne room of Elohim. The 72 pentagrams, when connected by 6 points, form an enormous hexagram connecting the Roman gods in the Apotheosis.

The number 72 combined with these signs are claimed to be traced back to a text originally written by Solomon, although the writings appear to derive from mystery teachings of Kabbalah. The book, known as *The Lesser Key of Solomon*, is divided into 5 parts. The Ars Goetia contains descriptions of 72 demons that Solomon allegedly evoked along with the magic symbols he used as seals.

The use of pentagrams and hexagrams in those symbols was intimately involved in summoning and controlling those demons. Tradition holds that King Solomon used a two-sided seal, known as The Seal of Solomon, to summon demons. On one side was the pentagram and the other side was the hexagram. They are symbols associated with opening and closing spiritual gates.

Of course, when we consider the architecture of Washington, D.C., the phallus of Nimrod/Osiris must penetrate those gates so that the seed can pass through. This is exactly what the Nephilim did when they descended from the heavenly realm and inserted themselves into the daughters of men. They passed through gates.

Standing on top of the dome is the Roman goddess, Minerva, essentially confirming that the dome represents the female genitive while the phallus represents the male. She stands on a globe with the phrase emblazoned "E Pluribus Unum" – "out of many one." Again, YHWH divided mankind, and the kingdom they had established through the Nephilim at Babel. So Babylon is the "union" that is intended to be restored and made "one."

As if there is any question of the source of this seed, on the tip of the Washington Monument is an aluminum cap that states: "Laus Deo." Laus Deo is a phrase repeated by those in the "camp" of the Scottish Rite Masons. It is usually understood to mean: "Praise God." That leads to the question: "What god?" The term "Deo" is actually used in sun worship and can reference the cult of Osiris, Isis and Horus. This is clearly seen in the *First Hymn of Isidorus to the Great Goddess Isis* from the Temple of Isis-Hermouthis-Renenutet at Narmouthis.

The culmination of this sexual union leads to the promised son Tammuz/Horus. That son is provided a house from which to rule – the White House. The White House is the focus of the inverted pentagram formed by the design of Washington, DC. The inverted pentagram is the head of Baphomet. The Baphomet is a hybrid Nephilim being, worshipped as the "Great Architect of the Universe" by the Masons - G.A.O.T.U. Baphomet is commonly depicted with a goat head on a winged, mixed human torso, with goat legs.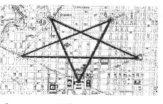

Even the Supreme Court of the United States depicts the Roman goddess Libertas at the apex of the frieze on the front of the building. The apex on the back side displays Moses with two blank documents. It depicts figures from throughout history, including Mohammed. Amazingly, in this so-called Christian nation, there are no depictions of Yahushua anywhere. The government is thoroughly Roman. Even when they used to depict the Ten Commandments, they depicted them with Roman numerals.

The messages are there in plain sight for those who have eyes to see. America is not, nor was it ever, a Christian nation. The freedom of religion so cherished by Americans permitted every religion to exist and florish. It assured that America would be a pagan nation. The Babylonian corruption has been perpetrated and disemminated through the revived Roman Empire – the United States of America.

Now in this discussion of America we have focused on two savior gods – Tammuz and Horus. These were "sons of god." They specifically reveal the connection between Babylon and the United States. There are many other names depicting the same messages in the cultures and religions throughout time and around the world. They all derive from the same source – Babylon.

So this grand illusion perpetrated upon mankind since Nimrod and Babylon has culminated into a world completely directing mankind toward the serpent from the garden. This deception has been orchestrated to establish the kingdom of the serpent (dragon) from the garden, and bring mankind under the judgment and wrath of Elohim.

The architecture and governmental institutions of America are littered with pagan symbols, statues and messages – too numerous to detail here. They all point to the Babylonian roots of the nation. As if there were any question about this all we need to do is examine the messages

contained within the Great Seal of the United States of America. As with Solomon's seal, this too is a 2 sided seal. It is found on the back of every one dollar bill and it is filled with messages and imagery. There is a hexagram consisting of 13 stars above the eagle, originally depicted as a phoenix.

Interestingly, there is a pyramid on the other portion that clearly directs us to Egypt. There are 72 stones on the pyramid. Interestingly, legend holds that the number of languages emanating from the Tower of Babel was 72. Also, Osiris was enclosed in a coffin by 72 evil disciples and accomplices of Set. We know that Solomon married Pharaoh's daughter, and it appears that this was the source of his knowledge. 1 Kings 3:1. This is the source of much Masonic mythology involving the master builder of the Temple of YHWH named Hiram Abiff.

Now back to the seal, above this 72 stone pyramid representing the tomb of Osiris we see the "son of god"

represented by the eye of Horus. Horus is seen descending as the chief capstone "rosh pina" in the *Novus Ordo Seclorum* – the New Order of the Ages, otherwise known as the New World Order. The Chief Capstone (Rosh Pina) is the function and title given to the Messiah (Psalm 118:22)

So we see that this New World Order will be established by and through the seed of Nimrod. That seed desires to open those 72 gates, and assume control of those gates. Amazingly, the architecture of the United States continues to reveal that message. The Pentagon building is the source of the military power for the United States of America. It was specifically designed in the shape of a pentagon, and each of the internal angles that would result in a pentagram is 72 degrees. You cannot make this up, nor can you simply explain it as coincidence.

This brief summary is simply scratching the surface, but it should be evident that the Nephilim have been designing and building an alternative kingdom for their offspring, and they are using America to establish that kingdom. It is directly opposed to the Kingdom of Elohim that was originally supposed to be established on earth by Adam and his sons. Anyone familiar with Yahushua knows that He holds the keys, and gives His disciples the power to bind and loose. (Matthew 16:19). In fact, this is an often overlooked aspect of spiritual warfare that will become increasingly more important as we approach the end of the age.

For now, it is important to understand that what the Nephilim were planning before the flood is about to become a reality once again with the willing participation of mankind. It will also be accompanied by judgment. This is perfectly consistent with what Nimrod started in Babylon. Nimrod established a kingdom in direct defiance to YHWH.

He built the Tower of Babel as a gate to the heavens. This may explain why the Scriptures state *"he began to be a mighty one."* He likely colluded with the Nephilim and changed.

It is quite possible that he was promised to be resurrected in the end. That might be a promise being fulfilled as we speak. It is believed that the United States has been refining cloning and transhumanism technologies for

decades through DARPA and other agencies. United States military forces purportedly claimed the remains of Nimrod for purposes that can only be left to the imagination.

Now all of this may come as a shock to an individual brought up to believe that that America is a Christian nation. It should be no surprise at all when we understand that the religion of Christianity was created by the Roman Empire, and is represented by the Roman Catholic Church.

When we examine the architecture of the Roman Catholic Church we see the exact same architecture and symbolism as Washington, DC. At the Vatican we see the phallus of Osiris, brought by Caligula from Heliopolis, Egypt - the ancient city of On. It stands in the midst of a sun wheel before the womb of Isis, represented by the dome of Saint Peter's Basilica.

The phallus in St. Peter's square has a cross afixed to the top. Interestingly, the cross or "tau" is seen throughout sun worship as the sign of Tammuz, who is the Babylonian version of the Egyptian god Horus. Inside the Basillica is filled with pagan imagery and even contains an enormous statue of Jupiter, that has been renamed Peter to make it acceptable.

The Catholic Church has always followed the practice of synchretism when seeking to convert various people and cultures. In other words, it typically incorporates pagan practices and icons and blends in pagan beliefs in order to make conversion easier. For instance, most would object to a statue of the sun god Jupiter, but when it is renamed Peter, the people line up to kiss the foot of this pagan statue.

Of course, this depiction of Jupiter, looks incredibly

the same as the ancient god named Baal Hammon. The point is that they all trace back to the dieties of Babylon, and revolve around the worship of the sun, the moon and the stars. Babylon directs worship to the "fallen stars" the Nephilim. These Nephilim were once in the Kingdom of Elohim commissioned with the worship of YHWH. There came a time when they desired their own kingdom and their own worship.

As with the government of the United States, the Roman Catholic Church has incorporated numerous pagan  elements – too numerous to mention here. The mitre of the Pope derives from the Priests of Dagon. It noticeably looks like the mouth of a fish because Dagon was a fish god. In fact, Dagon was a chief god of the Philistines, a people in direct conflict with Yisrael. Notice in the picture of Pope Benedict, the mitre also contains a hexagram.

While this book is being written, Pope Francis is easing restrictions and doctrines in order to open the way for greater acceptance and "tolerance." Tolerance is just another word for compromise and diluting what you believe. It makes for a very wide "gate" that leads to destruction. The Messiah instructed us to enter through the narrow "gate" that leads to life. (Matthew 7:13).

Now it should be stated that the observations in this book should not be viewed as an attack against individual Catholics. I have many Catholic friends and acquantances who are sincerely trying to serve YHWH the best that they can, according to what they have been taught. I view this the same as patriotic Americans who love their country, unaware of the true inner workings of their government. It is not up to me to judge these individuals, nor is it my intent. Rather, I make these observations about the systems in the hope that the individuals can make informed decisions regarding their associations.

That having been said, what we see through these combined governments and religious systems is a restored Babylon. It would seem that Babylon has come full circle and found its ultimate fulfillment in the United States of America, and the Christian religion deriving from Rome. How appropriate then, that the United States would host the United Nations. The United States is furthering and facilitating its goal of "E Pluribus Unum" to encompass the entire world and establish the New World Order. This entire process is meant to reunite and  restore that which YHWH divided and confused at the Tower of Babel.

The seat of the United Nations is located in New York City, one of the great economic powers of the world. It is intimately connected with another financial powerhouse –  London. Interestingly, the City of London is actually a city within greater London, founded by the Roman Empire, that is supposedly guarded by two giants – Gog and Magog. New York City, originally named New Amsterdam, was later named after York, another City in England founded by the Romans. So we can see that these powers and institutions trace back to the Roman Empire, and it all eventually flows back to Babylon.

Interestingly, after the attacks on September 11, 2001 when the Twin Towers were both destroyed, they were replaced with one single building. The Freedom Tower was

intentionally designed to represent an obelisk. So now New York City also contains an enormous phallus, directly across from the enormous goddess Isis – The Queen of Heaven - commonly called "The Statue of Liberty," that is seated on an 11 pointed star.

Of course, this is none other than another depiction of the seal of Solomon that contained a hexagram (6 points) on one side and a pentagram (5 points) on the other side. It is meant to symbolize a gate. As with Jupiter in the Vatican, all the illuminated ones do is place nice unassuming names on these pagan idols, and people flock to them in adoration.

As a result, we can see the religion of Babylon extend through Christianity, and the Christian nation of America.

The people of America have been led by their goddesses of Liberty, Democracy, Justice and Columbia to achieve their supposed "Manifest Destiny" from God. They have zealously spread their culture and religion throughout the world. That culture is epitomized by Las Vegas, where essentially anything goes. That licentious "gospel" message is then broadcast throughout the world through Hollywood, and the music industry.

We perpetuate that culture by paying off other countries, and our war machine, both funded by Congress. Is it any wonder that the Roman god of war named Mars stands guard outside the Congress of the United States of America. The message is crystal clear. The

culture being perpetrated is not a culture directing worship to YHWH. In fact, YHWH has been removed from all government institutions. Prayer has been banned from schools, and the freedom of religion has morphed into the freedom from the Christian religion as Scriptural beliefs are now being vilifies as intolerance, hatred and phobia. In fact, Rome is renowned for their diversity of religions, they were a polytheistic culture and worshipped the gods – the Nephilim.

While it is true that the early settlers, often called Puritans, were a covenant people interested in serving the Elohim of the Scriptures, well over a century passed until the United States was founded. The early settlers such as William Penn had a strong belief in Elohim and the Scriptures, but they were soon overwhelmed by Illuminists - those who sought to develop a nation that would "suit the needs" of the Nephilim. While those early settlers intended to serve Elohim, the government that was later formed serves a different god and is building a different kingdom.

This would explain the rapid decline in morality and lack of respect for life in America. The United States of America currently permits and condones the slaughter of millions of unborn babies every year. This equates to the child sacrifice of ancient pagan cultures where the helpless innocents were offered up to the gods in exchange for blessings. Indeed, it is no different than people sacrificing their children to Cronos or Molech in exchange for the god relieving them of their worldly cares.

Referring to the City of Carthage, Diodorus Siculus stated: "There was in their city a bronze image of Cronus extending its hands, palms up and sloping toward the ground, so that each of the children when placed thereon rolled down and fell into a sort of gaping pit filled with fire." (Bib. Hist. 20.14.6).

Interestingly, in Greek mythology Cronos was a

Titan depicted with a sickle or a Scythe that he used to castrate his father Uranus. Clearly, the intent was to cut off the seed, as Canaan likely did with Noah. Cronos was later melded into the Roman god Saturn. To this day, pagan cultures such as America continue to revere Saturn. The only day that YHWH ever named was the seventh day – The Sabbath. Pagan cultures have  replaced the Sabbath with Saturday, literally Saturn's Day.

Indeed, it is not simply Saturday that was named after a pagan god, all the days of the week are named after pagan gods, as are most of the months and the planets. We see our entire culture immersed in paganism, and most people fail to recognize it for what it is. It seems people are under a strong delusion.

That same delusion veils the mutilation and torture of unborn children as simple birth control. The spirit of abortion that pervades America is absolutely the same "spirit" that existed in days past, as women willingly place themselves on altars, called operating tables, to offer up their babies to the god of "self."

Most women do it because they do not want to be inconvenienced. It is all about them. This is the same motivation as the ancients, even prior to the flood according to the Book of Yasher 2:19-20. They want things to be better for themselves so they offer up these tiny "images of Elohim," and help the serpent kingdom de-populate mankind at the same time. This is especially tragic as so many American couples desire to adopt children, but these mothers do not even want to be inconvenienced for less than a year.

This is a terrible sign for this nation, and the mark of a society that has completely turned its back on YHWH. This depraved, self centered, materialistic culture is much of what America is spreading throughout the world. Sadly, there are millions of well meaning citizens who completely disagree with what is happening, but are compelled to pay their taxes and support this system. They have become slaves, as Yisrael once found itself in Egypt. The reason for these connections will become obvious further on in this discussion.

For now, it is important to understand that this nation is headed exactly as it was planned, not by the Puritans, but by the "founders." It is naïve to believe that the "founding fathers" were all purposed on serving YHWH. This is a myth that is spread to help portray America as a Christian nation. Many of the founding fathers were Illuminists and Masons, and their intention was to bring  about a new order of the ages. Many of them were deceived into believing that Satan, who they refer to as Lucifer, was actually "the enlightened one" and YHWH is the evil god.

Illuminists believe that the masses are deceived, and they are the ones who understand the "mysteries." Albert Pike, one of the preeminent Masonic philosophers, and the Grand Commander Sovereign Pontiff of Universal Freemasonry was very clear about the fact that "Lucifer" was the god that Masons worshipped, although that is not fully understood or revealed until members reach the higher degrees – 30th, 31st, 32nd and 33rd.

Men like Thomas Paine, Thomas Jefferson and Benjamin Franklin were well aware of this fact. They were actually building the dream of the New Atlantis as espoused by Francis Bacon. Thomas Jefferson, who is thought to have been a Mason, actually wrote *The Jefferson Bible* also known as *The Life and Morals of Jesus of Nazareth*. In that text he omits all of the supernatural elements of the Messiah, including the virgin birth, the miracles, the resurrection, and ascension. He also renounces the miracles of Yahushua in certain letters. His friend and fellow founding father, John Adams, noted that a source of his religious belief was found in the Brahman book called Shasta.

Thomas Paine, an Englishman, was the author of works such as *Common Sense* and *The Age of Reason*. He is often credited as the inspiration for the Declaration of Independence and the American Revolution. It is claimed by many sources that the Declaration of Independence was actually written on white lambskin – a Masonic apron. Thomas Paine actually wrote a book on Free Masonry, and was very much opposed to Christian doctrine. He is noted as stating that the word of God would better be described as the word of a demon. He was encouraged by his friend Benjamin Franklin to come to America and help start the revolution. He went on aid in the French Revolution. Both of these revolutions advocated reason and philosophy, not YHWH. Only 6 people attended his funeral because he was so ostracized for his ridicule of Christianity.

We know that Franklin was a Jew, born to Josiah and Abiah Franklin in Boston. Although he contributed to the Mikveh Israel Congregation in Philadelphia, he did not practice Judaism. In fact, he was very much an occultist, and a member of many secret societies including the infamous "Hellfire Club" that mocked traditional religion, conducted orgies and practiced satan worship.

Franklin was also deeply involved in masonry and aggressively advanced Masonry throughout the colonies. Many of the other founding fathers such as Paul Revere and Alexander Hamilton were Masons. Of course, the most famous Mason in America is the first president, George Washington. These men were a far cry from the Puritans. They were not Christians and they had not desire to make America a Christian nation. In fact, George Washington drafted Article XI of the Treaty of Tripoli of 1797 which specifically declared: " . . . the government of the United States is not, in any sense, founded on the Christian religion. . ." The Treaty received the unanimous consent of the US Senate. , and was signed by then President John Adams

The United States of America has become an incubation nation where the seeds of the Nephilim have been

planted and nurtured to bring about the serpent kingdom, known as the New World Order. While you may read "In God We Trust" throughout the country, that statement should not necessarily give you comfort. It does not refer to YHWH, but rather the "god" Nimrod. This revived Roman Empire is intent on leading the world back to Babylon. Is it any wonder that the 1st Marine Expeditionary Force built the military base known as "Camp Alpha" on the ruins of Babylon after the invasion of Iraq. The message was clear that the United States of America was the new Babylon.

While the American government has moved the world toward Babylon, it clearly identifies with the Roman Republic, and stands poised to completely mimic the Roman Empire. It shares many of the same gods and symbols that are

intentionally displayed to reveal that connection.

The Roman fasces, the symbol of Roman power and authority, is displayed at the Temple" known as the Lincoln

Memorial. Two large fasces are prominently displayed on either side of the American flag behind the rostrum in the House of Representatives. The message is painfully obvious – the United States is an extension of the Roman Empire. The fasces was even on older coins that clearly reveals the Roman origins of the US. The mercury dime depicted the Roman god Mercury on one side, and the Roman fasces on the other side.

This connection with Rome has been continued by certain fascist regimes in the 20th Century, and it is well known that the United States actually imported many Nazi scientists and intellectuals after World War II under the guise of Operation Paperclip. This was done to continue their research in areas such as eugenics and other sciences in order to continue the American space program and industrial war machine. Hitler was consumed with engineering what Nietzsche described as the Übermensch – the Overman. That was part of his obsession with Aryan purity and his desire to annihilate the Jews.

It is alleged by researchers such as Edwin Black and Jim Marrs, that the Third Reich essentially went underground and has operated through corporations and the acquisition of conglomerates as they work to establish the Fourth Reich or the New World Order. This fact will become more significant as we continue.

For now, it is important to recognize that as America has expanded its influence and power throughout the world, it has actually been helping build a kingdom in direct opposition to YHWH. It is literally transforming into a fascist regime. What a deception that the systems and religions that purport to represent the Messiah, have been

specifically used to build a system that will likely empower and enthrone the seed of the serpent - the one that has attempted to destroy mankind from the very beginning.

The deception is of the highest order and we should expect nothing less. According to the Book of Revelation, the dragon "deceives the nations." (Revelation 20:3 and 8) When referring to times of tribulation, the Messiah clearly stated that there would be great deception so as to deceive, if possible, even the elect. (Matthew 24:11, 24) Clearly, a veil has been drawn over many people's eyes, and a great cover-up has been orchestrated to mask the true nature and origins of America, as well as other powers of the world.

The deception runs even deeper still. It appears that America did indeed have a  manifest destiny that was specifically tied to the serpent. America was actually called Amaruca, named after the Peruvian serpent god Amaru. There are similar Aztec and Mayan derivations of this ancient serpent god. America (Amaruca) literally means: "Land of the Plumed Serpents" or better yet "Land of the winged Serpents."[101] This sounds a lot like a dragon, and as we shall see, the Scriptures specifically speak of the dragons making war against the children of YHWH. This is not a metaphor - these things are real.

We can actually see this drama played out in the stars as the new 13th constellation - Ophiuchus. The new constellation was recently added after apparent pole shifts in the earth. How incredible that this new constellation would be added at this time. The constellation actually depicts a man wrestling with the serpent as it attempts to attain the crown. This man is also depicted as trampling on a scorpion.

This is what the Messiah meant when He stated: "*Behold, I give you the authority to trample on serpents and scorpions, and over all the power of the enemy, and nothing shall by any means hurt you.*" Luke 10:19. This is the sign of the culmination of the battle between the seed of the woman and the seed of the serpent. We will be discussing that battle more as the discussion continues.

Just as the truth is not readily revealed regarding the significance of this sign, or any of the signs of the zodiac for that matter, so too much of the history of this planet has been hidden and suppressed. While many have been taught that America was named after Amerigo Vespucci, an Italian explorer and cartographer, the source of the name is far more ancient. America actually has a very ancient history that spans thousands of years before the European explorers claiming to "discover" it.

Throughout the "Americas" we find many dragon and serpent symbols. In fact, the State of Ohio actually contains a 1,348 foot long prehistoric effigy mound known as the Great Serpent Mound. It is the largest serpent effigy in the world.

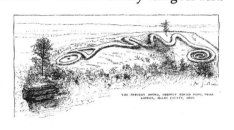

THE SERPENT MOUND, SERPENT MOUND PARK, NEAR
LOUDEN, ADAMS COUNTY, OHIO.

There is abundant evidence that America was a land filled with great civilizations and giants. That history has been wiped clean by institutions such as The Smithsonian. This, of course, is nothing new. Jean-Jacques Rousseau is well known for proclaiming: "The falsification of history has done more to mislead humans than any single thing known to mankind."[102]

We will be discussing world powers further on in this

discussion. For now, we can clearly see through this very brief analysis that the confusion of the languages did not squelch the false religious, political and economic system of Babylon that unified mankind. YHWH temporarily disintegrated and divided the world government established by the "antichrist" Nimrod.

I use the word "antichrist" while referring to Nimrod, because he surely was intent upon usurping the Kingdom of YHWH and establishing the serpent's kingdom. This is, after all, the spirit of "antichrist." The subject of "antichrist" is often misunderstood and applied to a man in the future. The word "antichrist" is only found in the Epistles of John, and John was clear that there were many "antichrists." (1 John 2:18) In fact, John states: *He is antichrist who denies the father and the son.*" 1 John 2:22 He also states that "antichrist" was in the world when he was alive. (see 1 John 4:3)

So there have always been antichrists, and Nimrod was a prime example of one of them. Despite the division that resulted after the Babel incident, mankind still maintained their rebellious beliefs, although they were separated by newly divided continents and languages. It is believed that the Babel incident not only divided the people into different languages, but it also involved the physical separation of their lands. This marked the beginning of the "nations."[103]

Prior to Babel, all of mankind spoke one language, and that language was Hebrew. Regardless of this disruption, it appears from historical and archaeological records that mankind continued their sun worship in their new languages and cultures. They likely continued to be guided by their "gods" the Nephilim.

YHWH later chose a man and called him out of Babylon. There are even traditions that speak of Nimrod's persecution of the man. Again, we do not find anything

regarding this conflict in the Scriptures, but there are sources that speak of Nimrod turning against YHWH.

According to another account, when Nimrod was eighteen years old, war broke out between the Hamites, his kinsmen, and the Japhethites. The latter were at first victorious, but Nimrod, at the head of a small army of Cushites, attacked and defeated them, after which he was made king over all the people on earth, appointing Terah his minister. It was then, elated by so much glory, that Nimrod changed his behavior toward YHWH and became the most flagrant idolater. When informed of Abraham's birth he requested Terah to sell him the newborn child in order that he might kill it.[104]

The Book of Yasher states that Terah hid Abraham and in his stead brought to Nimrod the child of a slave, which Nimrod dashed to pieces. This is similar to later accounts of rulers such as Pharaoh and Herod who tried to kill the chosen Messenger of YHWH. Despite the alleged efforts of Nimrod, the infant escaped death and grew up to enter into a Covenant with YHWH that would establish the line for the Messiah and the path for restoration. Through the life of this man we would be given the pattern of the Covenant that would be the framework within which YHWH would restore mankind.

As with the genealogy from Adam to Noah, there was a righteous line continuing from Noah that walked according to the ways of YHWH. That line descended through Shem for another ten (10) generations until the Covenant was developed and revealed through the life of Abram.

4

Covenants

As we read about Abram, the son of Terah, we see a man born into Babylon, the city and system from which originate the rebellious and adulterous religions which act contrary to the ways of YHWH. Abram was called out of Babylon by YHWH, out of those pagan surroundings, and promised a new land and a better future for his descendants. From Noah we saw the Covenant providing deliverance and protection from judgment  and death. Now through Abram we see a Covenant family being established - a family that would grow into nations.

The life of Abram reveals the pattern of the Covenant path that we all must walk. That is the path to life. To reject that Covenant essentially means you have made a covenant with death and hell. It is a rejection of the path to redemption, salvation and restoration provided by YHWH for mankind. This is important to remember as we continue this discussion.

As YHWH entered into a Covenant relationship with Abram, we see that the life of this man is very instructive, and provides a prophetic pattern of the Covenant walk. So let us examine it from the beginning.

When Abram was in Babylon he was immersed in a

pagan system. YHWH spoke to Abram and told him: "*Get out of your country, from your family and from your father's house.*" (Beresheet 12:1). A person who desires to be in Covenant with YHWH must "come out of Babylon" and "cross over." The word for "cross over" is "eber" (ﬡﬠﬡ), and it is the source for the word "Hebrew." A Hebrew is one who comes out of Babylon and crosses over. In this case, he had to cross over the Euphrates River and likely also the Jordan River to get into the land of Canaan.

Once Abram fully obeyed and entered into the Land of Canaan at Shechem we read: "*Then YHWH appeared to Abram and said 'To your descendants I will give this land.' And there he built an altar to YHWH, Who appeared to him.*" Beresheet 12:7

The building of an altar is significant. Blood was shed and, as with Noah, the promise made by YHWH was sealed with blood. Abram then moved to the mountain east of Bethel and west of Ai. Bethel means "House of El" and Ai means:  "ruinous heap." Actually, while the English text seems to refer to Ai as a city, the Hebrew refers to "ha'Ai" (ﬡﬨﬣ) - "the heap."

So Abram had a promise of land, but it was not immediate. He had left his fathers house in the east, and was headed to the House of El in the west. He was now residing between "the heap," representing the Babylon from which he had come out. In fact, when one thinks of "the heap" in the east standing in juxtaposition to the House of El, it clearly symbolizes the Tower of Babel, the unfinished heap of mud bricks.

Abram was on his way to the House of El, but the journey was not complete. He was at the place of the altar. He was still "east of Eden" so to speak. The symbolism of the geography is incredible. So it is clear that the physical locations where Abram pitched his tent had great symbolic significance. The pattern was clear, the life of Abram would provide the path from Babylon to the House of El – from the ruinous heap that leads to death, to paradise that contains the Tree of Life.

There came a time when famine struck the land, so Abram moved to Egypt. He went there to escape famine, but during his time in Egypt, his bride was taken captive by the Pharaoh. A series of plagues upon the Pharaoh led to the release of his bride, and Abram was provided great wealth when he departed Egypt. He left Egypt very rich, and he also left with a woman named Hagar. Her name is literally "ha'ger" (אֹגֹר) in Hebrew, which means: "the stranger." The gematria value for "hager" is 208. This has significance when we later learn the name of the promised son of the Covenant.

So we see Abram depart Egypt with his freed bride and another woman. This "stranger" became part of his family, and would later become his bride. This entire process has profound prophetic symbolism relative to his Covenant seed who would later become enslaved in Egypt.

After exiting Egypt, something very interesting occurs. We read in English the following account: "*3 And he went on his journey from the South as far as ◁☉-Bethel, to ◁☉-the place where his tent had been at the beginning, between Bethel and the heap (ha'Ai), 4 to the place of the altar which he had made there at first. And there Abram called on the Name of YHWH.*" Beresheet 13:3-4.

In the Hebrew text there is much more going on. For instance, Abram placed his tent where it had been "in the beginning." This was a return, a "shub" ($ꟼYW$). The cycle was complete, and Egypt was an important part of the cycle.

Abram returned to the place of the altar between Bethel and ha'Ai, between the House of El and "the heap." Only now something was different. In the Hebrew we see a very interesting distinction. We see an "ad" ($◁☉$) attached to the House of El and "the place." The "ad" ($◁☉$) was not present during the previous mention, but after the return from Egypt we see: $YYꟼY-◁☉\ /⨍-X⅂ꟼ-◁☉$.

Now one might justify a grammatical reason why the ad ($◁☉$) is attached to this word here, but the application would not be consistent with the previous portion. The "ad" ($◁☉$) consists of an "ayin" ($☉$) which is an "eye" and means "see." The "dalet" ($◁$) is a "door." So the ayin dalet ($◁☉$) is telling us – "see the door." At this place, east of the House and west of the heap. At the place of the altar, the place of the beginning, at the completion of the cycle – see the door.

We also see the word "shem" ($ꟼW$) four times in the text. Now "shem" ($ꟼW$) commonly means: "name," but only once in the text is the word translated as "name" - when Abram called on the Name of YHWH. In all the other instances it is translated as "there," but when you read the Hebrew there is no doubt that there is an emphasis on the Name (shem), and it was also emphasized to "see the door."

It was at this point in the journey that Abram had to separate from Lot. It appeared from the beginning that Abram was to completely separate from his family, but Lot had been with him thus far. Separation is part of walking in the Covenant. The Covenant requires participants to make distinctions, and to be "set apart" (qodesh). Once the separation was completed YHWH was ready to continue the Covenant journey with Abram.

"*14 And YHWH said to Abram, after Lot had separated*

from him: 'Lift your eyes now and look from the place where you are: northward, southward, eastward, and westward; [15] for all the land which you see I give to you and your descendants forever. [16] And I will make your descendants as the dust of the earth; so that if a man could number the dust of the earth, then your descendants also could be numbered. [17] Arise, walk in the land through its length and its width, for I give it to you.' [18] Then Abram moved his tent, and went and dwelt by the terebinth trees of Mamre, which are in Hebron, and built an altar there to YHWH." Beresheet 13:14-18

So we read that YHWH was starting to get more specific about the land that would be given. The descendants of Abram would be very numerous - like the dust of the earth. Abram then set out to walk the boundaries of the land and eventually settled in Hebron. Interestingly, the root of Hebron is "eber" (𐤏𐤁𐤓). It means: "cross over, beyond, on the other side." It is the same root as the word for Hebrew, and Abram became known as a Hebrew because of how he lived and where he dwelled - Hebron. (see Beresheet 14:13) Specifically, he dwelled by the terebinth trees of Mamre, the Amorite.

There came a time, after Abram and Lot separated, that Lot was taken captive after certain local kings were defeated in the Valley of Sodom. Abram actually had an army consisting of 318 trained fighting men.[105] These were not mercenaries, they were born in his house. As a result, he was able to hunt down the captors and retrieve Lot, along with the plunder taken from the local kings. So Abram was a travelling nation with a standing army, more powerful than the people he dwelled amongst.

After his return, we read about one of the most mysterious events in the Scriptures as Abram meets Melchizedek. "[18] *Then Melchizedek king of Salem brought out bread and wine; he was the priest of Elohim Most High. [19] And he blessed him and said: 'Blessed be Abram of Elohim Most High,*

Possessor of heaven and earth; [20] *And blessed be Elohim Most High, Who has delivered your enemies into your hand.' And he gave him a tithe of all.*" Beresheet 14:18-20

This is the only direct mention of the mysterious Melchizedek in the Hebrew Scriptures, except for Psalms 110:4. The word "melchizedek" means: "righteous king." This was a priest and a king and was a hint to a future righteous priestly king from Jerusalem – the Messiah.

"*After these things the Word of YHWH came to Abram in a vision, saying, Do not be afraid, Abram. I am your shield, your exceedingly great reward.*" Beresheet 15:1. This is quite an interesting passage, because we assume the Word of YHWH, Debar-YHWH (𐤀𐤉𐤇𐤆-𐤓𐤁𐤃), was something audible. From the text we see that it is connected to YHWH. We know that YHWH previously spoke to Abram, but now we have the Word of YHWH speaking "in a vision."

The word for "vision" is "machazah" (𐤄𐤆𐤇𐤌), and can mean "vision" or "light." It is something gazed at, seen and perceived. So this "Word" was something audible, and it was something visible. The "word" has always been something of a mystery. The Aramaic Targums actually refer to "the Memra" of YHWH. So it has been understood that The Word, or the Memra, was a special and unique manifestation of YHWH.

After he was given this promise, Abram was concerned because he had no child. He did not understand how his heirs would inherit the land if he had no children. He thought that maybe his servant Eliezer would be his heir. Here is the response that he received:

"[4] *And behold, the Word of YHWH came to him, saying, 'This one shall not be your heir, but one who will come from your own body shall be your heir.'* [5] *Then He brought him outside and said, 'Look now toward heaven, and sepher the stars if you are able* to *sepher* them.' And He said to him, 'So shall your descendants be.' ⁶ And he believed in YHWH, and He accounted it to him for righteousness. ⁷ Then He said to him, 'I am YHWH, who brought you out of Ur of the Chaldeans, to give you this land to inherit it.' ⁸ And he said, 'Master YHWH, how shall I know that I will inherit it?' ⁹ So He said to him, 'Bring Me a three-year-old heifer, a three-year-old female goat, a three-year-old ram, a turtledove, and a young pigeon.' ¹⁰ Then he brought all these to Him and cut them in two, down the middle, and placed each piece opposite the other; but he did not cut the birds in two. ¹¹ And when the vultures came down on the carcasses, Abram drove them away. ¹² Now when the sun was going down, a deep sleep fell upon Abram; and behold, horror and great darkness fell upon him. ¹³ Then He said to Abram: 'Know certainly that your descendants will be strangers in a land that is not theirs, and will serve them, and they will afflict them four hundred years. ¹⁴ And also the nation whom they serve I will judge; afterward they shall come out with great possessions. ¹⁵ Now as for you, you shall go to your fathers in peace; you shall be buried at a good old age. ¹⁶ But in the fourth generation they shall return here, for the iniquity of the Amorites is not yet complete.' ¹⁷ And it came to pass, when the sun went down and it was dark, that behold, there appeared a smoking oven and a fire (*esh*) torch that passed between those pieces. ¹⁸ On the same day YHWH made a Covenant with Abram, saying: 'To your descendants I have given this land, from the river of Egypt to the great river, the River Euphrates - ¹⁹ the Kenites, the Kenezzites, the Kadmonites, ²⁰ the

Hittites, the Perizzites, the Rephaim, ²¹ the Amorites, the Canaanites, the Girgashites, and the Jebusites." Beresheet 15:4-21

One cannot help but recognize the emphasis placed on this passage. Here the Word of YHWH (𐤉𐤄𐤅𐤄) was speaking to Abram, but now we are instructed to "behold." There was a promise found in the stars in the heavens.

Many translations provide that Abram was to "count" the stars, but the Hebrew provides "sepher" (𐤓𐤐𐤎) which literally means: "scroll." So the text really seems to be telling Abram to "read" the stars. The constellations were literally revealing history, including his descendants.[106]

Notice all of the lands belonging to people groups designated as "ites" – 9 in all. There is one additional group that stands apart – the Rephaim. These Rephaim are not listed like the other tribes because they were different. They were not men - they were offspring of the Nephilim. They are often described as "giants." Like Nimrod, they were "gibor." Their name is actually very interesting because it derives from "heal" as well as "shades or ghosts." So the Rephaim were likened to the resurrected dead.

This is important to understand because Abram had left the land of Nimrod and now he was being promised a land filled with giants. We know this to be the case from an earlier account of the Elamite King Chedorlaomer who battled the various giants throughout the region. (Beresheet 14:5)

Regardless, Abram was not afraid. He did not refuse to go into the land for fear of these giants. Abram believed this promise, and YHWH accounted it to him as righteousness. We also see a great promise of land with very specific and large boundaries - from the great river of Egypt, which is no doubt the Nile River to the Euphrates River.

So the western boundary falls in the middle of Egypt and the eastern boundary falls in the middle of Babylon. How incredible that this promised land would be couched between Egypt and Babylon. This has great future significance.[107] It is also worthy to note that the river Nile is not mentioned by name, but the River Euphrates is. In fact the Euphrates River is known as "Perath" (𐤗𐤗𐤗) in Hebrew.

This promise was sealed in and through a Covenant. What makes this Covenant unique was that it was unconditional and unilateral. In other words, after expressing belief and making the preparations for the Covenant, Abram was not an active participant in the actual Covenant ceremony. Just as with Noah, an active faith was required, while YHWH actually fulfilled the Promise of the Covenant.[108]

Typically, in a blood covenant, both parties would walk through the blood of the slaughtered pieces, symbolizing the penalty associated with breaking the covenant. In this case there were three animals divided in two, and two birds that were not divided. So there was blood shed from five animals. These would be the clean animals used later in the Temple. Three of them were divided in half and the birds were set opposite each other, which amounted to eight pieces total.[109]

The number eight is extremely significant in this covenant relationship. It is the numerical equivalent of the Hebrew character "het" (𐤇), which again, looks like an untwisted DNA strand.

It is the "ladder" that connects us to the Father, and as we shall see later, it connects heaven and earth. This Covenant is all about repairing our DNA so we can ascend back into the family of YHWH and into His House. Amazingly, when we look at the Appointed Time of the 8th

day, known as Shemini Atzeret, we are given insight into "when" this will occur.[110]

When you combine five and eight you get thirteen. Thirteen is actually the gematria for the word "echad" (ᐊᕼᐊ) - one. The first time we saw this word was when the night and the day were unified and became as "one" (ᐊᕼᐊ). This Covenant event was taking place at the exact time that the day and night were unified - often called "twilight" or "between the evenings." This is evident from the time described between Beresheet 15:12, when the sun was going down, to Beresheet 15:17 when the sun went down and it was dark. This has always been an important time in the Covenant process as we see with the Passover.[111] The other connecting point, known as "the dawning of the day" is also important.

This Covenant process was a very traumatic event for Abram. He was in a "deep sleep" (tardemah), the same condition as Adam when Hawah was taken from him. He experienced "horror" and "great darkness." It sounds like he died and went to Sheol or even saw Gehenom - Hell.[112]

Of important note was the fact that Abram did not walk between the pieces and through the blood. This was, after all, a blood covenant. In a typical blood covenant, both parties were expected to walk through the blood since both would be subject to the penalty of breaking the covenant.

Instead, only the "smoking oven and fire torch" passed through. This is another mystery imbedded within the Covenant, revealed as YHWH led the Children of Yisrael by day with a pillar of smoke and at night with a pillar of fire. The smoke and the fire in the Covenant represented the One Who watches over and leads Yisrael, the Children of the Covenant. So neither Abram nor his descendants were subject to any penalty for breaking this Covenant, only the One Who passed through the pieces.

When Abram was 86 years old he had a son named Yishmael through Hagar. While it appeared that the promise would flow through Yishmael, YHWH had chosen the womb of Sarai for the seed to be planted. The promised son would come through her, thirteen years later.

"*¹ When Abram was ninety-nine years old, YHWH appeared to Abram and said to him, 'I am Almighty Elohim; walk before Me and be blameless. ² And I will make My Covenant between Me and you, and will multiply you exceedingly.' ³ Then Abram fell on his face, and ✕✦ Elohim talked with him, saying: ⁴ 'As for Me, behold, My Covenant is with you, and you shall be a father of many nations. ⁵ No longer shall your ✕✦-name be called Abram, but ✦⟨⟩✦ your name shall be Abraham; for I have made you a father of many nations. ⁶ I will make you exceedingly fruitful; and I will make nations of you, and kings shall come from you. ⁷ And I will establish My ✕✦- Covenant between Me and you and your descendants after you in their generations, for an everlasting Covenant, to be Elohim to you and your descendants after you. ⁸ Also I give to you and your descendants after you ✕✦ the land in which you are a stranger ✕✦ all the land of Canaan, as an everlasting possession; and I will be their Elohim.' ⁹ And Elohim said to Abraham: 'As for you, you shall keep ✕✦ My Covenant, you and your descendants after you throughout their generations. ¹⁰ This is My Covenant which you shall keep, between Me and you and your descendants after you: Every male child among you shall be circumcised; ¹¹ and you shall be circumcised ✕✦ in the flesh of your foreskins, and it shall be a sign of the Covenant between Me and you. ¹² He who is eight days old among you shall be circumcised,* every male child in your generations, he who is born in your house or bought with money from any foreigner who is not your descendant. [13] He who is born in your house and he who is bought with your money must be circumcised, and My Covenant shall be in your flesh for an everlasting Covenant. [14] And the uncircumcised male child, who is not circumcised in the flesh of his foreskin, that person shall be cut off from his people; he has broken My Covenant.' [15] Then Elohim said to Abraham, 'As for Sarai your wife, you shall not call her ✕ꗞ-name Sarai, but Sarah shall be her name. [16] And I will bless her and also give you a son by her; then I will bless her, and she shall be a mother of nations; kings of peoples shall be from her.' [17] Then Abraham fell on his face and laughed, and said in his heart, 'Shall a child be born to a man who is one hundred years old? And shall Sarah, who is ninety years old, bear a child?' [18] And Abraham said to Elohim, 'Oh, that Yishmael might live before You!' [19] Then Elohim said: 'No, Sarah your wife shall bear you a son, and you shall call his name Isaac (Yitshaq); I will establish My Covenant with him for an everlasting covenant, and with his descendants after him. [20] And as for Yishmael, I have heard you. Behold, I have blessed him, and will make him fruitful, and will multiply him exceedingly. He shall beget twelve princes, and I will make him a great nation. [21] But My ✕ꗞ-Covenant I will establish with ✕ꗞ-Isaac (Yitshaq), whom Sarah shall bear to you at the Appointed Time (moad) next year.' [22] Then He finished talking with him, and Elohim went up from Abraham. [23] So Abraham took Yishmael his son, all who were born in his house and all who were bought with his money, every male

among the men of Abraham's house, and circumcised the flesh of their foreskins that very same day, as Elohim had said to him. ²⁴ *Abraham was ninety-nine years old when he was circumcised in the flesh of his foreskin.* ²⁵ *And Yishmael his son was thirteen years old when he was circumcised in the flesh of his foreskin.* ²⁶ *That very same day Abraham was circumcised, and his son Yishmael;* ²⁷ *and all the men of his house, born in the house or bought with money from a foreigner, were circumcised with him."*
Beresheet 17:1-27

Notice that the names of both individuals were changed. In fact, this was like a creation event as we read that the name would "exist" (𐤄𐤆𐤄). Each name had a "hey" (𐤄) attached. The "hey" (𐤄) represents a person with their arms upstretched. It literally means: "behold." The "hey" (𐤄) also represents "breath" or "spirit," and it is believed that this was similar to the garden of Eden. So from this event we see something marvelous coming from the union of Abraham and Sarah.

It did not just involve one man, but it was a Covenant involving a specific man and a specific woman. The intention was to produce fruit – offspring. Elohim breathed life into the man and the woman and they became new creations for the purpose of bearing the promised son of the Covenant.

This was a sort of recreation for both Abraham and Sarah. Just as Adam was made in the image of Elohim, that image was breathed into Abraham and Sarah which likely was a restoration of their DNA. This would explain why the Covenant was in the flesh and marked by the shedding of blood on the male organ – the conduit for the seed.

The circumcision was to occur on the eighth day and we again see the "het" (𐤇), the DNA, being emphasized. So we see that the plans and purposes of YHWH point to the union of two becoming one - echad. Through this physical and spiritual union the Covenant is established. The Covenant between Elohim and man is, after all, a Marriage Covenant.

This was a prophetic event, and it had as much to do with the spiritual as it did the physical. It was very much about his seed - the descendants of promise. As we saw the Aleph Taw (✗✕) repeatedly included in the text we recognize that this is not just about the promised son Yitshaq.

In fact, only some of the instances of the Aleph Taw (✗✕) are displayed above, there are many others in the text. We see the Covenant of Circumcision wherein the seed of the man passes through the cutting of the Covenant on his body, just as the smoke and the fire torch passed through the cuttings.

Circumcision is a sign of the Covenant. Both the act of circumcising the male child on the eighth day, and the subsequent mark are the sign. It is a visible act, and a visible mark - both are meant to be seen. While many cultures circumcise their children, only those in Covenant with YHWH specifically circumcise on the eighth day. Again, the number eight is an important part of the Covenant and we can start to see how circumcision becomes the focus of the mysterious Appointed Time that occurs on the "eighth day," known as Shemini Atzeret.[113]

The text literally reads that you will "cut off ✗✕ the flesh of the foreskin." The Hebrew word for "circumcise" is "muwl" (ל ומ), and it involves removing the covering of flesh from a male organ. The removed flesh forms a circle, and one cannot ignore the similarity with the crescent moon and rainbow. All of these signs are circular, and there is a distinct connection between light and blood.[114]

So the sign of circumcision is made in the Children of

Light, the Children of the Covenant. Therefore, circumcision is a visible sign of light. It also speaks to another spiritual circumcision, the circumcision of the heart. The heart is the major organ that transmits the blood through the body. Again, the Covenant is intimately involved with the blood.

Abraham and all of the males in his household were immediately circumcised. They had to bear the sign of the Covenant if they were to dwell in the midst of a Covenant people. Abraham and Sarah were given the name of the promised son. His name would be Yitshaq, which has the gematria value 208 – the same as Hagar "the stranger." These connections have profound implications. Remember that Abram was uncircumcised when he entered into Hagar, but he was nevertheless in Covenant with YHWH. Later, after he was circumcised, Abraham entered into Sarah and she produced Yitshaq within the context of the Covenant of Circumcision.

The Covenant of Circumcision is interesting because it marks the male child born into the Covenant, but that mark is actually a sign of the obedience of the parents. In other words, the child is helpless in determining whether it occurs on the 8th day or not. This is where people get confused concerning the significance of circumcision. It is a sign that is perpetuated through the generations, but it is the responsibility of the parents, not the one receiving the mark. Only when a person enters the Covenant as an adult is the mark the responsibility of the recipient.

We later read of a time when YHWH came to visit Abraham while he was residing in Hebron. *"¹ Then YHWH appeared to him by the terebinth trees of Mamre, as he was sitting in the tent door in the heat of the day. ² So he lifted his eyes and looked, and behold, three men were standing by him; and when he saw them, he ran from the tent door to meet them, and bowed himself to the ground . . ."* Beresheet 18:1-2

Abraham entices YHWH and His companions to stop and rest. He offers "a little water" and "a morsel of bread." He ends up preparing a small feast. YHWH actually sits down and has a meal with Abraham. During the course of their time together YHWH informed Abraham ". . . *at the Appointed Time I will return to you, according to the time of life, and Sarah shall have a son.*" Beresheet 18:14.

The son was the missing piece to the Covenant promise. The son had previously been given a name, but it was not clear how he would be born. We read that while YHWH appeared and ate with Abraham He provided the timing of the son's birth. Interestingly, YHWH was on His way to judge four wicked cities near the Dead Sea. So the revelation of the son was given in the context of judgment.

Abraham knew that his nephew Lot lived in one of those cities and had already saved him once. During the encounter with YHWH Abraham actually negotiated for his life. He was counting on the fact that Lot was considered to be righteous, and we see an important principle that YHWH does not judge the righteous with the unrighteous. Even more compelling is the time selected for the judgment, the deliverance of Lot and the date of the birth of the promised son – Passover.

The Appointed Time of the son's birth was just that – an Appointed Time. It was a specific date and we can glean from the evidence that it was likely the time of Passover. The reason is because Abraham had prepared "cakes" and there is no indication that they were unleavened. Presumably, the next day or soon thereafter the messengers of YHWH arrived in Sodom to seek out Lot.

The interchange is very interesting. Lot bows before the messengers with his face to the ground. He asks them to go to his house, wash their feet, spend the night so they could get up early and leave. Not a very warm welcome, but he was

obviously concerned for their safety. After putting pressure on them he made them a feast and baked them unleavened bread.

The next morning, at dawn, the messengers essentially dragged Lot, his wife and two of his daughters out of the city. The text makes a point to reveal that it was the mercy of YHWH that resulted in their deliverance, not necessarily because they were righteous. Lot clearly was expressing righteous conduct in his attempt to protect the "strangers." This is something near and dear to the heart of YHWH. Regardless, his offer to give up his virgin daughters seems almost inexpicable. Even in the midst of the pending judgment Lot negotiated his escape which was supposed to be to the mountains. Instead he was permitted to go to Zoar, which was spared as a result.

Lot's wife was turned into a pillar of salt because she apparently could not detach from her life in Sodom. Interestingly, Lot later left Zoar and ended up going to the mountains after all. He lived in a cave. His daughters committed incest with him which resulted in two children: Moab and Ben-Ammi. These two boys later became the Moabites and the Ammonites.

After the destruction of the cities on the plain Abraham moved South to Gerar, between Kadesh and Shur. Here again we see him dwelling between two places, and one should expect to find special meaning. Typically, if you only read the text in English you will not see the underlying message contained in the passage. This is how the Hebrew Scriptures describe the two locations: "bein-qadesh v'bein shur" (ⴹⵢⵙ ⵢⵣⵘⵢ ⵙⴷⵟ-ⵢⵣⵘ). Interestingly there is a "bein" (ⵢⵣⵘ) at each location, which translates as "perceive." So we are directed in the Hebrew to perceive something.

The question is: What are we supposed to perceive?

The circumcised Abraham moved in between Qadesh, which essentially means: "holy, set apart," and Shur which means: "journey." The life of Abraham was a pattern for the Covenant path. His life, therefore, was a holy, or rather, set apart journey that all in the Covenant can follow.

In the midst of this "set apart journey" we are told that Abraham lived in a place called Gerar, which derives from the word "stranger" - ger (ﭏﭏ). Remember the name of his wife Hagar, also spelled Hager – the ger. "Gerar" means: "to pull or drag away, as in fish in a net." The significance is profound when we consider the journey of the Covenant, and perceive that the promises of Abraham and Sarah involved their offspring becoming kings and royalty.

The plan was to draw together the chosen people from around the world, like fish in a net, into the kingdom. These people would be apparent "strangers" engrafted and joined into the Covenant. This is clear when we read the prophets such as Jeremiah (Yirmeyahu)[115] who later proclaimed: *"Behold I will send for many fishermen, says YHWH, and they shall fish them . . ."* (Yirmeyahu 16:16) We also know that the Messiah sought out "fishers of men" in furtherance of this prophecy.

While in Gerar we read about another Egypt-like experience involving Abimelech, the King of Gerar. Abimelech means: "father of the King" and like Pharaoh, he took Sarah. Abimelech was told that Sarah was Abraham's brother, which was a half-truth. YHWH protected Sarah and cursed Abimelech who eventually released her and blessed Abraham. He sarcastically rebuked Sarah by proclaiming *"Behold I have given your **brother** a thousand pieces of silver."* Beresheet 20:16

These stories are encouraging because they reveal the imperfections of the patriarchs and matriarchs of the faith. They reveal that YHWH remains faithful to his promises even when we make unwise decisions and lack the requisite faith. Even so, YHWH was still with Abraham. He prayed to Elohim and Abimelech and all of his house were healed. They were then able to bear children. This event was uniquely timed since we next read about Sarah finally being able to bear a child.

"*¹ And YHWH visited* ✕𝋲*-Sarah as He had said, and YHWH did for Sarah as He had spoken. ² For Sarah conceived and bore Abraham a son in his old age, at the Appointed Time of which Elohim had spoken to him. ³ And Abraham called* ✕𝋲*-the name of his son who was born to him - whom Sarah bore to him - Yitshaq. ⁴ Then Abraham circumcised his son* ✕𝋲*-Yitshaq when he was eight days old, as Elohim had commanded him.*" Beresheet 21:1-4

In the Hebrew we see an emphasis on the Aleph Taw (✕𝋲) and the Word (𝋴𝋸𝋰) "spoken" by YHWH regarding the promised son Yitshaq. Yitshaq was born at an Appointed Time, and we continue to see the lives of these individuals as they become integrated with time itself. Creation begins to get realigned as the Covenant people come into synchronicity with YHWH and His cycles of time, known as the Appointed Times (moadim).[116]

It is interesting because YHWH clearly actively participated in this conception. Now the promised son was finally born in the old age of Abraham and Sarah. Yitshaq was the firstborn son of the Covenant. Others in the household of Abraham joined the Covenant through Circumcision at any age, but Yitshaq, by the hands of Abraham was the first that we know of to be circumcised on the 8th Day, which began this Covenant ritual that would continue into perpetuity.

Based upon the previously mentioned hints regarding the birth of Yitshaq it is very likely he was born at the Appointed Time of Passover that occurs every year on Day

14 of Month 1.

As a result, he would have been circumcised on the 8th day, which is Day 21 of Month 1. It was the 6th day on the Omer Count and it was also the last day of the Feast of Unleavened Bread. This is a High Sabbath and would be a great day in the deliverance of his Covenant decendants, as we shall soon see.

So we can see through this firstborn son of the Covenant, referred to as the "only son" of Abraham, the patterns surrounding the Appointed Times that are essentially a blueprint for the Plan of YHWH leading to the end of time. These patterns established in the past through the Torah and lived out by the patriarchs are all prophetic in nature with profound future implications.

In what is likely the most mysterious and profound event of this Covenant family, YHWH later told Abraham to take Yitshaq, the promised son, and sacrifice him. It appears at this time that Abraham was residing in Beersheba, which means: "well of seven." This was the place were Abraham dug a well, planted a tree and gave Abimelech seven lambs.

Here is what happened: *"So Abraham rose early in the morning and saddled his* X𝚼-*donkey, and took* X𝚼-*two of his young men with him,* 𝚼X𝚼 *and* X𝚼 *Yitshaq his son; and he split the wood for the burnt offering, and arose and went to the place of which the Elohim had told him."* Beresheet 22:3 Notice the existence of the Aleph Taw (X𝚼) throughout the text. We see the Aleph Taw (X𝚼) brought to the place of sacrifice on a donkey. We also see the Aleph Taw (X𝚼) standing alone, affixed by the "waw" or "vav" (𝚼) – the stake, associated with the two men and the promised son Yitshaq. This was a foreshadow of the future work to be performed by the Messiah.

Abraham took his son to the mountains of Moriah,

which was in the region of Jerusalem, where Melchizedek reigned. So the place where the righteous king reigns, the Promised Son must die.

It was there that he took his son, built an altar and prepared to slaughter him. The thing that most people miss when reading this story is the fact that Abraham fully expected his son to be resurrected. That was the only way that the promises of the Covenant could be fulfilled. It was evident from the directives that he gave to the young men who accompanied him to the mountain. *"Stay here with* עֹ- *the donkey; the lad and I will go yonder and worship, and we will come back to you."* Beresheet 22:5. Notice the "am" (עֹ) attached to the donkey that stays behind. "am" means: "congregation." It is worth noting that worship involved shedding blood.

When the father and son walked up the hill, Yitshaq prophetically carried the wood on his back. When asked about the sacrifice Abraham prophetically stated: *"Elohim will provide Himself the Lamb."* Beresheet 22:8. Abraham erected the altar, placed the wood and bound his son. As he was about to slaughter Yitshaq, the Messenger of YHWH called out from heaven and told him not to harm his son. YHWH then provided a ram caught in a thicket by its horns. This was a prophetic picture of how YHWH would provide His son as the sacrifice. The ram was caught by the horns. Those horns would become two shofars after the sacrifice.

So through the life of this one man we see the Covenant path actually lived out. From the uncircumcised Abram who came out of Babylon, and later Egypt, to the circumcised Abraham who could populate the Kingdom. That was, after all, the promise - nations and kings – a lot of them.

When he was uncircumcised the promise involved numerous descendants likened to the dust of the earth, and the land was that which he could see in the Land of Canaan. (Beresheet 13) Later, he was promised descendants as numerous as the stars in the sky, and the borders ranged from the Nile to the Euphrates River. (Beresheet 15) When his name was changed to Abraham and he received the Covenant of Circumcision, the promise was that he would be a father of many nations and the borders consisted of the Land of Canaan. (Beresheet 17)

Finally, after he offered up the promised son to be slaughtered the promise was that his descendants would be multiplied as the stars of the heavens and the sand of the seashore. Also, all the nations of the earth would be blessed through his seed. (Beresheet 22) These are often overlooked distinctions with profound prophetic significance.

We were also provided patterns of his travels. When he came out of Babylon he delayed in Haran, which was to the north of Canaan, along the Euphrates River. He finally went to the land of Canaan. The first place in Canaan that he went was Shechem. This seems to be the entry point to the Land, as we shall see repeated.

This Covenant journey continued through the Covenant children of Abraham. We learn important lessons from the life of Yitshaq and his bride. The selection of the Bride for the Promised Son of the Covenant has great prophetic significance.

After we read about the presentation of the promised son and the Lamb of Elohim - the Messianic death and resurrection event - Yitshaq essentially disappears from the text. It is while Yitshaq is absent that the father goes about preparing a bride for his son.

In fact, the text very abruptly transitions from the event on the mountain in Moriah, to a lineage of Abraham's brother Nahor. The only way that the covenant promise can be fulfilled is if the promised son finds a wife.

Abraham chose his servant for the task – likely Eliezer. This was significant and important to both of these men. Abraham had originally thought Eliezer would be his heir. So he was very close to Abraham – like a son. The name Eliezer actually means: "El helps." The message here is that Elohim would find the bride. In fact, the text is very clear on that point.

"*² So Abraham said to the oldest servant of his house, who ruled over all that he had, Please, put your hand under my thigh, ³ and I will make you swear by YHWH, the Elohim of heaven and the Elohim of the earth, that you will not take a wife for my son from the daughters of the Canaanites, among whom I dwell; ⁴ but you shall go to my country and to my family, and take a wife for my son Yitshaq. ⁵ And the servant said to him, Perhaps the woman will not be willing to follow me to this land. Must I take your son back to the land from which you came? ⁶ But Abraham said to him, Beware that you do not take ✕✦-my son back there. ⁷ YHWH Elohim of heaven, who took me from my father's house and from the land of my family, and who spoke to me and swore to me, saying, To your descendants I give this ✕✦-land,' He will send His angel before you, and you shall take a wife for my son from there. ⁸ And if the woman is not willing to follow you, then you will be released from this oath; only do not take my son back there. ⁹ So the servant put ✕✦-his hand under the thigh of Abraham his master, and swore to him concerning this matter.*" Beresheet 24:2-9

So YHWH would send a messenger before Eliezer to find a bride for the promised son. The union is all about the Land and the Covenant. The English translation is not as graphic as the Hebrew. Eliezer did not place his hand under Abraham's thigh, but rather on his genitals, the place of the circumcision. By having Eliezer place his hand on the circumcision, Abraham was emphasizing that this task was all about the Covenant.

Interestingly, a servant was sent out of the Promised

Land to find a bride. Yitshaq did not go. He stayed in the Covenant Land. The Land of Canaan was, after all, an integral part of the Covenant of Circumcision. The Bridegroom would not go out to the bride, but rather the servant would go and gather the bride back to the Covenant Land where the Bridegroom was waiting. This is an extremely important detail when we consider how the messiah will gather His Bride at the end of the age.

Eliezar went north, to a region he was familiar with. He crossed the Euphrates and ventured into Paddan Aram, where some of Abram's family resided. When he came to the City of Nahor, also called Haran, he stopped at a well and prayed. After praying he was shown Rebekah, in Hebrew her name is Ribkah (𐤀𐤒𐤏𐤀). So at the well he found the bride for the son of the Covenant. He negotiated a price and Ribkah was given a choice. Ribkah agreed to marry Yitshaq. The passage is profound in the Hebrew.

"*59 So they sent away* X𐤊*-Ribkah their sister and her* X𐤊*-nurse, and Abraham's* X𐤊*-servant and his* X𐤊*-men. 60 And they blessed* X𐤊*-Ribkah and said to her: Our sister, may* X𐤊 *exist the mother of thousands of ten thousands; and may your descendants possess* X𐤊 *the gates of those who hate them. 61 Then Ribkah and her maids arose, and they rode on the camels and followed the man. So the servant took* X𐤊*-Ribkah and departed.*" Beresheet 24:59-61

Notice the literal translation taken from the Hebrew. Actually, the blessing was that Aleph Taw (X𐤊) would exist in enormous numbers through her. This is a mysterious and appropriate blessing for a woman who would wed the promised son of the Covenant that involved enormous descendants. The presence of the Aleph Taw (X𐤊) throughout the text reveals that this is truly establishing a pattern for the Bride of YHWH. Through this Bride the Covenant promise would multiply.

So Eliezer would fetch a bride and bring her back from the north, across the Euphrates River on 10 camels. Only after the bride is sought out by the messenger of the father, "purchased" and brought back to the Land does the Groom, Yitshaq, reappear in the text. While the Bride comes from the north, the groom comes from the south. The text describes Yitshaq coming from Beer Lahai Roi, the well between Kadesh (sanctuary) and Bered (hail).

Beer Lahai Roi was the spring where Hager, the stranger, fled after being despised by Sarai. It was there that she was met by the Messenger of YHWH, and told she was bearing the child of Abram. The text indicates that it was YHWH Who spoke to her and promised: "*I will multiply your* ×‹*-descendants exceedingly, so that they shall not be counted for multitude.*" Beresheet 16:10 This is where she called the Name of YHWH Who appeared to her "You are the El Who sees."

It became a well and was the place where Yitshaq dwelled after the death of Abraham. (Beresheet 25:11) So the bride, Ribkah, was found at a well and the groom, Yitshaq, lived at a well. The well, a place of water and life, was the connection between the bride and the groom. This entire event and the geography had profound prophetic significance.[117]

Eliezer brought back Ribkah, Yitshaq immediately took her into Sarah's tent. "*Then Yitshaq brought her into his mother Sarah's tent; and he took Ribkah and she became his wife, and he loved her. So Yitshaq was comforted after his mother's death.*" Beresheet 24:67

This is interesting because Sarah was obviously dead, so why was her tent erected. This was the place where Yitshaq was conceived and born. Her tent was passed on to Ribkah as the place where the Covenant seed would be passed. Like Sarah, Ribkah too was barren and she did not immediately bear children.

Eventually, through the cutting of the eighth day circumcision, she became pregnant and produced twins. The two brothers, Esau and Jacob (Yaakob) were clearly not identical twins based upon their described physical differences. There are actually two different ways that twins can be born. With identical twins, one fertilized egg replicates and divides after which both cells, containing identical genetic information, develop into children. In the case of fraternal twins, the woman produces two eggs, which are both fertilized by different sperm that each develop into children.

When these fraternal twins were born, Yaakob was actually grabbing on to the heel of his brother Esau while Esau was born. As a result, Esau was technically the first to be born, thus he was entitled to all the rights and privileges of the firstborn.

Yaakob ultimately obtained that birthright from both his brother and his father through questionable means and even outright deception. As a result, he fled Beersheba and headed north to the place called Paddan Aram. "The term was perhaps more especially applied to that portion which bordered on the Euphrates, to distinguish if from the mountainous districts in the north and northeast of Mesopotamia."[118]

En route to Paddan Aram, before leaving the Promised Land, he stayed at Luz, and named it Beit El (Bethel) – the House of El. The word "luz" is associated with an almond tree, and some believe that the Tree of Life was an almond tree.[119] How appropriate then for this place to be called the House of Elohim, representing the Garden of Eden.

While Yaakob slept, he dreamed, and YHWH spoke to him in the dream. YHWH affirmed the Covenant with him. *"[11] So he came to a certain place and stayed there all night,* *because the sun had set. And he took one of the stones of that place and put it at his head, and he lay down in that place to sleep. ¹² Then he dreamed, and behold, a ladder was set up on the earth, and its top reached to heaven; and there the messengers of Elohim were ascending and descending on it. ¹³ And behold, YHWH stood above it and said: I am YHWH Elohi of Abraham your father and the Elohi of Yitshaq; the land on which you lie I will give to you and your descendants. ¹⁴ Also your descendants shall be as the dust of the earth; you shall spread abroad to the west and the east, to the north and the south; and in you and in your seed all the families of the earth shall be blessed. ¹⁵ Behold, I am with you and will keep you wherever you go, and will bring you back to this land; for I will not leave you until I have done what I have spoken to you."* Beresheet 28:11-15.

Those were much needed words of reassurance as he was in the process of leaving the Land. He was headed north and would cross over the Euphrates, back the way Abram had come, but at the same time he was given the promises of Abraham. He would eventually return the same route that Abraham had come. The pattern of departing to the north and returning has implications that transcend to the end of this present age.

The event is commemorated by the vision of the ladder, often referred to as "Jacob's Ladder." The ladder should immediately make us think of the "het" (ח), which has the numeric value of 8 – the number associated with the Covenant and the culmination of time. This "ladder" was the connecting point between the heaven's and the earth. It was an intra-dimensional portal whereby man can transcend from the physical to the spiritual.

When he awoke from his sleep he made a very profound declaration: *"¹⁶ . . . surely YHWH is in this place, and I did not know it. ¹⁷ And he was afraid and said, How awesome is this place! This is none other than the House of Elohim, and <u>this is</u>*

the gate of heaven!" Beresheet 28:16-17

Now we know the place is called Beth El, so his declaration that it is the House of Elohim is no surprise. The intriguing part of his comment is that it is "the gate of heaven." So now we understand that there is a significant connection between the House of YHWH and the gate of heaven. The House of Elohim of earth connected to the heavens. This is the very gate that Nimrod was trying to open at the Tower of Babel.

After Yaakob awoke he was a changed man – at least his priorities had changed. While he had previously sought to build his own house through deception, he was now prepared to build the House of Elohim through the Covenant.

"*18 Then Yaakob rose early in the morning, and took* ✕✔- *the stone (aben) that he had put at his head, set it up as a pillar, and poured oil on top of it. 19 And he called the name of that place Bethel; but the name of that city had been Luz previously. 20 Then Yaakob made a vow, saying, 'If Elohim will be with me, and keep me in this way that I am going, and give me bread to eat and clothing to put on, 21 so that I come back to my father's house in peace, then YHWH shall be my Elohim. 22 And this stone which I have set as a pillar shall be Elohim's house, and of all that You give me I will surely give a tenth to You.*" Beresheet 28:18-22

This act had great prophetic significance. Incredibly, the Aleph Taw (✕✔) is attached to the stone. This is the "aben" (✔𝟗✔) in Hebrew, which was previously mentioned. By no coincidence the word "aben" (✔𝟗✔) is a combination of "father" – ab (𝟗✔) and "son" – ben (✔𝟗). Yaakob then raised up the aben as a pillar in the House of El and anointed it with oil. This is the first place in the Scriptures that we read about oil and anointing something with oil. The word for "anoint" is "moshiach" (𝋾W𝟿) which is where we get the word "messiah." We will later see that you anoint kings and priests, both of which are represented in Melchizedek.

Remember that the gematria value for aben ($\textrm{אבן}$) is 53, which is the same as "garden" – gan ($\textrm{גן}$), and "the jubilee" – ha'yobel ($\textrm{היובל}$). All of these concepts united in the Beit El – the House of Elohim. So this "stone" (Messiah) joins together this time (the Jubilee) and this space (Garden).

Yaakob raised a family and prospered greatly while living in his Uncle Laban's service as a veritable slave. Laban did not want Yaakob to leave because he knew YHWH prospered him because of Yaakob. He told Yaakob to name his wages, so he did. Yaakob struck a deal that he "tend and keep" the flocks of Laban. He would retain all of the speckled and spotted sheep, dark lambs and the spotted and speckled goats. Essentially, all of the pure white ones would belong to Laban and the mixed or dark ones would belong to Yaakob.

Interestingly, the word for "white" is "laban" ($\textrm{לבן}$). So Laban would keep the pure "laban" flocks. After they struck the deal and separated from one another Yaakob took some very peculiar steps.

Here is what we read in the text: "*37 Now Yaakob took for himself rods of moist poplar and of the almond and chestnut trees, peeled white strips in them, and exposed the white which was in the rods. 38 And the rods which he had peeled, he set before the flocks in the gutters, in the watering troughs where the flocks came to drink, so that they should conceive when they came to drink. 39 So the flocks conceived before the rods, and the flocks brought forth streaked, speckled, and spotted. 40 Then Yaakob separated the lambs, and made the flocks face toward the streaked and all the brown in the flock of Laban; but he put his own flocks by themselves and did not put them with Laban's flock. 41 And it came to pass, whenever the stronger livestock conceived, that Yaakob placed the rods before the eyes of the livestock in the gutters, that they might conceive among the rods. 42 But when the flocks were feeble, he did not put them in; so the feebler were Laban's and the stronger*

Yaakob's. *⁴³ Thus the man became exceedingly prosperous, and had large flocks, female and male servants, and camels and donkeys."* Beresheet 30:31-42

This process sounds bizarre but notice the emphasis on the white. What Yaakob is doing involves breeding and genetics. Through this process involving breeding the flocks while they are drinking water in front of peeled white rods, Yaakob strengthened his numbers while diminishing Laban's.

As it turns out, Yaakob was shown what to do in a dream, and he was told when to leave by the Messenger of YHWH. *"¹⁰ And it happened, at the time when the flocks conceived, that I lifted my eyes and saw in a dream, and behold, the rams which leaped upon the flocks were streaked, speckled, and gray-spotted. ¹¹ Then the Messenger of Elohim spoke to me in a dream, saying, Yaakob. And I said, Here I am. ¹² And He said, Lift your eyes now and see, all the rams which leap on the flocks are streaked, speckled, and gray-spotted; for I have seen all that Laban is doing to you. ¹³ I am the Elohim of Bethel, where you anointed the pillar and where you made a vow to Me. Now arise, get out of this land, and return to the land of your family."* Beresheet 31:10-13

Interestingly, YHWH identified Himself directly with the vow that Yaakob had previously made at Bet El – the House of Elohim. That vow involved a return to the Land and a tithe of his wealth. The focal point of that vow was the anointed stone – the Moshiach Aben.

When it finally came time for Yaakob to return home, he crossed the Euphrates River as he traveled from Paddan Aram in the North to the Land of Canaan in the South.

Just before he crossed over the Jordan River into the Promised Land, he had a mysterious encounter and received a name change, like his grandfather Abraham. We read that while on his way the messengers of Elohim met with him. When Yaakob saw them he said *"this is Elohim's Camp and he*

called the place Machenah (ꓺꓺꓺ)." (Beresheet 32:1-2)

The significance of this place might be lost, unless it is connected with the "camp" or rather "camps" (ꓺꓺꓺꓺ) later described in Bemidbar 5:3 which has the numerical equivalence of 153. Remember that "beni ha'Elohim" also equals 153. This passage references "their ✗𝄪-camps" in the midst where YHWH dwells.

What happens next should be seen as a prophetic event with future implications. While Yaakob met messengers of Elohim, we are not provided any information concerning a conversation. Instead we read about Yaakob sending messengers ahead of him to speak to his brother Esau, who is coming to meet him.

Yaakob received word back that Esau was coming to meet him with four hundred men. We read the following: *"So Yaakob was greatly afraid and distressed; and he divided ✗𝄪-the people that-✗𝄪 were with him, and ✗𝄪-the flocks and ✗𝄪-herds and camels, into two companies."* Beresheet 32:7. He did this to protect his family from being completely annihilated by Esau and his army, believing that Esau was ready for battle.

Interestingly, Yaakob did not turn and flee. He did not refuse to return to the Land of promise – even though he was in great distress and fear of impending doom. He divided his house into two companies – two camps (✗ꓺꓺꓺ). He prayed for deliverance and then invoked the Covenant promise that YHWH would make his: *"✗𝄪-seed as the sand of the sea."* Beresheet 32:12

He then took from his blessings and gave a gifts to Esau. The word for "gift" is "minchah" (ꓺꓺꓺꓺ) which means: "a tribute, gift or offering." This is the same word used to describe the offerings made to YHWH, and it appears to be in the form of a tithe, because it was calculated pursuant to the blessings he received while outside of the

Land. It was almost like an entrance fee to get back into the Promised Land.

He sent the offerings ahead of him in waves and each time the servants were to refer to Esau as "Lord" – Adonai (𐤉𐤄𐤀𐤊). Yaakob stayed that night behind in "the camp." Yaakob (𐤉𐤒𐤏𐤉) then arose that same night, and brought his family over the ford of Yabok (𐤒𐤉𐤆). This is a word play on Yaakob's name (𐤉𐤒𐤏𐤉). He sent everything and everyone else across so that he alone was left behind. At this mysterious place we see the bet (𐤉), the house, replacing the ayin (𐤏) in the word play. So we are being told to "see the house."

Here is what we read in English. "*And he arose that night and took his two wives, his two female servants, and his eleven sons, and crossed over the ford of Yabok.*" Beresheet 32:22. In the Hebrew we see the Aleph Taw (X𐤊) affixed to the "two" wives (𐤉𐤔𐤉 𐤉XW-X𐤊), the "two" servants (𐤉X𐤇𐤏W 𐤉XW-X𐤊) and "eleven" sons (𐤉𐤃𐤋𐤉 𐤀WO 𐤃𐤇𐤊-X𐤊). The Aleph Taw (X𐤊) also stands alone between "crossed over" and "ford of Yabok." The phrase "crossed over" is "eber" (𐤃𐤏𐤉), the same word as Hebrew – "ebriy" (𐤉𐤃𐤏𐤏). The only difference is the "yud" (𐤉). In fact, the word for "ford" (𐤉𐤃𐤏𐤉) is essentially the same word also.

So the Aleph Taw (X𐤊) is in the midst of the "crossing over" – becoming a Hebrew. After they all crossed over, Yaakob then "sent them over the brook." (see Beresheet 32:23). The Aleph Taw (X𐤊) was intimately involved in that process when you examine the Hebrew. Only then, when Yaakob was alone, did he wrestle with a mysterious Man.

Here again we see a word play with the name of Yaakob. The word for wrestle is "yabek" (𐤒𐤉𐤊𐤉). At the center of this wrestling event is "ab" (𐤉𐤊) – father. The life of this man Yaakob, who wrestled with life from the womb, was now coming full circle. His return (shub) to the land was a completion of the cycle. He is essentially wrestling with the "power ($\boldsymbol{\mathsf{K}}$) of the house ($\boldsymbol{\mathsf{9}}$)." He is no longer wrestling with his physical family (ie. Esau, Yitshaq, Laban), he is now wrestling with his spiritual father.

The text describing the name change is full of mystery. Now in an English translation it appears simple enough. Yaakob wrestled a man until the breaking of the day and the man said: "*Your name shall no longer be called Jacob, but Israel; for you have struggled with Elohim and with men, and have prevailed.*" Beresheet 32:28.

When we read the text in the Hebrew, it is filled with information that is not translated in the English. The reason that it is not included in the English is because the translators often do not know how to translate mysteries. Here is a translation with some of the missing information. "*Your name shall no longer be called Yaakob, but $\boldsymbol{\mathsf{ZY}}$ $\boldsymbol{\mathsf{YK}}$-Yisrael; for you have $\boldsymbol{\mathsf{ZY}}$-struggled ($\boldsymbol{\mathsf{XZ9W}}$) with $\boldsymbol{\mathsf{Y\odot}}$-Elohim and with $\boldsymbol{\mathsf{YK}}$-men, and have prevailed.*" Beresheet 32:28.

Now we could write a book concerning the mysteries contained in this single passage of Hebrew text. Here only a few words have been highlighted. For instance, Yaakob was not simply named Yisrael, but rather em-Yisrael. The word "em" ($\boldsymbol{\mathsf{YK}}$) literally means: "mother." So as with the name changes involving Abraham and Sarah, something was being birthed through Yisrael. This event demonstrated a transformation from physical to spiritual, as had occurred with Abraham and Sarah.

This fact was crystalized with the inclusion of the word "Sarai" ($\boldsymbol{\mathsf{Z9W}}$) followed by the taw ($\boldsymbol{\mathsf{X}}$), which means: "covenant." The word $\boldsymbol{\mathsf{XZ9W}}$ is translated as "struggle," but there is the word for prince ($\boldsymbol{\mathsf{Z9W}}$) followed by the taw ($\boldsymbol{\mathsf{X}}$). The focus is clear in the Hebrew. Notice that Elohim is preceded by the word "am" which means: "a flock, a people, a tribe, a nation." The same word precedes "men." This is a prophecy imbedded within the text, but it can only be seen in the Hebrew.

The word "kee" (𐤉𐤊) means: "to brand, scar or burn." The first time that "kee" (𐤉𐤊) is referred to in the Scriptures is when Elohim called the Light at the beginning "good." In fact, He called it "kee-tob" (𐤉𐤅𐤈-𐤉𐤊). So it seems hidden in the text is the branding of this man with the Light.

An important part of this wrestling event involved the name change and the blessing. It also focused on a very intimate and sensitive covenant event - circumcision. Most common English translations provide that the man "touched the socket of his thigh." The word used for thigh is "yarek" (𐤊𐤋𐤉) in Hebrew.

As with Abraham and Eliezer, the "thigh" is likely a euphemism for his genitals. (Beresheet 24:2, 9). Both instances involve a significant Covenant event, and the mystery here involves a circumcision of light. It was a necessary step as he crossed over into the Promised Land with his new name and identity. This surely would have accounted for his limp.

Amazingly, Yaakob named the place of this event Peniel (𐤋𐤀𐤉𐤍𐤐). He stated: *"For I have seen Elohim face to face, and my life is preserved."* Beresheet 32:30. The term "face to face" infers a deep and intimate knowledge. A man and a woman commune intimately "face to face," and we will later read about a special man named Mosheh who communed "face to face" with YHWH.

Immediately after he named the location we read: *"Just as he crossed over (eber)* 𐤕𐤀-Penuel (𐤋𐤀𐤅𐤍𐤐-𐤕𐤀) *the sun rose on him . . ."* Beresheet 32:31. Notice that the word Penuel (𐤋𐤀𐤅𐤍𐤐) is different from the previous name Peniel (𐤋𐤀𐤉𐤍𐤐). There is a vav (𐤅) inserted in the middle instead of the yud (ℸ). So the man - vav (Y) is connected with the arm - yud (ℸ). The yud representing an arm can easily be seen in the most ancient pictograph - ᴗ. There is also an Aleph Taw (X𝐊) connected with Penuel.

This encounter involved his intimate parts pointing to a birthing process that was part of the Covenant. The change of name involved a new identity, a blessing and the crossing over of a people, and the Aleph Taw (X𝐊) was directly involved in the process.

After this vital Covenant event, Yaakob then crossed over into the Land and made amends with Esau. He presented himself with humility to Esau, referring to Esau as "my lord" and himself as "your servant." After being restored with his brother and his family, and returning to the Land "Yisrael" he then went to Succot, where he built a house for himself and succas for his livestock.

This was a very prophetic event as Succot is one of the important Appointed Times on the Creator's Calendar. It is a time that occurs every year in the Seventh month. A time when we are to meet with YHWH at His House. Here again we see the Covenant people merging time and space providing prophetic pictures and patterns for future generations.[120]

Yisrael was joined together at Succot - a place within the eastern boundary of the Land Promised to Abraham - west of the Euphrates River. Yisrael lived in a house while the livestock live in succas - tents or other temporary dwellings. This was a prophetic event. It was a rehearsal that was to occur throughout time by the Covenant people foreshadowing a future return.

When the Kingdom of YHWH is established we see that there are those who will dwell in the House and those that will dwell in succas. Currently, those in the Covenant who celebrate Succot dwell in succas. The hope is to some day dwell in the House of YHWH. The point is evident – Yisrael is the one who dwells in the House.

Once Yisrael crossed over the Jordan River into the Land of Canaan he did as Abram had done – he went to Shechem. He purchased land in Shechem where things went awry. Elohim told him to go to Beit El, live there and build an altar. Interestingly, Elohim talks to him and affirms the Covenant. He confirms the name change of Yaakob to Yisrael. Yisrael built an altar and set up an aben as a pillar. He then anointed the pillar with wine <u>and</u> oil. (See Beresheet 35).

The altar of Abraham stood between man, and the House of YHWH. Now the Altar of Yisrael was erected within the House of Elohim – Beit El (Bethel). This was the place where the aben was anointed (moshiach). The aben was an unhewn stone, and the altar was built from unhewn stones. In other words it was not a creation of man, but a creation of YHWH. It was bloody and had 4 horns. It was the place where the holy fire (esh qodesh) was present and consumed the offerings of men. This was the point where a man did business with YHWH.

The altar represented the sacrifice needed to bring man into relationship with YHWH. Amazingly, an ancient breed of sheep called Jacob's Sheep have four horns. So the altar with 4 horns physically represents the Lamb of Elohim of the Covenant patterned through the lives of the patriarchs.

We can clearly see the redemptive plan of YHWH through the Covenant, and the patterns of the lives of those who entered into that Covenant. The Covenant established through Noah was with all of creation. Those eight (8)

beings in the Ark set the stage for the Covenant relationship that YHWH had in store for His people.

Ten generations from Noah led us to a man named Abram. Abram was given a promise and he acted upon that promise. His life was a pattern for the person desirous of entering into a Covenant relationship. YHWH was once again, building a House (Ark). Through the Covenant process YHWH was now building a family to fill that House.

Instead of simply creating beings and placing them in paradise, YHWH was now going to include those who freely chose Him and His ways. The Covenant process was how YHWH would communicate with mankind through a relationship. He made promises with blessings and consequences. He gave gifts and drew men to Himself. He did all of this through a man and a promised son to reveal how He would build a family to populate His Kingdom. The Kingdom of YHWH would consist of those within the Covenant family – an assembly of people called Yisrael.

5

Yisrael

The Assembly of Yisrael was the result of an individual born into the Covenant, renewed and transformed into a family, a tribe, a nation and then a Kingdom. Yisrael was the conduit for the Covenant made with Abraham. Through that Covenant YHWH has been building a Kingdom that can be restored to the Garden – His House. The Covenant continues to this day.

If you can understand this concept then you can understand what the Scriptures are describing from the beginning through to the end of time. Everything occurs within the context and confines of the Covenant. The Covenant is the path back into the Kingdom – the Kingdom that YHWH originally gave to Adam in Paradise. When this Kingdom is once again established on earth, it will be ruled by the Last Adam – the Messiah.

The patterns of this Earthly Kingdom transcend to the Heavenly Kingdom. Adam was to be a King and Priest over Creation – Melchizedek. He was to establish and rule over the Kingdom of YHWH on the earth. He failed and YHWH has been rebuilding His Kingdom through the Covenant. The Scriptures describe this Covenant progression that is not only a historical record, but also a pattern for us to learn from and follow. It connects both Heaven and Earth.

So far, we have read about YHWH entering into a Covenant relationship with certain individuals with the goal

of restoring creation. He communicated with them, we even read how Abraham was actually refered to as the friend of YHWH (Isaiah 41:8). So YHWH built relationships and friendships with His Creation.

After the man Yisrael returned to the Covenant Land with his family another son was born – Benjamin. We read about the twelve sons of Yisrael in the Land, with a great emphasis on Joseph and Judah (Yahudah). Joseph was actually given powerful dreams relative to his fate. In fact, this was how YHWH communicated to Joseph – through his dreams.

"*⁵ And Joseph dreamed a dream, and he told it to his brethren: and they hated him yet the more. ⁶ And he said unto them, Hear, I pray you, this dream which I have dreamed: ⁷ For, behold, we were binding sheaves in the field, and, lo, my sheaf arose, and also stood upright; and, behold, your sheaves stood round about, and made obeisance to my sheaf. ⁸ And his brethren said to him, Shalt thou indeed reign over us? or shalt thou indeed have dominion over us? And they hated him yet the more for his dreams, and for his words. ⁹ And he dreamed yet another dream, and told it his brethren, and said, Behold, I have dreamed a dream more; and, behold, the sun and the moon and the eleven stars made obeisance to me. ¹⁰ And he told it to his father, and to his brethren: and his father rebuked him, and said unto him, What is this dream that thou hast dreamed? Shall I and thy mother and thy brethren indeed come to bow down ourselves to thee to the earth? ¹¹ And his brethren envied him; but his father observed the saying.*"
Beresheet 37:5-11

Now if you only read this in the English you would miss something very important. When the text speaks of his brethren envying him, it also provides that his father "guarded" (shomar) "𐤕𐤀-the Word" (𐤓𐤁𐤃𐤄-𐤕𐤀). So we see the Aleph Taw (𐤕𐤀) attached to "the Word." These dreams therefore had great Messianic significance.

As the man Yisrael brought his family into the Promised Land we see the patterns of Abraham repeated. Only now there were eleven sons born across the Euphrates and later brought into the Land. There was another son, Benjamin, who was actually born in the Land. Yisrael purchased land at Shechem. He also built an altar there to YHWH, just as Abram had done when  he ventured from Padam Aram, across the Euphrates River and into the Land.

The Scriptures record that Joseph, the 11th son of Yaakob, was favored as a firstborn son. This was the result of the failures of the other sons, but they ended up becoming jealous of Joseph. He was given a robe, often referred to as a "coat of many colors." This was a royal robe setting him apart as a prince. All of the brothers, except for Reuben, plotted to kill him. The remaining brothers ultimately decided to sell him into slavery when his father sent him to check on them at Dothan, near Shechem.

The event was prophetic. The father sent "the prince," the firstborn son, as his representative to check on his brothers. Instead of focusing on their work and gladly receiving their brother, they were consumed with their own petty concerns and jealousies. When the son arrived, the first thing they did was strip him of his royal vestige. The account in Hebrew is quite profound. Here is the English with some Hebrew words not seen in the translation. "*So it came to pass, when Joseph had come to his brothers, that they stripped* 𐤕𐤀-

Joseph of his ✗‍☧-tunic, ✗‍☧-tunic of many colors that was on him." Beresheet 37:23

Notice the Aleph Taw (✗‍☧) associated with Joseph and the tunic. We see the Aleph Taw (✗‍☧) repeatedly associated with Joseph throughout the rest of the account. After stripping Joseph, at the behest of Reuben, they then threw him into a pit instead of immediately killing him. Joseph, naked in the pit, was in a symbolic state of death.

Unbeknownst to Reuben, the physical firstborn son, the other brothers sold Joseph into slavery. When Reuben returned to the pit to rescue Joseph we read: "ᵧ‍ᴢ‍☧-Joseph in the pit . . ." (Beresheet 37:29) Joseph did not exist (ᵧ‍ᴢ‍☧) in the pit. This was a type of resurrection.

Blood was shed by these 10 brothers who betrayed Joseph. The fact that there were 10 brothers associated with this event is prophetic concerning the future work of the Messiah ben Joseph concerning 10 tribes of Yisrael.[121] The brothers tore the royal robe and slaughtered one of their father's flock, a goat. They then dipped ✗‍☧-robe into the blood of the goat, and told their father that Joseph was dead.[122]

Joseph ended up a slave in Egypt, and then a prisoner. Despite this apparent downward spiral he was miraculously elevated to Vice Regent of Egypt, second only to Pharaoh, when he was 30 years old. (Beresheet 41:46). Interestingly, this was the age when a priest could begin his service. It was symbolic of the Messiah, the only Son of YHWH, being second to the Father reigning over the earth.

Joseph was able to interpret the dreams of the Pharaoh. This allowed Pharaoh to prepare during seven years of prosperity for seven future years of famine. Those who did not prepare sold everything they had to buy food from Pharaoh – their livestock, their possessions, their land and themselves. It was likely one of the greatest transfers of wealth in history. It later involved forced relocation and heavy taxation by Pharaoh. (Beresheet 47)

Through this process, Joseph saved many of the inhabitants of the region from starvation. It also set the stage for Pharaoh to acquire everything – even the people.

Joseph was responsible for this empowering of Pharaoh. After all, he was the one responsible for making preparations and implementing the plan. It is important to discern another important pattern revealed by this event. The text provides: "*Joseph gathered very much grain (ᎯᎩ), as the sand of the sea, until he stopped counting, for it was immeasurable.*" Beresheet 41:49. The word for "grain" is "bar" (ᎯᎩ) which actually means "son" in Hebrew.[123] So Joseph was prophetically gathering "sons" as the sand of the sea.[124]

This was the promise given to Abraham after he offered Yitshaq – his only son on the mountains of Moriah. It was the same promise given to Yaakob. "*For You said, I will surely treat you well, and make your ✗✗-descendants as the sand of the sea, which cannot be numbered for multitude.*" Beresheet 32:12 So this gathering in Egypt would play an important part in the Covenant process.

The Scriptures record that the famine was all over the earth. As a result, all countries came to Joseph in Egypt to buy grain. (Beresheet 41:56-57) He was known as Zaphnath-paaneah. As a result, he was hidden by an Egyptian name. Through this process of worldwide famine, all the nations were drawn to Joseph, including his family. It is interesting that Joseph never set about to find his family. He stayed in Egypt, even when given a great position and power.

It was only when famine struck and there was a lack of food in the land, that his brothers were drawn to Egypt. Abram had also gone to Egypt during a famine. His life lived through the Covenant provided the framework for what would later occur with the children of Yisrael.

At first, the brothers did not recognize their brother. He looked like an Egyptian and he spoke like an Egyptian - he even had an Egyptian name. Essentially, he appeared in every respect to be a pagan Egyptian. Despite being confronted by him, the brothers failed to recognize Joseph. It was only at the appointed time that he revealed himself to his brothers. This was likely an Appointed Time of YHWH, and a prophetic event to be sure.[125]

Joseph revealed himself during the second year of the seven year famine. He told his brothers that Elohim had sent them before his brothers for this exact time and for a specific purpose. *"And Elohim sent me before you to preserve a posterity for you in the earth, and to save your lives by a great deliverance."* Beresheet 45:7. So their lives would be saved from famine and death by a "great deliverance." In the Hebrew we read "pelitah gadolah" (𐤀𐤋𐤃𐤂 𐤄𐤈𐤋𐤐). It literally means: "great escape."

Joseph indicated that he would give them a place to live, and provide for them during the rest of the famine. He sent the brothers back to their father with clothes, food, wagons and donkeys loaded with the best of Egypt. When the brothers returned and told their father Yaakob, that Joseph was alive we read a very interesting account.

"[25] Then they went up out of Egypt, and came to the land of Canaan to Yaakob their father. [26] And they told him, saying, Joseph is still alive, and he is governor over all the land of Egypt. And Yaakob's heart stood still, because he did not believe them. [27] But when they told him all the words which Joseph had said to them, and when he saw the carts which Joseph had sent to carry him, the spirit of Jacob their father revived. [28] Then Yisrael said, It is enough. Joseph my son is still alive. I will go and see him before I die." Beresheet 45:25-28

Notice what happened here. Before he was informed that Joseph was alive, their father was called Yaakob. When he heard that Joseph was alive his "heart stood still." When he heard Joseph's words, and saw Joseph's gifts, his spirit was "revived." He then was called Yisrael. So we see a prophetic death and resurrection. Through that process Yaakob is transformed into Yisrael and the revelation of Joseph, the firstborn, was central to the event.

The weekly Torah portion that contains this account is called "Va'Yigeash" and the Haftarah portion is Ezekiel 37:15-28. This is a very important prophecy that will be discussed further in the text. It speaks of a future time when the two sticks of the divided Yisrael would be joined together. For now, it is important to understand that the revelation of Joseph is not simply something from the past. Rather, it has future significance as well.

The entire tribe of Yisrael ended up leaving the Promised Land and moving to Egypt. Yisrael and his family originally went into Egypt as honored guests of Pharaoh, but they ended up becoming slaves. This was foretold to Abram during the Covenant process. It was also a pattern rehearsed by Abram. After the allotted time Mosheh was sent to redeem Yisrael, the Bride, from the clutches of Pharaoh. Egypt is Mitsrayim in Hebrew and means bondage. YHWH delivered His Bride from bondage, along with the mixed multitude. This was exactly what occurred with Hager, the stranger, only on a grander scale.

The message was clear. The stranger was welcome to join in the Covenant with Yisrael. In fact, Yisrael was the conduit for the nations to be restored to YHWH. The Covenant was not meant to include just "Jews"[126] as is often taught.

In fact, Abraham was not even a Jew. He was a Hebrew – one who "crossed over" from death to life. Only later, when the Covenant promise passed through Yaakob, did the Covenant people become known as Yisrael.

Yisrael was not chosen because they were greater than the other nations. In fact, they were the least. (Debarim 7:7). He chose them as a demonstration that He is concerned with the least. He then placed them within the most powerful nation in the world. While they were in Egypt, the Children of Yisrael grew in number, but they also became defiled by their pagan environment.

Egypt was a culture that worshipped the sun. Listen to the Word of YHWH as related by Ezekiel concerning their condition in Egypt. "*⁵ On the day when I chose Yisrael and raised My Hand in an oath to the descendants of the House of Yaakob, and made Myself known to them in the land of Egypt, I raised My hand in an oath to them, saying, I am YHWH your Elohim. ⁶ On that day I raised My Hand in an oath to them, to bring them out of the land of Egypt into a land that I had searched out for them, flowing with milk and honey, the glory of all lands. ⁷ Then I said to them, Each of you, throw away the abominations which are before his eyes, and do not defile yourselves with the idols of Egypt. I am YHWH your Elohim. ⁸ But they rebelled against Me and would not obey Me. They did not all cast away the abominations which were before their eyes, nor did they forsake the idols of Egypt. Then I said, I will pour out My fury on them and fulfill My anger against them in the midst of the land of Egypt. ⁹ But I acted for My Name's sake, that it should not be profaned before the Gentiles among whom they were, in whose sight I had made Myself known to them, to bring them out of the land of Egypt*." Ezekiel 20:5-9

Yisrael was not delivered from Egypt because of their righteousness. In fact, they would not stop their abominations, known as "shiquwts" (ᴚYᕼW) in Hebrew. Shiquwts is defined as: "filthy or disgusting." It is usually something having to do with idolatry, although it is not the idol itself. Notice the distinction made in verse 8 between the "abominations" and the idols.

Regardless of their rebellion in Egypt, YHWH made

an oath, and He was going to keep that oath "for His Name's sake." This is an interesting perspective that is not always examined. We know that Yisrael was enslaved in Egypt, but we do not always recognize that they were involved in idolatry and rebellion while in Egypt.

This too is a pattern. When YHWH allows His Covenant people to mix with the nations, they tend to become infected by those cultures. YHWH uses this mixing to draw out the nations along with His people when He gathers them for His Name's sake – when they return (shub) to Him.

As a result of the mixing, YHWH had to get His people out of Egypt and onto the Covenant path. In fact, the entire deliverance process in Egypt was about revealing the Name of YHWH to the world.[127]

"*13 Then YHWH said to Mosheh, Rise early in the morning and stand before Pharaoh, and say to him, Thus says YHWH Elohim of the Hebrews: 'Let My people go, that they may serve Me, 14 for at this time I will send all My plagues to your very heart, and on your servants and on your people, that you may know that there is none like Me in all the earth. 15 Now if I had stretched out My Hand and struck you and your people with pestilence, then you would have been cut off from the earth. 16 But indeed for this purpose I have raised you up, that I may show My power in you, and that My Name may be declared in all the earth.*" Shemot 9:13-16

Pharaoh was raised up so YHWH could reveal His Name to the World. YHWH sent Moses and Aharon as two witnesses to testify before Pharaoh. They confronted the most powerful ruler in the world and orchestrated the plagues upon that world kingdom as YHWH revealed His Name and delivered His people. Through judgment upon this Kingdom standing in opposition to YHWH, He would deliver His Bride and bring her home to the marital residence – the

Promised Land. We can expect this pattern to be repeated in the end, as YHWH once again redeems and delivers His people.

The various plagues rendered upon Egypt were a direct affront on the gods of Egypt, revealed by each particular plague. The final plague culminated with the death of the firstborn and was directed against Pharaoh, who was thought to be a god. Pharaoh had ordered the death of the sons of the Hebrews, now YHWH would strike the firstborn of Egypt, including the son of Pharaoh – thought to be the son of god.

In order to be spared from this final plague, those in Covenant with YHWH needed to carry the sign of the Covenant – the sign of circumcision. They needed to slaughter a lamb for a house and place that blood onto the doorposts of their houses as a covering. They then needed to eat the Passover meal. That blood would protect the firstborn in the homes who partook of the meal.

Interestingly, it was not until the final plague that this Covenant process of redemption was completed. In fact, it may be that the plagues on Egypt were as much about coaxing Yisrael and others to observe the Passover and enter into Covenant as it was to punish Egypt. Once redeemed, those in Covenant were then ready to be delivered.

This is an important pattern to remember as we currently see YHWH's people practicing idolatry and committing abominations. YHWH will always keep His promise for His Name's sake. Yisrael was chosen for a purpose. That purpose was to reflect the light and truth of YHWH to the nations and draw men back to Him.

They were chosen for a task. Not just for themselves, but for all of the Nations. Yisrael was not just the end, but also the means. Anyone who wanted to join the Covenant could do so. They would actually become grafted into

Yisrael. They would no longer be Gentiles, they would be part of Yisrael. You see, the terms "nations" and "gentiles" are used interchangeably. The Hebrew word is "goyim" (𐤉𐤆𐤉𐤍), and it typically means: "heathen." The word refers to someone outside the Covenant. You cannot remain a heathen if you join the Covenant. To continue to attribute the label "Gentile" to those in the Covenant is confusing, divisive and erroneous.[128]

The life of Joseph was a pattern for an even greater fulfillment in the future – one involving the Nations. Because Joseph suffered and overcame, the nation of Egypt, and many of the surrounding nations were spared from famine. Joseph's family ended up moving into Egypt. While they received favor at first, they eventually became slaves until the promise of the Covenant previously made with Abram was ready to be continued.[129]

The Children of Yisrael grew into a great nation while they were in Egypt. It seems as though Egypt ultimately ends up being a place of great blessing for the Covenant people, even when it does not initially appear that way.

Just as Abram and Sarai went to Egypt to escape famine and Sarai had become a captive of Pharaoh, the same occurred with their descendants. Just as the Pharaoh was cursed and Abram and Sarai were released and blessed with great wealth, the same would occur with their descendants. YHWH uses the lives of the Covenant people as patterns for the future. This too is a pattern that will once again be repeated in the future.

In fact, the future fulfillment will be incredible because it involves the Nations – "the Goyim." Remember how Abram came out of Egypt with Hager – "the Ger." So too, when the Children of Yisrael were led out of Egypt by Mosheh, they were accompanied by a "mixed multitude."

(Shemot 12:38) People from the Nations (Goyim) who were formerly strangers (ger) to the Covenant.

In Hebrew, the "mixed multitude" is described as the "ereb rab" (𝘠𐤓 𝘠𐤓𐤏). Essentially, it is the same two words repeated except for the addition of the ayin (𐤏) to the rab (𝘠𐤓), which makes it "mixed." The ayin (𐤏) represents the eye and means "see." The gematria value of the ayin (𐤏) is 70, and 70 represents "the nations."[130] This mixed multitude represented the nations gathered into the Covenant Assembly of Yisrael. This was a prophetic event with a future fulfillment.[131]

Prior to departing from Egypt, all of Yisrael had observed the Passover and their homes were protected by the blood of the Lamb. This was another profound pattern demonstrated through the Covenant people for a future fulfillment. Those who were redeemed from Egypt were then brought to the Mountain of YHWH, where YHWH would elevate the relationship to a very intimate level – marriage.

Remember the theme of the house from "the beginning." YHWH was building a house, and filling it through the Covenant. He protects the house by the blood, which represents the blood of the Covenant. This Covenant family, the soon to be Bride of YHWH, marched out of Egypt like a conquering army, carrying great wealth that was plundered from the Egyptians.

The exodus from Egypt is closely connected with the Jubilee. We can discern this through a clue hidden in the Hebrew text. Here is a common English translation of the Scriptures that describes their exodus from Egypt. *"So God led the people around by way of the wilderness of the Red Sea. And the children of Israel went up in orderly ranks out of the land of Egypt."* Shemot 13:18

The word translated as "orderly ranks" is "hamesheem" (𐤇𝘔W𐤆𝘔) in Hebrew. The word "hamasheem" (𐤌𐤉𐤔𐤌𐤄) actually means "fifty" or "fifties." It can also mean "fiftieth."[132] Therefore the verse would better read: *"So Elohim led the people around by way of the wilderness of the Red Sea. And the children of Yisrael went up in fifties out of the land of Egypt."* Shemot 13:18

So either they went out in groups of 50 or they went out in the 50th, which would be a Jubilee Year. If our calculations are correct they actually departed Egypt in Month 1 of the Year 1437 BCE.* This was not a Jubilee year, but they were almost there. The Jubilee would begin less than 6 months later on Day 10 of Month 7 in that same year. So they were in the 49th year of the 50 year Jubilee cycle which makes perfect sense. Every seventh year is called "the year of release" while the Jubilee year is called the "restoration of all things."

During the year of release Hebrew men and women were released from their servitude and debts were forgiven.[133] Therefore this was a very appropriate time for the Hebrews to be delivered from bondage. This is especially true since it was the seventh Shemitah year in the Jubilee cycle – year 49. This will also be an ideal time for a future deliverance if the patterns are repeated. Incredibly, 49 is the gematria value for "ha'dam" (𐤌𐤃𐤄) – "the blood."

At this point, it is significant to point out that a Jubilee Year begins on Day 10 of Month 7. The children of Yisrael began their exodus on Day 15 of Month 1 and actually left the Land of Egypt on Day 21 of Month 1, which was the last day of the Feast of Unleavened Bread.

After leaving Egypt they traveled to Mount Sinai where they were preparing to enter into a Marriage Covenant with YHWH. It is at Sinai that we see another mystery in the text that confirms the fact that this was pointing to a Jubilee. Here is what we read in the English: *"Not a hand shall touch him, but he shall surely be stoned or shot with an arrow;*

whether man or beast, he shall not live. When the trumpet (𐤋𐤉𐤆𐤀) *sounds long, they shall come near the mountain."* Shemot 19:13

Interestingly, the Hebrew text does not state "trumpet," but rather "the yobel" (𐤋𐤉𐤆𐤀). "Yobel" is Hebrew for "Jubilee," and the instrument that was sounded at the Jubilee was the shofar (𐤓𐤐𐤅𐤔).[134]

So this was a shofar, not a trumpet and it was specifically called "the yobel." Interestingly, tradition holds that this was the Feast of Shabuot, which occurs in Month 3. Remember that Shabuot was the culmination of the grain harvest when the first fruit of the grain (sons) are presented before YHWH. In fact, the Torah describes a very interesting process where two leavened loaves are waved before YHWH.[135]

The assembling at Sinai was a wedding ceremony, and the focus on the Jubilee may be hinting to a future wedding at a future Jubilee. So this blast, which is likened to the voice of YHWH, is related directly to the Yobel – the Jubilee. This would have been a time when the Yobel was blasted throughout the Land. Since this was not a Jubilee, it implies that there would be another wedding with Yisrael as the Bride – a Jubilee wedding.

To fully appreciate this prophetic concept, it is important to understand the ancient ceremonies regarding a marriage. The instance of Abraham finding a bride for his promised son is a good example of a wedding agreement. Often, the father or a representative would bring wealth and goods to strike a deal.

Negotiations would take place and if an agreement were reached, the future bride would either consent or reject the offer. If the bride consented, they would seal the agreement with wine, a meal and the payment of the bride price. A written contract, called a "ketubah," would be signed. At that point, the bride and the groom may have never met "face to face," but they are considered to be husband and wife, and the relationship could only be severed by divorce.

The bride had been bought with a price, and she belonged to her husband. It is a marriage contract called "betrothal" although the relationship does not actually turn into a blood covenant until blood has been shed when the two become one.

That event may occur after the passage of time, depending upon their age and preparations. The groom may come to fetch his bride or, as in the case of Ribkah, the bride may be brought to meet the groom. The precise timing would be up to the groom and his father, once the necessary preparations have been completed.

Between the time of the agreement and the physical joining, the bride prepares herself for the husband. She clearly must remain a virgin and she would keep herself "spotless" for her husband. She would also prepare herself to be a good wife. She must know how to take care of the house once she is brought to live in the house.

Once the bride and the groom are brought together, they go and consummate the marriage. If the bride was a virgin, her blood would be shed during their union. The blood shed by the bride as the husband pierced the veil of her hymen would complete the covenant process.[136] The blood spilled on the sheet would actually be held as proof. It was a sign and bore witness to the marriage covenant.

This has a clear connection with the chuppa. Many get married under a chuppa, which is a prayer shawl or sheet used as a "covering" or "tent" over the bride and groom while they exchange their vows. This is the legal part of the relationship that preceded the union of the couple. It involved the reading of the terms of the marriage. This was as far as

Yisrael got at Sinai.

The bride and the groom would later lie on a sheet where the blood was spilled during their physical union. If there were no blood, the covenant would not be complete, so the blood on the sheet would be the sign of the covenant.

During this process there was a wedding banquet filled with guests celebrating the union. The wedding feast would last for seven days and was a time of joy. One cannot ignore the connection with the Appointed Time of Succot.[137]

Clearly during this Feast there is a distinction between the bride, the bridegroom and the guests. While the guests are there to celebrate the wedding, they do not share the intimate covenant relationship that the bride and the groom share. This is an important distinction to remember as we discuss a future wedding with Yisrael.

With that understanding we can see what was occurring at Sinai. Yisrael was a bride redeemed from slavery, brought out of Egypt with a mixed multitude. She was bought for a price. She was corporately washed in the waters of the Red Sea, and then each individual washed before the ceremony at Sinai. Yisrael, along with the mixed multitude, was preparing to be the Bride of the Circumcision. The Land was the House that had been prepared, and the Torah was the Ketubah, - the wedding contract.

Throughout the deliverance process, YHWH used Mosheh as a mediator. Mosheh was the one who would mediate the Covenant that was culminating into a wedding ceremony at Sinai. Here was the proposal made by YHWH: "*5 Now therefore, if you will obey My voice indeed, and keep My Covenant, then you shall be a peculiar treasure unto Me above all people: for all the earth is mine: 6 And you shall be unto Me a kingdom of priests, and an holy (set apart) nation.*" Shemot 19:5-6

Mosheh presented the offer before the elders of Yisrael and the answer was an equivocal acceptance. The

Bride, Yisrael, answered as one voice – "I do." As a bride prepares for her wedding, Yisrael was told to prepare for her Husband to meet with her. All of the people were to cleanse themselves and remain pure as YHWH appeared before them at Sinai on the third day.

On a "third day" in the third month the children of Yisrael gathered together for the wedding ceremony.[138] YHWH covered the mountain with a thick cloud like a huppa. He spoke the words of the Ketubah – the marriage contract.

It was truly an awesome and terrifying event. *"[16] And it came to pass on the third day in the morning, that there were thunders and lightnings, and a thick cloud upon the mount, and the voice of the shofar (ꤥꤢꤥ) exceeding loud; so that all the people that was in the camp trembled. [17] And Mosheh brought forth the people out of the camp to meet with Elohim; and they stood at the nether part of the mount. [18] And mount Sinai was altogether on a smoke, because YHWH descended upon it in fire: and the smoke thereof ascended as the smoke of a furnace, and the whole mount quaked greatly. [19] And when the voice of the shofar (ꤥꤢꤥꤢ) sounded long, and waxed louder and louder, Mosheh spake, and Elohim answered him by a voice (ꤢꤢꤢ)."* Shemot 19:16-19

There are many interesting things in this passage. Obviously, this is the first time that we are given a description of YHWH appearing and speaking in such a fashion. The fire and smoke should draw our attention to the fire and smoke that passed through the blood of the Covenant with Abram. The thunder is "qowlote" (ꤢꤢꤢꤢ) in Hebrew. It can mean "voices" or "thunders." We can see from the passage that the sound (ꤢꤢ) of the shofar is equated with the thunder. This will be significant when we consider seven thunders that will sound at the end.[139]

These sounds describe the voice (ꤢꤢꤢ) of YHWH as the voice of a "shofar." Interestingly, when used directly to refer to YHWH, a "vav" (𐤅) was added to both "voice" (𐤒𐤅𐤋) and "shofar" (𐤔𐤅𐤐𐤓). The "vav" (𐤅), of course, stands between each "hey" (𐤄) in the Name of YHWH (𐤉𐤄𐤅𐤄).

Now again, most people read the word "trumpet" in their English Bibles, but this is an important distinction. When you read the word "trumpet" you think of a metallic instrument, but the Hebrew word "shofar" (𐤔𐤅𐤐𐤓) specifically refers to a "ram's horn." Correcting the translation from Hebrew to English is important in order to gain a proper understanding of what is actually being described in the text.

YHWH then proceeded to speak to the Assembly of Yisrael.

> "1 *And Elohim spoke all these words, saying,* 2 *I am YHWH your Elohim, which have brought thee out of the land of Egypt, out of the house of bondage.* 3 *Thou shalt have no other gods before Me.* 4 *Thou shalt not make unto thee any graven image, or any likeness of any thing that is in heaven above, or that is in the earth beneath, or that is in the water under the earth:* 5 *Thou shalt not bow down thyself to them, nor serve them: for I YHWH your Elohim am a jealous Elohim, visiting the iniquity of the fathers upon the children unto the third and fourth generation of them that hate Me;* 6 *And showing mercy unto thousands of them that love Me, and keep My commandments.* 7 *You shall not take the Name of YHWH your Elohim in vain; for YHWH will not hold him guiltless that takes His Name in vain.* 8 *Remember the Sabbath day, to keep it set apart.* 9 *Six days shalt thou labor, and do all thy work:* 10 *But the seventh day is the Sabbath of YHWH your Elohim: in it you shall not do any*

work, you, nor your son, nor your daughter, your manservant, nor your maidservant, nor your cattle, nor your stranger that is within your gates: *¹¹ For in six days YHWH made heaven and earth, the sea, and all that in them is, and rested the seventh day: wherefore YHWH blessed the Sabbath day, and set it apart. ¹² Honor your father and your mother: that your days may be long upon the land which YHWH your Elohim gives you. ¹³ You shall not murder. ¹⁴ You shall not commit adultery. ¹⁵ You shall not steal. ¹⁶ You shall not bear false witness against your neighbor. ¹⁷ You shall not covet your neighbor's house, you shall not covet your neighbor's wife, nor his manservant, nor his maidservant, nor his ox, nor his ass, nor any thing that is your neighbor's.*" Shemot 20:1-17

After YHWH spoke what are referred to as the Ten Words we read the following account. "*¹⁸ And all the people saw* ✗✗-*the thunderings, and* ✗✗-*the lightnings, and* ✗✗ *the voice of the shofar, and* ✗✗ *the mountain smoking: and when the people saw it, they removed, and stood afar off. ¹⁹ And they said unto Mosheh, Speak thou with us, and we will hear: but let not Elohim speak with us, lest we die. ²⁰ And Mosheh said unto the people, Fear not: for Elohim is come to prove you, and that His fear may be before your faces, that you sin not. ²¹ And the people stood afar off, and Mosheh drew near unto the thick darkness where Elohim was.*" Shemot 20:18-21

The spoken Word of YHWH was so powerful that they actually saw the sound. The text specifically describes that "*all the people saw the thunderings . . . and the voice of the shofar.*" This was probably similar to what occurred at creation, only there were no people around to hear <u>and</u> <u>see</u> the voice of YHWH. As with creation we can see the Aleph Taw (✗✗) present during this event.

As a result of the enormity of this event that clearly overwhelmed their senses, the people requested that Mosheh hear the words and transmit them to the people. YHWH agreed to this request and He would no longer speak directly to the Children of Yisrael in such a fashion. Those Ten Words stand apart from all others spoken by YHWH and recorded in written form.

Now remember that the Marriage process was not yet complete. While the Passover meal initiated the process that led to the ceremony at Sinai, the full Ketubah still needed to be transmitted to the Bride. Only now, it would be done by a mediator instead of the Groom. In order to receive the words, Mosheh needed to ascend up the mountain.

YHWH spoke words on the Mountain that were then written down by Mosheh onto a Scroll. *"¹ And He said unto Mosheh, Come up unto YHWH, you, and Aharon, Nadab, and Abihu, and seventy of the elders of Yisrael; and worship you afar off. ² And Mosheh alone shall come near YHWH: but they shall not come nigh; neither shall the people go up with him. ³ And Mosheh came and told the people all the words of YHWH, and all the judgments: and all the people answered with one voice, and said, All the words which YHWH hath said will we do. ⁴ And Mosheh wrote all the words of YHWH, and rose up early in the morning, and builded an altar under the hill, and twelve pillars, according to the twelve tribes of Yisrael. ⁵ And he sent young men of the children of Yisrael, which offered burnt offerings, and sacrificed peace offerings of oxen unto YHWH. ⁶ And Mosheh took half of the blood, and put it in basons; and half of the blood he sprinkled on the altar. ⁷ And he took the Scroll of the covenant, and read in the audience of the people: and they said, All that YHWH hath said will we do, and be obedient. ⁸ And Mosheh took* ✕✕*-the blood, and sprinkled it on the people, and said, Behold this is the blood of the Covenant, which YHWH hath made with you concerning all these words."* Shemot 24:1-8

So we see the legal portion of the Marriage ceremony completed with the Children of Yisrael. It was a Covenant of blood – the blood of the Aleph Taw (X𐤊). This is a great mystery and reveals that the blood of the Messiah would need to be sprinkled upon them. Just as the Blood of the Passover Lamb was sprinkled on the door posts, the Blood of the Aleph Taw (X𐤊) was sprinkled upon the people.

They were sprinkled with blood of the Aleph Taw (X𐤊), and the Scroll of the Covenant was the Ketubah – Marriage Contract. The Scroll of the Covenant contained the Words transmitted from YHWH to Mosheh. Mosheh not only spoke the Words, but he also wrote all the Words on a scroll. In fact, it is those very words, written in a scroll, that we have been quoting thus far.

Notice that YHWH instructed Mosheh and 73 others to come up. Now it would seem that they were going up the mountain, but there was still a separation. The cloud was covering something that was there.[140]

"*9 Then Mosheh went up, also Aaron, Nadab, and Abihu, and seventy of the elders of Yisrael, 10 and they saw X𐤊 Elohim of Yisrael. And there was under His feet as it were a paved work of sapphire stone, and it was like the very heavens in its clarity.*" Shemot 24:9-10 It is as if they could look up through the sapphire stone and see YHWH. The sapphire stone is strongly associated with the Throne of YHWH.[141]

They were somehow seeing the Throne of YHWH. It is possible that the very Throne of YHWH had descended upon that mountain and was covered by the darkness in order to protect the people. So YHWH, the King of all the Universe had actually arrived on top of the Mountain for the wedding ceremony. He arrived as the Aleph Taw (X𐤊) on His Heavenly Mountain – Mount Zion.

There were 74 individuals instructed to come up, but it appears that Yahushua also went up, since he went up even further with Mosheh to get the tablets. This is a great mystery because when you add Yahushua you have 75 people. The Hebrew word for "priest" is "kohen" (𐤊𐤄𐤍) and it has the gematria value of 75.

Amazingly, the first time that we read the word "kohen" (𐤊𐤄𐤍) in the Scriptures is used to describe the Melchizedek, the priest of El Most High. (Beresheet 14:18) This reveals a great mystery surrounding Joshua (Yahushua),[142] particularly in light of the fact that he ascended nearer to YHWH as Mosheh went up further to receive the tablets.

YHWH then instructed Mosheh to come up and receive tablets. *"And YHWH said unto Mosheh, Come up to Me into the mount, and be there: and I will give thee tables of stone, and the Torah, and commandments which I have written; that you may teach them."* Shemot 24:12

So after Mosheh wrote the Scroll of the Covenant, YHWH would inscribe the Words spoken to the Children of Yisrael onto tablets of stone. The Scroll would be the Ketubah given to men, the stone tablets would be a witness before YHWH.

After feasting with the elders the two witnesses, Mosheh and Yahushua, left the elders behind. (Shemot 24:13) The glory (kabod) of YHWH rested on the mountain, and the cloud covered the mountain for 6 days and on the 7th day YHWH called Mosheh into the cloud.

"17 The sight of the glory (kabod) of YHWH was like a consuming fire on the top (rosh) of the mountain in the eyes of the children of Yisrael. 18 So Mosheh went into the midst of the cloud and went up into the mountain. And Mosheh was on the mountain forty days and forty nights." Shemot 24:17-18 So the "kabod" (𐤃𐤅𐤁𐤊) of YHWH was on the top of the mountain. Mosheh appears to have entered some sort of portal that brought him up to YHWH. Mosheh was away from the

people for 40 days and 40 nights where YHWH spoke to him.[143]

During this period of time YHWH gave Mosheh plans for His House and the furnishings that would go in the House. He also gave instructions for the clothing to be worn in the House by the Kohenim, the children of Aharon. He also told Mosheh the names of the individuals anointed to build all of the items. At the end of the instructions YHWH affirmed the Sabbath as the sign of the Covenant. If He was going to dwell with them in His House, they needed to live the sign of the Sabbath.

"[13] *Speak also to the children of Yisrael, saying: 'Surely My Sabbaths you shall keep, for it is a sign between Me and you throughout your generations, that you may know that I am YHWH who sanctifies you.* [14] *You shall keep the Sabbath, therefore, for it is holy to you. Everyone who profanes it shall surely be put to death; for whoever does any work on it, that person shall be cut off from among his people.* [15] *Work shall be done for six days, but the seventh is the Sabbath of rest, holy to YHWH. Whoever does any work on the Sabbath day, he shall surely be put to death.* [16] *Therefore the children of Yisrael shall keep the Sabbath, to observe the Sabbath throughout their generations as a perpetual covenant.* [17] *It is a sign between Me and the children of Yisrael forever; for in six days YHWH made the heavens and the earth, and on the seventh day He rested and was refreshed.* [18] *And when He had made an end of speaking with him on Mount Sinai, He gave Mosheh two tablets of the Testimony, tablets of stone, written with the finger of Elohim.*" Shemot 31:13-18

So after YHWH spoke all the words to Mosheh, He wrote on two tablets and gave them to him. There is a great mystery surrounding these tablets of stone, because it is the first time that we read about YHWH writing something. Not only did YHWH write words, but He was also communicating an important prophetic truth through a visual aid involving the tablets of stone. In Shemot 24:12 the tablets are referred to as "et-lechet h'aben" (𐤉𐤀𐤊𐤀 𐤗𐤇𐤋-𐤗𐤊).

The Aleph Taw (𐤗𐤊) is attached to the tablets (𐤗𐤇𐤋), and tablets (𐤗𐤇𐤋) were made of "aben" (𐤉𐤁𐤊) – stone. Now remember the "aben" (𐤉𐤁𐤊) that was raised up and anointed by Yaakob in the House of El. This is another picture of the Messiah. The picture becomes even more profound when we follow those tablets.

They represented the Marriage Contract – the words of the Marriage Covenant. While Mosheh was up on the Mountain receiving instructions, the Children of Yisrael grew impatient. They decided to construct an image, the golden calf, and declare of Feast to YHWH. They essentially began worshipping YHWH as the pagans in Egypt worshipped their gods. While YHWH was giving instructions for His Bride regarding their marital residence, she was busy fornicating.

As a result of that conduct, Mosheh came down from the Mountain and broke the Tablets. Now when you view these Tablets as the Messiah, the centerpiece of the marriage Covenant, that breaking has profound implications. It would seem to reveal that the Messiah Himself would be broken. Now that is perfectly consistent with the pattern of the Lamb of Elohim, whose blood is shed to protect those in the Covenant, and the fact that YHWH would bear the penalty for the Covenant made with Abram. So the "smoke and the fire" was now represented by the "aben" – the two tablets that were broken.

Interestingly, there were 2 tablets, and not just one. This would synchronize with the existence of the Aleph Taw (𐤗𐤊) two times in Beresheet 1:1. So the Aleph Taw (𐤗𐤊) is identified with these stones - stones that came directly from the mountain of YHWH. They belonged to Him, and He wrote upon them with His own finger.[144]

He wrote the Words that He had spoken. (Debarim 9:10) These stones were intimately connected with YHWH. The Tablets were broken, and the golden calf was destroyed. It is at this point that we read about a Scroll of YHWH – a Scroll that YHWH has written. Mosheh intervenes and asks that he be blotted out of YHWH's Scroll in the event YHWH will not forgive Yisrael.

YHWH was prepared to destroy the people and finish the Covenant through Mosheh and his offspring. Mosheh implored YHWH to relent and actually negotiated for Yisrael. "*[32] Yet now, if thou wilt forgive their sin; and if not, blot me, I pray thee, out of your Scroll which you have written. [33] And YHWH said unto Mosheh, Whosoever hath sinned against Me, him will I blot out of My Scroll.*" Shemot 32:32-33 In other words, those who sinned will be responsible for their own actions. YHWH has a Scroll and your name is either in it, or not. Rest assured, you want your name to be in His Scroll.

We then read of a request when Mosheh asks that YHWH show him "the way" (ᕼᎩ᭳ᗑ-ᗢᕼ). YHWH then agreed to do "the Word" (ᕀᎽᗑᕀ-ᗢᕼ). Mosheh then requested that YHWH show him His "glory" (ᗑᎽᎩ-ᗢᕼ). YHWH proclaimed that He would make all His goodness pass before Mosheh. He would be "*gracious upon whom* (ᕀᎳᕼ-ᗢᕼ) *He would be gracious and show mercy upon whom* (ᕀᎳᕼ-ᗢᕼ) *He would show mercy.*" Shemot 33:19

YHWH told Mosheh that he could not see His face (ᎽᎩᎫ-ᗢᕼ), but that He would cover Mosheh with His Hand. When He passed by, YHWH would take away His Hand (ᎽᎫᎩ-ᗢᕼ), and Mosheh would see His "back parts" (Ꮍᕀᕼᕼ-ᗢᕼ). During this exchange, one cannot ignore all of the allusions to the Aleph Taw (ᗢᕼ) when describing attributes of YHWH.

Immediately after Mosheh was permitted to see the

"back parts" of YHWH, Mosheh was then informed that the Covenant would be renewed. YHWH would allow the Covenant to be renewed, only this time, Mosheh the mediator had to cut the stone tablets and carry them up the mountain.

"*¹ And YHWH said unto Mosheh, Hew thee two tables of stone like unto the first: and I will write upon these tablets the words that were in the first tablets, which you broke. ² And be ready in the morning, and come up in the morning unto mount Sinai, and present yourself there to Me in the top of the mount. ³ And no man shall come up with you, neither let any man be seen throughout all the mount; neither let the flocks nor herds feed before that mount. ⁴ And he hewed two tablets of stone like unto the first; and Mosheh rose up early in the morning, and went up unto mount Sinai, as YHWH had commanded him, and took in his hand the two tablets of stone. ⁵ And YHWH descended in the cloud, and stood with him there, and proclaimed the Name of YHWH. ⁶ And YHWH passed by before him, and proclaimed, YHWH, YHWH El, merciful and gracious, longsuffering, and abundant in goodness and truth, ⁷ Keeping mercy for thousands, forgiving iniquity and transgression and sin, and that will by no means clear the guilty; visiting the iniquity of the fathers upon the children, and upon the children's children, unto the third and to the fourth generation. ⁸ And Mosheh made haste, and bowed his head toward the earth, and worshipped. ⁹ And he said, If now I have found favour in your sight, O Master, let my Master, I pray thee, go among us; for it is a stiffnecked people; and pardon our iniquity and our* sin, and take us for thine inheritance. ¹⁰ And He said, Behold, I make a Covenant: before all your people I will do marvels, such as have not been done in all the earth, nor in any nation: and all the people among which you are shall see the work of YHWH: for it is a terrible thing that I will do with you. ¹¹ Observe you that which I command you this day: behold, I drive out before you the Amorite, and the Canaanite, and the Hittite, and the Perizzite, and the Hivite, and the Jebusite. ¹² *Take heed to yourself, lest you make a covenant with the inhabitants of the land whither thou goest, lest it be for a snare in the midst of you:* ¹³ *But you shall destroy their altars, break their images, and cut down their groves:* ¹⁴ *For you shall worship no other god: for YHWH, whose Name is Jealous, is a jealous El:* ¹⁵ *Lest you make a covenant with the inhabitants of the land, and they go a whoring after their gods, and do sacrifice unto their gods, and one call thee, and you eat of his sacrifice;* ¹⁶ And you take of their daughters unto your sons, and their daughters go a whoring after their gods, and make your sons go a whoring after their gods. ¹⁷ You shall make thee no molten gods. ¹⁸ The Feast of Unleavened Bread shall you keep. Seven days you shall eat unleavened bread, as I commanded thee, in the time of the month of the Abib: for in the month of the Abib thou camest out from Egypt. ¹⁹ All that openeth the matrix is mine; and every firstling among thy cattle, whether ox or sheep, that is male. ²⁰ But the firstling of an ass you shall redeem with a lamb: and if you redeem him not, then you shall break his neck. All the firstborn of thy sons you shall redeem. And none shall appear before me empty. ²¹ Six days thou shall work, but on the seventh day you shall rest: in earing time and in harvest you shall rest. ²² And you shall observe the Feast of Weeks, of the firstfruits of wheat harvest, and the Feast of Ingathering at the year's end. ²³ Three times in the year shall all your males appear (𐤆𐤉𐤍-𐤕𐤀) before Master YHWH, the Elohim of Yisrael. ²⁴ For I will cast out the nations before thee, and enlarge thy borders: neither shall any man desire thy land, when you shall go up to appear before YHWH your Elohim three times in the year. ²⁵ You shall not offer the blood of My sacrifice with leaven; neither shall the sacrifice of the Feast of the Passover be left unto the morning. ²⁶ The first of the firstfruits of your land you shall bring unto the House of YHWH your Elohim. You shall not seethe a kid in his mother's milk. ²⁷ And YHWH said unto Mosheh, Write you these words: for after the tenor of these words I have made a Covenant with you and with Yisrael. ²⁸ And he was there with YHWH forty days and forty nights; he did neither eat bread, nor drink water. And He wrote upon the tablets the words of the Covenant, the Ten Commandments. ²⁹ And it came to pass, when Mosheh came down from Mount Sinai with the two tablets of testimony in Mosheh's hand, when he came down from the mount, that Mosheh did not know that the skin of his face shone while he talked with Him. ³⁰ And when Aharon and all the children of Yisrael saw Mosheh, behold, the skin of his face shone; and they were afraid to come nigh him. ³¹ And Mosheh called unto them; and Aharon and all the rulers of the congregation returned unto him: and Mosheh talked with them. ³² And afterward all

the children of Yisrael came nigh: and he gave them in commandment all that YHWH had spoken with him in mount Sinai." Shemot 34:1-32

So YHWH wrote the same words upon those second Tablets. The aben reappeared and was essentially resurrected. We also read that Mosheh told Yisrael all the Words that YHWH spoke to him on the mountain. This was previously mentioned prior to the first set of Tablets when YHWH had told Mosheh about the Torah and the commandments.

So their actions could have invalidated the wedding process, but YHWH agreed to renew the Covenant. Things would not be as originally intended. YHWH would live separate from Yisrael. Only the Levites, as representatives of the firstborn would be permitted to serve in His House. The rest of Yisrael would be allowed to visit, but on a limited basis. This was not the intimate marriage relationship desired by YHWH.

This was the reason for the hints of a future wedding at a Jubilee. Just as we saw the Aleph Taw (✕𐤟) emphasized with Ribkah, the Bride of the Promised Son of the Covenant, we see the need for the Aleph Taw (✕𐤟), the Messiah, to perfect the wedding with the Bride Yisrael.

Tradition holds that Mosheh descended with the second set of Tablets on Yom Kippur.[145] Now we know that the year Yisrael left Egypt was 1,437 BCE. Again, it was the 49th year in the 50 year Jubilee cycle. On Day 10 of Month 7, the Day of Atonement, when Mosheh came down Mount Sinai for the third time with the second set of Tablets, it was essentially new years day for Jubilee Year 51.[146]

Up to this point we have mentioned the Jubilee, but it is important to know the significance of the 50 year cycle. Here is the command concerning this important time that was later given to Yisrael.

"[1] *And YHWH spoke to Mosheh on Mount Sinai,*

saying, ² Speak to the children of Yisrael, and say to them: When you come into the land which I give you, then the land shall keep a Sabbath to YHWH. ³ Six years you shall sow your field, and six years you shall prune your vineyard, and gather its fruit; ⁴ but in the seventh year there shall be a Sabbath of solemn rest for the land, a sabbath to YHWH. You shall neither sow your field nor prune your vineyard. ⁵ What grows of its own accord of your harvest you shall not reap, nor gather the grapes of your untended vine, for it is a year of rest for the land. ⁶ And the Sabbath produce of the land shall be food for you: for you, your male and female servants, your hired man, and the stranger who dwells with you, ⁷ for your livestock and the beasts that are in your land - all its produce shall be for food. ⁸ And you shall count seven Sabbaths of years for yourself, seven times seven years; and the time of the seven sabbaths of years shall be to you forty-nine years. ⁹ Then you shall cause the shofar of the Jubilee to sound on the tenth day of the seventh month; on the Day of Atonement you shall make the shofar to sound throughout all your land. ¹⁰ And you shall consecrate the fiftieth year, and proclaim liberty throughout all the land to all its inhabitants. It shall be a Jubilee for you; and each of you shall return to his possession, and each of you shall return to his family. ¹¹ That fiftieth year shall be a Jubilee to you; in it you shall neither sow nor reap what grows of its own accord, nor gather the grapes of your untended vine. ¹² For it is the Jubilee; it shall be set apart to you; you shall eat its produce from the field. ¹³ In this Year of Jubilee, each of you shall return to his possession. ¹⁴ And if you sell anything to your neighbor or buy from your neighbor's hand, you shall not oppress one another. ¹⁵ According to the number of years after

the Jubilee you shall buy from your neighbor, and according to the number of years of crops he shall sell to you. ¹⁶ According to the multitude of years you shall increase its price, and according to the fewer number of years you shall diminish its price; for he sells to you according to the number of the years of the crops. ¹⁷ Therefore you shall not oppress one another, but you shall fear your Elohim; for I am YHWH your Elohim. ¹⁸ So you shall observe My statutes and keep My judgments, and perform them; and you will dwell in the land in safety. ¹⁹ Then the land will yield its fruit, and you will eat your fill, and dwell there in safety. ²⁰ And if you say, 'What shall we eat in the seventh year, since we shall not sow nor gather in our produce? ²¹ <u>Then I will command My blessing on you in the sixth year, and it will bring forth produce enough for three years.</u> ²² And you shall sow in the eighth year, and eat old produce until the ninth year; until its produce comes in, you shall eat of the old harvest. ²³ <u>The land shall not be sold permanently, for the land is Mine; for you are strangers and sojourners with Me.</u> ²⁴ And in all the land of your possession you shall grant redemption of the land. ²⁵ If one of your brethren becomes poor, and has sold some of his possession, and if his redeeming relative comes to redeem it, then he may redeem what his brother sold. ²⁶ Or if the man has no one to redeem it, but he himself becomes able to redeem it, ²⁷ then let him count the years since its sale, and restore the remainder to the man to whom he sold it, that he may return to his possession. ²⁸ But if he is not able to have it restored to himself, then what was sold shall remain in the hand of him who bought it until the Year of Jubilee; and in the Jubilee it shall be released, and he shall return to his possession. ²⁹ If a man sells a house in a walled city, then he may redeem it within a whole year after it is sold; within a full year he may redeem it. ³⁰ But if it is not redeemed within the space of a full year, then the house in the walled city shall belong permanently to him who bought it, throughout his generations. It shall not be released in the Jubilee. ³¹ However the houses of villages which have no wall around them shall be counted as the fields of the country. They may be redeemed, and they shall be released in the Jubilee. ³² Nevertheless the cities of the Levites, and the houses in the cities of their possession, the Levites may redeem at any time. ³³ And if a man purchases a house from the Levites, then the house that was sold in the city of his possession shall be released in the Jubilee; for the houses in the cities of the Levites are their possession among the children of Yisrael. ³⁴ But the field of the common-land of their cities may not be sold, for it is their perpetual possession. ³⁵ If one of your brethren becomes poor, and falls into poverty among you, then you shall help him, like a stranger or a sojourner, that he may live with you. ³⁶ Take no usury or interest from him; but fear your Elohim, that your brother may live with you. ³⁷ You shall not lend him your money for usury, nor lend him your food at a profit. ³⁸ I am YHWH your Elohim, who brought you out of the land of Egypt, to give you the land of Canaan and to be your Elohim. ³⁹ And if one of your brethren who dwells by you becomes poor, and sells himself to you, you shall not compel him to serve as a slave. ⁴⁰ As a hired servant and a sojourner he shall be with you, and shall serve you until the Year of Jubilee. ⁴¹ And then he shall depart from you - he and his children with him - and shall return to his own family. He shall return to the possession of his fathers. ⁴² For they are My servants, whom I brought out of the land of

Egypt; they shall not be sold as slaves. ⁴³ You shall not rule over him with rigor, but you shall fear your Elohim. ⁴⁴ And as for your male and female slaves whom you may have - from the nations that are around you, from them you may buy male and female slaves. ⁴⁵ Moreover you may buy the children of the strangers who dwell among you, and their families who are with you, which they beget in your land; and they shall become your property. ⁴⁶ And you may take them as an inheritance for your children after you, to inherit them as a possession; they shall be your permanent slaves. But regarding your brethren, the children of Yisrael, you shall not rule over one another with rigor. ⁴⁷ Now if a sojourner or stranger close to you becomes rich, and one of your brethren who dwells by him becomes poor, and sells himself to the stranger or sojourner close to you, or to a member of the stranger's family, ⁴⁸ after he is sold he may be redeemed again. One of his brothers may redeem him; ⁴⁹ or his uncle or his uncle's son may redeem him; or anyone who is near of kin to him in his family may redeem him; or if he is able he may redeem himself. ⁵⁰ Thus he shall reckon with him who bought him: The price of his release shall be according to the number of years, from the year that he was sold to him until the Year of Jubilee; it shall be according to the time of a hired servant for him. ⁵¹ If there are still many years remaining, according to them he shall repay the price of his redemption from the money with which he was bought. ⁵² And if there remain but a few years until the Year of Jubilee, then he shall reckon with him, and according to his years he shall repay him the price of his redemption. ⁵³ He shall be with him as a yearly hired servant, and he shall not rule with rigor over him in your sight. ⁵⁴ And if he is not redeemed in these years,

then he shall be released in the Year of Jubilee - he and his children with him. ⁵⁵ For the children of Yisrael are servants to Me; they are My servants whom I brought out of the land of Egypt: I am YHWH your Elohim."
Vayiqra 25:1-55

We can see from this text that there is a count leading up to the Jubilee Year. It is essentially a 50 year cycle. The count begins with six years followed by a seventh year of rest - a sabbath. This year count is patterned after the week count initiated at creation. Because of this, it is reasonable to assume that this count also began in the beginning.

Every seven years the land was to rest. Incredibly, every sixth year the land would produce enough for three years – the seventh, the eighth and the ninth years. This would provide an abundance of food that would also account for the fact that the 50ᵗʰ Year - the Jubilee year - was also a Sabbath. So after seven Sabbath years, the 50ᵗʰ year was also a Sabbath year. That would result in two Sabbath years in a row.

The Jubilee concerns both land and time. There is a connection between the two, and both time and land are important. It was a homecoming, so no one could permanently lose their land. They could permanently sell their homes, but not their land.

Interestingly, this text makes it clear that YHWH owns the land. The people were given an allotment of land to use depending upon which tribe they belonged to. Their use of the land was conditioned upon remaining in the Covenant relationship. If they obeyed, then the land would produce for them. They would be allowed to continually dwell in the land and receive the blessings of the Covenant.

So the Jubilee was a time of restoration and return. It was essentially a reset button for finances and property use that culminated every fifty years. Vows were also calculated

from one Jubilee to another. (Vayiqra 27:14-25)

It is important to understand that there was an existence before Day 1 described in Berseheet 1:3-5. It was known as "The World that Was" or Olam She'avar. There was a disruption that involved the rebellion of satan and the messengers that followed him – the watchers. The rebellion resulted in one third of the "stars" being cast down to the earth. (Revelation 12:4).

The pattern of the Jubilee was built into creation from the beginning to point to a future and final restoration. So creation progresses through the Jubilee Cycles until the final completion of the cycles. The Jubilee is often overlooked, but it is a very powerful event. It has been called "the restoration of all things," which is code for the Jubilee.

When you are not in a Jubilee year, every year should be a countdown toward the next Jubilee. The focus of time should always be the Jubilee cycle. In fact, there is a yearly Appointed Time that reminds us of the Jubilee count. Often known as the "omer count" there is a fifty day count that encompasses the barley harvest and the wheat harvest.

After the Passover, there is a "first" (resheet) offering of barley made by the priest that begins a seven week count. The day after the seven week count leads to the 50th day, which is Shabuot – the Feast of Firstfruits (bikkurim). It is on Shabuot that all of the people throughout the land bring their firstfruits of the grain harvest to the House of YHWH. So this 50 day count is a sort of mini-Jubilee cycle within the grain harvest.

Just as we count days and weeks to Day 50 - Shabuot, we count years and weeks of years to Year 50 – the Jubilee. We are therefore reminded every year to count the Jubilee. Incredibly, the 50 year Jubilee occurs on Day 10 of Month 7 – the Day of Atonement – a day most commonly associated with repentance (return), judgment and suffering (affliction).

So once every 50 years, this typically very somber day is marked by the sound of shofars, and it becomes an incredible day of rejoicing. Imagine the implications. You get back land and belongings that your ancestors sold. You are able to return to your inheritance just days before the most joyous Appointed Time – the Feast of Succot.

Interestingly, during the last two years in the Jubilee cycle there would be no firstfruits, because they are both Sabbath years and there was no harvest. So leading up to the Jubilee in year 49, and through year 50, there would be no firstfruit offering at Shabuot or Succot. This has important implications when we consider the time leading up the end of the age, which is fashioned around the Jubilee cycle of time.

Within the context of the 7,000 year plan we have a framework of 140 Jubilee years. Interestingly, the Hebrew word "the qahal" (ל ﬡ ﬡ ﬡ ﬡ) which means "the assembly" has a gematria value of 140. The qahal refers to the set apart assembly of Yisrael.[147] Based upon this pattern we should expect a restoration in a Jubilee Year by the Sabbath millennium, and a final restoration at the end of the Sabbath millennium. This entire process of time is about gathering the Assembly of Yisrael.

This is confirmed by another hinted Jubilee when the Yisraelites eventually entered the Land and conquered the city of Jericho. That entrance would be delayed 40 years due to their unbelief.

Incredibly, Yisrael was redeemed in a miraculous way from the shackles of slavery. They underwent an awesome Marriage Covenant procedure at Mount Sinai, and they were even given a second chance to have the Covenant renewed after they broke the Covenant by their fornication. They were promised a home and they were given the gift of the Torah.

"Torah" is another word, like "shofar," that you will

likely never read in an English translation of the text. Sadly, it was one of the greatest gifts given to Yisrael through this wedding process. It is extremely misunderstood by many because it is often improperly translated as "The Law."

The word "Torah" (ⴀⴀⵖⵝ) in Hebrew means: "utterance, teaching, instruction or revelation from Elohim." It comes from "horah" (ⴀⴀⵖⴀ) which means: "to direct, to teach" and derives from the stem "yara" (ⴀⵖⵣ) which means: "to shoot or throw." Therefore there are two aspects to the word Torah: 1) aiming or pointing in the right direction, and 2) movement in that direction. This gives a much different sense than the word "Law."

So Mosheh wrote the words spoken to him by YHWH. He wrote those words on a Scroll. YHWH wrote the words that He spoke to Yisrael on two tablets of stone. Both of these writings signified the marriage contract. Both were kept with the Ark of the Covenant, also known as the witness, which was later constructed and placed within the Tabernacle. It is believed that the Tablets were placed inside the Ark while the Scroll was placed beside the Ark.

The people were supposed to take the Torah with them into the Promised Land. It was a guide to show them how to be blessed in the Land. Sadly, they refused to enter the Land. After hearing the bad report from 10 out of 12 who spied out the Land, the people inclined toward the majority, an error that modern Judaism continues to this day.[148]

The report brought back was that they saw the Nephilim. Apparently they saw the descendants of Anak, who came from the Nephilim. Thus they called the inhabitants of the land the Nephilim. That part of the report was true. Caleb, who was a giant killer, encouraged the people to go up at once and take possession. He stated that they were able to overcome them. (Bemidbar 13:30).

The reason that the 10 gave a bad report was because

they contradicted Caleb. They specifically stated that they could not go up because the people in the land were stronger than they were. *"³² And they gave the children of Yisrael a bad report of the land which they had spied out, saying, The land through which we have gone as spies is a land that devours its inhabitants, and all the people whom we saw in it are men of great stature. ³³ There we saw the Nephilim (the descendants of Anak came from the Nephilim); and we were like grasshoppers in our own sight, and so we were in their sight."* Bemidbar 13:32-33

There were giants throughout the Promised Land, just as there had been during the days of Noah. We read this summary from Debarim where YHWH details the giants that were cleared out of the surrounding lands. *"¹⁹ And when you come near the people of Ammon, do not harass them or meddle with them, for I will not give you any of the land of the people of Ammon as a possession, because I have given it to the descendants of Lot as a possession. ²⁰ That was also regarded as a land of giants; giants formerly dwelt there. But the Ammonites call them Zamzummim, ²¹ a people as great and numerous and tall as the Anakim. But YHWH destroyed them before them, and they dispossessed them and dwelt in their place, ²² just as He had done for the descendants of Esau, who dwelt in Seir, when He destroyed the Horites from before them. They dispossessed them and dwelt in their place, even to this day. ²³ And the Avim, who dwelt in villages as far as Gaza - the Caphtorim, who came from Caphtor, destroyed them and dwelt in their place."* Debarim 2:19-23 (see also Debarim 2:10-12)

It appears that YHWH had herded the giant races from the surrounding areas into the Promised Land, and He was going to use Yisrael to wipe out these hybrid beings. Sadly, most of the people feared the giants in the Land - as if YHWH had brought them that far just to let them be devoured by the giants. This was the same as a bride getting married and refusing to live with her husband in the house he had specially prepared. Even worse, it was a wife stating that her husband is unable to protect her and provide for her. It was a slap in the face to YHWH.

Because of the presence of the Nephilim, the land was corrupted. The occupants were descended from Anak who was of the Nephilim. As a result, the land needed to be cleansed and YHWH desired for His Bride to share in the cleansing process. They were going to do a little house cleaning, but Yisrael refused.

They did not trust YHWH so the generation that rejected the Land also lost the privilege of living under the Torah, and receiving the blessings associated with obedience. There would be no further Passover meals until that generation died off and their children entered into the Land.

As they dwelled in the wilderness they camped around the Tent of YHWH. They were close, but they could not go inside the House. And the House was buffered by the Kohenim and the Levites who were essentially mediators. The Levites appear to have been exempted from the ban since they did not send a spy. They were also excluded from the numbering of the children of Yisrael at Horeb. The punishment specifically applied to "[29] . . . *all of you who were numbered, according to your entire number, from twenty years old and above.* [30] *Except for Caleb the son of Jephunneh and Joshua the son of Nun, you shall by no means enter the land which I swore I would make you dwell in.*" Bemidbar 14:29-30

Interestingly, the 10 who brought the bad report died immediately from a plague. This is an important lesson for those who would think to speak against the plan of YHWH, or discourage people from following the way of YHWH.

Instead of entering into the land, Yisrael travelled around the borders of the land. In the text of Debarim we read the following: "[6] *"YHWH our Elohim spoke to us in Horeb, saying: You have dwelt long enough at this mountain.* [7] *Turn and*

take your journey, and go to the mountains of the Amorites, to all the neighboring places in the plain, in the mountains and in the lowland, in the South and on the seacoast, to the land of the Canaanites and to Lebanon, as far as the great river, the River Euphrates." Debarim 1:6-7

This summary of the travels of Yisrael is a very different description than the maps displayed in the backs of many Bibles. They typically show Yisrael wandering around the Sinai Peninsula. Of particular note is the last place mentioned before they entered the Promised Land was the great River Euphrates. Again, this location and pattern continues to be significant when discussing a return to the Land.

Their travels were bitter sweet. While YHWH dwelled in their midst the Yisraelites were not allowed in His house. While they were traversing the Land, they were not allowed to enter in. They lived nomadic lives and were unable to settle into homes until the 40 year period of punishment had ended. The parents were essentially biding their time until they died, and their children would then enter into the Land.

They camped a total of 42 places from the time they left Egypt until they were about to enter into the Promised Land. When they would move two silver trumpets were used to call and direct the movement of the camp.

"¹ And YHWH spoke to Mosheh, saying: ² Make two silver trumpets for yourself; you shall make them of hammered work; you shall use them for calling the congregation and for directing the movement of the camps. ³ When they blow both of them, all the congregation shall gather before you at the door of the Tabernacle of Meeting. ⁴ But if they blow only one, then the leaders, the heads of the divisions of Israel, shall gather to you. ⁵ When you sound the advance, the camps that lie on the east side shall then begin their journey. ⁶ When you sound the advance the second time, then the camps that lie on the south side shall begin *their journey; they shall sound the call for them to begin their journeys.* [7] *And when the assembly is to be gathered together, you shall blow, but not sound the advance.* [8] *The sons of Aaron, the priests, shall blow the trumpets; and these shall be to you as an ordinance forever throughout your generations.*" Bemidbar 10:1-8

When it was finally time to enter in, only 2 individuals from the generation that left Egypt would enter into the Promised Land - Joshua and Caleb. They "had a different spirit." They were fearless warriors – giant slayers. This is a trait that we see is pleasing to YHWH.

Under Joshua (Yahushua) they would enter the Land and perform the task that their parents refused to do. They were also given a roadmap to follow and this new generation needed to get back on the Covenant path. Whenever Yisrael gets derailed, the Appointed Times are the reentry point. They get the Covenant people back into synchronicity with the Creator.

In this case the new generation essentially needed to repeat the rehearsal of their parents. They underwent the corporate immersion, but now instead of exiting Egypt through the divided waters of the Red Sea they were entering the Promised Land through the divided waters of the Jordan.

Their parents were circumcised and then exited bondage. This generation would enter into freedom and then get circumcised. Once they crossed the Jordan, they were circumcised at Gilgal so that they could partake in the Passover meal.[149]

We have already mentioned the Appointed Times, and we saw how they integrate with the Jubilee. They are annual appointments that reveal patterns through time. They are particularly related to the Covenant path that leads to restoration.

After the passage of the 40 year period of punishment,

Yisrael cycled to another Passover when they crossed over the Jordan River and were circumcised in the Promised Land. They ate the Passover and prepared to conquer the center of moon worship – Jericho.

Jericho is considered by many to be one of the oldest cities in the world. Interestingly, according to the Jewish Encyclopedia it was widely known as the "city of the giants." Apparently, there was a large population of giants in this walled city, as there were in many of the walled cities in the land of Canaan.

The name of the city actually derives from the word for "moon" which is "yerach" (𐤉𐤓𐤇). Yeracho (𐤉𐤓𐤇𐤅) was the primary place where the moon god was worshiped in the land of Canaan. Of course today we see a revival of moon worship through the religion of Islam. Islam calls their god Allah, but Allah was actually one of many gods worshipped in the pagan pantheon known as the Kaaba located in Mecca. History reveals that the Meccans took over the idol Hubal from the Moabites. Hubal and Allah are identical. While the moon god Allah may be the god of Islam, he is not YHWH. He is the Ba'al of the Moabites.

So we saw Yisrael in the past battling the same gods that exist today. In fact, those who worship the moon are in a desperate battle to regain the land once occupied by their ancestors. Even today, Jericho is occupied and controlled by Palestinians who primarily worship Allah.

The conquest of Jericho was specifically directed by YHWH through "the Prince" (sar) of the army of YHWH. (see Joshua 5:14) YHWH gave very explicit instructions concerning the conquest of the center of moon god worship in the Promised Land.

All the men of war were to march around Jericho once for six days. Seven priests were to carry seven shofars before the Ark of the Covenant. Interestingly, in the Hebrew, those

shofars were specifically referred to as Jubilee Shofars
(𐤔𐤅𐤐𐤓𐤕 𐤉𐤅𐤁𐤋𐤉𐤌). On the seventh day they were
to march around the city seven times.

   *"It shall come to pass, when they make a long blast with the
ram's horn, (horn jubilee) and when you hear the sound of the
shofar, that all the people shall shout with a great shout; then the
wall of the city will fall down flat. And the people shall go up every
man straight before him."* Joshua 6:5

   In the Hebrew we read about the "horn yobel" or the
"Jubilee Horn." The text literally states: "when you hear the
voice (et-qol) shofar." This was another hint of a future
Jubilee – a future fulfillment. Remember that this had only
been 40 years since the last Jubilee when the second set of
Tablets had been delivered to the Children of Yisrael and the
Covenant was renewed on Yom Kippur – Day 10 of Month 7
in the year 1,437 BCE.*

   So this was not a Jubilee year. As we previously saw
the hint of a future Jubilee wedding, it seems that this too
was hinting to a future event. It appears that there will be a
future Jubilee when the worship of the moon god would be
destroyed, and YHWH would send out His Voice as the
sound of a shofar to fight for His people. As we proceed with
our discussion this is one of many possibilities at the end of
the age.

   Anyone familiar with the worship of Allah should
think of the Hajj, when pilgrims from all over the world
travel to Mecca. One of the many rituals accociated with the
Hajj is the Tawaf, which involves walking seven times
around the Kaaba. These two events share much in common,
and seem to be pointing to an end time conflict between
YHWH and Allah.

   For Yisrael, at that point in time, the Covenant
relationship had come full circle from the Garden. Just as
Adam had been charged to tend and guard the Garden, the

Covenant family of Yisrael was supposed to tend and guard the commandments. As they entered the Land they were reminded of the significance of the number seven.

The reason is because they were also given a sign of the seventh day. This special day was given a name - the Sabbath, better known as Shabbat (**Χ𝑌W**) in Hebrew.[150]

> *"Therefore the children of Yisrael*
> *shall keep the Sabbath, to observe the Sabbath*
> *throughout their generations as a perpetual Covenant."*
> Shemot 31:16

YHWH could have chosen any day, but He did not. He chose the 7th day – the day when He rested, and the day that He set apart from the very beginning. He was now connecting His set apart people, his family, with the set apart time. He was connecting this Marriage Covenant with His Creation Covenant made in the beginning. Yisrael would be the Bride of YHWH, and she would fill the House. Just as Adam was to rest from tending and guarding the Garden, so too Yisrael was to rest from their work on Shabbat.

Now the sign was not some light in the heavens or in the sky. The sign was the Covenant Children observing the set apart day. Not only was the day a sign, but so were the Children of Yisrael. They became the Children of Light.

They would not only rest every seven days, but as we saw, to some extent every seven years since they would not be harvesting crops. The Land was to rest on these Sabbath days and Sabbath years, and the people and the Land were supposed to be connected.

This Covenant Family was also given instructions for building a House for YHWH. Since the Golden Calf "affair" the Levites were chosen to represent the firstborn of all Yisrael. Traditionally, the firstborn would function in the priestly role for their family. Now the Levites would fulfill that function before YHWH in the Tabernacle.

The pattern was established that you must be a firstborn to enter in to the Covenant House. The pathway was also patterned by the seven articles of furniture: 1) The Ark; 2) The Mercy Seat; 3) The Table of Showbread; 4) The Menorah; 5) The Brazen Altar; 6) The Altar of Incense; and 7) The Laver. The entire tent structure was intended to represent a person, with YHWH and His Commandments enthroned within them. This is the Shema. (Debarim 6:4-6)

For the time being, the Tabernacle would be placed in the center of the camp of Yisrael. It would provide a pattern for the people to learn how to dwell with YHWH. It was training camp for the return to Paradise. As with the Sabbath Day, the Covenant people were being taught by and through their actions, which were blended with both time and space.

This House would now be at the center of their relationship with YHWH. The Tabernacle "X𐤊-ahal" (𐤋𐤄𐤊-X𐤊) was set up at Shiloh within the tribal boundaries of Ephraim. (Yahushua 18:8). The males were commanded to meet with YHWH three times a year. Through these Pilgrimage Feasts, and the remaining Appointed Times, the people were supposed to be living set apart lives, synchronized with their Husband. Those Words written on stone, and on the Scroll, were manifesting through Yisrael.

We do not presently have the tablets of stone, because we do not know where the Ark of the Covenant is located. We do, however, have copies of the Scroll that Mosheh transcribed, known as the Torah. So the Torah is essentially the Book, or rather, the Scroll of the Covenant. While the Torah is contained in one scroll – "sepher" (𐤓𐤐𐤎), it is understood to be divided into 5 separate books. This is why it is sometimes referred to as the Pentateuch.

The 5 books are intended for those in Covenant with YHWH, an Assembly or Congregation known as Yisrael. All who desire to be in Covenant with YHWH must join this Assembly, and walk in the way of the Torah. The Torah applies to everyone in the Covenant, regardless of where they originated.[151]

Now this Covenant was initially established with a single man named Abram, but it was no small thing in the Universe. In fact, it was unprecedented. This was something that was about restoring Creation itself. *"For ask now concerning the days that are past, which were before you, since the day that Elohim created man on the earth, and ask from one end of heaven to the other, whether any great thing like this has happened, or anything like it has been heard."* Debarim 4:32

YHWH already had a Kingdom in the Heavens, but He was building His Kingdom on this Earth through the Covenant Assembly Yisrael. *"And you shall be to Me a kingdom of priests and a holy nation."* Shemot 19:6 The purpose of Yisrael was to establish that Kingdom.

6

The Kingdom

No kingdom is complete without a king. YHWH was to be the Husband of the Bride Yisrael, and the King of the Kingdom of Yisrael populated with the Covenant family. We saw that things did not start well for this Covenant Assembly when they originally came out of Egypt. The ideal marriage relationship did not occur, because Yisrael committed adultery in the midst of the wedding process. Yisrael broke the Covenant and because of her fornication she would not yet operate as a kingdom of priests. Instead, the Levites were chosen to represent them in the House of YHWH. The other tribes were not allowed to serve in the House.

Imagine being invited to your father's house for a festive engagement, and having to stand in the front yard – not permitted into the house. You could bring the food and you could watch it being cooked, but you had to eat your food in the front yard. You could not go in the house, sit at the dinner table and eat with him. This must have been an awkward and humbling experience. It was a constant reminder of the sin at Sinai.

Even worse, they had to wait 40 years until they could actually enter the Land. It was all their choosing, and things clearly were not ideal. Instead of the bride moving into the House after a pleasant honeymoon, their honeymoon consisted of 40 years in the wilderness camping in tents waiting for an entire generation to die. While in the wilderness they experienced various trials, rebellions, plagues and judgments.

Once their period of punishment expired – 40 years for 40 days[152] – they could begin the process of entering the Land of Promise. They first destroyed the stronghold of moon worship, and needed to destroy the inhabitants in the Land, including the Nephilim.

They first camped at Gilgal as they began their various campaigns. One unique encounter occurred when they went to defend Gibeon from 5 armies. The king of Jerusalem persuaded 4 other kings to attack the Gibeonites because they had made a Covenant with Yisrael. The king of Jerusalem was named Adonai-Tsedeq, which literally means: "Lord of Righteousness." This was not the same as the Melichzedek that Abram communed with.

The king and the others received special treatment from YHWH. He hurled large hailstones from the heavens upon them. The Scriptures record that more died from the hailstones than the children of Yisrael killed with the sword. This was not the only thing special that happened that day.

The Scriptures record the following: "*[12] Then Yahushua spoke to YHWH in the day when YHWH delivered up the Amorites before the children of Yisrael, and he said in the sight of Yisrael: 'Sun, stand still over Gibeon; and Moon, in the Valley of Aijalon.' [13] So the sun stood still, and the moon stopped, till the people had revenge upon their enemies. Is this not written in the Scroll of Yasher? So the sun stood still in the midst of heaven, and did not hasten to go down for about a whole day. [14] And there has been no day like that, before it or after it, that YHWH heeded the voice of a man; for YHWH fought for Yisrael.*" Joshua 10:12-14

There are a variety of theories regarding what happened ranging from the summer solstice, which is refered to as a "perfect day," to a close encounter with the planet Mars. That would also account for the hailstones, which were large meteors. The Scriptures certainly seem to validate the Scroll of Yasher, also known as the Upright Book. That text describes the event as follows: "*And YHWH hearkened to the voice of Yahushua, and the sun stood still in the midst of the heavens, and it stood still six and thirty moments, and the moon also stood still and hastened not to go down a whole day.*" (Jasher 88:63-64) Some attribute this to a 32 degree pole shift accounting for the sun and the moon standing still.

Whatever the explanation, YHWH fought with Yisrael as they conquered the Land. We specifically read that under Yahushua, they cleared the Land of the giants, except for the region of the Philistines. "*²¹ And at that time Joshua (Yahuhsua) came and cut off the Anakim from the mountains: from Hebron, from Debir, from Anab, from all the mountains of Yahudah, and from all the mountains of Yisrael; Yahushua utterly destroyed them with their cities. ²² None of the Anakim were left in the land of the children of Yisrael; they remained only in Gaza, in Gath, and in Ashdod.*" Yahushua 11:21-22

We read of Caleb, the giant killer, taking possession of the land of the mightiest of the Anakim. "*¹³ And Yahushua blessed him, and gave Hebron to Caleb the son of Yephunneh as an inheritance. ¹⁴ Hebron therefore became the inheritance of Caleb the son of Yephunneh the Kenizzite to this day, because he wholly followed YHWH Elohim of Yisrael. ¹⁵ And the name of Hebron formerly was Kirjath Arba (Arba was the greatest man among the Anakim).*" Joshua 14:13-15

Through this process of taking the Land, YHWH said He would send His Messenger before them to lead them and give them the Land. "*²⁰ Behold, I send an Angel before you to keep you in the way and to bring you into the place which I have prepared. ²¹ Beware of Him and obey His voice; do not provoke Him, for He will not pardon your transgressions; for My Name is* in Him. [22] *But if you indeed obey His voice and do all that I speak, then I will be an enemy to your enemies and an adversary to your adversaries.* [23] *For My Angel will go before you and bring you in to the Amorites and the Hittites and the Perizzites and the Canaanites and the Hivites and the Jebusites; and I will cut them off.*" Shemot 23:20-23

YHWH would fight with them, and He promised them victory. All that the Yisraelites needed to do was destroy the pagan symbols and get rid of the false gods. Their task was the same as Adam's in the garden. If they guarded and tended the Torah, the instructions and the Land, they would receive incredible blessings.

YHWH would bless their X𐤊-bread and their X𐤊-water. As a result, there would be no sickness in their midst and women would not miscarry. (Shemot 23:25-26) Clearly, when they destroyed the foreign gods and focused on YHWH, the Aleph Taw (X𐤊) would be responsible for blessing their food, and in turn their health and their offspring.

Their move into the Land would be a gradual process, not all at once. "[27] *I will send My X𐤊-fear before you, I will cause confusion among X𐤊-all the people to whom you come, and will make X𐤊-all your enemies turn their backs to you.* [28] *And I will send X𐤊-hornets before you, which shall drive out X𐤊-the Hivite, X𐤊-the Canaanite, and X𐤊-the Hittite from before you.* [29] *I will not drive them out from before you in one year, lest the land become desolate and the beasts of the field become too numerous for you.* [30] *Little by little I will drive them out from before you, until you have increased, and you inherit the land.* [31] *And I will set your bounds from the Red Sea to the sea, Philistia, and from the desert to the River. For I will deliver the inhabitants of the land into your hand, and you shall drive them out before you.*" Shemot 23:27-31

Notice the Aleph Taw (X𐤊) is directly involved with removing the pagan inhabitants from the Land. The point was to drive them out ahead of the Yisraelites so when they arrived, there were homes, vineyards and fields ready and waiting for them, lawns mowed, dishes washed, beds made – a turnkey transition. What an incredible blessing that must have been.

They did not have to build houses or clear land to plant crops. It was all there provided for them. All they needed to do was cleanse the Land of the filth and abominations that the locals were committing.

Notice though the dimensions of the boundaries. They would only be moving into a portion of the overall land promised to Abram. The full Covenant promise would be fulfilled at another wedding during a future renewal.

At that time they had no king. Yahushua was their leader and Eliezer was the High Priest. They were acting as representatives of YHWH. Since YHWH dwelled in their midst in a tent, He was their true King.

His tent was first pitched at Gilgal[153] and it stayed there for seven years. It was later moved to Shiloh within the boundaries of the Tribe of Ephraim. It is important to remember that Ephraim received the rights of the firstborn status that originally belonged to Reuben. The Scriptures are perfectly clear on this point, and this YHWH dwelled in the land of Ephraim. (1 Chronicles 5:1; Beresheet 48) It stayed in Shiloh for the period of time detailed in the Book of Judges.[154]

During this period, the people were divided and fell away from YHWH. Without a king, they turned to idolatry and fell under the curses of the Covenant. At times, YHWH would raise up a Judge who would lead the Yisraelites to victory over their enemies, but the people would eventually drift back into idolatry. This was because they never completely cleansed the land when they first entered.

A good example of one of these Judges can be found in Gideon. The Yisraelites were greatly oppressed and impoverished by their neighbors, particularly the Midianites. At that time a Messenger of YHWH came to Gideon while he was threshing wheat in a winepress. He was doing this in order to hide his food from the Midianites. The timing is interesting because this would have been after the barley and in the midst of the wheat harvest, before Shabuot.

The Messenger proclaimed to Gideon: "*YHWH is with you, you mighty man of valor.*" Judges 6:12. He was described as "mighty" which is "gibowr" (ᕠᖻᔕᖋ) in Hebrew. Next the text says "*YHWH turned to him*" and told him that he would "*save* ✕ᔮ-*Yisrael.*" Judges 6:14

Gideon was from the tribe of Manasseh, the oldest son of Joseph and he asked "*how can I save* ✕ᔮ-*Yisrael?*" Judges 6:15. Throughout his encounter with the Messenger of YHWH there is every indication that Gideon is meeting with the Aleph Taw (✕ᔮ) – the Messiah.

Gideon thereafter tore down the altar of Baal in the midst of his town, and used the wood to offer his father's second bull to YHWH. After this the Midianites, Amalekites and people of the East gathered together in the Valley of Jezreel. Then "*the Spirit of YHWH came upon* ✕ᔮ-*Gideon; then he blew the shofar.*" Judges 6:34. Thereafter, four of the northern tribes from the House of Yisrael gathered behind him, namely Manasseh, Asher, Zebulun and Naphtali.

Gideon then sought confirmation that YHWH was with him by using a fleece on a threshing floor. So he used a wine press as a threshing floor, and now he was using a threshing floor with the skin of an animal for confirmation from YHWH.[155] After receiving dual confirmations involving the fleece, he gathered with 32,000 people. (Judges 6:36-40)

As they prepared to confront their enemies, YHWH indicated that there were too many. Two thirds (22,000) were

afraid and they were dismissed. The 10,000 remaining were still too many. They scaled it down to 300 men based upon how they drank water.

Those 300, along with Gideon, went out to fight the enemy. Interestingly there are many profound connections that we can see through the gematria value of 301. For instance, the word "qara" (𐤊𐤓𐤐) refers to the voice of Elohim "calling" or naming the day and the night in Beresheet 1:5. The word "esh" (𐤅𐤊) refers to the "fire" of Elohim passing through the cuttings of the Covenant with Abram in Beresheet 15:17. The word "ha'tswur" (𐤓𐤅𐤌𐤄) refers to "the rock" that Mosheh struck at Horeb that provided water to Yisrael. (Shemot 17:6)

So the 301 readied themselves and took their "𐤗𐤊-provisions" and their "𐤗𐤊-shofars." (Judges 7:8) This was a clear indication that Aleph Taw (𐤗𐤊) would be fighting this battle. In fact, all they used was a shofar, a torch and an empty water pitcher. YHWH placed fear in the hearts of the camp ahead of time. At nighttime, at the beginning of the middle watch, they smashed their pitchers, held torch in their left hand and their shofar. They all shouted *"the sword of YHWH and of Gideon"* and blew their shofars.

The enemy then proceeded to kill each other with their swords and then fled. The Israelites from Naphtali, Asher, and all Manasseh then pursued the Midianites and retook a portion of their land. After capturing the leaders of the Midianites the text provides: *"So Gideon arose and killed Zebah and Zalmunna, and took the crescent ornaments that were on their camels' necks."* Judges 8:21

The crescent moon ornaments hint of moon worship. Indeed, these enemies encroaching upon the Land of the Northern Tribes of the House of Yisrael were moon-worshipping Ishmaelites – descendants of Abram. So, once again, we read about Yisrael doing battle with the moon god.

Gideon took the plunder of gold from the earrings of the Ishmaelite's. He made an ephod and set it up in his city of Ophrah. An "ephod" can be a priestly garment or an image. We do not know why he did such a thing, but Yisrael often struggles with their gold. It became a snare to Gideon and his house because "*all Yisrael played the harlot with it there.*" Judges 8:27 It seems that whenever men go beyond the commandments of YHWH they get themselves into trouble. A snare is something that catches, and will not let go until death occurs. You need to avoid snares – they are a trap set to destroy you.

Under Gideon, the Midianites were subdued and things were peaceful for forty years.[156] Regardless, the hearts of the people were not set toward YHWH. "*So it was, as soon as Gideon was dead, that the children of Yisrael again played the harlot with the Baals, and made Baal-Berith their god.*" Judges 8:33 This was a direct affront to their Covenant relationship with YHWH.

Baal means: "master or husband." Berith means: "covenant." So "Baal-Berith" was the "husband of the covenant." This was supposed to be the role of YHWH. Yisrael was involved in a covenant with another husband. Once again, she proved herself as an unfaithful bride. This pattern of unfaithfulness continued throughout the period of the Judges.

We have in the Tanak a very interesting and prophetic text called the Book of Ruth. It describes another time during the period of the Judges when there was a famine in the Land. Of course, famine was indicative of a curse so clearly things were not going well for Yisrael as she chased after other husbands.

Because of the famine, a certain family left the Promised Land and returned to the land of Moab. Whenever we read about the Covenant people leaving the land it usually means that they will be joined with the nations in some fashion that is meant to expand the Covenant. We saw this with Abram and Hagar. We also saw this with Yisrael and the mixed multitude.

The husband, Elimelech, and the wife Naomi, had two sons, Mahlon and Chilion who married Moabite women - Ruth and Orpah. Mahlon means: "sick" and Chilion means: "destruction." The husband and both of the sons died in the land of Moab, leaving Naomi, Ruth and Orpah.

Naomi decided to return to the land of Yisrael and Ruth decided to stay with her. In fact, the text says "she clung to her." Ruth declared to Naomi: "Your people shall be my people and your Elohi my Elohi." By doing this she was entering into the Covenant, and on the path to join the Assembly of Yisrael.

They returned to Bethlehem, which was the ancestral home of Elimelech, who was from the Tribe of Yahudah. They arrived at the beginning of the barley harvest, which would have been after Passover. Ruth gleaned in the fields of Boaz, a close relative of Naomi. She gleaned through the barley harvest and then through the wheat harvest. She visited Boaz at the "X𐤊-threshing floor" (𐤉𐤒𐤍-X𐤊) when he was sleeping during the time of threshing the barley. (Ruth 3:2) She had prepared herself to be his bride, and Boaz set about to take care of the legal prerequisites of redeeming her as a kinsman redeemer.

This all took place during the grain harvest, which is prophetic and points to a future grain harvest. Not only would this lead to the physical line of the eventual king of Yisrael, it also provided a pattern for how foreigners enter the Covenant and are redeemed by a kinsman redeemer. Ruth could have stayed in the land of Moab, which is something her counterpart Orpah actually did, but she decided to cling to the Elohim of Yisrael. As a result, she became a bride and

the matriarch of the royal bloodline of Yisrael. This is the pattern for a future bride who will return to the Land and be redeemed.

Throughout the period of the Judges, the relationship between Yisrael and YHWH was in shambles. The priesthood was corrupted, and the High Priesthood had transferred from the line of Eliezar to the line of Ithamar, Aharon's youngest son. The Yisraelites lost the Ark of the Covenant to the Philistines and the High Priest Eli and his two sons died. It was during this time that the final Judge, Shemuel, essentially functioned as a Priest, a Prophet and a King.

There apparently remained a functioning priesthood, but the Tabernacle had been moved about and the Ark was no longer located within the Tabernacle. The Ark, which represented the Throne of YHWH, had been treated as a sort of good luck charm. Yisrael did not know how to live with YHWH as their King. It was time to give them something they could understand and accept - a man as their king. Shemuel was the man who would see to the transfer of power. He was a very unique and powerful man who YHWH used to anoint the first two kings of Yisrael.

It was during this transition period that YHWH eventually moved out of the Land of Ephraim and made arrangements to relocate to the Tribe of Yahudah. We read the following summary in Psalm 78: "*67 Moreover He rejected the tent of Joseph, and did not choose the tribe of Ephraim, 68 But chose the Tribe of Yahudah, Mount Zion which He loved. 69 And He built His sanctuary like the heights, like the earth which He has established forever. 70 He also chose David His servant, and took him from the sheepfolds; 71 From following the ewes that had young He brought him, to shepherd Yaakob His people, and Yisrael His inheritance. 72 So he shepherded them according to the integrity of his heart, and guided them by the skillfulness of his hands.*" Psalm

78:67-72

So YHWH moved out of the Land of Ephraim, and eventually relocated to Yahudah. Notice the reference to Mount Zion. We know that Mount Zion is a Heavenly dwelling place but the text reveals that there is a mountain in Yahudah that will reveal the heavenly patterns.

The shepherd being referred to is David, the second King of Yisrael. Saul was the first King, from the Tribe of Benjamin, but he did not follow YHWH wholeheartedly. Therefore, while Saul was still alive, David was anointed as King. He awaited the death of Saul until he would eventually lead Yisrael. This was similar to the generation that eventually would enter the Promised Land under Yahushua having to wait for the former generation to die off.

Interestingly, David was the youngest son of Jesse – the 8th son. Typically a king would be the firstborn son, but by doing this YHWH was demonstrating that physical appearance and stature was not the deciding factor for a King of Yisrael. He was revealing that the heart is what makes a king. (1 Shemuel 16:7) By choosing the last He was demonstrating a very important requisite trait – humility. Recall that Mosheh was considered to be more humble than all men who were on the face of the earth. (Bemidbar 12:3)

So a man had to be humble to be a King of His people. In fact, it was tradition that the kings of Yisrael would actually ride on donkeys, rather than horses as the kings of other nations did. David was not only the 8th son, but he was also a shepherd and a servant. So this 8th son of Jesse was the ideal choice for YHWH, but not necessarily an obvious choice in the eyes of men.

The number 8, as has already been mentioned, is closely connected with the Covenant. This King was revealing the pattern of a Covenant King – the eighth son circumcised on the 8th day. He would provide many patterns

for a future Covenant King – the Anointed One Who would fulfill the Covenant on the Eighth Day.

Here is the text describing the anointing of David. *"Then Shemuel took the ✗𝐊-horn of oil and anointed him in the midst of his brothers; and the Spirit of YHWH came upon David from that day forward. So Samuel arose and went to Ramah."* 1 Shemuel 16:13

Notice the Aleph Taw (✗𝐊) affixed to the horn. In the Hebrew we see read: "et-qeren" (✗𝐊-𝟰𝟵𝟵). The word for "horn" is "qeren" (𝟰𝟵𝟵). It has a gematria value of 350 and shares the same value with the word "qaran" (𝟰𝟵𝟵) used to describe Mosheh when he came down from Mt. Sinai with the Tablets of the Covenant. In that case the word is translated as "shine" although it is spelled the same as "horn."

"Now it was so, when Mosheh came down from Mount Sinai (and the two tablets of the Testimony were in Moses' hand when he came down from the mountain), that Moses did not know that the skin of his face shone (𝟰𝟵𝟵) while he talked with Him." Shemot 34:29

Remember, that event occurred on Day 10 of Month 7, which is Yom Kippurim – the Day of Atonements. The word "atonements" (𝟰𝟮𝟰𝟳𝟰) also has the gematria value of 350. These connections reveal that atonement will be made through the anointed King Who will mediate the Covenant. This all points to the Messiah.

This anointing event involving the horn has profound significance. Interestingly, the horn is really a shofar. In this case a shofar filled with oil. While the shofar represents an instrument for the voice of YHWH, when it is used as a container, it holds the oil, which represents His Spirit and the reflection of His glory (kabod).

The horn of Shemuel was a shofar used to hold oil rather than to emit sound. How profound that the horn is an integral part of "anointing." Only when the oil is poured out can the horn be used for sound. So the oil being poured upon David and the Spirit of YHWH coming upon him was a "messiah" event.

The word "messiah" is "moshiach" (ﬤﬧWﬤ) in Hebrew. It actually means: "anoint." In fact, an anointed one is a messiah. Priests and Kings are anointed by Prophets, all fulfilling prophetic patterns pointing to The Prophet and The Messiah. In fact, after being anointed, the text states that: *"the Spirit of YHWH came upon David from that day forward . . . but the Spirit of YHWH departed from Saul."* 1 Shemuel 16:13-14

Even though David was anointed by Samuel, he did not immediately begin to reign as King. Incredibly, he went back to shepherding for some time. After the Spirit departed Saul, a distressing spirit from YHWH troubled him. He needed someone to play the harp, so he sent messengers to Jesse and told him *"send me your son David who is with the sheep."* 1 Shemuel 16:19

David would serve the king, and also feed his fathers flocks in Bethlehem. There came a time when the Philistines and the armies of Yisrael came together at the Valley of Elah. They encamped on each side of the Valley.

The Philistines sent out their champion named Goliath. He went into the valley and challenged the armies of Yisrael to send out a man to fight him. He actually presented himself and set forth his challenge for forty mornings and forty evenings.

Interestingly, instead of using the word "boker" (ﬧﬨﬧ) for "morning" the word "shechem" (ﬤשּׁW) is used. Recall that Shechem (ﬤשּׁW) is actually a place. In fact, it was the place where YHWH appeared to Abram, and the location of the first altar built by Abram in the land of Canaan. Obviously the mention of the number 40 is also significant.

David brought supplies to the army and was incensed that Goliath, "*the uncircumcised Philistine . . . should defy the armies of the living Elohim.*" 1 Shemuel 17:26 King Saul sent for David and David volunteered to fight the Philistine. Saul tried to discourage him, but David recounted instances when he killed a lion and a bear while protecting his sheep. He believed that YHWH Who delivered him from the "paw" (hand) of the lion and the bear would also deliver Goliath into his hands.

Saul offered David the use of his armor, but David declined – not because it did not fit him, but because he had not tested it in battle. (1 Shemuel 17:39) David then took his staff, and placed 5 smooth stones from the brook, and put them in a shepherd's bag along with his sling.

So what we have is a shepherd walking out to battle a giant. A giant fully armed with three different weapons: 1) a sword, 2) a spear, and 3) a javelin. He also had three different defenses: 1) a helmet, 2) a coat of mail, and 3) bronze armor on his legs. (1 Shemuel 17:4-7) Interestingly, the height of Goliath is described as: "*six cubits and a span.*" 1 Shemuel 17:4

A "span" is "zereth" (𐤗𐤘𐤓) in Hebrew which is "the spread of the fingers." Goliath was of the Rephaim, and a trademark of those born of the "giant" (𐤓𐤉𐤓) was the fact that they had six fingers and six toes. (2 Shemuel 21:20) Further, the iron spearhead of Goliath weighed six hundred shekels, and he carried six implements of battle.

So we see the number six strongly associated with this giant. This has significance when we consider the prophetic implications of the event. The shepherd of Yisrael anointed, but not yet reigning as king, faces the "beast" in the valley. The shepherd struck the giant with a stone (aben). The giant fell on his face, and then the shepherd took the sword of the giant and killed him with his own weapon. This is actually a pattern to be repeated by the Messiah.

Notice that the stone knocked down the giant, but it did not kill him. David actually used Goliath's own sword to cut off his head. He brought the head to Jerusalem, and took the armor to his tent. (1 Shemuel 17:48-54) So David was shepherd and a giant killer who was destined to be the king of Yisrael, but that would still have to wait. Despite the fact that David married Saul's daughter, Saul became jealous of David. He eventually sought to kill David, forcing him into exile.

David ended up living on the fringe of society, in the wilderness as an outcast with a small band of followers. This established a pattern for the future Messiah Who would be an anointed King, but would live in the wilderness. Only after the death of Saul did David begin to reign.

After the death of Saul, David was anointed by the House of Yahudah. *"Then the men of Yahudah came, and there they anointed David king over the House of Yahudah . . ."* 2 Shemuel 2:4

This reveals how fractured Yisrael was at the time. Since David was from the Tribe of Yahudah, the Southern Tribes apparently readily accepted him. The House of Yahudah consisted primarily of 2 Tribes – Yahudah and Benjamin. The reason for this connection derives from the fact that Yahudah offered himself in the place of Benjamin when they were before Joseph in Egypt. (Beresheet 44:32). Interestingly, one would expect Joseph and Benjamin to be united since they were both of the same mother, Rachel. Nevertheless, the event in Egypt incident clearly bound Yahudah and Benjamin together.

So the first King of Yisrael came from Benjamin, now the second King was from Yahudah and he ruled over the Yahudah and Benjamin. David reigned from Hebron, and after seven years the Northern Tribes accepted him as their king.

"*Therefore all the elders of Yisrael came to the king at Hebron, and King David made a covenant with them at Hebron before YHWH. And they anointed David king over Yisrael.*" 2 Shemuel 5:3 Interestingly, while the House of Yahudah merely anointed the King, the House of Yisrael made a covenant with him <u>and</u> anointed him.

The Kingdom of Yisrael was united under David and only when Yisrael was united did he move the Capital to Jerusalem. At that time the Ark of the Covenant was located in the house Abinadab at Kirjath Jearim where it had been placed sometime after being returned by the Philistines.

David thereafter brought the Ark to Jerusalem and placed it within a Tabernacle that he had constructed – the Tabernacle of David. This apparently was not the Tabernacle, "ahal" (𐤋𐤄𐤀) of Mosheh that was still standing in Gibeon and being serviced by Zadok. We can presume this since the Tabernacle was still in Gibeon at the time that Shlomo assumed the throne.

So David may have had a different Tabernacle, more like a "succa," constructed at Jerusalem. In fact, the prophet Amos specifically referred to "the 𐤗𐤊-succot (𐤗𐤉𐤎-𐤗𐤊) of David."[157] A "succa" (𐤀𐤉𐤉𐤅) is a temporary dwelling built by Yisraelites every year for the Feast of Succot. It was in this succa that the Ark was placed.

David was very much concerned with establishing the House of YHWH. In fact, it was when he contemplated building a House for YHWH that He was promised a perpetual throne. Clearly, his heart was in the right place and so YHWH made an unconditional Covenant with David within the context of the Covenant with Yisrael.

Here is that Covenant related through the Prophet Nathan.

"*[10] Moreover I will appoint a place for My people Yisrael, and will plant them, that they may dwell in a place of their own and move no more; nor shall the sons of wickedness oppress them anymore, as previously, [11] since the time that I commanded judges to be over My people Yisrael, and have caused you to rest from all your enemies. Also YHWH tells you that He will make you a house. [12] When your days are fulfilled and you rest with your fathers, I will set up your seed after you, who will come from your body, and I will establish his kingdom. [13] He shall build a house for My name, and I will establish the throne of his kingdom forever. [14] I will be his Father, and he shall be My son. If he commits iniquity, I will chasten him with the rod of men and with the blows of the sons of men. [15] But My mercy shall not depart from him, as I took it from Saul, whom I removed from before you. [16] And your house and your kingdom shall be established forever before you. Your throne shall be established forever."* 2 Shemuel 7:10-16

As with much in the life of David, this Covenant contained a prophecy concerning the Messiah. He could not build the House because his hands had too much blood on them from his violent past. He could make the plans and gather the supplies, but the building was left to his son Solomon (Shlomo).

David reigned for 40 years, 7 over the House of Yahudah and 33 over the United Kingdom of Yisrael. Only when Shlomo built the permanent Temple did the Ark finally rest in the House of YHWH and the proper priestly line, that of Zadok, was reestablished. All of the chaos of the past had been set in order. Sadly, that order did not last for long.

While Shlomo has been considered one of the wisest men to ever live, he failed to heed the commandments found in the Torah concerning the Kings of Yisrael.

"[1] But King Shlomo loved many foreign women, as well

as the daughter of Pharaoh: women of the Moabites, Ammonites, Edomites, Sidonians, and Hittites ² from the nations of whom YHWH had said to the children of Yisrael, You shall not intermarry with them, nor they with you. Surely they will turn away your hearts after their gods. Shlomo clung to these in love. ³ And he had seven hundred wives, princesses, and three hundred concubines; and his wives turned away his heart. ⁴ For it was so, when Shlomo was old, that his wives turned his heart after other gods; and his heart was not loyal to YHWH his Elohim, as was the heart of his father David. ⁵ For Shlomo went after Ashtoreth the goddess of the Sidonians, and after Milcom the <u>abomination</u> of the Ammonites. ⁶ Shlomo did evil in the sight of YHWH, and did not fully follow YHWH, as did his father David. ⁷ Then Shlomo built a high place for Chemosh the <u>abomination</u> of Moab, on the hill that is east of Jerusalem, and for Molech the <u>abomination</u> of the people of Ammon. ⁸ And he did likewise for all his foreign wives, who burned incense and sacrificed to their gods. ⁹ So YHWH became angry with Shlomo, because his heart had turned from YHWH Elohim of Yisrael, Who had appeared to him twice, ¹⁰ and had commanded him concerning this thing, that he should not go after other gods; but he did not keep what YHWH had commanded. ¹¹ <u>Therefore YHWH said to Shlomo, Because you have done this, and have not kept My Covenant and My statutes, which I have commanded you, I will surely tear the kingdom away from you and give it to your servant.</u> ¹² Nevertheless I will not do it in your days, for the sake of your father David; I will tear it out of the hand of your son. ¹³ However I will not tear away the whole kingdom; I will give one tribe to your son for the sake of My servant David, and for the sake

of Jerusalem which I have chosen." 1 Kings 11:1-13

Imagine such a man blessed with wisdom, privileged to build the House of YHWH and see the "glory" (kabod) of YHWH. He was the King of a united Kingdom and was blessed with great wealth. It was originally recorded that he loved YHWH (1 Kings 3:3), but he failed to obey the commandments concerning kings. He actually practiced and promoted the worship of the foreign gods of the surrounding nations. Notice that all of the male gods are referred to as the "abomination" (שׁקֻץ). This will be important concerning future prophecies.

Here is what Mosheh previously instructed Yisrael for the time when they finally would have a king: *"¹⁶ But he shall not multiply horses for himself, nor cause the people to return to Egypt to multiply horses, for YHWH has said to you, You shall not return that way again. ¹⁷ Neither shall he multiply wives for himself, lest his heart turn away; nor shall he greatly multiply silver and gold for himself. ¹⁸ Also it shall be, when he sits on the throne of his kingdom, that he shall write for himself a copy of this Torah in a scroll, from the one before the priests, the Levites. ¹⁹ And it shall be with him, and he shall read it all the days of his life, that he may learn to fear YHWH his Elohim and be careful to observe all the words of this Torah and these statutes, ²⁰ that his heart may not be lifted above his brethren, that he may not turn aside from the commandment to the right hand or to the left, and that he may prolong his days in his kingdom, he and his children in the midst of Yisrael."* Debarim 17:16-20

We do not know whether Shlomo copied his own Torah scroll, but he ended up violating all of the other prohibitions, and in his old age he was involved in some of the worst abominations imaginable.

Wisdom alone does not necessarily get you into the Kingdom or keep you in the Kingdom. Again, YHWH desires our obedience and faithfulness. Shlomo reigned over

the united Kingdom of Yisrael for 40 years. Sadly, the unity was short lived.

Nevertheless, this was not a surprise to YHWH and a pattern was established in the physical realm that would have tremendous spiritual ramifications. YHWH had revealed through the cycles of time how he would separate in order to build His Kingdom. He also showed how His Son would build a permanent House and establish the Kingdom.

Shlomo went the way of all men who do not obey the Torah. He was definitely not the Promised Son. So the Covenant made with David had much further reaching implications. Now that the pattern was concluded it was time for YHWH to set the stage for His Son to come and fulfill the prophetic patterns. First, the kingdom that was united 73 years earlier was now destined for division.[158]

7

Division

The sins of King Shlomo are the reason for the division of the Kingdom of Yisrael. He blatantly disobeyed the commandments, and the Kingdom would suffer as a result. Before his death, it was prophesied by Ahiyah of Shiloh that the Kingdom would be torn apart.

The prophet confronted the servant of Shlomo, Jereboam, as he was leaving Jerusalem. Ahiyah took a new cloak, and tore it into twelve (12) pieces. He told Jereboam to take 10 pieces and spoke the following to him:

"³¹ See, I am going to tear the kingdom out of Shlomo's hand and give you ten (10) tribes. ³² But for the sake of My servant David and the city of Jerusalem, which I have chosen out of all the tribes of Yisrael, he will have one (1) tribe. ³³ I will do this because they have forsaken Me and worshiped Ashtoreth the goddess of the Sidonians, Chemosh the god of the Moabites, and Molech the god of the Ammonites, and have not walked in My ways, nor done what is right in My eyes, nor kept My statutes and laws as David, Shlomo's father, did. ³⁴ But I will not take the whole kingdom out of Shlomo's hand; I have made him ruler all the days of his life for the sake of David My servant, whom I chose and who observed My commands and statutes. ³⁵ I will take the kingdom from his son's hands and give you ten tribes. ³⁶ I will give one tribe to his son so that David My servant may always have a lamp before

Me in Jerusalem, the city where I chose to put My Name.
³⁷ However, as for you, I will take you, and you will rule
over all that your heart desires; you will be king over
Yisrael. ³⁸ If you do whatever I command you and walk in
My ways and do what is right in My eyes by keeping My
statutes and commands, as David my servant did, I will be
with you. I will build you a dynasty as enduring as the one
I built for David and will give Yisrael to you. ³⁹ I will
humble David's descendants because of this, but not
forever." 1 Kings (Melakim) 11:31-39.

This was an incredible prophecy given to Jereboam –
an Ephraimite. The Scriptures record that Jereboam was a
mighty man of valor - he was a powerful man. Shlomo
recognized this and placed him in charge of the whole labor
force of the House of Joseph.

Jeroboam eventually rebelled against the throne of
Shlomo. His people, the House of Yisrael, were being
oppressed, and YHWH chose Jeroboam to punish Shlomo's
house for the idolatry and sin committed by Shlomo.

YHWH also gave Jeroboam great promises, if he
would only do what Shlomo failed to do – be like David. In
other words, this Ephraimite would be a great king over
Yisrael if he would simply obey and guard (shamar) the
commands, walk in His ways and do what was right.[159] So the
Kingdom of Yisrael was to continue through the Northern
Tribes not the House of Yahudah.

After the death of King Shlomo, the prophecy given
by Ahiyah came to pass. The House of Yisrael, also known as
the Northern Kingdom, petitioned Solomon's son, King
Rehoboam, essentially asking for tax relief. In the past, King
Shlomo, had put a heavy burden on the people amassing great
wealth and building mighty structures.

Instead of taking the advice of the elders, Rehoboam
took the advice of his young friends, and responded to the

apparent reasonable request with a vulgar reference to the size of his father's genitals. (see 1 Kings 12:10). He then proceeded to state: *"My father laid on you a heavy yoke - I will make it even heavier. My father scourged you with whips - I will scourge you with scorpions."* 1 Kings (Melakim) 12:11

His "unwise" response resulted in the prophesied split in the Kingdom of Yisrael. Under the rule of King Shlomo, Yisrael had broken the Covenant with YHWH, so they suffered the punishment of breaking the Covenant. Yisrael was split in two – as was pictured by the pieces in the Covenant process involving Abram. They were united through the flow of blood in between the "pieces." That was the path taken by the Messiah. Only the Messiah will re-united the divided Kingdom.

The House of Yisrael, which consisted of the ten northern Tribes, aligned with Jeroboam, son of Nebat. The House of Yahudah, which consisted of the southern Tribes, aligned with Rehoboam. While the House of Yahudah maintained the worship of YHWH in Jerusalem, the northern Tribes set up their own false worship system. This is where things started to go very bad for the House of Yisrael.

Jeroboam feared that if the people from his kingdom, the House of Yisrael, continued to go to Jerusalem they would eventually join back with the House of Yahudah and reunite the Kingdom of Yisrael. This notion was unfounded, self-serving and contrary to the promise given to him by YHWH. His fear and concern demonstrated that he did not believe the promise of YHWH, so he took matters into his own hands.

After seeking some bad advice he set up pagan worship in the north.

"26 Jeroboam thought to himself, the kingdom will now likely revert to the house of David. 27 If these

people go up to offer sacrifices at the House of YHWH in Jerusalem, they will again give their allegiance to their master, Rehoboam king of Yahudah. They will kill me and return to King Rehoboam. [28] *After seeking advice, the king made two golden calves.* He said to the people, 'It is too much for you to go up to Jerusalem. Here are your gods, O Yisrael, who brought you up out of Egypt. [29] one he set up in Bethel, and the other in Dan.' [30] And this thing became a sin; the people went even as far as Dan to worship the one there. [31] *Jeroboam built shrines on high places and appointed priests from all sorts of people, even though they were not Levites.* [32] *He instituted a festival on the fifteenth day of the eighth month, like the festival held in Yahudah, and offered sacrifices on the altar.* This he did in Bethel, sacrificing to the calves he had made. And at Bethel he also installed priests at the high places he had made. [33] *On the fifteenth day of the eighth month, a month of his own choosing, he offered sacrifices on the altar he had built at Bethel.* So he instituted the festival for the Yisraelites and went up to the altar to make offerings." 1 Kings (Melakim) 12:26-33

This is really quite incredible because Jeroboam was already promised a perpetual throne like David's if he would simply obey. He had originally built up the Covenant sites of Shechem and Penuel. (1 Kings 12:25) Instead of trusting the Word of YHWH, he tried to hold onto power using his own intellect and setting up his own system of worship in direct contravention to the ways of YHWH.

Jeroboam not only established new places of worship, he also established different appointed times and set up a false priesthood. Notice that he chose a familiar place to offer sacrifices. Beth El was, after all, the "House of El." It was the place where Yaakob, and later Yisrael, built altars and offered sacrifices. Now Jeroboam was setting up idols and profaning these important landmarks.

The sin of Jeroboam was even worse than the sin of his predecessors at Sinai. YHWH immediately sent a prophet to warn him of the error of his way. (see 1 Kings 13). Despite the warnings, Jeroboam refused to repent. As a result of this great sin, Yisrael was scheduled for punishment. It was not a mystery that they would be punished, Mosheh had told them long ago, but they apparently did not remember or they simply did not care. His new priests likely neglected to teach the curses associated with their actions to the people.

As you might imagine, not everyone in this new breakaway kingdom was pleased with the idolatry that was introduced by Jeroboam. While most likely appreciated the tax relief, they needed to choose whether the trade was worth it or not – they had a choice to make.

The Scriptures record the following: "*13 And from all their territories the priests and the Levites who were in all Yisrael took their stand with him (Rehoboam). 14 For the Levites left their common-lands and their possessions and came to Yahudah and Jerusalem, for Jeroboam and his sons had rejected them from serving as priests to YHWH. 15 Then he appointed for himself priests for the high places, for the goat and the calf idols which he had made. 16 And after them, those from all the tribes of Yisrael, such as set their heart to seek YHWH Elohim of Yisrael, came to Jerusalem to sacrifice to YHWH Elohim of their fathers. 17 So they strengthened the kingdom of Yahudah, and made Rehoboam the son of Shlomo strong for three years, because they walked in the way of David and Shlomo for three years." 2 Chronicles 11:13-17*

This tells us that at least the Levites from the Northern Kingdom left and went to dwell with Yahudah. While others from the Northern Kingdom "*came to Jerusalem* to *sacrifice*" we do not know for certain if they moved there. We can safely assume from the language that the statement: "*they strengthened the kingdom of Yahudah*" means that they were added to the kingdom by moving to region Judea. This is important to recognize, because it is highly likely that the Southern Kingdom ended up becoming a mixture of all of the tribes, although primarily Yahudah, Benyamin and Levi. So the present day people known as "Jews" are the descendants of the House of Yahudah and they likely have a mixture of all the tribes.

Sadly, the entire ordeal stemmed from a continuing sibling rivalry between Ephraim and Yahudah. Jeroboam, after all, was from the tribe of Ephraim (Joseph) and Rehoboam was from the tribe of Yahudah. We see this as a continuing theme throughout the Scriptures. It is a very important concept to understand – the battle between the first born and the rulership – because it continues to this day. Joseph was elevated to the firstborn while Yahudah was given the rulership.[160]

The matter was aptly summarized in 1 Melakim 12:19: "*So Yisrael has been in rebellion against the house of David to this day.*" The split in the kingdom was no accident, as proclaimed by Shemayah, the man of Elohim, when Rehoboam was about to suppress the rebellion of the House of Yisrael. "*This is what YHWH says: 'Do not go up to fight against your brothers, the Yisraelites. Go home, every one of you, for this is My doing. So they obeyed the Word of YHWH and went home again, as YHWH had ordered.'*" 1 Melakim 12:24 YHWH had a plan for this division which was much greater than people could imagine, and it was all about the Covenant.

As we read from the Scriptures, neither King followed good advice and both Kingdoms ended up getting into trouble. The audacity of the sin of the House of Yisrael resulted in a more immediate and severe judgment.

Ultimately, both Kingdoms ended up receiving the promised curses of YHWH that are found within the Torah. Since they were divided, and acting independently of one another, YHWH treated them differently. They committed different sins, and were given different punishments. The House of Yisrael started out worshipping Egyptian gods while the House of Yahudah ended up incorporating Babylonian worship.

The House of Yahudah staved off judgment as they drifted in and out of idolatry throughout the succession of many kings. Both ended up suffering the punishment foretold by Mosheh. They were evicted from the House, which was physical expulsion from the Land.

The fact that Yisrael was initially divided in two is not shocking. That separation was nothing new. These were the ancient divisions that existed in Yisrael, and David was only able to unify the north and the south after having reigned for seven years.

Since David was promised an everlasting throne and since he was responsible for building the House, his line was given Jerusalem and those tribes associated with Jerusalem – Yahudah and Benjamin. The territory of those two tribes actually divided Jerusalem. So the House of Yahudah primarily consisted of 2 tribes plus the Levites, while the House of Yisrael consisted of the other 10 Tribes.

Jeroboam was given the greater Kingdom. Since he was from Ephraim, and Ephraim received the double portion of the firstborn. YHWH had previously moved His House from Ephraim to Yahudah. Jerusalem was the issue that perplexed Jeroboam this posed a quandary, or at least that is what he thought. His kingdom did not include Jerusalem and the House of YHWH. So the males in his kingdom needed to make pilgrimage to another kingdom three times a year. This would also include Jeroboam if he was going to continue

serving YHWH.

With this logistical issue and the subsequent great transfer of wealth that would occur due to those pilgrimage feasts, Jeroboam decided to create his own system of worship. Like his predecessors who came out of Egypt, Jeroboam set up golden calf as a representation of YHWH. Instead of just one – he set up two. One calf was at Dan and the other was at Beth El. He also set up goat gods. At Beth El, they offered up sacrifices to the calf. Imagine this significant place of the Covenant being defiled in such a fashion. Jeroboam had incorporated the gods of Egypt into the worship of YHWH. He also changed the times of worship from the seventh month to the eighth month.

Now YHWH had established Appointed Times for the people to meet with Him at His House. Even though the Yisraelites were not allowed into the House because of the sin at Sinai, it was still a privilege and an honor to keep the Appointed Times.

Incredibly, the House of Yisrael repeated the very sin that kept them out of the House of YHWH. How ironic that they committed this fornication at the House of El (Beth El) – the very gateway to heaven. The House of Yisrael profaned the Feasts and used them to commit idolatry. This was highly offensive to YHWH. Instead of keeping the appointed "dates" with her Husband YHWH, the House of Yisrael was whoring after other gods.

YHWH was not pleased with how Jeroboam and subsequent kings of the House of Yisrael profaned His Torah and the Appointed Times. Several prophets related this displeasure through time.

The prophet Amos stated: *"⁵ But do not seek Beth El, nor enter Gilgal, nor pass over to Beersheba; For Gilgal shall surely go into captivity, and Beth El shall come to nothing. ⁶ Seek YHWH and live, lest He break out like fire in the house of Joseph, and* devour it, with no one to quench it in Beth El . . . ²¹ I hate, I despise *your feast days, and I do not savor your sacred assemblies.* ²² *Though you offer Me burnt offerings and your grain offerings, I will not accept them, nor will I regard your fattened peace offerings.* ²³ *Take away from Me the noise of your songs, for I will not hear the melody of your stringed instruments."* Amos 5:6-6, 21-23

Amos also reflected the heart of the House of Yisrael toward the weekly Sabbath and the New Moon Festivals. *"⁴ Hear this, you who swallow up the needy, and make the poor of the land fail ⁵ Saying: When will the New Moon be past, that we may sell grain? And the Sabbath, that we may trade wheat? Making the ephah small and the shekel large, falsifying the scales by deceit, ⁶ That we may buy the poor for silver, and the needy for a pair of sandals - even sell the bad wheat?"* Amos 8:4-6

In other words, they could not wait for the Sabbath and the New Moon days to get over so they could continue to rob people. We can only imagine that if they could even honor the weekly Sabbath, there is no way they would honor the yearly Sabbath – the Shemittah Year. The special days and years set apart for the Covenant people were nothing but a nuisance that hampered their corrupt activities.

They did not delight in YHWH and His Times. In fact, they corrupted these set apart Appointed Times, because they were being observed to the Baals – not YHWH. *"¹¹ I will also cause all her mirth to cease, her feast days, her new moons, her sabbaths - all her appointed feasts. ¹² And I will destroy her vines and her fig trees, of which she has said, These are my wages that my lovers have given me. So I will make them a forest, and the beasts of the field shall eat them. ¹³ I will punish her for the days of the Baals to which she burned incense. She decked herself with her earrings and jewelry, and went after her lovers; but Me she forgot, says YHWH."* Hosea 2:11-13

The Scriptural Appointed Times were the Feasts of YHWH, and they revolved around the harvests. They were supposed to be time when the people appeared before YHWH and acknowledged the blessings that YHWH had bestowed upon them. Instead, the people were attributing the produce of the Land to Baal.

Notice that they are "her" feast days, "her" new moons, "her" Sabbaths and all "her" appointed feasts. In Vayiqra 23 YHWH specifically states: "*Speak to the children of Yisrael, and say to them: The Appointed Times of YHWH, which you shall proclaim to beset apart gatherings, these are My Appointed Times.*" Vayiqra 23:2 When we change His times we make them our own. By doing so we profane them, and YHWH refers to them as "dung." (see Malachi 2:3) This is why it is imperative to diligently observe His times.[161]

So the House of Yisrael had departed the ways of YHWH and was worshipping Baal. YHWH sent prophets to warn them, but they failed to repent and turn back to Him. During this period of division we also read about two very unique prophets - Elijah and Elisha. Elijah spent a great deal of time addressing the sin of the House of Yisrael, specifically under the rulership of King Ahab.

Of Ahab we read the following: "*[30] Now Ahab the son of Omri did evil in the sight of YHWH, more than all who were before him. [31] And it came to pass, as though it had been a trivial thing for him to walk in the sins of Jeroboam the son of Nebat, that he took as wife Jezebel the daughter of Ethbaal, king of the Sidonians; and he went and served Baal and worshiped him. [32] Then he set up an altar for Baal in the temple of Baal, which he had built in Samaria. [33] And Ahab made a wooden image. Ahab did more to provoke* ✕✔-*YHWH Elohi of Yisrael to anger than all the kings of Yisrael who were before him.*" 1 Kings 16:30-33

Elijah spoke against Ahab and his wife Jezebel and strongly confronted the Baal worship that they promoted. In one incident he challenged 450 priests of Baal, and called down fire from heaven at Mount Carmel. (1 Kings 18:20-40)

Elijah was told to anoint Jehu as King when Ahab died, but it does not appear that he ever did it. At the same time Elijah was told to anoint Elisha as a prophet in his place. (1 Kings 19:16)

Since Elijah did not anoint Jehu, Ahaziah succeeded King Ahab. When King Ahaziah was later injured from a fall, he inquired of Baal-zebub, the god of Ekron. Elijah was sent to inform the King that he was going to die. After relating the bad news, the king sent for Elijah. Here is the account.

"⁹ Then the king sent to him a captain of fifty with his fifty men. So he went up to him; and there he was, sitting on the top of a hill. And he spoke to him: Man of Elohim, the king has said, Come down! ¹⁰ So Elijah answered and said to the captain of fifty, If I am a man of Elohim, then let fire come down from heaven and consume you and your fifty men. And fire came down from heaven and consumed him and his fifty. ¹¹ Then he sent to him another captain of fifty with his fifty men. And he answered and said to him: Man of Elohim, thus has the king said, Come down quickly! ¹² So Elijah answered and said to them, If I am a man of Elohim, let fire come down from heaven and consume you and your fifty men. And the fire of Elohim came down from heaven and consumed him and his fifty. ¹³ Again, he sent a third captain of fifty with his fifty men. And the third captain of fifty went up, and came and fell on his knees before Elijah, and pleaded with him, and said to him: Man of Elohim, please let my life and the life of these fifty servants of yours be precious in your sight. ¹⁴ Look, fire has come down from heaven and burned up the first two captains of fifties with their fifties. But let my life now be precious in your sight. ¹⁵ And the angel of YHWH said to Elijah, Go down with him; do not be afraid of him. So he arose and went down with him to the king. *¹⁶ Then he said to him, Thus says YHWH: Because you have sent messengers to inquire of Baalzebub, the god of Ekron, is it because there is no Elohim in Yisrael to inquire of His word? Therefore you shall not come down from the bed to which you have gone up, but you shall surely die. ¹⁷ So Ahaziah died according to the word of YHWH which Elijah had spoken."* 2 Kings 1:9-17

We already saw from his treatment of the prophets of Baal that he was able to call down fire from heaven. (1 Kings 18) This will prove significant when we later examine a future appearance of two witnesses.

What is particularly noteworthy about the above referenced passage are the numbers. There were 50 plus 1 captain, then 50 plus 1 captain and finally 50 plus 1 captain. All tolled there were 153 that came to Elijah. He called down fire on the first two groups and only 1/3 were spared. What makes this so profound is the number 153 as has already been mentioned several times. Remember that the gematria value of 153 is "beni ha'Elohim" (𐤅𐤉𐤄𐤋𐤊𐤄 𐤉𐤍𐤁) – "the sons of Elohim."

So there is a connection between Elijah and judgment by fire upon the House of Yisrael. Also there is a message that 1/3 of the sons of Elohim will escape the fire. We will examine this further on in the text as we examine the two witnesses prophesied to come at the end of the age. They will be given the power to call down fire from heaven.

After Ahaziah died, Jehoram became King. During the reign of Jehoram, Elijah apparently commissioned Elisha who, in turn, commissioned another prophet to finally go anoint Jehu as King of Yisrael. After the anointing people blew shofars announcing that Jehu had been anointed King of the House of Yisrael. Jehu then proceeded to massacre many people – well beyond his original mandate to wipe out the line of Ahab. While he appeared to do the will of YHWH, he continued the sins of Jeroboam - so went the House of Yisrael.

Elijah and Elisha were unique in the sense that they operated within this wicked kingdom ruled by wicked kings. They walked in incredible power, probably because they needed it to survive. While many prophets spoke the Word of YHWH, these two individuals performed feats reminiscent of Mosheh. They called down fire, raised the dead, healed the sick, controlled the weather, commanded animals, multiplied food, parted waters and even anointed foreign kings, along with other feats.

Elijah and Elisha really must be looked at together since Elisha followed Elijah, and actually wore the mantel of Elijah. He also walked in a double anointing. (2 Kings 2). When you examine their Hebrew names you see an incredible mystery. Elijah in Hebrew is Eliyahu (𐤉𐤄𐤅𐤋𐤀) which means: "My El is YHWH." Elisha (𐤏𐤅𐤋𐤀) means: "My El is Salvation." When these two names are combined we see that "Eli" is what connects the two. When you remove "Eli" from each and combine them you have "Yahushua." So the mystery of these two miracle working prophets is Eli Yahushua - "My El is Yahushua." Yahushua, of course, is the name of the Messiah.

So these two prophets, sent to the House of Yisrael, in great power also carried a message within their very names. Indeed, when we read that Elijah was to anoint Elisha in his place we read 𐤕𐤀-Elisha (𐤏𐤅𐤋𐤀-𐤕𐤀). (1 Kings 19:16) So we see the Aleph Taw (𐤕𐤀) associated with Elisha who operated in a double portion of the spirit of Elijah. (2 Kings 2:9-15) Despite the actions of these men, the House of Yisrael stubbornly refused to repent and turn back to YHWH. They continued to worship their calves and the gods of the

surrounding people.

Mosheh had warned the people that they would be punished if they turned from the Covenant. Remember that this was a marriage Covenant. The Bride was to remain faithful to her Husband. The House of Yisrael committed adultery. She was repeating the sins of Sinai. YHWH was patient, but He has His limits. YHWH sent prophets to warn them, but instead of returning to YHWH the House of Yisrael committed worse acts.

This was not just a single act of adultery - she had become a prostitute. She had gone even further. Instead of receiving money, or performing her acts of prostitution pro gratis, she actually paid her lovers! (see Ezekiel 37) This was simply unheard of in the history of prostitution. Yisrael had degraded herself to such an extent that she was vile – putrid in the eyes of YHWH.

YHWH sent the prophet Hosea to the House of Yisrael. Through his life, marriage and family YHWH revealed what would happen to them. Hosea actually married a harlot named Gomer to demonstrate the relationship between YHWH and the House of Yisrael. They had three children who were aptly named to reveal the deterioration of the relationship.

We are first introduced to Hoshea by being told when he was a prophet. *"The word of YHWH that came to Hoshea son of Beeri during the reigns of Uzziah, Jotham, Ahaz and Hezekiah, kings of Yahudah, and during the reign of Jeroboam son of Yahoash king of Yisrael."* Hoshea 1:1 Therefore, Hoshea was a prophet while both kingdoms were still in the Land.

YHWH instructed Hoshea to find a wife who would represent the House of Yisrael. He told Hoshea to: *"² Go, take to yourself an adulterous wife and children of unfaithfulness, because the land is guilty of the vilest adultery in departing from YHWH. ³ So he married Gomer daughter of Diblaim, and she* conceived and bore him a son. *⁴ Then YHWH said to Hoshea, Call him Yezreel, because I will soon punish the house of Jehu for the massacre at Yezreel, and I will put an end to the kingdom of Yisrael. ⁵ In that day I will break Yisrael's bow in the Valley of Yezreel."* Hoshea 1:2-5

Yezreel means both "Elohim scatters" and "Elohim sows." As He "scattered" them under Jehu, and finally by the Assyrian deportation, so He will "sow" them again. So we know that the Kingdom of Yisrael would come to an end and would be scattered.

We first read about Jehu, who was supposed to rid the land of King Ahab, his descendents and the Baal worship that they promoted. He actually committed a massacre that, on its face, appeared to be performing the will of YHWH, but he never intended to follow YHWH. Here is what the Scriptures provide: *"²⁹ However Jehu did not turn away from the sins of Jeroboam the son of Nebat, who had made Yisrael sin, that is, from the golden calves that were at Bethel and Dan. ³⁰ And YHWH said to Jehu, Because you have done well in doing what is right in My sight, and have done to the house of Ahab all that was in My heart, your sons shall sit on the throne of Yisrael to the fourth generation. ³¹ But Jehu took no heed to walk in the Torah-YHWH Elohi-Yisrael with all his heart; for he did not depart from the sins of Jeroboam, who had made Israel sin."* 2 Kings 10:29-31

So the first son of Hoshea and Gomer dealt with the bloodguilt associated with what happened at Jezreel. The text describes a second child between between the two.

"⁶ Gomer conceived again and gave birth to a daughter. Then YHWH said to Hoshea, Call her Lo-Ruhamah, for I will no longer show love to the House of Yisrael, that I should at all forgive them. ⁷ Yet I will show love to the House of Yahudah; and I will save them - not by bow, sword or battle, or by horses and horsemen, but by YHWH their Elohim." Hoshea 1:6-7

The definition for the name "Lo-Ruhamah is given in

the passage. In essence it means "no pity, no mercy, no compassion." In other words, YHWH was going to show restraint while the House of Yisrael was scattered and suffering – He would stop showing love to them for a time. At the same time, He would continue to show love to the House of Yahudah, and would save them in a way that they could not take credit.

After Gomer had weaned Lo-Ruhamah, she gave birth to another son. *"Then YHWH said, Call him Lo-Ammi, for you are not My people, and I am not your Elohim."* Hoshea 1:9 It could not get much worse than this. Not only would the Kingdom of Yisrael come to an end and be scattered, they would no longer be loved by YHWH. Finally, they would no longer be considered to be His people. In other words, they would be put away from YHWH because they were adulterous.

YHWH would no longer have mercy on the House of Yisrael and would utterly remove her from the Land. Finally, He would sever the Covenant relationship with them. They would no longer be His people, and He would no longer be their Elohim. The classic Covenant identification language is "they shall be My people and I will be their Elohim." So the Covenant was terminated and the House of Yisrael would be out of relationship with YHWH. This meant a literal divorce for the House of Yisrael.

This was confirmed by the Prophet Jeremiah who later provided the following: *"Then I saw that for all the causes for which backsliding Yisrael had committed adultery, I had put her away and given her a certificate of divorce; yet her treacherous sister Yahudah did not fear, but went and played the harlot also."* Jeremiah 3:8

Notice that the House of Yahudah also played the harlot and was called a treacherous sister. In fact, both the House of Yisrael and the House of Yahudah were likened to

2 lewd sisters: Oholah and Oholibah. (Ezekiel 23) The only difference between the two was that YHWH would still have mercy on the House of Yahudah. For the sake of David, He would not divorce the House of Yahudah.

As we discussed, the House of Yisrael failed to heed the warnings of Hosea and were eventually punished.

"¹ Say of your brothers, 'My people,' and of your sisters, 'My loved one.' ² Rebuke your mother, rebuke her, for she is not my wife, and I am not her husband. Let her remove the adulterous look from her face and the unfaithfulness from between her breasts. ³ Otherwise I will strip her naked and make her as bare as on the day she was born; I will make her like a desert, turn her into a parched land, and slay her with thirst. ⁴ I will not show my love to her children, because they are the children of adultery. ⁵ Their mother has been unfaithful and has conceived them in disgrace. She said, I will go after my lovers, who give me my food and my water, my wool and my linen, my oil and my drink. ⁶ Therefore I will block her path with thorn bushes; I will wall her in so that she cannot find her way. ⁷ She will chase after her lovers but not catch them; she will look for them but not find them. Then she will say, I will go back to my husband as at first, for then I was better off than now. ⁸ She has not acknowledged that I was the one who gave her the grain, the new wine and oil, who lavished on her the silver and gold-which they used for Baal. ⁹ Therefore I will take away my grain when it ripens, and my new wine when it is ready. I will take back my wool and my linen, intended to cover her nakedness. ¹⁰ So now I will expose her lewdness before the eyes of her lovers; no one will take her out of my hands. ¹¹ I will stop all her celebrations: her yearly festivals, her new moons, her sabbath days - all her appointed feasts. ¹² I will ruin her vines and her fig trees, which she said were her pay from her lovers; I will make them a thicket, and

wild animals will devour them. ¹³ I will punish her for the days she burned incense to the Baals; she decked herself with rings and jewelry, and went after her lovers, but me she forgot, declares YHWH." Hoshea 2:1-13

YHWH vividly illustrates the adulterous conduct of the House of Yisrael through her idolatry – chasing after other gods. When things start to go bad, Yisrael thinks that she can simply return to YHWH, but it is too late. All of the curses start to come upon her. She specifically lost her appointed times when the people are supposed to meet with YHWH. This is a vivid demonstration of the separation that she would experience. She was a wife, but she whored. She chose Baal Peor over YHWH. She would be like a barren woman. (see Hoshea 9)

The punishment rendered upon the House of Yisrael came from the north by the Assyrians. The Assyrians controlled a large portion of Mesopotamia as they expanded their empire from around 911 BCE to around 627 BCE when they eventually started to decline. It was during their period of expansion that YHWH used them to punish the House of Yisrael.

The Assyrians were an advanced but brutal culture. The Northern Tribes essentially whored with Assyria and the Assyrian gods. (Ezekiel 23). Of course, at that time the Assyrian Empire controlled the entire region commonly referred to as Babylon, and the 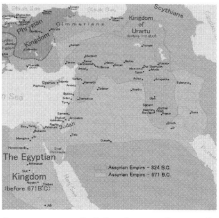 influence of Babylon could be seen and felt throughout the

Northern Tribes. So where they started with Egyptian gods, they also mingled Babylonian gods. It is all sun worship, and the source is the same. In fact, we see Yisrael startled between Egypt and Assyria – moving back and forth between relationships.

Let us first read what happened to the House of Yisrael during the reign of a king named Hoshea:

"*¹ In the twelfth year of Ahaz king of Yahudah, Hoshea son of Elah became king of Yisrael in Samaria, and he reigned nine years. ² He did evil in the eyes of YHWH, but not like the kings of Yisrael who preceded him. ³ Shalmaneser king of Assyria came up to attack Hoshea, who had been Shalmaneser's vassal and had paid him tribute. ⁴ But the king of Assyria discovered that Hoshea was a traitor, for he had sent envoys to So king of Egypt, and he no longer paid tribute to the king of Assyria, as he had done year by year. Therefore Shalmaneser seized him and put him in prison. ⁵ The king of Assyria invaded the entire land, marched against Samaria and laid siege to it for three years. ⁶ In the ninth year of Hoshea, the king of Assyria captured Samaria and deported the Yisraelites to Assyria. He settled them in Halah, in Gozan on the Habor River and in the towns of the Medes. ⁷ All this took place because the Yisraelites had sinned against YHWH their Elohim, who had brought them up out of Egypt from under the power of Pharaoh king of Egypt. They worshiped other gods ⁸ and followed the practices of the nations YHWH had driven out before them, as well as the practices that the kings of Yisrael had introduced. ⁹ The Yisraelites secretly did things against YHWH their Elohim that were not right. From watchtower to fortified city they built themselves high places in all their towns. ¹⁰ They set up sacred stones and Asherah*

poles on every high hill and under every spreading tree.
¹¹ At every high place they burned incense, as the nations
whom YHWH had driven out before them had done.
They did wicked things that provoked YHWH to
anger. ¹² They worshiped idols, though YHWH had
said, 'You shall not do this. ¹³ YHWH warned Yisrael
and Yahudah through all his prophets and seers: Turn
from your evil ways. Observe My commands and
decrees, in accordance with the entire Torah that I
commanded your fathers to obey and that I delivered to
you through My servants the prophets.' ¹⁴ But they
would not listen and were as stiff-necked as their
fathers, who did not trust in YHWH their Elohim.
They rejected His decrees and the Covenant He had
made with their fathers and the warnings He had given
them. They followed worthless idols and themselves
became worthless. They imitated the nations around
them although YHWH had ordered them, 'Do not do as
they do,' and they did the things YHWH had forbidden
them to do. ¹⁶ They forsook all the commands of
YHWH their Elohim and made for themselves two
idols cast in the shape of calves, and an Asherah pole.
They bowed down to all the starry hosts, and they
worshiped Baal. ¹⁷ They sacrificed their sons and
daughters in the fire. They practiced divination and
sorcery and sold themselves to do evil in the eyes of
YHWH, provoking Him to anger. ¹⁸ So YHWH was
very angry with Yisrael and removed them from His
presence. Only the tribe of Yahudah was left, ¹⁹ and
even Yahudah did not keep the commands of YHWH
their Elohim. They followed the practices Yisrael had
introduced. ²⁰ Therefore YHWH rejected all the people
of Yisrael; He afflicted them and gave them into the
hands of plunderers, until He thrust them from His

presence. ²¹ When He tore Yisrael away from the house of David, they made Jeroboam son of Nebat their king. Jeroboam enticed Yisrael away from following YHWH and caused them to commit a great sin. ²² The Yisraelites persisted in all the sins of Jeroboam and did not turn away from them ²³ until YHWH removed them from His presence, as He had warned through all His servants the prophets. So the people of Yisrael were taken from their homeland into exile in Assyria, and they are still there." 2 Melakim 17:1-24

The Assyrians actually removed all of the House of Yisrael from the Land. This is a fact debated by some, but the Scriptures clearly state that *"YHWH rejected ALL the people of Yisrael"* and *"ONLY the Tribe of Yahudah was left."* Remember that a remnant of the Northern Tribes, along with the Levites, likely "moved in" with the House of Yahudah after Jeroboam set up his idolatrous system of worship.
Therefore, while Assyria removed the Northern Tribes from their Land, there was probably a remnant of these Tribes who lived in Judea and joined the Tribe of Yahudah.

Known for displacing their captives, the Assyrians actually removed all of the House of Yisrael from their land and relaocated them elsewhere. By removing them from their land, the prophesy of Hoshea came to pass. The House of Yisrael lost their connection with the Covenant Land and the Elohim of the Covenant. They ultimately lost their identity. The House of Yisrael was replaced by strangers from other parts of the Assyrian Empire.

"²⁴ The king of Assyria brought people from Babylon, Cuthah, Avva, Hamath and Sepharvaim and settled them in the towns of Samaria to replace the Yisraelites. They

took over Samaria and lived in its towns. ²⁵ When they first lived there, they did not worship YHWH; so He sent lions among them and they killed some of the people. ²⁶ It was reported to the king of Assyria: The people you deported and resettled in the towns of Samaria do not know what the Elohi of that country requires. He has sent lions among them, which are killing them off, because the people do not know what He requires. ²⁷ Then the king of Assyria gave this order: 'Have one of the priests you took captive from Samaria go back to live there and teach the people what the Elohi of the land requires.' ²⁸ So one of the priests who had been exiled from Samaria came to live in Bethel and taught them how to worship YHWH. ²⁹ Nevertheless, each national group made its own gods in the several towns where they settled, and set them up in the shrines the people of Samaria had made at the high places. ³⁰ The men from Babylon made Succoth Benoth, the men from Cuthah made Nergal, and the men from Hamath made Ashima; ³¹ the Avvites made Nibhaz and Tartak, and the Sepharvites burned their children in the fire as sacrifices to Adrammelech and Anammelech, the gods of Sepharvaim. ³² They worshiped YHWH, but they also appointed all sorts of their own people to officiate for them as priests in the shrines at the high places. ³³ They worshiped YHWH, but they also served their own gods in accordance with the customs of the nations from which they had been brought. ³⁴ To this day they persist in their former practices. They neither worship YHWH nor adhere to the decrees and ordinances, the Torah and commands that YHWH gave the descendants of Yaakob, whom He named Yisrael. ³⁵ When YHWH made a Covenant with the Yisraelites, He commanded them: 'Do not worship any other gods or bow down to them, serve them or sacrifice to them. ³⁶ But YHWH, who brought you up out of Egypt with mighty *power and outstretched arm, is the One you must worship. To Him you shall bow down and to Him offer sacrifices. [37] You must always be careful to keep the decrees and ordinances, the Torah and commands He wrote for you. Do not worship other gods. [38] Do not forget the Covenant I have made with you, and do not worship other gods. [39] Rather, worship YHWH your Elohim; it is He who will deliver you from the hand of all your enemies.' [40] They would not listen, however, but persisted in their former practices. [41] Even while these people were worshiping YHWH, they were serving their idols. To this day their children and grandchildren continue to do as their fathers did."* 2 Melakim 17:24-41

Notice that YHWH sent lions to destroy these new settlers from Babylon and other regions of the Assyrian Empire. This was because they too were not worshipping Him. As a result, the King of Assyria sent back a priest to instruct the foreigners how to serve YHWH, which they did <u>along</u> with their

pagan worship. We can see this very day the foreigners who still live in Samaria.

The Samaritans currently practice a hybrid religion, centered at Mount Gerizim. Their religion is based primarily upon the Torah, which retains the Paleo Hebrew Script, although it includes a certain amount of deviation. This has resulted in ancient and underlying tensions between the Samaritans and those from the House of Yahudah who eventually returned from their own exile.

Just as was prophesied, the House of Yisrael was removed during 5 successive exiles beginning in 723 BCE. There was a second in 722 BCE and a third in 720 BCE. Then

beginning in 716 BCE there was a three year siege of Samaria that ended in 714 BCE. That 3 year siege was described in 2 Kings 18:11-12.[162]

The prophet Ezekiel was from the House of Yahudah. He was taken into exile by the Babylonians. During his exile he physically demonstrated the period of punishment for both houses. For now, pay particular attention to the House of Yisrael. *"4 Lie also on your left side, and lay the iniquity of the House of Yisrael upon it. According to the number of the days that you lie on it, you shall bear their iniquity. 5 For I have laid on you the years of their iniquity, according to the number of the days, three hundred and ninety days; so you shall bear the iniquity of the House of Yisrael. 6 And when you have completed them, lie again on your right side; then you shall bear the iniquity of the House of Yahudah forty days. I have laid on you a day for each year."* Ezekiel 4:4-6

So the House of Yisrael was destined to be punished for 390 years. We know that YHWH had previously told them, through Mosheh, that they would be exiled and later returned. (Debarim 30:3-40). If their punishment was restricted to 390 years then one would expect to see them return to the Land around 333 BCE to 324 BCE.

This did not occur and we understand that the House of Yisrael failed to repent for their sins. As a result, we must recognize that their punishment must have been multiplied seven times as foretold by Mosheh.

All of Yisrael was previously told that if they disobeyed the Torah they would be defeated and exiled. *"And after all this, if you do not obey Me, then I will punish you seven times more for your sins."* Vayiqra 26:18 Therefore, we should expect to see the punishment over the House of Yisrael to last for 2,730 years and end somewhere around the years 2007 to 2016. At the time that this book is being written the punishment period is coming to an end.

As we previously read in Jeremiah, the House of Yahudah was no better than the House of Yisrael. In fact, the House of Yahudah watched as the punishment was rendered on the House of Yahudah but she failed to learn the lesson. While there were good Kings who led the people back to YHWH, those periods of return were brief and did not last.

Jeremiah prophesied specifically to the House of Yahudah of their impending exile. *"[10] When you tell these people all this and they ask you, Why has YHWH decreed such a great disaster against us? What wrong have we done? What sin have we committed against YHWH our Elohim? [11] then say to them, It is because your fathers forsook Me, declares YHWH, and followed other gods and served and worshiped them. They forsook Me and did not keep My Torah. [12] But you have behaved more wickedly than your fathers. See how each of you is following the stubbornness of his evil heart instead of obeying me. [13] So I will throw you out of this land into a land neither you nor your fathers have known, and there you will serve other gods day and night, for I will show you no favor."* Yirmeyahu 16:10-13

He went on to proclaim: *"[1] Yahudah's sin is engraved with an iron tool, inscribed with a flint point, on the tablets of their hearts and on the horns of their altars. [2] Even their children remember their altars and Asherah poles beside the spreading trees and on the high hills. [3] My mountain in the land and your wealth and all your treasures I will give away as plunder, together with your high places, because of sin throughout your country. [4] Through your own fault you will lose the inheritance I gave you. I will enslave you to your enemies in a land you do not know, for you have kindled My anger, and it will burn forever."* Yirmeyahu 17:1-4

The hearts of those in the House of Yahudah had become like stone. Instead of the Torah being enscribed on them, as it was with the tablets of stone presented by Mosheh, their sins were inscribed on their hearts, which were stone. Just as Mosheh smashed the tablets, and later renewed

the Covenant at Sinai, Yahudah needed to have the Covenant renewed because they had broken the Covenant - only this time the Torah would be written on their hearts.

Jeremiah was prophesying prior to, through and beyond the Babylonian exile. While in exile, Ezekiel was actually taken in a vision to Jerusalem and shown the abominations that were going on there. He was also told to look north and observe abominations that the House of Yisrael was committing. Now the House of Yisrael had already been exiled, but this seems to be linking the sins of Beth El and Jerusalem.

While he sat in his house with the elders of Yahudah, he was met by a marvelous being appearing like fire and brightness. The being took Ezekiel by his tzitzit and brought him between heaven and earth.[163] This is an interesting place that is strongly associated with the Messiah as we saw from the first sentence of Beresheet.

Here is an account of the vision. *"3 . . . the Spirit lifted me up between earth and heaven, and brought me in visions of Elohim to Jerusalem, to the door of the north gate of the inner court, where the seat of the image of jealousy was, which provokes to jealousy. 4 And behold, the glory of the Elohim of Yisrael was there, like the vision that I saw in the plain. 5 Then He said to me, Son of man, lift your eyes now toward the north. So I lifted my eyes toward the north, and there, north of the altar gate, was this image of jealousy in the entrance. 6 Furthermore He said to me, Son of man, do you see what they are doing, the great abominations that the house of Yisrael commits here, to make Me go far away from My sanctuary? Now turn again, you will see greater abominations. 7 So He brought me to the door of the court; and when I looked, there was a hole in the wall. 8 Then He said to me, Son of man, dig into the wall; and when I dug into the wall, there was a door. 9 And He said to me, Go in, and see the wicked abominations which they are doing there. 10 So I went in and saw, and there - every sort of* creeping thing, abominable beasts, and all the idols of the House of Yisrael, portrayed all around on the walls. " And there stood before them seventy men of the elders of the House of Yisrael, and in their midst stood Jaazaniah the son of Shaphan. Each man had a censer in his hand, and a thick cloud of incense went up. ¹² Then He said to me, Son of man, have you seen what the elders of the House of Yisrael do in the dark, every man in the room of his idols? For they say, YHWH does not see us, YHWH has forsaken the land. ¹³ And He said to me, Turn again, and you will see greater abominations that they are doing. ¹⁴ So He brought me to the door of the north gate of YHWH's House; and to my dismay, women were sitting there weeping for Tammuz. ¹⁵ Then He said to me, Have you seen this, O son of man? Turn again, you will see greater abominations than these. ¹⁶ So He brought me into the inner court of YHWH's house; and there, at the door of the Temple of YHWH, between the porch and the altar, were about twenty-five men with their backs toward the Temple of YHWH and their faces toward the east, and they were worshiping the sun toward the east. ¹⁷ And He said to me, Have you seen this, O son of man? Is it a trivial thing to the House of Yahudah to commit the abominations which they commit here? For they have filled the land with violence; then they have returned to provoke Me to anger. Indeed they put the branch to their nose. ¹⁸ Therefore I also will act in fury. My eye will not spare nor will I have pity; and though they cry in My ears with a loud voice, I will not hear them." Ezekiel 8:3-18

So Ezekiel was taken first to the House of Yisrael. Notice the mention of 70 elders. This was the same number of elders that were on Mount Sinai during the Covenant process. The number 70 is significant because it is the gematria value for the word "muwl" ($\ell\,\mathbf{Y}$) which means: "circumcision."

The number 70 is also associated with "the nations." The word "ha'hekal" ($\ell\,\mathbf{Y}\,\mathbf{Z}\,\mathbf{A}\,\mathbf{A}$) also has the gematria value of 70. It refers to "the House" or "The Temple" of YHWH.

We can see at Sinai, and through the House of Yisrael, how "the nations" will be circumcised into the Covenant through the mixing of the House of Yisrael through the nations. Through this process the nations will be brought to the House of YHWH.

After being shown the House of Yisrael, Ezekiel was brought to the House of YHWH in Jerusalem. There he was shown that the House of Yahudah committed even greater abominations that the House of Yisrael.

So both of the divided kingdoms rebelled and would be punished, but they were treated differently and punished separately. The House of Yisrael was first, because their fall was more immediate and pronounced. After the decline of the Assyrian Empire, the Empire of Babylon rose up as a world power. YHWH would use the Babylonian King Nebuchadnezzar to punish the House of Yahudah.

Through the prophet Jeremiah YHWH pleaded with Yahudah to return to Him. His words were like a shofar blast, and he used the shofar in his prophecies. It was a warning to repent, and find shelter in YHWH.

"¹ If you will return, O Yisrael, says YHWH, Return to Me; and if you will put away your abominations out of My sight, then you shall not be moved. ² And you shall swear, YHWH lives, in truth, in judgment, and in righteousness; The nations shall bless themselves in Him, and in Him they shall glory. ³ For thus says YHWH to the men of Yahudah and Jerusalem: Break up your fallow ground, and do not sow among thorns. ⁴ Circumcise yourselves to YHWH, and take away the foreskins of your hearts, you men of Yahudah and inhabitants of Jerusalem, lest My fury come forth like fire, and burn so that no one can quench it, because of the evil of your doings. ⁵ Declare in Yahudah and proclaim in Jerusalem, and say: Blow the

shofar in the land; Cry, Gather together, and say, Assemble yourselves, and let us go into the fortified cities. ⁶ Set up the standard toward Zion. Take refuge! Do not delay! For I will bring disaster from the north, and great destruction. ⁷ The lion has come up from his thicket, and the destroyer of nations is on his way. He has gone forth from his place to make your land desolate. Your cities will be laid waste, without inhabitant. ⁸ For this, clothe yourself with sackcloth, lament and wail. For the fierce anger of YHWH has not turned back from us. ⁹ And it shall come to pass in that day, says YHWH, That the heart of the king shall perish, and the heart of the princes; the priests shall be astonished, and the prophets shall wonder. ¹⁰ Then I said, Ah, Master YHWH! Surely You have greatly deceived this people and Jerusalem, Saying, You shall have peace, whereas the sword reaches to the heart. ¹¹ At that time it will be said to this people and to Jerusalem, A dry wind of the desolate heights blows in the wilderness toward the daughter of My people - not to fan or to cleanse - ¹² A wind too strong for these will come for Me; now I will also speak judgment against them. ¹³ Behold, he shall come up like clouds, and his chariots like a whirlwind. His horses are swifter than eagles. Woe to us, for we are plundered! ¹⁴ O Jerusalem, wash your heart from wickedness, that you may be saved. How long shall your evil thoughts lodge within you? ¹⁵ For a voice declares from Dan and proclaims affliction from Mount Ephraim: ¹⁶ Make mention to the nations, Yes, proclaim against Jerusalem, that watchers come from a far country and raise their voice against the cities of Yahudah. ¹⁷ Like keepers of a field they are against her all around, because she has been rebellious against Me, says YHWH. ¹⁸ Your ways and your doings have procured these things for you. This is your wickedness, because it is bitter, because it reaches to your heart. *¹⁹* O my soul, my soul! I am pained in my very heart! My heart makes a noise in me; I cannot hold my peace, because you have heard, O my soul, the sound of the shofar, the alarm of war. *²⁰* Destruction upon destruction is cried, for the whole land is plundered. Suddenly my tents are plundered, and my curtains in a moment. *²¹* How long will I see the standard, and hear the sound of the shofar? *²²* For My people are foolish, they have not known Me. They are silly children, and they have no understanding. They are wise to do evil, but to do good they have no knowledge. *²³* I beheld the earth, and indeed it was <u>without form, and void</u>; and the heavens, they had no light. *²⁴* I beheld the mountains, and indeed they trembled, and all the hills moved back and forth. *²⁵* I beheld, and indeed there was no man, and all the birds of the heavens had fled. *²⁶* I beheld, and indeed the fruitful land was a wilderness, and all its cities were broken down at the presence of YHWH, by His fierce anger. *²⁷* For thus says YHWH: The whole land shall be desolate; yet I will not make a full end. *²⁸* For this shall the earth mourn, and the heavens above be black, because I have spoken. I have purposed and will not relent, nor will I turn back from it. *²⁹* The whole city shall flee from the noise of the horsemen and bowmen. They shall go into thickets and climb up on the rocks. Every city shall be forsaken, and not a man shall dwell in it. *³⁰* And when you are plundered, what will you do? Though you clothe yourself with crimson, though you adorn yourself with ornaments of gold, though you enlarge your eyes with paint, in vain you will make yourself fair; Your lovers will despise you; they will seek your life. *³¹* For I have heard a voice as of a woman

in labor, the anguish as of her who brings forth her first child, the voice of the daughter of Zion bewailing herself; She spreads her hands, saying, Woe is me now, for my soul is weary because of murderers!" Jeremiah 4:1-31

YHWH was calling for the Yahudim to circumcise their hearts. That is, after all, what He always desired from Yisrael. Mosheh clearly indicated this prior to them entering the Land. (Debarim 10:16; 30:6) A husband wants his wife to be pure, and he wants her heart to be true and faithful toward him.

If they would heed the warning of the shofar, purify their hearts and remove the wickedness, then they could be restored. They refused and would ultimately experience the judgment of exile.

Notice the reference to the beginning – when the earth was without form and void. (v. 23). In the Hebrew we read "tohu v'bohu" (𐤅𐤄𐤁𐤅 𐤅𐤄𐤕). This was the same language from Beresheet 1:2 describing the Earth that had undergone a previous judgment when everything was wiped out leaving it void and in darkness.[164]

In fact, YHWH clearly stated that He did not create the earth "tohu" (𐤅𐤄𐤕) (Isaiah 45:18). So earth was originally created in perfection, but became "without form and void" to judgment. Therefore, this language was used because the House of Yahudah was about to experience judgment.

Jeremiah even provided the duration for the punishment upon the House of Yahudah, as well as upon Babylon. *"And this whole land shall be a desolation and an astonishment, and these nations shall serve the king of Babylon seventy years."* Jeremiah 25:11 *"Then it will come to pass, when seventy years are completed, that I will punish the king of Babylon and that nation, the land of the Chaldeans, for their iniquity, says*

YHWH; and I will make it a perpetual desolation." Jeremiah 25:12 "For thus says YHWH: After seventy years are completed at Babylon, I will visit you and perform My good word toward you, and cause you to return to this place." Jeremiah 29:10

There would actually be two separate seventy year periods. The first seventy years would be the time until Babylon would be judged. The second would be the period when the House of Yahudah would be exiled from the Land.

Jeremiah actually referred to those exiled in Babylon as "good figs" while those left behind in the land were "bad figs." (see Jeremiah 24) From this we can assume that the House of Yahudah can be likened to a fig tree that produces either good or bad fruit. This will be more significant as we look further into the future.

The Book of Jeremiah provides a vivid description of the period of time leading up to and beyond the exile of the House of Yahudah. The Babylonians exiled captives from Jerusalem through seven separate exiles in three different stages.

In an early campaign around 618 BCE, the prophet Daniel was among the Yahudim taken to Babylon. A second attack against the city occurred in 610 BCE, when many more captives were taken. Ezekiel was likely taken captive at this time. Then in the extensive campaign of 601 BCE - 599 BCE, Nebuchadnezzar destroyed Jerusalem and took most of the remaining inhabitants into exile.[165] Through it all, the Prophet Jeremiah was prophesying, and he was never taken captive by the Babylonians.

So the Bride of YHWH was divided in two and ejected from the Land. This was a repeat of the pattern seen in the Garden. Yisrael was supposed to restore what was lost, but they failed to obey as did Adam and Hawah. YHWH used the Prophet Mosheh to inform the Yisraelites what would happen if they failed to obey the Torah.

YHWH also sent prophets to warn them, and turn the hearts of the people back to Him. Ultimately, all of Yisrael fell away, but that was not the end of the story. Those prophets provided much more than warnings of punishment, they provided promises of hope. We will now continue the discussion by examining the promises of hope provided through Prophets.

8

Prophets

The division of the Kingdom of Yisrael, and then the subsequent exile of both Houses would appear to have been the end. Certainly any nation that experienced such things would appear to be doomed – erased from existence and left to the annals history. This was not just any nation or Kingdom though, this people represented a bride in Covenant relationship with YHWH. While both Houses had been ejected from the Land and one House divorced, none of this was irreparable. In fact, Mosheh had already indicated that this would happen, and he also stated that that Yisrael would be regathered.

"*¹ Now it shall come to pass, when all these things come upon you, the blessing and the curse which I have set before you, and you call them to mind among all the nations where <u>YHWH your Elohim</u> drives you, ² and you return to <u>YHWH your Elohim</u> and obey His voice, according to all that I command you today, you and your children, with all your heart and with all your soul, ³ that <u>YHWH your Elohim</u> will bring you back from captivity, and have compassion on you, and gather you again from all the nations where <u>YHWH your Elohim</u> has scattered you. ⁴ If any of you are driven out to the farthest parts under heaven, from there <u>YHWH your Elohim</u> will gather you, and from there He will bring you. ⁵ Then <u>YHWH your Elohim</u> will bring you to the land which your fathers possessed, and you shall possess it. He will prosper you and multiply you more than your fathers. ⁶ And <u>YHWH your Elohim</u> will*

circumcise your heart and the heart of your descendants, to love <u>*YHWH your Elohim*</u> *with all your heart and with all your soul, that you may live.*" Debarim 30:1-6

This was a great promise, but likely hard to imagine after all of the curses that had befallen the divided and exiled kingdom. While there were numerous prophets throughout the history of Yisrael, most of their words were not recorded. We do have certain prophecies provided in the Tanak that provided hope consistent with Mosheh.

Despite the devastating prophecy given to the House of Yisrael through Hoshea that they would no longer be His people, that prophecy actually continued with a message of hope. "*¹⁰ Yet* <u>*the Yisraelites will be like the sand on the seashore,*</u> *which cannot be measured or counted. In the place where it was said to them, You are not my people,' they will be called 'sons of the living Elohim.* ¹¹ *The people of Yahudah and the people of Yisrael will be reunited, and they will appoint one leader and will come up out of the land, for great will be the day of Yezreel.*" Hosea 1:10-11

This is consistent with the promise given through Mosheh. Notice how many times Mosheh used the phrase "YHWH your Elohim" – eight times in that passage. Of course it has been mentioned how the number eight is uniquely associated with the Covenant. Remember that "YHWH your Elohim" is Covenant language. It reveals a relationship and provides identification. Because this is about a relationship, those in the Covenant must have their heart circumcised by "YHWH their Elohim" so they can truly love Him within the context of the marriage Covenant.

The prophecies cited above describe a restored relationship with YHWH when He is their Elohim and they are His people. Hoshea specifically uses the language of the Covenant promise describing Yisrael as numerous as "the sand on the seashore."

The problem was that YHWH had not been their

Elohim. They had chased after other gods. Incredibly, not only would the House of Yisrael be restored to the status of "sons of Elohim," they would also be reunited with Yahudah and be too numerous to count.

Before this great promise would occur, the House of Yisrael would literally lose their identity. YHWH describes this progression from rejection to restoration through the family of Hoshea. Gomer represented the then, present day House of Yisrael, and her children represented the future House of Yisrael.

YHWH continued to detail how He would restore His relationship with the House of Yisrael. *"[14] Therefore I am now going to allure her; I will lead her into the desert and speak tenderly to her. [15] There I will give her back her vineyards, and will make the Valley of Achor a door of hope. There she will sing as in the days of her youth, as in the day she came up out of Egypt. [16] In that day, declares YHWH, you will call Me 'my husband' - you will no longer call Me 'my master.' [17] I will remove the names of the Baals from her lips; no longer will their names be invoked. [18] In that day I will make a covenant for them with the beasts of the field and the birds of the air and the creatures that move along the ground. Bow and sword and battle I will abolish from the land, so that all may lie down in safety. [19] I will betroth you to me forever; I will betroth you in righteousness and justice, in love and compassion. [20] I will betroth you in faithfulness, and you will acknowledge YHWH. [21] In that day I will respond, declares YHWH - I will respond to the skies, and they will respond to the earth; [22] and the earth will respond to the grain, the new wine and oil, and they will respond to Yezreel. [23] I will plant her for Myself in the land; I will show My love to the one I called "Not My loved one." I will say to those called 'Not My people,' 'You are My people' and they will say, 'You are my Elohim.'"* Hoshea 2:14-23

YHWH states that He will take the House of Yisrael in the desert as when she was redeemed from Egypt. So then, there will be another redemption as in the days of the exodus and just as the song of Mosheh was sung at the exodus from Egypt, the House of Yisrael will sing a song at their redemption.

Also, just as Yisrael was married to YHWH at Sinai after the exodus from Egypt, the House of Yisrael will be remarried to YHWH after they are redeemed. The names of the Baals that they once worshipped will be removed from their lips, and YHWH will make a covenant between them and the animals.

Hoshea continues: *"¹ Then YHWH said to me, Go again, love a woman who is loved by a lover and is committing adultery, just like the love of YHWH for the children of Yisrael, who look to other gods and love the raisin cakes of the pagans. ² So I bought her for myself for fifteen shekels of silver, and one and one-half omers of barley. ³ And I said to her, You shall stay with me many days; you shall not play the harlot, nor shall you have a man - so, too, will I be toward you. ⁴ <u>For the children of Yisrael shall abide many days without king or prince, without sacrifice or sacred pillar, without ephod or teraphim. ⁵ Afterward the children of Yisrael shall return and seek YHWH their Elohim and David their king. They shall fear YHWH and His goodness in the latter days.</u>"* Hoshea 3:1-4

We have actually seen the passage of much time since these words were spoken. Indeed, at the time of the writing of this book, the punishment period described by Ezekiel is nearing completion. As a result, many are looking for a fulfillment of this prophecy as we approach the end of this age.

The "latter days" are marked by Yisrael returning to YHWH. *"¹ O Yisrael, return to YHWH your Elohim, for you have stumbled because of your iniquity; ² Take words with you, and return to YHWH. Say to Him, Take away all iniquity; receive us graciously, for we will offer the sacrifices of our lips. ³ Assyria shall not save us, we will not ride on horses, nor will we say anymore to* the work of our hands, 'You are our gods.' For in You the fatherless finds mercy. ⁴ I will heal their backsliding, I will love them freely, for My anger has turned away from him. ⁵ I will be like the dew to Yisrael; He shall grow like the lily, and lengthen his roots like Lebanon. ⁶ His branches shall spread; His beauty shall be like an olive tree, and his fragrance like Lebanon. ⁷ Those who dwell under his shadow shall return; They shall be revived like grain, and grow like a vine. Their scent shall be like the wine of Lebanon. ⁸ Ephraim shall say, What have I to do anymore with idols? I have heard and observed him. I am like a green cypress tree; Your fruit is found in Me. ⁹ Who is wise? Let him understand these things. Who is prudent? Let him know them. For the ways of YHWH are right; The righteous walk in them, but transgressors stumble in them." Hosea 14:1-9

So clearly the House of Yisrael would be restored to YHWH, but it would not be for a long time. We saw from Ezekiel that the punishment is in the process of ending. One thing is certain, the restoration of the House of Yisrael has not yet occurred.

The Promises of a return are too numerous to detail in one chapter of a book, but here is a sample of some significant prophecies concerning the House of Yisrael.

"¹¹ For thus says the Master YHWH: Indeed I Myself will search for My sheep and seek them out. ¹² As a shepherd seeks out his flock on the day he is among his scattered sheep, so will I seek out My sheep and deliver them from all the places where they were scattered on a cloudy and dark day. ¹³ And I will bring them out from the peoples and gather them from the countries, and will bring them to their own land; I will feed them on the mountains of Yisrael, in the valleys and in all the inhabited places of the country. ¹⁴ I will feed them in good pasture, and their fold shall be on the high mountains of Yisrael. There they shall lie down in a good fold and feed in rich pasture on the mountains of Yisrael. ¹⁵ I will feed My flock, and I will make them lie down, says the Master YHWH. ¹⁶ I will seek what was lost and bring back what was driven away, bind up the broken and strengthen what was sick; but I will destroy the fat and the strong, and feed them in judgment. ¹⁷ And as for you, O My flock, thus says the Master YHWH: Behold, I shall judge between sheep and sheep, between rams and goats. ¹⁸ Is it too little for you to have eaten up the good pasture, that you must tread down with your feet the residue of your pasture - and to have drunk of the clear waters, that you must foul the residue with your feet? ¹⁹ And as for My flock, they eat what you have trampled with your feet, and they drink what you have fouled with your feet. ²⁰ Therefore thus says the Master YHWH to them: Behold, I Myself will judge between the fat and the lean sheep. ²¹ Because you have pushed with side and shoulder, butted all the weak ones with your horns, and scattered them abroad, ²² therefore I will save My flock, and they shall no longer be a prey; and I will judge between sheep and sheep. ²³ I will establish one shepherd over them, and He shall feed them - My servant David. He shall feed them and be their shepherd. ²⁴ And I, YHWH, will be their Elohim, and My servant David a prince among them; I, YHWH, have spoken. ²⁵ I will make a Covenant of peace with them, and cause wild beasts to cease from the land; and they will dwell safely in the wilderness and sleep in the woods. ²⁶ I will make them and the places all around My hill a blessing; and I will cause showers to come down in their season; there shall be showers of blessing. ²⁷ Then the trees of the field shall yield their fruit, and *the earth shall yield her increase. They shall be safe in their land; and they shall know that I am YHWH, when I have broken the bands of their yoke and delivered them from the hand of those who enslaved them. *²⁸ *And they shall no longer be a prey for the nations, nor shall beasts of the land devour them; but they shall dwell safely, and no one shall make them afraid. *²⁹ *I will raise up for them a garden of renown, and they shall no longer be consumed with hunger in the land, nor bear the shame of the Gentiles anymore. *³⁰ *Thus they shall know that I, YHWH their Elohim, am with them, and they, the House of Ysrael, are My people, says the Master YHWH. *³¹ *You are My flock, the flock of My pasture; you are men, and I am your Elohim, says the Master YHWH."* Ezekiel 34:11-31

YHWH will shepherd His people. Though He scattered the House of Yisrael from the Land, He will once again regather them to their Land – the Mountains of Yisrael. He will feed them, and they will dwell in safety. This analogy of sheep is important to remember. The flock of sheep will place their entire trust in the shepherd. He leads them to food and water, and he protects them. All the sheep have to do is follow, and stay close to the shepherd.

"¹⁶ Again the word of YHWH came to me: ¹⁷ Son of man, when the people of Yisrael were living in their own land, they defiled it by their conduct and their actions. Their conduct was like a woman's monthly uncleanness in my sight. ¹⁸ So I poured out My wrath on them because they had shed blood in the land and because they had defiled it with their idols. ¹⁹ <u>I dispersed them among the nations, and they were scattered through the countries; I judged them according to their conduct and their actions. ²⁰ And

wherever they went among the nations they profaned My set apart Name, for it was said of them, These are YHWH's people, and yet they had to leave his land. ²¹ *I had concern for My set apart Name, which the House of Yisrael profaned among the nations where they had gone.* ²² *Therefore say to the House of Yisrael, This is what the Sovereign YHWH says: It is not for your sake, O House of Yisrael, that I am going to do these things, but for the sake of My Set Apart Name, which you have profaned among the nations where you have gone.* ²³ *I will show the holiness of My great Name, which has been profaned among the nations, the name you have profaned among them. Then the nations will know that I am YHWH, declares the Sovereign YHWH, when I show Myself set apart through you before their eyes.* ²⁴ <u>*For I will take you out of the nations; I will gather you from all the countries and bring you back into your own land.*</u> ²⁵ *I will sprinkle clean water on you, and you will be clean; I will cleanse you from all your impurities and from all your idols.* ²⁶ <u>*I will give you a new heart and put a new spirit in you; I will remove from you your heart of stone and give you a heart of flesh.*</u> ²⁷ <u>*And I will put My Spirit in you and move you to follow My decrees and be careful to keep My laws.*</u> ²⁸ <u>*You will live in the land I gave your forefathers; you will be My people, and I will be your Elohim.*</u> ²⁹ *I will save you from all your uncleanness. I will call for the grain and make it plentiful and will not bring famine upon you.* ³⁰ *I will increase the fruit of the trees and the crops of the field, so that you will no longer suffer disgrace among the nations because of famine.* ³¹ *Then you will remember your evil ways and wicked deeds, and you will loathe yourselves for your sins and* detestable practices. [32] *I want you to know that I am not doing this for your sake, declares the Sovereign YHWH. Be ashamed and disgraced for your conduct, O House of Yisrael!* [33] *Thus says the Master YHWH: On the day that I cleanse you from all your iniquities, I will also enable you to dwell in the cities, and the ruins shall be rebuilt.* [34] *The desolate land shall be tilled instead of lying desolate in the sight of all who pass by.* [35] *So they will say, This land that was desolate has become like the Garden of Eden; and the wasted, desolate, and ruined cities are now fortified and inhabited.* [36] *Then the nations which are left all around you shall know that I, YHWH, have rebuilt the ruined places and planted what was desolate. I, YHWH, have spoken it, and I will do it.* [37] *Thus says the Master YHWH: I will also let the House of Yisrael inquire of Me to do this for them: I will increase their men like a flock.* [38] *Like a flock offered as set apart sacrifices, like the flock at Jerusalem on its Appointed Times, so shall the ruined cities be filled with flocks of men. Then they shall know that I am YHWH."* Ezekiel 36:16-38

This entire prophecy hints of a repeat of the exodus from Egypt. Remember that the judgment upon Egypt, and the redemption and deliverance of the Children of Yisrael, was for the sake of the set apart Name of YHWH.[166]

This time though, the people will be sprinkled with clean water and they will receive a new spirit so they can truly obey YHWH. They will rebuild the ruins and it will be like the Garden of Eden. They will live in the Covenant Land and YHWH will be their Elohim and they will be His people.

Again, we see the House of Yisrael referred to as flocks – very large numbers. You see the scattering of the

House of Yisrael was YHWH actually sowing them throughout the planet. *"Then I will sow her for Myself in the earth, and I will have mercy on her who had not obtained mercy; Then I will say to those who were not My people, You are My people! And they shall say, 'You are my Elohim!"* Hosea 2:23.

Only when you have planted something for yourself can you truly understand the ways of YHWH and Creation. He multiplies when He sows. So the sowing of the House of Yisrael would result in an incredible multiplication of the House of Yisrael. This was the prophecy spoken over Joseph's children by their father Yisrael while they were still in Egypt.

"¹⁴ Then Yisrael stretched out his right hand and laid it on Ephraim's head, who was the younger, and his left hand on Manasseh's head, guiding his hands knowingly, for Manasseh was the firstborn. ¹⁵ And he blessed Joseph, and said: Elohim, before whom my fathers Abraham and Yitshaq walked, the Elohim who has fed me all my life long to this day, ¹⁶ The Messenger Who has redeemed me from all evil, bless ✗✦-the lads; Let my name be named upon them, and the name of my fathers Abraham and Yitshaq; and let them grow into a multitude in the midst of the earth. ¹⁷ Now when Joseph saw that his father laid his right hand on the head of Ephraim, it displeased him; so he took hold of his father's hand to remove it from Ephraim's head to Manasseh's head. ¹⁸ And Joseph said to his father, Not so, my father, for this one is the firstborn; put your right hand on his head. ¹⁹ But his father refused and said, I know, my son, I know. <u>He also shall become a people, and he also shall be great; but truly his younger brother shall be greater than he, and his descendants shall become a multitude of nations.</u> *²⁰ So he blessed them that day, saying, By you Yisrael will bless, saying, May Elohim make you as Ephraim and as Manasseh!* <u>And thus he set Ephraim before Manasseh.</u> *²¹ Then Yisrael said to Joseph, Behold, I am dying, but Elohim will be with you and bring you back to the land of your fathers. ²² Moreover* <u>I have given to you</u>

one portion above your brothers, which I took from the hand of the Amorite with my sword and my bow." Beresheet 48:14-22

Through this event we can see that Yisrael adopted the sons of Joseph. Both sons had the Aleph Taw (**X⟨**) associated with them. They were both born in Egypt to an Egyptian mother. Through the adoption, Yisrael made his grandsons into his sons. They were transformed from Egyptians to Hebrews. This was prophetic as the divorced House of Yisrael, represented by Joseph, is now scattered throughout the world – literally hidden in plain sight. They need the Aleph Taw (**X⟨**) to redeem them and deliver them so they be grafted back into Yisrael.

Ephraim, the youngest son of Joseph, became the firstborn of all Yisrael entitled to a double portion. His name actually means: "fruitful" as described by Joseph. "*And the name of the second he called Ephraim: For Elohim has caused me to be fruitful in the land of my affliction.*" Beresheet 41:52.

In fact, the blessing over Ephraim is quite profound. The English "*become a multitude of nations*" is "yahayah mala ha'goyim" (**ﬠﬨﬡﬡ-ﬥﬤ ﬡﬨﬡ**). It literally means that through Ephraim would "exist or become the fullness of the nations." The word for "exist" (**ﬡﬨﬡ**) is the same word used to describe the process of creation. In fact, it is the first recorded word spoken by Elohim when He said: "*Exist light.*" Beresheet 1:3. The word for "fullness" (**⟨ﬥﬤ**) is used to refer to a winepress, threshing floor or vessel when they are full of the fruits of the harvest.[167]

Of course, the implications are profound when you consider that the Appointed Times of YHWH are centered around the harvests. In fact, remember when the text described Joseph as gathering very much grain – "son" (**ﬡﬤ**). (Beresheet 41:49). We can begin to see how the House of Yisrael being regathered through the harvest cycles would restore the "sons of Elohim" to YHWH.

The astute observer may recognize the similarity between the name "Ephraim" (𐤅𐤉𐤀𐤓𐤐), and the word "Rephaim" (𐤅𐤉𐤀𐤐𐤓). Incredibly, they both contain the exact same Hebrew characters and share the same gematria value of 331. As a result we see a connection between Ephraim and giants. They both are "great" (gibor) only Ephraim (𐤅𐤉𐤀𐤓𐤐) derives from "apher" (𐤓𐤐𐤀) which is "ashes." Abraham described himself as but "dust" (𐤓𐤐𐤏) and "ashes" (𐤓𐤐𐤀) - literally, apher v'apher. (Beresheet 18:27). In Job 26:5 the word "rapha" (𐤀𐤐𐤓) in rendered the dead. So while the source of Ephraim is the same ashes and dust as Adam and Abraham, the Rephaim are the "dead." That is why they are also referred to as "shades and ghosts." As it turns out, Ephraim will be the resurrected dead, and the mighty ones of YHWH. This will become evident as the discussion continues.

First, look at the meaning of the actual firstborn son of Joseph – Manasseh. *"Joseph called the name of the firstborn Manasseh: For Elohim has made me forget all my toil and all my father's house."* Beresheet 41:51 Instilled in the names of these sons we see the eventual prophetic path of the House of Yisrael through Joseph. They would "forget their fathers's house" – Yisrael. They would also become "fruitful" in Egypt. We see from our review of history that this is what happened to the House of Yisrael. After they were scattered and sown throughout the planet, they have become fruitful, but they have forgotten that they are the House of Yisrael!

Now read the famous prophecy given by Ezekiel concerning the revival of the House of Yisrael. Revive is a term bantered about very much in Christianity. This is a true vision of revival. *"¹ The hand of YHWH came upon me and brought me out in the Spirit of YHWH, and set me down in the midst of the valley; and it was full of bones. ² Then He caused me to pass by them all around, and behold, there were very many in the* open valley; and indeed they were very dry. ^{3} And He said to me, Son of man, can these bones live? So I answered, "O Master YHWH, You know. ^{4} Again He said to me, Prophesy to these bones, and say to them, O dry bones, hear the Word of YHWH! ^{5} Thus says the Master YHWH to these bones: Surely I will cause breath to enter into you, and you shall live. ^{6} I will put sinews on you and bring flesh upon you, cover you with skin and put breath in you; and you shall live. Then you shall know that I am YHWH. ^{7} So I prophesied as I was commanded; and as I prophesied, there was a noise, and suddenly a rattling; and the bones came together, bone to bone. ^{8} Indeed, as I looked, the sinews and the flesh came upon them, and the skin covered them over; but there was no breath in them. ^{9} Also He said to me, Prophesy to the breath, prophesy, son of man, and say to the breath, Thus says the Master YHWH: <u>Come from the four winds, O breath, and breathe on these slain, that they may live.</u> ^{10} So I prophesied as He commanded me, and breath came into them, and they lived, and stood upon their feet, an exceedingly great army. ^{11} Then He said to me, Son of man, <u>these bones are the whole House of Yisrael. They indeed say, Our bones are dry, our hope is lost, and we ourselves are cut off!</u> ^{12} Therefore prophesy and say to them, Thus says the Master YHWH: Behold, O My people, <u>I will open your graves and cause you to come up from your graves, and bring you into the land of Yisrael.</u> ^{13} Then you shall know that I am YHWH, when I have opened your graves, O My people, and brought you up from your graves. ^{14} <u>I will put My Spirit in you, and you shall live, and I will place you in your own land.</u> Then you shall know that I, YHWH, have spoken it and performed it, says YHWH." Ezekiel 37:1-15

One cannot ignore the fact that these bones are in a valley. The Hebrew word for "valley" is "biqah" (𐤀𐤏𐤒𐤁), and it generally refers to a wide level plain between mountains. Is this valley a metaphor or an actual place? No one knows for sure, but the prophecy of Hosea certainly comes to mind.

"⁵ It shall come to pass in that day that I will break the bow of Yisrael in the Valley of Jezreel . . . ¹⁰ And it shall come to pass in the place where it was said to them, You are not My people, there it shall be said to them, You are sons of the living Elohim. ¹¹ Then the children of Yahudah and the children of Yisrael shall be gathered together, and appoint for themselves one head; And they shall come up out of the land, for great will be the day of Jezreel!" Hosea 1:5, 10-11

It appears that both Ezekiel and Hosea may be speaking of the same place – the Valley of Jezreel. They both seem to referring to a transformation involving the Spirit of YHWH when the House of Yisrael would become "sons of Elohim."

Both of these prophecies also tell us that Yahudah and Yisrael will be joined back together. Ezekiel provides a vivid description of this event after the prophecy concerning the "dry bones."

"¹⁵ Again the word of YHWH came to me, saying, ¹⁶ As for you, son of man, take a stick for yourself and write on it: For Yahudah and for the children of Yisrael, his companions. Then take another stick and write on it, For Joseph, the stick of Ephraim, and for all the House of Yisrael, his companions. ¹⁷ Then join them one to another for yourself into one stick, and they will become one in your hand. ¹⁸ And when the children of your people speak to you, saying, Will you not show us what you mean by these? ¹⁹ say to them, Thus says Master YHWH: Surely I will take the stick of Joseph, which is in the hand of Ephraim, and the tribes of Yisrael, his companions; and I will join them with it, with the stick of Yahudah, and make them one stick, and they will be one in My hand. ²⁰ And the sticks on which you write will be in your hand before their eyes. ²¹ Then say to them, Thus says Master YHWH: Surely I will take the children of Israel from among the nations, wherever they have gone, and will gather them from every side and bring them into their own land; ²² and I will make them one nation

in the land, on the mountains of Yisrael; and one king shall be king over them all; they shall no longer be two nations, nor shall they ever be divided into two kingdoms again. [23] *They shall not defile themselves anymore with their idols, nor with their detestable things, nor with any of their transgressions; but I will deliver them from all their dwelling places in which they have sinned, and will cleanse them.* <u>*Then they shall be My people, and I will be their Elohim.*</u> [24] *David My servant shall be king over them, and they shall all have one shepherd; they shall also walk in My judgments and observe My statutes, and do them.* [25] *Then they shall dwell in the land that I have given to Yaakob My servant, where your fathers dwelt; and they shall dwell there, they, their children, and their children's children, forever; and My servant David shall be their prince forever.* [26] *Moreover I will make a covenant of peace with them, and it shall be an everlasting covenant with them; I will establish them and multiply them, and I will set My sanctuary in their midst forevermore.* [27] *My tabernacle also shall be with them; indeed* <u>*I will be their Elohim, and they shall be My people.*</u> [28] *The nations also will know that I, YHWH, sanctify Yisrael, when My sanctuary is in their midst forevermore."* Ezekiel 37:15-28

This was the great promise provided to the whole House of Yisrael. They would have a reunited kingdom ruled by a righteous king – the Messiah. We can see from the language that this reunification is clearly within the context of a renewed Covenant.

Notice the distinction between the stick of Yahudah representing the House of Yahudah, and the stick of Ephraim, representing the House of Yisrael. The stick of Yahudah includes the children of Yisrael, his companions. The Hebrew word for "children" is "beni" (ㄱㄚㄚ) and it means literal offspring. The word "companion" is "chabar" (ㄱㄚㄖ) and it literally means: "to join, fellowship, associate, community." So the stick of Yahudah represents the physical descendents of Yisrael and all those who have joined with

them. In other words the House of Yahudah.

The stick of Ephraim represents the House of Yisrael – those who have been scattered to the four corners and mixed in with the nations. When the House of Yahudah is drawn out of the nations, as Yisrael was previously drawn out of Egypt, the House of Yisrael will bring "companions" – just as the "mixed multitude" came out of Egypt with Yisrael.

The Covenant at Sinai with the Children of Yisrel and the mixed multitude revealed the pattern for the future. The renewal at Sinai allowed the possibility for a future renewal. This is what both Jeremiah and Ezekiel described would happen to Yisrael and Yahudah. First we will look at what Jeremiah prophesied concerning a renewal of the covenant that was, once again, broken. In fact, Jeremiah specifically provided that there would be a renewal of the Covenant.

"*31* The time is coming, declares YHWH, when I will make a _renewed_ covenant with the House of Yisrael and with the House of Yahudah. *32* It will not be like the covenant I made with their forefathers when I took them by the hand to lead them out of Egypt, because they broke my covenant, though I was a husband to them, declares YHWH. *33* This is the Covenant I will make with the House of Yisrael after that time, declares YHWH. I will put My Torah in their minds and write it on their hearts. _I will be their Elohim, and they will be My people._ *34* No longer will a man teach his neighbor, or a man his brother, saying, Know YHWH, because they will all know me, from the least of them to the greatest, declares YHWH. For I will forgive their wickedness and will remember their sins no more. *35* This is what YHWH says, He Who appoints the sun to shine by day, Who decrees the moon and stars to shine by night, Who stirs up the sea so that its waves roar -

YHWH Almighty is His Name: *³⁶ Only if these decrees vanish from My sight, declares YHWH, will the descendants of Yisrael ever cease to be a nation before Me.* *³⁷ This is what YHWH says: Only if the heavens above can be measured and the foundations of the earth below be searched out will I reject all the descendants of Yisrael because of all they have done, declares YHWH.* *³⁸ The days are coming, declares YHWH, when this city will be rebuilt for Me from the Tower of Hananel to the Corner Gate.* *³⁹ The measuring line will stretch from there straight to the hill of Gareb and then turn to Goah.* *⁴⁰ The whole valley where dead bodies and ashes are thrown, and all the terraces out to the Kidron Valley on the east as far as the corner of the Horse Gate, will be set apart to YHWH. The city will never again be uprooted or demolished.*" Jeremiah 31:31-40

Notice how Jeremiah indicates that there will be a time when the Covenant would be renewed with both Houses, but He then goes on to describe the Covenant with the House of Yisrael. The reason is because the House of Yisrael is divorced and needs to return to the Covenant.

Ezekiel indicated that this renewed covenant with the House of Yisrael would occur when they were regathered. Their hearts would be circumcised and their spirit renewed.

"*¹⁴ The word of YHWH came to me: ¹⁵ Son of man, your brothers - your brothers who are your blood relatives and the whole House of Yisrael - are those of whom the people of Jerusalem have said, They are far away from YHWH; this land was given to us as our possession. ¹⁶ Therefore say: This is what the Sovereign YHWH says: Although I sent them far away among the nations and scattered them among the countries, yet for a little while I have been a sanctuary for them in the countries where they have gone. ¹⁷ Therefore say: This is what the Sovereign YHWH says: I will gather you from the* *nations and bring you back from the lands where you have been scattered, and I will give you back the land of Yisrael again. ¹⁸ They will return to it and remove all its vile images and detestable idols. ¹⁹ I will give them an undivided heart and put a new spirit in them; I will remove from them their heart of stone and give them a heart of flesh. ²⁰ Then they will follow My decrees and be careful to keep My judgments. They will be My people, and I will be their Elohim. ²¹ But as for those whose hearts are devoted to their vile images and detestable idols, I will bring down on their own heads what they have done, declares the Sovereign YHWH. ²² Then the cherubim, with the wheels beside them, spread their wings, and the glory of the Elohim of Yisrael was above them. ²³ The glory of YHWH went up from within the city and stopped above the mountain east of it. ²⁴ The Spirit lifted me up and brought me to the exiles in Babylonia in the vision given by the Spirit of Elohim. Then the vision I had seen went up from me, ²⁵ and I told the exiles everything YHWH had shown me." Yehezqel 11:14-25*

There will be a return to the Land, but it is premised upon being cleansed from the defilements of idolatry and obedience to the Covenant. This return involves a transformation, specifically a "heart transplant." YHWH will take away their divided hearts and give them a unified (echad) heart. Just as YHWH is unified (echad) so with Yisrael. (Debarim 6:4).

In fact, the heart of YHWH will yearn for Ephraim, the prodigal son. Ephraim will repent and return to YHWH.

"¹⁶ Thus says YHWH: Refrain your voice from weeping, and your eyes from tears; For your work shall be rewarded, says YHWH, and they shall come back from the land of the enemy. ¹⁷ There is hope in your future, says YHWH, that your children shall come

back to their own border. [18] I have surely heard Ephraim
bemoaning himself: You have chastised me, and I was
chastised, like an untrained bull; Restore me, and I will
return, for You are YHWH my Elohim. [19] Surely, after
my turning, I repented; and after I was instructed, I
struck myself on the thigh; I was ashamed, yes, even
humiliated, because I bore the reproach of my youth. [20]
Is Ephraim My dear son? Is he a pleasant child? For
though I spoke against him, I earnestly remember him
still; Therefore My heart yearns for him; I will surely
have mercy on him, says YHWH. [21] Set up signposts,
make landmarks; Set your heart toward the highway,
the way in which you went. Turn back, O virgin of
Yisrael, turn back to these your cities. [22] How long will
you gad about, O you backsliding daughter? For
YHWH has created a new thing in the earth - A
woman shall surround a man (𐤂𐤁𐤓). [23] Thus says
YHWH of hosts, the Elohim of Yisrael: They shall
again use this speech in the land of Yahudah and in its
cities, when I bring back their captivity: YHWH bless
you, O home of justice, and mountain of holiness! [24] And
there shall dwell in Yahudah itself, and in all its cities
together, farmers and those going out with flocks. [25] For
I have satiated the weary soul, and I have replenished
every sorrowful soul. [26] After this I awoke and looked
around, and my sleep was sweet to me. [27] Behold, the
days are coming, says YHWH, that I will sow the
House of Yisrael and the House of Yahudah with the
seed of man and the seed of beast. [28] And it shall come to
pass, that as I have watched over them to pluck up, to
break down, to throw down, to destroy, and to afflict, so
I will watch over them to build and to plant, says
YHWH. [29] In those days they shall say no more: The
fathers have eaten sour grapes, and the children's teeth

are set on edge. ³⁰ But every one shall die for his own iniquity; every man who eats the sour grapes, his teeth shall be set on edge." Jeremiah 31:16-30

So just as YHWH plucked and removed the House of Yisrael and the House of Yahudah, so He will replant them back in the Land. Notice the reference to the "virgin Yisrael." This is important because only in this renewed state can Yisrael be restored to the position of the Bride. Also, the reference to the "new thing" is referencing when Yisrael will embrace her strong One – "gibor" (**ꓷꓘꓶ**). Instead of Yisrael running away from Elohim, she will be drawn to Him and embrace Him. This surely will be a new thing as history records her repeated and continuous fornication and running after foreign gods. For her to be a faithful bride surely will be a new thing.

Only when restored to the position of the Bride can Yisrael then reenter the Covenant Kingdom – the Promised Land. This replanting is reiterated by the prophet named Amos.

*"⁹ For surely I will command, and will sift the House of Yisrael among all nations, as grain is sifted in a sieve; Yet not the smallest grain shall fall to the ground. ¹⁰ All the sinners of My people shall die by the sword, Who say, The calamity shall not overtake nor confront us. ¹¹ On that day I will raise up the tabernacle (**ꓫꓬ╪-ꓫꓘ**) of David, which has fallen down, and repair its damages; I will raise up its ruins, and rebuild it as in the days of old; ¹² That they may possess the remnant of Edom, and all the Nations (goyim) who are called by My Name, says YHWH who does this thing. ¹³ Behold, the days are coming, says YHWH, When the plowman shall overtake the reaper, and the treader of grapes him who sows seed; The mountains shall drip with sweet wine, And all the hills shall flow with it. ¹⁴ I will bring back the captives of My people Yisrael; They shall build the waste cities and inhabit them; They shall plant vineyards and drink wine from them;*

They shall also make gardens and eat fruit from them. ¹⁵ I will plant them in their land, and no longer shall they be pulled up from the land I have given them, says YHWH your Elohim." Amos 9:9-15

It appears from these prophecies that the people of YHWH will return they way that they left. The question of the ages is how and when this will happen. That will be discussed in detail further in the text. We know that it will occur in a more spectacular fashion than occurred when Yisrael left Egypt.

"<u>*¹⁴ Therefore behold, the days are coming, says YHWH, that it shall no more be said, YHWH lives who brought up the children of Yisrael from the land of Egypt, ¹⁵ but, YHWH lives who brought up the children of Yisrael from the land of the north and from all the lands where He had driven them.*</u> *For I will bring them back into their land which I gave to their fathers. ¹⁶ Behold, I will send for many fishermen, says YHWH, and they shall fish them; and afterward I will send for many hunters, and they shall hunt them from every mountain and every hill, and out of the holes of the rocks. ¹⁷ For My eyes are on all their ways; they are not hidden from My face, nor is their iniquity hidden from My eyes. ¹⁸ And first I will repay double for their iniquity and their sin, because they have defiled My land; they have filled My inheritance with the carcasses of their detestable and abominable idols. ¹⁹ O YHWH, my strength and my fortress, my refuge in the day of affliction, the Gentiles shall come to You from the ends of the earth and say, Surely our fathers have inherited lies, worthlessness and unprofitable things. ²⁰ Will a man make gods for himself, which are not gods? ²¹ Therefore behold, I will this once cause them to know, I will cause them to know My hand and My might; and they shall know that My Name is YHWH.*" Jeremiah 16:14-21

The great significance that the Name of YHWH has in the restoration and regathering of the House of Yisrael cannot be emphasized enough. In fact, it is because of the Name that all this will occur. Again, one cannot ignore the

connection with the exodus from Egypt. The text commonly
called "Exodus" is "Shemot" in the Tanak. Shemot means:
"Names." So the purpose of the exodus was really about the
Name of YHWH. This was made clear in the text. YHWH
reveals Himself and His Name to Mosheh. He then proceeds
to reveal it to Pharaoh and the entire world.

The same will occur in the future. This world that
ignores the Creator and His Commandments will some day
be forced to acknowledge Him and His set apart Name. This
will occur through great judgment and through that judgment
Yisrael will be regathered.

Once Yisrael is regathered there is a great promise
concerning the Name. *"So I will make My Set Apart Name
known in the midst of My people Yisrael, and I will not let them
profane My Set Apart Name anymore. Then the nations shall know
that I am YHWH, the Holy One in Yisrael."* Ezekiel 39:7

One of the great mysteries is just how YHWH will
regather His people. *"[6] I will strengthen the House of Yahudah,
and I will save the House of Joseph. I will bring them back, because
I have mercy on them. They shall be as though I had not cast them
aside; for I am YHWH their Elohim, and I will hear them. [7] Those
of Ephraim shall be like a mighty man (gibor), and their heart shall
rejoice as if with wine. Yes, their children shall see it and be glad;
Their heart shall rejoice in YHWH. [8] I will whistle for them and
gather them, for I will redeem them; and they shall increase as they
once increased. [9] I will sow them among the peoples, and they shall
remember Me in far countries; They shall live, together with their
children, and they shall return. [10] I will also bring them back from
the land of Egypt, and gather them from Assyria. I will bring them
into the land of Gilead and Lebanon, until no more room is found for
them. [11] He shall pass through the sea with affliction, and strike the
waves of the sea: all the depths of the River shall dry up. Then the
pride of Assyria shall be brought down, and the scepter of Egypt
shall depart. [12] So I will strengthen them in YHWH, and they shall*

walk up and down in His name, says YHWH." Zecheriah 10:6-12

So this regathering will come from the East – Assyria and the West – Egypt. It is important to understand what Egypt and Assyria represent. Remember that Yisrael entered into Egypt as honored, invited guests. They were initially highly esteemed and lived in the most fertile region of Eqypt.

Over time they became slaves. The word for Egypt in Hebrew is Mitsrayim (ﬦﬧﬔﬡﬔ) and it means: "bondage." So the people of YHWH will be in a system of bondage where their strength and resources are being tapped to feed Pharaoh, or Uncle Sam – whatever you want to call it.

Assyria represents a system that takes away the identity of their captives. They would conquer a people, uproot them and transplant them so that they would not have any connection with their land. As a result, the House of Yisrael lost their identity as a covenant people, they forgot YHWH, and they lost their connection with the Promised Land.

This actually sounds a lot like the majority of Christians who do not use the name of YHWH. They do not have any identity with Yisrael, the Covenant or the Promised Land – yet they are drawn to the Elohim of Abraham, Yitshaq and Yaacob. Could it be that those who call themselves Christians are actually the lost sheep of the House of Yisrael – those who the Messiah came to redeem. We will be examing that more as we continue the discussion.

For now, it is important to recognize that the regathering will surround the land commonly known as the Modern State of Israel. It will actually involve the ancient boundaries promised to Abram.

Notice that the language of a return is similar to the Exodus. They shall "pass through the sea of affliction" and "all the depths of the River shall dry up." Remember that the Exodus from Egypt involved passing through the Red Sea,

and then 40 years later, crossing the waters of the river. This sounds like another exodus from the lands where they have been scattered. This time we read about them gathering in Lebanon and Gilead until they run out of room. Lebanon, of course, lies to the north and Gilead is the region of Gad and Reuben to the east of the Jordan River.

In fact, this is clearly the case as we read in Jeremiah. *"¹ Woe to the shepherds who destroy and scatter the sheep of My pasture! says YHWH. ² Therefore thus says YHWH Elohim of Yisrael against the shepherds who feed My people: You have scattered My flock, driven them away, and not attended to them. Behold, I will attend to you for the evil of your doings, says YHWH. ³ But I will gather the remnant of My flock out of all countries where I have driven them, and bring them back to their folds; and they shall be fruitful and increase. ⁴ I will set up shepherds over them who will feed them; and they shall fear no more, nor be dismayed, nor shall they be lacking, says YHWH. ⁵ Behold, the days are coming, says YHWH, That I will raise to David a Branch of righteousness; A King shall reign and prosper, and execute judgment and righteousness in the earth. ⁶ In His days Yahudah will be saved, and Yisrael will dwell safely; Now this is His Name by which He will be called: 'YHWH our righteousness.' ⁷ Therefore, behold, the days are coming, says YHWH, that they shall no longer say, As YHWH lives who brought up the children of Yisrael from the land of Egypt, ⁸ but, As YHWH lives who brought up and led the descendants of the House of Yisrael from the north land and from all the land where I had driven them. And they shall dwell in their own land."* Jeremiah 23:1-8

So YHWH will bring back Yisrael from the north, and all the lands where they were driven. These seem to be two different places - one being land in a specific direction and the other is simply a general reference to land. Is this to assume that all the nations where the House of Yisrael was scattered are geographically north of the Promised Land? No,

while the House of Yisrael was originally taken north by the Assyrians, they were eventually scattered to the four corners of the earth. (Isaiah 11:12)

The Hebrew word for "north" is "tsephon" (𐤑𐤐𐤅𐤍). It is an interesting word for many reasons. It actually occurs 153 times in the Scriptures.[169] We already saw that 153 is the gematria value for "camps where YHWH dwells" and "the sons of Elohim." So now we have the "north" associated with the camps of YHWH, and the sons of Elohim.

When you examine the origins of the word "tsephon" (𐤑𐤐𐤅𐤍) you also find it connected with "Baal Tsephon" - Baal of the North, also known as Baal of Winter. This is actually the source of much of the pagan elements in the Christmas celebration. Most Christians celebrate the birth of their christ on the date of the ancient winter solstice – December 25. This is the birth date for sun gods deriving from Babylonian worship. The birth dates for gods such as the Babylonian Tammuz and the Egyptian Horus were celebrated on December 25. The integration of Santa Claus into the christ mass involves none other than Baal Tsephon. How interesting that Santa Claus is eternal and all knowing and lives at the "North" pole.

How amazing that we see a modern connection between Christianity and the lost sheep of the House of Yisrael. In fact, many believe that Christians constitute a majority of the House of Yisrael as YHWH has cast them, like a net, throughout the world in anticipation of a future regathering.

"Tsephon" also means "dark," and can be used to refer to the northern quarter. So while it may mean that the House of Yisrael will return from the direction of the north, it also seems to indicate a return from Baal worship – idolatry.[170] That certainly is consistent with the notion of the House of Yisrael being immersed in Christianity. While most

Christians sincerely believe in the Messiah of Yisrael, their religious system has been corrupted by Babyolnian sun worship.

The House of Yisrael needs to taken out of Babylon, and Babylon needs to be taken out of them. We saw this process occur through the previous exodus from Egypt, and the connection with the future regathering of the House of Yisrael cannot be ignored. After the Passover in Egypt had occurred, and the Children of Yisrael were about to leave Egypt by crossing the Red Sea, we read the following account:

"*¹ Now YHWH spoke to Mosheh, saying: ² Speak to the Children of Yisrael, that they turn and camp before Pi Hahiroth, between Migdol and the sea, in the face of Baal Tsephon; you shall camp before it by the sea. ³ For Pharaoh will say of the Children of Yisrael, They are bewildered by the land; the wilderness has closed them in. ⁴ Then I will harden Pharaoh's heart, so that he will pursue them; and I will gain honor over Pharaoh and over all his army, that the Egyptians may know that I am YHWH. And they did so.*"
Shemot 14:1-4

So when the Children of Yisrael were about the leave Egypt, along with the mixed multitude, they were facing Baal Tsephon. This could provide a clue for the actual crossing point, because there it was obviously a geographic location. While there are many theories regarding the place of the crossing, they must fit within the Scriptural account, and here we know that the children of Yisrael were literally facing Baal Tsephon.[171] This also appears to be a connection and a hint for a future exodus.

Hosea also describes the return of the House of Yisrael, specifying it is from Egypt and Assyria. "*¹⁰ They shall walk after YHWH. He will roar like a lion. When He roars, then His sons shall come trembling from the west; ¹¹ They shall come like a startled (trembling) bird from Egypt, like a dove from the land of*

Assyria. And I will let them dwell in their houses," Says YHWH." Hosea 11:10-11

The Hebrew word for "tremble" is "harad" (◁◀ḥ). It can mean "tremble" but it is the idea of being "startled," like at the "sound of a trumpet" or a shofar.[172] So there will be an incredible sound when YHWH "roars" like a lion, and they will suddenly come flying from the west. We will examine this sound further in the Book of Revelation.

Just how they will be flying remains a mystery, but it starts to become clear how this return will make the Exodus from Egypt pale in comparison. In fact, this makes us think of the statement that YHWH made that appears to be prophetic. *"You have seen what I did to the Egyptians, and how I bore you on eagles' wings and brought you to Myself."* Shemot 19:4

So in the future there may actually be a winged exodus from all over the world back to YHWH. It will also involve passing through waters. *"[10] And in that day there shall be a Root of Jesse, Who shall stand as a banner to the people; For the Gentiles shall seek Him, and His resting place shall be glorious.* [11] *It shall come to pass in that day YHWH shall set His hand again the second time to recover the remnant of His people who are left, from Assyria and Egypt, from Pathros and Cush, from Elam and Shinar, from Hamath and the islands of the sea.* [12] *He will set up a banner for the nations, and will assemble the outcasts of Yisrael, and gather together the dispersed of Yahudah from the four corners of the earth.* [13] *Also the envy of Ephraim shall depart, and the adversaries of Yahudah shall be cut off; Ephraim shall not envy Yahudah, and Yahudah shall not harass Ephraim.* [14] *But they shall fly down upon the shoulder of the Philistines toward the west; together they shall plunder the people of the East; they shall lay their hand on Edom and Moab; and the people of Ammon shall obey them.* [15] *YHWH will utterly destroy the tongue of the Sea of Egypt; with His mighty wind He will shake His fist over the River, and strike it in the seven streams, and make men cross over dryshod.* [16]

*There will be a highway for the remnant of His people who will be
left from Assyria, as it was for Yisrael in the day that he came up
from the land of Egypt.*" Isaiah 11:10-16

So there is absolutely going to be a physical return of
the House of Yisrael to the Land of Yisrael. The prophecy
specifically speaks of a "second time." It will be an incredible
"exodus" from all over the world, far greater than the
previous exodus from Egypt led by Mosheh and Aharon.
Very interestingly, one of the places they will be gathered
from is "Shinar." It is spelled "v'mashinar" (ꟼ⊙ᖯWᖯY),
and has the gematria value of 666. Remember that Shinar was
the land that Nimrod established his kingdom, and it was the
land that Abram was taken out of – Babylon. Interestingly,
the Sumerian counting system was actually based upon 6.

So in the future, the House of Yisrael will be removed
from Babylon, and this particular Kingdom is directly
associated with the number 666. This will be significant as
we explore the end of the age described in the Book of
Revelation.

The remnant will be returning from Egypt and
Assyria. "*[12] And it shall come to pass in that day that YHWH will
thresh, from the channel of the River to the Brook of Egypt; And
you will be gathered one by one, O you children of Yisrael. [13] So it
shall be in that day: The great shofar will be blown; they will come,
who are about to perish in the land of Assyria, and they who are
outcasts in the land of Egypt, and shall worship YHWH in the set
apart mountain at Jerusalem.*" Isaiah 27:12-13

I grew up in a religious system that was centered upon
itsself. I was a Christian and the handling of prophecy was
often very haphazard, to say the least. Passages were
frequently taken out of their historical context and
spiritualized to apply to the so-called Christian Church.
Especially those that were considered to be apocalyptic or end
times related. All of the bad prophecies were attributed to

"ancient" Yisrael. All of the good prophecies were essentially rendered upon the Christian Church, which did not even exist at that time, except in the variant forms of Babylonian sun worship found throughout the ages.

As a result, I grew up with many deep-seeded assumptions regarding the end times. Mainly, I was taught and believed that the end times would be all about Christians. For instance, I assumed that there would be a seven year period of tribulation before the return of the Messiah. That period was divided in half between the first 3½ years of tribulation followed by another 3½ years called the Great Tribulation.

I assumed that the Temple in Jerusalem needed to be rebuilt so that certain periods described by the prophet Daniel could be fulfilled. I also assumed that all of the Seals, Trumpets and Vials described in the Book of Revelation had to occur within that seven year period of time.

Those assumptions were based upon countless sermons and books presented from a Christian perspective that saw the Christian Church as "Spiritual Israel," and therefore the focus of all or most of the prophecies attributed to the end of the age.

I hope that by now, the reader understands that Yisrael was and remains the Covenant Assembly of YHWH. Therefore, it is important to view the prophecies given by the Prophets of Yisrael within their proper context. It is also critical to recognize that most prophecies in the Tanak were made over 2,500 years ago. Those prophets were dealing with issues of the day along with future events. Some things have been fulfilled while others remain unfulfilled.

There are two major camps dealing with Scriptural prophecy, namely preterists and futurists. The preterists tend to believe that all prophecy has already been fulfilled, while futurists look to future fulfillments of prophecies. I do not

subscribe to one camp or the other. I believe that each prophecy must be looked at within the context of the Scriptures. Some prophecies clearly have been fulfilled while others have not. Even some prophecies that had a past fulfillment may have a future fulfillment.

Now it should be clear that when referring to these prophecies we are talking about the texts in the Tanak from the major and the minor prophets, collectively known as "The Prophets," or better yet the "Nebi'im" (𐤍𐤁𐤉𐤀𐤉𐤌). While there were many prophecies and prophetic patterns provided throughout the Scriptures, those commonly attributed to the end times are found within The Prophets.

Those "Prophets" are typically categorized as major and minor prophets, not based upon importance, but rather size. The major prophets Isaiah, Ezekiel and Jeremiah including Lamentations, are much longer than the other prophetic text. The Book of Daniel, while similar in length to Hosea and Zechariah, is found in the major prophets in Christian Bibles, but it is contained within the Writings (Ketubim) in the Tanak.

Most of the major and minor prophets lived and prophesied during a specific span of time starting before the exile of the House of Yisrael, and ending shortly after the return of the House of Yahudah. There were clearly prophets who lived throughout all time. Most are never mentioned in the Scriptures while others have their prophecies written down and compiled within the Prophets or the Writings.

The prophets who are included within the Tanak with specific texts attributed to them were often focused on a divided Yisrael. They warned of the punishments that would be rendered as well as the promise of a return. Most also contain both obvious and veiled references to the needed Messiah.

This is where it is important to understand the

context of the passages. Again, these prophecies were given to a divided Covenant people who had strayed from the Covenant. They were made within the context of that Covenant, and revealed the need for a messiah to restore the Covenant.

When these prophecies were given, the Messiah had not yet come and after the House of Yahudah had been exiled by the Babylonians, the Temple was also destroyed. So these prophecies would have been focused on those punishments inflicted upon the divided Houses of Yisrael and Yahudah as well as their restoration of the Kingdom and the appearance of the Messiah.

Some prophecies, such as Jeremiah 50 speak of the reunited Houses of Yisrael along with the punishment of Babylon. This particular prophecy reveals the major difference between preterists and futurists. The preterists believe that this entire passage was fulfilled in the past, the futurists apply the entire passage to a future destruction of Babylon, which requires a rebuilding and restoration of Babylon.

Much of the debate rests upon whether or not Babylon was completely desolated in accordance with the various prophecies found in Isaiah and Jeremiah. While Babylon was clearly defeated and eventually overtaken and left desolate, there are those, like Isaac Newton, who believe that there must be a future destruction that completely complies with the prophecies. Again, there are arguments to be made on both sides and the answer may lie somewhere in the middle. There may have been partial fulfillments and there may be other matters remaining for future fulfillment.

There is a very significant Messianic prophecy already partially cited that specifically speaks to that point. Interestingly, when it refers to the Messiah reuniting the Tribes of Yisrael, it is when He reaches out His Hand a

second time. This fits perfectly with the notion that the Messiah came first as the Messiah ben Joseph, and would be returning a second time as Messiah ben David.

Read this passage from Isaiah very carefully: "*¹ There shall come forth a Rod from the stem of Jesse, and a Branch shall grow out of his roots. ² The Spirit of YHWH shall rest upon Him, the Spirit of wisdom and understanding, the Spirit of counsel and might, the Spirit of knowledge and of the fear of YHWH. ³ His delight is in the fear of YHWH, and He shall not judge by the sight of His eyes, nor decide by the hearing of His ears; ⁴ But with righteousness He shall judge the poor, and decide with equity for the meek of the earth; He shall strike the earth with the rod of His mouth, and with the breath of His lips He shall slay the wicked. ⁵ Righteousness shall be the belt of His loins, and faithfulness the belt of His waist. ⁶ The wolf also shall dwell with the lamb, the leopard shall lie down with the young goat, the calf and the young lion and the fatling together; and a little child shall lead them. ⁷ The cow and the bear shall graze; Their young ones shall lie down together; and the lion shall eat straw like the ox. ⁸ The nursing child shall play by the cobra's hole, and the weaned child shall put his hand in the viper's den. ⁹ They shall not hurt nor destroy in all My set apart mountain, for the earth shall be full of the knowledge of YHWH as the waters cover the sea. ¹⁰ And in that day there shall be a Root of Jesse, Who shall stand as a banner to the people; for the Gentiles shall seek Him, and His resting place shall be glorious. ¹¹ It shall come to pass in that day that Master shall set His hand again the second time to recover the remnant of His people who are left, from Assyria and Egypt, from Pathros and Cush, from Elam and Shinar, from Hamath and the islands of the sea. ¹² He will set up a banner for the nations, and will assemble the outcasts of Yisrael, and gather together the dispersed of Yahudah, from the four corners of the earth. ¹³ Also the envy of Ephraim shall depart, and the adversaries of Yahudah shall be cut off; Ephraim shall not envy Yahudah, and Yahudah shall not harass Ephraim. ¹⁴ But they shall fly down upon the shoulder of the Philistines toward the west; together they shall plunder the people of the East; they shall lay their hand on Edom and Moab; and the people of Ammon shall obey them. ¹⁵ YHWH will utterly destroy the tongue of the Sea of Egypt; With His mighty wind He will shake His fist over the River, and strike it in the seven streams, and make men cross over dryshod. ¹⁶ There will be a highway for the remnant of His people who will be left from Assyria, as it was for Yisrael in the day that he came up from the land of Egypt."* Isaiah 11:1-16

This text is filled with amazing information. It involves the role of the Messiah in the rebuilding of the Kingdom. Particularly it mentions two appearances and the second time would be the regathering of the people from the four corners of the planet through a great Exodus, like the time when the Children of Yisrael were brought out of Egypt. This time they will be flying and plundering until the cross over dry ground into the Land.

Two of those things already occurred in history. The House of Yahudah was allowed to return and rebuild the Temple in Jerusalem after the seventy year Babylonian capitivity was complete. Also, the Messiah did indeed come when, where and how it was prophesied.¹⁷³ Both of these will be discussed in the following chapter.

The primary event that has not occurred at any time in history is the regathering of the exiled House of Yisrael and the restoration of the divided Kingdom under One Ruler – the Messiah.

It is because of this fact that many Jews reject the Christian Jesus as the Messiah. They proclaim that because Jesus did not restore the Kingdom then he could not have been the Messiah. Of course, the Christian religion has badly misrepresented the Messiah Yahushua and his teachings so it is easy to understand how Jews reject the Christian christ.

Regardless, Yahushua is the only One qualified to be

the Messiah and if He is not the Messiah then the prophets were wrong. Thankfully, the problem lies in the Jews expectations of the Messiah, and the Christian representation of the Messiah, not in the Prophets or Yahushua. Yahushua came as the Messiah ben Joseph first, and through His death and resurrection freed us all from the curse of death imposed upon mankind after the fall.

He also made a way for the divided House of Yisrael to become like a clean virgin so she could become the Bride of YHWH. The House of Yahudah was also now able to be restored. Some day in the future Yahushua will come again as Messiah ben David. It is the distinction between these two roles that has many confused concerning end time prophecies.

While there are some who recognize that many of the prophecies have already been fulfilled, others view the prophecies through strictly an "end times" lense as if all prophecies have a fulfillment at the end of the age. Still others believe that many prophecies have dual fulfillments. As a result, we must be careful to examine prophecies within their historical context.

This chapter has included lengthy Scripture citations but it is important to realize that these are merely a small sample of the prophecies concerning the division, punishment and restoration of the House of Yisrael and the House of Yahudah. It is because of the great importance of this issue that I wanted the reader to see the actual prophecies, not just my thoughts regarding the prophecies on this subject.

This is not a topic that is taught in most mainline religions that base their faith upon the Scriptures. Sadly, if you fail to understand this information you will not understand the plan of YHWH and the work of the Messiah. Both the House of Yisrael and the House of Yahudah were

given durations for their exiles. As we shall examine in the next chapter, the House of Yahudah returned to the Land precisely according to schedule while the House of Yisrael remained in exile. Their exile was not to end for quite sometime.

Despite these many promises, the House of Yisrael had a long wait until their return. During this process, YHWH would sow them among the nations and multiply them. Then when their punishment is complete, in a promised return, YHWH would draw the nations in and through them.

Once you place these prophecies into context and recognize which were fulfilled and which await a future fulfillment we then must examine them within the prophetic framework of the Appointed Times.

So we see from the prophets who lived during the punishments of Yisrael that they provided hope for the future. There would be a renewal of the Covenant, a return to the Land and a Restoration of the Kingdom.

One unique prophet actually lived during the completion of the first punishment on the House of Yahudah. He witnessed the fulfillment of the two seventy year punishments rendered upon Babylon and Yahudah. He was also provided specific and additional information concerning the end of the age. As with Ezekiel, he was taken captive and exiled into the Land of Babylon. His Babylonian name was Belteshazzar, but his Hebrew name was Daniel.

9

Daniel

It is helpful to continue our examination of prophecy by separately examining the transitional prophet named Daniel. The text of Daniel is quite unique. Christians place Daniel with the major prophets in the "Old Testament."[174] In the Tanak, it is located with the collection of texts known as the Writings (Ketubim). The placement of Daniel shows the different ways that the text is viewed. Christians typically love this text and give it great weight while many in Judaism minimize it. Some even go so far as to question the authenticity of the text.[175]

The reason why Christians tend to favor this text is because, in English versions, it is the one book in the Tanak that specifically translates the Hebrew word "moshiach" (ᕼ𝟤ᘜ𝟆) as Messiah. (see Daniel 9:25 and 26) As mentioned, "moshiach" is a word that literally means: "anointed." It can be used to describe persons such as kings and priests, although in Daniel there is no mistake that "moshiach" is referring to The Messiah.

In fact, Daniel actually gives very specific timing regarding the rebuilding of the Temple, and the appearance of the Temple. These were the two great expectations concerning the fractured Kingdom of Yisrael. The House of Yisrael had been exiled and divided. The House of Yahudah was subject to a 70 year period of punishment. They had been partially exiled by the Babylonians who had destroyed the Temple and sacked Jerusalem.

The issues addressed in Daniel are particularly poignant to the House of Yahudah. Daniel was, after all, from the House of Yahudah and was himself exiled into Babylon. There are many mysteries associated with this text, one of which involves language.

Throughout this book, we have shown the Paleo-Hebrew characters when examining the language. It was some time after the division of the Kingdom and the exile of the House of Yahudah that they adopted a hybrid form of the Hebrew language known as Modern Hebrew. The character set is often referred to as Chaldean Flame Letters. Those from the House of Yahudah continue to use this derivative language that was not the language of the patriarchs.[76]

With that understanding, it is important to point out the fact that the Book of Daniel is written in two different languages – Aramaic and Modern Hebrew. From the beginning to chapter 2, verse 3, the text is written in Modern Hebrew. From chapter 2, verse 4 through the end of chapter 7 it is written in Aramaic. Chapters 8 through 12 are again, written in Modern Hebrew.

Prior to the Babylonian exile, the Yisraelites all used one language, often described as Paleo Hebrew. At some point during or after the Babylonian captivity, the House of Yahudah began using the Modern Hebrew script. We do not know how or when Daniel was written in two different languages, but that is what we presently have. It appears to have significance when we compare the contents of each portion.

For instance, in Daniel 2, written in Aramaic, there is a description of an image that represents world kingdoms from Babylon through the Roman Empire leading up to the Messiah. In Daniel 7, written in Modern Hebrew, there is a

description of different systems and powers that will exist at the end of the age.

Chapter 1, written in Modern Hebrew, begins with an introduction that tells how Daniel was taken by the Babylonians during one of the captivities of the House of Yahudah.

Read the following account at the beginning of Daniel: "*¹ In the third year of the reign of Jehoiakim king of Yahudah, Nebuchadnezzar king of Babylon came to Jerusalem and besieged it. ² And YHWH gave Jehoiakim king of Yahudah into his hand, with some of the articles of the House of Elohim, which he carried into the land of Shinar to the house of his god; and he brought the articles into the treasure house of his god. ³ Then the king instructed Ashpenaz, the master of his eunuchs, to bring some of the children of Yisrael and some of the king's descendants and some of the nobles, ⁴ young men in whom there was no blemish, but good-looking, gifted in all wisdom, possessing knowledge and quick to understand, who had ability to serve in the king's palace, and whom they might teach the language and literature of the Chaldeans. ⁶ Among these were some from Yahudah: Daniel, Hananiah, Mishael and Azariah. ⁷ The chief official gave them new names: to Daniel, the name Belteshazzar; to Hananiah, Shadrach; to Mishael, Meshach; and to Azariah, Abednego.*" Daniel 1:1-7

Daniel was from the tribe of Yahudah and descended from nobility. It is important to understand that Daniel was taken into captivity by the Babylonians after the northern Kingdom of Yisrael had been removed through the Assyrian captivity. He was one of the best and the brightest. He was one of the "good figs" described by Jeremiah.

True to the prophecies, the Kingdom of Yahudah was indeed conquered by the Babylonian King Nebuchadnezzar after a series of sieges and exiles that culminated in the destruction of Jerusalem. Along with the captivity of King Jehoiachin, King of the House of Yahudah, many of the royal family and nobility were forced into Nebuchadnezzar's service. Nebuchadnezzar conquered Yahudah over a period of twenty four (24) years, in which people of Yahudah were taken captive in seven different captivities. In the very first captivity, four young men from Yahudah were taken named Daniel, Hananiah, Mishael and Azariah.[177]

The Babylonian kingdom ruled by Nebuchadnezzar was not the same Babylon that was ruled by Nimrod. Some scholars refer to this empire as the 10th Dynasty of Babylon, or the Neo Babylonian Empire. New or not, it still contained the same pagan roots as old Babylon. Interestingly, the names of the four young Hebrew men mentioned in Daniel 1:6-7 all contained the Name of YHWH or the title Elohim. Once they entered into the pagan culture, they were assimilated and given new names attributed to the gods of the land.

The name Daniel ($\ell \mathsf{K} \mathsf{Z} \mathsf{Y} \mathsf{d}$) means: "El is my judge" in Hebrew. His new name Belteshazzar means: "Bel protects his life." Bel Marduk was originally the patron deity of the City of Babylon and eventually became the supreme deity of Babylonia, the sun god. Bel Marduk was credited with bringing order to an otherwise chaotic universe, and his exploits are described in the ancient text known as the Enuma Elish.

The name Haniniyah ($\mathsf{Y} \mathsf{Z} \mathsf{Y} \mathsf{Y} \mathsf{H}$) means: "Yah has favored" in Hebrew. His new name Shadrach means: "command of Aku." Aku was the Sumerian moon god. The name Mishael ($\ell \mathsf{K} \mathsf{W} \mathsf{Z} \mathsf{Y}$) means: "Who is El" in Hebrew. His new name Meshach means: "Who is Aku" and it was clearly in direct opposition to his Hebrew name. Aku was the Babylonian god of the moon.

The name Azaryah ($\mathsf{Y} \mathsf{Z} \mathsf{Y} \mathsf{Z} \mathsf{O}$) means: "Yah has helped" in Hebrew. His new name Abednego means:

"Servent of Nego." Nego, also known as Nebo and Nabu. This was the Babylonian god of wisdom - worshipped as the son of Marduk. Thus he was the "son of god" to the Babylonians. His mother was a moon goddess Sarpanit, often depicted as being pregnant, and is considered to be the same goddess as Easter (Ishtar).

Imagine being a Torah observant Yisraelite who serves YHWH, given a name exalting an abominable pagan god. The objective was to snuff out the remembrance of the god of the captives, in this case YHWH, and enforce the worship of the victor's gods. YHWH had other plans, and He actually used Nebuchadnezzar as His servant to accomplish His purposes.

Despite the fact that these individuals were captives, the Scriptures record that Daniel greatly excelled in Babylon. "*[17] As for these four young men, Elohim gave them knowledge and skill in all literature and wisdom; and Daniel had understanding in all visions and dreams. [18] Now at the end of the days, when the king had said that they should be brought in, the chief of the eunuchs brought them in before Nebuchadnezzar. [19] Then the king interviewed them, and among them all none was found like Daniel, Hananiah, Mishael, and Azariah; therefore they served before the king. [20] And in all matters of wisdom and understanding about which the king examined them, he found them ten times better than all the magicians and astrologers who were in all his realm.*" Daniel 1:17-20

The reason they excelled was because they maintained their Torah observance while in captivity. It was also because of the favor, blessings and giftings bestowed upon them by YHWH.

The rise of Daniel is similar to that of Joseph. Daniel came into captivity as a slave, but due to the giftings of YHWH he excelled in the Babylonian court of Nebuchadnezzar. In fact, he was not only able to interpret the dreams of the ruler, he was actually able to tell him what he dreamed. Unlike Pharaoh, Nebuchadnezzar had a dream and he greatly desired the interpretation. He knew that his advisors would likely lie to him if they did not know the correct interpretation. He therefore required that they tell him the dream and the interpretation or they would all be killed.

While all of the wise men were in the process of being killed, Daniel asked the king for time. He then went to his three friends and they all sought mercy from Elohim that he might make known the King's demand and save them and all the wise men of Babylon. Their prayers were answered and Daniel was able to tell the King his dream and the interpretation.

Here is the account. *"27 Daniel answered in the presence of the king, and said, The secret which the king has demanded, the wise men, the astrologers, the magicians, and the soothsayers cannot declare to the king. 28 But there is a Elah in heaven who reveals secrets, and He has made known to King Nebuchadnezzar what will be in the latter days. Your dream, and the visions of your head upon your bed, were these: 29 As for you, O king, thoughts came to your mind while on your bed, about what would come to pass after this; and He who reveals secrets has made known to you what will be. 30 But as for me, this secret has not been revealed to me because I have more wisdom than anyone living, but for our sakes who make known the interpretation to the king, and that you may know the thoughts of your heart. 31 You, O king, were watching; and behold, a great image! This great image, whose splendor was excellent, stood before you; and its form was awesome. 32 This image's head was of fine gold, its chest and arms of silver, its belly and thighs of bronze, 33 its legs of iron, its feet partly of iron and* partly of clay. ³⁴ <u>You watched while a stone (aben) was cut out without hands, which struck the image on its feet of iron and clay, and broke them in pieces.</u> ³⁵ <u>Then the iron, the clay, the bronze, the silver, and the gold were crushed together, and became like chaff from the summer threshing floors; the wind carried them away so that no trace of them was found. And the stone (aben) that struck the image became a great mountain and filled the whole earth.</u> ³⁶ This is the dream. Now we will tell the interpretation of it before the king. ³⁷ You, O king, are a king of kings. For the Elah of heaven has given you a kingdom, power, strength, and glory; ³⁸ and wherever the children of men dwell, or the beasts of the field and the birds of the heaven, He has given them into your hand, and has made you ruler over them all - you are this head of gold. ³⁹ But after you shall arise another kingdom inferior to yours; then another, a third kingdom of bronze, which shall rule over all the earth. ⁴⁰ And the fourth kingdom shall be as strong as iron, inasmuch as iron breaks in pieces and shatters everything; and like iron that crushes, that kingdom will break in pieces and crush all the others. ⁴¹ Whereas you saw the feet and toes, partly of potter's clay and partly of iron, the kingdom shall be divided; yet the strength of the iron shall be in it, just as you saw the iron mixed with ceramic clay. ⁴² And as the toes of the feet were partly of iron and partly of clay, so the kingdom shall be partly strong and partly fragile. ⁴³ <u>As you saw iron mixed with ceramic clay, they will mingle with the seed of men; but they will not adhere to one another, just as iron does not mix with clay.</u> ⁴⁴ <u>And in the days of these kings the Elah of heaven will set up a kingdom which shall never be destroyed; and the kingdom shall not be left to other people; it shall break in pieces and consume all these kingdoms, and it</u>

shall stand forever. *45 Inasmuch as you saw that the stone (aben) was cut out of the mountain without hands, and that it broke in pieces the iron, the bronze, the clay, the silver, and the gold - the great Elah has made known to the king what will come to pass after this. The dream is certain, and its interpretation is sure. 46 Then King Nebuchadnezzar fell on his face, prostrate before Daniel, and commanded that they should present an offering and incense to him. 47 The king answered Daniel, and said, Truly your Elah is the Elah of Elohin, the Lord of kings, and a revealer of secrets, since you could reveal this secret. 48 Then the king promoted Daniel and gave him many great gifts; and he made him ruler over the whole province of Babylon, and chief administrator over all the wise men of Babylon. 49 Also Daniel petitioned the king, and he set Shadrach, Meshach, and Abed-nego over the affairs of the province of Babylon; but Daniel sat in the gate of the king." Daniel 2:27-49*

Interestingly, this information concerning the future was given to the ruler of Babylon, referred to as the servant of YHWH (Jeremiah 25:9). He was a unique king, called a king of kings (Daniel 2:37; Ezekiel 26:7). He actually wrote an entire chapter in the Book of Daniel. (see Daniel 4) He was humbled by YHWH, and as a result, he praised and extolled Him as the King of the heavens (Daniel 4:37). He humbly realized that there was a greater King with a greater Kingdom. *"His kingdom is an everlasting kingdom, and His dominion is from generation to generation."* Daniel 4:3

The Kingdom of Babylon under Nebuchadnezzar is described as fine gold. It was esteemed above all earthly kingdoms. So wee see in Babylon the best of man's kingdoms on Earth. From that point on, all others would differ and diminish in quality. While Babylon, under Nebuchadnezzar, would initially serve YHWH and extol Him, future

Kingdoms, particularly the final Kingdom of men, would oppose Him.

So Nebuchadnezzar, having the greatest kingdom, was given a dream concerning the remaining kingdoms through time. He described a great "image" which is "tselem" (צלם) in Hebrew. This is the same word that we read in Beresheet describing Elohim making man in His image. (see Beresheet 1:26-27) The fact that YHWH would reveal a series of kingdoms as one combined image is quite profound and revealing as we shall see.

It turns out that the head of fine gold represented Nebuchadnezzar's Chaldean Empire. The breast and arms of silver represented the Medo-Persian Empire. The belly and thighs of brass represented the Grecian Empire.

While most agree that the fourth kingdom is the Roman Empire, confusion lies with the toes. Is this a separate kingdom, an extension of the Roman Empire or a fifth Kingdom? As it turns out, the legs of iron represented the Roman Empire that was divided into two Empires, east and west, ruled from Rome and Constantinople. The feet and toes mixed with iron and clay are an extension of the Roman Empire, but different.

The fact that man was essentially made from clay makes man a very important part of this last kingdom, and it is this mixture of man that actually makes the kingdom weak. There is a mystery hidden in the Torah regarding how the nations are divided. In the Septuagint and the Dead Sea Scrolls we read ". . . *He established the boundaries of the people according to the Sons of El.*" (Debarim 32:8)

So it appears that the nations are ruled by "angelic" forces. While man sees the physical aspect to these earthly kingdoms, there are powers and principalities assigned to the nations. In this final kingdom we will see a complete consolidation and merging of man and these fallen angels as

they cross dimensions and join forces in absolute rebellion against YHWH. This the mixing of iron and clay involves the mixing of iron (spiritual beings) and clay (man). This will be a repeat of what occurred before the flood, and the Nephilim offspring were taking over the planet. Man and the spiritual beings will not be completely united.

At the end we will see the Kingdom of Elohim destroy this mixed kingdom. Remember that Adam, the first man, was supposed to set up the Kingdom of Elohim of earth. Now we see the final culmination of the rebellion of the fallen angels and man, establishing a world kingdom directly opposed to Elohim.

Even though the Roman Empire seemed to fall we should be able to trace the kingdoms represented in this image up to the the end of the age, since the interpretation clearly reveals that the final kingdom mixed with iron and clay will be broken into pieces and consumed by the Kingdom of Elohim. (see Daniel 2:44) The Kingdom of Elohim will thereafter stand through the ages.

We know this because the final kingdom will be destroyed by the "aben" stone – the stone cut without hands. This stone is clearly a reference to the stone standing in the House of Elohim (Beth El). It should also make us think about the tablets provided to Mosheh that were later broken. All of these lead us to the Messiah.

The stone should also make us think of the Altar that stands before the door of the House of YHWH. The Altar of YHWH must be made with uncut stones. (Shemot 20:22, Debarim 27:5). The Altar is the place where offerings are made and presented before YHWH. The Altar is the place where worship occurs between men and YHWH. The Altar of YHWH was made from uncut stone and situated directly on a threshing floor. (2 Samuel 24:18)

Understanding this connection provides a very

interesting clue in this vision concerning when Messiah, the aben stone, will destroy the kingdoms of the earth. Recall that the entire image will crumble when the aben strikes the feet. The image will be crushed together and become *"like chaff from the summer threshing floors."* All of these kingdoms are connected through time becaue they are made from the same mold – Babylon.

This is describing what occurs during the grain harvest between the Feast of Unleavened Bread and Shabuot. After the grain is harvested from the fields, the tares are burned and the sheaves are brought to the threshing floor. They are then either beaten or trampled by oxen.[178]

The treading continues until the cereal grain is loosened from the scaly, inedible chaff that surrounds it. Once separated, the winnowing occurs where the chaff and the straw is blown away and the grain falls to the threshing floor. So while the kingdoms of men will blow away like chaff, the grain will remain at the threshing floor – at the Altar of YHWH.

So the final Kingdom that undergoes this process will be a continuation of Rome. It can certainly be agrued that Rome still exists today through the Holy Roman Empire. It is important to note that the political center of the Roman Empire was the city of Rome, but the center of the Holy Roman Empire was Germany. Today we see the spiritual headquarters in Vatican City, a city built on seven hills (Rome), and the undeniable power of the European Union being Germany.[179]

With the allusion to 10 toes one cannot ignore the relationship with the 10 Tribes of the House of Yisrael that were scattered and mixed with these European nations.[180] This relationship becomes even clearer when we compare the contents that they are made from with a prophecy from Ezekiel.

After describing the abominations of the House of Yisrael here is what is said through Ezekiel: "*¹⁸ . . . the House of Yisrael has become dross to Me; they are all bronze, tin, iron, and lead, in the midst of a furnace; they have become dross from silver. ¹⁹ Therefore thus says the Master YHWH: Because you have all become dross, therefore behold, I will gather you into the midst of Jerusalem. ²⁰ As men gather silver, bronze, iron, lead, and tin into the midst of a furnace, to blow fire on it, to melt it; so I will gather you in My anger and in My fury, and I will leave you there and melt you. ²¹ Yes, I will gather you and blow on you with the fire of My wrath, and you shall be melted in its midst. ²² As silver is melted in the midst of a furnace, so shall you be melted in its midst; then you shall know that I, YHWH, have poured out My fury on you.*" Ezekiel 22:18-22

Notice the absence of gold and silver. The House of Yisrael was the dross from the fine metal silver. So then, the later kingdoms appear to be related to the House of Yisrael that went north and mixed with the northern kingdoms. The kingdoms revealed through the image would span the time from Nebuchadnezzar to the time when the Messiah (aben) would destroy the kingdoms of the earth and establish an eternal kingdom.

This is an important point to understand. The vision was given to Daniel while he was in Babylon, but Babylon was not the first world empire in the region that we call Mesopotamia. While it was the first empire in the image, it was actually the third world empire after Egypt and Assyria. So when we consider the image we are dealing with the third, fourth, fifth and sixth empires. The number 6 being associated with the final empire being split by 1 leg and 5 toes – 6, and 1 leg and 5 toes – 6.

Years later when Belshazzar was King of Babylon Daniel had a vision that provided more detail regarding the future kingdoms. Instead of one image representing four

kingdoms, Daniel's vision involved four beasts representing these four kingdoms.

Here is the vision: *"² Daniel spoke, saying, I saw in my vision by night, and behold, the four winds of heaven were stirring up the Great Sea. ³ And four great beasts came up from the sea, each different from the other. ⁴ The first was like a lion, and had eagle's wings. I watched till its wings were plucked off; and it was lifted up from the earth and made to stand on two feet like a man, and a man's heart was given to it. ⁵ And suddenly another beast, a second, like a bear. It was raised up on one side, and had three ribs in its mouth between its teeth. And they said thus to it: Arise, devour much flesh! ⁶ After this I looked, and there was another, like a leopard, which had on its back four wings of a bird. The beast also had four heads, and dominion was given to it. ⁷ After this I saw in the night visions, and behold, a fourth beast, dreadful and terrible, exceedingly strong. It had huge iron teeth; it was devouring, breaking in pieces, and trampling the residue with its feet. It was different from all the beasts that were before it, and it had ten horns. ⁸ I was considering the horns, and there was another horn, a little one, coming up among them, before whom three of the first horns were plucked out by the roots. And there, in this horn, were eyes like the eyes of a man, and a mouth speaking pompous words. ⁹ I watched till thrones were put in place, and the Ancient of Days was seated; His garment was white as snow, and the hair of His head was like pure wool. His throne was a fiery flame, Its wheels a burning fire; ¹⁰ A fiery stream issued and came forth from before Him. A thousand thousands ministered to Him; Ten thousand times ten thousand stood before Him. The court was seated, and the scrolls were opened. ¹¹ I watched then* because of the sound of the pompous words which the horn was speaking; I watched till the beast was slain, and its body destroyed and given to the burning flame. ¹² As for the rest of the beasts, they had their dominion taken away, yet their lives were prolonged for a season and a time. ¹³ *I was watching in the night visions, and behold, One like the Son of Man, coming with the clouds of heaven! He came to the Ancient of Days, and they brought Him near before Him.* ¹⁴ *Then to Him was given dominion and glory and a kingdom, that all peoples, nations, and languages should serve Him. His dominion is an everlasting dominion, which shall not pass away, and His kingdom the one which shall not be destroyed.* ¹⁵ I, Daniel, was grieved in my spirit within my body, and the visions of my head troubled me. ¹⁶ I came near to one of those who stood by, and asked him the truth of all this. So he told me and made known to me the interpretation of these things: ¹⁷ Those great beasts, which are four, are four kings which arise out of the earth. ¹⁸ *But the set apart ones of the Most High shall receive the kingdom, and possess the kingdom forever, even forever and ever.* ¹⁹ *Then I wished to know the truth about the fourth beast, which was different from all the others, exceedingly dreadful, with its teeth of iron and its nails of bronze, which devoured, broke in pieces, and trampled the residue with its feet;* ²⁰ and the ten horns that were on its head, and the other horn which came up, before which three fell, namely, that horn which had eyes and a mouth which spoke pompous words, whose appearance was greater than his fellows. ²¹ *I was watching; and the same horn was making war against the saints, and prevailing against them,* ²² *until the Ancient of Days came, and a judgment was made in favor of the set apart ones of the Most High, and the*

time came for the set apart ones to possess the kingdom.
²³ *Thus he said: The fourth beast shall be a fourth kingdom on earth, which shall be different from all other kingdoms, and shall devour the whole earth, trample it and break it in pieces.* ²⁴ *The ten horns are ten kings who shall arise from this kingdom. And another shall rise after them; He shall be different from the first ones, and shall subdue three kings.* ²⁵ *He shall speak pompous words against the Most High, shall persecute the saints of the Most High, and shall intend to change times and law. Then the saints shall be given into his hand for a time and times and half a time.* ²⁶ *But the court shall be seated, and they shall take away his dominion, to consume and destroy it forever.* ²⁷ *Then the kingdom and dominion, and the greatness of the kingdoms under the whole heaven, shall be given to the people, the saints of the Most High. His kingdom is an everlasting kingdom, and all dominions shall serve and obey Him."* Daniel 7:2-27

The word for "beast" in Daniel is different than in other portions of the Scriptures. Typically when refering to an animal the Hebrew word for "beast" is "hai" (ᚑᒾᕼ). The word literally means: "living thing." Interestingly, when Elohim "created" every "𐤎𐤊-living thing (ᚑᒾᕼ) He made each according to its kind. (Beresheet 1:24)

In Daniel, each "beast" is referred to as "hewah" (ᚑᎩᒾᕼ). Notice the addition of the "vav" (Ꭹ). The "vav" (Ꭹ) has the gematria value of 6 and is typically associated with man. So each "beast" in Daniel is intimately associated with man.

The text describes four "beast" kingdoms leading up to the end of the age and the Messiah. It is interesting to note the several instances where the text speaks of this eternal kingdom being "possessed" by the set apart ones. So Messiah, the aben stone, will destroy the mysterious fourth kingdom, which is the 6th and 7th serpent kingdom. The fourth actual transforms from Rome to the New World Order. The set apart ones will then "possess" (𐤔𐤟𐤟) the eternal kingdom, which means to "to hold in occupancy."

Just as the fourth kingdom in the image revealed to Nebuchedzezzar was perplexing, the vision of Daniel reveals how this kindgom was different from the others. Daniel was particularly disturbed by the fourth kingdom that would devour the whole earth. Instead of simply a kingdom that rose and fell, this kingdom transformed and extended through time. It ended up being mixed with man and angels and that kingdom is more specifically described in the Book of Revelation.

We already mentioned that the fourth kingdom began with the Roman Empire and then transitioned into a world empire. Just as with the ten toes in Nebuchadnezzars dream we see ten horns in Daniel vision. Because they are horns, and horns represent powers, we can discern that these ten horns represent ten kingdoms deriving from the Roman Empire  that was divided in two and then transformed. We know from history that the ten kingdoms of Rome were Britannia, Gallia, Hispania, Italia, Africa, Pannonia, Moesia, Thracia, Asiana and Oriens.

It is through this divided kingdom that we see the ten horns and the little horn with eyes and a mouth that speaks "pompous" words. The word "pompous" is not in the original text. Rather, this "little horn" speaks "words as an adversary against the Most High." The "little horn" is likened to an individual, rather than an impersonal kingdom. It sees and speaks like a man, and will speak against YHWH.

Interestingly, it will actually intend "to change the appointed times and the Torah." It also makes war against the set apart ones of YHWH until a judgment was rendered in their favor and the time came for them to possess the kingdom.

In the midst of this vision, Daniel actually sees the Throne of YHWH as was described by Ezekiel. There are certain proceedings occurring in the Court of Heaven while the little horn exists. There are additional thrones being set up and scrolls are opened. This scene will be elaborated further in a later Revelation given by the Messiah to His disciple named John.

For now, it is important to understand that this is a heavenly Court, and judgment is about to be rendered upon the kingdoms of the earth. It is during this proceeding that Messiah is given dominion over all the earth, that He, in turn, gives to His set apart ones to possess.

The "little horn" will be discussed further, but it is important to recognize that it is not the fourth beast, only a part of the beast. Many believe that it is describing the papacy ruling from Vatican City in Rome.

Interestingly, we currently see Europe as the dominant entity in the region, and the countries that make up the European Union are believed to be the descendents of the Northern Tribes of the House of Yisrael.[181] Some of those tribes eventually migrated to America. So there is a link between America and Europe. They both appear to be collaborating together in this quest to establish the New World Order.

We already mentioned the connection between the United States and Rome. Interestingly, the Club of Rome, formed in 1968 in the city of Rome is believed to be one of orginizations working to establish a one-world government. Their report entitled *Regionalized and Adaptive Model of the Global World System*, divides the world into ten political and

economic regions.

Remember that the kingdoms revealed to Nebuchadnezzar and Daniel were focused on Europe and the Near East. While there were certainly other civilizations around the planet, the context of Daniel was the City of Jerusalem and the Temple, and the empires that impacted those specific places. As a result, that is why we may not see every country in the world mentioned through the Scriptural prophecies.

Interestingly, the fourth beast empire in Daniel, which is really the 6th and 7th kingdoms, was different from all others. In fact, *"it will devour the whole earth, trample it and break it in pieces."* So we should not expect to see an empire looking like the others, at least not at the end. In fact, today we see numerous governments, organizations, groups and cabals working together behind the scenes and in public to establish a one world government – a new world order. We specifically saw how the United States  of America was essentially founded to bring about the New World Order. It is a revived Roman Empire and is likely a part of this 4th beast.

So it appears that the many nations of the earth will combine together to form this beast. We saw the symbols in America that connect it with the beast. Indeed, the entire concept of Europe, symbolized by the entity Europa, seems to fit well into popular end times expectations of the beast. For instance, the European Parliamentary building in Strasburg, France is modeled upon the popular painting of *The Tower of Babel* by Pieter Brueghel. Thus Europe appears to be mimicking ancient Babylon in many ways.

The ancient myth of Europa involves a woman being abducted by the sun god Zeus, in the form of a white bull.

Europa has been linked with the Canaanite goddess Astarte as well as the Egyptian goddess Hathor. In either case the source is Babylon. As a result of the mythology, Europa has even been portrayed as a woman riding a beast – symbology adopted by the European Union and even placed on its currency. So clearly there is a connection with Europe and the fourth beast or kingdom in the vision of Daniel.

Remember, in the ancient city of Babylon we saw mankind coming together unified in a religious, political and economic system in defiance to the kingdom of YHWH. This was a three part kingdom centered upon man. Since man was created on the 6th day, the number 6 is often attributed to man. This final world "beast" empire will be reviving Babylon, and unifying mankind in the very act of defiance and rebellion that resulted in the previous scattering. This will become even more evident when we examine "Mystery Babylon" in the Book of Revelation. In fact, this final kingdom will take center stage at the end of the age.

A very interesting comment often overlooked concerning this final kingdom is a mixing of seed. "*^{42} And as the toes of the feet were partly of iron and partly of clay, so the kingdom shall be partly strong and partly fragile. ^{43} As you saw iron mixed with ceramic clay, <u>they will mingle with the seed of men;</u> but they will not adhere to one another, just as iron does not mix with clay.*" Daniel 2:42-43 Again, this will likely be the recurrence of the mixing that took place when the Watchers mingled with the seed of men in the Days of Noah. This will be the final push for the serpent to establish his kingdom on earth. Just as YHWH judged the earth then, He will judge it again – possibly under similar conditions.

It was after the flood that the nations were established through the offspring of Noah. Now the kingdoms of the earth will be established by the stone (aben) *that was cut out of the mountain without hands.*" Daniel 2:34 This language is remiscent of the Tablets provided by YHWH on Sinai. The Tablets upon which His spoken words were written were originally cut from the Mountain by YHWH, likely taken from the Throne itself. This was a pattern for what Daniel describes occurring in the future. When Yahsuhua goes before the Heavenly Court and is given dominion, He will not be broken, but this time He will be the One doing the breaking.

The "aben" ($\mathcal{Y}\mathcal{I}\mathcal{K}$) in the vision of Daniel is none other than the Messiah given authority to destroy the earthly kingdoms so that He can establish the Kingdom of YHWH on the planet. The "aben" ($\mathcal{Y}\mathcal{I}\mathcal{K}$) will destroy the final empire of man that rules the earth at the end of the age.

So through the Babylonian King Nebuchadnezzar, an image of future governments was provided. While Daniel was under Babylonian dominion, he was then given a vision depicting those four kingdoms as four beasts. (Daniel 7) He was later given another vision providing even more detail regarding the fall of the Medo-Perisan Empire, and the rise of the Grecian Empire under Alexander. (Daniel 8) On either 10 or 11 June 323 BC, Alexander died in the palace of Nebuchadnezzar II, in Babylon, at age 32. After his death in the city of Babylon, his empire was divided by his 4 generals: 1) Lysimachus in the north, 2) Seleucus in the east, 3) Cassander in the west, and 4) Ptolemy in the south.

Remember that the image and the vision of the four beasts historically pick up at neo-Babylon. There had been previous kingdoms after the disbursion from Babel, including Egypt and Assyria that had all been dealt with by YHWH. The purpose of the information in Daniel was to relate the remaining kingdoms that would exist prior to the Kingdom of YHWH being restored on the planet. This would all occur

within the seven day (millennium) patterns established in the beginning.

These kingdoms ultimately became opposed to YHWH. Nebuchadnezzar of the Babylonian Empire and Cyrus of the Medo-Persian Empire were each considered servants of YHWH. Cyrus was even called an "anointed servant." (Isaiah 45:1) They appear to be exceptions. Most kingdoms did not properly honor YHWH as the One and Only Elohim, although they did serve Him exactly as He needed them. As with the Assyrians punishing the House of Yisrael, the Babylonians were used to punish the House of Yahudah.

Just as the Assyrians were later punished after being used as a tool for punishing the House of Yisrael, so too the Babylonians would also be punished after being used to punish the House of Yahudah. In fact, it was the punishment of Babylon that triggered some of the most mysterious revelations provided through the Book of Daniel.

Remember that prior to the exile of the House of Yahudah, the Prophet Jeremiah had prophesied two different 70 year periods of punishment – one for Babylon and one for the House of Yahudah. The prophecy provided 70 years until Babylon would be punished and also provided a 70 year duration for the punishment of the House of Yahudah.

Daniel actually witnessed the punishment upon Babylon during the famous "handwriting on the wall" incident. (Daniel 5) While the Babylonian King Belshazzar was busy profaning the Temple vessels taken by Nebuchadnezzar, a hand appeared and wrote on the wall. Daniel was able to translate the words that predicted the fall of Babylon. That very night the Medo-Persians conquered Babylon.

Babylon was indeed punished after 70 years. They were conquered by Cyrus, the Medo-Persian ruler. The very night that Belshazzar saw the handwriting on the wall. Cyrus lowered the water of the Euphrates River, allowing his troops to enter into the City of Babylon unhindered. The gates of the city were then opened up from the inside allowing Cyrus to conquer the city without besieging and destroying it.

Incredibly, the prophet Isaiah had foretold this event centuries earlier. He actually named Cyrus and indicated that he would rebuild the City of Jerusalem and the Temple. Cyrus would even be called the "anointed" (moshiach) of YHWH.

"44:28 Who says of Cyrus, He is My shepherd, and he shall perform all My pleasure, saying to Jerusalem, 'You shall be built, and to the temple, "Your foundation shall be laid. 45:1 Thus says YHWH to His anointed, To Cyrus, whose right hand I have held - To subdue nations before him and loose the armor of kings, To open before him the double doors, so that the gates will not be shut: 2 I will go before you and make the crooked places straight; I will break in pieces the gates of bronze and cut the bars of iron. 3 I will give you the treasures of darkness and hidden riches of secret places, that you may know that I, YHWH, Who call you by your name, Am the Elohi of Yisrael. 4 For Yaakob My servant's sake, and Yisrael My elect, I have even called you by your name; I have named you, though you have not known Me." Isaiah 44:28-45:4

Many speculate that Daniel actually approached Cyrus and read this prophecy to him as he entered the city of Babylon. This would have certainly made Cyrus predisposed to favor Daniel, and to actually rebuild the City of Jerusalem and the Temple.

As a result of seeing the fulfillment of the 70 year prophecy concerning the punishment of Babylon, along with the hope for the rebuilding of the City and the Temple, Daniel greatly desired to know when the exile of the House of Yahudah would end.

The problem was that the House of Yahudah

experienced 7 different Babylonian exiles over a span of many years. So the question would be: When did the 70 years begin, and when would it end? Would the clock start running with the first exile or with the last and final exile? As the 70 years was approaching, Daniel was praying about the subject.

That is the context of the famous "70 Week" prophecy actually given to Daniel from the Messenger Gabriel. This is another of the many unique distinctions attributed to Daniel. He was given different information while he was in different kingdoms. After the fall of Babylon he transitioned into the second beast – the silver portion of the image.

The context of Daniel is extremely important to understand in order to grasp the information provided to him. You must understand the order of historical events as well as the subject of his prayers and the responses given to those prayers.

Daniel was from the House of Yahudim. He was from the best and the brightest of the Yahudim, from the royal courts. He was given special favor and giftings from YHWH, probably due to his diligent obedience to the commandments as can be read in the beginning of the text. As a result, he was elevated within the Babylonian Kingdom. He knew the Scriptures and specifically he was keeping track of time. He knew that Jeremiah had previously provided that Babylon would be punished after seventy years, and that the House of Yahudah would be exiled for 70 years. (see Yirmeyahu 25:11-12 and 29:10)

Therefore, he was interested in the fate of his people – the House of Yahudah. He was also interested in the City of Jerusalem and the temple of YHWH that had been destroyed. As a result, the information provided to him was primarily limited to those subjects.

Interestingly, while he was praying about a 70 year

period, he was given a vision concerning 70 weeks. This should make one wonder about the significance of the number 70. The word for circumcise is "muwl" (𐤋𐤅), and the gematria value for "muwl" is 70. It is helpful to think of circumcision when we examine these passages concerning the number 70. The Scriptures speak primarily of two circumcisions – the circumcision of the flesh and the circumcision of the heart.

The circumcision of the flesh was the preliminary circumcision as an outward sign of the Covenant made with Abraham. It is a one time event that does not reflect the condition of a person's heart. The circumcision of the flesh was supposed to be followed by the circumcision of the heart, which was a second circumcision.

The circumcision of the heart is spiritual, and it is the circumcision of the Messiah Yahushua. In fact that was hinted to after the Children of Yisrael crossed the Jordan and entered into the Promised Land. The Yisraelites had been circumcised before they left Egypt so that they could partake of the Passover in Egypt. After experiencing 40 years of wandering, a new generation needed to be circumcised so they could partake of the Passover in the Promised Land.

Here is the text describing that event. "*At that time YHWH said to Joshua (Yahushua), Make flint knives for yourself, and circumcise* ✗𐤊*-sons of-Yisrael again the second time.*" Joshua 5:2 Notice the Aleph Taw (✗𐤊) as the One Who circumcises the sons of Yisrael "a second time." This is a prophetic passage concerning the circumcision performed by the Messiah in the Land - not the one in Egypt. The eighth day circumcision is a prophetic picture of the prophetic fulfillment of the 8th Day Feast, after the seven day Feast of Succot. It is when those who are circumcised in their hearts are adopted by YHWH and become sons of Elohim. (see Hoshea 1)

As discussed previously, the number 70 is also associated with "the Nations" since this was the number attributed the original nations that developed from the offspring of Noah. It is also significant because seventy (70) is the number of souls mentioned from the House of Yaakob who went into Egypt.

"*26 All the persons who went with Yaakob to Egypt, who came from his body, besides Jacob's sons' wives, were sixty-six persons in all. 27 And the sons of Joseph who were born to him in Egypt were two persons. All the persons of the house of Yaakob who went to Egypt were seventy.*" Beresheet 46:26-27 So 70 from the House of Yaakob went into Egypt and later the Children of Yisrael were delivered from bondage. This has great prophetic significance.

Interestingly, the Hebrew word for "wine" is "yayin" (ילל) that has a gematria value of 70. So too is the word for "the doorpost" – "ha'mezuzah" (הזוזמה). Both of these words and concepts become important when we examine the wine harvest at the Appointed Time of Succot, and the process of becoming a servant at the doorpost.[183]

When we examine the number 70 detailed in Daniel we see that the 70 years were a period of punishment, while the 70 weeks provided a solution. It was directly related to the circumcision of Yahushua. We then see through the numbers, related concepts combined with time. This shows how the Hebrew Language is multi-dimensional. It was, after all the language of creation and transcends space and time.

Now this ties in with the interpretation of the 70 weeks that has confounded many. Daniel may have only been inquiring into the end of the exile, but the answer provided much more. It is important to recognize that Daniel was diligently praying for an answer to a specific question.

He undersood the Covenant, and the fact that YHWH keeps His Covenant and shows mercy to those "*who*

love Him and keep His commandments." That is an important point which we will revisit as we examine those who overcome in the end.

Read what he was specifically referring to when he prayed. *". . . I, Daniel, understood by the scrolls the number of the years specified by the word of YHWH through Jeremiah the prophet, that He would accomplish seventy years in the desolations of Jerusalem."* Daniel 9:2 He understood that the House of Yahudah had been punished, and Jerusalem had been desolate for seventy years. So this desolation resulted from an attack. It was not a one-time event, but rather a condition that lasted for the entire 70 year period of punishment.

Daniel recounts the following answer to his petition: *"20 Now while I was speaking, praying, and confessing my sin and the sin of my people Yisrael, and presenting my supplication before YHWH my Elohay for the set apart mountain of my Elohay, 21 yes, while I was speaking in prayer, the man Gabriel, whom I had seen in the vision at the beginning, being caused to fly swiftly, reached me about the time of the evening offering. 22 And he informed me, and talked with me, and said, O Daniel, I have now come forth to give you skill to understand. 23 At the beginning of your supplications the command went out, and I have come to tell you, for you are greatly beloved; therefore consider the matter, and understand the vision: 24 Seventy weeks are determined for your people and for your set apart city, to finish the transgression, to make an end of sins, to make atonement (רפך) for iniquity, to bring in everlasting righteousness, to seal up vision and prophecy, and to anoint the Most Holy. 25 Know therefore and understand, that from the going forth of the command to restore and build Jerusalem until Messiah the Prince, there shall be seven weeks and sixty-two weeks; the street shall be built again, and the wall, even in troublesome times. 26 And after the sixty-two weeks Messiah shall be cut off, but not for Himself; and the people of the prince who is to come shall destroy the city and the sanctuary. The end of it shall be*

with a flood, and till the end of the war desolations are determined.
²⁷ Then he shall confirm a covenant with many for one week; but in
the middle of the week he shall bring an end to slaughtering and
meal offering. And on the wing of abominations shall be one who
makes desolate, even until the consummation, which is determined,
is poured out on the desolate." Daniel 9:20-27

We know that the evening offering occurred at
sunset, so Daniel continued to offer up prayer and praise at
this important time of day despite the absence of a Temple.
When the messenger Gabriel appeared he gave Daniel skill to
understand. Then he provided Daniel, not only a time frame
for the appearance of the Messiah, but a detailed list of items
that the Messiah was to accomplish.

He provided Daniel with a framework of seventy (70)
"weeks" in which these matters would be completed. In
Hebrew we read "shabuyim shabuyim" (שבעים
שבעים). These words are exactly the same. The text
actually reads "seventy sevens." These periods of sevens are
then divided into 7 "weeks," 62 "weeks" and 1 "week"
providing a total of seventy "weeks." These seventy (70)
weeks were specifically related to the people and the set apart
city. The time period would begin with a decree and after the
seven (7) and the sixty two (62), Messiah the Prince would be
revealed. The remaining week involves a covenant.

People have poured over these numbers for centuries
wondering about their meaning. There are a variety of issues
that need to be resolved to understand this passage, including
the starting point. One very important question is: When
was the going forth of the command or word? Was it the
petition of Daniel, was it the command from heaven that
resulted from Daniel's request, or was it some decree made by
a ruler?

Also how do we deal with these various periods of
time? Are they the same lengths or are they different? It is

generally understood that the "weeks" are seven (7) year periods, but if Gabriel had wanted to give Daniel a number of years he could have simply told him 49 years, 434 years and 7 years. And if they were all consecutive, Gabriel could have simply told Daniel there were 490 years. He was obviously telling Daniel a mystery that needed skill to understand. What takes understanding is the fact that these periods of 7 were necessarily years. Those that were years were not arbitrary years - they were likely Shemitah years or rather Shemitah cycles.

The command concerning the Shemitah year has already been mentioned, but it bears repeating. *"10 For six years you are to sow your fields and harvest the crops, 11 but during the seventh year let the Land lie unplowed and unused. Then the poor among your people may get food from it, and the wild animals may eat what they leave. Do the same with your vineyard and your olive grove."* Shemot 23:10-11 (see also Debarim 15)

Every seventh year the Yisraelites were supposed to let the Land rest. Thus, there was a Sabbath for the Land every seven years. Just as the seven day count began at creation, so too did the seven (7) year Shemitah count. The Shemitah year would begin on the first day of the seventh month on Yom Teruah, which marks the beginning of physical Creation. From this day until the following Yom Teruah there would be no official harvest.

This cycle of sevens would occur within another cycle of sevens – The Jubilee Cycle. At the end of the seventh Shemitah year there would be a 9 day period between Yom Teruah until Yom Kippur, which would then mark the beginning of the Jubilee Year – the fiftieth year.

Amazingly, Yisrael failed to obey the command concerning the Shemitah year, and that was the reason why Yahudah was in exile for 70 years. YHWH was giving His Land the rest that He had commanded. (2 Chronicles 36:21)

So there is a powerful connection between the 70 year period of punishment concluding at the same time the 70 "week" period concerning the Messiah was revealed. They were directly connected to one another.

It is important to recognize that the Shemitah cycles are intimately connected with the Jubilee (yobel). *"³ For six years sow your fields, and for six years prune your vineyards and gather their crops. ⁴ But in the seventh year the Land is to have a Sabbath of rest, a Sabbath to YHWH. Do not sow your fields or prune your vineyards. ⁵ Do not reap what grows of itself or harvest the grapes of your untended vines. The Land is to have a year of rest. ⁶ Whatever the Land yields during the sabbath year will be food for you - for yourself, your manservant and maidservant, and the hired worker and temporary resident who live among you, ⁷ as well as for your livestock and the wild animals in your land. Whatever the Land produces may be eaten. ⁸ Count off seven Sabbaths of years - seven times seven years - so that the seven Sabbaths of years amount to a period of forty-nine years. ⁹ Then have the shofar sounded everywhere on the tenth day of the seventh month; on the Day of Atonement sound the shofar throughout your Land. ¹⁰ Consecrate the fiftieth year and proclaim liberty throughout the land to all its inhabitants. It shall be a Jubilee (Yobel) for you; each one of you is to return to his family property and each to his own clan. ¹¹ The fiftieth year shall be a Jubilee (Yobel) for you; do not sow and do not reap what grows of itself or harvest the untended vines. ¹² For it is a jubilee and is to be holy for you; eat only what is taken directly from the fields."* Vayiqra 25:3-12

The imagery of the Jubilee is reminiscent of the Feast of Shabuot, sometimes referred to as Pentecost. Shabuot involves this same count in days, and it occurs every year to remind us of the Jubilee. With that foundation being laid, let us now look at various aspects of the 70 "weeks" or "sevens" prophecy, and see if we can discern just what and when Gabriel is referring to.

From the information given to Daniel by Gabriel, we discern that there is a command issued "to restore and rebuild Jerusalem." We further know that from the issuance of that command until Messiah the prince shall be 7 "sevens" and 62 "sevens." We are further told *"after the sixty-two weeks Messiah shall be cut off, but not for Himself."* Sometime after the Messiah is "cut off" the city and the Temple would be destroyed. There is also a 1 "seven" where a Covenant is "confirmed." No clear indication is given as to when this 1 "seven" takes place.

Therefore, according to Gabriel, we should be looking at a cycle consisting of a period of time consisting of seven (7) multiplied by seven (7), which should lead us either to Shabuot, a cycle of 7 weeks, or the Jubilee, a cycle of 7 Shemitah years. We should also be focusing on a period of time consisting of sixty-two (62) multiplied by seven (7).

For the clock to begin, we need to look for the specific word or decree that was issued concerning restoring and rebuilding Jerusalem, not simply the Temple. This would obviously be linked with the end of the 70 year period of exile that was the very reason why Daniel was praying in the first place.

There is very specific information in the Scriptures concerning a governmental decree that seems to meet the criteria. We read in Ezra the following account: *" Now in the first year of Cyrus king of Persia, that the Word of YHWH by the mouth of Yirmeyahu might be fulfilled, YHWH stirred up the spirit of Cyrus king of Persia, so that he made a proclamation throughout all his kingdom, and also put it in writing, saying, ² 'Thus says Cyrus king of Persia: All the kingdoms of the Earth YHWH Elohim of heaven has given me. And He has commanded me to build Him a House at Jerusalem which is in Yahudah. ³ Who is among you of all His people? May his Elohim be with him, and let him go up to Jerusalem which is in Yahudah, and build the House of*

YHWH, Elohim of Yisrael (He is Elohim), which is in Jerusalem. *And whoever is left in any place where he dwells, let the men of his place help him with silver and gold, with goods and livestock, besides the freewill offerings for the house of Elohim which is in Jerusalem. *Then the heads of the fathers' Houses of Yahudah and Benjamin, and the priests and the Levites, with all whose spirits Elohim had moved, arose to go up and build the House of YHWH which is in Jerusalem. *And all those who were around them encouraged them with articles of silver and gold, with goods and livestock, and with precious things, besides all that was willingly offered. *King Cyrus also brought out the articles of the House of YHWH, which Nebuchadnezzar had taken from Jerusalem and put in the temple of his gods; *and Cyrus king of Persia brought them out by the hand of Mithredath the treasurer, and counted them out to Sheshbazzar the prince of Yahudah."* Ezra 1:1-8

This decree of Cyrus to return and rebuild the House was issued in the first year of his reign in 526 BCE.* What an amazing event, the King of a pagan nation declared YHWH to be Elohim. He then took on the responsibility of rebuilding the House of YHWH, returning all of the treasures that had been taken from the House by the Babylonians, and allowing the captives of Yahudah to return to their Land.

Notice that it was only those from the Tribes of Yahudah, Benjamin and the Levites who returned. That was because these were the Tribes constituting the House of Yahudah, taken captive by the Babylonians. The other tribes from the House of Yisrael had been removed from the Land and taken by the Assyrians who moved them into the regions of the north. They were not scheduled to return to the Land as their punishment would not be completed until between 2007 and 2016 CE.

The issuance of the decree of Cyrus was no doubt a wonderful part of the fulfillment of the second 70 year prophecy by allowing the Yahudim to return. Regardless, they still had a long and difficult road ahead of them. Over time, the decree lost its force, until it was later found and readdressed. Artaxerxes I, the third King of the Persian Empire and grandson of Darius I, reissued the decree and advanced funds to finish the House in 461 BCE.* He later decreed the rebuilding of Jerusalem in 443 BCE.*

As a result of these different decrees, and because of the funding problems, the rebuilding of the Altar and the Temple experienced great delays, and was fraught with difficulties. Seventy years passed from the original decree to rebuild the Second Temple by Cyrus in 526 BCE,* to its completion in 456 BCE.* It was during this period that we read certain prophets such as Haggai and Zechariah giving encouragement and direction to those who returned.

We know from historical records that while the original decree was given in the first year of Cyrus, there were numerous subsequent decrees that followed. So the question is which one of those decrees, if any, would start the count on Daniel's 70 weeks. There was only one that would qualify, because all others were tied specifically with the Temple. The decree we are looking for involved rebuilding Jerusalem. (See Daniel 9:25).

Artaxerxes I, in the 7th year of his reign in 456 BCE decreed that the Judeans could return under Ezra. Here is the decree as provided in the text of Ezra.

"*7* Some of the Yisraelites, including priests, Levites, singers, gatekeepers and Temple servants, also came up to Jerusalem in the seventh year of King Artaxerxes. *8* Ezra arrived in Jerusalem in the fifth month of the seventh year of the king. *9* He had begun his journey from Babylon on the first day of the first month, and he arrived in Jerusalem on the first day of the fifth month, for the gracious Hand of his Elohim was on him. *10* For Ezra had devoted himself to the study and observance of the Torah of YHWH, and to teaching its decrees and laws in Yisrael. [11] This is a copy of the letter King Artaxerxes had given to Ezra the priest and teacher, a man learned in matters concerning the commands and decrees of YHWH for Yisrael: [12] Artaxerxes, king of kings, To Ezra the priest, a teacher of the Law of the Elah of heaven: Greetings. [13] Now I decree that any of the Yisraelites in my kingdom, including priests and Levites, who wish to go to Jerusalem with you, may go. [14] *You are sent by the king and his seven advisers to inquire about Yahudah and Jerusalem with regard to the Torah of your Elah, which is in your hand.* [15] Moreover, you are to take with you the silver and gold that the king and his advisers have freely given to the Elah of Yisrael, whose dwelling is in Jerusalem, [16] together with all the silver and gold you may obtain from the province of Babylon, as well as the freewill offerings of the people and priests for the Temple of their Elah in Jerusalem. [17] With this money be sure to buy bulls, rams and male lambs, together with their grain offerings and drink offerings, and sacrifice them on the altar of the Temple of your Elah in Jerusalem. [18] You and your brother Yahudim may then do whatever seems best with the rest of the silver and gold, in accordance with the will of your Elah. [19] Deliver to the Elah of Jerusalem all the articles entrusted to you for worship in the Temple of your Elah. [20] And anything else needed for the Temple of your Elah that you may have occasion to supply, you may provide from the royal treasury. [21] Now I, King Artaxerxes, order all the treasurers of Trans-Euphrates to provide with diligence whatever Ezra the priest, a teacher of the Torah of the Elah of heaven, may ask of you - [22] up to a hundred talents of silver, a hundred cors of wheat, a hundred baths of wine, a hundred baths of olive oil, and salt without limit. [23] Whatever the Elah of heaven has prescribed, let it be done

with diligence for the Temple of the Elah of heaven. Why should there be wrath against the realm of the king and of his sons? [24] *You are also to know that you have no authority to impose taxes, tribute or duty on any of the priests, Levites, singers, gatekeepers, Temple servants or other workers at this house of Elah.* [25] *And you, Ezra, in accordance with the wisdom of your Elah, which you possess, appoint magistrates and judges to administer justice to all the people of Trans-Euphrates - all who know the laws of your Elah. And you are to teach any who do not know them.* [26] *Whoever does not obey the laws of your Elah and the law of the king must surely be punished by death, banishment, confiscation of property, or imprisonment."*
Ezra 7:12-26

Notice the mention of Jerusalem nine times in this passage alone.[184] Interestingly though, the decree only dealt with the Temple. Despite this great decree given to Ezra, by the 20th year of Artaxerxes I, we read about Nehemiah requesting help from this same king. One day the King noticed that the countenance of Nehemiah, his cup bearer, was down and he inquired regarding the problem. Nehemiah responded concerning the difficulties that his people were experiencing in Jerusalem.

"[1] And it came to pass in the month of Nisan, in the 20th year of King Artaxerxes, when wine was before him, that I took the wine and gave it to the king. Now I had never been sad in his presence before. [2] *Therefore the king said to me, Why is your face sad, since you are not sick? This is nothing but sorrow of heart. So I became dreadfully afraid,* [3] *and said to the king, May the king live forever! Why should my face not be sad, when the city, the place of my fathers' tombs, lies waste, and its gates are burned with fire?* [4] *Then the king said to me, What do you request? So I prayed to the Elohim of heaven.* [5] *If it pleases the king and if your servant has found favor in his sight, let him send me to the city in Yahudah*

where my fathers are buried so that I can rebuild it. [6] *Then the king, with the queen sitting beside him, asked me, How long will your journey take, and when will you get back? It pleased the king to send me; so I set a time.* [7] *I also said to him, If it pleases the king, may I have letters to the governors of Trans-Euphrates, so that they will provide me safe-conduct until I arrive in Yahudah?* [8] *And may I have a letter to Asaph, keeper of the king's forest, so he will give me timber to make beams for the gates of the citadel by the Temple and for the city wall and for the residence I will occupy? And because the gracious hand of my Elohim was upon me, the king granted my requests.* [9] *So I went to the governors of Trans-Euphrates and gave them the king's letters. The king had also sent army officers and cavalry with me."* Nehemiah 2:1-9

So this was this decree, in 443 BCE to rebuild Jerusalem, that initiated the count in Daniel's 70 "seven's" prophecy. From the decree to rebuild Jerusalem in the twentieth year of Artaxerxes I (Nehemiah 2:1-9) until Messiah the Prince, Daniel was told there would be seven (7) weeks and sixty-two (62) weeks (Daniel 9:25). *"[25] Know and understand this: From the issuing of the decree to restore and rebuild Jerusalem until the Messiah the Prince, there will be seven sevens and sixty two sevens. It will be rebuilt with streets and a trench, but in times of trouble.* [26] *After the sixty-two sevens, the Anointed One will be cut off and will have nothing."* Daniel 9:25-26

The fact that these two divisions are mentioned separately could lead one to reasonably assume that they are different time periods. They could either be different measurements of time, or they simply might not be continuous.

Daniel was looking for the restoration of the city of Jerusalem, which obviously included the House of YHWH. He was asking about a literal rebuilding of the city, and he was given a literal time frame. This count historically began in the 20th of Artaxerxes according to Nehemiah 2:1-9. This was well understood and accounted for by Sextus Julius Africanus in his 5 volume work, written in the 2nd century CE, entitled *Chronographiai*. The double dated Elephantine Letters place Artaxerxes ascension in Egypt in 465 BCE. That would place the 20th of Artaxerxes in Egypt in 445 BCE, but his reign in Persia began in 443 BCE.[185]

Some believe that the seven weeks involved seven Shemittah cycles, or 49 years, when Malachi prophesied leading to a sealing up of vision, and end of prophesy concerning the Messiah and the renewed Covenant.[186] This may be, but the first 7 sevens seem to be directly related to the streets and walls being rebuilt. We know that Nehemiah finished rebuilding the walls on Day 25 of Month 6. (Nehemiah 6:15) Interestingly, in the year 445 BCE there were seven Sabbaths included between Day 3 of Month 5 when the work began, to Day 25 of Month 6, when the work was completed.

Whatever count involved the 7 sevens, what can be said with certainty is that 62 Shemitah cycles, with eight (8) intervening Jubilee years, covers a span of 443 years. All scholars would agree that 443 years reckoned from the 20th of Artaxerxes, would bring one to around the turn of the millennium when we would anticipate seeing the Messiah.

Indeed, we know that Yahushua was born on September 11, 3 BCE.[187] This was Yom Teruah, a day when shofars were blasted around the land. This was right when we would expect to see the Messiah according to the timeline provided through Daniel. Artaxerxes I acceded to the throne of Persia in 463 BCE, two years after acceding to the throne of Egypt under his father Xerxes I. The 20th year of Artaxerxes I, king of Persia was therefore in 443 BCE, and it was in month 1 of this year that Artaxerxes made a decree for Nehemiah to go to Jerusalem as governor to rebuild "the city

of my father's tombs" – Jerusalem. (Nehemiah 2:5)

The spring of 443 BCE was in year 1 of Shemittah Cycle 497 and counting to the 62nd Sabbath year of the 62nd Shemittah Cycle takes one to Yom Teruah in 2 BCE, which begins year 7 of Shemittah Cycle 558 on the Messiah's first birthday. This was likely the day that the Magi "anointed" the "prince" whom they declared had been born King of the Yahudim. (Matthew 2:1-12).[188]

The Magi actually came to the "house" where the "young child" was located according to Matthew 2:11. Many students of Scripture have noted that the account in Matthew 2:11 describes a different place and a different time than the circumstances of the Messiah's birth in Bethlehem described in Luke 2:7-20. So we can see that the 62 "weeks" were completed when the Messiah was "anointed" and after this time we would expect the Messiah to be cut off.

If we again look at the prophecy in Daniel we should note that it states: "*after the sixty-two (62) weeks Moshiach will be cut off.*" Daniel 9:26 The Hebrew text uses the word "karath" (ХЧҮ) for "cut off." The word "karath" means "cut" or "covenant." Through the Prophets, YHWH revealed His plan to restore the Kingdom by His Servant, His Right Arm - the Messiah. The Covenant made with Abraham and mediated by Mosheh at Sinai had been broken by Yisrael.

Through the Covenant made with Abraham, we see that the One that passed through the pieces was subject to the penalty of death. The death of that One would atone just as was shown through the pattern of Abraham and Yitshaq. YHWH would provide the Lamb, His only Son, who would be cut off during Passover.

Therefore, the information given to Daniel was good news coupled with bad news. It started with a decree to return and rebuild, followed by the Messiah, but then then it revealed that the Messiah would be cut off and the City and

the Temple would be destroyed.

Those 70 weeks are divided into 3 different increments – 7 weeks, 62 weeks and 1 week. The question is how these weeks are calculated. There is no denying the relationship between these weeks and the Sabbatical year, also known as the Shemitah Cycle. The reason why the House of Yahudah was punished for 70 years was due to their failure to observe the Sabbatical Year for 490 years. Therefore, we can safely assume that this 70 week period of restoration would revolve, in some way, around the Shemitah Cycle.

Indeed, we see the first seven and sixty two week periods were actually "weeks of years" that began with the command to rebuild Jerusalem, and concluded with the appearance of Yahushua. Now interpreting these weeks as "weeks of years" makes sense since the period involves the restoration of the Land.

"*Know and understand that* from the going forth of the command to restore and build Jerusalem until Messiah the Prince, *There shall be* seven weeks and sixty-two weeks;" Daniel 9:25. So couched within this text we have a beginning point - the going forth of the command, and and end point – the cutting off of Messiah the Prince.

We know that Yahushua was born on September 11, 3 BCE. This was Yom Teruah, a day when shofars were blasted around the land. We also know that Yahushua was crucified on Passover Day, Wednesday, March 24, 34 CE at 3:00 pm. The 7 "sevens" and the 62 "sevens" were fulfilled by the birth and anointing of the Messiah. That leaves us with one week left to accomplish those things provided in Daniel 9:24.

Many believe this last week is also a week of years, and is a future event. There is nothing in Daniel that would force us to that conclusion. Remember that the Messiah had

many functions and we are told certain things in Daniel that are encompassed within a specific timeframe – the restoration of Jerusalem and the subsequent destruction of Jerusalem.

He was shown three different segments of time – those led up to the rebuilding of the Temple and the City of Jerusalem. The final time segment of one week was to occur after the rebuilding, but before the subsequent destruction.

The work described within that week is nothing more than the Aleph Taw (✗𝙆) doing the work necessary to restore creation. What they fail to realize is that the work being described is a restoration of creation. Just as creation occurred within one week of days, such was the duration of the work of Messiah to restore Creation – the final week of His life. There have been and false teachings concerning this final week that lead many to try to believe that there is a seven year period of tribulation in the end concluding with the return of the Messiah. As we shall see, this is not necessarily the case

We know Daniel was praying about the Covenant. Specifically he was praying about the Covenant people who were in exile, the City of Jerusalem and the Temple. He was given an answer within the context of the Covenant of YHWH. Incredibly, many interpret Daniel 9:27 as meaning that the antichrist will confirm some unknown covenant for seven years. This interpretation is not suitable given the context of the entire passage, which is the Covenant with Yisrael.

Let us look at that passage again: *"Then he shall confirm a covenant with many for one week; but in the middle of the week he shall bring an end to slaughtering and meal offering. And on the wing of abominations shall be one who makes desolate, even until the consummation, which is determined, is poured out on the desolate."* Daniel 9:27

The word for "confirm" is "gaber" (ﬧﬨ﬩ﬧ), which means: *"to elevate or make superior."* That is exactly what Yahushua did during His final week. (Hebrews 7:22, 8:6) He was crucified on a Wednesday, in the middle of a week, after He renewed and elevated the Covenant at the Passover meal. He was then resurrected on Shabbat, the last day of the week.

Therefore, it would appear that the "he" confirming the "covenant" in the 70th week was the Messiah during a literal week, renewing the Covenant between YHWH and Yisrael.

Here is what was supposed to happen within the 70 weeks. *"Seventy weeks are determined for your people and for your holy city, to finish the transgression, to make an end of sins, to make atonement (kippur) for iniquity, to bring in everlasting righteousness, to seal up vision and prophecy, and to anoint (moshiach) the Most Holy."* Daniel 9:24

We know that the Messiah was the Covenant. He was given by YHWH as a Covenant to the people – a light to the Nations. (Isaiah 42:5-6) So Messiah was the Covenant and we saw Him as the smoke and the fire that passed between the pieces and through the blood. This final week in the prophecy was not specified to be at the end of the age. In fact, the 70 weeks would include "sealing up" vision and prophecy that we understand would be unsealed at the end of the age. (Daniel 12:4; Revelation 6-8)

The vision and the prophecy was that concerning the Messiah and the Covenant. The sealing up vision and prophecy would not occur at the end of the age. Rather, it is at the end of the age that the vision and prophecy would later be unsealed and fulfilled.

So people have assumed that this 70th week remains open and unfulfilled when, in fact, that 70th week has long since been fulfilled by the Messiah. While we will talk extensively about the Messiah in the next chapter, for the

sake of dealing with Daniel we will briefly look at the final week of the life of Yahushua.

We know that during the Passover meal, Yahushua renewed the Covenant through His flesh and blood. (Matthew 26:28; Mark 14:24; Luke 22:20) This renewed Covenant was superior to the prior Covenant that had been broken. (Hebrews 7:22, 8:6). The year Yahushua was crucified, the Passover fell on a Tuesday evening. This began Day 4 of the Scriptural week. Remember that the Scriptural Day begins in the evening. Yahushua died on Wednesday afternoon. While this was a different day on the solar calendar, it was the same day, Day 4, on the Scriptural calendar. Therefore, Yahushua was "cut off" in the midst of the week.

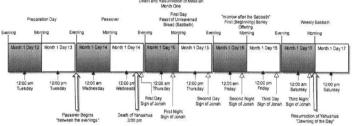

While modern popular teaching attributes the covenant of the 70th week to an "anti-christ," earlier understanding always recognized that Covenant as the promised renewed Covenant.[189] In fact, it was evident that the Covenant had to be renewed with the House of Yisrael and the House of Yahudah in order to reconcile the divided Kingdom. Sadly, Christianity has so misunderstood the Covenant and the required renewal, that the work of the Messiah is often attributed to the so-called "anti-christ."

A text that can properly be attributed to an "anti-christ" or "prince who is to come" is typically translated as follows: "And on the wing of abominations shall be one who makes desolate, even until the consummation, which is determined, is *poured out on the desolate.*" Daniel 9:27b In a translation from the Septuigant we read: "*and on the temple [shall be] the abomination of desolations; and at the end of time an end shall be put to the desolation.*"

It is in this rendering that we first read about "the abomination of desolations." This is something that Yahushua will later refer to, but for now it is important to recognize that the One Who makes the Covenant is Yahushua. It is the people of "the prince who is to come" who destroyed the City of Jerusalem, and made it desolate, after the death and resurrection of Yahushua. That desolation would continue until the end of the age.

The "abomination of desolations" referred to in that passage occurred in 70 AD when the Roman army under the leadership of Titus destroyed the Temple and burned the city. Later, around 135 AD, the Roman army, under the leadership of Hadrian completely razed the city of Jerusalem. It essentially vanished from existence, and was replaced by a pagan city called Aelia Capitolina.

"Jerusalem was still in ruins from the First Jewish-Roman War in 70. Josephus, a contemporary, reports that Jerusalem . . . was so thoroughly razed to the ground by those that demolished it to its foundations, that nothing was left that could ever persuade visitors that it had once been a place of habitation. When the Roman Emperor Hadrian vowed to rebuild Jerusalem from the wreckage in 130, he considered reconstructing Jerusalem as a gift for the Jewish people. The Jews awaited with hope, but then after Hadrian visited Jerusalem, he decided to rebuild the city as a Roman colony which would be inhabited by his legionnaires.[2] Hadrian's new plans included temples to the major regional deities, and certain Roman gods, in particular Jupiter Capitolinus. Jews secretly started putting aside arms from the Roman munitions workshops; soon after, a revolt broke out under

Simeon ben Kosiba. This Bar Kokhba revolt, which the Romans managed to suppress, enraged Hadrian, and he came to be determined to erase Judaism from the province. Circumcision was forbidden, Iudaea province was renamed Syria Palaestina and Jews (formally all circumcised men) were banned from entering the city on pain of death."[190]

So the Roman Empire, the 4th empire, made the Temple and the City into a desolation, and then set up an abomination over it all. This would lead to the eventual punishment of the fourth kingdom, by the aben stone, in the end.

Again, this is the focus of Daniel - the events of the rebuilding and subsequent destruction. How upsetting this must have been to him. Here the Temple had been destroyed by the Babylonians. He was hoping for good news about the rebuilding and he was given information about its eventual destruction. The only good news was that of the Messiah, but even that news was tempered by the fact that He would be cut off.

The abomination of desolation is a key event in Daniel. Here is what we read about in Daniel 11 and Daniel 12. First in Daniel 11 we read: "*And forces shall be mustered by him, and they shall defile the sanctuary fortress; then they shall take away the daily sacrifices, and place there the abomination of desolation.*" Daniel 11:31 In Daniel 12 we read: "*And from the time that the daily sacrifice is taken away, and the abomination of desolation is set up, there shall be one thousand two hundred and ninety days.*" Daniel 12:11

Now these are not the same event. The abomination of desolation in Daniel 11 takes place within the historical context of that passage. Daniel 11 is actually the longest prophetic verse in the Scriptures. It is very likely that everything in Daniel 11 occurred over 2,000 years ago. This is not to say that prophetic patterns cannot repeat themselves –

they clearly do at times. It is simply a fact that the events described in Daniel 11 have already occurred in the past.

In fact, the "abomination of desolation" in Daniel 11 was likely attributed to the actions of Antiochus IV Epiphanes. He was a Greek king of the Seleucid Empire from 175 BCE until his death in 164 BCE. Believing himself to be a manifiestation of Zeus he greatly persecuted the Yahudim.

He forbid Torah observance, he plundered and burned the city of Jerusalem, killed many Yahudim, and on the 15th day of Kislev in 167 BCE set up an image and altar to Zeus upon the Temple Altar. He also allegedly sacrificed swine upon it. Therefore, at face value it would be reasonable to believe that his actions were "the abomination of desolation"

spoken by Daniel. This position is reinforced by the reference found in the apocryphal text of Maccabees. (see 1 Maccabees 1:54)

While these events certainly were egregious, profane and an abomination that defiled the Temple, there would be another even greater "abomination of desolation." It is important to understand that while the word "abomination" can refer to an idol, this is a secondary meaning. "Hence, there is nothing in Daniel 9:27 . . . to warrant the idea that those prophecies speak of idol worship being set up in some Jewish temple."[191]

Indeed, the Maccabean Revolt commemorated by Hannukah actually resulted in a cleansing of the Temple and restoration of services. Neither the Temple nor the City of Jerusalem were made completely

desolate by Antiochus IV, and mere idol worship does not seem to completely fit the bill. This was the desolation of the third kingdom as provided in Daniel 8.

Accordingly, it seems far more likely that the actions of the Roman Empire, the fourth Kingdom that extends to the end and will be punished in the end, was responsible for the abomination of desolation. This was the "abomination of desolation" described in Daniel 9.

There are two more references in the text: 1) "the abomination of desolation" in Daniel 11:31, and 2) "abomination of desolation" in Daniel 12:11. There is no definite article (ie. "the") before the Daniel 12:11 reference. So "the abomination of desolation" in Daniel 12:11 reference might more properly be rendered "an abomination of desolation."[192]

Again, it is important to recognize the context of the Book of Daniel. It spans the entire Babylonian exile of the House of Yahudah, and the focus was the rebuilding of the City of Jerusalem and the Temple, the appearance of the Messiah and the subsequent destruction of the Temple.

Only a small portion of Daniel mentions any time after the destruction of the rebuilt Temple. Here is a portion of what we read:

"*¹ At that time Michael shall stand up, the great prince who stands watch over the sons of your people; and there shall be a time of trouble, such as never was since there was a nation, even to that time. And at that time your people shall be delivered, every one who is found written in the scroll. ² And many of those who sleep in the dust of the earth shall awake, some to everlasting life, some to shame and everlasting contempt. ³ Those who are wise shall shine like the brightness of the firmament, and those who turn many to righteousness like the stars forever and ever. ⁴ But you, Daniel, shut up the words, and seal the scroll until the time of the end; many shall run to and fro, and knowledge shall increase. ⁵ Then I, Daniel,* looked; and there stood two others, one on this riverbank and the other on that riverbank. *⁶ And one said to the man clothed in linen, who was above the waters of the river, How long shall the fulfillment of these wonders be? ⁷ Then I heard the man clothed in linen, who was above the waters of the river, when he held up his right hand and his left hand to heaven, and swore by Him who lives forever, that it shall be for a time, times, and half a time; and when the power of the set apart people has been completely shattered, all these things shall be finished. ⁸ Although I heard, I did not understand. Then I said, My adonai, what shall be the end of these things? ⁹ And he said, <u>Go your way, Daniel, for the words are closed up and sealed till the time of the end.</u> ¹⁰ Many shall be purified, made white, and refined, but the wicked shall do wickedly; and none of the wicked shall understand, but the wise shall understand. ¹¹ <u>And from the time that which is continual (tamiyd) is taken away, and the abomination of desolation is set up, there shall be one thousand two hundred and ninety days.</u> ¹² Blessed is he who waits, and comes to the one thousand three hundred and thirty-five days. ¹³ But you, go your way till the end; for you shall rest, and will arise to your inheritance at the end of the days."* Daniel 12:1-13

There will be a time when Michael will "stand up." At that time there will be a time of trouble as there has not been since there was a nation. It is clearly at the end of the age, at the point of the millennial kingdom, because there is a resurrection of the dead who are written in the Scroll of Life. But that time is not the entire focus of the text. There are some general comments being made about the end, that Daniel did not understand. So Daniel was told to seal up those things that pertain to the end.

Interestingly, couched within an instruction to Daniel to "go your way until the end" is the other reference to an "abomination of desolation" providing specific numbers of days. In fact it provides a span of 1,290 days, or 3 ½ years, between two different events. This is the same length of time as the *time, times, and half a time.*

What has caused great confusion is whether this is a third and separate "abomination of desolation" at the end of the age, or whether this was simply giving another detail for a previously mentioned "abomination of desolation" (ie. Daniel 9 or Daniel 11). Since Daniel was told to seal up the matters at the end of the age, this was likely not a future "abomination of desolation," otherwise it would have been sealed.

Therefore, many are anticipating another future "abomination of desolation" which would require, at the very least, setting up an altar and initiating some type of service. To do this, the ashes of the red heifer would be required. Some believe that finding the Ark of the Covenant would initiate such an event. There was no Ark in the Temple of Zerubbabel, and there is no reason to think that the Ark would be necessary to restart an Altar service in the future. Also, some believe that a Temple would need to be built, but the Tabernacle built by Mosheh would certainly suffice.

Now maybe such an event will occur in the future, but it does not seem to be necessary. As we shall see, it appears that the times given to Daniel were actually applicable to the "abomination of desolation" that occurred in 70 CE.

The first event that triggers the count is often thought to be the daily sacrifice taken away, but the Hebrew text does not specifically state that. We read "tamiyd" (◁ㄥ𐤘X) in the Hebrew, which simply means: "continuous."

There are a lot of things that were continuous relating to the Temple, including daily sacrifices and the three perpetual Pilgrimage Feasts - the Appointed Times of Unleavened Bread, Shabuot and Succot. Interestingly, the priests also offered a continuous sacrifice to the Roman Emperor.

"In 39 CE, the emperor Gaius Caligula (37-41CE), who

thought he was a god, ordered the Jews to place a golden statue in the Temple. They refused, since it was a clear violation of the second commandment (Exodus 20:4-5). According to Josephus (Wars, II, 10, 4, ed. Simhoni, p. 146) Caligula sent Petronius to get the job done. The Jews engaged in civil disobedience and refused to let him proceed to Jerusalem. (6) <u>They told him 'that they sacrifice twice a day sacrifices for the welfare of the Emperor and the Roman people.'"</u>[193]

So for some time, the Yahudim had been offering regular or "continuous" sacrifices in the Temple of YHWH for the head of the Roman Empire, who was considered a god. It is very possible that this was the "continuous" thing in the Temple that needed to be stopped that would begin the count to the abomination of desolation.

The Daniel 12 reference to "abomination of desolation" does not say "the," but rather "an" abomination of desolation." As a result, it is thought by some to be different because it is not referred to as "the abomination of desolation." The context of Daniel 12 is different from Daniel 11. In fact, both of these chapters are part of the same conversation that Daniel was having with a very unique man described as "One-man."

When Daniel received this information he was in mourning for three weeks and this vision appears to be connected to the previous prayer that he had made concerning the seventy years. At that time Gabriel appeared and told him about the seventy weeks. Now Daniel was receiving additional information, still relating to his inquiry concerning the Temple and the City of Jerusalem.

"*²In those days I, Daniel, was mourning three full weeks. ³I ate no pleasant food, no meat or wine came into my mouth, nor did I anoint myself at all, till three whole weeks were fulfilled. ⁴Now on the twenty-fourth day of the first month, as I was by the side of* the great river, that is, the Tigris, ⁵ I lifted my eyes and looked, and behold, One Man (aish-echad) clothed in linen, whose waist was girded with gold of Uphaz! ⁶ His body was like beryl, his face like the appearance of lightning, his eyes like torches of fire, his arms and feet like burnished bronze in color, and the sound of his words like the voice of a multitude. ⁷ And I, Daniel, alone saw ✕✦-the vision, for the men who were with me did not see ✕✦-the vision; but a great terror fell upon them, so that they fled to hide themselves. ⁸ Therefore I was left alone when I saw this great ✕✦-vision, and no strength remained in me; for my vigor was turned to frailty in me, and I retained no strength. ⁹ Yet I heard the ✕✦-voice (sound) of his words; and while I heard the ✕✦-voice (sound) of his words I was in a deep sleep on my face, with my face to the ground. ¹⁰ Suddenly, a hand touched me, which made me tremble on my knees and on the palms of my hands. ¹¹ And he said to me, O Daniel, man greatly beloved, understand the words that I speak to you, and stand upright, for I have now been sent to you. While he was speaking this word to me, I stood trembling." Daniel 10:2-11

This beautiful messenger is likely also Gabriel, but it is interesting the detail of the description given. We know that Gabriel appeared to Daniel previously, in the third year of Belshazzar. (Daniel 8:1). At that time Gabriel spoke information commanded by the "voice of a man." (Daniel 8:16)

Here is what happened at that appearance. "¹⁷ So he came near where I stood, and when I came I was afraid and fell on my face; but he said to me, 'Understand, son of man, that the vision refers to the time of the end.' ¹⁸ Now, as he was speaking with me, I was in a deep sleep with my face to the ground; but he touched me, and stood me upright. ¹⁹ And he said, Look, I am making known to you what shall happen in the latter time of the indignation; for at the Appointed Time (moad) the end shall be." Daniel 8:17-19

Interestingly, that particular revelation described

Alexander the Great and the successive 4 kingdoms. It paid particular attention to Antiochus IV. The events clearly were fulfilled over 2,000 years ago. As a result, while the events were in the future from Daniel's perspective, they are in our distant past. So the use of the phrase "time of the end" or "latter days" does not necessarily speak to the end of all time or the end of this present age. One needs to view time in cycles. That, after all, is how YHWH views time. In fact, if we consider the harvest cycles it helps to understand these phrases better. For instance, "the end of days" can mean the end of a harvest cycle.

With that understanding we will continue with another revelation that begins in Daniel 10, and continues to the end of the text. The Messiah appears to be involved in this process. One cannot miss the presence of the Aleph Taw (𐤀𐤕) attributed to the voice. Also, the description of the "One Man" is the same as the description of the Aleph Taw (𐤀𐤕) that we will later discuss in Revelation 1:12-17.

The entire revelation provided in Daniel 10 through 12 was given to Daniel as an answer to prayer. The information was to inform Daniel what would befall his people "in the latter days." Again, many people believe that this term only applies to the end of time, but that is not the case. It is about what would befall the House of Yahudah within a certain period of time. Those events are specifically provided in the text.

The information provided to Daniel was given in sequence, beginning with Darius the Mede – the then living sovereign. It actually overlaps with the information provided in Daniel 8, although Daniel 8 was just an outline. The information in Daniel 11 is very specific. We can actually trace historical events as Alexander the Greats kingdom gets divided into four kingdoms and then consolidated into two: 1) The Seleucid kings in the north, and 2) The Pyolemaic kings in the south. As we read through the struggles between the king of the north and the king of the south, it is these two kingdoms being described.

The text leads up to Antiochus IV coming to power in the Seleucid kingdom. Antiochus forced the High Priest Onais III, "the prince of the covenant," from his position and replaced him with the Hellenized Jason. (Daniel 11:21-22) Antiochus then set his sights on the king of the south and went against Ptolemy VI in Egypt.

He attacked Egypt, made an agreement with Ptolemy VI, and returned home with great riches. On his return from Egypt he quashed a revolt in Jerusalem led by Jason, who had previously been deposed by Antiochus, and replaced by Menelaus. He killed thousands of Judeans and sold many into slavery. He also entered the Temple and removed the set apart furnishings and treasures and returned to Antioch. (Daniel 11:28)

Later in Egypt, the brothers Ptolemy VI and Ptolemy VII reconciled with each other and agreed to share power. This nullified the alliance made between Antiochus IV and Ptolemy VI and caused Antiochus IV to lose control over the Ptolemaic kingdom. This resulted in him returning to Egypt with his army. (Daniel 11:29)

During this period, as Antiochus and his army marched toward Alexandria, he was met by the Romans and humiliated by them. Forced to withdraw from Egypt, on his return to Syria, he surrounded and attacked Jerusalem in a rage. (Daniel 11:30)

It was at this point that we read about "the abomination of desolation." "*And forces shall be mustered by him, and they shall defile the sanctuary fortress; then they shall take away the daily sacrifices, and place there the abomination of desolation.*" Daniel 11:31 This is exactly what happened, Antiochus desecrated the Temple, stopped the sacrifices, built a pagan altar and placed an image of Zeus Olympius upon it. Ten days later on the 25th day of Kislev, swine's flesh was offered on the altar to Zeus. Antiochus then essentially outlawed Torah observance and killed anyone caught observing the Torah. He even commanded the cities of Yahudah to offer pagan sacrifices.

These actions led to the Maccabean revolt against Antiochus IV and the Hasmonean Dynasty being established in the Land. The Temple was cleansed and rededicated, which is where we derive the festival of Hannukah. The rule of the Hasmoneans lasted from around 168 BCE until about 37 BCE. We then read the following passage in Daniel 11:35: "*And some of those of understanding shall fall, to refine them, purify them, and make them white, until the time of the end; because it is still for the Appointed Time.*" The time of the end being refered to is the end of the 69 weeks in the 70 week prophecy.

The text in Daniel 11 then proceeds to reveal a new king – not a king of the north or a king of the south. This reference to a king is clearly speaking of Herod, the Idumean. Herod derived his power from the Roman Empire. He was first appointed as tetrarch in 41 BCE, and later King of Judea in 37 BCE. Daniel 11:36 to 39 describe his ascension.

Finally in Daniel 11:40 to 43 very accurately describe the final remnants of Alexander's Kingdom fighting one last battle. Mark Anthony aligned with Cleopatra is the king of the south, and Octavius is the king of the north. Octavius won and from that point forward Rome dominated the region of Judea. Daniel 11:44-45 return to detail Herod and his demise.[194]

In fact there seems to be a direct connection between Daniel 11:44 and Matthew chapter 2, when Herod heard reports from the Magi from the east who later found the Messiah in the north. The Magi actually found the Messiah and anointed Him as a child precisely at the completion of the 7 weeks and the 62 weeks – on the Appointed Time of Yom Teruah. This is why Herod ordered the slaughter of children under the age of 2 years old. (Matthew 2:16)

So it should be evident that the substance of Daniel's prophetic visions were fulfilled within the time frame revealed through Gabriel. Everything included within Daniel 11 occurred within the 7 weeks and the 62 weeks leading up to the appearance and anointing of the Messiah.

Daniel 12 then jumps forward to what many believe to be the end of time. Again, it is important to read it within the context of the subject matter – the people of Yahudah, Jerusalem and the Temple.

Here is what we read in most English translations: "*⁵ Then I, Daniel, looked; and there stood two others, one on this riverbank and the other on that riverbank. ⁶ And one said to the man clothed in linen, who was above the waters of the river, How long shall the fulfillment of these wonders be? ⁷ Then I heard* ✕✶- *the man clothed in linen, who was above the waters of the river, when he held up his right hand and his left hand to heaven, and swore by Him who lives forever, that it shall be for a time, times, and half a time; and when the power of the set apart people has been completely shattered, all these things shall be finished. ⁸ Although I heard, I did not understand. Then I said, My adonai, what shall be the end of these things? ⁹ And he said, Go your way, Daniel, for the words are closed up and sealed till the time of the end. ¹⁰ Many shall be purified, made white, and refined, but the wicked shall do wickedly; and none of the wicked shall understand, but the wise shall understand. ¹¹ And from the time that which is "continual" is taken away, and the abomination of desolation is set up, there shall be one thousand two hundred and ninety days. ¹² Blessed is he who waits, and comes to the one thousand three hundred and thirty-five days. ¹³ But you, go your way till the end; for you shall rest, and will arise to your inheritance at the end of the days.*" Daniel 12:5-13

The question that is posed is how long shall the

fulfillment of these wonders be? The answer is: *"it shall be for a time, times, and half a time."* In the Hebrew we read "l'moad moadim v'hatzi" (ΖℋϤ ℋℤ◁⊙ΥΥ ◁⊙Υℋ𝑙) – literally "Appointed Time, Appointed Times half." We then read the final reference to "the abomination of desolation." There is a time span of 1,290 days between that which is continual being taken away and the abomination of desolation.

It seems clear that the abomination of desolation in Daniel 11 preceded the abomination of desolation in Daniel 12. The Daniel 11 event involved Antiochus IV, while the Daniel 12 event involved the Roman Empire, and was the same abomination mentioned in Daniel 9.

This will become even clearer when we examine Yahushua's later comment on the abomination of desolation in the next chapter. At that point we will also show just how the 1,290 fulfilled by the Roman Empire – the fourth empire.

Daniel was previously instructed to seal up the scroll. *"But you, Daniel, shut up the words, and seal the scroll until the time of the end . . ."* Daniel 12:4 We currently have the Book of Daniel opened and available, so that begs the question: What was sealed? It was not the Book of Daniel, but rather a scroll that will be unsealed at a later date – the "time of the end" (Χ⊙-◁⊙). That scroll will be discussed further in this book.

While some things were sealed, we were given certain information identifying the rebuilding, and the destruction of the Temple and Jerusalem. We were also given information concerning the appearance and the purpose of the Messiah. Certain information concerning the end was sealed in a scroll to be opened at a future time.

Through the Book of Daniel we see the emphasis on the transfer from the Kingdom of Yisrael to the great kingdoms of man that would span through the ages to the

end of the age. Daniel II provided very specific information concerning these kingdoms leading up to the Messiah. We also read about the kingdoms of men that will ultimately be smashed by the Messiah, Who would establish the Kingdom of YHWH on earth.

Now let us look at the One identified as the Son of Elohim, Who would function as the role of the Messiah. We will examine what He taught and how he fulfilled the prophecy given to Daniel. The Messiah came at the exact time prescribed and the first words that we read are about the Kingdom – the Kingdom of YHWH.

10

The Messiah

The Messiah was the long anticipated One Who would restore the divided Kingdom. As was discussed, "messiah" literally means: "anointed." There were many anointed in the history of Yisrael, even Cyrus was called "anointed" by YHWH. Generally, priests and kings were anointed, but there was an anticipation of the coming Annointed One – The Messiah.

The Messiah was generally thought to be King, but a Priest was first needed to mediate a renewed Covenant with YHWH and attend to the sin that plagued man since the Garden. So the Messiah would function as both King and High Priest.

It was understood that He would bring justice to the Gentiles according to the prophet Isaiah: *"Behold! My Servant whom I uphold, My Elect One in whom My soul delights! I have put My Spirit upon Him; He will bring forth justice to the Gentiles."* Isaiah 42:1.

The word for "gentiles," as we already mentioned, is "goyim" (𐤉𐤆𐤉𐤂) in Hebrew. It means: "nations" or "heathens." Essentially, the "goyim" are those outside of the Assembly of Yisrael. So the Messiah was not just coming to deal with Yisrael, but the entire planet.

As we saw through the life of Abraham, the Messiah would be the Promised Son of Elohim. He would be the

Lamb of Elohim and His life would fulfill the patterns of the Appointed Times. The Prophet Daniel was given specific timing concerning the rebuilding of the Temple and the coming of the Messiah.

Through Daniel we saw a period of seven weeks of Shemitah cycles that led to the restoration of the Temple and the City. This, in fact occurred as foretold so the next anticipated event was the return of the Messiah and the restoration of the Kingdom, although things did not proceed as many anticipated.

The return from exile was hampered with problems and the rebuilding of the City and the Temple was filled with delays. The builders would be attacked while they were building causing each to carry a sword.

Here is the account provided through Nehemiah: *"17 Those who built on the wall, and those who carried burdens, loaded themselves so that with one hand they worked at construction, and with the other held a weapon. 18 Every one of the builders had his sword girded at his side as he built. And the one who sounded the trumpet was beside me. 19 Then I said to the nobles, the rulers, and the rest of the people, "The work is great and extensive, and we are separated far from one another on the wall. 20 Wherever you hear the sound of the shofar, rally to us there. Our Elohim will fight for us."* Nehemiah 4:17-20

The people were armed for battle as they rebuilt the walls and they would rally to the sound of the shofar. Eventually the work was complete, but we know from certain accounts and prophets that their hearts strayed. They took foreign wifes and eventually became distracted building their own homes, rather than the House of YHWH.

An interesting event occurred when Ezra read the Torah to the entire congregation. *"Now all the people gathered together as one man in the open square that was in front of the Water Gate; and they told Ezra the scribe to bring the Book of the*

Torah of Mosheh, which YHWH had commanded Yisrael."
Nehemiah 8:1 This should draw us back to the
commandment given by Mosheh before the Children of
Yisrael entered the Promised Land.

"*10* And Moses commanded them, saying: At the end of
every seven years, at the Appointed Time in the year of release, at
the Feast of Tabernacles, *11* when all Yisrael comes to appear before
YHWH your Elohim in the place which He chooses, you shall read
this Torah before all Yisrael in their hearing. *12* Gather the people
together, men and women and little ones, and the stranger who is
within your gates, that they may hear and that they may learn to
fear YHWH your Elohim and carefully observe all the words of
this Torah, *13* and that their children, who have not known it, may
hear and learn to fear YHWH your Elohim as long as you live in
the land which you cross the Jordan to possess." Debarim 31:10-13

So they were in a seventh year – a Shemitah year
when they were reading the Torah. This was "the year of
release" when all Hebrew slaves were set free every seven
years. This is perfectly consistent with the "weeks" shown to
Daniel. We also saw through Daniel a period of sixty-two
"weeks" that led to the Messiah Yahushua.

The mystery concerning the prophecies found in
Daniel indicated that Messiah would be cut off. This seemed
to conflict with the notion that He would restore the
Kingdom. As a result, many were looking for two different
Messiah's – Messiah son of Joseph and Messiah son of
David.

It was clear that the Messiah would come in the form
of a man, the Son of Elohim. "Therefore YHWH Himself will
give you a sign: Behold, the virgin shall conceive and bear a Son,
and shall call His name Immanuel." Isaiah 7:14 Interestingly, in
the Hebrew text we see Immanuel appear as two words:
"Amanu El" (𐤋𐤀 𐤉𐤄𐤅𐤏). The Book of Matthew
specifically provides that the virgin birth of the Messiah

Yahushua was a fulfillment of the Isaiah prophecy. (see Mathew 1:22-23)

So the Messiah was Elohim in the flesh. This is a highy debated issue – the so-called "divinity" of the Messiah. It really should not be when we have a proper understanding of man in Creation. We know from the beginning that man was made in the image of Elohim, according to His likeness. "*Then Elohim said, Let Us make man in Our image, according to Our likeness.*" Beresheet 1:26

This is a very powerful statement with profound implications. It is particularly poignant when we read the vision of Ezekiel concerning the image of YHWH. "[26] *And above the firmament over their heads was the likeness of a throne, in appearance like a sapphire stone; on the likeness of the throne was a likeness with the appearance of a man high above it.* [27] *Also from the appearance of His waist and upward I saw, as it were, the color of amber with the appearance of fire all around within it; and from the appearance of His waist and downward I saw, as it were, the appearance of fire with brightness all around.* [28] *Like the appearance of a rainbow in a cloud on a rainy day, so was the appearance of the brightness all around it. This was the appearance of the likeness of the glory of YHWH.*" Ezekiel 1:26-28

The word for "likeness" is "d'muwt" (XY𐤌𐤃) and we understand that man was created to resemble the likeness of YHWH seated on the throne. So man exists in Creation to rule and to reign, just like the Creator. Man is created to look, act and function like YHWH. That is what it means to be in the Image of Elohim. It was like a parent and child relationship.

This was actually specifically provided from the very beginning when man was conceived. "[26] . . . *let them have dominion over the fish of the sea, over the birds of the air, and over the cattle, over all the earth and over every creeping thing that creeps on the earth.* [27] *So Elohim created man in His own image; in* the image of Elohim He created him; male and female He created them. ²⁸ Then Elohim blessed them, and Elohim said to them, Be fruitful and multiply; fill the earth and subdue it; have dominion over the fish of the sea, over the birds of the air, and over every living thing that moves on the earth." Beresheet 1:26-28

This is a critical understanding. When one steps back and observes mankind on the earth, what is seen is the likeness of YHWH, the likeness of the Creator of the Universe and the Ruler of all things. This is what the powers of darkness see, and those who hate YHWH attack the likeness of YHWH.

The prophecy from Isaiah provides that the One on the Throne would come down to Earth and exist in the flesh among those who were made in His likeness. This was what makes the Messiah unique among all of the other fleshly beings. So of course the Messiah was "divine." That was the very purpose of the Messiah. YHWH would appear in flesh to guide and instruct His likeness in His ways. He showed them how to live.

While the Torah, the Prophets and the Writings all pointed to the Messiah, we must look to other ancient writings for their fulfillment – namely those texts called The Gospels[195] in the New Testament. The title New Testament is really quite misleading as the information contained therein does not describe a "brand new" Covenant, but rather a renewed Covenant with Yisrael through the Messiah.

Some of the following information was gleaned from the Walk in the Light series book entitled *The Messiah*, but it bears repeating here as we first examine the timing of the birth of the Messiah.

The New Testament texts describe a candidate for the Messiah of Yisrael. The English translations call Him Jesus, but His actual name was Yahushua. Once you understand that the name of Yahushua has been misrepresented

throughout the centuries, you should probably ask, as I did, if there is anything else about this individual that has been changed.

With a little investigation, it is easy to discern that there are many more errors that must be corrected in order to obtain a clear understanding of life and purpose of Yahushua. It turns out that it is not just His name that has been changed. His teachings, and even the chronology of His life, have been filtered through multiple lenses of tradition, history and linguistics.

As a result, we will now turn our discussion to the life of Yahushua and where better to start then at the beginning – His birth. While most of the world celebrates his birth on December 25, no one seriously believes that He was actually born on that date. After all, December 25 was the traditional pagan date for the birth and rebirth of sun gods long before the birth of Yahushua.

The date of December 25 was attributed to such savior gods as Tammuz, Horus, Apollo, Mithras, Bacchus and Dionysus, among others. The reason is because December 25 was the ancient date for the winter solstice by 405 BCE.* The winter solstice is the shortest day of the year, after which the sun is "resurrected" from death to new life. Therefore, to pagans, it represents the birth and rebirth of their sun deities.

The tradition of attributing December 25 to the birth of Jesus is an example of how the Christian religion has adopted pagan concepts and traditions. While most recognize December 25 as a fictitious birth date, there is great debate over the actual time of Yahushua's birth. Any investigation into the correct date must logically begin in the New Testament although, at first glance, there appear to be conflicts between those texts.

The Book of Matthew places the birth "during the time of King Herod" who has traditionally been thought to have died in 4 BCE. We know that Herod ordered the death of children two years old and younger after learning of the birth of Yahushua. This was apparently because when he heard about the birth from the wise men it was possible that Yahushua had been alive for up to two years prior. So, based upon the information in Matthew, the birth of Yahushua would be before 6 BCE.

The Book of Luke ties the birth of Yahushua with the census of Quirinius, which is traditionally thought to have occurred in 6 CE. This would seem to create an eleven year difference between the two accounts (there is no year zero), which is certainly a problem. As it turns out, neither Matthew nor Luke are wrong, rather the commonly accepted dates of the events that they refer to are incorrect. The date of Herod's death was not 4 BCE, but more probably 1 BCE, and the census of Quirinius was likely not in 6 CE. Both of these dates will be discussed further in this examination.

With that understanding, let us begin our investigation by looking at Luke 2:1, which provides that Yahushua's birth was during the reign of Augustus Caesar. Augustus Caesar reigned from 44 BC to his death on August 19, 14 CE. The method of measuring time in the ancient Roman world was based on the reigns of the Emperors. Thus the early "Church fathers" of Christianity dated the birth of Yahushua according to the accepted method used by the Romans, arriving at similar dates. Irenius states that it was in the 41st year of Augustus's reign, which would place it at 4/3 BCE depending on how you date the beginning of Augustus's reign. Clement of Alexandria dates it November 18, 3 BCE. Tertullian provides the date of 3/2 BCE. Julius Africanus provides the date of 3/2 BCE. Eusebius of Caesarea provides the date of 3/2 BCE. Hypolotus of Rome provides the date of 3/2 BCE. Epiphanius provides the date of 3/2 BCE.[196]

Due to the above, there appears to be agreement from

earlier historical records that Yahushua was born around 3 BCE, although this is widely disputed, again, largely because of the accepted dating of Herod's death and the census of Quirinius. So how do we reconcile these matters?

There is actually another way, besides historical accounts, that we can make this determination from the Scriptures. In Beresheet 1:14 we read: *"And Elohim said, Let there be lights in the expanse of the sky to separate the day from the night, and let them serve as signs to mark seasons and days and years."* Days and years are clear, but what exactly is meant by "signs" and "seasons"?

A sign is something that is visibly observable – a signal. The Hebrew word for sign is "owt" (𐤗𐤅𐤀), and it is used to describe the signs or marks of the Covenants made with YHWH. For instance, the rainbow, circumcision and the Sabbath are all signs of YHWH's Covenants and they are all visible.

The English word "seasons" is actually the Hebrew word "moadim" (𐤌𐤉𐤃𐤏𐤅𐤌) in the text. The Hebrew word "moadim" (𐤌𐤉𐤃𐤏𐤅𐤌) refers specifically to the "Appointed Times" of YHWH. These moadim are set forth throughout the Torah. They are often erroneously referred to as Jewish Holidays, because the religion of Judaism celebrates them along with various other days not set forth in the Scriptures. YHWH specifically stated that they were His days and they belonged to Him, not Yisrael or any particular group or religion. (Vayiqra 23:2,4)

The moadim are considered to be rehearsals, and they all teach about the plan that YHWH has to restore His Creation, and get His chosen people back into a right relationship with Him. So the moadim are there to teach about the future. In fact, they are critical to our understanding of the life and ministry of the Messiah. You cannot fully recognize the Messiah without understanding

the moadim.

As the restoration of all things is centered around the Messiah, it should not be any surprise that The Appointed Times are intimately related to the Messiah. They are sequentially enumerated in the text of Vayiqra 23 as follows: 1) Passover; 2) The Feast of Unleavened Bread; 3) Shavuot; 4) Yom Teruah; 5) Yom Kippur; 6) Succot; and 7) Shemini Atzeret.

The first two Appointed Times based on the moon occur in the first month, refered to as the month of the Aviv. The Feast of Shavuot occurs 50 days after Day 16 of Month 1, and the final four Appointed Times based upon the moon occur in the seventh month.

Remember the discussion regarding the difference between eastern and western thought. Hebrew is an eastern language and culture. These Appointed Times provide a continuous loop which repeat, and when a person enters into the life and faith expressed in the Hebrew Scriptures, they need to enter this cycle of life and participate in the moadim. Through this process we synchronize with creation and the Creator.

According to the Creator's Calendar, the months of the year are numbered "one" through "twelve." It is believed that creation actually began at what is now considered month seven. When YHWH called Yisrael out of Egypt YHWH told Mosheh, prior to the Passover – *"This month shall be your beginning of months; it shall be the first month of the year to you."* Shemot 12:2.

We see here that a sort of dimensional shift occurred, and at that moment a significant change took place. At that new moon (rosh chodesh) when Yisrael left Egypt, the numbering of the months changed and time, in essence, shifted. The seventh month effectively became the first month. (Shemoth 12:2) Those of the Jewish faith currently recognize two different calendars to recognize this change. They designate them the civil calendar and the religious calendar. Sadly, they currently follow a man made calculated calendar rather than the Scriptural Calendar that operates around the sun and the moon.[197]

The "civil calendar" begins on the first day of the seventh month that begins with the sighting of the seventh crescent moon. This marks the beginning of creation and the original calendar. The "religious calendar," on the other hand, begins on the first day of the first month as it was designated prior to the time of the Exodus. This shift was not a matter confined to the religion of Judaism. It was ordained by YHWH for the Covenant Assembly of Yisrael, and it is an important concept to understand as we examine the birth of Yahushua.

With an accurate understanding of the Scriptural Calendar, we can look at the Messianic writings in the New Testament, and recognize certain information that directs us to the birth date of Yahushua. Our investigation continues with a comment in the Book of Luke that helps us discern what year Yahushua was born. The passage indicates that Yahushua began His work "about 30 years of age."

According to Luke "*¹ In the fifteenth year of the reign of Tiberius Caesar - when Pontius Pilate was governor of Judea, Herod tetrarch of Galilee, his brother Philip tetrarch of Iturea and Traconitis, and Lysanias tetrarch of Abilene - ² during the high priesthood of Annas and Caiaphas, the Word of Elohim came to Yahanan son of Zechariah in the desert.*" We are also told around this time that Yahushua "*was about thirty years old when He began his ministry.*" Luke 3:1-2 and 23

Luke provides an incredible amount of historical data when "*The Word of Elohim*" came to Yahanan . . . in the desert." Remember the connection between "The Word" and the Aleph Taw (✗✗). The text is not only giving us a way to date the event, it is also linking Yahushua with the Aleph Taw (✗✗) as The Word going to Yahanan when he was "about thirty years old."

The fifteenth year of Tiberius Ceasar has been much debated by modern scholars, and many theories have been advanced. We know that Tiberius became Emperor of Rome on September 17 in the year 14 CE. Since the Romans were pagans, they did not use the Creator's Calendar that operated on a lunar system. They worshipped the sun, and therefore they used a solar calendar. The fact that we still operate on a calendar derived from Rome demonstrates that much of the world continues under the 4th Kingdom.

Roman scholars who lived when Luke was writing, such as Tacitus or Suetonius, generally dated the first regnal year of a Roman ruler from January 1 of the year following the date of accession. It is most probable that Luke would have reckoned the years of Tiberius Ceasar in this manner. The first year of Tiberius would therefore be reckoned from January 1 to December 31, 15 CE and his fifteenth year would have been reckoned between January 1 to December 31, 29 CE.[199]

Yahushua would have been 30 ½ years old in the spring of 29 CE. If we count back 30 years we see that Yahushua was likely born in the fall of 3 BCE, just as was stated by the early Christians. This year can be further confirmed by some additional information contained in the Messianic writings. The account of Luke provides the following dating at the time of His birth: *"¹ In those days Caesar Augustus issued a decree that a census should be taken of the entire Roman world. ² (This was the first census that took place while Quirinius was governor of Syria.) ³ And everyone went to his*

own town to register." Luke 2:1-3

"Caesar Augustus reigned as emperor of the Roman empire from 27 [BCE] to 14 [CE] . . . 41 years in all. The grandnephew of Julius Caesar (100 - 44 [BCE]), his real name was Gaius Octavius and he lived from 63 [BCE] to 14 [CE] Because Julius Caesar had legally adopted Octavius as his son, Octavius took the name 'Caesar' from Julius, which in later years became a name almost equivalent to 'emperor.' 'Augustus' is a Latin term that means 'worthy of reverence.' Caesar Augustus's reign was marked by peace and security - the famous Pax Romana - as well as by lavish building projects throughout the empire. In addition, according to Paul Maier, Augustus had such an intense interest in religion within his realm that, if not for his other great achievements, he might have gone down in history as a religious reformer. In his day, belief in the traditional Greco-Roman pantheon had decreased dramatically as philosophical skepticism grew and a growing number joined the foreign mystery religions. Augustus was convinced that belief in the old gods had made Rome great so he set out to encourage his subjects to return to the worship of these gods. He restored eighty-two temples in Rome alone! He became the pontifex maximus (highest priest) in the state cult."[200]

So we see that Augustus revived the pagan religious systems in the Empire. While he was not technically an emperor, he was highly esteemed and after his death in 14 CE, the Roman senate declared him a god. We know that Augustus issued a decree for a census on three different occasions during his reign, namely 28 BCE, 8 BCE and 14 CE. Since these were empire-wide decrees, they likely took time to implement, so Luke was probably referring to the second decree in 8 BCE.

This appears to pose a problem by the fact that Quirinius was governor of Syria in the years 6 CE to 7 CE. How could the comment in Luke be correct which states: *"This was the first census that took place while Quirinius was governor of Syria."* There are various plausible explanations for this apparent discrepancy. The Greek word that has been translated as "first" is *prote* which can mean "prior to" or "before." Therefore, Luke was likely referring to the second census of Augustus (8 BCE) which occurred "before" Quirinius was Governor rather than the third census of Augustus which occurred after he became governor.

There is also evidence that Quirinius served an earlier tour of duty in Syria, and that this census was actually from a later tour of duty, when the people of the Roman Empire were required to take an oath when Augustus was being named Pater Patriae. The oath would likely have been obtained in 3 BCE as the honor was bestowed upon Augustus in 2 BCE.[201]

All of this information seems to confirm that 3 BCE was indeed the year of the birth of Yahushua. Later in this chapter we will see a final proof that makes it an absolute certainty.

We know that Miryam, the mother of Yahushua, was betrothed to a man named Joseph. Joseph essentially adopted Yahushua, which is incredibly profound since Yahushua was coming as the Messiah son of Joseph. He literally fulfilled the prophetic expectation.

Joseph and Miryam were both descendants of David, and were of royal lineage. As a result, they both would have been required to swear allegiance to Augustus and would have been mandated to participate in the "census." This meant that they both needed to go to Bethlehem, their town of origin – the birth place of David in the region of Judea. They were, after all, from the tribe of Yahudah.

If you had to go to Bethlehem and you lived in the Galilee this was no small trip. If you knew that you were going to an obligatory Feast in Jerusalem three times a year, which was extremely close to Bethlehem you would probably try to combine these trips. Only males were required to make the trek to Jerusalem three times a year for the Appointed Times, but we know that Miryam was in Bethlehem when she gave birth to Yahuhsua. The census perfectly explains why a pregnant woman would travel such a distance?

Since Bethlehem is literally "House of Bread" and the birthplace of David, the event was also an incredible fulfillment of the expectation of the Messiah son of David.

All Yisraelite women would have surely remembered the travails of Rachel as she gave birth to Benjamin while traveling from Bethel to Ephratah. Ephratah was the name for Bethlehem in Yaakob's time. Rachel died on her way to Bethlehem, which was undoubtedly on the mind of Miryam the entire trip. Miryam likely would not have gone on such a journey under normal circumstances.

Thus, we see both Joseph and Miryam traveling to Bethlehem around the seventh month, right before the birth of Yahushua. Interestingly, Luke says that they were "betrothed" or "engaged," but there is no mention that they were married at this time. This is because they did not actually "know" one another until after the birth of Yahushua, and it is that sexual union that ultimately seals the marriage. Up until that time they were still "engaged."

This was surely a very awkward situation for both of them. Traveling together in such a fashion while not being married was not typical, and with Miryam so far along in her pregnancy, the appearance of impropriety must have been enormous. They probably did not bother explaining themselves since the story of the conception would have been a bit more than most people were prepared to accept.

Yahushua was born while they were in Bethlehem. The following is the account of his birth: "*⁴ So Joseph also went up from the town of Nazareth in Galilee to Judea, to Bethlehem the town of David, because he belonged to the house and line of David. ⁵ He went there to register with Miryam, who was pledged to be married to him and was expecting a child. ⁶ While they were there, the time came for the baby to be born, ⁷ and she gave birth to her firstborn, a son. She wrapped him in cloths and placed him in a manger, because there was no room for them in the Inn.*" Luke 2:4-7.

Yahushua was born while his mother was unmarried and her husband was not his father. If this fact would have been known, it would put the status of Yahushua in a difficult state. Some may have deemed him a "mamzer" as a result. In other words, he would have been treated as a bastard, which would have made him an outsider in the community.

Interestingly, the text states that there was no room at the Inn. The "Inn" was not a motel or a bed and breakfast, but more likely a guestroom in the home of a family member or friend. We do not know why it was occupied, but we can deduce that this was likely one of the three times that males were commanded to travel to Jerusalem to celebrate a festival to YHWH.

It has been taught by some that Yahushua was born around the time of the Feast of Succot, which occurs in the seventh month during what is commonly referred to as the fall season. The book of Luke describes the infant being placed in a "manger" which can mean a feeding trough. How symbolic that in the feeding trough was placed the bread of life - the living manna - born in the House of Bread.

Some mistranslate manger as "tabernacle" or "succa" because they want Yahushua to be born during the Feast of Succot. This seems to work well with the phrase from the

Gospel of John 1:14 that states He "tabernacled among us." This could also be styled that he "pitched his tent" with us. As a result, some people believe that Yahushua was actually born in a succa during the Feast of Succot, also known as the Feast of Tabernacles. It is important to recognize that Succot is not the only Appointed Time to occur in Month 7. Within the two week period preceding Succot there are the Appointed Times of Yom Teruah on Day 1 and Yom Kippur on Day 10.

It would probably not be uncommon for those coming to Jerusalem for Succot to come early and celebrate all of the Appointed Times of the seventh month namely: Yom Teruah, Yom Kippur, Succot and Shemini Atzeret. Since there was no room in the "Inn" and people were supposed to be living outside in succas during the Feast of Succot, then there is a distinct possibility that the birth occurred earlier in the seventh month.

There is no commandment to be in Jerusalem during Yom Teruah or Yom Kippur, and it is also important to point out that Yahushua was born in Bethlehem - not Jerusalem. While the two are both geographically close in proximity, they are not the same. It would not have been appropriate to build a succa and celebrate Succot in Bethlehem rather than Jerusalem. If Yahushua was born during Succot, then he would have been in Jerusalem.

In the year 3 BCE Yom Teruah, also known as the Feast of Trumpets, occurred on Day 1 of Month 7 at the sighting of the New Moon on the Gregorian date of September 11. This is an extremely significant day because Yom Teruah was traditionally considered to be the birthday of Creation. It is the day that Elohim said: *"Let there be light."* It was also the day from which the ancient kings of Yahudah reckoned their regnal years. This procedure was followed consistently in the time of Solomon, Yirmeyahu and Ezra.[202]

It is a day of blowing shofars, announcing the birth of creation and the king of Yahudah. What an appropriate day for the Messiah to be born.

Therefore, Yom Teruah in 3 BCE appears to be the definitive date for the birth of the Messiah – the Annointed King of Yahudah. As people were rehearsing this moadi by blowing shofars, they were actually fulfilling the prophetic purpose of the Feast by announcing the birth of Messiah Yahushua.

This leads us to a very interesting and often misunderstood event involving "wise men." According to the Book of Matthew there were "wise men" who knew about this birth by looking at the stars – one star in particular. We know from modern technology that prior to September 11, 3 BCE there were spectacular "signs" in the sky.

Remember that the constellations and the planets were created for specific purposes. The Sages were well aware of this fact, and Job clearly spoke of certain constellations in his writings. While the occult and pagans have taken these concepts and twisted them, it is important to remember that the Creator of the Universe also created these things for His glory and His purpose.

One of these purposes is to provide a "sign" for the coming of the Messiah. The Book of Matthew speaks of "wise men" or "magi" from the East who came because they saw "the star."

"*¹ Now after Yahushua was born in Bethlehem of Judea in the days of Herod the king, behold, wise men from the East came to Jerusalem, ² saying, Where is He who has been born King of the Yahudim? For we have seen His star in the East and have come to worship Him. ³ When Herod the king heard this, he was troubled, and all Jerusalem with him. ⁴ And when he had gathered all the chief priests and scribes of the people together, he inquired of them where the Messiah was to be born. ⁵ So they said to him, In*

Bethlehem of Judea, for thus it is written by the prophet: [6] But you, Bethlehem, in the Land of Yahudah, are not the least among the rulers of Yahudah; for out of you shall come a Ruler Who will shepherd My people Yisrael. [7] Then Herod, when he had secretly called the wise men, determined from them what time the star appeared. [8] And he sent them to Bethlehem and said, go and search carefully for the young Child, and when you have found Him, bring back word to me, that I may come and worship Him also. [9] When they heard the king, they departed; and behold, the star which they had seen in the East went before them, till it came and stood over where the young Child was. [10] When they saw the star, they rejoiced with exceedingly great joy. [11] And when they had come into the house, they saw the young Child with Miryam His mother, and fell down and worshiped Him. And when they had opened their treasures, they presented gifts to Him: gold, frankincense, and myrrh. [12] Then, being divinely warned in a dream that they should not return to Herod, they departed for their own country another way." Matthew 2:1-12

The wise men appeared after Yahushua was born, they did not appear the night that he was born. Their appearance was really quite an amazing event because we have these "wise men" approaching Herod, the supposed "king" of Yahudah, telling him that they have come to see the real King of Yahudah. It was a blatant assertion that the kingship of Herod was illegitimate, but notice how he played along. They said that they saw "His Star" meaning the "King of the Yahudim's star."

This would have certainly brought remembrance to the word spoken from Balaam to Balak: "[17] I see Him, but not now; I behold Him, but not near. A star will come out of Yaakob; a scepter will rise out of Yisrael. He will crush the foreheads of Moab, the skulls of all the sons of Sheth. [18] Edom will be conquered; Seir, his enemy, will be conquered, but Yisrael will grow strong. [19] A ruler will come out of Yaakov and destroy the survivors of the

city." Bemidbar 24:17-19.

Herod was an Edomite, and the word indicated that a ruler would come out of Yaakob and Edom would be conquered. He took this event "deadly" serious because it was an affront to his reign. He took it so serious that he later ordered the death of all children two years and younger (Matthew 2:16). Why two years and younger? Because the wisemen came to Yahushua after a significant period of time from when they first saw the star. Herod understood from the timing that the Messiah could have been two years old.

So contrary to popular belief these wise men, called Magi, did not come to the baby while He was in the manger - they came much later. The only witnesses to the birth of the infant, according to the Scriptures, were the shepherds. (Luke 2:12). Most traditional manger scenes are inaccurate when they show the baby Jesus in a manger with the "Three Wise Men" looking over Him.

In fact, the Scriptures do not mention three wise men, but rather three gifts: gold, frankincense, and myrrh. There were most likely many more than three of them, and they probably would have had a large entourage to carry and protect the gifts and supplies necessary for such a long journey. This is particularly true since they were coming from the Parthian Kingdom in the east. Relations between the Parthians and the Romans were tense. The two were in a veritable détente. The fact that Herod "was troubled and all Jerusalem with him" was probably indicative that their entourage was a small army. (Matthew 2:3).

There is considerable evidence to support the fact that the "wise men" found Yahushua in the Galilee - not in Bethlehem. One significant reason is because after the Messiah was circumcised on the eighth day in accordance with the Torah and after the days of purification were completed, Yoseph and Miryam took Him to Jerusalem to

present Him before YHWH and *"to offer a sacrifice according to what is said in the Torah of YHWH, a pair of turtledoves or two young pigeons."* Luke 2:34.

What Luke is telling us is that they presented a sacrifice which a *poor person* would bring to the Temple. According to the Torah: *"⁶ When the days of her purification are fulfilled, whether for a son or a daughter, she shall bring to the priest a lamb of the first year as a burnt offering, and a young pigeon or a turtledove as a sin offering, to the door of the tabernacle of meeting.⁷ Then he shall offer it before YHWH, and make atonement for her. And she shall be clean from the flow of her blood. This is the Torah for her who has born a male or a female. ⁸ And if* <u>*she is not able to bring a lamb, then she may bring two turtledoves or two young pigeons*</u> *- one as a burnt offering and the other as a sin offering. So the priest shall make atonement for her, and she will be clean."* Vayiqra 12:6-8.

Since they did not bring a lamb, they must have been poor. This is inconsistent with the myth that Yahushua and his family were loaded up with gold and other gifts on the night he was born. The wise men were nowhere near the manger in Bethlehem because the Scriptures later record: <u>"And coming into the House</u>, *they saw the Child with Miryam His mother, and fell down and did reverence Him . . ."* Matthew 2:11.

The wise men appeared at the "House" - not at the manger when Yahushua was a "child" - not a baby.

Their journey likely took many months and they did not arrive to see the infant, which is "brephos" in the Greek, but rather a toddler "paidion," indicating that the birth itself had been some years before. When they finally located *"the Child"* Yahushua in the Galilee, they anointed Him King of Yahudah and gave Him the riches of His Kingdom. This could have very possibly occurred on His first birthday, Yom Teruah in the year 2 BCE, a date from which Kings of Yahudah would reckon their reigns.²⁰³

It was only then that they worshipped him and gave Him gifts. It was after that point that they were warned in a dream not to return to Herod. (Matthew 2:12). Herod had already learned from the wise men exactly what time the star appeared. That is why, when he learned that he had been duped by them he ordered all children two years old and younger to be killed. Joseph was also warned in a dream to flee to Egypt, and he could now afford the trip, because he had just been given the resources necessary for the journey. (Matthew 2:13).

Just who were these "wise men" seems to be the mystery of the ages, although it is possible to piece together their identity through a historical analysis. At the time of the birth of Yahushua, the Roman Empire and the Parthian Empire were experiencing somewhat of a détente. While the Roman Empire ruled the west, the Parthian Empire ruled the east.

The wise men described in the Scriptures were likely Parthians from Persia, members of the Megistanes, who were very high officials in the Parthian Empire.[204] The historian Josephus strongly implies that these Parthians may have been Yisraelites formerly deported by the Assyrian Empire, which was later replaced by the Parthian Empire.[205]

It is important to remember that Daniel was a "wise man" and was placed in charge of the "wise men" in the Babylonian Kingdom. Later, he was elevated in the Medo-Persian Empire. He was no doubt a wealthy and powerful man with no known heir due to the fact that he was a eunuch. He also happened to have incredible insight into the coming of the Messiah. It is highly probable that these "wise men" from the East brought with them the wealth of Daniel.

Being a Prophet of the Most High he was given wisdom, knowledge and revelation beyond any man of his time. He was also told to *"close up and seal the words of the*

scroll until the time of the end." (Daniel 12:4) Daniel likely knew when the Messiah would come, or at least the signs to look for, since he was one prophet that was given very specific time frames for prophetic events.

As such, it is believed by some that he passed on his riches through his eventual successors, the Parthian Magi, with instructions to bring his wealth to the Messiah when the sign of His birth was seen in the Heavens. Since the Magi were a priestly line they may have actually been priests of Yisrael. When the Magi saw the sign, they knew that it signaled the birth of the Hebrew Messiah. Since the prophecies indicated where the Messiah would be born (Micah 5:2-5) and where He would dwell (Isaiah 9:1), they knew where to look for Him.

The specific purpose of the "wise men" was to find the King of Yahudah, because they saw "his star." So what was this star, this sign that made them come looking for the King of the Yahudim. Incredibly, with the advent of computers and technology we can now see what they saw.

They first indicated that they saw the star in the east. In other words, they first saw it when they were at their home in the east. This star first appeared at a certain time. (Matthew 2:7) After conferring with Herod we read the following account. *"⁹ After they had heard the king, they went on their way, and the star they had seen in the east went ahead of them until it stopped over the place where the child was. ¹⁰ When they saw the star, they were overjoyed."* Matthew 2:9-11

Many people believe that this was some sort of light bobbing around in the sky like tinker bell in a Disney movie, but that is not the case. This was clearly a heavenly body that was moving in such a way as to provide a sign.

There were numerous celestial events that occurred prior to and after the birth of Yahushua, including nine major conjunctions that occurred between May 19, 3 BCE and

August 26, 2 BCE.[206] One particular event occurred that would have certainly attracted attention on August 12, 3 BCE. On that day Jupiter rose as a morning star in conjunction with Venus.

Astronomically, Jupiter was said to represent the father of the gods. When we talk about the planets and the stars as signs it is important to remember that they were originally created to transmit information about the plan of YHWH.[207]

The pagans took these created signs and twisted them to fit their own myths – thus the name Jupiter. The Hebrew name for this planet is Tzedeq. It is the King Planet, and it means: *righteousness.* Therefore, we see the planet Jupiter representing the King of Righteousness - Melchizedek.

Astronomically, Venus is symbolic of the Virgin. So the King Planet coming into conjunction with the Virgin signaled a royal birth. The Hebrew name for this planet is Nogah, which indicates brightness, illumination and splendor. Twenty days later, Mercury, which represented the messenger of the gods, came into conjunction with Venus. Known as Kochav, in Hebrew it actually means: "star." Thus this "star" left its position with the Sun and positioned itself into close conjunction with Venus. This took place when the sun had just entered the constellation of Virgo – The Virgin.

Mercury and Venus were then in the constellation of Leo, which represents the Lion – Yahudah. Jupiter was just then entering Leo. This would certainly lead one to the final words of Malachi referring to the Messiah as "the sun of righteousness."

Throughout this period Jupiter was also moving above Regulus, known as the King Star, and actually made a loop or crowning motion over Regulus. Regulus is the brightest star in the constellation of Leo. The track of Jupiter appeared to move in its normal path, then it appeared to stop and move in the opposite direction. Astronomers call this backwards movement retrograde movement. After a certain amount of retrograde motion of Jupiter around Regulus, Jupiter then stopped a second time and continued to proceed on its original course. In this way Jupiter appeared to circle around Regulus, symbolizing the birth of a King to the Magi. This event is likely what the magi were referring to when they talked about His star.[208]

All of these celestial events culminated with the great

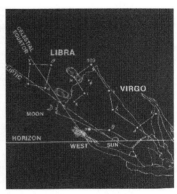

sign that occurred in the heavens on September 11, 3 BCE shown below. Amazingly, this is the sign which was specifically provided in the Book of Revelation as follows: "*1 Now a great sign appeared in heaven: a woman clothed with the sun, with the moon under her feet, and on her head a garland of twelve stars. 2 Then being with child, she cried out in labor and in pain to give birth.*"

Revelation 12:1-2

This has long been a mystery to those who did not realize that a celestial event was being described. The woman is obviously Yisrael, represented through the constellation of the Virgin, known as Bethula, in Hebrew.

Thanks to the precision afforded by technology we can discern the moment that the sign in Revelation 12 occurred. Up to this point we could approximate from the text of the Messianic Writings the date of Yahushua's birth and now we know that the sign confirms the fact that Yahushua was born at sunset, the beginning of September 11, 3 BCE – the Appointed Time of Yom Teruah.

At the moment of his birth, shofars, were blasting throughout the Land of Yisrael. It was the fulfillment of a rehearsal that had occurred for centuries in anticipation of this very moment – to announce the birth of the Messiah.

So Yahushua was born on Yom Teruah in 3 BCE, and anointed by the wise men in 2 BCE, precisely as provided through Daniel. While frankincense and myrhh are resins, they are often turned into oils. It is possible that Yahushua was actually anointed with these two oils, because He was the King of the Yahudim and He was also functioning as a priest – thus two oils for two roles. He "came" and was anointed before 6 CE, the time when the Scepter departed from Yahudah.

It is important to understand that Yahushua was not some theoretical or self-proclaimed king. He was actually the King of Yahudah. That is the context that one must view his time on Earth in order to properly understand His actions and teachings. This is why the Messianic Scriptures provide the lineage of both the mother and the adoptive father of Yahushua. (see Matthew 1:1-16; Luke 3:23-38)

In either case, Yahushua was a descendant of David and an heir to the throne of Yahudah. Joseph was a direct descendant of Solomon who was the fifth son of David and Bathsheba. Mary was a direct descendant of Nathan who was the fourth son of David and Bathsheba.

The rulership of the Northern Kingdom had been taken away from David's line. Therefore, if Yahushua was the Messiah, son of David, he would be able to lead the House of Yahudah, but that was only part of the work to be accomplished. There was still the issue of the Northern Kingdom.

Based simply upon these facts, Yahushua is the only qualified and known candidate for the Messiah. In fact, I know of no other historical figure who meets the criterion established by Gabriel in the Book of Daniel and the prophecy given by Yaakob that the Scepter would not depart from Yahudah until Shiloh (Messiah) comes. (Beresheet 49:10). As a result, if Yahushua is not the Messiah then prophecy has failed and there is no Messiah.

Thankfully, we can easily discern from His life, teachings, death and subsequent resurrection that Yahushua was indeed the Messiah. Like David, He was originally anointed without an earthly kingdom. David was first anointed King by Shemuel and later anointed as the King of the House of Yahudah. After those anointings he was anointed as the King of the House of Yisrael. Only when the Kingdom was united would the seat of the United Kingdom be established in Jerusalem. This was the context of the life of Yahushua.

He was there to unite a divided Kingdom. Like David, Yahushua was anointed before He actually served as king. Later, when Yahushua was 30, the age when a priest was eligible to serve, He was anointed by the Spirit from the Father. (Acts 10:38). We read about this event as the Prophet John the Immerser immersed Yahushua in the Jordan River at the point where Yisrael crossed the Jordan.[209]

Here are the accounts of that even as described in the New Testament. *"When He had been baptized, Yahushua came up immediately from the water; and behold, the heavens were opened to Him, and He saw the Spirit of Elohim descending like a dove and alighting upon Him."* Matthew 3:16 *"And immediately, coming up from the water, He saw the heavens parting and the Spirit descending upon Him like a dove."* Mark 1:10 *"And the set apart Spirit descended in bodily form like a dove upon Him, and a voice came from heaven which said, You are My beloved Son; in You I am well pleased."* Luke 3:22 *"And Yahanan bore witness, saying, I saw the Spirit descending from heaven like a dove, and He remained upon Him."* Yahanan 1:32

His first recorded teachings placed the focus squarely on the Kingdom. In fact, His message was all about the

Kingdom. John the Immerser first came proclaiming the Kingdom, and Yahushua followed bringing the Kingdom. In fact, their message was the same.

"¹ In those days John the Immerser came preaching in the wilderness of Judea, ² and saying, Repent, for the kingdom of heaven is at hand!" Matthew 3:1-2 After John was imprisoned by Herod, Yahushua took over. *"From that time Yahushua began to preach and to say, Repent, for the kingdom of heaven is at hand."* Matthew 4:17

Notice both of these passages come from the Book of Matthew, a text originally written in the Hebrew language.[210] The emphasis was clearly on the Kingdom. All throughout the Gospel of Matthew we read Yahushua teaching the principles of the Kingdom of Heaven. The mystery was that Yahushua was speaking of a heavenly Kingdom that would be brought down upon the earth. Most of the people who heard Him could only think in terms of an earthly kingdom.

Remember that the Kingdom was divided. The House of Yisrael was exiled and divorced. According to Ezekiel and Mosheh, their punishment would last 2,730 years. Therefore, the work of the Messiah was twofold.

As the Second Adam, He would make an atonement for sin originating from the First Adam, so that Creation would be restored. This restoration and population of the restored planet would occur through the Covenant Assembly of Yisrael. Both Houses needed to be cleansed and restored. The House of Yisrael still needed to be regathered and restored into the marriage relationship.

This, of course, was why that point in time was chosen. He specifically stated that He was the Good Shepherd. (John 10:11, 14) He sent His disciples out to the Lost Sheep of the House of Yisrael, and He stated that He came for the Lost Sheep of the House of Yisrael. (Matthew 10:6, 15:24) This was revealing that He would fulfill the

Prophecy of Ezekiel that the Master YHWH would search for and seek out the scattered sheep of the House of Yisrael. (Ezekiel 34)

He was rebuilding the Kingdom and preparing to establish the Kingdom of YHWH on earth. With that in mind, we can read that He spoke in parables teaching the principles of the Kingdom. In fact, He taught His disciples to pray for the Kingdom.

"*8 Therefore do not be like them. For your Father knows the things you have need of before you ask Him. 9 In this manner, therefore, pray: Our Father in heaven, Hallowed be Your name. 10 Your kingdom come. Your will be done on earth as it is in heaven. 11 Give us this day our daily bread. 12 And forgive us our debts, as we forgive our debtors. 13 And do not lead us into temptation, but deliver us from the evil one. For Yours is the kingdom and the power and the glory forever.*" Matthew 6:9-13

So the grand design is to establish the Kingdom of Elohim "on earth as it is in heaven." If that is the case then it is important to know how and where we fit into this kingdom on earth. There are various roles to be filled in any kingdom. First and foremost is the royal family. You do not have a kingdom without a king and the king needs a queen, a bride. This was another important topic of parables. Yahuhsua spoke concerning the bride and the wedding. That is because one of the significant things that this King needed was a Bride to help Him populate His Kingdom.

In fact, Yahushua made it clear that He was going, but would be returning. As a Bridegroom would make the Marriage Contract and then return to His home to prepare a place for this bride, this is exactly what Yahushua said He would do.

"*2 In My Father's house are many mansions; if it were not so, I would have told you. I go to prepare a place for you. 3 And if I go and prepare a place for you, I will come again and receive you to*

Myself; that where I am, there you may be also." John 14:2-3

This is clear marriage language. Remember the progressive stages of the wedding covenant. Yahushua, as the Son of Elohim, was mediating the renewed Covenant with Yisrael as Mosheh had done at Sinai. Only this time, the living arrangements would be different. Now the Bride would be permitted in the House to become one with her Husband.

So Yahushua indicated that He would be returning for His Bride. When we think about how YHWH redeems and delivers His Bride we should remember the plagues rendered upon Egypt - both when Sarai was held captive and later when Yisrael was held captive. This will be a repeating pattern for the further deliverance of the Bride of the Covenant that will be discussed further in the book.

So restoring the Bride was a primary concern, and Yahushua would make a way for the House of Yisrael to be remarried to YHWH. Through this marriage the Bride, the House of Yisrael, would reenter the Kingdom. By cleansing and restoring these relationships, Yahushua would be able to reunite the Kingdom. Yahushua, as the Arm of YHWH, would make a way for the House of Yisrael to be reunited to YHWH and restore both Houses.

He made it clear that Yisrael remained divided while He walked among the people. While in the Land speaking to the Yahudim and the House of Yahudah, He made the specific statement about other sheep. *"And other sheep I have which are not of this fold; them also I must bring, and they will hear My voice; and there will be one flock and one shepherd. John 10:16* In other words, I have other sheep from another house – the House of Yisrael.

He even instructed His disciples: *"But go rather to the lost sheep of the House of Yisrael."* Matthew 10:6 Could it be any clearer? Yahushua came to restore the House of Yisrael to the

Covenant.

His actions and teachings were intended to demonstrate the compassion and forgiveness that would be shown to the adulterous women - Yisrael. There is a particular incident when Yahushua left Judea and went to the city of Samaria that has profound prophetic significance.

"⁵ So He came to a city of Samaria which is called Sychar, near the plot of ground that Yaacob gave to his son Joseph. ⁶ Now Yaacob's well was there. Yahushua therefore, being wearied from His journey, sat thus by the well. It was about the sixth hour. ⁷ A woman of Samaria came to draw water. Yahushua said to her, Give Me a drink. ⁸ For His disciples had gone away into the city to buy food. ⁹ Then the woman of Samaria said to Him, How is it that You, being a Yahudi, ask a drink from me, a Samaritan woman? For Yahudim have no dealings with Samaritans. ¹⁰ Yahushua answered and said to her, If you knew the gift of Elohim, and who it is who says to you, Give Me a drink, you would have asked Him, and He would have given you living water. ¹¹ The woman said to Him, Sir, You have nothing to draw with, and the well is deep. Where then do You get that living water? ¹² Are You greater than our father Yaakob, who gave us the well, and drank from it himself, as well as his sons and his livestock? ¹³ Yahushua answered and said to her, Whoever drinks of this water will thirst again, ¹⁴ but whoever drinks of the water that I shall give him will never thirst. But the water that I shall give him will become in him a fountain of water springing up into everlasting life. ¹⁵ The woman said to Him, Sir, give me this water, that I may not thirst, nor come here to draw. ¹⁶ Yahushua said to her, Go, call your husband, and come here. ¹⁷ The woman answered and said, I have no husband.

Yahushua said to her, You have well said, I have no husband, [18] for you have had five husbands, and the one whom you now have is not your husband; in that you spoke truly. [19] The woman said to Him, Sir, I perceive that You are a prophet. [20] Our fathers worshiped on this mountain, and you Yahudim say that in Jerusalem is the place where one ought to worship. [21] Yahushua said to her, <u>Woman, believe Me, the hour is coming when you will neither on this mountain, nor in Jerusalem, worship the Father.</u> [22] You worship what you do not know; we know what we worship, for salvation is of the Yahudim. [23] But the hour is coming, and now is, when the true worshipers will worship the Father in spirit and truth; for the Father is seeking such to worship Him. [24] Elohim is Spirit, and those who worship Him must worship in spirit and truth. [25] The woman said to Him, <u>I know that Messiah is coming. When He comes, He will tell us all things.</u> [26] Yahushua said to her, <u>I who speak to you am He.</u> [27] And at this point His disciples came, and they marveled that He talked with a woman; yet no one said, What do You seek? or, Why are You talking with her? [28] The woman then left her waterpot, went her way into the city, and said to the men, [29] Come, see a Man who told me all things that I ever did. Could this be the Messiah? [30] Then they went out of the city and came to Him." Yahanan 4:5-30

Notice that this took place in Samaria – the former Capital of the House of Yisrael. It was also where Ahab transcended beyond the sins of Jeroboam and erected a Temple and altar to Baal. (1 Kings 16) It was near the plot of ground that Yaakob gave to his son Joseph. So this was land belonging to Joseph, it was called Yaakob's well.

This woman was with different men, but she was not married. This was the condition of the House of Yisrael.

Remember that Yisrael had been divorced so she could pursue her lovers. Despite her depraved condition, Yahushua expressed his willingness to reveal Himself to her.

In fact, what happens next is extremely important. She went and testified to the Samaritans and many "believed." Yahushua then stayed with them for 2 days and many more believed. Notice they did not convert to some new religion, they simply believed the teaching and testimony of Yahushua.

They believed that Yahushua was the Messiah, and they believed what He taught. One of those significant teachings was that "the hour is coming when you will neither on this mountain, nor in Jerusalem, worship the Father." Remember that the location of worship was what originally divided the Kingdom. Now Yahushua was revealing that they would not worship Yahushua in Jerusalem. This should make us recall where the Throne of YHWH is located – on the Heavenly Mountain known as Mount Zion.[211]

There was another important event recorded in the Scripures involving an unfaithful woman. In this case, the woman was actually caught in the act of adultery and Yahushua was sought out to consider His judgment.

"² *Now early in the morning He came again into the Temple, and all the people came to Him; and He sat down and taught them.* ³ *Then the scribes and Pharisees brought to Him a woman caught in adultery. And when they had set her in the midst,* 4 *they said to Him, Teacher, this woman was caught in adultery, in the very act.* ⁵ *Now Mosheh, in the Torah, commanded us that such should be stoned. But what do You say?* ⁶ *This they said, testing Him, that they might have something of which to accuse Him. But Yahushua stooped down and wrote on the ground with His finger, as though He did not hear.* ⁷ *So when they continued asking Him, He raised Himself up and said to them, He who is without sin among you, let him throw a stone at her first.* ⁸ *And again He* *stooped down and wrote on the ground. ^{9} Then those who heard it, being convicted by their conscience, went out one by one, beginning with the oldest even to the last. And Yahushua was left alone, and the woman standing in the midst. ^{10} When Yahushua had raised Himself up and saw no one but the woman, He said to her, Woman, where are those accusers of yours? Has no one condemned you? ^{11} She said, No one, Lord. And Yahushua said to her, Neither do I condemn you; go and sin no more."* John 8:2-11

So He did not come to condemn the adulterous bride Yisrael, but rather to provide forgiveness and to Renew the Covenant as was described by Jeremiah. The admonishment to *"go and sin no more"* essentially meant to repent and walk according to the righteous instructions in the Torah.

Another event occurred when Yahushua was asked to raise a 12 year old girl from the dead. A ruler from the synagogue came fell at His feet and begged Him to heal his daughter. His daughter had just died and Yahushua was on His way to resurrect her from the dead.

"^{20} And suddenly, a woman who had a flow of blood for twelve years came from behind and touched <u>the hem of His garment</u>. ^{21} For she said to herself, If only I may touch His garment, I shall be made well. ^{22} But Yahushua turned around, and when He saw her He said, <u>Be of good cheer, daughter</u>; your faith has made you well. And the woman was made well from that hour." Matthew 9:20-22 (see also Mark 5:25-34, Luke 8:43-48)

These seemingly different situations are actually intimately connected. One cannot ignore the number 12 and the connection with Yisrael. Interestingly, 12 is the age when a daughter in ancient Israel could be married. This potential bride was dead.

The woman with the flow of blood for 12 years was in a perpetual state of "niddah." She was unclean for 12 years, and could not have relations with a man. In this condition she could not go to the House of YHWH. She certainly

should not be touching a man, let alone a kosher Rabbi.

The woman was intent of taking hold of the "hem" of His garment. The word for "hem" in the Greek is "krespedon" (κράσπεδον). It actually refers to the tzitzit on His garment. Yahushua was, after all, a Torah observant Yisraelite from the tribe of Yahudah. The tzitzit represented the commandments. So this unclean woman taking hold of the tzitzit of the Messiah was an incredible image.

This event makes one think of a future event when the House of Yisrael and the House of Yahudah will be restored. *"Thus says YHWH of hosts: In those days ten from every language of the nations (goyim) shall grasp the tzitzit (kanaf) of a Yahudi, saying, Let us go with you, for we have heard that Elohim is with you."* Zechariah 8:23

Incredibly, this may be the only recorded miracle that Yahuhsua did not initiate. Her faith drew power out of Him and she was healed. The implication is that our faith in the healing power of the Messiah can heal us. Instead of getting angry at the woman for doing such a thing, He told her to be of good cheer. He was happy that she had been healed.

With these two individuals we are given an incredible picture of how Yahushua will treat His bride. He will heal the unclean woman and raise from the dead the virgin bride. Both were called daughters, representing "daughters of Zion."

Indeed, all of His acts of compassion were symbolic and prophetic. Healing sick, lame, blind, lepers and even raising the dead. These were symbolic of the condition and need of the House of Yisrael. So while He came as a King to the House of Yahudah there was more work to be done. He was functioning as a Priest, healing the people, cleansing them and restoring them to YHWH. This is how we know that Yahushua was the Melchizedek.

While there was a physical priesthood operating

through the Levitic line, Yahushua was of a priesthood that transcended the physical priesthood. You could say that it was interdimensional, that is why He spent much time casting out spirits. He operated with authority and He was revealing that we need to deal with the spiritual realm.

There came a time when He brought His disciples to the city of Banias, formerly known as Panias. In the Scriptures the city is referred to as Caesarea Philipi. The origin of the name Panias was due to the worship of Pan. Pan was a vile Nephilim hybrid entity. It was a combination between a goat and a man, similar to the Baphomet that dominates the gate of Washington, DC. It was a dreadful, spiritually dark city, where the people worshipped demons and committed some of the most abominable sexual perversions imaginable involving men, women and animals.

Yahushua brought his disciples there to teach them a very important lesson regarding gates. You see Banias is one

 of the many places throughout the earth believed to contain a "gate to hell" or a gate to the underworld. Amazingly, it is at the base of Mount Hermon – the location where the 200 Watchers descended to earth according to 1 Enoch.

Here is the account from Matthew: *"[15] He said to them, But who do you say that I am? [16] Simon Peter answered and said, You are the Messiah, the Son of the living Elohim. [17] Yahushua answered and said to him, Blessed are you, Simon Bar-Jonah, for flesh and blood has not revealed this to you, but My Father who is in heaven. [18] And I also say to you that you are a stone (aben), and on this rock I will build My House of Prayer, and the gates of Gehenna (hell) shall not prevail against it. [19] And I will give you*

the keys of the kingdom of heaven, and whatever you bind on earth will be bound in heaven, and whatever you loose on earth will be loosed in heaven." Matthew 16:15-19

The revelation spoken by Simon Peter was that Yahushua was "*the Messiah the Son of the living Elohim.*" This is what the returning House of Yisrael would be called "*sons of the living El.*" Interestingly, the Hebrew Gospel of Matthew provides more information. It details Peter as stating "*You are the Messiah . . . the Son of the living Elohim, who has come into this world.*" So Peter was acknowledging that Yahushua came from another world into this world. In other words, Yahushua came into this dimension from another dimension.

Here they were at a gate when this profound revelation was made. Yahushua called Simon Peter a stone (aben), and on that spoken foundation Yahushua would build His House. This would be the House for His Bride. Like the Garden, it will have gates – 12 to be exact. (Ezekiel 48:31-34; Revelation 21:21) Gates were generally made to keep someone out, or possibly to keep someone in.

As a result, this statement by Yahushua was quite interesting. First, He was stating that there were "gates" that led to Gehenna, not just one. Second, He was stating that those gates would not stay closed. The reason was that Yahushua had the keys to the Kingdom of Heaven, and He would give those keys to His followers. He then stated that whatever they bind on earth will be bound in heaven, and whatever they loose on earth will be loosed in heaven.

Therefore He was making a direct correlation between things on this earth and the things in heaven. The gates were the portals that connect the two together. This particular "gate of hell" stands in contrast to the "gate of heaven" at Beth El. While the gate of heaven had a staircase or ladder leading up, the gate of hell at Banias is a cave that leads into the depths of Mount Hermon.

This teaching from Yahushua, concerning these gates with keys, is misunderstood by many. He is telling His followers that He is going to resolve the problem that has plagued mankind since they were expelled from the Garden. While Gehenna was made for the fallen angels, sinful man is also doomed to Gehenna. Yahushua indicated that those in the Covenant could not be restrained by the gates of Gehenna. He would hold the keys to death and Gehenna, and He would also have the keys to the gates of the Kingdom.

He would give them keys, and they should be binding and loosing things here on this earth that are directly connected to the heavens. Binding and loosing is directly connected to interpreting the Torah. Implementing the heavenly instructions here in Earth. So not only was Yahushua functioning in multiple dimensions, those in the Covenant should be doing the same.

Remember that the Covenant was intended to restore the earth and establish the Kingdom of YHWH on earth. A promise was made to Abraham that his decendants would possess the gates of their enemies. (Beresheet 22:17). The word for "gate" in Hebrew is "shar" (ꀄꄱ), and it is connected with "shamar." It is something to be guarded and protected. If you possess the gates of your enemy you have taken control of that territory. We previously read that there was a gate to Eden. That is what Adam was commanded to "guard" (shamar). Man was expelled through that gate and, as a result, he also lost connection with the heavenly dimension.

Yahushua operated in both the spiritual realm and the physical realm. He understood how to command the spirit realm and He taught His disciples how to exercise authority over evil spirits. Remember that Enoch I described evil spirits as the disembodied spirits of the former giants. This gives a different take on what Yahuhsua was doing. He may have

been commanding those very beings that had previously tried to destroy mankind and assume His position.

There is a particular incident a bit south of this gate of hell at Banias. It occurred in the region of the Gergesenes, near a Decapolis City called Hippos. It was there that they likely worshipped Dionysus, a messianic savior god born on December 25, very similar to the Christian Jesus. The sacrificing of pigs was prevelant in Dionysus worship. He was also a version of Bacchus, known for turning water into wine.

It was within this context that Yahushua was met by two demon possessed men who came out of tombs. They are described as being "exceedingly fierce." Upon seeing Yahushua, here is their response: *"And suddenly they cried out, saying, What have we to do with You, Yahushua, You Son of Elohim? Have You come here to torment us before the time?"* Matthew 8:29 It was not unusual for the spirits to recognize Yahushua, and they called Him "son of Elohim." So here was the Son of Elohim confronting the likely offspring of the "sons of Elohim." What is particularly interesting is their statement of whether He came to torment them "before the time."

The word for "time" in the Greek is "kairos" (καιροῦ). We know from the Septuigant that the Hebrew equivalent is "moed" (𐤃𐤏𐤅𐤌). The Hebrew word "moed" (𐤃𐤏𐤅𐤌) means: "Appointed Time." So they knew that He was coming at an Appointed Time to judge the wicked. They even seemed to know the Appointed Time, because they were indicating that He was early. We already examined some of the patterns involving the Appointed Times pointing to the Messiah. Through His life, we also see Him fulfilling the Appointed Times. This passage leads us to believe that His future appearance will also revolve around the Appointed Times. In fact, you cannot understand His second coming

unless you recognize the fact that Yahushua is fulfilling the patterns of the Appointed Times.

In another account of this event, the demon is described as Legion because there was a large amount of demons and they begged Him that He would not command them to go into the abyss. The abyss, as we already saw, was the holding place for angelic beings awaiting judgment. They clearly did not want to go there, and Yahushua clearly had the authority to tell them where to go. They ended up going into a herd of pigs, about 2,000 of them. The herd then ran down into the sea and drowned. This likely put a damper on Dionysus worship for awhile, and the symbolism is profound. The sea is often likened to the abyss, so that is likely where these demons ended up after all.

So understanding the connection between these two realms and the authority that Yahushua gives to those in the Covenant is critical. Yahushua demonstrated His authority and His intention was to instruct those in the Covenant to exercise that same authority. Yahushua is at the center of the Covenant. In fact, He is the Covenant, and He is the One Who was foretold would unite the Heavens and the Earth. The second Aleph Taw (✗𐤊) in the Scriptures revealed the connection between the Heavens and the Earth (𐤓𐤀𐤊𐤀 ✗𐤊𐤉 𐤅𐤆𐤉𐤌𐤔𐤀).

Remember that Abram was uncircumcised when the blood Covenant was executed. He represented the "ger" (𐤓𐤂), the stranger, coming from the "nations" (𐤌𐤆𐤉𐤂𐤓). In this uncircumcised state he crossed over and became a Hebrew. He then entered into Covenant with the Messiah. The Messiah, as the representative of YHWH in the Covenant, was the smoke and the fire that passed through the trench of blood. He was the only One who passed through the Covenant pieces. That blood with the eight pieces represented the DNA of those in the Covenant. He

had to bear the penalty of death so that the "ger" could enter the Covenant. This is how the Covenant would be renewed with the House of Yisrael.

Through the regathering of the House of Yisrael, the nations could join the Covenant and proceed to be circumcised. They then could enter into an intimate relationship with YHWH. The death required from this Covenant being broken was focused on the Passover. That was why Yahushua needed to die, representing the Lamb of Elohim.

Incredibly, it was His own House - the House of Yahudah - that wanted Him dead. It was prophesied by Ezekiel that the ger would join with Yisrael and be given an inheritance.

"*²¹ Thus you shall divide this land among yourselves according to the tribes of Yisrael. ²² It shall be that you will divide it by lot as an inheritance for yourselves, and for the strangers (ger) who dwell among you and who bear children among you. They shall be to you as native-born among the children of Yisrael; they shall have an inheritance with you among the tribes of Yisrael. ²³ And it shall be that in whatever tribe the stranger (ger) dwells, there you shall give him his inheritance, says the Master YHWH.*" Ezekiel 47:21-23

Therefore, this Scripture passage stands in stark contrast to the common held teaching of the Jews through their "oral torah."²¹² Those who consider themselves genetically descended from ancient Yisraelites leave little room for any others who desire to join the Covenant. In fact, it is fairly common for Jews to discourage Gentiles from following the Torah. They teach that the Torah was meant for those of Jewish descent, which is simply untrue. Thus, Judaism finds itself in direct contravention with the express desire of YHWH to include the "ger." The modern State of Israel specifically describes itself as a "Jewish State." Those from the House of Yisrael are not welcome to return to their allotted land if they cannot prove "Jewish" lineage or submission to the religion of Judaism.

Thankfully, you do not need to convert to Judasim to enter into the Covenant that Yahushua renewed with the House of Yisrael and the House of Yahudah. Further, if Yahushua wants you to return to the Land, it will happen, regardless of any governmental policy.

The religious leaders found Yahushua's emphasis on the "sinners" and the lost to be offensive. In fact, here is what they said about Yahushua: *"Look, a glutton and a winebibber, a friend of tax collectors and sinners!"* Matthew 11:19 The religious leaders were not concerned about the lost in their own midst, and they certainly were not interested in their brethren from the House of Yisrael. They were not prepared to accept the stranger (ger) into Yisrael, contrary to the plan and purpose of YHWH.

They ended up being diametrically opposed to Yahushua. They were building their own kingdom while Yahushua was building the Kingdom of YHWH. They eventually decided to kill Him.

Amazingly, once they made the decision to kill Yahushua He stopped appearing in public. Yahushua went to a city called Ephraim after the Jews agreed to kill him. *"[53] Then, from that day on, they plotted to put Him to death. [54] Therefore Yahushua no longer walked openly among the Yahudim, but went from there into the country near the wilderness, to a city called Ephraim, and there remained with His disciples."* John 11:53-54

Imagine the significance of the statement. He went to a city called Ephraim <u>near the wilderness</u>. He could not have made the point any clearer! They wanted to kill Him so He was going to the lost sheep of the House of Yisrael. Ephraim was like sheep lost in the wilderness. The House of Yisrael

had been divorced, but it was promised that she would be restored. This was the focus of the Messiah.

He came exactly when Daniel was told that He would come, and He did exactly what was needed at the time. The punishment period for the House of Yisrael still had a long way to go, so He was not going to reunite the Kingdom at that point in time. That was for the future.

That is why there were two different Messianic expectations, and two different appearances. Those who reject Yahushua as Messiah because He did not reunite the Kingdom are either ignorant or intentionally ignoring the prophecies that specifically point to His first coming.

Instead of restoring the Kingdom of Yisrael, at the end of His work, He rode into Jerusalem on a donkey with a colt. The kings of Yisrael rode donkeys – not horses. Now anybody can ride a donkey, so that simple act would not have been significant.

What makes the act so important was that it did not just include a donkey, it involved two animals according to the prophecy of Zechariah. Here is the prophecy. *"Rejoice greatly, O daughter of Zion! Shout, O daughter of Jerusalem! Behold, your King is coming to you; He is just and having salvation, lowly and riding on a donkey, a colt, the foal of a donkey."* Zechariah 9:9

Notice the two animals described in the prophecy. Here is the instruction that Yahushua gave to His disciples prior to entering Jerusalem: *"Go into the village opposite you, and immediately you will find a donkey tied, and a colt with her. Loose them and bring them to Me."* Matthew 21:2

So there were two animals, not just one. His conduct consisted of specific actions intended to fulfill the prophecy in Zecheriah. Yahushua was fulfilling prophecy and specifically making the statement that He was the promised King.

This event has caused no small controversy because of the apparent contradictions in the accounts. Let us start by looking closer at the Hebrew text of Zechariah. The phrase *"on a donkey, and a colt, the foal of a donkey"* is "al-chamowr b'al-eyer ben-ethnote" (ХҮ⅄Х⅄-⅄⅁   ⅁⅄⊙-(⊙Ү ⅁Ү⅏Ⱶ-(⅄).

The word "al" means: "the highest." The word "chamowr" means: "donkey," and one should recall the Aleph Taw (Х⅄) affixed to the donkey that transported the sacrifice of Abraham to the site at Moriah. Here now we have "the highest" ((⅄) affixed to the donkey and associated with the Aleph Taw (Х⅄).

Now that is straighforward and simple to understand. The next words are actually quite profound. The words "and a colt" are "b'al-eyer" in the Hebrew. Again, "al" means: "highest." The word "eyer" actually means: "city." So the Messiah will be coming on the "highest city." This is a hint to another prophecy concerning a future return when He comes in the clouds. This will make more sense further in the discussion.

Finally, the phrase translated as: "the foal of a donkey" is "ben-atonote." The word "ben" means "son." The word "atonote" means: "female donkeys." This would refer to a colt. Therefore there is a donkey and a colt, and hidden between these to animals is a reference to Him also riding a "highest city."

So the prophecy describes two different animals and has deeper meaning than just the animals. It speaks to his various entrances as King. An entrance in the present time involving two animals, followed by another in the future involving "the highest city" – the New Jerusalem. Indeed, riding on two animals represents His two roles – Messiah ben Joseph and Messiah ben David.

Now let us read the account from Luke. "²⁹ *And it came*

to pass, when He drew near to Bethphage and Bethany, at the mountain called Olivet, that He sent two of His disciples, *30* saying, Go into the village opposite you, where as you enter you will find a colt tied, on which no one has ever sat. Loose it and bring it here. *31* And if anyone asks you, Why are you loosing it?'thus you shall say to him, Because the Lord has need of it. *32* So those who were sent went their way and found it just as He had said to them. *33* But as they were loosing the colt, the owners of it said to them, Why are you loosing the colt? *34* And they said, The Master has need of him. *35* Then they brought him to Yahushua. And they threw their own clothes on the colt, and they set Yahushua on him. *36* And as He went, many spread their clothes on the road. *37* Then, as He was now drawing near the descent of the Mount of Olives, the whole multitude of the disciples began to rejoice and praise Elohim with a loud voice for all the mighty works they had seen, *38* saying: Blessed is the King who comes in the Name of YHWH! Peace in heaven and glory in the highest! *39* And some of the Pharisees called to Him from the crowd, Teacher, rebuke Your disciples. *40* But He answered and said to them, I tell you that if these should keep silent, the stones would immediately cry out. *41* Now as He drew near, He saw the city and wept over it, *42* saying, If you had known, even you, especially in this your day, the things that make for your peace! But now they are hidden from your eyes. *43* For days will come upon you when your enemies will build an embankment around you, surround you and close you in on every side, *44* and level you, and your children within you, to the ground; and they will not leave in you one stone upon another, because you did not know the time of your visitation." Luke 19:29-44

Here is the account from John. "*12* The next day a great multitude that had come to the Feast, when they heard that Yahushua was coming to Jerusalem, *13* took branches of palm trees and went out to meet Him, and cried out: Hosanna! Blessed is He who comes in the Name of YHWH! The King of Yisrael! *14* Then Yahushua, when He had found a young donkey, sat on it; as it is written: *¹⁵ Fear not, daughter of Zion; Behold, your King is coming, Sitting on a donkey's colt. ¹⁶ His disciples did not understand these things at first; but when Yahushua was glorified, then they remembered that these things were written about Him and that they had done these things to Him."* John 12:12-16

It is believed by some that there were actually two different entries - one on the sixth day before Passover and one on the fourth day before Passover.[213]

This cannot be proven but would account for the description of Yahushua seated on two different animals as well as the fact that in one instance people were throwing their clothes down on the road before Him while in the other, they were waving palm branches. The idea of two different triumphal entries could be consistent with the accounts in Matthew and Mark.

The first entry might have only involved the disciples before the throngs had all arrived for the Feast. They declared him a King and proclaimed peace. Afterward He wept over Jerusalem. The second entry could have involved the multitudes who had arrived for the Feast. They declared Him King of Yisrael, not just Yahudah.

This parallels the two different roles of the Messiah as King of the House of Yahudah first, and later over the King of the House of Yisrael and a united Kingdom. In the first entry He would have come into Jerusalem on Day 8 of Month 1. The eighth day is the day of circumcision and it is essential to the Covenant. Remember that Yahushua walked between the 8 pieces in the Covenant with Abram. The Feast of the Eighth Day following Succot is the most mystical Appointed Time and the culmination of the Plan of YHWH as set forth in the Appointed Times. During His first coming He would not be recognized by all.

The second Triumphal entry would have occurred on Day 10 of Month 1. The Feasts of the First and Seventh months interestingly parallel one another except there is no specific Appointed Time on Day 10 of Month 1. Instead, it is "lamb selection day." It is the day when people would select their lamb to slaughter at Passover. If you do not choose an unblemished lamb on that day, then you do not have a lamb for the Passover to cover the firstborn of the house. This is an important parallel to Day 10 of Month 7 – Yom Kippur. It is a day when blood is shed and atonement is made for the Assembly of Yisrael.

There is a very important Appointed Time on Day 10 of Month 7, the Month when it is believed Yahushua will return to judge and rule over the earth. Day 10 of Month 7 is the Day of Atonements – Yom Ha'kippurim. It is a day when the blood of the goat of YHWH is shed.

During His first appearance Yahushua died at Passover as the Lamb of Elohim. It is by the blood that He shed during His first appearance that the redeemed firstborn of the House of YHWH will be delivered from death. He will also be shedding much blood as the wrath of the Lamb is poured out upon the earth. More on that as we continue.

Understanding the symbolism of His actions and their prophetic implications is important. In fact, waving of palm branches at His second entry provides a clue regarding the timing of His second Coming. Those in Covenant are commanded to wave palm branches during Succot, a Feast of the Seventh month. (Vayiqra 23:40) In ancient times it was common to lay down palm branches before kings and newlyweds. Newlyweds were treated as royalty after their wedding, especially during their 7 day wedding feast. This was all symbolic of a future wedding.

The failure to discern the meaning of His actions is one of the major problems that many Jews have with Yahushua. They claim that He did not restore the divided Kingdom, but they fail to understand the dual nature of His

role as the anointed High Priest and the anointed King.

After dying as the Passover Lamb, Yahushua had to come again and fulfill the pattern of the Messiah ben David. The conquering King Who would rule the World with righteous judgment (Revelation 19:11-21). He repeatedly spoke of His return, although it seems clear that those statements were not immediately understood by those who heard Him. People had expectations that the Messiah would come and deliver the Yisraelites from their Roman oppressors. As a result, people wanted Yahushua to "save now" - Hosanna

They failed to realize that He needed to die. Despite the fact that it was clearly set forth in the Scriptures, the people were consumed with their own expectations. In fact that was not necessarily made clear until two days before Yahushua was crucified when He plainly stated: *"You know that after two days is the Passover, and the Son of Man will be delivered up to be crucified."* Matthew 26:2

Prior to that time things seemed to be on track for the advent of the Messianic Age with Yahushua at the healm. He even made statements about when He would return, although this was not necessarily understood at the time. It was not necessarily apparent that He must die first. In fact, this was inconceivable to most, due to their expectations.

Those statements were couched within other prophetic statements, and while they were likely misunderstood by many in the past, they are also misunderstood by people today.

One of the most detailed statements of the future was made by Yahushua in what is known as the Olivet Discourse. It is called the Olivet Discourse because it was spoken by Yahushua on the Mount of Olives, shortly before His death. The most comprehensive depiction is found in Matthew 24, but there is another similar account in Mark 13. Luke 21 is often grouped with these passages, although that

passage begins in the Temple and probably was spoken exclusively in and about the Temple. They all add to our understanding, and it is helpful to look at all of them in order to recognize the full meaning.

Many misunderstand the substance of the "discourse" because they fail to read it in context. We will now examine that very important prophetic statement. First we will look at the entire portion of Matthew 24, and then we will examine that text along with the related passages in the other Gospels.

"¹ Then Yahushua went out and departed from the Temple, and His disciples came up to show Him the buildings of the Temple. ² And Yahushua said to them, 'Do you not see all these things? Assuredly, I say to you, not one stone shall be left here upon another, that shall not be thrown down.' ³ Now as He sat on the Mount of Olives, the disciples came to Him privately, saying, '<u>Tell us, when will these things be? And what will be the sign of Your coming, and of the end of the age?</u>' ⁴ And Yahushua answered and said to them: Take heed that no one deceives you. ⁵ For many will come in My Name, saying, 'I am the Messiah,' and will deceive many. ⁶ And you will hear of wars and rumors of wars. See that you are not troubled; for all these things must come to pass, but the end is not yet. ⁷ For nation will rise against nation, and kingdom against kingdom. And there will be famines, pestilences, and earthquakes in various places. ⁸ All these are the beginning of sorrows. ⁹ Then they will deliver you up to tribulation and kill you, and you will be hated by all nations for My Name's sake. ¹⁰ And then many will be offended, will betray one another, and will hate one another. ¹¹ Then many false prophets will rise up and deceive

many. ¹² And because lawlessness will abound, the love of many will grow cold. ¹³ But he who endures to the end shall be saved. ¹⁴ And this gospel of the kingdom will be preached in all the world as a witness to all the nations, and then the end will come. ¹⁵ Therefore <u>when you see the 'abomination of desolation,' spoken of by Daniel the prophet, standing in the set apart place</u> ¹⁶ <u>then let those who are in Judea flee to the mountains.</u> ¹⁷ Let him who is on the housetop not go down to take anything out of his house. ¹⁸ And let him who is in the field not go back to get his clothes. ¹⁹ But woe to those who are pregnant and to those who are nursing babies in those days! ²⁰ And pray that your flight may not be in winter or on the Sabbath. ²¹ For then there will be great tribulation, such as has not been since the beginning of the world until this time, no, nor ever shall be. ²² And unless those days were shortened, no flesh would be saved; but for the elect's sake those days will be shortened. ²³ Then if anyone says to you, 'Look, here is the Messiah!' or 'There!' Do not believe it. ²⁴ For false messiahs and false prophets will rise and show great signs and wonders to deceive, if possible, even the elect. ²⁵ See, I have told you beforehand. ²⁶ Therefore if they say to you, 'Look, He is in the desert!' do not go out; or 'Look, He is in the inner rooms!' do not believe it. ²⁷ For as the lightning comes from the east and flashes to the west, so also will the coming of the Son of Man be. ²⁸ For wherever the carcass is, there the eagles will be gathered together. ²⁹ 'Immediately after the tribulation of those days the sun will be darkened, and the moon will not give its light; the stars will fall from heaven, and the powers of the heavens will be shaken. *³⁰ Then the sign of the Son of Man will appear in heaven, and then all the tribes of the earth will mourn, and they will see the Son of Man coming on the clouds of heaven with power and great glory. ³¹ And He will send His messengers with a great sound of a blast, and they will gather together His elect from the four winds, from one end of heaven to the other.* ³² Now learn this parable from the fig tree: When its branch has already become tender and puts forth leaves, you know that summer is near. ³³ So you also, when you see all these things, know that it is near - at the doors! ³⁴ Assuredly, I say to you, this generation will by no means pass away till all these things take place. ³⁵ Heaven and earth will pass away, but My words will by no means pass away. ³⁶ But of that day and hour no one knows, not even the angels of heaven, but My Father only. *³⁷ But as the days of Noah were, so also will the coming of the Son of Man be.* ³⁸ For as in the days before the flood, they were eating and drinking, marrying and giving in marriage, until the day that Noah entered the ark, ³⁹ and did not know until the flood came and took them all away, so also will the coming of the Son of Man be. ⁴⁰ Then two men will be in the field: one will be taken and the other left. ⁴¹ Two women will be grinding at the mill: one will be taken and the other left. ⁴² Watch therefore, for you do not know what hour your Master is coming. ⁴³ But know this, that if the master of the house had known what hour the thief would come, he would have watched and not allowed his house to be broken into. ⁴⁴ Therefore you also be ready, for the Son of Man is coming at an hour you do not expect. ⁴⁵ 'Who then is a faithful and wise servant, whom his master made ruler over his household, to give them food in due season? *46* Blessed is that servant whom his master, when he comes, will find so doing. *47* Assuredly, I say to you that he will make him ruler over all his goods. *48* But if that evil servant says in his heart, 'My master is delaying his coming,' *49* and begins to beat his fellow servants, and to eat and drink with the drunkards, *50* the master of that servant will come on a day when he is not looking for him and at an hour that he is not aware of, *51* and will cut him in two and appoint him his portion with the hypocrites. There shall be weeping and gnashing of teeth." Matthew 24:1-51

Again, to properly understand the information being conveyed by Yahushua, it is important to recognize the context. Yahushua had previously made the triumpal entry into Jerusalem as prophesied by Zechariah. He rode into Jerusalem lowly, humble on a donkey and a colt. He was functioning as the Messiah, Son of Joseph.

The people recognized Him as the Messiah, Son of David - The King of Yahudah. As such, the people expected Him to restore the Kingdom. In fact, it appeared as though that was exactly what He was going to do. He proceeded to cleanse the Temple. He healed the lame and the blind. He was teaching and speaking in the Temple, and had just finished the famous woes to the Scribes and Pharisees.

It looked as though everything was set for Him to assume control. Then He made the following statement. "*37* O Jerusalem, Jerusalem, the one who kills the prophets and stones those who are sent to her! How often I wanted to gather your children together, as a hen gathers her chicks under her wings, but you were not willing! *38* See! Your house is left to you desolate; *39* for I say to you, you shall see Me no more till you say, 'Blessed is He who comes in the Name of YHWH!' " Matthew 23:37-39

Yahushua made a reference to "your house" being left "desolate." He then stated that they would see Him no more until they said, *"Blessed is He who comes in the name of YHWH!"* The people had actually just said that the previous day during the triumphal entry (Matthew 21:9). So the disciples were understandably confused. They had just arrived, and it appeared that Yahushua was getting ready to reign. Now He said that He would not return until there was a repeat of what had just happened.

Clearly the disciples were interested in when this would be. They wanted Yahushua to establish the Messianic Kingdom. Before leaving the Temple we read that *"some spoke of the Temple how it was adorned with beautiful stones and donations."* Luke 21:5 Instead of assuming His reign in Jerusalem, they left the Temple and the City. It seemed like everything was set for the Messianic Age to begin, and now Yahushua was leaving the Temple.

As they left, the disciples were trying to redirect Yahushua's attention back to the Temple. We read the following: *"His disciples came up to show Him the buildings of the Temple"* Matthew 24:1 *"Teacher, see the manner of stones and what buildings are here!"* Mark 13:1.

He just left the Temple, why did they feel the need to *"show Him the buildings."* They were directing His attention to the Temple as if to say – "Where are you going? Here it is - your Temple. Let's go get started with the Kingdom."

Yahushua's response to that was: *"Do you not see all these things? Assuredly, I say to you, not one stone shall be left here upon another, that shall not be thrown down."* So they were showing Him the Temple, and He indicated that the days were coming when it would be totally destroyed.

Yahushua then went away to the Mount of Olives. This was the perfect place to view the Temple complex. As they sat on the Mount of Olives the Temple would dominate their view. It was at this point that His disciples came to Him privately and asked Him about His statement.

The Temple was clearly the focus of their question as the Gospel of Mark provides "*3 Now as He sat on the Mount of Olives opposite the Temple, Peter, James, John and Andrew asked Him privately, 4 'Tell us, when will these things be? And what will be the sign when all these things will be fulfilled?'*" Mark 13:3-4. So we read 2 questions from these 4 disciples. They wanted to know 1) when the Temple would be destroyed, and 2) what would be the sign?

In Luke 21 we read: "*. . . Teacher, but when shall this be? And what is the sign when this is about to take place?*" Luke 21:7. Here again, 2 specific questions are posed to Yahushua concerning the timing and the signs associated with the destruction of the Temple.

The observant reader might have noticed that the passage from Matthew actually involved 3 questions: 1) *when will these things be? 2) what will be the sign of Your coming? and 3) what will be the sign of the end of the age?* These are really loaded questions based upon their expectations of how things would occur. Remember that the context of the questions was focused on the then standing Temple.

Now the disciples likely believed that question 2 and 3 were one and the same, because they believed the end of their present age would lead into the new age – the Age of the Messiah. So if the Temple was going to be destroyed, when was it going to happen and when would Yahushua come to begin the Age of the Messiah? With the vantage of hindsight we understand that the destruction of the Temple would not coincide with the reign of Messiah, but they did not.

In all of the Gospel accounts, Yahushua answered them within the context and the subject of the conversation – the destruction of Temple. We know that the destruction of the Temple occurred in 70 CE. History is replete with records of the very events foretold by Yahushua. The Scriptures speak of some of the tribulation experienced by the disciples. They were killed and persecuted. Yahushua told them that they would be hated for His Name, and they were. (Acts 5:28, 5:40, 9:21, 15:26)

When He said those who *"endure to the end would be saved,"* He was not referring to the end of the world. He was referring to the end of their lives. In other words, do not get discouraged and give up. Finish the race and keep the good faith to the end of your life. At the end of your life you will be saved. This is when the salvation of our soul occurs, at the end, not when we say a prayer or ask Jesus into our hearts. This will be discussed further on in the text.

He could also have meant that the lives of those who endured until the end of the Roman siege would be saved. Salvation can either mean a deliverance from physical death or deliverance of the soul from death.

We know that there was extensive lawlessness at that time, which was disobedience to the commandments. Yahushua repeatedly spoke to this before He was crucified. There were many false messiahs who appeared along with many false prophets. What was very significant about the Yahudim prior to the destruction of the Temple was their divisions. There was incredible strife and murder occurring between the various seditious groups of Yahudim as the "love of many grew cold."

Historians such as Suetonius, Tacitus and Seneca provide ample evidence confirming the wars and rumors of wars, the famines, pestilence and earthquakes leading up to 70 CE. We also have recorded the history and tradition regarding the disciples spreading the Gospel throughout the world before the "end."

The word "end" in this context is does not mean the "end of the age." The disciples asked about the "end" in

Matthew 24:3, and there the word was "sunteleia" (συντελείας) which means: "entire completion." Yahushua's words in verses 6 and 14 when He refers to the "end" are translated as "telos" (τέλος) which is "the point aimed at as a limit." So while the disciples were focused on "the end of the age," Yahushua was focused on the end of His statement – the destruction of the Temple. Yahushua was answering the question correctly. The disciples had asked the wrong question.

Again, it appears that those asking the questions believed these events to be the same, but Yahushua was very clear that they were not. While He was describing the events leading up to the destruction of the Temple, He was very clear that He would not be returning immediately.

One particular event has caused great confusion for people in this present day. Specifically, Yahushua stated: *"when you see the 'abomination of desolation' spoken of by Daniel the Prophet standing in the set apart place then let those in Judea flee to the mountains."* (Matthew 24:16)

As discussed previously in the Daniel chapter, many believe that the "abomination of desolation" had already occurred under Antiochus IV around 168 BCE. Recall that was the event described in Daniel 11. Now we read Yahushua stating specifically when you see *"the abomination of desolation spoken of by Daniel."* In other words, there was another and we know that it must refer to the one in Daniel 9 and Daniel 12.

This seems to be absolutely confirmed by the fact that Yahushua was making this statement during the 70th week. The very week that He would "confirm the Covenant," and bring an end to sacrifice and offering by offering Himself in the middle of the week, on Passover Day. The fulfillment of this 70th week in Daniel was the same passage that described the "abomination of desolation."

"And He shall confirm a Covenant with many for one week; but in the middle of the week He shall bring an end to sacrifice and offering. And on the wing of abominations shall be one who makes desolate, even until the consummation, which is determined, is poured out on the desolate."
Daniel 9:27

Many translations begin this passage with "then," as if this passage needed to take place after all of the events described in Daniel 9:26. The verse actually begins with a "vav" (Y), which means "and." Therefore, the verse describing the 70th week connects that week with the previously described 62 weeks.

This is incredible how Yahushua tied it all together at this very important time. While Yahushua was referring to the "abomination of desolation" as a future event, at that point in time, it was still well into the future. Many today continue to interpret this as a future event that still must be fulfilled. Again, that might require the building of yet another Temple prior to the return of Yahushua, and the setting up of some pagan idol or the "anti-christ" as some believe. At the very least an altar would need to be built for sacrifices. The question we should ask is why would YHWH restore the sacrificial system if the messiah brought an end to sacrifice and offering with His life?

The problem with the belief that this is a future event from this present day is the fact that Yahushua was speaking to His disciples alive in the first century CE. He specifically instructed them *"when you see"* the abomination of desolation then get out of Judea. In fact, when read in conjunction with the Daniel 12 "abomination of desolation" they were given a specific timeline within which to flee. These events were a precursor of the destruction about to come, and it was the trigger event that was a signal for those followers of

Yahushua to leave, for their own protection.

We can glean some clarity concerning this "abomination" from a previous event in Yisraelite history. *"³ And Jonathan attacked the garrison of the Philistines that was in Geba, and the Philistines heard of it. Then Saul blew the shofar throughout all the land, saying, Let the Hebrews hear! ⁴ Now all Yisrael heard it said that Saul had attacked a garrison of the Philistines, and that Yisrael had also become an abomination to the Philistines. And the people were called together to Saul at Gilgal."* 1 Samuel 13:3-4.

Yisrael, under the leadership of Saul, the first king of Yisrael, had become an "abomination" to the Philistines. He was attacking and becoming a stench to his adversaries. This was used in the context of warfare. The word in Hebrew is "ba'ash" (W✗𐤙). It is different from the "shiqquts" (✲Y𐤒W) in Daniel 11 and 12, but nevertheless the context is similar.

Notice the shofar. It is an instrument to get the attention of the Hebrews. All of Yisrael heard the shofar. In the future the shofar will again call the Hebrews and all Yisrael will hear it – the voice of YHWH. Yahushua was providing a warning to His followers – like a shofar blast.

While the "abomination of desolation" continues to baffle people because they strictly look at it as a future event, Luke 21 actually provides greater clarity. Remember that the only questions posed in Luke 21 involved the destruction of the Temple. Yahushua answered those questions up until verse 24 when He indicated that Jerusalem would be trampled *"until the time of the Gentiles are filled."* After that point He discussed the signs of His return.

Prior to that point His statements were directed to the upcoming destruction of the Temple by the Romans. In Luke 21:20 we read Yahushua stating: *"When you see Jerusalem surrounded by armies, then know that its desolation is near."* In

other words, desolation would result from the pagan army surrounding Jerusalem. That desolation would continue until "*the times of the Gentiles are filled.*" (Luke 21:24)

Another way of saying the abomination of desolation is "the abomination that lays waste." Often abomination refers to idolatry and the "laying waste" or "desolation" refers to the abolition of the Temple service and the destruction of the City and the Temple.

What many fail to recognize is that destruction of the Temple was a foretold curse if Yisrael did not obey, and that punishment was referred to as "a desolation." In Vayiqra 26 we read: "*[29] You shall eat the flesh of your sons, and you shall eat the flesh of your daughters. [30] I will destroy your high places, cut down your incense altars, and cast your carcasses on the lifeless forms of your idols; and My soul shall abhor you. [31] I will lay your cities waste and bring your sanctuaries to desolation, and I will not smell the fragrance of your sweet aromas. [32] I will bring the land to desolation, and your enemies who dwell in it shall be astonished at it.*" Vayiqra 26:29-32

This is probably a good point to, once again, address the third mention of an "abomination of desolation" in the Book of Daniel. (Daniel 12:11) Remember that the first mention was made in Daniel 9 and was specifically tied in with the timing of the Messiah, the Temple and Jerusalem. It clearly was linked to the destruction of the Temple, and we know that event occurred in 70 CE by the Romans. The second instance was found in Daniel 11, during the same revelation given through Daniel 12. This revelation was sequential and the Daniel 11 mention was clearly tied to Antiochus IV, around 170 BCE.

We can assume that the Daniel 12 mention occurred after the Daniel 11 mention. The reference in Daniel 12 must also be read in context. Daniel was concerned about Jerusalem, the Temple and the Messiah. He asked: "*Why lord, what shall be the end of these things?"* Daniel 12:8 The answer was then given *"And from the time you see that which is continuous and the abomination is set up there shall be 1,290 days.* ¹² *Blessed is he who waits, and comes to the 1,335 days."* Daniel 12:11

He was asking about the end of <u>these things</u>. Based upon the context there is every reason to believe that this abomination of desolation being referred to is the same one referred to in Daniel 9, involving the Roman invasion.

So what do we make with the time frames of the 1,290 days and the 1,335 days. It is not difficult to determine, when it is placed within proper historical context. We have very detailed accounts of the Roman invasion from the works of Josephus.

We know that in the year 66 CE Cestius arrived at Gabao on Day 22 of Month 7. This was a High Sabbath, an Appointed Time known as the Eighth Day or Shemini Atzeret. Remember that Daniel was previously told that the 1,290 days was literally *"Appointed Times, Appointed Times half."* (Daniel 12:7) This was not simply another way of stating 1,290 days, it was a clue involving the Appointed Times.

On Day 30 of Month 7 he entered the City of David, and on Day 5 of Month 8 he broke through the Temple wall, and then retreated for no known reason. This all occurred in the year 66 CE – 3 ½ years before 70 CE.

Another event in 66 CE involved Eliazer ben Hanania, a leader of the Yahudim during the revolt against the Romans. "Eliazar was the son of the High Priest Hanania ben Nedebai and hence a political figure of the 1st century Judaea Province. Eliazar worked as a high-positioned Temple clerk in Jerusalem. At the outbreak of the rebellion in 66 CE and following the initial outbreak of the violence in Jerusalem convinced the priests of the Jewish Temple to stop service of sacrifice for the Emperor. The action, though

largely symbolic, was one of the main milestones to bring a full-scale rebellion in Judea."[214]

The reason this is significant is because the sacrifice on behalf of the Roman Emperor was something "continuous." That was one of the key events that fueled the revolt of the Yahudim. Many interpret Daniel 12:11 to specifically refer to the Temple service, but that is not what the text says. Again, this popular misunderstanding supports belief that the Temple in Jerusalem must be rebuilt and sacrifices must begin and end before the count begins in the future.

We can see from history that the "continuous" sacrifice for the Roman Emperor in the Temple ceased around 3 ½ years prior to the destruction. Now this does not mean that prophecies cannot or will not be repeated in the future, but it is very likely that the count began sometime in 66 CE, when the sacrifice for the Roman Emperor was "taken away."

Around 3 ½ years later Titus, commanding the 10th Roman Legion, invaded and then completely surrounded Jerusalem on the Day 4 of the Month 3 in 70 CE. The Temple was later destroyed on the Day 9 of Month 5 – Tisha B'Av. The destruction of the Temple and Jerusalem by the Romans was so complete that it is the very definition of the word desolation. *"Jerusalem . . . was so thoroughly laid even with the ground by those that dug it up to the foundation, that there was left nothing to make those that came thither believe it had ever been inhabited."*[215]

We can see that the events surrounding the revolt and subsequent destruction of Jerusalem and the Temple could have fulfilled the time frames discussed in Daniel. Again, this does not preclude another fulfillment in the future – that is always a possibility. The point is that there was very likely a fulfillment in 70 CE, and people who are anticipating the

return of Messiah may be waiting for one or more "necessary" events that may not occur, because they already occurred in the past. As a result, they may find themselves asleep and unprepared.

The evidence seems to indicate that the "abomination of desolation" prophecy in Daniel 12 was fulfilled in 70 CE. If the point could not be any clearer, the destruction of the Temple by the Romans under the command of Titus is traditionally understood to have occurred on the same day as the destruction of the Temple by the Babylonians under the command of Nebuchadnezzar – the 9ᵗʰ of Av (Day 9 of Month 5). Therefore, Solomon's Temple and Zerubbabel's Temple were both destroyed on the same day, essentially completing the prophecies given to Daniel that were not sealed.

The eye witness accounts of the invasion of Jerusalem and the destruction of the Temple by Josephus confirm the horrifying nature of what occurred.[216] In fact, the statement that "*unless YHWH shortened those days no flesh would be saved*" was clearly applicable to that time of desolation. All of the Yahudim in Jerusalem would have been wiped out if Titus continued his siege.

During the siege, the inhabitants of Jerusalem were killing themselves inside the city while they were also starving to death. Dead bodies were strewn throughout the city and the Temple. Disease was rampant. There were even reports of people eating the dead. All of the inhabitants of the city would have died if the siege were not ended. The days of the siege were shortened for the sake of the elect – the chosen ones who were present, those who did not flee as warned by Yahushua.

Now many take the position that this cannot be referring to the destruction of 70 CE because of the preceding statement. "*For then there will be great tribulation, such as has not* been since the beginning of the world until this time, no, nor ever shall be." Matthew 24:21 No doubt there will be a time of trouble in the future (Daniel 12:1), but that will likely be upon all the nations of the world. The context of Matthew 24 was the city of Jerusalem and the Temple

As a result people believe that the entire passage must be referring to the future, because surely there will be greater tribulation in the end. What they fail to remember is the context of the passage – Jerusalem and the Temple and the people of Yahudah. While there will surely be great tribulation around the world at the end of the age, Yahushua was referring to a specific place and a specific people.

He was declaring judgment on the House of Yahudah and Jerusalem because they did not know the time of their visitation. (Luke 19:41-44) From the description provided by Josephus, there may have never been such a horrendous time for the City, the Temple and Jerusalem. Since 70 CE, Jerusalem has been trampled by the Gentiles, so there likely will not be a time of tribulation upon the people and the City since they need to be returned, and there currently is no Temple in existence in Jerusalem.

Now refering back to the Olivet discourse in Matthew 24, Yahushua then digressed from the destruction of the Temple to the sign of His coming. That was the second question posed by the disciples: "What will be the sign of your coming." Matthew 24:3

He made a specific point that He would not be coming when the Temple was destroyed. He told them not to go looking for Him in the desert or the inner rooms. He indicated that when He returns, it will be like lightening flashes from the east to the west.

Yahushua then shifted back to the Temple and tells of signs that would occur "immediately after the tribulation of those days." Matthew 24:29. In other words, "immediately after the

tribulation concerning the destruction of Jerusalem and the Temple.

He used very interesting language concerning the sun, the moon the stars and the heavens. He is not talking about actual signs in the heavens. This was actually a very Hebraic way of declaring judgment upon a nation. It is the same language that Ezekiel used when declaring judgment upon Pharaoh and Egypt. *"When I put out your light, I will cover the heavens, and make its stars dark; I will cover the sun with a cloud, and the moon shall not give her light."* Ezekiel 32:7

It also is a direct reference to the punishment of Babylon prophesied by the Prophet Isaiah. *"For the stars of heaven and their constellations will not give their light; the sun will be darkened in its going forth, and the moon will not cause its light to shine."* Isaiah 13:10

In other words "lights out!" This was no coincidence since it was Babylon that was the previous kingdom to destroy the Temple, and Babylon was punished for what she had done.

Again, the destruction of the Temple by the Romans was on the same day as the desctruction by the Babylonians. This was another punishment upon the House of Yahudah, now by the Roman Empire – the last Empire. The conclusion of things will involve punishment upon that empire.

In Luke there is a bit more detail that adds additional support to the fact that these predictions were focused around the destruction of Jerusalem in 70 CE. Referring to the distress in the Land and the wrath upon His people He declared that *"they will fall by the edge of the sword and be led captive into all of the nations."* (Luke 21:24) If this were the end of the world, there would not be any nations to be led away captive. We know from history that the survivors of the Jerusalem siege in 70 CE were, in fact, taken captive into the nations.

As we already mentioned, Yahushua then stated: *"And Jerusalem will be trampled by the Gentiles until the times of the Gentiles are fulfilled."* (Luke 21:24) Again, the context involves the destruction of the Temple, and the punishment on the ones who destroyed the Temple. The Gentiles are the "nations" and that will be the focus of the end of the age and the return of the Messiah – the punishment of the Nations that constitute the final world empire.

Therefore, Yahushua seems to be indicating that Jerusalem would remain trampled by the nations until the punishment of the Nations. Very interestingly, the City of Jerusalem is currently unofficially considered "corpus separatum" by the United Nations resolutions 181 and 194. The UN believes that Jerusalem should be placed under a special international regime. That position is supported by the European Union, and the Holy See of the Roman Catholic Church.

If we believe that the Scriptures provide patterns for the future, then the conclusion of the punishment of the House of Yisrael is likely to coincide with the punishment of the Nations. Just as Egypt was plagued while Yisrael was set free, so the Nations will be plagued when the House of Yisrael is delivered in the future. This will likely relate to the return of the Messiah as He comes as the Son of David – the conquering King Who unites the divided Kingdom of Yisrael. Of course, this should also center on Jerusalem.

After describing the final judgment language upon the House of Yahudah and Jerusalem up to Luke 21:26, which parallels Matthew 24:29, Yahushua proceeded to answer the third question concerning the sign of the end of the age. *"[30] Then the sign of the Son of Man will appear in heaven, and then all the tribes of the earth will mourn, and they will see the Son of Man coming on the clouds of heaven with power and great glory. [31] And He will send His angels with a great sound of a trumpet (shofar),*

and they will gather together His elect from the four winds, from one end of heaven to the other." Matthew 24:30-31

Yahushua had already described how He would come. *"For as the lightning comes from the east and flashes to the west, so also will the coming of the Son of Man be."* Matthew 24:27 *"For as the lightning that flashes out of one part under heaven shines to the other part under heaven, so also the Son of Man will be in His day."* Luke 17:24

So the sign of Yahushua will appear in heaven and everyone on earth will mourn. You mourn when someone dies. It is possible that they think this is some "planet killer" asteroid or an alien invasion. The people of the earth are clearly distraught by what they see coming in the heavens. They will see the Son of Man in the clouds of heaven with power and great glory. At that point: *". . . He will send His angels with a great sound of a shofar, and they will gather together His elect from the four winds, from one end of heaven to the other."* Matthew 24:31 This does not say that Yahushua will come to earth at that time. His messengers will gather the elect from the entire planet.

Notice that Yahushua referred to the great sound. The text is specifically referring to a shofar, not a trumpet. There are four basic shofar blasts: 1) Tekiah - a long single blast, 2) Shevarim - three short blasts, 3) Teruah - nine staccato blasts of alarm, and 4) Tekiah ha-Gadol - a great long blast. So Yahushua was referring to a Tekiah ha-Gadol.

Remember that when the shofar sounded long Yisrael could approach the mountain for the wedding with YHWH. (Shemot 19:13) This long shofar at that time was called the Yobel, so it was hinting at the Jubilee Shofar. We should take special note that the shofar blast at Sinai occurred on the Appointed Time of Shabuot. This is when the firstfruits of the grain harvest are gathered to the House of YHWH from all over the land. Here Yahushua will be gathering the

firstfruits from all over the earth.

After providing a description of His coming in the clouds, Yahushua goes on to provide a parable of the fig tree. This takes us back to the progression of the signs He ascribed to the destruction of the Temple. Of course, the parable echoes the figs spoken of by Jeremiah after the Babylonian destruction of Jerusalem. The good figs were the ones taken captive while the bad figs were the ones left in the Land. (Jeremiah 24)

The focus on figs is clearly not a coincidence. Yahushua had just previously cursed a fig tree for not bearing fruit.[217] Yahushua was invoking the curse upon Jerusalem and the Temple. After all, He had spent years teaching and speaking truth to them, and they did not repent. Instead, they plotted to kill Him so they would be judged.

This is exactly what He foretold in the parable of the fig tree. "*[6] . . . A certain man had a fig tree planted in his vineyard, and he came seeking fruit on it and found none. [7] Then he said to the keeper of his vineyard, 'Look, for three years I have come seeking fruit on this fig tree and find none. Cut it down; why does it use up the ground?' [8] But he answered and said to him, 'Sir, let it alone this year also, until I dig around it and fertilize it. [9] And if it bears fruit, well. But if not, after that you can cut it down.'*" Luke 13:6-9

It is important to remember that YHWH did not dwell in the Temple. His Throne, the Mercy Seat upon the Ark of the Covenant, was not found in the Holy of Holies. It had been absent since the Temple was destroyed by the Babylonians.[218] Yahushua was therefore indicating that it was time to, once again, punish the House of Yahudah. The Babylonian destruction, and the Roman destruction were intimately connected, and this statement was made within the 70 weeks determined "*for your people and your holy city.*" (Daniel 19:24)

The Yahudah was allowed to return after the Babylonian destruction but it was a conditional return limited in time. That is why Yahushua indicated that "this generation" would not pass away until all those things took place. Again, He was speaking to His disciples, and the generation that would see the destruction of the Temple.

So it appears that without a proper understanding of this passage, many may be looking for certain events to happen in the future that have already occurred in the past. They are erroneously assuming that the signs of the impending destruction of Jerusalem are the signs of the end of the age.

This will take some by surprise and seems to be confirmed by the fact that Yahushua connected His return with the days of Noah. (Matthew 24:37; Luke 17:26) Clearly the days of Noah and the return of Yahushua are linked with a judgment rendered upon the entire planet. The times leading up to the judgment are also similar. Apparently everyday life will be going on as usual when Yahushua returns.

"*26 And as it was in the days of Noah, so it will be also in the days of the Son of Man: 27 They ate, they drank, they married wives, they were given in marriage, until the day that Noah entered the ark, and the flood came and destroyed them all. 28 Likewise as it was also in the days of Lot: They ate, they drank, they bought, they sold, they planted, they built; 29 but on the day that Lot went out of Sodom it rained fire and brimstone from heaven and destroyed them all. 30 Even so will it be in the day when the Son of Man is revealed.*" Luke 17:26-30

So when the Messiah is revealed, mankind will be in a depraved condition, although it appears they will carry on as normal – oblivious to the signs. They may be looking for signs that will never appear, because they already occurred.

It is very interesting to note that the description of

what people will be doing also happens to be the major actions of the Nephilim offspring against mankind. They were "marrying" the women, and eating flesh and drinking the blood. (1 Enoch 7:4-7; Jubilees 5:2) So there are different ways to interpret this saying with very different expectations.

The reason Yahushua is coming will be to restore the Kingdom. The earthly kingdom had thus far failed under man. Adam, the first ruler of the world had sinned, and his righteous son Hebel had been killed.

Thus, mankind needs the Son of Adam to restore creation and rule over the world. The Kingdom of Yisrael had been united by David. He too had sinned, as did his son, which resulted in the Kingdom being divided. Thus the Kingdom needed a son of David. Therefore, the Messiah could not simply be a Son of Man, He also needed to be the Son of Elohim.

This concept was well understood and accepted by the Yahudim as demonstrated by The Aramaic "son of God" Text from Qumran Cave 4 (4Q246). Only in the role of the Son of Elohim could Yahushua fulfill the Covenant and make way for mankind to re-enter the Garden and partake of the Tree of Life. He needed to place His blood on the doorposts.

This is the largely overlooked and misunderstood fuction of Yahushua. Atoning for sin, which allows for the restoration of the Kingdom. The restoration involved re-gathering those who were scattered. Remember the pattern provided by David – the Shepherd King fighting the Rephaim giant.

The remnant is now in the Nations that are holding the outcasts of Yisrael. The re-gathering should occur around the time when the signs of His coming begin. In fact, in Luke, He stated: "Now when these things begin to happen, look up

and lift up your heads, because your redemption draws near." Luke
21:28

Notice that Yahushua states: *"when these things begin to happen."* So we should be looking for our redemption at the beginning of the signs, at the end of the time of the Gentiles. *"Jerusalem will be trampled by Gentiles until the times of the Gentiles are fulfilled."* The "times of the Gentiles" is often misunderstood. Another way of saying it is "the fullness of the Gentiles" or rather "the fullness of the Nations." This was actually the prophecy made over Ephraim by Yisrael – *"his seed is to become the fullness of the nations."* Beresheet 48:19

So the entire time of the "fullness of the nations" is essentially an incubation period for Ephraim, while the House of Yisrael is mixed within the nations. This is the same thing that occurred when the Children of Yisrael were in Egypt. The fullness of the Nations will be completed at a specific time – the Day of YHWH. (Ezekiel 30:3)

We can see the culmination of the end of the age involving the regathering of the House of Yisrael and the Day of YHWH. It is a time of deliverance mixed with judgment. The redemption does not necessarily occur at the same moment as the gathering to Yahushua. Remember that Yisrael was redeemed while Egypt was plagued, they were covered by the blood of the Lamb and delivered from bondage. They were then brought to Sinai for the wedding agreement. After that time they were supposed to enter into the Land, the marital residence. They refused and were punished on none other than the 9th of Av. So we can see the continued connection with the Covenant, and dwelling in the Land with YHWH.

Now let reexamine the conclusion of the Olivet discourse provided in Matthew 24. After describing all of the events leading up to the destruction of the Temple, Yahushua then described the sign of the end of the age in answer to the

third question posed by His disciples.

It is similar to the other account provided in Mark 13:26-27. Here is a common translation of His answer. *"³⁰ Then the sign of the Son of Man will appear in heaven, and then all the tribes of the earth will mourn, and they will see the Son of Man coming on the clouds of heaven with power and great glory. ³¹ And He will send His messengers with a great sound of a blast, and they will gather together His elect from the four winds, from one end of heaven to the other."* Matthew 24:30-31

By beginning the passage with "then," it leads the reader to believe that the sign of the Son of Man immediately follows the previously described events. This is what causes many to interpret the entire passage as describing His second coming. When you recognize this as a separate response and look at the Greek, you can see that it simply follows in order. Yahushua is actually just answering the third question in order. He is not providing a specific length of time.

In other words, the Messiah will not be coming until after all of the previous events, and He does not say how soon that will be – He only provides signs. In fact, there is every indication that He will tarry longer than people expect, as we shall soon see in a parable involving 10 virgins.

The sign of the Son of Man will be something that all will see. Interestingly, the text does not say that Yahushua will actually come to the earth at that time. In fact, it is very clear that He will not. He will be in the "clouds" – "nephelen" (νεφελῶν). He will send His messengers with a great blast, a shofar blast, to the "4 winds" to gather His elect.[219]

The 4 winds refer to the 4 corners of the Earth, as was seen in numerous Scriptures describing where Yisrael and Yahudah had been scattered. In fact, it is a type of code that we need to understand. According to Daniel 11, the kingdom of the mighty King was scattered to the 4 winds. Also, the

Prophet Jeremiah proclaimed that the Kingdom of Elam would be scattered throughout the entire planet. They would also be brought back in the end.[220]

Most importantly, the House of Yisrael was scattered to the 4 winds – the 4 corners of the earth. So Yahushua was referring to a regathering of His people, both the House of Yisrael and the House of Yahudah, from all around the Earth through His messengers after a blast.

This was already made clear by the prophets. In Isaiah we read: "*He will set up a banner for the nations, and will assemble the outcasts of Yisrael, and gather together the dispersed of Yahudah from the four corners of the earth.*" Isaiah 11:12

Zechariah provides the following: "*[6] Up, up! Flee from the land of the north, says YHWH; for I have spread you abroad like the four winds of heaven, says YHWH. [7] Up, Zion! Escape, you who dwell with the daughter of Babylon. [8] For thus says YHWH of hosts: He sent Me after glory, to the nations which plunder you; for he who touches you touches the apple of His eye. [9] For surely I will shake My hand against them, and they shall become spoil for their servants. Then you will know that YHWH of hosts has sent Me. [10] Sing and rejoice, O daughter of Zion! For behold, I am coming and I will dwell in your midst, says YHWH. [11] Many nations shall be joined to YHWH in that day, and they shall become My people. And I will dwell in your midst. Then you will know that YHWH of hosts has sent Me to you. [12] And YHWH will take possession of Yahudah as His inheritance in the Holy Land, and will again choose Jerusalem. [13] Be silent, all flesh, before YHWH, for He is aroused from His holy habitation!*" Zechariah. 2:6-13

The question of the ages is how, where and when this great regathering will be accomplished. Some attribute this to a "rapture" event, while others believe it will be a miraculous physical regathering. It is important to note that Yahushua will be sending messengers to gather the sheep. There is often a belief that Yahushua will be returning to regather His elect, but this passage makes it clear that messengers will be gathering the elect to Yahushua.

The use of messengers brings to mind the manner in which YHWH delivered Lot and his family from Sodom and Gomorrah prior to judgment. In fact, Yahushua specifically mentioned "the days of Lot" linkened to the time of His return. (Luke 17:28) It is also important to note the references to people working and one being taken. (Matthew 24:40-42) This event would not occur on a Feast Day, or a Sabbath, since work is prohibited on these days. Notice also that there is one out of two that will be taken - 50 percent.

This leads us directly to another parable provided by Yahushua concerning 10 virgins: "*¹ Then the kingdom of heaven shall be likened to ten virgins who took their lamps and went out to meet the bridegroom. ² Now five of them were wise, and five were foolish. ³ Those who were foolish took their lamps and took no oil with them, ⁴ but the wise took oil in their vessels with their lamps. ⁵ But while the bridegroom was delayed, they all slumbered and slept. ⁶ And at midnight a cry was heard: Behold, the bridegroom is coming; go out to meet him! ⁷ Then all those virgins arose and trimmed their lamps. ⁸ And the foolish said to the wise, Give us some of your oil, for our lamps are going out. ⁹ But the wise answered, saying, No, lest there should not be enough for us and you; but go rather to those who sell, and buy for yourselves.' ¹⁰ And while they went to buy, the bridegroom came, and those who were ready went in with him to the wedding; and the door was shut. ¹¹ Afterward the other virgins came also, saying, Master, Master, open to us! ¹² But he answered and said, Assuredly, I say to you, I do not know you. ¹³ Watch therefore, for you know neither the day nor the hour in which the Son of Man is coming.*" Matthew 25:1-13

Now there were 10 virgins, which should make us think about the 10 Tribes of the House of Yisrael. They were virgins, and they were going to a wedding – their wedding.

Notice that they all slept and slumbered. This event should make us think of Passover, especially the last Passover of Yahushua often called "The Last Supper." It was indeed a Passover meal, which is a watch night. Just as the Yisraelites in Egypt stayed up all night as the firstborn of Egypt were judged, so those in the Covenant stay up all night.

Yahushua, as the firstborn of YHWH, was up all night fulfilling prophecy. *"He who watches (shamar) over Yisrael shall neither sleep nor slumber."* Psalm 121:4 The Lamb of Elohim stayed up before being slaughtered on Passover Day. Despite His repeated exhortations to watch (shamar) – His disciples slept and slumbered.

Sadly, in the parable, 5 of the virgins were foolish, and they were not prepared. As a result, they missed the wedding. It appears that if the Bridegroom had not delayed they would have been ready, but because He delayed they were not ready. While He was coming, they had to go meet Him. Remember when Messiah said He was coming in the clouds. He did not say He was coming to earth to fetch His Bride. His messengers would actually be gathering the Bride.

Also notice that the 5 foolish virgins eventually made it to the Feast location. The problem was that they were late. The Bridegroom already "knew" (yada) His Bride, and the seven day Feast was underway. This will be another one week period when the Messiah finishes the work performed in the week involving His death and resurrection.

There are many who want to go to the wedding who will not be allowed. So it appears that we can "know "(ginosko) many things, but that we will not intuitively "know" (oida) the exact day and hour when the Son of Man will return.[221] Therefore, we must be prepared.

As with this parable and most of the parables given by Yahushua, they were meant to teach about the Kingdom. He even taught His disciples to pray for the Kingdom. *"⁹ In this manner, therefore, pray: Our Father in heaven, set apart be Your Name.* [10] *Your kingdom come. Your will be done on earth as it is in* <u>*heaven.*</u> [11] *Give us this day our daily bread.* [12] *And forgive us our debts, as we forgive our debtors.* [13] *And do not lead us into temptation, but deliver us from the evil one.* <u>*For Yours is the*</u> <u>*kingdom and the power and the glory forever. Amen.*</u>" Matthew 6:9-13

The Kingdom of YHWH that exists in the Heavens is coming to the physical realm. The Kingdom on earth is established through Yisrael. "*And you shall be to Me a*　*kingdom of priests and a holy nation. These are the words which you shall speak to the children of Yisrael.*" Shemot 19:6 The Hebrew word for "kingdom" is "mamlekah" (ᗄYᏝᎩᎩ), and it implies that a "king" (melek) will rule over it.

As with any Kingdom, there is a royal family and there are the subjects. The Tabernacle provides an incredible pattern for this Kingdom. The Gentiles are those who do not follow the Torah of YHWH, they live outside of the Kingdom. They are strangers (ger).

The stranger is welcome to join the Kingdom if they follow the commands. Just because they live in the Kingdom does not mean that they are in the Covenant. To be in the Covenant, blood must be shed – this is the pattern of the circumcision. It is the sign which someone takes upon themselves when they enter the Covenant. They then continue to live the sign of the Covenant – the Sabbath. (Shemot 31:13, 17)

"[1] *Thus says YHWH: Keep justice, and do righteousness, for My salvation is about to come, and My righteousness to be revealed.* [2] *Blessed is the man who does this, and the son of man who lays hold on it; who keeps from defiling the Sabbath, and keeps his hand from doing any evil.* [3] *Do not let the son of the foreigner who has joined himself to YHWH speak, saying, YHWH has utterly separated me from His people, nor let the eunuch say, Here I am, a* dry tree. *⁴ For thus says YHWH: To the eunuchs who keep My Sabbaths, and choose what pleases Me, and hold fast My Covenant, ⁵ Even to them I will give in My house and within My walls a place and a name better than that of sons and daughters; I will give them an everlasting name that shall not be cut off. ⁶ Also the sons of the foreigner who join themselves to YHWH, to serve Him, and to love the Name of YHWH, to be His servants - Everyone who keeps from defiling the Sabbath, and holds fast My Covenant - ⁷ Even them I will bring to My holy mountain, and make them joyful in My House of prayer. Their burnt offerings and their sacrifices will be accepted on My altar; For My House shall be called a House of prayer for all nations. ⁸ The Master YHWH, who gathers the outcasts of Yisrael, says, Yet I will gather to him others besides those who are gathered to him."* Isaiah 56:1-8

Notice the status of "*better than sons and daughters.*" The only relationship better than sons and daughters is the bride. So we can see through the analogy of the House that we have different levels of relationships between those in and around the House.

There is the Husband and the Wife – they are the King and the Queen and the mother and the father. There are then the seed of the relationship – the sons and the daughters. Then there are the servants who work in the house. Finally, there are the guests who only come to the house when invited. They can visit the house and maybe dwell there temporarily, but they are not permanent residents.

This, of course is the entire message of the Appointed Times. The Appointed Times provide the pattern for coming and visiting at the times of invitation. Those visitations also provide the path to become servants, sons and daughters and ultimately the Bride. Not all will reach the Holy of Holies – that is reserved for the Bride.

This, of course, is the Kingdom of YHWH that Yahushua, as the arm of YHWH, came to establish. This is

why He emphasized the Kingdom. That Kingdom is established within the context of the Covenant. In fact, everything Yahushua did was in the context of the Covenant and the Kingdom. He taught the Kingdom and revealed mysteries concerning the Kingdom. In fact, He stated: "*It has been given to you to know the mysteries of the Kingdom of Elohim.*" Luke 8:10; Matthew 13:11

One of the mysteries of the Kingdom involves the wedding of the King with the Queen. Here is the promise that the Bride will be restored. See if you can discern the House of Yisrael and the House of Yahudah in this passage.

"*¹ Sing, O barren, You who have not borne! Break forth into singing, and cry aloud, you who have not labored with child! For more are the children of the desolate than the children of the married woman, says YHWH. ² Enlarge the place of your tent, and let them stretch out the curtains of your dwellings; Do not spare; lengthen your cords, and strengthen your stakes. ³ For you shall expand to the right and to the left, and your descendants will inherit the nations, and make the desolate cities inhabited. ⁴ Do not fear, for you will not be ashamed; neither be disgraced, for you will not be put to shame; For you will forget the shame of your youth, and will not remember the reproach of your widowhood anymore. ⁵ For your Maker is your Husband, YHWH of hosts is His Name; and your Redeemer is the Holy One of Yisrael; He is called the Elohim of the whole earth. ⁶ For YHWH has called you like a woman forsaken and grieved in spirit, Like a youthful wife when you were refused, Says your Elohim. ⁷ For a mere moment I have forsaken you, but with great mercies I will gather you. ⁸ With a little wrath I hid My face from you for a moment; but with everlasting kindness I will have mercy on you, Says YHWH, your Redeemer. ⁹ For this is like* the waters of Noah to Me; For as I have sworn that the waters of Noah would no longer cover the earth, so have I sworn that I would not be angry with you, nor rebuke you. *10* For the mountains shall depart and the hills be removed, but My kindness shall not depart from you, nor shall My Covenant of peace be removed, says YHWH, who has mercy on you. *11* O you afflicted one, tossed with tempest, and not comforted, Behold, I will lay your stones with colorful gems, and lay your foundations with sapphires. *12* I will make your pinnacles of rubies, Your gates of crystal, and all your walls of precious stones. *13* All your children shall be taught by YHWH, and great shall be the peace of your children. *14* In righteousness you shall be established; You shall be far from oppression, for you shall not fear; and from terror, for it shall not come near you. *15* Indeed they shall surely assemble, but not because of Me. Whoever assembles against you shall fall for your sake. *16* Behold, I have created the blacksmith Who blows the coals in the fire, who brings forth an instrument for his work; and I have created the spoiler to destroy. *17* No weapon formed against you shall prosper, and every tongue which rises against you in judgment you shall condemn. This is the heritage of the servants of YHWH, and their righteousness is from Me, says YHWH." Isaiah 54:1-17

Notice this description of the Bride sounds like a City. This was the pattern revealed by Jerusalem. The Bride is Jerusalem - the renewed Jerusalem, the restored Garden. Yahushua is described as the Last Adam. As a result, the Bride is the Last Eve. Just as Adam was pierced and shed His blood so that Hawah, his Bride could come out of him, so Yahushua's side was pierced and His blood was shed for His Bride. Only through this renewal can the Bride be brought back into the Garden.

The Husband and Wife will rule and reign from the restored Garden – the Renewed Jerusalam. This is all about the Kingdom being established and restored through the Covenant.

The Bride is a neglected and often misunderstood subject, but it is actually the focus of the entire planet. The planet we call Earth was meant to be a dwelling place for the Son and His Bride.

Here is an often overlooked quote from Yahushua. *"[16] The Torah and the prophets were until John. Since that time the Kingdom of Elohim has been preached, and everyone is pressing into it. [17] And it is easier for heaven and earth to pass away than for one tittle of the Torah to fail."* Luke 16:16-17 Before John, it was about the earthly Kingdom that was the pattern for the Kingdom of YHWH. John came announcing the Messiah and the Kingdom of Heaven. Yahushua came proclaiming and revealing the Kingdom of Heaven.

This text clearly reinforces the continued significance of the Torah, much like His statement in Matthew. *"[17] Do not think that I came to destroy the Torah or the Prophets. I did not come to destroy but to fulfill. [18] For assuredly, I say to you, till heaven and earth pass away, one jot or one tittle will by no means pass from the Torah till all is fulfilled. [19] Whoever therefore breaks one of the least of these commandments, and teaches men so, shall be called least in the Kingdom of Heaven; but whoever does and teaches them, he shall be called great in the Kingdom of Heaven. [20] For I say to you, that unless your righteousness exceeds the righteousness of the Scribes and Pharisees, you will by no means enter the Kingdom of Heaven."* Matthew 5:17-20

Here we see a direct link to the Kingdom and according to the passage in Luke, Yahushua seems to be indicating that John the Baptist was a turning point. John preached *"Repent for the Kingdom of heaven is at hand."* (Matthew 3:2) In fact Yahushua preached the same thing.

(Matthew 4:17)

After Yahushua, the Temple was destroyed and Jerusalem was literally wiped off the map. The Kingdom would not be restored until Messiah came to bring the Kingdom of Heaven to the Earth. We can see this demonstrated in the first sentence of the Scriptures as the Aleph Taw (𐤗𐤗) literally connects *"the heavens and the earth"* (𐤅𐤘𐤗𐤗 𐤗𐤗𐤉 𐤅𐤆𐤅𐤅𐤔𐤗).

The Torah transcends both Kingdoms through the Messiah. The earthly Kingdom of Yisrael had a Torah written on stone and scrolls. The heavenly Kingdom has the living Torah who writes the Torah on the hearts and minds of those in the Kingdom.

If you look closely we see that Yahushua spoke a lot about the Kingdom. He provided an extensive teaching of the Kingdom on the Sabbath.

"¹⁰ Now He was teaching in one of the synagogues on the Sabbath. ¹¹ And behold, there was a woman who had a spirit of infirmity eighteen years, and was bent over and could in no way raise herself up. ¹² But when Yahushua saw her, He called her to Him and said to her, Woman, you are loosed from your infirmity. ¹³ And He laid His hands on her, and immediately she was made straight, and glorified Elohim. ¹⁴ But the ruler of the synagogue answered with indignation, because Yahushua had healed on the Sabbath; and he said to the crowd, There are six days on which men ought to work; therefore come and be healed on them, and not on the Sabbath day. ¹⁵ The Master then answered him and said, Hypocrite! Does not each one of you on the Sabbath loose his ox or donkey from the stall, and lead it away to water it? ¹⁶ So ought not this woman, being a daughter of Abraham, whom Satan has bound - think of it - for eighteen years, be loosed from this bond on the Sabbath?

¹⁷ And when He said these things, all His adversaries were put to shame; and all the multitude rejoiced for all the glorious things that were done by Him. ¹⁸ Then He said, What is the kingdom of Elohim like? And to what shall I compare it? ¹⁹ It is like a mustard seed, which a man took and put in his garden; and it grew and became a large tree, and the birds of the air nested in its branches. ²⁰ And again He said, To what shall I liken the kingdom of Elohim? ²¹ It is like leaven, which a woman took and hid in three measures of meal till it was all leavened. ²² And He went through the cities and villages, teaching, and journeying toward Jerusalem. ²³ Then one said to Him, Master, are there few who are saved? And He said to them, ²⁴ Strive to enter through the narrow gate, for many, I say to you, will seek to enter and will not be able. ²⁵ When once the Master of the house has risen up and shut the door, and you begin to stand outside and knock at the door, saying, Master, Master, open for us and He will answer and say to you, I do not know you, where you are from, ²⁶ then you will begin to say, We ate and drank in Your presence, and You taught in our streets. ²⁷ But He will say, I tell you I do not know you, where you are from. Depart from Me, all you workers of iniquity. ²⁸ There will be weeping and gnashing of teeth, when you see Abraham and Yitshaq and Yaakob and all the prophets in the kingdom of Elohim, and yourselves thrust out. ²⁹ They will come from the east and the west, from the north and the south, and sit down in the Kingdom of Elohim. ³⁰ And indeed there are last who will be first, and there are first who will be last. ³¹ On that very day some Pharisees came, saying to Him, Get out and depart from here, for Herod wants to kill You. ³² And He said to them, Go, tell that fox, Behold, I cast out demons and perform cures today and tomorrow, and the

third day I shall be perfected. [33] Nevertheless I must journey today, tomorrow, and the day following; for it cannot be that a prophet should perish outside of Jerusalem." Luke 13:10-33

Yahushua gave many more teachings about the Kingdom, and often made the connection between the Kingdom and the Sabbath.[222] With the proper understanding of time, one can understand that the Kingdom will be restored in the Sabbath millennium. Remember the time limit given at the time of the flood - 120 "shanah" meaning 120 cycles. This refers to 120 Jubilees which is 6,000 years. So after 6,000 years we should expect the Kingdom to be restored, and a part of that restoration will involve a Jubilee.

The Jubilee actually begins on Day 10 of Month 7 – a day typically associated with judgment. That day is called the Day of Atonement and is marked by the blasting of shofars. With all of His talk about the Kingdom, people expected that Yahushua was going to usher in the Kingdom of YHWH. As Christians do today, many Yahudim back then had forgetten their history.

The House of Yisrael was being punished, and could not be redeemed until that period of punishment was over. Remember the 5 exiles between 723 BCE and 714 BCE? Also remember that Ezekiel prophesied 390 years for the House of Yisrael. Mosheh had said that the punishment would be multiplied by 7. The failure of the House of Yisrael to repent after the passage of 390 years resulted in the multiplication of that punishment to 2,730 years. As a result, the punishment could not end until between 2007 and 2016 CE.

So Yahushua came as the King of the House of Yahudah, but He could not restore both Houses into a united Kingdom until the punishment over the House of Yisrael was satisfied. This, of course, fits the pattern perfectly. Just as David initially was King of the House of Yahudah and

later became the King of the United Kingdom of Yisrael, this was a pattern for the Messiah – the son of David.

After Yahushua entered Jerusalem as the King of Yahudah He was anointed two days before Passover.[223] His feet had previously been anointed and at the Passover meal He washed the feet of His disciples – on the same day that He was crucified.[224]

The Passover meal occurred after sunset on Day 14 of Month 1 and Yahushua was crucified the following afternoon on Passover Day.[225] The washing of the feet was specifically intended to focus on the fact that He came as a servant. So Yahushua was clearly fulfilling the expectation of a suffering servant. (see Isaiah 53)

On that very important Passover Day He renewed the Covenant. The twelve disciples present represented the whole House of Yisrael. Again, remember the pattern of David. David was anointed when he became King of Yahudah. Seven years later, the covenant was "cut" with the House of Yisrael before He was anointed. In other words, blood was shed before David was anointed king over the House of Yisrael.

Of course that was prophetic. With the House of Yisrael divorced from YHWH, blood was required to be shed, and a covenant cut, before the House of Yisrael could be restored and remarried. That was why Yahushua was killed on Passover.

This was also the pattern provided back from the Garden through Abraham. Yahushua, the Lamb of Elohim, came as a son of Adam, the son of David and presented Himself as the sacrifice to atone for the sin of the House of Yisrael and all mankind.

We know from the Gospels that Yahushua renewed the Covenant at the Passover meal that occurred after the sun had set on Day 14 of Month 1 (March 23, 34 CE). He was then crucified the following afternoon, which was a Wednesday – the middle of the week. This is exactly what was prophesied by Daniel. The text indicates: *"He shall "confirm a Covenant."* Daniel 9:27

Remember, the word in Daniel often translated as "confirm" is "gabir" (ヿ⅄⅄ㄱ). It shares the same root as "gibor" (ㄱ⅄⅄ㄱ) which means: "great, mighty, strengthen or superior." So the "he" will make the Covenant "superior or better." It is not about making a new covenant, but rather renewing by making the former one better – elevating the Covenant.

This was prophesied by the Prophet Jeremiah concerning the Covenant between YHWH, and both the House of Yisrael and the House of Yahudah. *"Behold, the days are coming, says YHWH, when I will make a renewed Covenant with ✗⅄-House of Yisrael and ✗⅄-House of Yahudah."* Jeremiah 31:31. The text clearly reveals that the Aleph Taw (✗⅄), the Messiah, will be renewing a Covenant. It is also the subject of much of the Book of Hebrews. (see Hebrews 8:6)

Incredibly, in Christian prophetic circles there is almost unanimous opinion that the so-called anti-christ will be the one confirming the Covenant. Some attempt to tie this with the so-called "covenant with death" found in Isaiah 28. That is a stretch as the covenant is with "death and sheol" not with the anti-christ. There is absolutely no Scriptural connection.

Other than the obscure reference to "the covenant with death and sheol," the entire focus of the Scriptures is the Covenant between YHWH and His people. So why on earth would people connect this covenant in Daniel with the so-called antichrist? Daniel, after all, was focused on the Messiah and the Covenant through a specific period of time.

We know that Yahushua spent His final days in

Jerusalem where He was crucified on an execution stake on Passover day, which was a Wednesday.[226]

Wednesday is day 4 of a 7 day week, and therefore Yahuhsua was "cut off" in the midst of a week. He was raised after three days and three nights which means He was raised in day 7 – the Sabbath.

So when we read about the Messiah being cut off in the midst of a week - it is an actual 7 day week. This fact dispels the need for a 7 year tribulation which dominates Christian eschatology. There are still other time periods provided in other prophecies that are yet to be fulfilled though. Those will be discussed further on.

By that act of being cut off, Yahushua fulfilled the pattern of Abraham and Yitshaq. The promised Son was the Lamb of Elohim. The blood of this Lamb was shed to redeem the firstborn – the firstfruits. He also completed the unsealed revelation provided to Daniel.

Now the redemption was only part of the plan. The shedding of blood allowed entrance into the Covenant, and allowed us to walk in the Covenant way. That way leads to life and the Garden. If Yahushua had remained dead, then the hope of a conquering king would have vanished and there would be no way that the Tribes could be regathered and restored. Elohim only had One Son after all, and Yahushua had repeatedly been proclaimed to be the Son of Elohim.

Thankfully, after three days and three nights Yahushua arose from the grave. He did not just arise, others in the past had risen from the grave, but they eventually died again. So Yahushua was not simply raised from the dead, He was transformed into a renewed body and He never died. While He began His work by spending 40 days in the wilderness, now He spend 40 days during the Counting of the Omer leading up to Shabuot. (Acts 1:3)

During this time of counting the Omer, when the

grain was being harvested throughout the land, He appeared to His disciples. They were not harvesting grain. Rather they were fishing in a little boat at night near the shore. That means they were fishing for small fish – sardines.

Here is their encounter with Yahushua: "*³ . . . They went out and immediately got into the boat, and that night they caught nothing. ⁴ But when the morning had now come, Yahushua stood on the shore; yet the disciples did not know that it was Yahushua. ⁵ Then Yahushua said to them, Children, have you any food? They answered Him, No. ⁶ And He said to them, Cast the net on the right side of the boat, and you will find some. So they cast, and now they were not able to draw it in because of the multitude of fish. ⁷ Therefore that disciple whom Yahushua loved said to Peter, It is the Master! Now when Simon Peter heard that it was the Master, he put on his outer garment (for he had removed it), and plunged into the sea. ⁸ But the other disciples came in the little boat (for they were not far from land, but about two hundred cubits), dragging the net with fish. ⁹ Then, as soon as they had come to land, they saw a fire of coals there, and fish laid on it, and bread. ¹⁰ Yahushua said to them, Bring some of the fish which you have just caught. ¹¹ Simon Peter went up and dragged the net to land, full of large fish, 153, and although there were so many, the net was not broken." John 21:3-11*

Here we see the fulfillment of the significance of the 153 in a powerful way. Remember the gematria value for "sons of Elohim" is 153. When Yahushua first met His disciples He told them that He would make them into fishers of men. (Matthew 4:9; Mark 1:17) Here the disciples were fishing for small fish, and He showed them how to gather large fish in their nets. Those 153 large fish represented "the sons of Elohim." The message was clear. Instead of fishing for sardines, these disciples were supposed to be fishing for men.

This, of course, was to fulfill the prophecy given

through Jeremiah concerning a future regathering of Yisrael.

"*[14] Therefore behold, the days are coming, says YHWH, that it shall no more be said, YHWH lives who brought up the children of Yisrael from the land of Egypt, [15] but, YHWH lives who brought up the children of Yisrael from the land of the north and from all the lands where He had driven them. For I will bring them back into their land which I gave to their fathers. [16] Behold, I will send for many fishermen, says YHWH, and they shall fish them; and afterward I will send for many hunters, and they shall hunt them from every mountain and every hill, and out of the holes of the rocks. [17] For My eyes are on all their ways; they are not hidden from My face, nor is their iniquity hidden from My eyes. [18] And first I will repay double for their iniquity and their sin, because they have defiled My land; they have filled My inheritance with the carcasses of their detestable and abominable idols. [19] O YHWH, my strength and my fortress, My refuge in the day of affliction, the Gentiles shall come to You from the ends of the earth and say, Surely our fathers have inherited lies, worthlessness and unprofitable things. [20] Will a man make gods for himself, which are not gods? [21] Therefore behold, I will this once cause them to know, I will cause them to know My hand and My might; and they shall know that My Name is YHWH."* Jeremiah 16:14-21

Yahushua had offered Himself as the Lamb of Elohim, known as the Passover – "ha'pesach" (月丰刀刄). (Shemot 12:21) The gematria for "ha'pesach" (月丰刀刄) is 153. The connection is clear. The Passover was killed for "the sons of Elohim." Hoshea prophesied that the regathered House of Yisrael would be called "sons of the living El." Hoshea 1:10

He ascended into the Heavens and was seated on the right hand of the Father in the throne room in the Heavens. He is awaiting His Bride who will sit enthroned with Him when He establishes the Kingdom of YHWH on earth. He had previously told His disciples: "*[2] In My Father's house are* many mansions; if it were not so, I would have told you. I go to prepare a place for you. ³ And if I go and prepare a place for you, I will come again and receive you to Myself; that where I am, there you may be also." John 14:2-3

Since His resurrection and ascension, He has been preparing a place for His Bride. This was the proper order of the Wedding process. Yahushua renewed the Covenant with Yisrael at the Passover. That Covenant is the Torah. He completed the necessary work to make way for the Bride to dwell with YHWH. The House that He is preparing is the New Jerusalem. It is in the heavens, and Yahushua will be coming in the clouds to meet the redeemed who will be gathered to Him. The marriage will occur before the Heavenly Court in the Throne Room of YHWH, just as Mount Zion had descended upon Mount Sinai for the previous wedding. Only this time, the Bride will be on Mount Zion, not below Sinai.

The Gospels are filled with parables and teachings of Yahushua concerning the wedding feast. This was to prepare His Bride for the future Feast that must occur when He comes for His Bride.

His first recorded miracle was incredibly profound. The act of turning water into wine at Cana was not the central point. The word "Cana" is "qanah" (ٱ 𐤉 𐤒) in Hebrew, and the only direct reference to "qanah" in the Tanak is a river that runs between Ephraim and Manasseh toward the sea. (see Joshua 16:8, 17:9). This river actually connected the two tribes of Joseph into one - echad.

The root of "qanah" means "acquired" and it is actually quite prophetic. The "quf" (𐤒) represents the back of the head. This should make us think of the "back" of YHWH, described as the "et-achowr" (𐤓𐤅𐤇𐤀-𐤕𐤀) revealed to Mosheh. Notice the Aleph Taw (𐤕𐤀) being visible when YHWH removed His "hand." So Mosheh saw the Messiah, the physical manifestation of YHWH on Mount Sinai. This was the part of YHWH that man can see without dying. (Shemot 33:19-23).

The "nun" (𐤍) represents "the quickened life of the Spirit," and actually looks like sperm. The "hey" (𐤄) means: "behold" and represents the "breath or spirit." So "qanah" literally represents: "the Messiah quickening His seed to give us life." This will happen to the Bride at His Wedding Feast, when the Messiah and His Bride become one - echad.

So this wedding at Cana was symbolic of a wedding involving the House of Yisrael. While Yahushua came as a guest at this wedding, the prophetic picture was about a future wedding when He would "acquire" or "redeem" His Bride. That was the emphasis, along with the water needed to flow through the House of Yisrael. Now let us read from John what actually happened.

"*¹ On the third day there was a wedding in Qanah of Galilee, and the mother of Yahushua was there. ² Now both Yahushua and His disciples were invited to the wedding. ³ And when they ran out of wine, the mother of Yahushua said to Him, They have no wine. ⁴ Yahushua said to her, Woman, what does your concern have to do with Me? My hour has not yet come. ⁵ His mother said to the servants, Whatever He says to you, do it. ⁶ Now there were set there six waterpots of stone, according to the manner of purification of the Yahudim, containing twenty or thirty gallons apiece. ⁷ Yahushua said to them, Fill the waterpots with water. And they filled them up to the brim. ⁸ And He said to them, Draw some out now, and take it to the master of the feast. And they took it. ⁹ When the master of the feast had tasted the water that was made wine, and did not know where it came from (but the servants who had drawn the water knew), the master of the feast called the bridegroom. ¹⁰ And he said to him, Every man at the beginning sets out the good wine, and when the guests have well drunk, then the inferior. You have kept the good wine until now! ¹¹ This beginning* of signs Yahushua did in Qanah of Galilee, and manifested His esteem; and His disciples believed in Him." John 2:1-11

Notice the text says this was "the beginning" of signs. If you read this in Hebrew it would be "resheet" the "first." This should make us think of the first (resheet) barley offering presented during Passover. Those who planned this wedding feast had failed. Through this miracle, Yahushua actually stepped up and filled the role as the "master of the feast."

Yahushua told Miryam that it was not yet His time, because the entire event was pointing toward a future wedding. While He came as a servant, only in the future would He come as a King, and a Bridegroom, to marry His Bride. The wedding in Qanah would point to the process leading up to that future wedding.

Notice also that the water was specifically placed in the stone jars used for water of purification. These stone jars were very large, and there have been numerous archaeological finds of stone jars this size around the land of Israel.[227] The stone jars were empty because the bride of that wedding likely just immersed in them as preparation for the wedding they were attending. A Bride must wash and make herself pure for her wedding. She must not be in her "niddah" period, which is a monthy condition of ritual impurity. This should also make us think of the mysterious Red Heifer sacrifice made outside the camp. Those ashes, when mixed with water, made what were called "the waters of niddah" – "mei niddah" (𐤉𐤃𐤉 𐤆𐤉). (Bemidbar 19:9)

The central focus is the symbolic meaning of the water and the blood needed to complete the wedding feast. This traditional seven day joyous occasion would have been a bust had Yahushua not intervened. This also points to the most joyous time of the Creator's Calendar – the seven day Feast of Succot, when we are actually commanded to rejoice

and drink. The reason is because it is a rehearsal for a future Wedding Feast when the Messiah marries His Bride.

So he was connecting the waters of purification with the blood of the Passover. That was the mystery that He revealed at His final Passover. *"For this is My blood of the renewed Covenant, which is shed for many for the remission of sins."* Matthew 26:28 (see also Mark 14:24 and Luke 22:20) His blood is the blood of the Renewed Covenant promised through Jeremiah and Ezekiel.

Remember the "hard saying" of Yahushua that drove many away from Him? *"⁵³ Then Yahushua said to them, Most assuredly, I say to you, unless you eat the flesh of the Son of Man and drink His blood, you have no life in you. ⁵⁴ Whoever eats My flesh and drinks My blood has eternal life, and I will raise him up at the last day. ⁵⁵ For My flesh is food indeed, and My blood is drink indeed. ⁵⁶ He who eats My flesh and drinks My blood abides in Me, and I in him."* John 6:53-56

His blood is the wine of the Passover, and His flesh is the unleavened bread – representing the Bread of Life. He was the Lamb of Elohim. Therefore, we must partake of the Passover Lamb of Elohim to enter into the Renewed Covenant and follow Him into eternal life. Whenever we do this, (ie. the Passover), we now do it in remembrance of Him. (Luke 22:19) Yahushua did not create some new ritual called Eucharist or Communion. He was revealing a fulfillment of the Passover.

The life of the body is in the blood. (Vayiqra 17:11) Therefore, without the blood of Messiah we cannot have eternal life. This is why the First Adam died. He sinned and could no longer receive life from the Tree of Life.

The point should be very clear. There will be another wedding, and the Bride is the House of Yisrael. She was divorced from YHWH, but through the death and resurrection of the Son, she will be regathered and remarried through the Covenant renewed by the Son. He paid for the Bride with His own blood. The Torah is the Ketubah and His blood is the Bride price. When He regathers the Bride she will come to the Wedding Feast with the riches of the world, just as Yisrael plundered Egypt as they left for Sinai.

That is why there was unique language used by Jeremiah pertaining to each house. *"[31] Behold, the days are coming, says YHWH, when I will make a Renewed Covenant with the House of Yisrael and with the House of Yahudah [32] not according to the Covenant that I made with their fathers in the day that I took them by the hand to lead them out of the land of Egypt, My Covenant which they broke, though I was a husband to them, says YHWH. [33] But this is the Covenant that I will make with the House of Yisrael after those days, says YHWH: I will put My Torah in their minds, and write it on their hearts; and I will be their Elohim, and they shall be My people."* Jeremiah 31:31-33

This is the fulfillment of the Prophecy given by Hoshea. *"Yet the number of the children of Yisrael shall be as the sand of the sea, which cannot be measured or numbered. And it shall come to pass in the place where it was said to them, You are not My people, There it shall be said to them, You are sons of the living Elohim."* Hosea 1:10

Again, this redemption and restoration needed to wait for the punishment to expire until He could fulfill prophecy. That necessary fulfillment could be found in the prophecy of Isaiah.

"[1] Listen, O coastlands, to Me, and take heed, you peoples from afar! YHWH has called Me from the womb; From the matrix of My mother He has made mention of My name. [2] And He has made My mouth like a sharp sword; In the shadow of His hand He has hidden Me, and made Me a polished shaft; In His quiver He has hidden Me. [3] And He said to me, You are My servant, O Yisrael, in whom I will be glorified. [4]

Then I said, I have labored in vain, I have spent my strength for nothing and in vain; Yet surely my just reward is with YHWH, and my work with my ✗𝋾-Elohi. ⁵ And now YHWH says, Who formed Me from the womb to be His Servant, To bring Yaakob back to Him, so that Yisrael is gathered to Him (For I shall be glorious in the eyes of YHWH, and My Elohi shall be My strength), ⁶ Indeed He says, It is too small a thing that You should be My Servant to raise up the tribes of Yaakob, and to restore the preserved ones of Yisrael; I will also give You as a light to the Gentiles, that You should be My salvation to the ends of the earth. ⁷ Thus says YHWH, the Redeemer of Yisrael, their Holy One, to Him whom man despises, to Him whom the nation abhors, to the Servant of rulers: Kings shall see and arise, Princes also shall worship, because of YHWH who is faithful, The Holy One of Yisrael; And He has chosen You. ⁸ Thus says YHWH: In an acceptable time I have heard You, and in the day of salvation I have helped You; I will preserve You and give You as a Covenant to the people, to restore the earth, to cause them to inherit the desolate heritages; ⁹ That You may say to the prisoners, Go forth, To those who are in darkness, Show yourselves. They shall feed along the roads, and their pastures shall be on all desolate heights. ¹⁰ They shall neither hunger nor thirst, neither heat nor sun shall strike them; For He who has mercy on them will lead them, even by the springs of water He will guide them. ¹¹ I will make each of My mountains a road, and My highways shall be elevated. ¹² Surely these shall come from afar; Look! Those from the north and the west, and these from the land of Sinim. ¹³ Sing, O heavens! Be joyful, O earth! And break out in singing, O mountains! For YHWH has comforted His

people, and will have mercy on His afflicted. *14* But Zion said, YHWH has forsaken me, and my Master has forgotten me. *15* Can a woman forget her nursing child, and not have compassion on the son of her womb? Surely they may forget, yet I will not forget you. *16* See, I have inscribed you on the palms of My hands; Your walls are continually before Me. *17* Your sons shall make haste; Your destroyers and those who laid you waste shall go away from you. *18* Lift up your eyes, look around and see; all these gather together and come to you. As I live, says YHWH, You shall surely clothe yourselves with them all as an ornament, and bind them on you as a bride does. *19* For your waste and desolate places, and the land of your destruction, will even now be too small for the inhabitants; and those who swallowed you up will be far away. *20* The children you will have, after you have lost the others, will say again in your ears, The place is too small for me; Give me a place where I may dwell. *21* Then you will say in your heart, Who has begotten these for me, since I have lost my children and am desolate, a captive, and wandering to and fro? And who has brought these up? There I was, left alone; but these, where were they? *22* Thus says the Master YHWH: Behold, I will lift My hand in an oath to the nations, and set up My standard for the peoples; They shall bring your sons in their arms, and your daughters shall be carried on their shoulders; *23* Kings shall be your foster fathers, and their queens your nursing mothers; They shall bow down to you with their faces to the earth, and lick up the dust of your feet. Then you will know that I am YHWH, For they shall not be ashamed who wait for Me. *24* Shall the prey be taken from the mighty, or the captives of the righteous be delivered? *25* But thus says YHWH: Even the captives of the mighty

444

shall be taken away, and the prey of the terrible be delivered; For I will contend with him who contends with you, and I will save your children. ²⁶ I will feed those who oppress you with their own flesh, and they shall be drunk with their own blood as with sweet wine. All flesh shall know that I, YHWH, am your Savior, and your Redeemer, the Mighty One of Yaakob."
Isaiah 49:6-25

We see that this is a Messianic reference detailing the Messiah as the Hand of YHWH. YHWH saves and redeems through His Hand, and the Messiah is the Covenant. He is a Light to the Gentiles that Yisrael was supposed to be, and He will bring the Gentiles into the Covenant through the regathering of Yisrael.

This is why He spent so much time in the Galilee. It was the region where the Northern Tribes used to reside before they were exiled. His actions fulfilled prophecy concerning the Messiah.

"¹ Nevertheless the gloom will not be upon her who is distressed, as when at first He lightly esteemed the land of Zebulun and the land of Naphtali, and afterward more heavily oppressed her, by the way of the sea, beyond the Jordan, In Galilee of the Gentiles. ² The people who walked in darkness have seen a great light; Those who dwelt in the land of the shadow of death, upon them a light has shined. ³ You have multiplied the nation and increased its joy; They rejoice before You according to the joy of harvest, as men rejoice when they divide the spoil. ⁴ For You have broken the yoke of his burden and the staff of his shoulder, the rod of his oppressor, as in the day of Midian. ⁵ For every warrior's sandal from the noisy battle, and garments rolled in blood, will be used for burning and fuel of fire. ⁶ For unto us a Child is born, Unto us a Son is given; And the government will be upon His shoulder. And His name will be called Wonderful, Counselor, Mighty Elohim, Everlasting Father, Prince of Peace. ⁷ Of the increase of

His government and peace there will be no end, upon the throne of David and over His kingdom, to order it and establish it with judgment and justice from that time forward, even forever. The zeal of YHWH of hosts will perform this." Isaiah 9:1-7

So Yahushua went to the lost sheep of the House of Yisrael who were scattered in the Nations. He was the manifestation of His Father YHWH there to restore His Bride and His Kingdom. By allowing the House of Yisrael to be mixed with the nations, they would grow in number as the Children of Yisrael had while in Egypt.

This is the process by which He would populate His Kingdom, and this is the context for the end of the age. Interestingly, the entire prophetic passage that was previously cited in Isaiah 49 actually begins at Isaiah 47 and it is addressing the "virgin daughter of Babylon."

This is not the ancient Kingdom of Nimrod nor would it appear to be neo-Babylon. Rather it appears to be some offspring of Babylon, posed as a virgin. YHWH used this "daughter of Babylon" to punish His people, but she will receive sudden punishment when His people are regathered.

Only when you understand the culmination of these events does the end make sense. In fact, this information given to Isaiah is much of the focus of the end of the age. After His resurrection Yahushua provided further information concerning this "mystery Babylon" as well as how and when He would establish the Kingdom. This was provided by Yahushua to His disciple John in what is popularly called the Book of Revelation.

II

The Revelation

The Book of Revelation is actually the revelation of Yahushua. It was revelation given by Yahushua to His disciple John, while he was exiled on the Island of Patmos. This text is a mysterious book filled with symbolism and incredible visions. The English word "revelation" comes from the Greek word "apocalypse" (Ἀποκάλυψις) which literally means: "revealing, unveiling, a laying bare."[228] One could even say that it is an "unsealing."

It is important to understand the meaning of the name attributed to the text in order to discern its purpose. It is also important to know the time period in which it was given and written to gain a proper context. The Book is generally dated near the end of the First Century, around 96 CE.

Yahushua had already provided guidance to his disciples concerning the destruction of Jerusalem. He did this before His death and resurrection. The Temple was later destroyed in 70 CE, and those words were fulfilled. Those who heeded His words were protected and those who did not likely suffered great tribulation by the Romans.

Now that the Temple was destroyed, Yahushua was giving guidance through to the end of the age and His Second Coming. He had already revealed the sign of His coming. Now He would provide the details of events leading up to His return and beyond.

So this was the Revelation given by Yahushua to John after He was resurrected, and after the Temple was destroyed. John had seen all of this and he was about to see more. It is believed that he was the last living disciple of the original 12. He was writing this text in times of tribulation.

In the first chapter we read: *"I, John, both your brother and companion in the tribulation and kingdom and patience of Messiah Yahushua, was on the island that is called Patmos for the word of Elohim and for the testimony of Messiah Yahushua."* Revelation 1:9

He was imprisoned by the Romans, and he was writing to Assemblies within the Roman Empire who were also being persecuted. It is highly likely that it was written at the very end of the First Century CE during the reign of Domitian.[229]

He specifically described the text as: *"The Revelation of Messiah Yahushua, which Elohim gave Him to show His servants - things which must shortly take place."* Revelation 1:1. Notice that he is detailing "things which must shortly take place." As a result, we must understand that at least some of the things described in the Revelation likely took place centuries ago.

As with other prophecies we must step back and examine whether they have been fulfilled in the past, or await a future fulfillment. If the text is true, then at least some of the Revelation was fulfilled shortly after it was given. The key is to understand what, if anything, remains to be fulfilled.

We already examined that Yahushua gave information leading up to the destruction of the Temple before He was crucified. The Temple was destroyed and the various assemblies were being persecuted. As a result, Yahushua appeared to John to give words to certain persecuted assemblies. This would be followed by certain visions concerning events beyond that time.

After having reviewed the history of the Covenant and the promises provided through the Prophets and the Messiah, we are left with one final prophetic outline provided by the Messiah Himself. He revealed the end to us. It ties together the remaining prophecies from the Tanak and there are actually many similarities between those prophecies and the Revelation of Yahushua, as we should expect.

Read how He appeared to John. *"[12] Then I turned to see the voice that spoke with me. And having turned I saw seven golden lampstands, [13] and in the midst of the seven lampstands One like the Son of Man, clothed with a garment down to the feet and girded about the chest with a golden band. [14] His head and hair were white like wool, as white as snow, and His eyes like a flame of fire; [15] His feet were like fine brass, as if refined in a furnace, and His voice as the sound of many waters; [16] He had in His right hand seven stars, out of His mouth went a sharp two-edged sword, and His countenance was like the sun shining in its strength. [17] And when I saw Him, I fell at His feet as dead. But He laid His right hand on me . . ."* Revelation 1:12-17

Notice that this description is similar to the aish-echad, the One Man, described by Daniel. The reaction of John is the same as Daniel, they both fell as dead at the appearance of the Aleph Taw (✗✝) until He touched them. He appeared in the midst of seven lampstands. A lampstand in this context is a menorah. The reason he appears in the midst of the seven lampstands is because He comes with the seven spirits of YHWH (Isaiah 11:1-2), and YHWH sent the Spirit to the Assemblies. (John 14:26; Acts 2) If these are seven menorahs then there would be 49 lights, with Yahushua in their midst – amounting to 50. This seems to connect Yahushua with His Assemblies that will be gathered at the Jubilee.

While in the midst of the Menorah, Yahushua identifies Himself as the Aleph Taw (✗✝). This explains the mystery of the Aleph Taw (X𐤟) found throughout the Tanak. Anyone familiar with the Aleph Taw (X𐤟) in the Hebrew then understands that Yahushua was "the common thread" woven throughout time and the text.

In fact, the Aleph Taw (X𐤟) was specifically represented by the blue thread of the tzitzit. We are commanded to wear tzitzit on the "four corners" of our garments. We are to look upon the tzitzit and X𐤟-remember all the commandments. "*39 And you shall have the tzitzit, that you may look upon it and remember all the commandments (XҐᵇ𐤟-ℓҮ-X𐤟) of YHWH and do them, and that you may not follow the harlotry to which your own heart and your own eyes are inclined, 40 and that you may remember and do all My commandments (ℤXҐᵇ𐤟-ℓҮ-X𐤟), and be set apart for your Elohim.*" Bemidbar 15:39-40

So when we see the thread of blue we see that the Aleph Taw (X𐤟) is tied to and intertwined with the commandments. The English word translated "blue" is "techelet" (XℓҮX) in Hebrew.

"Techelet" is not only the color of the thread in the tzitzit, but it is the color of the coverings for the items used in the Temple service. When the Tabernacle was moved, they are covered with "techelet" cloth. So when the "holy" furnishings that belonged in the House were taken out of the House and travelled with and among men, they were covered by "techelot." This was a picture of the Messiah leaving the House and walking among men.

What is particularly is interesting about this word is the fact that it contains the word "kol" (ℓҮ) surrounded by the taw (X) that represents the Covenant. The word "kol" (ℓҮ) means: "whole." So the blue thread of the tzitzit represents the Aleph Taw (X𐤟), and the commandments, coupled with the Messiah, represents the "whole" Covenant.

Many in Orthodox Judaism wear all white tzitzit,

lacking the blue thread. This is reflective of the fact that they do not believe in Yahushua the Messiah. As a result, when you have the Commandments without the Messiah you end up with a man-made religion that binds men and directs them away from the commandments of YHWH.

In contrast, Christians, who claim to have the Messiah, do not wear tzitzit at all. They have essentially forgotten the commandments, and when you forget the Torah you have lawlessness. Remember that Yahushua specifically rebuked and sent away those who claim to call Him "Lord" but practice lawlessness. (Matthew 7:21-23) He stated that He did not come to destroy the Torah or the Prophets, but to fulfill. He also stated: "*18 For assuredly, I say to you, till heaven and earth pass away, one jot or one tittle will by no means pass from the Torah till all is fulfilled. 19 Whoever therefore breaks (relaxes) one of the least of these commandments, and teaches men so, shall be called least in the kingdom of heaven; but whoever does and teaches them, he shall be called great in the kingdom of heaven.*" Matthew 5:18-19

There are many Christian pastors, teachers and leaders who are considered to be great in this world, but they will be least in the Kingdom because they teach against the Torah and direct people to disregard the Commandments. In fact, they may not get in at all because the word translated as "breaks" really means "relaxes."

I cannot tell you how many of these individuals I have heard scoff at commandments, such as the dietary instructions, by claiming that their Christian liberty affords them the ability to eat anything they want. Of course they consider this to be a trivial legalistic matter. They claim that God doesn't really care what they eat anyway.

Actually YHWH cares about everything that we do. That is why He gave us the Torah, so that we could live righteous lives and be blessed. You certainly can eat anything

that you want, but you also might die from a disease because of it. These individuals need to open their eyes and see society full of sick and dying people who are suffering specifically because of their disobedience. They need to repent, and stop sending the flock away from the blessings of the Torah.

Essentially, Yahushua will be in the midst of those Assemblies that operate in the Spirit and the Truth of the Torah. Many Christians quench the Spirit through their persistent lawlessness. Remember that the Spirit fell upon the early disciples who were in Jerusalem, because they were obedient. They were following the Torah.

When we see Yahushua identified with the menorah, we understand His position in the House of YHWH. The seven spirits are upon Him and we immediately recognize the fulfillment of the Messianic prophecy in Isaiah 11.

Here is what the prophecy provides:

"[1] There shall come forth a Rod from the stem of Jesse, and a Branch shall grow out of his roots. [2] The Spirit of YHWH shall rest upon Him, the Spirit of wisdom and understanding, the Spirit of counsel and might, the Spirit of knowledge and of the fear of YHWH. [3] His delight is in the fear of YHWH, and He shall not judge by the sight of His eyes, nor decide by the hearing of His ears; [4] But <u>with righteousness He shall judge the poor, and decide with equity for the meek of the earth; He shall strike the earth with the rod of His mouth, and with the breath of His lips He shall slay the wicked.</u> [5] Righteousness shall be the belt of His loins, and faithfulness the belt of His waist. [6] The wolf also shall dwell with the lamb, the leopard shall lie down with the young goat, the calf and the young lion and the fatling together; and a little child shall lead them. [7] The cow and the bear shall graze; Their young ones shall lie down

together; and the lion shall eat straw like the ox. [8] *The nursing child shall play by the cobra's hole, and the weaned child shall put his hand in the viper's den.* [9] *They shall not hurt nor destroy in all My set apart mountain, for the earth shall be full of the knowledge of YHWH as the waters cover the sea.* [10] *And in that day there shall be a Root of Jesse, Who shall stand as a banner to the people; for the Gentiles shall seek Him, and His resting place shall be glorious.* [11] *It shall come to pass in that day that the Master shall set His hand again the second time to recover the remnant of His people who are left, from Assyria and Egypt, from Pathros and Cush, from Elam and Shinar, from Hamath and the islands of the sea.* [12] *He will set up a banner for the nations, and will assemble the outcasts of Yisrael, and gather together the dispersed of Yahudah from the four corners of the earth.* [13] *Also the envy of Ephraim shall depart, and the adversaries of Yahudah shall be cut off; Ephraim shall not envy Yahudah, and Yahudah shall not harass Ephraim.* [14] *But they shall fly down upon the shoulder of the Philistines toward the west; together they shall plunder the people of the East; they shall lay their hand on Edom and Moab; and the people of Ammon shall obey them.* [15] *YHWH will utterly destroy the tongue of the Sea of Egypt; with His mighty wind He will shake His fist over the River, and strike it in the seven streams, and make men cross over dryshod.* [16] *There will be a highway for the remnant of His people who will be left from Assyria, as it was for Yisrael in the day that he came up from the land of Egypt.*" Isaiah 11:1-16

This prophecy is all about the Messiah reigning, regathering and judging the world. By emphasizing the root of Jesse, we understand this to be Messiah ben David. So this revelation sets the tone for the rest of the text. It is clearly revealing how Yahushua will fulfill the Messianic expectations as the counquering King. The One Who unites the Kingdom of Yisrael and restores them to the Land.

That having been said, it is critical to view the events described in the Revelation within the context of the Covenant, and the prophecies relating to the Covenant. It must be read from a Hebraic perspective, and it really is a book for Hebrews. Hebrews are those who have "crossed over" and follow YHWH. It is intended for servants, so it will not be understood by all. In fact, it begins by stating it is: *"The Revelation of Messiah Yahushua, which Elohim gave Him to show His servants - things which must shortly take place."* Revelation 1:1. A servant is one who obeys his master. So only those obeying the commandments will understand the Revelation.

Again, notice that it was revealing things that must shortly take place. That would mean that at least some of the contents in the text would have happened almost 2,000 years ago. Some people have a tendency to spiritualize the entire book of Revelation, and place it all in the future. If you believe the text, then that is an improper application. This should become evident as we proceed to examine it within the proper historical context. Having been revealed nearly 2,000 years ago, much time and history has passed since that time.

As a result, before we start applying every prophecy to our day, or the impending future, it is important to discern whether any or all of it has been fulfilled. Indeed, as with the Prophets, there is a wide spectrum of opinion concerning the Book of Revelation. There are those who believe that it was already fulfilled, because it was a coded prophecy specifically to the seven assemblies identified in the text.

Now the reader must understand that the text is specifically addressed to *"the seven assemblies which are in*

Asia." Revelation 1:4. Many believe that it was written to seven Christian "churches," but we know that there was no Christian religion in existence at this time. We also know that it was written to the "ekklesia" (ἐκκλησία), also known as the "qahal" (𐤋𐤄𐤒) in Hebrew, which was a set apart Assembly.

In the Greek we read "ekklesias" (ἐκκλησίαν) which means: "assembly." It is the same word as "qahal" (𐤋𐤄𐤒) in Hebrew and almost always refers to the assembly of Yisrael. So this was Yisrael in exile. Church is an English word improperly inserted in the text that distorts the meaning.

Therefore, it is critical to understand that this is a message to Yisrael, not to seven Christian churches as is often believed. Church is a fabricated word and because it is commonly associated with Christianity, Christians automatically believe these messages apply to them.

With this understanding we are able to place the text into its proper context. It is all about the covenant, the Kingdom and the Land. This revelation is the fulfillment of the Covenants with Abram and Abraham.

Many attempt to spiritualize these assemblies and apply the messages to the end times or throughout the ages, but the first application is to those actual assemblies.

Interestingly, the Book of Revelation was not even included within the Aramaic Peshitta, which shows that many in the east did not consider it to be Scripture. They may not have included it in their "canon" because it was not addressed to them. It was written to seven western assemblies in Asia, namely: Ephesus, Smyrna, Pergamos, Thyratira, Sardis, Philadelphia and Laodicea.

This message came directly from the throne: "⁴ . . . *Grace to you and peace from Him who is and who was and who is to come, and from the seven Spirits who are before His throne, ⁵ and from Messiah Yahushua, the faithful witness, the firstborn from the* dead, and the ruler over the kings of the earth. To Him who loved us and washed us from our sins in His own blood, ^{6} and has made us kings and priests to His Elohim and Father, to Him be glory and dominion forever and ever." Revelation 1:4b-6

This is written to those who are washed clean by the blood of Messiah who are made kings and priests to YHWH. This is the promise given to Yisrael. It is from YHWH, the seven Spirits and Yahushua the Messiah.

Now there are seven letters that have specific meaning to the angels of those assemblies located in Asia Minor. As with many prophetic passages, there is likely a layered message with a later relevance. Particulalry the portions that end with the phrase: *"He who has an ear let him hear what the Spirit says to the assemblies."* Here are the portions of those letters that provide promises given to overcomers.

To the assembly of Ephesus: *"He who has an ear, let him hear what the Spirit says to the assemblies.* <u>*To him who overcomes I will give to eat from the Tree of Life, which is in the midst of the Paradise of Elohim.*</u>" Revelation 2:7

To the assembly of Smyrna: *"He who has an ear, let him hear what the Spirit says to the assemblies.* <u>*He who overcomes shall not be hurt by the second death.*</u>" Revelation 2:11

To the assembly of Pergamos: *"He who has an ear, let him hear what the Spirit says to the assemblies.* <u>*To him who overcomes I will give some of the hidden manna to eat. And I will give him a white stone, and on the stone a new name written which no one knows except him who receives it.*</u>" Revelation 2:17

To the assembly of Thyratira: *"*^{26} <u>*And he who overcomes, and keeps My works until the end, to him I will give power over the nations -*</u> ^{27} *He shall rule them with a rod of iron; they shall be dashed to pieces like the potter's vessel - as I also have received from My Father;* ^{28} *and I will give him the morning star.* ^{29} *He who has an ear, let him hear what the Spirit says to the*

assemblies." Revelation 2:26-29

To the assembly of Sardis: "*⁵ He who overcomes shall be clothed in white garments, and I will not blot out his name from the Scroll of Life; but I will confess his name before My Father and before His angels. ⁶ He who has an ear, let him hear what the Spirit says to the assemblies.*" Revelation 3:5-6

To the Assembly of Philadelphia: "*¹² He who overcomes, I will make him a pillar in the Temple of My Elohim, and he shall go out no more. I will write on him the Name of My Elohim and the name of the city of My Elohim, the New Jerusalem, which comes down out of heaven from My Elohim. And I will write on him My new Name. ¹³ He who has an ear, let him hear what the Spirit says to the assemblies.*" Revelation 3:12-13

To the assembly of Laodicea: "*²¹ To him who overcomes I will grant to sit with Me on My throne, as I also overcame and sat down with My Father on His throne. ²² He who has an ear, let him hear what the Spirit says to the assemblies.*" Revelation 3:21-22

While some attempt to attribute these promises to different "church ages," it seems these are more universal promises that transcend time. In fact, while the preliminary critiques given in the various letters seem to be assembly specific, these promises to overcomers are each given to "the assemblies."

These promises show just how incredible the work of the Messiah was, and the blessings in store for those who believe in those promises. They are not for everyone – only overcomers.

Later on in the text we are provided the secret of the overcomers. "*And they overcame him by the blood of the Lamb and by the word of their testimony, and they did not love their lives to the death.*" Revelation 12:11 There is no assurance that a person will not be killed for their testimony. Many of us exist in a very self centered culture, and we have adopted doctrines and beliefs that nuture and support those selfish beliefs. Through

the Covenant we must follow the lead of the Messiah. As we die to self we may very well lose our lives. It is through this process that the overcomer finds eternal life. The promise is that: *"He who overcomes shall inherit all things, and I will be his Elohim and he shall be My son."* Revelation 21:1

So this sets the stage for the entire book – the identity and purpose of Yahushua, and the blessings to those who overcome. While the letters were addressed to the seven assemblies, the promises to overcomers were for all overcomers in all assemblies.

As we proceed through the Revelation, we will see some of the events that they will need to overcome. The information is a roadmap through time, and the key to the map is the Appointed Times.

One particular assembly needs further mention - the assembly of Philadelphia. *"9 . . . These things says He who is set apart, He who is true, He who has the key of David, He who opens and no one shuts, and shuts and no one opens 8 I know your works. See, I have set before you an open door, and no one can shut it; for you have a little strength, have kept My word, and have not denied My name. 9 Indeed I will make those of the synagogue of Satan, who say they are Yahudim and are not, but lie - indeed I will make them come and worship before your feet, and to know that I have loved you. 10 Because you have kept My command to persevere, I also will keep you from the hour of trial which shall come upon the whole world, to test those who dwell on the earth."* Revelation 3:7-10

This message contains a similar reference as the message to the angel of the Assembly of Smyrna. *"I know the blasphemy of those who say they are Yahudim and are not, but are a synagogue of Satan."* Revelation 2:9 Remember that there were those calling themselves Yahudim who were not in the Kingdom of Heaven. Plain and simple, they were outside the Covenant. Yahushua was very clear on this point. *"For I say*

to you, that unless your righteousness exceeds the righteousness of the scribes and Pharisees, you will by no means enter the kingdom of heaven." Matthew 5:20

Yahushua said that the Scribes and the Pharisees would not make it into the Kingdom, so they were not in the Covenant. Their definition of righteousness through their traditions and laws was not the righteousness required through the Torah. This essentially meant that they were not Yahudim. So while they assembled in the synagogue, that did not mean they were part of the Covenant Assembly. Yahushua referred to their assembly as the synagogue, or assembly of satan.

He rebuked them while He dwelled upon the earth and specifically identified their problem. "*⁶ He answered and said to them, "Well did Isaiah prophesy of you hypocrites, as it is written: This people honors Me with their lips, but their heart is far from Me. ⁷ And in vain they worship Me, teaching as doctrines the commandments of men. 8 For laying aside the commandment of God, you hold the tradition of men - the washing of pitchers and cups, and many other such things you do. ⁹ He said to them, All too well you reject the commandment of Elohim, that you may keep your tradition.*" Mark 7:6-9

They had chosen their traditions over the Torah. They were specifically commanded not to add to, or take away from, the Words of the Torah. (Debarim 4:2, 12:32) Through their traditions, this is exactly what they had done. This placed them at odds with the Torah of YHWH, and outside the Covenant. It is important to recognize that an individual only remained in the Covenant Assembly if they obeyed the Covenant. Refusal to obey the Covenant meant exile or death. So while you might be born into the Covenant, your continued obedience was required for you to remain in the Covenant.

Remember that the House of Yahudah was then the

only House in Covenant relationship with YHWH. The House of Yisrael had been divorced and was in exile. So for all intents and purposes the notion of being a Yisraelite became blended with the identity of those who remained in the House of Yahudah. The Yahudim considered themselves to be Yisrael. We see this even to this day as most Jews in Judaism believe that they constitute the assembly of Yisrael. The problem is that you must be in Covenant with YHWH to be a Yisraelite. It does not matter who your father or mother were. If you reject the Torah you reject YHWH and His Covenant.

So there were individuals and sects from the House of Yahudah, living in the region of Yahudah, who believed they were of the Assembly of Yahudah, but they were not. Rather, they were from the assembly of satan. It could not be any clearer as Yahushua specifically told the Scribes and the Pharisees that their father was the devil. (John 8:44)

This is revealing that YHWH has an assembly and the serpent has an assembly. The Assembly of YHWH is in the Covenant, and they keep the commandments of Elohim. The assembly of satan is outside the Covenant, opposed to the Covenant. They keep different commandments.

In fact, a certain statement made to the angel of the assembly of Philadelphia is very telling. *"Because you have kept My command to persevere, I also will keep you from the hour of trial which shall come upon the whole world, to test those who dwell on the earth."*

So specifically keeping His commands will be critical. This appears to be speaking of a time of tribulation at the end of the age. The duration is one hour. We will later see how this "one hour" period will distinguish between the two assemblies.

That, after all, is the purpose of the end of the age. It is interesting that Yahushua divides His assembly into seven

parts. This is to reveal that it is diametrically opposed to the beast system that, as we have seen and will continue to see, is also divided into seven parts.

In fact, immediately upon reading the text the reader is struck by the emphasis on sevens. We already mentioned the significance of the first seven words of Beresheet, as well as the significance of the number seven in time, and the Appointed Times. It only seems fitting that the age would culminate in sevens.

We also read about the seven Spirits, the seven assemblies, as well as seven angels, or messengers assigned to each assembly. The assemblies are presented as lampstands, or menorahs, and the angels are presented as stars. An important note is that these are messages written to the angels concerning each assembly, not the assemblies themselves.

We read about seven seals, seven "trumpets," seven plagues and seven thunders. These will all be mentioned as we proceed with this discussion. For those in a Covenant relationship with YHWH seven stands out as the sign of the Covenant. The Sabbath is the day when they demonstrate they are in Covenant with YHWH by their conduct.

By resting on the Sabbath, and obeying this command, they are visibly demonstrating that they are in the Covenant. Their conduct is the sign of the Covenant. Sadly, many in Judaism have followed the traditions of the Pharisees. While they claim to be observing the Sabbath, they are actually following the hundreds of man-made rules dictated by their traditions, which makes it a burden. This is clearly not the rest commanded by YHWH and provided by Yahushua. (Matthew 11:29) It is a rehearsal that those in the Covenant undergo every week. In fact, there are actually only seven commandments in the Torah concerning the Sabbath.

Those in Covenant with YHWH should also be

counting seven weeks every year to the Feast of Shabuot and seven weeks of years toward the Jubilee. Seven is intimately tied with the time of this created world, and so we see that the Book of Revelation is very much focused on the end of this age into the seventh millennium and beyond.

Remember the pattern of the seven day week that was established at the beginning of time. It is a constant reminder that time is established in sevens. We know that those seven days are actually a pattern for the seven thousand years that are the limit to this present existence. Time did not necessarily start at the beginning of our existence, nor does it end at seven thousand years. It actually transitions to the "eighth day." The eighth day is a mysterious day that leads to a renewed age for this Creation.

So after providing the messages to the assemblies to prepare them to be overcomers, the text picks up on prior prophecies, and provides a framework for time as it progresses to the end of the age and beyond.

Of course, throughout this book we have emphasized the fact that Yisrael and the Covenant is the focus of the end of the age. The regathering and restoration of all Yisrael were prophesied, and those prophecies have not yet been fulfilled.[230]

Yahushua came as the suffering servant. He was the Messiah ben Joseph. Just as Joseph was hidden from his brothers in Egypt, Yahshua has been hidden from the House of Yahudah. While the House of Yisrael generally sees the Messiah, they have hidden Him behind a pagan veil, including a pagan name and lawless teachings. At an Appointed Time, Yahushua, the Messiah ben Joseph will be seen by the House of Yahudah. This will occur when He comes as Messiah ben David – the conquering King.

With that foundation we will proceed to examine the rest of the Revelation. After the message to the assemblies, the entire text transitions. This is no longer Yahushua transmitting a message through John. Now John is taken to the heavens. *"After these things I looked, and behold, a door standing open in heaven. And the first voice which I heard was like a trumpet (shofar) speaking with me, saying, Come up here, and I will show you things which must take place after this."* Revelation 4:1

Remember that the voice of YHWH was likened to the sound of the shofar. The word translated as "door" is "thura" (θύρα) in Greek. It is actually a "portal" or a "gate." So John is taken through a portal into another dimension. He is immediately before the Throne of YHWH, and he describes the incredible proceedings that take place in the Throne Room. This is important to remember that John is relating things that are happening in the Throne Room of Heaven.

"¹ And I saw in the right hand of Him who sat on the Throne a scroll written inside and on the back, sealed with seven seals. ² Then I saw a strong angel proclaiming with a loud voice, Who is worthy to open the scroll and to loose its seals? ³ And no one in heaven or on the earth or under the earth was able to open the scroll, or to look at it. ⁴ So I wept much, because no one was found worthy to open and read the scroll, or to look at it. ⁵ But one of the elders said to me, Do not weep. Behold, the Lion of the tribe of Yahudah, the Root of David, has <u>prevailed</u> to open the scroll and to loose its seven seals." Revelation 5:1-5

Notice that this Scroll was sealed with seven seals, a number previously attributed to the assemblies, the Spirit and time itself. Notice also that the Scroll was written on both sides. This should make us think of the Scroll that was handed to Ezekiel.

"⁹ Now when I looked, there was a hand stretched out to me; and behold, a roll of a scroll was in it. ¹⁰ Then He spread it before me; and there was writing on the inside and on the outside,

and written on it were lamentations and mourning and woe."
Ezekiel 2:9-10

Ezekiel was told to eat ✗𝘬 the scroll and then speak ✗𝘬 the words to the House of Yisrael. (Ezekiel 3:1-2) He had a vision of the Throne of YHWH. After the passage of seven days he was commissioned as a watchman to warn the House of Yisrael.

Now the scroll given to Ezekiel was eaten and transmitted. The scroll of Ezekiel was not sealed though. When a scroll was sealed with writing on the outside, that indicated that there were legal prerequisites for opening those seals, like a land deed. (see Jeremiah 32) Therefore, the scroll could only be opened by One who was found worthy – that was the One Who actually gave the revelation. That is why we see Yahushua as the slain Lamb – Who had died but was resurrected as the "first" – the resheet cut off and waved before the Father. Through His death and resurrection He "prevailed" and was qualified to open the seals and thus reveal the contents to His disciple John.

There is another scroll that we read about in the Scriptures that was sealed. It was a scroll that was sealed for a future time – the Scroll of Daniel. The connection will become more evident as we proceed further.

For now we see a marvelous description of the Lamb of Elohim. "*6 And I looked, and behold, in the midst of the Throne and of the four living creatures, and in the midst of the elders, stood a Lamb as though it had been slain, having seven horns and seven eyes, which are the seven Spirits of Elohim sent out into all the earth. 7 Then He came and took the scroll out of the right hand of Him who sat on the throne.*" Revelation 5:6-7

Now let us examine what happens when He takes the scroll. "*8 Now when He had taken the scroll, the four living creatures and the twenty-four elders fell down before the Lamb, each having a harp, and golden bowls full of incense, which are the*

prayers of the set apart ones. ⁹ *And they sang a new song, saying: You are worthy to take the scroll, and to open its seals;* <u>*For You were slain, and have redeemed us to Elohim by Your blood out of every tribe and tongue and people and nation,*</u> ¹⁰ <u>*And have made us kings and priests to our Elohim; and we shall reign on the earth.*</u>"
Revelation 5:8-10

So we have an "elder" speaking to John, and there are 24 elders described in the Throne Room. As we already mentioned the Christian understanding of angelic hierarchy found in *De Coelesti Hierarchia, the Celestial Hierarchy* lists "thrones." In other words, the 24 elders are considered to be angelic beings. This does not necessarily conform with Scriptures. Yahushua specifically stated to His 12 disciples that: *"you also shall sit upon twelve thrones, judging the 12 tribes of Yisrael."* Matthew 19:28 There is reason to believe that the 24 elders are the 12 disciples and the 12 sons of Yisrael.

Notice what the elders sing: *"You were slain and have redeemed us to Elohim."* So the Elders have been redeemed and they are singing about regathering the redeemed. That would be the people of Yisrael gathered from throughout the planet in order to make them kings and priests so that they can reign upon the earth. Remember kings and priests are the anointed ones. So the Messiah is redeeming them so He can "anoint" (moshiach) them. The kings and the priests reign and serve in the Kingdom of YHWH. The redeemed will specifically reign upon the earth. So the notion of dying and going to heaven is not what the Scriptures reveal. The goal after death is to be redeemed, resurrected and reign upon the Earth.

In Revelation we read about the Lamb beginning to open the scroll. He opens four of the seals which results in four different horses being sent forth upon the earth. These horses were colored white, red, black and pale, which is likely a putrid greenish color.

These horses should make us think of Zechariah which actually identified the function of these horses. *"⁸ I saw by night, and behold, a man riding on a red horse, and it stood among the myrtle trees in the hollow; and behind him were horses: red, sorrel, and white. ⁹ Then I said, My master, what are these? So the messenger who talked with me said to me, I will show you what they are. ¹⁰ And the man who stood among the myrtle trees answered and said, These are the ones whom YHWH has sent to walk to and fro throughout the earth."* Zechariah 1:8-10

So these horses carry out various functions throughout the earth. They are often refereed to as the 4 Horsemen of the Apocalypse, as if they are released at the very end.

The horses and the riders are followed by the fifth seal being opened, and here we read about a specific group of servants – those who have been killed for the word of Elohim and their testimony.

"⁹ When He opened the fifth seal, I saw under the altar the souls of those who had been slain for the word of Elohim and for the testimony which they held. ¹⁰ And they cried with a loud voice, saying, How long, O Master, holy and true, until You judge and avenge our blood on those who dwell on the earth? ¹¹ Then a white robe was given to each of them; and it was said to them that they should rest a little while longer, until both the number of their fellow servants and their brethren, who would be killed as they were, was completed." Revelation 6:9-10

They were given white robes, these are robes of righteousness and purity. White robes were given to those who attended a wedding so it appears as though they will be attending a wedding. Note that they are called "servants" and others who will be joining them are "brethren." So there is a familial connection.

They are "souls" under the altar, because this is the purpose of an altar. The altar was the place where offerings were made to YHWH. When an animal was killed and it's blood was poured at the altar, the soul, or "nefesh" (𐤉𐤅𐤔) was essentially placed below the altar. The slaughtered animals represented those slaughtered for YHWH. These souls were offerings to YHWH.

It is generally understood that the soul goes to Sheol when one dies, so this is a very special waiting place for those killed for YHWH. Now we will see the focus of the Revelation shift from the Throne Room in the Heavens to the Earth. The events that occur on earth are directly related to what is occurring in the heavens.

Now the sixth seal provides a specific event on earth described as follows: "*12 I looked when He opened the sixth seal, and behold, there was a great earthquake; and the sun became black as sackcloth of hair, and the moon became like blood. 13 And the stars of heaven fell to the earth, as a fig tree drops its late figs when it is shaken by a mighty wind. 14 Then the sky receded as a scroll when it is rolled up, and every mountain and island was moved out of its place. 15 And the kings of the earth, the great men, the rich men, the commanders, the mighty men, every slave and every free man, hid themselves in the caves and in the rocks of the mountains, 16 and said to the mountains and rocks, Fall on us and hide us from the face of Him who sits on the throne and from the wrath of the Lamb! 17 For the great day of His wrath has come, and who is able to stand?*" Revelation 6:12-17

This is an incredible quake with signs in the sky. It appears to be triggered by some astronomical event. The text also says that the sky receded as a scroll when it is rolled up, and every mountain and island was moved out of its place. It actually sounds like a pole shift of some sort.

One cannot ignore the specific mention of the sun becoming "*black as sackcloth of hair*" and the moon becoming "*like blood.*" These are the same signs that Joel prophesied would occur before the Day of YHWH. "*The sun shall be turned into darkness, and the moon into blood, before the coming of the great and awesome day of YHWH."* Joel 2:31

At first glance, these signs appear to be two different 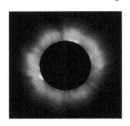 types of astronomical events. The first might involve a solar eclipse where the moon completely blocks the disk of the sun. All that is seen are flares from the sun that sometimes looks like hair. This sign is unique to our planet, and it reveals the precision in its creation. Here we see that the distance between the earth and the sun, the distance between the moon and the earth, as well as the size of the sun and the moon all play a part.

The second sign involving the moon becoming like blood is a different sign sometimes called a "blood moon." Typically, blood moons are simply the first full moon after the harvest moon, which is the full moon closest to the fall equinox. They do not have to look any different from another full moon. It is simply about timing. Others refer to reddish moons as blood moons.

Now at the time of writing this book there is a popular teaching concerning the "tetrad moons." The teaching essentially provides that there will be four blood moons on four consecutive full moon Feasts beginning Passover April 15, 2014, then Succot October 8, 2014, then Passover April 4, 2015 followed by Succot September 28, 2015. It is also noted that there will be a total eclipse on April 20, 2015 and a partial eclipse on September 13, 2015.

The problem is that the March 20, 2015 total solar eclipse will only be personally witnessed by a miniscule fraction of the world population. The only landfalls in that eclipse path are the Faroe Islands and Svalbard. The other solar eclipse is only partial, so that would not fit the description in the Revelation.

Regarding the lunar eclipses, one would think that they would be signs seen from Jerusalem, but the first three "blood moons" will not be seen from Jerusalem. Only the beginning of the fourth one will be visible in Jerusalem.

As a result, the so-called "tetrad moons" may be signs for those who are able to view them, but they do not appear to be the worldwide signs depicted in the Scriptures on or during the Day of YHWH.

The sun becoming black and the moon becoming blood may be caused by the same atronomical event. In fact, they both appear to occur simultaneously. They may be directly related to the great earthquake and the "stars falling from the sky." This could all occur with the appearance of a Planet X type object obstructing the sun, eclipsing the moon, disrupting the earth's gravitation and reigning a debris trail.

There are many who believe the governments of the world have been preparing for such an event. There are presently hundreds of miles of underground tunnels, shelters and even cities all around the world. The wealthy and the elite are preparing for some sort of doomsday event. Even average people are preparing shelters, so it appears that we actually are in a time when we can see a fulfillment of this passage concerning people hiding in "caves" and in the "rocks of the mountains."

Apparently, those shelters will not provide the expected relief, as people will want the rocks and mountains to fall on them to hide them from the Lamb. This seems to be a clue that the Lamb is directly involved, and the people know it.

Immediately after these incredible events we read about four angels who are given authority to harm the earth and the sea. They are described as standing on the 4 corners of the earth, and they are to hold back the wind, which is a Hebrew idiom for holding back the blessings during the following period of judgment. One cannot help but identify these 4 messengers of harm with the four messengers on the horses previously described.

The 4 messengers were instructed to wait until 144,000 individuals had been sealed on their foreheads. These 144,000 are described as "servants of Elohim," and represent the Tribes of Yisrael. While Dan is not mentioned in this list, the 144,000 are clearly intended to represent the combined tribes of Yisrael – the whole House of Yisrael. These are individuals in the Covenant.

This is very important to understand. These individuals keep the Commandments of YHWH, and are therefore under the protective blood of the Lamb of Elohom – Yahushua. If you are in Covenant with YHWH, then you must present the evidence of the Covenant – The Sabbath.

The Sabbath is called an "owt" (✕ Ɏ ✕), which is "a sign, a mark, a monument." (Shemot 31:13). Notice that that "sign" is the Aleph Taw (✕ ✕) surrounding a "vav" (Ɏ) – a man. The Sabbath is a sign that we demonstrate and exhibit through our lives. It is a sign that we willingly demonstrate each and every week. It is a matter of life and death. That is why YHWH rendered the death penalty for those who profane the Sabbath. If you do not bear the sign of the Covenant then do not expect to be sealed.

The Greek word for "seal" is "sphragizo" (σφραγίζω) which means: "to stamp or set a seal upon" or "to mark with a seal." So this mark is clearly intended to keep them secure, and protect them from the harm about to occur.

This "sealing" or "marking" is what previously occurred before YHWH judged Jerusalem. We can read about it in the prophecy of Ezekiel. *"¹ Then He called out in my hearing with a loud voice, saying, Let those who have charge over the city draw near, each with a deadly weapon in his hand. ² And suddenly six men came from the direction of the upper gate, which* faces north, each with his battle-ax in his hand. One man among them was clothed with linen and had a writer's inkhorn at his side. They went in and stood beside the bronze altar. *³ Now the glory of the Elohim of Yisrael had gone up from the cherub, where it had been, to the threshold of the Temple. And He called to the man clothed with linen, who had the writer's inkhorn at his side; ⁴ and YHWH said to him, Go through the midst of the city, through the midst of Jerusalem, and* put a mark on the foreheads of the men who sigh and cry over all the abominations that are done within it. *⁵ To the others He said in my hearing, Go after him through the city and kill; do not let your eye spare, nor have any pity. ⁶ Utterly slay old and young men, maidens and little children and women; but do not come near anyone on whom is the mark; and begin at My sanctuary. So they began with the elders who were before the temple. ⁷ Then He said to them, Defile the Temple, and fill the courts with the slain. Go out! And they went out and killed in the city. ⁸ So it was, that while they were killing them, I was left alone; and I fell on my face and cried out, and said, Ah, Master YHWH! Will You destroy all the remnant of Yisrael in pouring out Your fury on Jerusalem? ⁹ Then He said to me, The iniquity of the House of Yisrael and Yahudah is exceedingly great, and the land is full of bloodshed, and the city full of perversity; for they say, YHWH has forsaken the land, and YHWH does not see! ¹⁰ And as for Me also, My eye will neither spare, nor will I have pity, but I will recompense their deeds on their own head. ¹¹ Just then, the man clothed with linen, who had the inkhorn at his side, reported back and said, I have done as You commanded me."* Ezekiel 9:1-11

The Book of Revelation describes judgment upon the planet. It is the wrath of the Lamb. Before judgment befalls, the people in Covenant will receive a "mark." The Hebrew word for mark is "taw" (ΥX), and it means: "a mark or signature." It is literally symbolized by the last letter in the Hebrew alephbet, the "taw" (X). This should immediately make us think about the "mark" placed on the thresholds of

people's houses at the Passover. This mark was made with blood and provided a "covering."

It protected the Yisraelites from death before they were gathered and delivered from Egypt. The mark is the mark of the Covenant. It identifies those in Covenant and protects them from the judgment resulting from disobedience.

The principle is clearly established that "judgment begins in the House of YHWH." *"For the time has come for judgment to begin at the House of Elohim; and if it begins with us first, what will be the end of those who do not obey the good news of Elohim?"* 1 Peter 4:17 Make no mistake that YHWH will be judging His people, and this is the beginning of judgments seen in the Revelation.

This "mark" on the forehead was already revealed by the garments of the High Priest. The people of YHWH, represented by the High Priest bear the Name of YHWH. *"36 And you shall make a plate of pure gold, and grave upon it, like the engravings of a signet, HOLINESS TO YHWH. 37 And you shall put it on a blue lace, that it may be upon the mitre; upon the forefront of the mitre it shall be. 38 And it shall be upon Aaron's forehead, that Aaron may bear the iniquity of the set apart things, which the children of Yisrael shall hallow in all their set apart gifts; and it shall be always upon his forehead, that they may be accepted before YHWH."* Shemot 28:36-38

The Name of YHWH would protect the High Priest and the High Priest would, in turn, place the Name of YHWH on the people in what is commonly known as the Aaronic blessing. *"22 And YHWH spoke to Moses, saying: 23 Speak to Aaron and his sons, saying, This is the way you shall bless the children of Yisrael. Say to them: 24 YHWH bless you and keep you; 25 YHWH make His face shine upon you, and be gracious to you; 26 YHWH lift up His countenance upon you, and give you peace. 27 So they shall put My Name on the children of Yisrael, and*

I will bless them." Bemidbar 6:22-27

The blessing rests upon those who bear the Name of YHWH. That is why the Yisraelites were instructed to bind the words of YHWH on their hands, and as frontlets between their eyes. (Debarim 6:8, 11:18) We know that the seal on the foreheads was, in fact, the Name of YHWH from a later reference as follows: "*Then I looked, and behold, a Lamb standing on Mount Zion, and with Him one hundred and forty-four thousand, having His Father's Name written on their foreheads.*" Revelation 14:1 So not only are these 144,000 sealed and protected from judgment, they later stand on Mount Zion with the Lamb – the One Who opens the seals.

Remember that Mount Zion is located in the heavenly realm, another dimension. While an actual mountain in Jerusalem was intended to be a pattern, Jerusalem is going to be split asunder. These 144,000 are located with the Lamb on the mountain in heaven, in another dimension. In fact, it appears that these 144,000 will be delivered and brought "up" the mountain, as Mosheh had gone up for the previous wedding feast at Sinai, where he likely saw into Mount Zion above him.

We can see that YHWH seals and protects those in Covenant with Him prior to rendering judgment. These are the ones who are set apart. He will seal those who "sigh and cry over the abominations" being committed. The language in the Hebrew is actually quite poetic. The word for "sigh" is "anachim" (𐤌𐤉𐤇𐤍𐤀) while the word for "cry" is "anaqim" (𐤌𐤉𐤒𐤍𐤀). They actually sound very similar, and are different by only one letter. The word for "abomination" is "towebah" (𐤄𐤏𐤅𐤕). The ones who are sealed are the people who are in Covenant with YHWH immediately prior to the judgment falling upon earth.

After reading about the 144,000 we immediately are told about a great multitude of people. "⁹ *After these things I looked, and behold, a great multitude which no one could number, of all nations, tribes, peoples, and tongues, standing before the throne and before the Lamb, clothed with white robes, with palm branches in their hands,* [10] *and crying out with a loud voice, saying, Salvation belongs to our Elohim who sits on the throne, and to the Lamb!* [14] *. . . These are the ones who come out of (the) great tribulation, and washed their robes and made them white in the blood of the Lamb.* [15] *Therefore they are before the Throne of Elohim, and serve Him day and night in His Temple. And He who sits on the throne will dwell among them.* [16] *They shall neither hunger anymore nor thirst anymore; the sun shall not strike them, nor any heat;* [17] *for the Lamb who is in the midst of the Throne will shepherd them and lead them to living fountains of waters. And Elohim will wipe away every tear from their eyes."* Revelation 7:9-10, 14-17

This great multitude consists of those who come out of what is commonly called "The Great Tribulation." The problem with that description is the word "The." It does not provide for a good rendering. While many people believe this refers to a group that comes out of a future event known as "The Great Tribulation," it could also be referring to all who have come out of great tribulation throughout history.

In fact, translations such as the Douay-Rheims provide: *"These are they who are come out of great tribulation . . . "* That seems to be a better description. To think that all of these events occurring before the Throne were exclusively limited to those living and dying in the latter days is a bit constrained. It is important to remember that the Throne of YHWH is seated outside of our limited dimensional existence.

Many brethren in the past have gone through great tribulation. There is no reason to think they would be excluded, and only one generation from the end would be included. The fact that this is such a great multitude that cannot be counted seems to confirm that this multitude spans

all time. In fact, they come from all nations, all tribes, all peoples and all tongues. Clearly this is a culmination of people throughout time.

So this group could include those from a future tribulation, or all those who come out of tribulation experienced throughout time. Thus far we have not read about one "Great Tribulation," although there are many tribulation periods suffered by the people of YHWH described in the Scriptures and historical records. In fact, the only mention of a "Great Tribulation" was from the Messiah, and we have already discussed that event which occurred in 70 CE. (Matthew 24:21)

Now many mistake this multitude for the Bride, but that is not accurate. They are dressed in white robes, because they were invited to a wedding. They are not seated on the Throne with the Groom, nor are they standing next to the Throne. They are before the Throne where the guests would be standing.

Notice what they are saying. *"Salvation belongs to our Elohim who sits on the throne, and to the Lamb!"* This is a very interesting statement coming from this great multitude. Salvation is a concept that is misunderstood by many. In fact, Christians often treat salvation as a one time event that occurs when a decision is made. They confuse a decision to "accept Jesus" as salvation. This is a serious mistake.

To begin, the real Name of the Messiah is Yahushua. That Name specifically means: "YHWH saves" or "YHWH is salvation." The multitudes are therefore confirming that salvation belongs to YHWH and His Son. These multitudes have actually received salvation from YHWH, through His Son.

Salvation can mean deliverance from both physical death and more importantly, spiritual death. When we are born into this world, we are all destined for death and we need to be saved from that "death penalty." There is nothing we can do to avoid death, and therefore we need intervention from YHWH. YHWH sent His Son to save us through the Covenant He established with man. Therefore, salvation is provided through the Covenant.

That is why Yahushua had to shed His blood. The blood is what cleans, and provides the atonement from death. Right before Yahushua died on the execution stake, He proclaimed: "It is finished." He finished the work that He had come to accomplish.

The reason that the multitude specifically referred to the Lamb, is because Yahushua was the Lamb of Elohim. Yahushua shed His blood to save them from physical death, as we saw during the Passover, and to cover us and save us from the judgment, as we see at Yom Kippur. In each of these Appointed Time rehearsals, the shedding of blood alone did not accomplish the salvation.

The blood needed to be applied on the doorpost at Passover, and the mercy seat at Yom Kippur. It is that pure blood of Yahushua that we all need to transform our DNA, and cleanse us from the sin of the Garden. We literally need a blood transfusion of His DNA. When His DNA becomes our DNA then we are "adopted" by and through His blood into the Family of Elohim. We become transformed into Children of Light. That is the salvation that we need, and it is more than a simple prayer, the raising of a hand or a mental decision.

There are many being duped into believing that they are "eternally secure," because they said a prayer at some point in their life or because they "believe in God." They are told "once saved always saved" as if salvation was an event in the past.

Yaakob (James), the brother of Yahushua stated: "*19* . . . *even the demons believe and tremble* [20] *but . . . faith without works is dead.*" (Yaakob 2:19) Yaakob points to Abraham whos faith was made perfect by his actions – his walk. We must look to Abram who was brought forth out of Babylon. He believed and he acted. His belief in YHWH was counted as righteousness. (Beresheet 15:6). He did not stop there. He continued to walk out the Covenant path until he finished.

So the path to salvation is a process that begins with belief, leading to a future event. It begins with a free gift provided by the mercy and "grace" of Elohim, but that is only the beginning. We already saw the emphasis on becoming an overcomer. In fact, Paul reckoned it to running a race, and the point of a race is to finish. When you start the "race" your "track" is the Torah. You need to stay on the track to remain in the race, and the race is not over until you cross the finish line.

Paul further exhorted: *"work out your own salvation with fear and trembling."* Philippians 2:12 Salvation is something that will be inherited. (Hebrews 1:14) In fact, the salvation of your soul is the end of your faith, not the beginning. (1 Peter 1:9)

It is clearly expressed as follows: " . . . *so Messiah was offered once to bear the sins of many. To those who eagerly wait for Him He will appear a second time, apart from sin, for salvation."* Hebrews 9:28 Yahushua is salvation, and He brings salvation with Him. We cannot earn our salvation. It is freely given to those who join the Covenant. Yahushua shed His blood for the Renewed Covenant. We are justified by His blood (Romans 5:9), and He is the door to that Covenant. (John 10:9) If we are in the Covenant then we should live the life prescribed by the Covenant with assurance and hope of the promised salvation.

Now this multitude, declaring that salvation belongs to YHWH and to the Lamb, are those who are saved. They came out of tribulation, and they received the promised salvation. They called upon the Name of YHWH (Joel 2:32; Acts 2:21; Romans 10:13), and they endured to the end. (Matthew 24:13; Mark 13:13)

This is important to remember because in days of trouble we call upon YHWH, and He hears us. His makes His face to shine upon us, and that is how we are saved. (Psalm 80:3, 7, 19)

There is something very interesting about this multitude. They are holding palm branches. Now Christians might think that this is Palm Sunday, but they would be wrong. Palm Sunday is a misunderstanding of what is read in the triumphal entry accounts in the Gospels. Even though it was approaching Passover, the time for the Lamb of Elohim to die, the people thought it was time for the Messiah to rule and reign. That is why they cut palm branches. As was already mentioned, there is one one specific Appointed Time where the Covenant people are instructed to hold palm branches. That Appointed Time is Succot. (Vayiqra 23:40)

Sukkot is the time of joy when we anticipate building succas and dwelling with YHWH. The Passover is much more somber and we rehearse consider the blood and flesh of the Lamb of Elohim, bondage, plagues and the path to deliverance. Indeed, during the Passover, Yahushua was humiliated and His clothes were stripped from Him. He hung on the execution stake naked. This was the punishment that Adam deserved when his eyes were opened and he saw that he was naked. Instead, he was covered – atoned with blood.

So the palm branches held by the multitude before the Throne would seem to be a clue that Succot will play an important role in the future – at the second coming of Yahushua. Indeed, there is a tradition that if the people of YHWH call out to Him on the Last Day of Succot – the seventh day – He will save them.[231]

They are wearing white, which represents that they are there for the wedding. They are holding palm branches to lay down before the Bride and the Bridegroom. So at this point we are waiting for the Bride to be revealed.

As we proceed to the opening of the final seal we are told about seven angels with seven trumpets. Now it is important to understand that the Greek language does not have a specific word for the Hebrew word "shofar." That is why we do not read about any shofars in the English translation of the New Testament.

It is well understood that the "great trumpet" that Yahushua referred to in Matthew 24:31 was a shofar. The Greek word used was "salpigx" (σάλπιγγος). It was the same word used in the Greek Septuagint when referencing the Hebrew word "shofar." It is also the same word used to describe the "trumpets" in Revelation. Therefore, the seven "trumpets" that we read about are actually seven "shofars." This is another one of those items that are often "lost in translation," but it is highly significant to recognize.

The seventh seal leads us into the Heavenly Temple service. The one on earth was just a shadow of the one in Heaven. Just as there were priests in the Temple on Earth, the Heavenly Temple also has priests. Just as shofars are blown here on earth, so too they are blown in the Heavens.

Remember that the voice of YHWH is likened to the shofar, and it was that shofar blast, emanating from the Throne that brought the world into existence. We will read about various messengers acting as priests in the Heavenly Temple. Part of that service involves the blowing of shofars.

"*¹ When He opened the seventh seal, there was silence in heaven for about half an hour. ² And I saw the seven messengers who stand before Elohim, and to them were given seven shofars. ³ Then another messenger, having a golden censer, came and stood at the altar. He was given much incense, that he should offer it with the prayers of all the set apart ones upon the golden altar which was before the Throne. ⁴ And the smoke of the incense, with the prayers of the set apart ones, ascended before Elohim from the messenger's hand. ⁵ Then the messenger took the censer, filled it with fire from the altar, and threw it to the earth. And there were noises, thunderings, lightnings, and an earthquake. ⁶ So the seven messengers who had the seven shofars prepared themselves to sound.*" Revelation 8:1-6

Once the seventh seal was opened, the scroll could be fully opened and then read. This results in silence of ½ hour. Since this is all taking place in the Heavenly Temple we should look at the pattern for the earthly service for clues.

According to Alfred Edersheim, "On ordinary days the priests blew seven times, each time **three blasts** - a short sound, an alarm, and again a sharp short sound (Tekiah, Teruah, and Tekiah), or, as the Rabbis express it, 'An alarm in the midst and a plain note before and after it.' According to tradition, they were intended symbolically to proclaim the kingdom of God, Divine Providence, and the **final judgment**. The first three blasts were blown when the great gates of the Temple - especially that of Nicanor - were opened. Then, when the drink-offering was poured out, the Levites sung the psalm of the day in three sections. After each section there was a pause, when the priests blew three blasts, and the people worshipped. This was the practice at the evening, as at the morning sacrifice. On the eve of the Sabbath a threefold blast of the priests' trumpets summoned the people, far as the sound was carried over the city, to prepare for the holy day, while another threefold blast announced its actual commencement. On Sabbaths, when, besides the ordinary, an additional sacrifice was brought, and the 'Song of Moses' sung - not the whole every Sabbath, but divided in six parts, one for every Sabbath, - the priests sounded their trumpets additional three times in the pauses

of the Sabbath psalm.[232]

Therefore, the events described in the heavenly Temple are not random events being described. They are very specific rituals being performed with specific purpose and timing. The mention of ½ hour along with seven shofars, which are all part of the daily service, all seem to set this in the framework of one day.

Whether there is an earthly Temple or not, the Heavenly Temple is still functioning. That is why we saw Daniel in the habit of praying 3 times a day, including the time of the morning and evening offerings, also known as oblations. (Daniel 9:21) These would be the times when the people would assemble at the Temple and offer up their prayers. Daniel knew that his prayers were the incense offered up in the heavenly Temple.

The incense service is something done in the morning and the evening when the lamps on the menorah are tended. *"7 Aaron shall burn on it sweet incense every morning; when he tends the lamps, he shall burn incense on it. 8 And when Aaron lights the lamps at twilight, he shall burn incense on it, a perpetual incense before YHWH throughout your generations."* Shemot 30:7-8

On earth, the multitudes of people would gather at the Temple and be praying while the incense would be offered on the altar of incense. So we can see the connection between the prayers of the people and the incense. The incense symbolically carried the prayers up to YHWH. They would fill the House since this altar was located within the House. The silence would seem to mean that there was no praying taking place, and this makes sense when we understand what occurs before the incense is offered.

The first order of affairs in the Temple involved casting lots for the priestly service of the day. First the altar needed to be cleaned and prepared. Then the morning offering needed to be readied. The trumpet (shofar) would sound, and the doors of the Temple would be opened as the morning offering was killed. Only then did the people come in while the priests were preparing the sacrifice, salting it and placing it on the altar. After the sacrifice was presented on the altar, then the incense offering was presented.

Since the messenger with the incense took fire from the altar, it was the fire that consumed the morning sacrifice. In this case the Lamb of Elohim. The daily service in the Temple on earth was literally a shadow of what was happening in the heavens. Knowing this we can follow the progression of what is happening on earth when the shofars are blown.

After the incense offering the seven messengers sound their shofars. The first four shofars sound in succession resulting in great destruction throughout the earth.

"7 The first messenger sounded: And hail and fire followed, mingled with blood, and they were thrown to the earth. And a third of the trees were burned up, and all green grass was burned up. 8 Then the second messenger sounded: And something like a great mountain burning with fire was thrown into the sea, and a third of the sea became blood. 9 And a third of the living creatures in the sea died, and a third of the ships were destroyed. 10 Then the third messenger sounded: And a great star fell from heaven, burning like a torch, and it fell on a third of the rivers and on the springs of water. 11 The name of the star is Wormwood. A third of the waters became wormwood, and many men died from the water, because it was made bitter. 12 Then the fourth messenger sounded: And a third of the sun was struck, a third of the moon, and a third of the stars, so that a third of them were darkened. A third of the day did not shine, and likewise the night. 13 And I looked, and I heard an angel flying through the midst of heaven, saying with a loud voice, Woe, woe, woe to the inhabitants of the earth, because of the remaining

blasts of the shofar of the three messengers who are about to sound!"
Revelation 8:7-13

These events are largely associated with the destruction and diminisment of the physical creation. One cannot ignore the emphasis on the amount of one third (1/3). Although many die from the water, none of these shofars are directed specifically at men. That will be later.

Remember that the shofar is strongly connected with Yom Teruah (Vayiqra 23:24; Bemidbar 29:1) and the Yom Kippur Jubilee (Vayiqra 25:29). It is specifically blown on both of these days. The time in between these two Appointed Times are often referred to as the 10 Days of Awe. They span between Day 1 of Month 7 and Day 10 of Month 7. It is a time of repentance in contemplation of judgment every year. So the shofar is directly associated with repentance.

Every 50 years these "Days of Awe" also result in a type of time shift, as time essentially "stands still." As the 49th Shemittah Year ends at Day 1 of Month 7, the Jubilee Year does not begin until Day 10 of Month 7.

A very interesting tradition developed starting with the shofar blast of Rosh Chodesh (Day 1) of Month 6, often called the Month of Elul. This shofar blast marked the beginning of a 40 day reflection period leading up to Yom Kippur on Day 10 of Month 7. Since the shofar was sounded throughout Month 6, calling the people to repentance, the shofar sounded on Day 1 of Month 7 (Yom Teruah) was called "The Final Shofar." Then, after 10 days, the shofar sounded on Day 10 of Month 7 (Yom Kippur) was called "The Great Shofar," since at that time judgment was sealed.

So we can see the shofars blown by the messengers are intended to get people's attention in order for them to repent and turn to YHWH. The one third (1/3) makes more sense as we continue toward the culmination of events leading to the restoration of the "sons of Elohim."

The first four shofars are then followed by the remaining three shofars – all referred to as woes. These are directed toward the remaining inhabitants of the earth. Now one would expect YHWH to make a distinction between His people, and the ones subject to the final three woes.

In fact, He does through the Prophet Isaiah when describing woes upon the people. "*^{18} Woe to those who draw iniquity with cords of vanity, and sin as if with a cart rope; ^{19} That say, Let Him make speed and hasten His work, that we may see it; and let the counsel of the Set Apart One of Yisrael draw near and come, that we may know it. ^{20} Woe to those who call evil good, and good evil; Who put darkness for light, and light for darkness; Who put bitter for sweet, and sweet for bitter! ^{21} Woe to those who are wise in their own eyes, and prudent in their own sight! ^{22} Woe to men mighty at drinking wine, woe to men valiant for mixing intoxicating drink, ^{23} Who justify the wicked for a bribe, and take away justice from the righteous man! ^{24} Therefore, as the fire devours the stubble, and the flame consumes the chaff, so their root will be as rottenness, and their blossom will ascend like dust; because they have rejected the Torah of YHWH of hosts, and despised the word of the Holy One of Yisrael. ^{25} Therefore the anger of YHWH is aroused against His people; He has stretched out His hand against them and stricken them, and the hills trembled. Their carcasses were as refuse in the midst of the streets. For all this His anger is not turned away, but His Hand is stretched out still. ^{26} He will lift up a banner to the nations from afar, and will whistle to them from the end of the earth; surely they shall come with speed, swiftly.*" Isaiah 5:18-26

Notice the mention of four woes, and they are all directed at the people of YHWH. So it appears that up to this point, the four shofars have been woes intended to judge the people of YHWH. After those four woes, YHWH will lift up a banner, whistle for His people and gather them quickly. This event will apparently be intended to protect them from

the three woes that are about to come through the last three shofars.

The first four shofars provide a description of events occurring on the earth that are fairly straightforward. We have enough knowledge of the catastrophic effects of asteroids, volcanoes, tsunamis and the like to try to explain these events.

When the fifth angel sounds his trumpet, things begin to get very interesting. Instead of natural disasters, the events shift to the supernatural. *"¹ Then the fifth messenger sounded: And I saw a star fallen from heaven to the earth. To him was given the key to the bottomless pit. ² And he opened the bottomless pit, and smoke arose out of the pit like the smoke of a great furnace. So the sun and the air were darkened because of the smoke of the pit. ³ Then out of the smoke locusts came upon the earth. And to them was given power, as the scorpions of the earth have power. ⁴ They were commanded not to harm the grass of the earth, or any green thing, or any tree, but only those men who do not have the seal of Elohim on their foreheads. ⁵ And they were not given authority to kill them, but to torment them for five months. Their torment was like the torment of a scorpion when it strikes a man. ⁶ In those days men will seek death and will not find it; they will desire to die, and death will flee from them. ⁷ The shape of the locusts was like horses prepared for battle. On their heads were crowns of something like gold, and their faces were like the faces of men. ⁸ They had hair like women's hair, and their teeth were like lions' teeth. ⁹ And they had breastplates like breastplates of iron, and the sound of their wings was like the sound of chariots with many horses running into battle. ¹⁰ They had tails like scorpions, and there were stings in their tails. Their power was to hurt men five months. ¹¹ And they had as king over them the angel of the bottomless pit, whose name in Hebrew is Abaddon, but in Greek he has the name Apollyon."* Revelation 9:1-11

This is the first woe and the events described have

confounded many. The Greek word for "bottomless" is "abbussos" (ἀβύσσου) which means: "abyss." We already read about the "abyss" as the place where Azazel and his hosts were bound and held.

The Greek word for "pit" is "phrear" (φρέαρ). "Phrear" in Greek mythology is "an orcus, a deep chasm bound by a gulf where fallen angels are imprisoned."[233] So this "bottomless pit" is clearly the same "abyss" where Azazel was bound. It is another dimension, and there is a gate that requires a key. Indeed, at the heart of our Milky Way galaxy is a super dense black hole with intense gravitational forces. Some believe that the universe operates like a grand combination lock, and certain doors can be opened at precise alignments – all you need is the right key.

This should immediately make us recall the statement made by Yahushua at the "gate of hell" in Banias. Yahushua

said that He holds the keys, so He is apparently giving the key at a specific time to open the gate of the abyss. Interestingly, there is significant ancient tradition regarding "gods" travelling through these gates. One such gate from ancient Mayan archaeology remarkably resembles the particle collider built by CERN, the European Organization for Nuclear Research, in Switzerland.

The real purpose of CERN has been questioned by many. The fact that the logo for CERN contains an imbedded 666, intertwined with a rendering of the collider is one reason for concern. Experiments at

CERN's 27-kilometer circular lab, which lies 100 meters underground, identified what is believed to be the Higgs Boson, the long-sought maker of mass, theorized in the 1960s. As a result, two theoreticians, Peter Higgs and Francois Englert, were awarded the Nobel Physics award for discovering the so-called "God particle."

Many suspect that the CERN Large Hadron Collider (LHC) is modern man's attempt to open a gate. The similarity between ancient renderings and the CERN LHC cannot be ignored or discounted. It has been stated that the CERN "machine" may possibly create or discover previously unimagined scientific phenomena, or "unknown unknowns" – for  instance "an extra dimension." In fact, Sergio Bertolucci, who is Director for Research and Scientific Computing at CERN has said: "Out of this door might come something, or we might send something through it."[234]

The existence of a statue of Shiva at CERN seems to reveal their true intentions. Shiva is the ancient Hindu god of destruction. In the statue at CERN, Shiva is depicted as coming forth out of a stargate. This is not just any stargate, it is the gate at CERN. Interestingly, Shiva is specifically depicted as Nataraja, the cosmic dancer who performs his divine dance to destroy a weary  universe, and make preparations for the god Brahma to start the process of creation.

Whether CERN is a gate that will be opened, or whether it will play a part in opening a gate is yet to be determined. Nevertheless, the intent appears to be ominous. It is about the destruction of the universe to create a new world order. Some critics of CERN have even cautioned of the many dangers of continuiung to use the super collider, including the creation of black holes. So one cannot ignore the connection with the abyss mentioned in the text that emits a swarm locust, and their king, known as the destroyer.

Swarms of locust are always associated with a plague and destruction. They are never associated with anything good. The locust described in the text are clearly not normal locust. Locust eat vegetation, and these are specifically commanded not to eat food, but to torment men. To get a handle on this, it is important to recognize that the messengers, also called "angels," are often referred to as "stars." Here the Greek word for "star" is "astare" (ἀστέρα), and could be of the feminine gender.

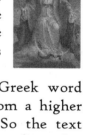

As a result, one cannot ignore the connection with Easter, also known as Astarte. She was the "queen of heaven" known as Semaramis in Babylon who was said to have descended to earth in a flying craft appearing like an egg, landing in the Euphrates River. Isis was also called the "Queen of Heaven."

Interestingly, instead of "falling," the Greek word "pipto" (πίπτω) could refer to: "descending from a higher place to a lower place" or "lighting upon." So the text literally reads "*I saw astare descending from heaven to the earth.*" Many in the Catholic religion refer to Mary as the "Queen of Heaven." They expect her to descend upon the earth and there are numerous eye witness accounts describing "apparitions" of Mary.

Now what is very profound in the mass sighting of the apparition of Mary at Fatima on October 13, 1917 where somewhere around 60,000 people witnessed a large silver-gray disk descend from the clouds. The worship of Mary is simply a repeat of the worship of Semaramis from Babylon. Remember that she too was called the "Queen of Heaven"  and the "mother of God." The connection with Islam cannot be ignored as Fatima was actually the name of the daughter of Mohammed, who is highly venerated in the religion of Islam.

So we see a connection with Mary and Fatima. In fact, in Islam, there is a stone believed to be a fallen star – a meteor. It is one of the most venerated objects in Islam known as the Kaaba Stone or al-Hajr al-Aswad. It almost appears to be of "alien" origin, and it is literally a "cornerstone" on the eastern corner of the monolithic structure known as the  Kaaba. Some believe that this is the same black stone associated with the worship of the goddess Cybele from Pergamum. That stone was also thought to be a "fallen star" and was eventually brought to Rome.

Cybele worship was the same as Diana worship. Both  are directly connected with Semaramis of Babylon, and both were associated with the crescent moon and the black stone. How interesting that we see these two objects associated with Islam. Of course, Islam also includes the phallus and the dome imagery in the mosques, as do the Christians and various governments around the world.

Typically each mosque will include a minaret from which the call to prayer is emitted. This will then gather the adherents into the mosque where they bow toward Mecca and pray toward the Kaaba and the Kaaba Stone. This sounds a lot like what Nebuchadnezzar did in Babylon, and it is plain to see the Babylonian elements mixed within all of these systems.

The point of all this is to recognize the actions of the angels and the fallen angels and how they both descend from the heavens to the earth in order to accomplish their tasks. Whoever or whatever this star is, it is given the key to open the abyss from which a great smoke emits. Also a special breed of beings, initially  described as locust, are released from their confinement. Many speculate as to the origin of these strange beings, but they are clearly linked with the Nephilim.

It is important to remember that the sexual sins described in 1 Enoch were not limited to women. According  to the Book of Giants, and other ancient texts, the Nephilim profaned all of creation. That is why the entire planet had to be wiped out, and only certain animals were saved from destruction. These "locust" are hybrid beings, but they are not of the flesh. They have been described as "demonic monsters" that fly like locusts (Shemot 10:12-20; Joel 1:4, 2:4-14), and sting like scorpions. (Ezekiel 2:6, Luke 11:12)[235]

They are actually very similar to the ancient creatures depicted in Sumerian renderings. These creatures are clearly not new to this world. The abyss is reserved for the angelic beings, so these are very likely demonic beings. These "demon" locust have a king. His name is Abaddon in Hebrew, and Apollyon in the Greek. Abaddon actually means "the destroyer." We see the Greek name of Apollyon very closely associated with Apollos, the Roman sun god. This is the same god as the Egyptian Osiris. Both are the same god in different cultures, believed to come from the constellation Orion. Apollyon will not be seeking worship, he will be terrorizing mankind.

This is not the first mention of Apollyon in history. In fact, Apollyon, or rather Apollos, was the "son of god"- the son of Zeus. He was said to communicate through the Oracle of Delphi. This prophetess of Apollos was located at the Temple of Apollo at the very site where Apollo was said to have killed the great serpent Python. Apollyon is no doubt one of the Nephilim, and he works through a false prophet or prophetess. We see a clear depiction of this through the Roman prophetess known as the Cumean Sybil. Apollo spoke through this prophetess who some believe is actually depicted with six fingers in the rendering by Michelangelo Buonarroti in the Sistine Chapel at the Vatican.

These powerful prophetesses speaking for the Nephilim should make us think of Jezebel, who was a harlot and a prophetess of Baal. She was the daughter of Ethbaal, king of the Sidonians. She married Ahab, the King of the House of Yisrael, and merged the Kingdom of Yisrael with Baal worship. Elijah was sent as a prophet of Elohim to witness against them and their Babylonian system. As we can see the parallels begin to emerge, especially in light of Isaiah 23 and 24, it is important to remember that much of the context of the end of days revolves around the House of Yisrael.

This destroyer that comes out of the abyss clearly seems to be referring to Azazel. He was, after all, the one who taught weaponry and warfare to men. His purpose was to destroy mankind, and thus he would aptly be described as "the destroyer." He was bound in the abyss with his hoards. It is possibly the very reason that he was bound – to keep him from destroying all of mankind.

He was destined for judgment on the Day of Judgment, which is the culmination of the Day of YHWH. The Day of YHWH is a one year period, so it seems that Azazel may be released until he is finally judged. The text provides that he and his locust swarm have power for 5 months.

Some attempt to interpret these entities released from the abyss as simply metaphors or a description of modern war machinery. Their origination point seems to define their identity. They are clearly not of this world. They are from another dimension, the abyss that restrains and contains angelic beings. Their appearance will definitely be one of those "know it when you see it events" as are most of the events that follow in the Revelation, although, since they are spiritual beings they may remain unseen.

John was allowed to see them because he was taken up in the spirit, but that does not mean that all of mankind will know what is happening. That may be why John was given the revelation. It may be to explain events occurring in the spirit realm that would otherwise be unexplained to the naked eye. We know that this entity preferred to speak through a prophetess so we may see the same pattern in the end. Maybe this time the prophetess will be an apparition of Mary, or some other false prophet or prophetess.

As we transiton to the sixth messenger and the sixth shofar, that does not mean that the Destroyer disappears. He is still unleashed and there is no mention that he has been judged. Now with the sounding of the sixth shofar, things escalate.

When the sixth messenger sounds his shofar we are

brought back to the Temple in heaven, and we read about the horns of the altar speaking. It is now that we read about judgment being rendered upon mankind – the second woe. *"[13] Then the sixth messenger sounded: And I heard a voice from the four horns of the golden altar which is before Elohim, [14] saying to the sixth messenger who had the shofar, Release the four messengers who are bound at the great river Euphrates. [15] So the four messengers, who had been prepared for the hour and day and month and year, were released to kill a third of mankind. [16] Now the number of the army of the horsemen was two hundred million; I heard the number of them. [17] And thus I saw the horses in the vision: those who sat on them had breastplates of fiery red, hyacinth blue, and sulfur yellow; and the heads of the horses were like the heads of lions; and out of their mouths came fire, smoke, and brimstone. [18] By these three plagues a third of mankind was killed - by the fire and the smoke and the brimstone which came out of their mouths. [19] For their power is in their mouth and in their tails; for their tails are like serpents, having heads; and with them they do harm. [20] But the rest of mankind, who were not killed by these plagues, did not repent of the works of their hands, that they should not worship demons, and idols of gold, silver, brass, stone, and wood, which can neither see nor hear nor walk. [21] And they did not repent of their murders or their sorceries or their sexual immorality or their thefts."* Revelation 9:13-21

Here again we see some apparently supernatural beings. While there may be two hundred million horsemen, it is not possible, at this point in time, to muster two hundred million horses. There are currently not anywhere near that number of horses on the earth. There were four angels bound at the Euphrates River for a specific hour, day, month and year to kill 1/3 of mankind. Again we see the precise timing of these events, and the sixth shofar was sounded at a very precise pre-planned time. Interestingly, the Euphrates River begins in Turkey, extends through Syria, Iraq and Iran.

These nations likely have dominions and powers over them. They are centered on the ancient land of Babylon, so it is possible that these angels were four Watchers bound during the time described in 1 Enoch.

This event suddenly describes an army of 200 million with very strange horses that render three plagues of fire, smoke and brimstone. The previous batch of beings released from the abyss did not kill men. These messengers send forth plagues that kill 1/3 of mankind. Incredibly, mankind still fails to repent. This reveals the purpose of the plagues – to lead mankind to repentance. So all of these terrible things are meant for the good of mankind. They are to lead men back to YHWH.

Now before we read about the seventh shofar, which is the third woe, we read about a "Mighty Angel." Remember that the word "angel" means: "messenger." Typically, a messenger is one coming from the Throne of YHWH bringing a message to men. See if you can identify this "messenger" by the description given.

"¹ I saw still another 'Mighty Messenger' coming down from heaven, clothed with a cloud. And a rainbow was on his head, his face was like the sun, and his feet like pillars of fire. ² He had a little scroll open in his hand. And he set his right foot on the sea and his left foot on the land, ³ and cried with a loud voice, as when a lion roars. When he cried out, seven thunders uttered their voices. ⁴ Now when the seven thunders uttered their voices, I was about to write; but I heard a voice from heaven saying to me, Seal up the things which the seven thunders uttered, and do not write them. ⁵ The messenger whom I saw standing on the sea and on the land raised up his hand to heaven ⁶ and swore by Him who lives forever and ever, who created heaven and the things that are in it, the earth and the things that are in it, and the sea and the things that are in it, that there should be delay no longer, ⁷ but in the days of the sounding of the seventh angel, when he is about to sound, the

mystery of Elohim would be finished, as He declared to His servants the prophets. *8 Then the voice which I heard from heaven spoke to me again and said, Go, take the little scroll which is open in the hand of the messenger who stands on the sea and on the earth. 9 So I went to the angel and said to him, Give me the little book. And he said to me, Take and eat it; and it will make your stomach bitter, but it will be as sweet as honey in your mouth. 10 Then I took the little scroll out of the messenger's hand and ate it, and it was as sweet as honey in my mouth. But when I had eaten it, my stomach became bitter. 11 And he said to me, You must prophesy again about many peoples, nations, tongues, and kings." Revelation 10:1-11*

This Mighty Messenger is described as standing "on" the sea and "on" the land. The Greek word is "epi" (ἐπι) which means: "over" or "above." This Messenger is "over" the sea and "over" the land. So we see the connection with Yahushua in the clouds, and this Messenger above the Earth.

Also, the rainbow is over His head. The rainbow was the sign that YHWH would never destroy the entire earth with a flood. This was a sign of the Covenant and a reminder of judgment. The seven colors of the rainbow represent the seven spirits of YHWH. We know from Isaiah that the Messiah has the seven spirits of YHWH resting upon Him. (Isaiah 11:2). The rainbow is also something directly related with the Throne Room. (Revelation 4:3).

Yahushua, as the Lamb, took the scroll and broke open the seven seals, now this messenger hands a scroll to John. Interestingly, we have seen a process of unsealing a scroll, and now we read about the seven thunders that were heard, but they were not written by John.

The word for "thunder" in Hebrew is either "qowl" (ᒪᕼᕠ) or "ra'am" (ᒧᐤᕤ). We can see the voice of YHWH described as He judges the earth in the following verse. *"The adversaries of YHWH shall be broken in pieces; From heaven He will thunder (ra'am) against them. YHWH will judge the ends of the earth. He will give strength to His king, and exalt the horn of His Anointed (Moshiach)."* 1 Samuel 2:10

The word "ra'am" can mean "thunder" as well as "crash" and "roar." That is really interesting because the roar of the lion was already discussed previously. The Messiah is often described as the Lion of the Tribe of Yahudah. So it will likely be His voice "thundering" or "roaring" for His people.

"They shall walk after YHWH. He will roar like a lion. When He roars, then His sons shall come trembling from the west." Hosea 11:10. *"YHWH also will roar from Zion, and utter His voice from Jerusalem; The heavens and earth will shake; but YHWH will be a shelter for His people, and the strength of the children of Yisrael."* Joel 3:16

We already saw the Lamb of Elohim with seven horns, eyes, and the seven spirits before the throne. The voice of YHWH has been likened to seven thunders. In fact, Psalms 29 actually describes the seven voices of YHWH. So the roar and the thunders appear to be eminating from the Throne of YHWH, and they mark the re-gathering and return of the outcasts of Yisrael.

This makes perfect sense when we consider the order of the shofars. The shofar was used to call the assembly and there is a tradition that after Yisrael left Egypt on their way to the Promised Land, every morning before they started on their journey, they would have seven shofars blown through the process of breaking camp. When the seventh shofar sounded – the final shofar – that meant it was time to move. So these shofars are intended for the Assembly of Yisrael. They are not some obscure "trumpets" blown for no known reason. They are shofar blasts specifically meant to call and assemble His people.

This is all very consistent with the many verses that describe Yahushua as "coming in the clouds" when He sends forth His messengers to gather His elect. Here, this Mighty Messenger is clothed with a cloud. This is Yahushua, the Lamb of Elohim – the One who was worthy to open the scroll. He now hands the open scroll to John who must eat it so that he can prophesy the remaining portion of the vision shown to Daniel.

Therefore, we should expect the rest of the Revelation to finish what began in Daniel. It should provide additional information concerning the final beast kingdom, and how the rock, the Messiah, will destroy that kingdom and establish the Kingdom of YHWH on earth. As we consider Yahushua the Messiah conquering the earth, we cannot ignore the pattern provided in the Scriptures involving Joshua, whose Hebrew name was Yahushua.

There are actually many patterns and parallels to discern from the conquering of the land by Joshua (Yahushua), and the Messiah Yahushua conquering the earth. Those patterns reveal how Yahushua brings his people out of the desert, through the parted waters and into the Land. He circumcises them so that they can partake of the Covenant meal, and then proceed to conquer the land so that they can enter into their inheritance. It appears to reveal that first on the agenda is the absolute destruction of the moon god. This places the religion of Islam squarely within the crosshairs of Yahushua at the end of the age.

As we proceed with Revelation chapter 11 we will also see many parallels with the Book of Zechariah. For instance, the passage begins with an instruction to measure. *"¹ Then I was given a reed like a measuring rod. And the angel stood, saying, Rise and measure the Temple of Elohim, the altar, and those who worship there. ² But leave out the court which is outside the Temple, and do not measure it, for it has been given to the Gentiles (Nations). And they will tread the set apart city underfoot for forty-two months."* Revelation 11:1-2

This is significant because at this point we are seeing a distinction between the inner courts and the outer courts. Those who belong in the House are counted. The outer courts, which will be filled by the Nations, are yet to be counted.

In Zechariah we read: *"¹ Then I raised my eyes and looked, and behold, a man with a measuring line in his hand. ² So I said, Where are you going? And he said to me, To measure Jerusalem, to see what is its width and what is its length. ³ And there was the angel who talked with me, going out; and another angel was coming out to meet him, ⁴ who said to him, Run, speak to this young man, saying: Jerusalem shall be inhabited as towns without walls, because of the multitude of men and livestock in it. ⁵ For I, says YHWH, will be a wall of fire all around her, and I will be the glory in her midst. ⁶ Up, up! Flee from the land of the north, says YHWH; for I have spread you abroad like the four winds of heaven," says YHWH. ⁷ Up, Zion! Escape, you who dwell with the daughter of Babylon. ⁸ For thus says YHWH of hosts: He sent Me after glory, to the nations which plunder you; for he who touches you touches the apple of His eye. ⁹ For surely I will shake My hand against them, and they shall become spoil for their servants. Then you will know that YHWH of hosts has sent Me. ¹⁰ Sing and rejoice, O daughter of Zion! For behold, I am coming and I will dwell in your midst, says YHWH. ¹¹ Many nations shall be joined to YHWH in that day, and they shall become My people. And I will dwell in your midst. Then you will know that YHWH of hosts has sent Me to you. ¹² And YHWH will take possession of Yahudah as His inheritance in the Set Apart Land, and will again choose Jerusalem. ¹³ Be silent, all flesh, before YHWH, for He is aroused from His Set Apart Habitation!"* Zechariah 2:1-13

This prophecy involved measuring the City of Jerusalem, and it is telling Zion to get out of Babylon. This is a theme that will continue in Revelation. While Zechariah was previously instructed to measure Jerusalem, John was

instructed to measure the Temple. The Court of the Gentiles was left open, because the House of Yisrael must be re-gathered from the Gentiles – the Nations.

Notice the final verse in Zechariah: "*Be silent, all flesh, before YHWH, for He is aroused from His set apart habitation!*" This is the ½ hour of silence that we previously read as YHWH is aroused from His House to begin concluding the service on Earth.

Now in the Revelation, John is told about two witnesses. "*³ And I will give power to My two witnesses, and they will prophesy one thousand two hundred and sixty days, clothed in sackcloth. ⁴ These are the two olive trees and the two lampstands standing before the Elohim of the earth. ⁵ And if anyone wants to harm them, fire proceeds from their mouth and devours their enemies. And if anyone wants to harm them, he must be killed in this manner. ⁶ These have power to shut heaven, so that no rain falls in the days of their prophecy; and they have power over waters to turn them to blood, and to strike the earth with all plagues, as often as they desire.*" Revelation 11:3-6

This verse actually provides a direct reference to Zechariah by describing the two witnesses as "*the two olive trees and the two lampstands standing before Elohim.*"

In Zechariah we read: "*¹ Now the angel who talked with me came back and wakened me, as a man who is wakened out of his sleep. ² And he said to me, What do you see? So I said, I am looking, and there is a lampstand of solid gold with a bowl on top of it, and on the stand seven lamps with seven pipes to the seven lamps. ³ Two olive trees are by it, one at the right of the bowl and the other at its left. ⁴ So I answered and spoke to the angel who talked with me, saying, What are these, my master? ⁵ Then the angel who talked with me answered and said to me, Do you not know what these are? And I said, No, my master. ⁶ So he answered and said to me: This is the word of YHWH to Zerubbabel: Not by might nor by power, but by My Spirit, Says YHWH of hosts. ⁷ Who are you, O great* mountain? Before Zerubbabel you shall become a plain! And he shall bring forth the capstone (✗✗-aben) with shouts of Grace, grace to it! *8* Moreover the Word of YHWH came to me, saying: *9* The hands of Zerubbabel have laid the foundation of this Temple; His hands shall also finish it. Then you will know that YHWH of hosts has sent Me to you. *10* For who has despised the day of small things? For these seven rejoice to see the plumb line in the hand of Zerubbabel. They are the eyes of YHWH which scan to and fro throughout the whole earth. *11* Then I answered and said to him, What are these two olive trees - at the right of the lampstand and at its left? *12* And I further answered and said to him, What are these two olive branches that drip into the receptacles of the two gold pipes from which the golden oil drains? *13* Then he answered me and said, Do you not know what these are? And I said, No, my master. *14* So he said, <u>These are the two anointed ones, who stand beside the Master of the whole earth.</u>" Zechariah 4:1-14

So we can see that the actual events involving Zerubabbel rebuilding the Temple, after the return of the House of Yahudah from Babylon, were prophetic toward the future rebuilding of the Temple by the Messiah.

The cornerstone is specifically called the "et-aben" (✗✗-✗✗). Therefore, the "first" stone, the Rosh Pina, is the Messiah, and the rest of the stones are His Bride. This is a Temple prepared in the heavens, that will be brought down to earth. So this act of measuring is like the Bride going to get fitted for her gown prior to the wedding. At this point in the text, we can see that we are getting very close to the wedding day.

The two witnesses are the anointed ones who stand beside the Master. Because they are associated with gold, we can discern that they belong inside the Temple. They will come to earth and prophesy 1,260 days in sackcloth, and with great power at their disposal. The word for "witness" in the Greek is "marturia" (μαρτυρία). A "witness" speaks what they know, and testify to what they have seen. (John 3:11) Their function is directly related to a prophet. The word "marturia" is where we get the word "martyr," because prophets were usually killed for their testimony.

So these "two witnesses" are two prophets. They will be providing testimony concerning things they know and have seen. Many people are awaiting the appearance of these two witnesses to begin the 1,260 day count. The problem with this is that we cannot rely upon mainstream media to make the announcement that day one of the 1,260 day count has begun. We should not expect a "two witnesses cam" to appear on our television screens. We do not know who exactly they will be testifying to, and whether they will be moving around or in one place.

Remember that when Mosheh and Aaron were going before Pharaoh as two witnesses on behalf of YHWH, not all of Egypt or the world knew when they began testifying. The same will likely hold true for these witnesses. While there clearly will be a time when the world knows about them, we may not necessarily know the exact timing. We can be certain that YHWH keeps His word, and they will indeed testify for the prophesied duration.

Therefore, these witnesses may be operating against the principalities and powers of the world, and most people could be oblivious to much of their conduct. This is exactly as it was in the days of Noah. While Noah was building the Ark and likely warning people, life went on as usual until the rains of judgment began to fall upon the earth.

This 1,260 day period comes right after the mention of 42 months that the Gentiles will trample the Holy City. Interestingly, 1,260 days is the same as 42 months of 30 days each month, but that is not something likely to happen so the 1,260 days points to about a 44 month duration of time. It is helpful to recall the hint in Daniel when a specific period of days was provided, and those days were linked with the "moadi" – the Appointed Times. It is likely that this day count spans between certain Appointed Times as a beginning and an end point.

We assume that they will end up in Jerusalem, because they are later killed in Jerusalem. *"And their dead bodies will lie in the street of the great city which spiritually is called Sodom and Egypt, where also our Master was crucified."* Revelation 11:8 Again, they are not simply witnesses, they are two prophets who are actually tormenting those who dwell on the earth. (Revelation 11:10) We do not exactly know what they will be stating, but we can assume that they will be warning of the impending judgment and the return of Yahushua. I would suspect that they will reveal many of the mysteries that remain concerning the end of the age – for those who have ears to hear.

Based strictly upon their descriptions one could speculate that these two witnesses are Mosheh and Elijah. These two witnesses testify to the Covenant – the Torah (Mosheh) and the Prophets (Elijah). The powers demonstrated by the two witnesses are the same powers demonstrated by both of these individuals in the Torah and the Prophets.

Indeed, these are the two individuals that Yahushua met with in what is commonly referred to at the Mount of Transfiguration. This event is traditionally believed to have occurred on Mount Tabor. Some believe it was actually on Mount Hermon, where a gate exists above the gate of hell at Banias. They both met with Yahushua, and can therefore testify to what they saw and what they know. They both have first hand knowledge of the Messiah.

Here is that meeting as described in Matthew. *"[1] Now after six days Yahushua took Peter, Yaakob, and John his brother, led them up on a high mountain by themselves; [2] and He was*

transfigured before them. His face shone like the sun, and His clothes became as white as the light. ³ And behold, Mosheh and Elijah appeared to them, talking with Him. ⁴ Then Peter answered and said to Yahushua, Master, it is good for us to be here; if You wish, let us make here three tabernacles: one for You, one for Mosheh, and one for Elijah. ⁵ While he was still speaking, behold, a bright cloud overshadowed them; and suddenly a voice came out of the cloud, saying, This is My beloved Son, in whom I am well pleased. Hear Him! ⁶ And when the disciples heard it, they fell on their faces and were greatly afraid. ⁷ But Yahushua came and touched them and said, Arise, and do not be afraid. ⁸ When they had lifted up their eyes, they saw no one but Yahushua only. ⁹ Now as they came down from the mountain, Yahushua commanded them, saying, Tell the vision to no one until the Son of Man is risen from the dead. ¹⁰ And His disciples asked Him, saying, Why then do the scribes say that Elijah must come first? ¹¹ <u>Yahushua answered and said to them, Indeed, Elijah is coming first and will restore all things.</u> ¹² But I say to you that Elijah has come already, and they did not know him but did to him whatever they wished. Likewise the Son of Man is also about to suffer at their hands. ¹³ Then the disciples understood that He spoke to them of John the Immerser."
Matthew 17:1-13

The question that most people should have is: What were they talking about? Interestingly, the Hebrew Shem Tob translation provides: "(Then) Mosheh and Elijah, while speaking with Him, (were revealed) to them and they told Yahushua all which would happen to Him in Jerusalem."²³⁶

Mosheh and Elijah were clearly alive and speaking when they met with Yahushua. They were particularly focused on events in Jerusalem, so this connects them perfectly with the two witnesses. We know from Malachi that Elijah is supposed to come before the Day of YHWH, and Yahushua reiterated that: "Elijah is coming and will restore all things."

This is an interesting point because although John the Immerser was likened to Elijah, he was not actually Elijah. He did not restore all things. He prepared the way for Yahushua, and as Gabriel stated: "*He will also go before Him in the spirit and power of Elijah, to turn the hearts of the fathers to the children, and the disobedient to the wisdom of the just, to make ready a people prepared for the Master.*" Luke 1:7

Mosheh led the Children of Yisrael out of Egypt, and we are expecting another greater exodus in the future. Elijah specifically operated in great power to confront Baal worship in the House of Yisrael. He closed the heavens from raining for 3 ½ years, and performed many miracles already discussed. Remember that he was the one who called down fire on 2/3 of the 153 – "sons of Elohim." It is possible that he will be invoking some or all of YHWH's wrath on the Nephilim. He was taken up to the heavens in a whirlwind and a chariot. (2 Kings 2:11)

According to the last words in the Tanak, spoken by Malachi, there is more to be done by Elijah.

"*¹ Behold, I send My messenger, and he will prepare the way before Me. And the Master, whom you seek, will suddenly come to His temple, even the Messenger of the Covenant, in whom you delight. Behold, He is coming, says YHWH of hosts. ² But who can endure the day of His coming? And who can stand when He appears? For He is like a refiner's fire and like launderers' soap. ³ He will sit as a refiner and a purifier of silver; He will purify the sons of Levi, and purge them as gold and silver, that they may offer to YHWH an offering in righteousness. ⁴ Then the offering of Yahudah and Jerusalem will be pleasant to YHWH, as in the days of old, as in former years. ⁵ And I will come near you for judgment; I will be a swift witness against sorcerers, against adulterers, against perjurers, against* those who exploit wage earners and widows and orphans, and against those who turn away an alien - because they do not fear Me, says YHWH of hosts. ⁶ For I am YHWH, I do not change; Therefore you are not consumed, O sons of Yaakob. ⁷ Yet from the days of your fathers you have gone away from My ordinances and have not kept them. Return to Me, and I will return to you, says YHWH of hosts. But you said, In what way shall we return? ⁸ Will a man rob Elohim? Yet you have robbed Me! But you say, In what way have we robbed You? In tithes and offerings. ⁹ You are cursed with a curse, for you have robbed Me, even this whole nation. ¹⁰ Bring all the tithes into the storehouse, that there may be food in My house, and try Me now in this, says YHWH of hosts, If I will not open for you the windows of heaven and pour out for you such blessing that there will not be room enough to receive it. ¹¹ And I will rebuke the devourer for your sakes, so that he will not destroy the fruit of your ground, nor shall the vine fail to bear fruit for you in the field, says YHWH of hosts; ¹² And all nations will call you blessed, for you will be a delightful land, says YHWH of hosts. ¹³ Your words have been harsh against Me, Says YHWH, Yet you say, What have we spoken against You? ¹⁴ You have said, It is useless to serve Elohim; What profit is it that we have kept His ordinance, and that we have walked as mourners before YHWH of hosts? ¹⁵ So now we call the proud blessed, for those who do wickedness are raised up; they even tempt Elohim and go free. ¹⁶ Then those who feared YHWH spoke to one another, and YHWH listened and heard them; so a scroll of remembrance was written before Him for those who fear YHWH and who meditate on His Name. ¹⁷ They shall be Mine, says YHWH of hosts, On the day that I

make them My jewels. And I will spare them as a man spares his own son who serves him. [18] Then you shall again discern between the righteous and the wicked, between one who serves Elohim and one who does not serve Him. [4:1] For behold, the day is coming, burning like an oven, and all the proud, yes, all who do wickedly will be stubble. And the day which is coming shall burn them up, Says YHWH of hosts, that will leave them neither root nor branch. [2] But to you who fear My Name the Sun of Righteousness shall arise with healing in His wings; and you shall go out and grow fat like stall-fed calves. [3] You shall trample the wicked, for they shall be ashes under the soles of your feet on the day that I do this, Says YHWH of hosts. [4] Remember the Torah of Mosheh, My servant, Which I commanded him in Horeb for all Yisrael, with the statutes and judgments. [5] Behold, I will send you Elijah the prophet before the coming of the great and dreadful day of YHWH. [6] And he will turn the hearts of the fathers to the children, and the hearts of the children to their fathers, lest I come and strike the earth with a curse."
Malachi 3:1-4:6

Interestingly, YHWH has a special scroll with the Names of those who meditate upon His Name. His Name is very important, as we can see throughout the Scriptures. There are many today who know His real Name, but refuse to use it. They see the issue of His Name as trivial and insignificant – even "legalistic." They are truly deluded as they insist upon using a fictitious and false name that they have inherited along with their pagan religious traditions. They will someday find out that this is no minor point as they stand before Him and give an account. Those who belong to Him are to bear His Name.

Malachi also specifically instructed us to remember

Mosheh. He then said that Elijah would come <u>before</u> the Great and Terrible Day of YHWH. While John the Immerser partially fulfilled the mandate of YHWH "to turn the hearts of the fathers to the children" he did not even have the mandate "*to turn the hearts of the children to their fathers.*"

As we have discussed throughout this text, the end of the age will culminate with the House of Yisrael turning back to the fathers, and the Covenant of the fathers, Abraham, Yitshaq and Yaakob. They will begin to understand their identity and be restored to the Covenant. This great restoration and re-gathering will be connected with the Day of YHWH.

The Day of YHWH is a day filled with many special signs, and we will examine that Day further in the text. The mention that Elijah would "restore all things" is a veiled reference to the Jubilee, which is known as "the restoration of all things." It also means that Elijah needs to appear before the end to set things straight.

Many believe that Enoch will be one of the two witnesses, simply because he walked with Elohim "and was not." (Beresheet 5:24) It is believed that he was translated into heaven because he was righteous. It is also traditional that he was born and translated on Shabuot, the Feast of Firstfruits which occurs on the 50th Day.

As such, it would seem to be more of a prophetic picture of a future harvest when Yahushua reaps the harvest of the Earth, and presents the firstfruits of that harvest before the Throne in the Heavens. Further, Yahushua specifically stated: "*No one has ascended to heaven, but He Who came down from heaven, that is, the Son of Man Who is in heaven.*" John 3:13

Whatever the identity of the two witnesses may be, sending them to the world is definitely an act of great mercy. According to Amos 3:7: "*Surely Adonai YHWH does nothing, unless He reveals His secret to His servants the prophets.*" Since the role of a prophet is to transmit information to the people, we can safely assume that these two prophets will be providing valuable testimony to mankind. They should be telling mankind everything that YHWH is planning to do, yet they will be despised and eventually killed.

Their bodies lie untouched for 3 ½ days when they are ultimately resurrected. There is another great earthquake that will be a defining waypoint for anyone watching and following the roadmap to the end provided through the Revelation. The second woe is now complete.

It is now time for the seventh shofar and the third woe. It is essentially "times up" for the kingdoms of the world. It is now time for the Kingdom of YHWH to come to earth. "*15 Then the seventh angel sounded: And there were loud voices in heaven, saying, The kingdoms of this world have become the kingdoms of our Master and of His Messiah, and He shall reign forever and ever! 16 And the twenty-four elders who sat before Elohim on their thrones fell on their faces and worshiped Elohim, 17 saying: We give You thanks, O YHWH El Shaddai, The One who is and who was and who is to come, because You have taken Your great power and reigned. 18 The nations were angry, and Your wrath has come, and the time of the dead, that they should be judged, and that You should reward Your servants the prophets and the saints, and those who fear Your Name, small and great, and should destroy those who destroy the earth. 19 Then the Temple of Elohim was opened in heaven, and the Ark of His Covenant was seen in His Temple. And there were lightnings, noises, thunderings, an earthquake, and great hail.*" Revelation 11:15-19

The doors of the Temple of Heaven are now opened and we can see the Ark, because there is no veil in front of the Holy of Holies. That was torn down when Yahushua died. (Matthew 27:51, Mark 15;38, Luke 23:45)

When we read about this seventh shofar we see an absolute transfer of power. The kingdoms of the earth now

are transferred to Yahushua. This final shofar should make us think about the great sound of the shofar that Messiah referenced during the Olivet discourse. (Matthew 24:31)

It should also make us think of Zechariah again: *"⁹ Rejoice greatly, O daughter of Zion! Shout, O daughter of Jerusalem! Behold, your King is coming to you; He is just and having salvation, lowly and riding on a donkey, a colt, the foal of a donkey. ¹⁰ I will cut off the chariot from Ephraim and the horse from Jerusalem; The battle bow shall be cut off. He shall speak peace to the nations; His dominion shall be from sea to sea, and from the River to the ends of the earth. ¹¹ As for you also, because of the blood of your Covenant, I will set your prisoners free from the waterless pit. ¹² Return to the stronghold, you prisoners of hope. Even today I declare that I will restore double to you. ¹³ For I have bent Yahudah, My bow, fitted the bow with Ephraim, and raised up your sons, O Zion, against your sons, O Greece, and made you like the sword of a mighty man (gibor). ¹⁴ Then YHWH will be seen over them, and His arrow will go forth like lightning. Adonai YHWH will blast the shofar, and go with whirlwinds from the south. ¹⁵ YHWH of hosts will defend them; they shall devour and subdue with slingstones. They shall drink and roar as if with wine; They shall be filled with blood like basins, like the corners of the altar. ¹⁶ YHWH their Elohim will save them in that day, as the flock of His people. For they shall be like the jewels of a crown, lifted like a banner over His land ¹⁷ For how great is its goodness and how great its beauty! Grain shall make the young men thrive, and new wine the young women."* Zechariah 9:9-16

The shofar is a warning, meant to prepare people for battle. This final shofar is when YHWH will defend His people. If you really read this passage carefully we see Yahudah as a bow, and Ephraim as arrows. The sons of Zion will be raised up like the sword of a mighty man (gibor). Remember how David raised up the sword of the mighty one (gibor) Goliath in order to cut off the head of the beast. So

these sons of Zion will be raised up like a sword. Then
YHWH will be seen over them, and His arrow will go forth
like lightening. This is how Yahushua described His
appearance.

Interestingly, the Revelation now takes a turn and
begins to recount the birth of the One Who, as our High
Priest, made a way for us to enter the Holy of Holies and sit
with Him on the Throne. We will discuss the remainder of
the text in the following chapter.

At this point we can see that the seals and the shofars
are the roadmap to the end of the age, the rest of the
Revelation fills in with more detail regarding the end, and
beyond. It is important to recognize that the seventh shofar is
not the last shofar that will ever be sounded. There is still a
Sabbath millennium ahead. We are only speaking of the final
shofar of the age that ushers in the next age, and the
Covenant of Peace.

If we view this book in the context of completing the
Prophecy given to Daniel, it makes much more sense. The
time frame covered by the book spans from the birth of
Messiah to the end of the seventh millennium, and into the
next age – the eighth day.

The scroll originally sealed up by Daniel has now
been opened and eaten by John. The reason a prophet eats a
scroll is so that they can prophesy the words on the scroll.
Finally, John can prophesy regarding the things that Daniel
was not permitted to speak. We will now examine the rest of
the Revelation as well as the many prophecies in the Tanak
that all speak to what will happen in the end.

12

In the End

Today we see various religions with differing perspectives concerning the end of the age. For those who believe the Hebrew Scriptures it is essential to understand the plan of restoration set forth within those texts. Sadly we see artificial labels and divisions created by men that cause confusion for those seeking to know truth.

It is important to understand the path demonstrated through the life of Abraham. He started in Babylon in an uncircumcised condition. He believed the promise of YHWH and left Babylon. He crossed over the Euphrates River, and then the Jordan River. He was called a Hebrew because he "crossed over." He "passed over" so that he could enter into Covenant with YHWH, and dwell in the Land promised to his descendants.

He went into Egypt, where his bride was held captive until the Pharaoh was plagued. Abram then left Egypt with his freed bride and the stranger – Hagar. He was later circumcised and promised a son. The promise of the Covenant would flow through that son, circumcised on the eighth day.

When we consider the concept of "the end" we must view it from a Hebraic perspective within the context of the Covenant. The typical western mindset thinks of the beginning on one end of a straight line that leads to the other end of the line. Thus a beginning point and an endpoint with

time pushing in one direction.

Time, from a Hebraic sense, operates in cycles. So there are many beginnings and many ends. In fact there is an "end of days" every year when the harvest cycle concludes. We must remember this when we consider the future end of the age leading to the return of Messiah. Recall that while Daniel was praying about <u>the end</u> of punishment, it also involved <u>the beginning</u> of the return.

During his time of praying about "the end," Daniel was shown the world powers that would reign from his time until the end of this age. The final beast empire was the feet of the image shown to Nebuchadnezzar that would be smashed by the Aben stone, the Messiah, at the seventh shofar. He will destroy that beast kingdom that is the final kingdom associated with man. He will then establish the reign of YHWH – the kingdom that would rule over the earth during the seventh day, the seventh millennium.

Daniel was also shown the timing for the appearance of the Messiah, to His being cut off and the destruction of the Temple. The Messiah indeed came at the time revealed and was cut off in the midst of a week, fulfilling the seventieth week in the prophecy of Daniel.

The Revelation given through John showed the path from the sealing of the Daniel's scroll to the unsealing through the establishment of the Kingdom of YHWH. After the description of the seventh shofar the Book of Revelation shifts gears.

It essentially describes the war between two kingdoms. Revelation 12 begins with the following: "*¹ Now a great sign appeared in heaven: a woman clothed with the sun, with the moon under her feet, and on her head a garland of twelve stars. ² Then being with child, she cried out in labor and in pain to give birth.*" Revelation 12:1-2.

This was the sign that appeared in the sky over

Jerusalem the moment that Yahushua was born on September 11, 3 BCE. On the Hebrew calendar it was Day 1 of Month 7 – Yom Teruah. It was a day of blasting shofars throughout the Land of Yisrael. At that time, the remnant of the House of Yahudah that had returned from the Babylonian exile hundreds of years earlier was unwittingly announcing the appearance of their King. The sign literally described the birth of the King Messiah from the constellation Virgo – known as Bethula in Hebrew.

After the sign of the birth of the Messiah we read about another sign in the heavens. "*³ And another sign appeared in heaven: behold, a great, fiery red dragon having seven heads and ten horns, and seven diadems on his heads. ⁴ His tail drew a third of the stars of heaven and threw them to the earth. And the dragon stood before the woman who was ready to give birth, to devour her Child as soon as it was born. ⁵ She bore a male Child who was to rule all nations with a rod of iron. And her Child was caught up to Elohim and His throne. ⁶ Then the woman fled into the wilderness, where she has a place prepared by Elohim, that they should feed her there one thousand two hundred and sixty days.*" Revelation 12:3-6.

The Dragon represents satan and, as with Bethula, it is a constellation intended to be a sign in the sky. Indeed there is one constellation called Draco that is to the north of the virgin. In the Greek we read "drakon" (δράκων) which means: "a fabulous kind of serpent" or "a dragon." Standing between Bethula and Draco is the Decan - Bootes. Bootes means: "the coming One" and  represents the Messiah born from the virgin. It is commonly depicted as a shepherd and a harvester, carrying a shepherds crook and a sickle. So the Son of the virgin is a gatherer, and the Dragon wants to destroy the Son.

There is actually another constellation with an ancient myth closely associated with this description. The constellation Cetus represents a sea monster and is located in the region of the sky known as "The Sea" – likened to the abyss. The myth surrounding Cetus was that it was slain by the Bridegroom before it could devour the Bride. So there are some very interesting constellations related to the sign in Revelation 12.

We see the time period of 1,260 days associated with the woman fleeing to a special place. It is the same exact duration that the two witnesses will be prophesying in the end (Revelation 11:3). This makes most people believe that this sign will occur at the end. If we knew the exact timing of this sign it could provide us with a key start date for the two witnesses.

On the other hand, it may have nothing to do with the future event of the two witnesses. It may be describing signs that "appeared" in the past. If the woman of this sign is the same as the woman in the sign describing the birth of the Messiah, then we are looking at Yahudah. The period of time is essentially 3 ½ years associated with the time when the woman flees into the wilderness. Remember that the Child, being the Messiah, came through the House of Yahudah – the woman. He was born and Herod tried to kill Him and His family was forced to flee "in the wilderness" as they journeyed to Egypt.

As conceded earlier, it is very possible that all of these events have a future fulfillment, but we also must consider that there has been a past fulfillment. In Daniel we saw that 1,290 days could have been the time span from the ceasing of "that which is continual" to the "abomination of desolation." (Daniel 12:11) We know from the Olivet Discourse that Yahushua warned His followers to flee when they saw the signs.

In fact, during this period, the believing Yahudim who lived in Jerusalem did exactly as Yahushua instructed. They fled to the wilderness east of Jerusalem. They fled to Pella, located in modern day Jordan. It is believed by some that this was fulfillment of the sign.[237] The 1,260 days is just one month shy of the 1,290 days that were likely fulfilled around 70 CE. The 1,260 days could have been the actual time that the Yahudim were cared for in the wilderness. So the events described in these constellations could have been fulfilled, or they may have a future fulfillment.

The text continues to reveal that there is a war between this dragon and the woman and her offspring. "*And the dragon was enraged with the woman, and he went to make war with the rest of her offspring, who keep the commandments of Elohim and have the testimony of Yahushua the Messiah.*" Revelation 12:17

We see in the constellations - the mazzaroth - Draco battling Orion, a Decan of Taurus – the Bull. The Tribal symbol of Ephraim is a bull and we can see a connection between Orion – "coming forth as Light" and Joseph who was a clear Messianic figure. The Revelation goes on to describe the war raging between the Dragon and the Son.

This story has been displayed in the scroll of the heavens for all to see from the beginning of Creation. Many Christians make the mistake of attributing these signs to astrology. It is important to remember that YHWH created them for signs. (Beresheet 1:14) The Revelation is affirming that these signs in the sky reveal truths concerning the conflict between two kingdoms – the kingdom of darkness and the Kingdom of YHWH.

We know from the Scriptures that Yahushua was manifested to destroy the serpent dragon and his rebellious kingdom. (Beresheet 3:15; 1 John 3:8). There have been wars in the heavens that will be played out on the earth in the future.

In fact, the earthly battle has essentially been a proxy war throughout time leading up to the end.

The serpent has been operating through the nations while Yisrael represents the Kingdom of YHWH. The text provides an important fact concerning the rebellion of the serpent. He drew 1/3 of the sons of Elohim with him as he formed a rebellion against YHWH. So this text is clearly linking certain constellations with the serpent. We can see other possible links with Cetus and Hydra.

Interestingly the phrase "fiery red dragon" in Revelation 12:3 is better translated "fiery serpent" or "serpent of fire." There is another constellation representing satan which is called Serpens. It specifically means: "the serpent." In fact, the text directly links the great dragon with the serpent of old – called *"the devil and satan."* (Revelation 12:9)

We see this "serpent" described with *"seven heads and ten horns, and seven diadems on his heads."* This is directly connected to the fourth beast empire that was shown to be the final empire in the Book of Daniel. The serpent makes war through this kingdom, and it is against a specific group – those *"who keep the commandments of Elohim and have the testimony of Yahushua the Messiah."* If you do not keep the commandments you are not in this group. In fact, the serpent is not concerned about those who do not keep the commandments, because their fate was already revealed by Yahushua.

Now the text turns from the heavens to the earth. The text specifically provides *"Then I stood on the sand of the sea . . ."* Revelation 13:1 The description that follows is the actual war depicted in the heavens through the constellations. This war will be occurring in the heavens and on the earth. It describes a beast empowered by the serpent. This is the continuing proxy war occurring on earth with man at the center of the struggle between two kingdoms. This struggle is

for the souls of mankind.

The beast is described as follows: "*¹ . . . And I saw a beast rising up out of the sea, having seven heads and ten horns, and on his horns ten crowns, and on his heads a blasphemous name. ² Now the beast which I saw was like a leopard, his feet were like the feet of a bear, and his mouth like the mouth of a lion. The dragon gave him his power, his throne, and great authority. ³ And I saw one of his heads as if it had been mortally wounded, and his deadly wound was healed. And all the world marveled and followed the beast. ⁴ So they worshiped the dragon who gave authority to the beast; and they worshiped the beast, saying, Who is like the beast? Who is able to make war with him?"* Revelation 13:1-4

The dragon uses the beast to direct worship to him. He has been doing this since mankind was corrupted. If he can get men to disobey the commandments and turn away from YHWH they are essentially serving him.

Even deeper, we already discussed that when satan looks at man – he sees Elohim, since man was made in the Image of Elohim. So if satan can get men to worship him, it is like getting Elohim to worship him. This, of course, is his ultimate desire.

Since the time of Babylon we have seen sun worship develop as a direct afront to YHWH. As the nations were divided they continued to oppose YHWH, until YHWH chose a man to enter into a Covenant relationship with. Through the seed of the man and the Covenant, YHWH would build a nation.

We already saw the description of the 4 beasts in Daniel 7. They came up out of the sea. Remember that the seas were created from the flood. They were the result of the judgment of the corruption that existed from the fallen angels and their progeny. The Nephilim existed both before and after the flood, and they have likely influenced these kingdoms – thus the title "beasts." These beasts would have

dominion over the earth in different forms, although when their dominion was taken away *"their lives were prolonged for a season and a time."* Daniel 7:12

So it appears that the 3 beasts would diminish, but not completely disappear. This helps to understand the fourth beast that is different from the others. It is directly empowered and enthroned by the serpent dragon. (Revelation 13:2).

Daniel described the fourth beast as follows: *"⁷ After this I saw in the night visions, and behold, a fourth beast, dreadful and terrible, exceedingly strong. It had huge iron teeth; it was devouring, breaking in pieces, and trampling the residue with its feet. It was different from all the beasts that were before it, and it had ten horns. ⁸ I was considering the horns, and there was another horn, a little one, coming up among them, before whom three of the first horns were plucked out by the roots. <u>And there, in this horn, were eyes like the eyes of a man, and a mouth speaking pompous words</u>."* Daniel 7:7-8

Daniel was given much information concerning the fourth beast. *"¹⁹ Then I wished to know the truth about the fourth beast, which was different from all the others, exceedingly dreadful, with its teeth of iron and its nails of bronze, which devoured, broke in pieces, and trampled the residue with its feet; ²⁰ and the ten horns that were on its head, and the other horn which came up, before which three fell, namely, that horn which had eyes and a mouth which spoke pompous words, whose appearance was greater than his fellows. ²¹ I was watching; and the same horn was making war against the saints, and prevailing against them, ²² until the Ancient of Days came, and a judgment was made in favor of the set apart ones of the Most High, and the time came for the saints to possess the kingdom. ²³ Thus he said: <u>The fourth beast shall be a fourth kingdom on earth, which shall be different from all other kingdoms, and shall devour the whole earth, trample it and break it in pieces.</u> ²⁴ The ten horns are ten kings who shall arise from this kingdom. And* *another shall rise after them; He shall be different from the first ones, and shall subdue three kings.* <u>^{25} He shall speak pompous words against the Most High, shall persecute the set apart ones of the Most High, and shall intend to change times and laws</u> (✗◁). *Then the saints shall be given into his hand for a time and times and half a time. ^{26} But the court shall be seated, and they shall take away his dominion, to consume and destroy it forever. ^{27} Then the kingdom and dominion, and the greatness of the kingdoms under the whole heaven, shall be given to the people, the saints of the Most High. His kingdom is an everlasting kingdom, and all dominions shall serve and obey Him."* Daniel 7:19-27

So the Revelation is now providing the progression of the fourth kingdom. This kingdom is the beast, and it will be in direct conflict with the elect of YHWH. Again, this will be the kingdom in existence when the Messiah comes to establish the Kingdom of YHWH on planet Earth. It will be directly opposed to the Messiah.

You should notice from the account in Revelation that it is a mixture of the three preceeding kingdoms, but it is incredibly more powerful. So how does the Roman Empire, which appeared to fragment and dissolve around 1,500 years ago actually  continue on to rule the world. That is part of the mystery of the end of the age.

We can actually see clues all around us. Interestingly, "in 102 BC, the Roman consul Gaius Marius decreed that the eagle would be the symbol of the Senate and the people of Rome. The eagle symbolized strength, courage, farsightedness and immortality. It is considered to be the king of the air and the messenger of the highest gods. Mythologically speaking, it is connected by the Greeks with the god Zeus, by the Romans with Jupiter, by the Germanic tribes with Odin and by Christians with God."[238]

We can see this eagle continue throughout time. It has represented sun gods, and was intimately involved in sun  worship. It is even used in powerful cultures such as the United States of America which, as previously discussed, clearly seems to be an extension of the Roman Empire. Interestingly, the American eagle began as a pheonix. It is well established that the bird on the Great Seal was originally designed as a pheonix. Of course the mythology of the phoenix is very appropriate for the Nation and the Empire that it represents.

The phoenix is related to the Egyptian solar bird known as the benu bird. In ancient mythology, the phoenix "is a long-lived bird that is cyclically regenerated or reborn. Associated with the sun, a phoenix obtains new life by arising from the ashes of its predecessor."[239] The symbology of the Great Seal, including the phoenix, is therefore very telling. It would seem  that the intention of the seal is to announce the fact that the United States of America would rise from the ashes and resurrect a former empire. Based upon the prevelant Roman symbology associated with the United States, it is clear that the United States is actually the resurrected Roman Empire in the process of transforming itself from the phoenix to the eagle.

In the Roman Empire, the eagle ultimately ended up representing the sun god and the emperor. This was the ultimate transformation of the Roman Empire from a republic to an autocracy, when the emperor was considered to be a god. Just as Rome began as a republic and transitioned into an autocracy, we see the United States transforming from a federal republic to an autocracy. The constitution, which is the framework for the Republic has become a meaningless document. Most all politicians are aligned with special interest groups that fund their campaigns and keep their political careers alive. The Supreme Court has departed from being a protector of the constitution to another political body advancing an ideology. The president is increasingly assuming more power and control, and the nation is one disaster away from becoming a military regime headed by an oligarch.

This eagle provides a common thread and continuation of the sun worship that has pervaded the satanic kingdoms of the earth. In fact, we can trace the breakup of the Roman Empire, and the subsequent kingdoms to the

nations of this present day. You see it is not simply the United States heading in this direction, it is the entire world. We saw this very same message being broadcast in the Olympic ceremonies held in London. There again, the phoenix was a highlight as the advent the New World Order was being announced to the entire world. Of course the Olympics originated in sun worship, and the Olympic torch has always represented the light of Zeus.

There is no doubt that the nations of the world have been joining together through such organizations as the United Nations and the European Union, among others. They are also bound together by certain religious organizations such as the Roman Catholic Church, and banking institutions, such as the World Bank and the IMF. There is even a world court known as the International Court of Justice located in The Hague, Netherlands. Through all of this we can see the sovereignty of individual nations increasingly eroded as the final world empire rises from the ashes. The flow of this river is rapidly leading mankind back to ancient Babylon. As the nations were once divided in Babylon, they will someday complete the cycle and be reunited in Babylon.

So we see that the kingdoms of the world have been the kingdoms of the serpent – the dragon. The seven heads could represent the serpent's dominion over the seven continents. It is believed that these seven continents were formed after the destruction and dispersion of the Tower of Babel. That was the beginning of the nations.

The mention of seven headed beast rising out of the sea should also make us think of Leviathan, an actual creature described throughout history. According to the New Unger's Bible Dictionary: "Since the discovery of the Ras Shamra religious texts in Syria on the site of ancient Ugarit, it has become evident that there is a parallel between the seven-headed Canaanite monster Lotan of prevailing mythology."

Isaiah even associated Leviathan with the final judgment of YHWH – the day of YHWH. "*In that day YHWH with His severe sword, great and strong, will punish Leviathan the fleeing serpent, Leviathan that twisted serpent; and He will slay the reptile that is in the sea.*" Isaiah 21:1 According to the Oxford Companion to the Bible, Leviathan is: "A mythological sea monster who is one of the primeval adversaries of the storm god. In the Ugaritic texts, Baal defeats Lothan . . . described as a seven-headed serpent . . ."

The Book of Job actually provides a very detailed description of Leviathan, and it is clearly describing a fire breathing dragon with armor like scales. Here is just a brief portion of the text: "*14 Who can open the doors of his face, with his terrible teeth all around? 15 His rows of scales are his pride, shut up tightly as with a seal; 16 One is so near another that no air can come between them; 17 They are joined one to another, they stick together and cannot be parted. 18 His sneezings flash forth light, and his eyes are like the eyelids of the morning. 19 Out of his mouth go burning lights; sparks of fire shoot out. 20 Smoke goes out of his nostrils, as from a boiling pot and burning rushes. 21 His breath kindles coals, and a flame goes out of his mouth. 22 Strength dwells in his neck, and sorrow dances before him. 23 The folds of his flesh are joined together; they are firm on him and cannot be moved.*" Job 41:14-23

Notice the phrase "*his eyes are like the eyelids of the morning.*" The word for "morning" is "shakar"(שחר) in Hebrew. It means: "the darkness before morning." Recall that this is what the adversary was called – "son of the morning" or rather "son of the dark." (Isaiah 14:12). So this Leviathan dragon is clearly associated with the adversary – the serpent – the dragon. Accordingly, the seven headed beast may be an actual creature that rises out of the water, often associated with the abyss. The beast has seven heads like the serpent, and will act on behalf of the serpent to conquer the kingdoms of men.

The 10 horns are ruled by this beast based upon Daniel 7:23-25. The 10 horns are 10 kings that arise in the future (Daniel 7:24). Remember that this beast kingdom is different from all others. This one covers the entire earth.

As a result, they could represent the ten regions of the planet as determined by the United Nations, and those planning the New World Order.[240] Very interestingly, there are also allegedly plans to divided the United States of

America into 10 regions. This future kingdom divided into 10 regions is the kingdom from which the second beast will arise.

As discussed previously, there were 10 kingdoms derived from the Roman Empire. The one that was different than the others appears to be the Roman Catholic Church. It was originally a creation of the State of Rome, and has always been the primary representative of the Christian religion. Indeed by Papal Bull it was declared that: "I acknowledge the Holy Catholic Apostolic Roman Church for the mother and mistress of all churches."[241]

The Roman Catholic Church remained a separate power as the State of Rome fractured and disintegrated. It later defeated the Vandals, Ostrogoths and the Heruli. "Beginning in A.D. 554, the Roman Empire became known as the *Holy* Roman Empire. Historians almost universally acknowledge that the Pope's crowning of *Justinian*, after he had defeated the Ostrogoths, signaled this change. Events in Europe, surrounding the Holy Roman Empire, rose and fell for many centuries. Periodically, new rulers appeared— *Charlamagne* (the Frankish head in A.D. 800)—*Otto the Great* (the German head crowned in A.D. 962)—followed by the Hapsburg Dynasty of *Charles V* (the Austrian head crowned in A.D. 1520)—which, in turn, was followed by *Napoleon's* reign (the French head crowned in A.D. 1805)—with the sixth head being that of Garibaldi's united Italian head from A.D. 1870-1945. This sixth resurrection of the Holy Roman Empire culminated in the defeat of Adolph Hitler and Benito Mussolini. Mussolini, after signing a secret agreement (Concordat) with the Vatican in 1929, united Ethiopia, Eritrea and Italian Somaliland back to Italy in 1935. He declared this union to be the Roman Empire re-established."[242]

This religious "Empire" of the Roman Catholic

Church is ruled by Popes who claim to be the "Vicar of Christ." As the Roman Emperors from Julius Ceasar onward were worshipped as gods, so the Popes continue a similar tradition through their status of "Vicar of Christ." Essentially they are deemed the "representative" of God, acting vicariously for Christ.

Another title for the papacy is "the Holy See." The word "see" derives from a "visionary" or a "prophet." So the Holy See could also be called the Holy Prophet. This is significant when we consider "the false prophet" who speaks for "the beast," often called the antichrist. (see Revelation 16:13, 19:20) In fact, Protestants throughout history have generally believed that the Roman Catholic Pope was the anti-christ.

The Roman Catholic Church ruled most of the civilized world throughout the Dark Ages. It persecuted all who opposed their doctrines through the Inquisition. In fact, it has been stated that: "The number of Christians whom the Catholic Church put to death during the Dark Ages is not known exactly, but some estimates run as high as 200 million. This makes the papacy the most cruel, persecuting power that has ever existed, surpassing Hitler, Stalin, and Mao . . . 'That the Church of Rome has shed more innocent blood than any other institution that has ever existed among mankind, will be questioned by no Protestant who has a competent knowledge of history.'"[243]

The Roman Catholic Church continues to exercise

great control over the world through the White Pope in the forefront and the Black Pope operating behind the scenes and controlling the Jesuits.[244] The current pope of the Roman Catholic Church is from the Jesuit Order, thus placing the White

Papacy directly under the control of the Black Pope.

So pervasive was the power and control of the Catholic Church that some of the founding fathers of America feared the influence of the Jesuits.[245] It appears that those fears were realized when President Abraham Lincoln actually blamed the civil war of the United States of America on the Jesuits.

"This war would never have been possible without the sinister influence of the Jesuits. We owe it to Popery that we now see our land reddened with the blood of her noblest sons. Though there were great differences of opinion between the South and North, on the question of slavery, neither Jeff Davis nor any one of the leading men of the Confederacy would have dared to attack the North, had they not relied on the promise of the Jesuits, that, under the mask of Democracy, the money and the arms of the Roman Catholics, even the arms of France, were at their disposal if they would attack us."[246]

The Roman Catholic Church operates consistently with the little horn of the final beast described in Daniel. It has actually developed its own calendar derived from the Roman sun calendar intimately associated with sun worship.[247] It has changed the Appointed Times, and actually forbidden those in the church to follow the Appointed Times in the Scriptures. There are even those who claim that Islam originated with the Vatican.[248]

Most notably, the Roman Catholic Church has indicated that it has the power to change the commandments of YHWH as provided in the Torah, the Prophets and the Writings. The "sign" of this authority was demonstrated by the act of changing the Sabbath to Sunday – the day most esteemed in sun worship.[249]

The Catholic Church actually refers to the Sunday sabbath as their "mark." Notice the word "dath" (✗◁) in

Daniel 7:25 used for "laws" that the beast will change. The "dalet" (◁) mean: "door" and the taw (✕) means: "mark or covenant." So this potential little horn of the final kingdom of man will actually change the "door and the mark of the covenant." The covenant promoted by the Roman Catholic Church is a different covenant than the Covenant with YHWH. Just as the Yahudim created a new religion through their traditions, so has the Roman Catholic Church. Therefore, we can actually see the transformation of the Roman Empire into the final beast kingdom described in Daniel.

There are others who believe that Islam better fits the descriptions in Daniel and Revelation. In fact, if those claiming that Islam originated with Roman Catholicism are correct, we could see a merging of these world religions through some supernatural event that would cause adherents to worship a beast. One thing that they both have in common is the expectation of a coming messiah.

In fact, both believe that Jesus is returning. Catholics anticipate Jesus the Christ, and Muslims anticipate Jesus the Prophet who will kill the anti-christ. The differences in titles may easily be worked out in a time of crisis. Since neither of these religions follow the Torah, they would both likely be susceptible to following a messiah that does not conform to the Scriptures, or should I say an anti-messiah (anti-christ).

Many Christians are taught and believe that Jesus did away with the Torah, which they call "The Law." Yahushua the Messiah is specifically associated with the Torah, as the Word that became flesh. Therefore, the Christian Jesus is essentially portrayed as an anti-christ. Also, it is very interesting, as previously discussed, that the Roman Catholic Church is making preparations for a future alien appearance.

So we can see through this enormous religious system that the stage is being set for the final kingdom, diametrically opposed to the Torah of YHWH. We can also see how the Nephilim can operate in conjunction with the Church to fulfill the prophecies concerning the end of the age.

Daniel was looking forward through time from neo-Babylon. That is why he saw 4 kingdoms leading to a final 5th beast kingdom. The Revelation given to John is including the entire history of the major kingdoms in that region of the world. That is why he lists seven heads and the ten horns are affixed to the last head – the transformed 4th kingdom of Daniel, which becomes a 5th kingdom. (see Revelation 17:3).

Now back to the description of the beast as described in Revelation. "*5 And he was given a mouth speaking great things and blasphemies, and he was given authority to continue for forty-two months. 6 Then he opened his mouth in blasphemy against Elohim, to blaspheme His Name, His tabernacle, and those who dwell in heaven. 7 It was granted to him to make war with the set apart ones and to overcome them. And authority was given him over every tribe, tongue, and nation. 8 All who dwell on the earth will worship him, whose names have not been written in the Book of Life of the Lamb slain from the foundation of the world.*" Revelation 13:5-8

So this kingdom is different from all others due to its enormous power, reach and control. Rather than one of the various organizations or religions that we have described, it will likely mix and merge them all together. Things will become clearer as the Revelation later provides more detail concerning this 7 headed beast and its origins.

The text provides a very important clue to those who dwell on the earth in those days. "*9 If anyone has an ear, let him hear. 10 He who leads into captivity shall go into captivity; he who kills with the sword must be killed with the sword. Here is the patience and the faith of the saints.*" Revelation 13:9-10

Notice the phrase "*if anyone has an ear to hear.*" This is the same phrase repeated to the assemblies regarding those

who would overcome. It appears to be stating that this is the Lamb's battle. Yahushua alone will protect His sheep and destroy the enemy. If anyone in the Lamb's Book of Life uses a sword he will die by the sword, if he takes enemies captive he will in turn be taken captive. This will not be a typical battle. YHWH will fight for His people.

This would appear to tie in directly with Ezekiel 38, which described an attack upon those dwelling in prosperity and safety after a return to the Land. We must remember that the Book of Revelation is an outline that should contain the prophecies found in the Tanak that remain unfulfilled. Recall all of the prophecies concerning the regathering of the outcasts of the House of Yisrael. When exactly this regathering occurs is of great importance.

The warning against refraining from war-like conduct in order to overcome seems to provide us with a clue. This would appear to describe the return of the House of Yisrael in the Land prophesied by Ezekiel. When Yisrael returns and dwells safely in the Land, Gog will attack the House of Yisrael from all directions.

Here is the word spoken to Gog: *"⁸ After many days you will be visited. In the latter years you will come into the land of those brought back from the sword and gathered from many people on the mountains of Yisrael, which had long been desolate; they were brought out of the nations, and now all of them dwell safely. ⁹ You will ascend, coming like a storm, covering the land like a cloud, you and all your troops and many peoples with you. ¹⁰ Thus says Adonai YHWH: On that day it shall come to pass that thoughts will arise in your mind, and you will make an evil plan: ¹¹ You will say, I will go up against a land of unwalled villages; I will go to a peaceful people, who dwell safely, all of them dwelling without walls, and having neither bars nor gates - ¹² to take plunder and to take booty, to stretch out your hand against the waste places that are again inhabited, and against a people gathered from the nations,* who have acquired livestock and goods, who dwell in the midst of the land. *13* Sheba, Dedan, the merchants of Tarshish, and all their young lions will say to you, Have you come to take plunder? Have you gathered your army to take booty, to carry away silver and gold, to take away livestock and goods, to take great plunder? *14* Therefore, son of man, prophesy and say to Gog, Thus says Adonai YHWH: On that day when My people Yisrael dwell safely, will you not know it? *15* Then you will come from your place out of the far north, you and many peoples with you, all of them riding on horses, a great company and a mighty army. *16* You will come up against My people Yisrael like a cloud, to cover the land. It will be in the latter days that I will bring you against My land, so that the nations may know Me, when I am hallowed in you, O Gog, before their eyes. *17* Thus says Adonai YHWH: Are you he of whom I have spoken in former days by My servants the prophets of Israel, who prophesied for years in those days that I would bring you against them? *18* And it will come to pass at the same time, when Gog comes against the land of Yisrael, says Adonai YHWH, that My fury will show in My face. *19* For in My jealousy and in the fire of My wrath I have spoken: Surely in that day there shall be a great earthquake in the land of Yisrael, *20* so that the fish of the sea, the birds of the heavens, the beasts of the field, all creeping things that creep on the earth, and all men who are on the face of the earth shall shake at My presence. The mountains shall be thrown down, the steep places shall fall, and every wall shall fall to the ground. *21* I will call for a sword against Gog throughout all My mountains, says Adonai YHWH. Every man's sword will be against his brother. *22* And I will bring him to judgment with pestilence and bloodshed; I will rain down on him, on his troops, and on the many peoples who are with him, flooding rain, great hailstones, fire, and brimstone. *23* Thus I will magnify Myself and sanctify Myself, and I will be known in the eyes of many nations. Then they shall know that I am YHWH." Ezekiel 38:8-23

Now things should start to come into perspective.

This is the same description this great multitude sounds like those from the fifth and sixth shofar blasts. Notice that they ascend and cover the land like a cloud. This sounds exactly like the locust coming up out of the abyss like smoke. So if that is the case we should expect the House of Yisrael to be returned and restored to the Land prior to the fifth shofar blast.

The mountains of Yisrael describe the region known as Samaria, which was the center of the House of Yisrael. Also known as the West Bank, this land is essentially desolate, containing only scattered Arab villages and some Jewish settlements.

Remember that the period of punishment is ending between 2007 and 2016. Since a restoration of Land is a fundamental part of the Jubilee many believe that a Jubilee will coincide with the return of the House of Yisrael.[250] Of course, it would begin at Yom Kippur, but noone knows for certain what, if anything will happen on that specific date (Day 10 of Month 7). It could prove to be an eventful year, because the Jubilee is just that – a year. So if this were a time for prophecies to be fulfilled, a restoration could happen throughout a period of one year.

The return of the House of Yisrael is promised to be a great and memorable process. The previous exodus from Egypt will pale in comparison. (Jeremiah 16:14-15) In fact people will no longer speak of the exodus from Egypt. This is important because every Passover we remember the Exodus, so the Passover seder will apparently change focus from that point onward. (Jeremiah 23:7-8)

If we consider the timing of the exodus from Egypt we understand that they were delivered from bondage at Passover in the 49th year, which was the seventh Shemittah cycle and the year of release. It took seven days, during the Feast of Unleavened Bread, for them to be delivered from

Pharaoh and ultimately exit Egypt through the parted waters of the Red Sea. It will be interesting to see a future fulfillment of that seven day period as the Assembly is regathered and delivered from bondage.

The redeemed Bride of Yisrael then proceeded to the wedding ceremony at Sinai on Shabuot. Were it not for the sin of the golden calf, they would have likely moved into the promised Land during Succot, five days after Yom Kippur, which marked the Jubilee year. Instead, they were given a second chance as Mosheh delivered a second set of Tablets on that Yom Kippur.

Interestingly, the inhabitants of the mountains of Yisrael will be very wealthy. This is another sign that they have made a great exodus. Remember the pattern of the exodus with Abram and Yisrael included a return to the Land with great wealth. In each event they carried great wealth out of Egypt. It appears that a future deliverance will involve the same transfer of wealth. Indeed, it is this great wealth that will be the hook in the jaw for Gog to attack. It will lure the nations into the trap set by YHWH, just as He lured Pharaoh and his army into the Red Sea with Yisrael as the bait.

YHWH will fight for His people after they return, but noticeably absent is mention of Yahudah and Jerusalem. Could it be that the return of the House of Yisrael is preceded by some devastating war in the Land of Yahudah? We may see the answer in Psalm 83.

Psalm 83 contains an often overlooked prophecy concerning a group of 10 nations/peoples that conspire to wipe out the nation of Yisrael. They include the Edomites, the Yishmaelites, the Moabites, the Hagarites, Gebal, Ammon, Amaleq, Pelesheth with the inhabitants of Tsor, and Assyria. These make a covenant against Elohim. These groups can actually be traced to the Palestinians as well as surrounding Arab and Persian terrorist groups and nations that currently exist today. According to the Psalm, these conspirators get wiped out, not Yisrael. So this could very likely be an event that clears the entire Covenant Land, from the Nile to the Euphrates, and opens up the possibility for the return of the House of Yisrael. It might also be an event that judges those inhabitants currently in the Land who are not in Covenant with YHWH.

Something dramatic needs to happen to change the current situation, because the passage in Ezekiel has all of the earmarks of a return to the Land after a great Exodus. It shares many of the aspects from the past exodus from Egypt. Remember that when the Children of Yisrael left Egypt, they were not alone. They left with a "mixed multitude" of people. The same may hold true in this future exodus, when the nations will be gathered to YHWH through the return of the House of Yisrael to the Land.

One major question involves when this attack will occur. Another involves the identity of Gog and Magog. Clearly Magog is a people and a region of land settled by the descendents of Japheth. Gog is described as a Prince of Rosh, Meshech and Tubal. Interestingly Meshech and Tubal were both brothers of Magog, but there is no mention of a son named Rosh in their lineage. It is more likely that Rosh is not a name of an individual, but rather part of a title.

While some attribute these roles to Russia, others believe that Gog is actually a demon king. This is gleaned from the Septuagint translation of Amos 7:1 which provides: *"Thus has Adonai YHWH showed me; and, behold, a swarm of locusts coming from the east; and, behold, one caterpillar, king Gog."*[251]

The locust clearly do not have a king according to the Scriptures. *"The locusts have no king, yet they all advance in ranks."* Proverbs 30:27 Interestingly, in the book of

Revelation, we read about the great hoard of mutant locust beings that pour out of the abyss. This could explain why we read about Gog both before and after the millennial reign of Messiah. (Revelation 20:8) The millennial reign will be discussed further in the text.

For now it is important to remember that there are spiritual powers operating in conjunction with the nations of the earth. Therefore, there are both spiritual and physical applications to the prophecies concerning the nations.

The premillenium Gog/Magog invasion is directly linked with the return of the House of Yisrael. Gog and his armies are drawn to the mountains of Yisrael, because they are jealous of the House of Yisrael who had apparently already returned and plundered the world through their exodus and return. Therefore they are invading to get their possessions. This is described as the hook in the jaw to draw them in.

Ezekiel 39 clearly demonstrates that this is in the context of a restored House of Yisrael. "*¹ And you, son of man, prophesy against Gog, and say, Thus says the Master YHWH: Behold, I am against you, O Gog, the prince of Rosh, Meshech, and Tubal; ² and I will turn you around and lead you on, bringing you up from the far north, and bring you against the mountains of Yisrael. ³ Then I will knock the bow out of your left hand, and cause the arrows to fall out of your right hand. ⁴ You shall fall upon the mountains of Yisrael, you and all your troops and the peoples who are with you; I will give you to birds of prey of every sort and to the beasts of the field to be devoured. ⁵ You shall fall on the open field; for I have spoken, says the Master YHWH. ⁶ And I will send fire on Magog and on those who live in security in the coastlands. Then they shall know that I am YHWH. ⁷ So I will make My Set Apart Name known in the midst of My people Yisrael, and I will not let them profane My Set Apart Name anymore. Then the nations shall know that I am YHWH, the Set Apart One in Yisrael. ⁸ Surely it*

is coming, and it shall be done, says the Master YHWH. This is the day of which I have spoken." Ezekiel 39:1-8

This is the day promised that YHWH would again fight for the House of Yisrael. YHWH does not just kill the individuals who are physically attacking, He also attacks their lands as far away as "the coastlands." So this is not an isolated judgment, it goes beyond the physical Land of Yisrael.

The judgment is rendered upon Gog and Magog, and through that judgment the Name of YHWH is exalted. Again, this was the pattern of the exodus from Egypt. All of the plagues upon Egypt were so that the nations would know the Name of YHWH. Throughout the Scriptures we see a repeating theme of judgment and the return of the House of Yisrael.

"[25] *Thus says the Master YHWH:* <u>*When I have gathered the House of Yisrael from the peoples among whom they are scattered, and am hallowed in them in the sight of the Nations, then they will dwell in their own land which I gave to My servant Yaakob.*</u> [26] *And they will dwell safely there, build houses, and plant vineyards; yes,* <u>*they will dwell securely, when I execute judgments on all those around them who despise them.*</u> *Then they shall know that I am YHWH their Elohim."* Ezekiel 28:25-26

So there will be a time when the House of Yisrael returns to their Land. They will be dwelling in safety while at that time YHWH will be judging the nations around them. Here is what YHWH said concerning the Land promised to Yaakob: *"*[13] *. . . I am YHWH Elohim of Abraham your father and the Elohim of Yitshaq; the land on which you lie I will give to you and your descendants.* [14] <u>*Also your descendants shall be as the dust of the earth; you shall spread abroad to the west and the east, to the north and the south; and in you and in your seed all the families of the earth shall be blessed."*</u> Beresheet 28:13-14

Through this return, the inhabitants of the Land will

expand and enlarge the border of the Land. Again we read about the promised return accompanied with a "mighy hand" and "an outstretched arm." "33 *As I live, says the Master YHWH, surely with a mighty hand, with an outstretched arm, and with fury poured out, I will rule over you.* 34 *I will bring you out from the peoples and gather you out of the countries where you are scattered, with a mighty hand, with an outstretched arm, and with fury poured out.* 35 *And I will bring you into the wilderness of the peoples, and there I will plead My case with you face to face.* 36 Just *as I pleaded My case with your fathers in the wilderness of the land of Egypt, so I will plead My case with you, says the Master YHWH.* 37 *I will make you pass under the rod, and I will bring you into the bond of the Covenant;* 38 *I will purge the rebels from among you, and those who transgress against Me; I will bring them out of the country where they dwell, but they shall not enter the Land of Yisrael. Then you will know that I am YHWH.* 39 *As for you, O House of Yisrael, thus says the Master YHWH: Go, serve every one of you his idols - and hereafter - if you will not obey Me; but profane My Holy Name no more with your gifts and your idols.* 40 *For on My Holy Mountain, on the mountain height of Yisrael, says the Master YHWH, there all the House of Yisrael, all of them in the Land, shall serve Me; there I will accept them, and there I will require your offerings and the firstfruits of your sacrifices, together with all your holy things.* 41 *I will accept you as a sweet aroma when I bring you out from the peoples and gather you out of the countries where you have been scattered; and I will be hallowed in you before the Gentiles.* 42 *Then you shall know that I am YHWH, when I bring you into the Land of Yisrael, into the country for which I raised My Hand in an oath to give to your fathers.* 43 *And there you shall remember your ways and all your doings with which you were defiled; and you shall loathe yourselves in your own sight because of all the evils that you have committed.* 44 *Then you shall know that I am YHWH, when I have dealt with you for My Name's sake, not according to your wicked ways nor according to your corrupt doings,*

O House of Yisrael, says the Master YHWH." Ezekiel 20:33-44

Again, the language used is reminiscent of the deliverance of Yisrael from Egypt. *"So YHWH brought us out of Egypt with a mighty hand and with an outstretched arm, with great terror and with signs and wonders."* Debarim 26:8 As Yisrael and the mixed multitude were brought out of a decimated Egypt, so too His people will be brought out of the Nations as a victorious and conquering assembly. This is the context of the end of the age.

It appears that through the deliverance process YHWH will sift His people and purge the rebels – not unlike what He did when they came out of Egypt and made their way to the Promised Land. The return of the House of Yisrael is actually described throughout the book of Ezekiel. Ezekiel is actually made a "watchman" over the House of Yisrael. (Ezekiel 33:7)

A watchman is supposed to stay awake and alert to see the danger coming and warn the people. The instrument for warning the assembly is the shofar. If you read the text in the English you will likely read the word "trumpet" but the Hebrew is clear, the watchman sounds the shofar (ꓱꓕꓶꓪ). If we look at the Greek Septuagint we see that the shofar (ꓱꓕꓶꓪ) in Ezekiel 33 was translated as "salpingi" (σαλπιγγι).

Those in Christianity familiar with the Book of Revelation are likely familiar with the seven "trumpets." Interestingly, the Greek manuscripts of the text use the same word as Ezekiel to describe the "trumpets." So, once again, it is clear that the trumpets in Revelation are actually shofars. This is one of the shofars that we read about in Joel. It is blasted from the Set Apart Mountain - Mount Zion to announce the Day of YHWH. (Joel 2)

With that in mind, it sheds some new light into the purpose of the shofar blasts sounded from the heavenly

Mountain in the Book of Revelation. We will discuss that in more detail later on. For now though we see that the shofar is a warning.

Ezekiel 34 is where we see the House of Yisrael originally being described as lost sheep after they were scattered. *"⁵ So they were scattered because there was no shepherd; and they became food for all the beasts of the field when they were scattered. ⁶ My sheep wandered through all the mountains, and on every high hill; yes, My flock was scattered over the whole face of the earth, and no one was seeking or searching for them."* Ezekiel 34:5-6

This was followed by a great promise. *"¹¹ For thus says the Master YHWH: Indeed I Myself will search for My X𐤊-sheep and seek them out. ¹² As a shepherd seeks out his flock on the day he is among his scattered sheep, so will I seek out My X𐤊-sheep and deliver them from all the places where they were scattered on a cloudy and dark day. ¹³ And I will bring them out from the peoples and gather them from the countries, and will bring them to their own land;* <u>I will feed them on the mountains of Yisrael</u>*, in the valleys and in all the inhabited places of the country. ¹⁴ I will feed them in good pasture, and their fold shall be on the high mountains of Yisrael. There they shall lie down in a good fold and feed in rich pasture on the mountains of Yisrael. ¹⁵ I will feed My flock, and I will make them lie down, says the Master YHWH. ¹⁶ I will seek what was X𐤊-lost and bring back what was X𐤊-driven away, bind up the broken and strengthen what was X𐤊-sick; but I will destroy X𐤊-the fat and X𐤊-the strong, and feed them in judgment. ¹⁷ And as for you, O My flock, thus says the Master YHWH: Behold, I shall judge between sheep and sheep, between rams and goats."* Ezekiel 34:11-17

So YHWH Himself would regather the lost sheep of the House of Yisrael. Notice the emphasis on the ownership of the sheep with the Aleph Taw (X𐤊). They have been redeemed by Him – bought with His blood. The Aleph Taw

(✗𝗞) is also associated with the restoration of the sheep as well as judging the sheep. Those who have grown fat while their brethren were not fed will be judged.

Notice also the geographic location where they will be settled – the mountains of Yisrael. This is not to mean that that they will simply dwell on mountains throughout the land of Yisrael, rather the mountains of Yisrael are specific to the land allotted to the House of Yisrael. So this is describing the Lost Sheep of the House of Yisrael being brought back to their Covenant Land.

Now many evangelical Christians attempt to link this with the formation of the modern State of Israel, but that is  not the case. The modern State of Israel is officially recognized as a "Jewish State." It consists of many from the House of Yahudah, known as Jews, although it is probably a mixture of all the tribes since some from the House of Yisrael joined with the House of Yahudah after the sin of Jereboam.

The Jewish State of Israel was founded upon the philosophy of Zionism, not the Torah and the Covenant. In fact, there were many powerful Illuminist families, such as the Rothschild's and the Rockefellers, and institutions involved in the formation of this State. It is very telling that the hexagram was selected as the national symbol.

If the Jewish State were interested in the Covenant, they would have kept control of the Temple Mount that they took along with Jerusalem in 1967. They also would have kept control of the Cave of the Patriarchs, also known as the Cave of Machpelah at Hebron.

While the formation of the modern State of Israel surely is within the plan of YHWH, it must not be confused with the restoration and return of the House of Yisrael. The modern State of Israel is a parliamentary democracy founded by Zionists. Zionists are focused on secular principles involving genetic Jews. They are not interested in restoring the Kingdom of YHWH. Most of the population is secular, and this is a critical distinction that people must understand, otherwise they get confused.

The prophecies speak of a return and a restoration. The people were exiled because of their disobedience. YHWH did not and will not allow people to live in the Promised Land who continue to defile the Land, otherwise the exile of the former inhabitants would not have been just. Some people believe that YHWH is just so happy to have some Jews back in the Land that the commandments and the prophecies have somehow been waived.

YHWH does not change. Just as He punished disobedience in the past, He will do so in the future. While there is a very small portion of the population observing the Shemittah year, and giving the Land rest in the 7th year, most ignore the commandments. While many in the modern State of Israel are genetically Jewish, most of them do not follow YHWH. Even the religious subscribe to the religion of Judaism, a religion developed by the Pharisees. Of course, the Messiah specifically condemned their doctrines and indicated that they would not be in the Kingdom of Heaven.

Interestingly, a significant portion of the population is not even Jewish. They are neither genetic Jews, nor do they subscribe to the religion of Judaism. These are the Arab citizens who are typically either Christian or Muslim. So there is quite a mix, and a disparity of beliefs.

What we currently see in the modern State of Israel is not what would be considered a Scriptural restoration. The people have not repented, nor have the collectively returned to YHWH and His Torah. In fact, those who actually desire to follow the Torah in spirit and in truth, as taught by

Yahushua are not permitted to live in the Land, other than to visit. The modern State of Israel specifically opposes a return of the House of Yisrael, because they are not considered to be Jews. This could be the undoing of the government of Israel, which currently stands in direct opposition to the restoration of the Tribes and the restoration of the Kingdom.

This is a very relevant fact as we contemplate possible end time scenarios, because the people in the Land will likely be given a choice. They must either repent or be taken out through some sort of judgment. They cannot continue to dwell in the Land, and defile the Land by their disobedience. When I first started writing this series I read about "rave" parties held in the deserts of Israel where youth would dance around a golden calf all night long. The reports of the sin and licentiousness in Tel Aviv and throughout the country have only gotten worse. They are shocking, to say the least. So if YHWH is just, there will be a judgment upon the people who currently live in the Modern State of Israel if they do not repent. That judgment will likely lead to many repenting and it will also pave the way for a return to the Land.

Interestingly, the Jewish State of Israel is struggling to control the so-called "occupied territories" also known as "The West Bank." These lands actually contain the mountains of Yisrael – the Land that is the inheritance of the House of Yisrael. So there will be a time when the lost sheep of the House of Yisrael will be gathered back home to the mountains of Yisrael – despite the prohibitions of the modern State of Israel. That roadblock will be removed by YHWH, likely through some sort of attack by neighboring nations.

In Ezekiel 36 we read of Ezekiel actually prophesying to the mountains of Yisrael. YHWH will breathe life into His people and revive them and then join the House of Yisrael and the House of Yahudah together. This was vividly portrayed through Ezekiel.

"*¹ The hand of YHWH came upon me and brought me out in the Spirit of YHWH, and set me down in the midst of the valley; and it was full of bones. ² Then He caused me to pass by them all around, and behold, there were very many in the open valley; and indeed they were very dry. ³ And He said to me, Son of man, can these bones live? So I answered, O Adonai YHWH, You know. ⁴ Again He said to me, Prophesy to these bones, and say to them, O dry bones, hear the word of YHWH! ⁵ Thus says Adonai YHWH to these bones: Surely I will cause breath to enter into you, and you shall live. ⁶ I will put sinews on you and bring flesh upon you, cover you with skin and put breath in you; and you shall live. Then you shall know that I am YHWH. ⁷ So I prophesied as I was commanded; and as I prophesied, there was a noise, and suddenly a rattling; and the bones came together, bone to bone. ⁸ Indeed, as I looked, the sinews and the flesh came upon them, and the skin covered them over; but there was no breath in them. ⁹ Also He said to me, Prophesy to the breath, prophesy, son of man, and say to the breath, Thus says Adonai YHWH: Come from the four winds, O breath, and breathe on these slain, that they may live. ¹⁰ So I prophesied as He commanded me, and breath came into them, and they lived, and stood upon their feet, an exceedingly great army. ¹¹ Then He said to me, Son of man, these bones are the whole House of Yisrael. They indeed say, Our bones are dry, our hope is lost, and we ourselves are cut off! ¹² Therefore prophesy and say to them, Thus says Adonai YHWH: Behold, O My people, I will open your graves and cause you to come up from your graves, and bring you into the land of Yisrael. ¹³ Then you shall know that I am YHWH, when I have opened your graves, O My people, and* brought you up from your graves. *¹⁴ I will put My Spirit in you, and you shall live, and I will place you in your own land. Then you shall know that I, YHWH, have spoken it and performed it, says YHWH.* *¹⁵* Again the word of YHWH came to me, saying, *¹⁶* As for you, son of man, take a stick for yourself and write on it: For Yahudah and for the children of Ysrael, his companions. Then take another stick and write on it, For Joseph, the stick of Ephraim, and for all the House of Yisrael, his companions. *¹⁷* Then join them one to another for yourself into one stick, and they will become one in your hand. *¹⁸* And when the children of your people speak to you, saying, Will you not show us what you mean by these? *¹⁹* say to them, Thus says Adonai YHWH: *Surely I will take the stick of Joseph, which is in the hand of Ephraim, and the tribes of Yisrael, his companions; and I will join them with it, with the stick of Yahudah, and make them one stick, and they will be one in My hand.* *²⁰* And the sticks on which you write will be in your hand before their eyes. *²¹* Then say to them, Thus says Adonai YHWH: *Surely I will take the children of Yisrael from among the nations, wherever they have gone, and will gather them from every side and bring them into their own land;* *²²* *and I will make them one nation in the land, on the mountains of Yisrael; and one king shall be king over them all; they shall no longer be two nations, nor shall they ever be divided into two kingdoms again.* *²³* They shall not defile themselves anymore with their idols, nor with their detestable things, nor with any of their transgressions; but I will deliver them from all their dwelling places in which they have sinned, and will cleanse them. *Then they shall be My people, and I will be their Elohim.* *²⁴* *David My servant shall be king over them, and they* *shall all have one Shepherd; they shall also walk in My judgments and observe My statutes, and do them.* [25] *Then they shall dwell in the land that I have given to Yaakob My servant, where your fathers dwelt; and they shall dwell there, they, their children, and their children's children, forever; and My servant David shall be their prince forever.* [26] Moreover I will make a Covenant of peace with them, and it shall be an everlasting Covenant with them; I will establish them and multiply them, and I will set My sanctuary in their midst forevermore. [27] My tabernacle also shall be with them; indeed I will be their Elohim, and they shall be My people. [28] The nations also will know that I, YHWH, sanctify Yisrael, when My sanctuary is in their midst forevermore." Ezekiel 37:1-28

Notice that "David shall be their prince." This is a Messianic reference that shows the Messiah as the Son of YHWH. YHWH is the King in the Kingdom of Heaven. The son is the Prince in that Kingdom. Yahushua came as a King of Yisrael and He, as the Son of Elohim, is a prince in the Kingdom of YHWH. He already came as the Messiah son of Joseph, and soon will come again as the Messiah Son of David – King over the united Kingdom of Yisrael.

We are certainly living in very interesting times. There is a sense of anticipation among many who believe that we are approaching the end of the age. Many are anticipating a messiah, although there are differing opinions as to the identity or purpose of that messiah. If we believe the Scriptures we should be anticipating a fulfillment of the prophecies concerning the return of the House of Yisrael. This, after all, is YHWH keeping His promise according to the Covenant.

It is because of this Covenant, referred to as the Covenant of Peace, that YHWH fights for His people who

are dwelling safely in the Land as previously shown in Ezekiel 39:1-8. Here is a description of what follows:

"*⁹ Then those who dwell in the cities of Yisrael will go out and set on fire and burn the weapons, both the shields and bucklers, the bows and arrows, the javelins and spears; and they will make fires with them for seven years. ¹⁰ They will not take wood from the field nor cut down any from the forests, because they will make fires with the weapons; and they will plunder those who plundered them, and pillage those who pillaged them, says the Master YHWH. ¹¹ It will come to pass in that day that I will give Gog a burial place there in Yisrael, the valley of those who pass by east of the sea; and it will obstruct travelers, because there they will bury Gog and all his multitude. Therefore they will call it the Valley of Hamon Gog. ¹² For seven months the House of Yisrael will be burying them, in order to cleanse the land. ¹³ Indeed all the people of the land will be burying, and they will gain renown for it on the day that I am glorified, says the Master YHWH. ¹⁴ They will set apart men regularly employed, with the help of a search party, to pass through the land and bury those bodies remaining on the ground, in order to cleanse it. At the end of seven months they will make a search. ¹⁵ The search party will pass through the land; and when anyone sees a man's bone, he shall set up a marker by it, till the buriers have buried it in the Valley of Hamon Gog. ¹⁶ The name of the city will also be Hamonah. Thus they shall cleanse the land. ¹⁷ And as for you, son of man, thus says the Master YHWH, Speak to every sort of bird and to every beast of the field: Assemble yourselves and come; gather together from all sides to My sacrificial meal which I am sacrificing for you, a great sacrificial meal on the mountains of Yisrael, that* you may eat flesh and drink blood. ^{18} You shall eat the flesh of the mighty, drink the blood of the princes of the earth, of rams and lambs, of goats and bulls, all of them fatlings of Bashan. ^{19} You shall eat fat till you are full, and drink blood till you are drunk, at My sacrificial meal which I am sacrificing for you. ^{20} You shall be filled at My table with horses and riders, with mighty men and with all the men of war, says the Master YHWH. ^{21} I will set My glory among the nations; all the nations shall see My judgment which I have executed, and My Hand which I have laid on them. ^{22} So the House of Yisrael shall know that I am YHWH their Elohim from that day forward. ^{23} The nations shall know that the House of Yisrael went into captivity for their iniquity; because they were unfaithful to Me, therefore I hid My face from them. I gave them into the hand of their enemies, and they all fell by the sword. ^{24} According to their uncleanness and according to their transgressions I have dealt with them, and hidden My face from them. ^{25} Therefore thus says the Master YHWH: Now I will bring back the captives of Yaakob, and have mercy on the whole House of Yisrael; and I will be jealous for My set apart Name ^{26} after they have borne their shame, and all their unfaithfulness in which they were unfaithful to Me, when they dwelt safely in their own land and no one made them afraid. ^{27} When I have brought them back from the peoples and gathered them out of their enemies' lands, and I am hallowed in them in the sight of many nations, ^{28} then they shall know that I am YHWH their Elohim, Who sent them into captivity among the nations, but also brought them back to their land, and left none of them captive any longer. ^{29} And I will not hide My face from them anymore; for I shall have poured out My Spirit on

the House of Yisrael, says the Master YHWH."
Ezekiel 39:9-29

So while YHWH will fight the battle, the House of
Yisrael will have some cleaning up to do. This is their Land,
but they need to cleanse the Land. There is a very special
procedure set in place that some ascribe to a radioactive
protocol. Many people have trouble understanding this as a
future event, because of the description of the weaponry,
which appears to be ancient – not modern.

Because these are not modern metallic materials the
weapons are used for fuel for seven years. As a result of this 7
year period of burning the weapons, many have difficulty
dating the event. We will discuss the timing further when we
examine the Battle referred to as Armageddon.

During the return and restoration of the House of
Yisrael, YHWH will pour out His Spirit on the House of
Yisrael as prophesied by the Prophets. Here are just a few.

"For I will pour water on him who is thirsty,
And floods on the dry ground;
I will pour My Spirit on your descendants,
And My blessing on your offspring."
Isaiah 44:3

"As for Me, says YHWH, this is My Covenant with them: My
Spirit Who is upon you, and My words which I have put in your
mouth, shall not depart from your mouth, nor from the mouth of
your descendants, nor from the mouth of your descendants'
descendants, says YHWH, from this time and forevermore."
Isaiah 59:21

"[28] And it shall come to pass afterward that I will pour out My
Spirit on all flesh; Your sons and your daughters shall prophesy,
your old men shall dream dreams, your young men shall see visions.

²⁹ And also on My menservants and on My maidservants I will pour out My Spirit in those days."
Joel 2:28-29

These prophecies describe the fulfillment of the Renewed Covenant - the one described by Jeremiah. *"³³ But this is the Covenant that I will make with the* ✗✦*-House of Yisrael after those days, says YHWH: I will put My Torah in their minds, and write it on their hearts; and I will be their Elohim, and they shall be My people. ³⁴ No more shall every man teach his neighbor, and every man his brother, saying, 'Know YHWH,' for they all shall know Me, from the least of them to the greatest of them, says YHWH. For I will forgive their iniquity, and their sin I will remember no more."* Jeremiah 31:33-34

Notice that this promise is made specifically with ✗✦-House of Yisrael. The House of Yisrael was purchased by the blood of the Lamb of Elohim. This is the renewed Covenant that the Messiah is making with the divorced House of Yisrael. YHWH will put His Torah in our minds and write it on their hearts!

This means that the Torah will be inside of them. The mind is part of us that we cannot see. Even if you perform an autopsy you will not see a persons mind. The heart is the organ that pumps the blood of life throughout the body.

This was the same promise provided to the House of Yisrael after they were regathered and returned to the Land. *"²⁵ Therefore thus says the Master YHWH: 'Now I will bring back* ✗✦*-captives of Yaakob, and have mercy on the whole House of Yisrael; and I will be jealous for My set apart Name ²⁶ after they have borne their shame, and all their unfaithfulness in which they were unfaithful to Me, when they dwelt safely in their own Land and no one made them afraid. ²⁷ When I have brought them back from the peoples and gathered them out of their enemies' lands, and I am set apart in them in the sight of many nations, ²⁸ then they*

shall know that I am YHWH their Elohim, who sent them into captivity among the nations, but also brought them back to their Land, and left none of them captive any longer. [29] *And I will not hide My face from them anymore; for I shall have poured out My Spirit on the House of Yisrael, says the Master YHWH.*" Ezekiel 39:25-29

YHWH will pour out His Spirit upon the House of Yisrael as He did on Shabuot, after the ascension of Yahushua. Now this entire scenario fits within the context of the final beast described in Daniel.

We left off describing the beast as a religious, political and economic system actually mimicking the ancient system of Babylon under Nimrod. This beast is unlike the other beasts because it is essentially a rebirth of ancient Babylon under Nimrod. It actually had seven heads like the serpent dragon.

Now back to more information regarding the beast in Revelation. We know that the serpent gave power to the beast. "[2] *Now the beast which I saw was like a leopard, his feet were like the feet of a bear, and his mouth like the mouth of a lion. The dragon gave him his power, his throne, and great authority.* [3] *And I saw one of his heads as if it had been mortally wounded, and his deadly wound was healed. And all the world marveled and followed the beast.* [4] *So they worshiped the dragon who gave authority to the beast; and they worshiped the beast, saying, "Who is like the beast? Who is able to make war with him?"* Revelation 13:2-4

So the beast with seven heads and ten crowns receives a deadly wound on one of his heads. That deadly wound was healed, and it is that process which apparently accelerates the rise and control of this beast, because people believe that it cannot be killed. He was given authority to continue for 42 months. Here is that number again, the number linked with the trampling of Jerusalem and the two witnesses. (Revelation 11:3). The beast speaks blasphemies against Elohim, His Name, His Tabernacle and those who dwell in heaven. He will make war against the set apart ones, and everyone whose name is not in the Scroll of Life of the Lamb will worship him.

As the Revelation continues we read about another beast. *"11 Then I saw another beast coming up out of the earth, and he had two horns like a lamb and spoke like a dragon. 12 And he exercises all the authority of the first beast in his presence, and causes the earth and those who dwell in it to worship the first beast, whose deadly wound was healed. 13 He performs great signs, so that he even makes fire come down from heaven on the earth in the sight of men. 14 And he deceives those who dwell on the earth by those signs which he was granted to do in the sight of the beast, telling those who dwell on the earth to make an image to the beast who was wounded by the sword and lived. 15 He was granted power to give breath to the image of the beast, that the image of the beast should both speak and cause as many as would not worship the image of the beast to be killed. 16 He causes all, both small and great, rich and poor, free and slave, to receive a mark on their right hand or on their foreheads, 17 and that no one may buy or sell except one who has the mark or the name of the beast, or the number of his name. 18 Here is wisdom. Let him who has understanding calculate the number of the beast, for it is the number of a man, its number is 666."* Revelation 13:11-18

The symbolism describing the second beast is quite profound. Here we read of another beast that comes out of the earth. The Greek uses the word "anabiano" (ἀναβαῖνο) which means: "to ascend, to climb, to arise." Adam came from the earth so this beast appears to be a man. He has two horns like a lamb. This is not the Lamb of Elohim that stands on Mount Zion with His marked servants. Clearly though, this second beast is trying to appear like the Lamb. This beast may look like the Lamb, but it speaks like a dragon. It speaks

for satan. It is a counterfeit meant to deceive many. This man beast exercises all of the authority of the first beast whose deadly wound was healed.

So here are the dynamics. We see the serpent dragon representing satan. He empowers the 7 headed beast that looks like him. Both of them are worshipped. There is an image of the first beast that is also worshipped, and then there is a second beast that speaks like a dragon. This is the mouthpiece of the serpent dragon that could be called the false prophet.

This man beast performs signs and directs worship toward the first beast. He instructs the people to construct an image of the first beast. He then makes the image come to life. It can speak and kill people who do not worship it, because it is the image of the first beast that is supposed to be worshipped by the entire world. This may be the realization of transhumanists, or it may be something completely supernatural. One cannot ignore the fact that Elohim made man in His image. This seems to be the serpent's progeny of some sort.

Not only must everyone worship the image and the first beast, they must also receive a mark. This is total control as Nebuchadnezzar attempted in Neo-Babylon. Read what happened there:

"*¹ Nebuchadnezzar the king made an image of gold, whose height was sixty cubits and its width six cubits. He set it up in the plain of Dura, in the province of Babylon.*" Notice the focus on six, as we saw with Goliath. Nebuchadnezzar then ordered all of the officials of his kingdom to come before the image that he erected. "*⁴ Then a herald cried aloud: To you it is commanded, O peoples, nations, and languages, ⁵ that at the time you hear the sound of the horn, flute, harp, lyre, and psaltery, in symphony with all kinds of music, you shall fall down and worship the gold image that King Nebuchadnezzar has set up; ⁶ and whoever*

does not fall down and worship shall be cast immediately into the midst of a burning fiery furnace." Daniel 3:4-6

This sounds like a modern day rock concert, and we can clearly see how society is susceptible to such a system of worship. Music lovers regularly attend worship sessions dubbed as concerts. They raise their hands and scream in adoration, directing their praise and worship toward their gods and goddesses on stage. Now many do not consider this conduct to be worship, simply entertainment. Nevertheless, the lines are clearly getting blurred.

There were three men from Yahudah who knew where to draw the line. They followed the Torah, and they could distinguish between righteous conduct and an abomination. They refused to worship the image of Nebuchadnezzar. They were the friends of Daniel previously mentioned. Their refusal enraged the king and he ordered them thrown into a burning fiery furnace. In the midst of the fire they were joined by a fourth – one *"like the Son of Elohim."* Daniel 3:25

This clearly demonstrated that YHWH is capable of saving His servants from the fires of the beast. This is good to know when we understand that the image will kill those who do not worship it. Interestingly the numbers associated with the image of Babylon apparently involved a 2 dimensional image. We are only given the height of 60 cubits and the width of 6 cubits – there is no depth measurement.

In contrast, the image of the first beast in Revelation will be a three dimensional image that is animated. It may look like a man, and the number of man is 6. So we should be looking for another number 6 associated with this image – possibly 600. Interestingly, the Hebrew word for "six" is "shesh" (**ＷＷ**). The gematria for the word "shesh" (**ＷＷ**) is 600. This emphasis on the number 6 leads us to what is commonly referred to as "the mark of the beast."

Not only will people be killed for not worshipping the beast, no one will be able to buy or sell without taking 1) the mark of the beast, or 2) the name of the beast, or 3) the number of his name.

The "mark" of the beast has intrigued many for centuries. Part of the reason for the confusion is understanding the beast being referred to and misleading translations. Many popular translations of Revelation 13:18 end with ". . . *his number is 666.*" As a result, many ascribe the number to the so-called anti-christ, or the second beast. The problem is that the beast being referred to is the first beast, not the second.

A literal translation of the passage actually reads: *"Here is the wisdom! He who is having the understanding, let him count the number of the beast, for the number of a man it is, and its* (αὐτοῦ) *number [is] 666."* Young's Literal Translation. The pronoun "autos" (αὐτοῦ) should be translated as "its" instead of "his."

With that understanding we can then look further at this "mark" of the first beast. The Greek word for "mark" is "charagma" (χάραγμα). There are actually three different "signs" that those who worship the beast can carry – 1) the mark, 2) the name of the beast, or 3) the number of the beast.

We are given a clue that if we have wisdom we can "calculate" the mark of the beast. The word for "calculate" is "psephizo" (ψηφισάτω) and means: "to count or compute." The number is actually three words in most Modern Greek texts: "ἑξακόσιοι ἑξήκοντα ἕξ." So it is actually spelled out in Greek as "Six Hundred (ἑξακόσιοι), Sixty (ἑξήκοντα), Six (ἕξ)."

While this is the modern standard, many older texts actually use three Greek characters – "chi (X)," "xi" (ξ) and "stigma" (ς). Therefore, as with gematria involving Hebrew letters, there are letters representing numbers in the Greek language as well. "Chi" (X) equals 600, "xi" (ξ) equals 60 and "stigma" (ς) equals 6.

This leads to a very interesting theory that these Greek letters are not only a number, but also a name. It has already been mentioned that the Name of the Messiah is Yahushua. The name Jesus is a fabricated name, essentially non-existent until the creation of the English language. There are some who suppose that the three Greek letters actually provide a name.

If you pronounce the Greek letters you read: "chezus." Is it possible that the text is providing a phonetic pronunciation for the pagan derived name Jesus? This, after all, is the incorrect name attributed to the Messiah of Yisrael. Since there was no "J" in the Greek or Hebrew languages, there was no way of specifically providing for the letter "J" sound, that would not be invented for another 1,500 years.

It is possible that this false name will play a part in the end time deception as the identity of the Messiah is blurred and misrepresented. Of course, the name Jesus, rendered Iesus in Greek, is connected with the worship of Zeus. So Jesus is a perfectly acceptable name to be used in a Babylonian religious system as we see it currently being used in the Christian religion.

Tammuz Wearing Crosses

Recognizing that the mark or "image" of Christianity is the cross, which is the same as the "tau" used in Babylonian Tammuz worship we can see the possibility for deception.

Imagine if Christians, the ones most concerned about this mark, being the ones actually deceived by this mark because of their refusal to give up their tradition of calling the Messiah Jesus. In fact, quite often when confronted with this issue Christians will retort: "You're not going to take away

MY Jesus." That really goes to the heart of the matter. They are not concerned with the truth, only their tradition. They are not willing to give up their traditions, even when presented with irrefutable evidence. This is the same sin as the Pharisees. They would not give up their traditions even while standing in the very presence of Truth.

 Now it is worth noting that not all texts reveal the number "666." In fact, one of the oldest fragments from the Oxyrhynchus Papyrion, known as P. Oxy. 4499, reveals 616 rather than 666. The three Greek letters are: "chi (X), "iota" (I) and "stigma" (ς). So there is no unanimity regarding the Greek characters or the number that they represent.

This is the number of the first beast, not the man beast, but it is the number of a man. The word "number" is found in the text 3 times. It is "arithmos" (ἀριθμὸν) in the Greek. The text warns people not to take that number on their hands or forehead.

We do not readily know the name or the mark, and it is the name that requires calculation. Many have tried to impute specific names to this number. It is clear that there are numerous ways to calculate names, and just about any name can be calculated to equal 666. There are some who believe that Prince Charles of Wales is a viable candidate due to the fact that his name calculates to 666, and his crest appears to display the beast symbology.[252]

Others believe that the mark has to do with the Sabbath. Observing the Sabbath is the "sign" of the Covenant of YHWH. The Roman Catholic Church, as a demonstration of its power, changed their sabbath to Sunday. The church actually calls Sunday their Sabbath, and it is their "mark" of authority. If people were forced to work and buy and sell on Shabbat, while observing a Sunday sabbath, this would be a plausible scenario, although it still does not calculate a name of the beast.

Others ascribe an Islamic symbol to the mark. They believe that the beast will be an Islamic Empire, the image will be the crescent moon, and the mark will involve the sword of Islam. In support of this claim they reference a passage from Codex Vaticanus that actually appears to provide the crossed swords, followed by the sign for Allah. 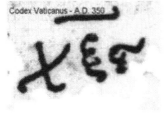 Thus, the number, mark and name of the beast combined.[253]

Still others believe that the mark will consist of a bar code, an RFID chip or some other type of biometric tattoo or implanted device. In a digital controlled society, these are certainly all plausible explanations. In fact, the connection with buying and selling is intimately connected with this "mark." We also see this commercial connection with mystery Babylon, so this "mark" will be intimately connected with the government of the beast, and the commercialization and idolatry associated with the harlot.

As we have discussed the attack on the genetic coding of man, the use of vaccinations cannot be ignored. Some believe that there may be an actual or contrived epidemic perpetrated upon the planet in the future. The "anti-christ" could appear as a benevolent individual prepared to save humanity. The beast system could provide the vaccine that prevents or heals the people from a virus.

That vaccine could alter the genetic coding of the recipients, and transform them into the "image" of the beast instead of the image of Adam. This could explain the severe punishment rendered upon those who take the mark. Their

blood has been defiled, and their genetic makeup has been altered.

Those who receive the vaccine may also receive a mark as evidence that the vaccine was administered. Those who do not receive the vaccine/mark may be quarantined and/or killed to prevent the spread of some "zombie apocalypse."

The mark could also constitute some genetic modification guised as a promise of immortality. The Nephilim may come promising the "god gene" that prepares mankind for their next evolutionary phase and transcendence into the New Age. These modified beings will no longer be creations in the image of Elohim, and therefore unable to become sons of Elohim. This may be similar to the transformation that took place with Nimrod. (Beresheet 10:8).

The possibilities are many, and only time will tell the precise scenario, or the actual name, number and mark of the beast. Some people obsess over this issue. I suggest that if this concerns you, it would be advisable to keep the commandments of YHWH and the testimony of Yahushua. Only if you start worshipping a false deity, and following false signs will you get into trouble. I know there are people who fear inadvertently taking the mark, but I do not see that as a possibility. The circumstances surrounding the taking of the mark should be quite obvious – it will be necessary to buy or sell in the beast system. If you find yourself in that situation, then you will likely have the answer.

The circumstances remind me of the Jews during World War II. Those in Nazi controlled countries were forced to wear a mark – the hexagram. They had to wear the hexagram in order to function in society. This seems very similar to the mark of the beast. In fact, it seems to be a precursor to the mark in Revelation. The selection of the

hexagram was really quite profound. It is often called a "star" and we know that angelic beings are often referred to as "stars." In fact, the hexagram has been called the Talisman of Saturn due to its association with the 6th planet Saturn.

The Israelites had previously worshipped the star of Saturn under different names. Here are two passages that reference their idolatry regarding the star. *"You also carried Sikkuth your king and Chiun, your idols, the star of your gods, which you made for yourselves."* Amos 5:26. *"You also took up the tabernacle of Moloch, and the star of your god Remphan, Images which you made to worship; and I will carry you away beyond Babylon."* Acts 7:43.

While hexagrams are visible, along with other pagan symbols in ancient synagogues that have been unearthed through archaeology, there was no known usage of it in Jewish circles until the 17th century when the cabalist, Isaac Luria, introduced it in Germany. It later became the insignia for Zionists. We already saw that Solomon used the hexagram in summoning demons. So the so-called "star of David" is better known for what it is, the star of Saturn on the seal of Solomon. It is a symbol used in Zionism, and it is not s Scriptural symbol condoned by YHWH.

The hexagram was associated with the occult, and Hitler was completely consumed with the occult. The selection of the hexagram was purposeful, and should have been a warning to the Jews. Of course, one cannot ignore the fact that it is strongly associated with the number 6 and the occult. Very interestingly, the modern State of Israel has adopted this mark as the image displayed on their national banner. One can only wonder if this symbol will somehow be used in the future as it was in the past.

One thing is certain, taking the mark of the beast will not be some accidental decision that some will mistakenly

make. Rather, it will be an obvious mark, purposefully taken by people in direct defiance and opposition to YHWH. It will be a form of worship in opposition to the Covenant of YHWH.

The mark is actually placed on the exact locations that those in Covenant are instructed to "bind the Words of the Covenant as a sign" – on the forehead and on the hand. (see Debarim 6:8, 11:18) Therefore, those who take the mark of the beast have essentially entered into covenant with the beast.

"*⁹ Then a third angel followed them, saying with a loud voice, If anyone worships the beast and its (αὐτοῦ) image, and receives his mark on his forehead or on his hand, ¹⁰ he himself shall also drink of the wine of the wrath of Elohim, which is poured out full strength into the cup of His indignation. He shall be tormented with fire and brimstone in the presence of the set apart messengers and in the presence of the Lamb. ¹¹ And the smoke of their torment ascends forever and ever; and they have no rest day or night, who worship the beast and his image, and whoever receives the mark of its (αὐτοῦ) name.*" Revelation 14:9-11

Those who worship the beast and the image and receive the mark stand in direct contrast to those with the seal of YHWH – the 144,000. In fact, to show the distinction between these two groups the 144,000 are immediately referenced in the text. Now some believe that this is a different 144,000, because they specifically have the Name of the Father on their forehead, but we have already established that to be the seal. Now they are in heaven before the Throne that appears to be on a heavenly Mount Zion.

"*¹ Then I looked, and behold, a Lamb standing on Mount Zion, and with Him one hundred and forty-four thousand, having His Father's Name written on their foreheads. ² And I heard a voice from heaven, like the voice of many waters, and like the voice of loud thunder. And I heard the sound of harpists playing their harps. ³ They sang as it were a new song before the Throne, before the four living creatures, and the elders; and no one could learn that song except the hundred and forty-four thousand who were redeemed from the earth. ⁴ These are the ones who were not defiled with women, for they are virgins. These are the ones who follow the Lamb wherever He goes. These were redeemed from among men, being firsts (aparche) to Elohim and to the Lamb. ⁵ And in their mouth was found no deceit, for they are without fault before the throne of Elohim."* Revelation 14:1-5

Notice how they are described. They are redeemed from the earth. They were initially on the earth when they were sealed and protected. Now they are on Mount Zion. The fact that they are "redeemed" seems to indicate that they were "taken up" or translated into the heavenly realm during the Feast of Unleavened Bread after Passover. That is why they are present with the Lamb.

They are virgins – "firsts" to Elohim and the Lamb. The word for "firsts" in Greek is "aparche." This is the same word found in the Septuagint to describe the Hebrew word "resheet." (X𝟕W𝐊𝟗) (Vayiqra 23:10). If we examine the "first" (resheet) offering in the Torah, we see that those "resheet" (X𝟕W𝐊𝟗) from the "X𝐊-harvest" (𝟗𝟗𝟕𝔹𝟗-X𝐊) consist of one "X𝐊-omer" (𝟗𝐲⊙-X𝐊). Notice the association with the Aleph Taw (X𝐊). The "X𝐊-omer" (𝟗𝐲⊙-X𝐊) is then waved by the priest before YHWH. When this is complete, the rest of the harvest continues through to Shabuot – 50 days later.

Prior to Shabuot, the grain is harvested throughout the land and the "first fruits" – "bikkurim" (𝐲𝟕𝟗𝐘𝐘𝟓) are then gathered from all over the land. They are brought before YHWH on Shabuot and waved before Him. Interestingly, this offering consists of two loaves mixed with leaven. Many confuse this "bikkurim" offering of Shabuot with the "resheet" offering during the Feast of Unleavened Bread. The distinction is very different. They are two different harvests of two different grain crops offered at two different times. The "resheet" offering during the Feast of Unleavened Bread consists of one omer presented without leaven. The "bikkurim" offering during Shabuot is two loaves, consisting of two omers, presented with leaven. (Vayiqra 23:17)

The "resheet" is the "first" offering of the entire harvest, and it is presented by the priest. It "begins" the harvest cycle, and also begins the 50 day omer count to Shabuot when everyone in the Covenant brings their "first fruits" after the harvest is over in order to present them before YHWH.

Now we start to see the Temple service combined with the Appointed Times. This is the Bride joined together with the Lamb. They are the "firsts," marked and sealed just as the "firsts" of the barley harvest are marked and sealed by the priest before they are harvested and waved before YHWH. The "first" offering is presented by the Priest at the very beginning of the harvest. These "firsts" will be the final fulfillment of the Passover, following the work of the their Husband, the Lamb of Elohim – the first if the firsts. They will be presented by their High Priest Yahushua, Who is the High Priest according to the Melchizedek order.

We read that no deceit or guile was found in them. This was also said of the Lamb. They are a worthy offering. They were without "fault" which means they were without "spot or blemish." We will soon see that this is a trademark of the "Bride of the Lamb." (Ephesians 5:25) We will also see that where they stand is a great and mighty mountain representing a city – New Jerusalem. The mountain is not on earth. John had to be carried away in the spirit to see it. (Revelation 21:10)

This was previously revealed by the prophet Micah. *"I will make the lame a remnant, and the outcast a strong nation; so YHWH will **reign over** them in Mount Zion from now on, even* *forever.*" Micah 4:7 So we see that YHWH will reign over the earth in this mountain city. This is a heavenly city that likely remains above the earth "in the clouds" until it has been completely prepared after the 1,000 year reign.

Yahushua said He is coming in the clouds. It appears that Mount Zion will be over us – in the clouds. Remember that place between heaven and earth where Ezekiel was brought. This is the place associated with the Messiah since the very beginning. The earth has not been fully cleansed from all of the abominations. Yahushua and His unblemished Bride will not necessarily dwell in or on a city or a land littered with dead men's bones and the blood of the wicked. That is why Yahushua went to prepare a place in the heavens for His Bride. Not until the planet is "koshered" by fire and renewed will it be a suitable dwelling place for the Bride on the eighth day.

Those who dwell within and make up the city are the barley offering – the first of the harvest. The firstfruits will follow as they are later gathered from all over the world and brought to the mountain.

So now we start to see the final cycles of the Appointed Times that likely begin at or during the Jubilee on Day 10 of Month 7 in the 120th Jubilee Year. Remember that the Jubilee count consists of seven periods of seven years, known as Shemittah cycles.

After the seventh year of the seventh Shemittah cycle we have the 50th year that is also the 8th year in that last cycle. That 8th year, the Jubilee year, follows the seventh year in the seventh Shemittah cycle and begins on Day 10 of Month 7, not Day 1 of Month 1.

Of course, this symbolizes the 8th day of the Covenant, so we should expect an important fulfillment on the Feast of the Eighth Day – Shemini Atzeret. Shemini Atzeret falls on the eight day after the beginning of the Seven

Day Feast of Succot – the Feast of Ingathering. This "eighth day" is actually Day 22 of Month 7.

Since every seventh year in the Shemittah Cycle is a Sabbath year, the 49th and 50th years combine as two consecutive Sabbath years. Every seventh year is called "the year of release." (Debarim 15:9) It is a year when Hebrews are released from bondage, and debts are forgiven at the end of the year. (Debarim 15:1-12) So we should expect to see a repeat of the pattern involving the exodus from Egypt in a 49th year preceding a Jubilee year.

Once the House of Yisrael has been released from their "debt" of punishment, and their period of bondage, they will then be ready to inherit their Land during the Year of Jubilee in the 50th year.

If it happens that there are 13 months in the Jubilee year we find ourselves 7 months later on Day 10 of Month 1 which is Lamb selection day. The Passover begins on Day 14 in the evening following the sunset of Day 13. The question is what has happened during the 7 month period from the beginning of the Jubilee year until Month 1, which marks a new Civil Year - possibly judgment and restoration at the same time. Indeed, we know that the end of the age culminates with the Day of YHWH. It is not only a "day" of judgments, but YHWH also fights for His people during this time.

We can read about the Day of YHWH in many different passages, including Zechariah.

"*¹ Behold, the day of YHWH is coming, and your spoil will be divided in your midst. ² For I will gather all the nations to battle against Jerusalem; the city shall be taken, the houses rifled, and the women ravished. Half of the city shall go into captivity, but the remnant of the people shall not be cut off from the city. ³ Then YHWH will go forth and fight against those*

nations, as He fights in the day of battle. ⁴ And in that day His feet will stand on the Mount of Olives, which faces Jerusalem on the east. And the Mount of Olives shall be split in two, from east to west, making a very large valley; half of the mountain shall move toward the north, and half of it toward the south. ⁵ Then you shall flee through My mountain valley, for the mountain valley shall reach to Azal. Yes, you shall flee as you fled from the earthquake in the days of Uzziah king of Yahudah. Thus YHWH my Elohim will come, and all the saints with You. ⁶ It shall come to pass in that day that there will be no light; the lights will diminish. ⁷ It shall be one day which is known to YHWH - Neither day nor night. But at evening time it shall happen that it will be light. ⁸ And in that day it shall be that living waters shall flow from Jerusalem, half of them toward the eastern sea and half of them toward the western sea; In both summer and winter it shall occur. ⁹ And YHWH shall be King over all the earth. In that day it shall be YHWH is One, and His Name One. ¹⁰ All the land shall be turned into a plain from Geba to Rimmon south of Jerusalem. Jerusalem shall be raised up and inhabited in her place from Benjamin's Gate to the place of the First Gate and the Corner Gate, and from the Tower of Hananel to the king's winepresses. ¹¹ The people shall dwell in it; and no longer shall there be utter destruction, but Jerusalem shall be safely inhabited. ¹² And this shall be the plague with which YHWH will strike all the people who fought against Jerusalem: Their flesh shall dissolve while they stand on their feet, their eyes shall dissolve in their sockets, and their tongues shall dissolve in their mouths. ¹³ It shall come to pass in that day that a great panic from YHWH will be among them. Everyone will seize the hand of his

neighbor, and raise his hand against his neighbor's hand; [14] Yahudah also will fight at Jerusalem. And the wealth of all the surrounding nations shall be gathered together: Gold, silver, and apparel in great abundance. [15] Such also shall be the plague on the horse and the mule, on the camel and the donkey, and on all the cattle that will be in those camps. So shall this plague be. [16] And it shall come to pass that everyone who is left of all the nations which came against Jerusalem shall go up from year to year to worship the King, YHWH of hosts, and to keep the Feast of Tabernacles. [17] And it shall be that whichever of the families of the earth do not come up to Jerusalem to worship the King, YHWH of hosts, on them there will be no rain. [18] If the family of Egypt will not come up and enter in, they shall have no rain; they shall receive the plague with which YHWH strikes the nations who do not come up to keep the Feast of Tabernacles. [19] This shall be the punishment of Egypt and the punishment of all the nations that do not come up to keep the Feast of Tabernacles. [20] In that day "HOLINESS TO YHWH" shall be engraved on the bells of the horses. The pots in YHWH's house shall be like the bowls before the altar. [21] Yes, every pot in Jerusalem and Judah shall be holiness to YHWH of hosts. Everyone who sacrifices shall come and take them and cook in them. In that day there shall no longer be a Canaanite in the House of YHWH of hosts."
Zechariah 14:1-21

This is a really amazing prophecy. First Jerusalem will be attacked and pillaged. All the nations shall be gathered to battle against Jerusalem. We previously mentioned when Babylon and Rome destroyed Jerusalem, but there has never been a time when <u>all the nations</u> battled against Jerusalem. They will partially succeed and commit atrocities, but

nothing to the extent that occurred in 70 CE.

YHWH will then fight for the City. The phrase "His feet will stand" on the Mount of Olives has confused many. This does not necessarily mean that the feet of YHWH will actually touch down on the Mount of Olives. He calls the earth "His footstool." (Isaiah 66:1) This is likely a poetic allusion to YHWH splitting the mountain and fighting for His people, as He did for David.

Read the song of David describing YHWH saving him from his enemies. "*7 In my distress I called upon YHWH, and cried out to my Elohim; He heard my voice from His Temple, and my cry entered His ears. 8 Then the earth shook and trembled, the foundations of heaven quaked and were shaken, because He was angry. 9 Smoke went up from His nostrils, and devouring fire from His mouth; coals were kindled by it. 10 He bowed the heavens also, and came down with darkness under His feet. 11 He rode upon a cherub, and flew; and He was seen upon the wings of the wind. 12 He made darkness canopies around Him, dark waters and thick clouds of the skies. 13 From the brightness before Him coals of fire were kindled. 14 YHWH thundered from heaven, and the Most High uttered His voice. 15 He sent out arrows and scattered them; Lightning bolts, and He vanquished them. 16 Then the channels of the sea were seen, the foundations of the world were uncovered, at the rebuke of YHWH, at the blast of the breath of His nostrils. 17 He sent from above, He took me, He drew me out of many waters.*" 2 Samuel 22:7-17

So the Mount of Olives will be as if YHWH stood on it, it will actually split in two. It does not necessarily mean that He will literally come down to earth at that time. In fact, He is clearly not there, because He tells His people to flee through the valley that He created. If He were present his people would have no need to flee.

Again, people link the passage in Zechariah with the description of the ascension of Yahushua in Acts 1. Here is what the text provides: "*⁹ Now when He had spoken these things, while they watched, He was taken up, and a cloud received Him out of their sight. ¹⁰ And while they looked steadfastly toward heaven as He went up, behold, two men stood by them in white apparel, ¹¹ who also said, Men of Galilee, why do you stand gazing up into heaven? This same Yahushua, who was taken up from you into heaven, will so come in like manner as you saw Him go into heaven.*" Acts 1:9-11

Because of this passage, people assume that Yahushua will be setting foot on the Mount of Olives when the event in Zechariah occurs. That is not what the text says. It was not referring to the location, but rather "the manner" in which Yahushua will be returning – "in the clouds."

Instead, He will fight from His Throne. We already saw how YHWH fights for His people in the examples of Joshua and Gideon. The same will likely occur here. The common translation of Zechariah can be misleading due to numerous translation errors. It appears to be saying that YHWH will come returning with His saints, but this scenario conflicts with the fact that the text is instructing His people to flee. Why would they be fleeing if YHWH had just set down on the Mount of Olives with His saints? The pertinent portion of Zechariah 14:5 says: "*Come YHWH all the set apart congregation.*" So the text does not necessarily describe what people interpret it to mean.

Remember He sends His messengers to gather His people. We previously saw the Lamb on Mount Zion in the Heavens with the 144,000. So it appears that Yahushua will be coming in the clouds on Mount Zion. This could be a portal or star gate being opened as Yaakob saw in His vision at Beth El.

Notice that YHWH will be King "over" the earth. The Hebrew is "al" (𐤋𐤏) and it means: "above, highest, the top." This is a fulfillment of "The Shema" - a fulfillment of the Covenant. "*And YHWH shall be King over all the earth. In*

that day it shall be - YHWH is one, and His Name one."
Zechariah 14:9

We know that this will occur before the Millennial Kingdom, because the text actually follows with some information concerning the celebration of the Feasts and sacrifices during that time. The people will be strictly judged if they disobey the commandments. This is how Messiah will be ruling with a rod of iron.

At that time Jerusalem will be a Set Apart City. We know this from the references of "Holiness to YHWH." This was the inscription on the breastplate of the High Priest as well as his crown. *"You shall also make a plate of pure gold and engrave on it, like the engraving of a signet: HOLINESS TO YHWH."* Shemot 28:36. *"Then they made the plate of the holy crown of pure gold, and wrote on it an inscription like the engraving of a signet: "HOLINESS TO YHWH."* Shemot 39:30

The Hebrew word for "signet" is "howtam" (𐤉𐤗𐤕𐤀𐤄) and it means: "seal." So the High Priest was sealed with the Name of YHWH. He was "holy" which is "qadosh" (𐤅𐤃𐤒) in Hebrew. It means: "set apart."

All of Yisrael was to be "sealed" and set apart unto YHWH. *"Yisrael was holiness to YHWH, the first fruits (resheet) of His increase."* Jeremiah 2:3 So we can see that the Capital City of the Millennial Kingdom will be set apart – Qadosh to YHWH.

If the pattern of the exodus is to be repeated, those in the Covenant will find themselves being re-gathered from the 4 corners of the earth. So we continue to see the patterns of the Appointed Times and their progressive fulfillment.

Now sequentially, in the Revelation we read that Babylon has fallen. Just as Egypt was plagued up to and including Passover, so Babylon will finally be decimated, when the Bride is redeemed out of Babylon. Those with the mark are then severely judged.

The roadmap back to the Land is through the Torah and the Appointed Times. "*Here is the patience of the saints; here are those who keep the commandments of Elohim and the faith of Yahushua.*" Revelation 14:12 Those who keep the Commandments will find their way. It will light their path, just as Yahushua described in the parable of the Ten Virgins. The righteous acts of the Bride are what set her apart. It is a true demonstration of her love. This is why when asked what was the greatest commandment, Yahuhsua stated: "*Shema Yisrael.*"

"*29 . . . The first of all the commandments is: 'Hear (Shema) Yisrael, YHWH our Elohim, YHWH is one. 30 And you shall love YHWH your Elohim with all your heart, with all your soul, with all your mind, and with all your strength.' This is the first commandment.*" Mark 12:29-30 Those who love YHWH obey Him, and through their obedience they will be in the right place at the right time when the Bride is called.

YHWH created all things and through creation we see that everything is cyclical. Therefore the end in Hebraic thought leads back to a beginning, the renewal of another cycle. The Appointed Times are described as "cycles of righteousness." (Psalms 23:3) Through these cycles of righteousness those in the Covenant will find the way back to the House. That is why Yahushua called Himself "the Way, the Truth and the Life." John 14:6 As Yahushua walked and lived the Torah He not only showed us how to live, He also fulfilled the requirements of the Covenant that would allow restoration to occur.

After the Passover, during the Feast of Unleavened Bread, when the First Barley offering is made it marks the beginning of the Omer Count. So during the 50th year, we start the count of seven sevens to the 50th day – Shabuot. It is during that 50 day period that the grain crops are harvested – the barley followed by the wheat. These grain first fruits are

gathered from all of the land, and brought to the House of YHWH where they are presented.

Here is how the earth will be harvested. "*14 Then I looked, and behold, a white cloud, and on the cloud sat One like the Son of Man, having on His head a golden crown, and in His hand a sharp sickle. 15 And another messenger came out of the Temple, crying with a loud voice to Him who sat on the cloud, Thrust in Your sickle and reap, for the time has come for You to reap, for the harvest of the earth is ripe. 16 So He who sat on the cloud thrust in His sickle on the earth, and the earth was reaped. 17 Then another messenger came out of the Temple which is in heaven, he also having a sharp sickle. 18 And another messenger came out from the altar, who had power over fire, and he cried with a loud cry to him who had the sharp sickle, saying, Thrust in your sharp sickle and gather the clusters of the vine of the earth, for her grapes are fully ripe. 19 So the messenger thrust his sickle into the earth and gathered the vine of the earth, and threw it into the great winepress of the wrath of Elohim. 20 And the winepress was trampled outside the city, and blood came out of the winepress, up to the horses' bridles, for one thousand six hundred furlongs.*" Revelation 14:14-20*

Notice there are two harvesters described with two different sickles. The first appears to be Yahushua sitting in the clouds. From this place above the earth He is harvesting the grain – likened to the "sons." The other angel came out and later harvests the grapes, those who will be thrown into the winepress.

So we see the grain harvest followed by the fruit harvest. The grain harvest was performed by Yahushua, which must be threshed and winnowed. That is why the House of YHWH was built on a threshing floor in Jerusalem. Yahushua will harvest the earth, and the grain will be threshed and winnowed. This process involves removing the outer husk to get to the kernel – the life source of the grain. Yahushua needs to remove our hearts of stone

and give us hearts of flesh. He will take away our corrupted flesh and give us new bodies so that we can live with Him in the House.

This is His harvest, and it is possible that during the 50 Day Omer Count, the promise of the 50 Year Jubilee is being fulfilled as the outcasts of Yisrael leaving their places of exile and returning to the Land.

Here is an interesting point to consider. Yahushua was resurrected during the Omer Count and ascended into the heavens on Day 41 of the Omer Count. Beginning at Succot, there were 41 camps that the Yisraelites stayed in after they left Egypt, and before they entered into the Promised Land. (Bemidbar 33) Therefore, if these patterns have future meaning, we may see 41 different "camps" around the earth while the people are being re-gathered.

This re-gathering will likely take place while judgments are rendered upon the planet, because it appears that the returning exiles will be on clean up duty. Something happened in the Land that opens the door for their return. This may possibly be the attack on Jerusalem by all the nations as described in Zechariah 12 or through the attack described in Psalm 83.

Right now, those who follow Messiah are not welcome to move into the Land – only to visit. There is a strong "anti-christ" spirit pervading the modern State of Yisrael. Therefore, we will likely see judgment befall those in the modern State of Yisrael who do not follow YHWH as a way of preparing the Land for the re-gathering of the exiles – those who have the testimony of Yahushua and obey the commandments.

After the grain harvest and the Feast of Shabuot, there is another harvest season leading up to the Feasts of the seventh month. The grape harvest described in the text was not performed by Yahushua. That harvest will occur before the seventh month. It is performed by a messenger with the sharp sickle. The harvest of the seventh month progresses toward Yom Teruah, Yom Kippur and culminates with Succot which is called the Feast of Ingathering.

While the grain was threshed and winnowed on a threshing floor to get to the kernel inside, the grapes are crushed in a winepress "outside the city." This event was described by Joel, and it describes the regathering associated with the reaping of the harvests and the Day of YHWH. It is a day of rendering judgment upon the nations.

"¹ For behold, in those days and at that time, when I bring back the captives of Yahudah and Jerusalem, ² I will also gather all nations, and bring them down to the Valley of Yehoshaphat; and I will enter into judgment with them there on account of My people, My heritage Yisrael, whom they have scattered among the nations; they have also divided up My land. ³ They have cast lots for My people, have given a boy as payment for a harlot, and sold a girl for wine, that they may drink. ⁴ Indeed, what have you to do with Me, O Tyre and Sidon, and all the coasts of Philistia? Will you retaliate against Me? But if you retaliate against Me, swiftly and speedily I will return your retaliation upon your own head; ⁵ Because you have taken My silver and My gold, and have carried into your temples My prized possessions. ⁶ Also the people of Yahudah and the people of Jerusalem you have sold to the Greeks, that you may remove them far from their borders. ⁷ Behold, I will raise them out of the place to which you have sold them, and will return your retaliation upon your own head. ⁸ I will sell your sons and your daughters into the hand of the people of Yahudah, and they will sell them to the Sabeans, to a people far off; For YHWH has spoken. ⁹ Proclaim this among the nations: Prepare for war! Wake up the mighty men, let all the men of war draw near, let them come up. ¹⁰ Beat your plowshares into swords and your pruning hooks into spears; Let the weak say, I am strong. ¹¹ Assemble and come, all you nations, and gather together all around. Cause Your mighty ones to go down

there, O YHWH. [12] *Let the nations be wakened, and come up to the Valley of Jehoshaphat; For there I will sit to judge all the surrounding nations.* [13] *Put in the sickle, for the harvest is ripe. Come, go down; For the winepress is full, the vats overflow - For their wickedness is great.* [14] *Multitudes, multitudes in the valley of decision! For the day of YHWH is near in the valley of decision.* [15] *The sun and moon will grow dark, and the stars will diminish their brightness.* [16] *YHWH also will roar from Zion, and utter His voice from Jerusalem; The heavens and earth will shake; but the YHWH will be a shelter for His people, and the strength of the children of Yisrael.*" Joel 3:1-16

The word "Yehoshaphat" means: "YHWH judged." The nations will be gathered in the valley to be judged. It is the valley of decision. Decisions will be made and the verdict will be rendered. This all directs us the the sounding of the final shofar.

After the messenger there was another great sign of heaven. (Revelation 15:1). This is likely Yom Teruah, the same day that the previous sign of the Messiah was seen. It is the day when the final shofar is traditionally sounded.

There are seven plagues leading up to Yom Kippur – the Day of Atonement. We know this from the following description of what is going on in the heavenly Temple. "*The Temple was filled with smoke from the glory of Elohim and from His power, and no one was able to enter the temple till the seven plagues of the seven angels were completed.*" Revelation 15:8

Yom Kippur is a time when no one is allowed in the Temple while the High Priest makes atonement. It is also a time associated with judgment. (See Vayiqra 16) So the 7 plagues of judgment will likely begin to be poured out on a future Yom Kippur.

Remember that once every 50 years Yom Kippur begins the Jubilee. It is a great day of joy as the Jubilee shofar is blasted marking the "restoration of all things." This has

been a prophetic rehearsal established since man was expelled from the Garden. It is a time when those with land rights have the ability to return to the Land of their inheritance.

The Jubilee cycle culminates with the completion of the last Shemittah year, and the beginning of the Jubilee year. So the Jubilee year is a one year period that begins at Yom Kippur and ends at Yom Kippur. So this year of restoration is couched between the Day of Atonements - a time specifically associated with judgment. Interestingly, the Day of YHWH is the culmination of the judgment of YHWH and it lasts for one year. Of course, judgment is what we read about next in the text.

"*¹ Then I heard a loud voice from the Temple saying to the seven angels, Go and pour out the bowls of the wrath of Elohim on the earth. ² So the first went and poured out his bowl upon the earth, and a foul and loathsome sore came upon the men who had the mark of the beast and those who worshiped his image. ³ Then the second angel poured out his bowl on the sea, and it became blood as of a dead man; and every living creature in the sea died. ⁴ Then the third angel poured out his bowl on the rivers and springs of water, and they became blood. ⁵ And I heard the angel of the waters saying: You are righteous, O Master, The One who is and who was and who is to be, because You have judged these things. ⁶ For they have shed the blood of set apart ones and prophets, and You have given them blood to drink. For it is their just due. ⁷ And I heard another from the altar saying, Even so, YHWH El Shaddai, true and righteous are Your judgments. ⁸ Then the fourth angel poured out his bowl on the sun, and power was given to him to scorch men with fire. ⁹ And men were scorched with great heat, and they blasphemed the Name of Elohim who has power over these plagues; and they did not repent and give Him glory. ¹⁰ Then the fifth angel poured out his bowl on the throne of the beast, and his kingdom became full of darkness; and they gnawed their tongues because of the pain. ¹¹ They blasphemed the Elohim of heaven because of their pains and their* sores, and did not repent of their deeds. ^{12} Then the sixth angel poured out his bowl on the great river Euphrates, and its water was dried up, so that the way of the kings from the east might be prepared. ^{13} And I saw three unclean spirits like frogs coming out of the mouth of the dragon, out of the mouth of the beast, and out of the mouth of the false prophet. ^{14} For they are spirits of demons, performing signs, which go out to the kings of the earth and of the whole world, to gather them to the battle of that great day of El Shaddai. ^{15} Behold, I am coming as a thief. Blessed is he who watches, and keeps his garments, lest he walk naked and they see his shame. ^{16} And they gathered them together to the place called in Hebrew, Armageddon. ^{17} Then the seventh angel poured out his bowl into the air, and a loud voice came out of the Temple of heaven, from the throne, saying, It is done! ^{18} And there were noises and thunderings and lightnings; and there was a great earthquake, such a mighty and great earthquake as had not occurred since men were on the earth. ^{19} Now the great city was divided into three parts, and the cities of the nations fell. And great Babylon was remembered before Elohim, to give her the cup of the wine of the fierceness of His wrath. ^{20} Then every island fled away, and the mountains were not found. ^{21} And great hail from heaven fell upon men, each hailstone about the weight of a talent. Men blasphemed Elohim because of the plague of the hail, since that plague was exceedingly great." Revelation 16:1-21

This text should dispel any notion of a pre-tribulation rapture. First of all, the bowls sound very similar to the plagues rendered upon Egypt. In fact, they are plagues. Just as the plagues were rendered upon the gods of Egypt, so these plagues are rendered upon the gods of the world. The serpent and the Nephilim who have made themselves gods are on the planet receiving their punishment along with those who worshipped them. This will be a fulfillment of the previous exodus from Egypt. It is the fulfimment of the prophecies concerning a greater exodus and a return for Yisrael.

Remember that while Egypt was undergoing the plagues, the Children of Yisrael were set apart. This will also occur in the end. Those who obey the commandments will remain set apart, and will not be harmed. This will likely draw the remnant of nations into the Covenant, just as occurred in Egypt.

Through these plagues, the Covenant people may be released from their captivity. Remember that the Nile will be dried up for the return of Yisrael in a future Exodus. (Isaiah 11:15-16). It appears that the Euphrates will be dried up to draw in the armies of the beast, using Yisrael as bait, just as was done with Pharaoh and his armies. Remember also that the city of Babylon and the Kingdom of Babylon were defeated by Cyrus when he lowered the Euphrates River. How appropos!

The future return of Yisrael and the eventual judgment upon the planet are intimately combined, just as they were in Egypt. There are certain key events that link Ezekiel 38, Zechariah 14 and Revelation 16 such as the great earthquake, an attack from a great army and YHWH fighting for His people using great hailstones. Also, men will be killing one another in great numbers in panic and confusion. They will be food for vultures. Of course, Yahuhsua indicated this would be an event at His return. (Matthew 24:28)

As with the exodus from Egypt, the purpose of the final plagues will also be so that the world will know the great Name of YHWH. This was the purpose of the demonstration of power against Gog and Magog. *"Thus I will magnify Myself and sanctify Myself, and I will be known in the eyes of many nations. Then they shall know that I am YHWH."* Ezekiel 38:23

Again, concerning Magog we read: *"⁶ And I will send fire on Magog and on those who live in security in the coastlands.*

Then they shall know that I am YHWH. ⁷ *So I will make My Set Apart Name known in the midst of My people Yisrael, and I will not let them profane My Set Apart Name anymore.* <u>*Then the nations shall know that I am YHWH, the Set Apart One in Yisrael.*</u> ⁸ *Surely it is coming, and it shall be done, says Adonai YHWH.* <u>*This is the day of which I have spoken.*</u>" Ezekiel 39:6-8

This is why many link the Gog/Magog attack with the Battle of Armageddon. While there are many similarities, there are also clear differences between the two events. They are not insurmountable, and those differences could certainly be resolved as time progresses. As most matters concerning the end of the age – time will tell.

The Battle of Armageddon is associated with a place called Armageddon. It is only referenced once in the Scriptures and is typically associated with "har'megiddo" – the mountain of Megiddo. How interesting that Megiddo was a stronghold for the House of Yisrael. It is literally a "mountain of Yisrael" where the Gog/Magog attack is supposed to occur.

Now many have trouble associating these to events together because of the timing. As previously discussed, there will be seven months of cleaning up dead bodies, and there will be seven years of burning the weapons for fuel after the Gog/Magog invasion. Those who have difficulty linking this battle to Armageddon cannot comprehend these activities occurring commensurate with the return of the Messiah. They mistakenly assume that the world will somehow be transformed upon the return of Yahushua, but this is not the case.

The world will have been devastated, and exist in a state of ruin. The condition will likely resemble the earth after the previous destruction, the "katabole" (καταβολῆς), referred to as *'foundation of the world."* The kingdoms of the world will have been utterly destroyed, but this will also lay the foundation and become the "birthing" for the Kingdom of YHWH. YHWH planted a garden and established His Kingdom on Earth after the previous "katabole." The world outside the Garden was in a state of destruction compared to the perfection in the Garden. Just as Adam was to rule over His Kingdom, Yahushua as the Son of Elohim and a son of Adam, the Last Adam, will establish the Kingdom in the 7th Millenium. It will be a time of "watching and tending" as mankind rebuilds. As the rebuilding previously began in the Garden, in the future it will begin in Jerusalem.

The "sons of the living El" will reign on earth, and have access to the Throne. Yahushua will reconnect the heavens and the earth as we saw the Aleph Taw ($\mathsf{X}\mathsf{\acute{K}}$) connecting the heavens and the earth in the first sentence in Beresheet. It is very likely that they will access the Throne from Beth El – the gate to the Heavens.

This is what the Prophet Isaiah was alluding to when he declared: "*² Now it shall come to pass in the latter days that the mountain of YHWH's House shall be established on the top of the mountains, and shall be exalted above the hills; and all nations shall flow to it. ³ Many people shall come and say, Come, and let us go up to the mountain of YHWH, to the House of the Elohim (Beth El) of Yaakob; He will teach us His ways, and we shall walk in His paths. For out of Zion shall go forth the Torah, and the word of YHWH from Jerusalem.*" Isaiah 2:2-3

The Mountain of YHWH's House is Mount Zion. Yahushua will be "coming in the clouds," and we will likely see Mount Zion above the Promised Land – "on the top of the mountains." This was what the New World Order envisioned, as seen in the seal of the United States of America.

It is important not forget, the Nephilim were the fallen Sons of Elohim. They previously had access to Mount Zion and the Throne. They had seen what Mount Zion looked like, and that is why they built pyramid shaped depictions of Mount Zion in their Babylonian system. They have been mimicking YHWH and setting up a counterfeit kingdom since their fall.

So in the future, if the sons of the living El want to "go up" to Mount Zion, they will likely go to Beth El and ascend through the gate up to Mount Zion. The sons of the living El will be taught the Torah, and they will then bring that Torah to the nations.

After the judgment, Yahushua will be rebuilding from the ruins. He will be doing this through His people who have been transformed into "sons of the living El." This will likely be a training period for these "sons" as they learn to rule and reign, replacing the previous sons of Elohim who were given power, authority and dominion over the nations. The people living on the earth will clearly need fuel for fire, and the 7 year period may be the much needed "sabbath" for the planet to regroup and regrow after the previous devestation.

That having been said, the people of YHWH will clearly be be present during this these prophesied battles. Notice the admonition between the sixth and the seventh plagues to "watch." The word in Hebrew is "shamar" and it means: "to guard and protect." This is what Adam was commanded and it is a specific allusion to the duty of the priest in the Temple to "watch" and "keep" the fire on the altar burning throughout the night. The fire from the altar needed to be ready for the services in the morning – specifically the morning offering and the incense offering. This is the very incense that we saw from the Temple service described in The Revelation.

It is imperative that the priest in charge of the altar at night stay awake and attend to his duties. He cannot fall asleep and let the fire go out. The High Priest comes in the night, before sunrise – like a thief in the night. If he finds the priest sleeping he will take embers from the altar and burn the clothes of the sleeping priest. That priest will then run out naked and ashamed, having failed to accomplish his task. They were not supposed to fall asleep and they were supposed to keep their fires burning. So this warning is given to the servants who are to become the "sons of the living El."

Yahushua repeatedly told His disciples to watch, and that was the point of the parable of the 10 virgins. The 10 virgins obviously represent the House of Yisrael - the 10 tribes who were previously divorced from YHWH. The only way that they can be restored to the Covenant, through marriage, is if they are restored to the status of virgins. The reason that they are virgins is because they have been "sprinkled" by the blood of the Lamb. (Isaiah 52:15 and Ezekiel 36:25). They have been made clean and pure. This is why there was a distinction made between the House of Yisrael and the House of Yahudah regarding the renewed Covenant in Jeremiah 31, when Ephraim is referred to as the virgin Yisrael returning from the ends of the earth.

YHWH renews the Covenant uniquely with the House of Yisrael through His Son. Those who trust in the Son will have the Torah written in their minds and on their hearts. These are the ones who have their hearts circumcised. These are the ones who will become the Bride. The male organ was circumcised in order to enter into the Covenant of Circumcision as a demonstration that it was about seed and a family. The Bride will be the partner in building the Kingdom of YHWH. She, therefore, must have a circumcised heart. This Bride must be known by the Bridegroom, and who she is will remain a mystery until the end.

There is another bride described as a mystery in the Revelation. She is the opposite of the Bride of YHWH, and is described as a Great Harlot. The Revelation goes to great

lengths to describe the Great Harlot, and the judgment to be rendered upon her. While she may believe that she is the true bride, she is not. She is actually the bride of the serpent.

Here is a description of the Great Harlot:

"¹ Then one of the seven angels who had the seven bowls came and talked with me, saying to me, Come, I will show you the judgment of the great harlot who sits on many waters, ² with whom the kings of the earth committed fornication, and the inhabitants of the earth were made drunk with the wine of her fornication. ³ So he carried me away in the Spirit into the wilderness. And I saw a woman sitting on a scarlet beast which was full of names of blasphemy, having seven heads and ten horns. ⁴ The woman was arrayed in purple and scarlet, and adorned with gold and precious stones and pearls, having in her hand a golden cup full of abominations and the filthiness of her fornication. ⁵ And on her forehead a name was written: MYSTERY, BABYLON THE GREAT, THE MOTHER OF HARLOTS AND OF THE ABOMINATIONS OF THE EARTH. ⁶ I saw the woman, drunk with the blood of the saints and with the blood of the martyrs of Yahushua. And when I saw her, I marveled with great amazement. ⁷ But the angel said to me, Why did you marvel? I will tell you the mystery of the woman and of the beast that carries her, which has the seven heads and the ten horns. ⁸ The beast that you saw was, and is not, and will ascend out of the bottomless pit (abyss) and go to perdition. And those who dwell on the earth will marvel, whose names are not written in the Scroll of Life from the foundation of the world, when they see the beast that was, and is not, and yet is. ⁹ Here is the mind which has wisdom: The seven heads are seven mountains on which the woman sits. ¹⁰ There are also

seven kings. Five have fallen, one is, and the other has not yet come. And when he comes, he must continue a short time. ¹¹ The beast that was, and is not, is himself also the eighth, and is of the seven, and is going to perdition. ¹² The ten horns which you saw are ten kings who have received no kingdom as yet, but they receive authority for one hour as kings with the beast. ¹³ These are of one mind, and they will give their power and authority to the beast. ¹⁴ These will make war with the Lamb, and the Lamb will overcome them, for He is Master of masters and King of kings; and those who are with Him are called, chosen, and faithful. ¹⁵ Then he said to me, The waters which you saw, where the harlot sits, are peoples, multitudes, nations, and tongues. ¹⁶ And the ten horns which you saw on the beast, these will hate the harlot, make her desolate and naked, eat her flesh and burn her with fire. ¹⁷ For Elohim has put it into their hearts to fulfill His purpose, to be of one mind, and to give their kingdom to the beast, until the words of Elohim are fulfilled. ¹⁸ And the woman whom you saw is that great city which reigns over the kings of the earth." Revelation 17:1-18

So this harlot is described as "mystery" - Babylon the Great. In other words, this Babylon is the greatest in rank, having outdone the Babylon of the past. Because it is a mystery, we can surmise that it is not the same Babylon of the past.

She is specifically identified with Babylon, a kingdom and a city, and she is a mother of harlots. So she has children that are harlots. This mystery kingdom appears to describe all of the Babylonian religions united. She includes *"peoples, multitudes, nations, and tongues."* This could include the Catholic Church, which actually incorporates countless apects of pagan religions, and all her offspring –

denominations throughout the world. She stands in stark contrast to the Bride of YHWH, identified with the City of Jerusalem. The Bride of YHWH has a different writing on her forehead. As we shall soon see, she is directly identified with YHWH.

This city of Mystery Babylon is on seven mountains, which represent kingdoms. We know this because the text immediately speaks of seven kings. Many people try to attribute this "city" to Rome, Jerusalem or Mecca, but it does not appear to be limited to one specific earthly city.

Again, we can speculate all we want, and there are numerous possibilities, but we may not know the ultimate fulfillment until the culmination of the end of the age. The point is that she will be directly opposed to YHWH, and the set apart ones, and she is carried by the beast.

There is now additional information provided about the seven headed beast. The beast *was, and is not, and will ascend out of the bottomless pit (abyss)."* We already discussed that Azazel and Abaddon were likely the same - "the destroyer." He was bound and locked in the abyss until his release at the fifth shofar. At the time the Revelation was written, just prior to the 1st century CE, the destroyer was in the past, he was not in the present because he was in the abyss. In the future he will ascend out of the abyss when the messenger with the key unlocks the gate. So now we can see how it will be like the days of Noah before the coming of the Messiah. The same Nephilim will be released back upon the earth. We also know that the destroyer is destined for perdition, so it seems to fit the description of the beast.

We also read of ten horns that are ten kings. The kings are likely front men empowered by the Nephilim. So while the Revelation describes everything that is actually occurring, all of mankind may not be aware of the actual identity of the beast and the powers behind these kings. In fact, it will likely only be those with wisdom and understanding who perceive what is actually happening. (Revelation 13:18, 17:9)

These kings are given power for one hour. Remember that this is the duration that the Assembly of Philadelphia would be preserved through tribulation, so we may be dealing with the same period. In fact, the Assembly of Philadelphia will be preserved through a time of testing that will cover the entire world. One hour is also the duration of the judgment that is rendered upon Babylon through these 10 kings. (Revelation 18:10, 17, 19) So again, it appears that all these events are occurring simultaneously in the same "hour."

As we continue in the text, we read that there is another angel who declares that Babylon has fallen, followed by an admonition. *"And I heard another voice from heaven saying, 'Come out of her, My people, lest you share in her sins, and lest you receive of her plagues.'"* Revelation 18:4 So there are people of Elohim who need to come out of the harlot or they will be judged along with her. Again, the Assembly of Philadelphia os preserved because they keep the command to persevere. Yahushua specifically tells this Assembly that He is coming quickly, so they are present in the end.

Likewise, the judgment of the harlot Babylon is swift. *"5 For her sins have reached to heaven, and Elohim has remembered her iniquities. 6 Render to her just as she rendered to you, and repay her double according to her works; in the cup which she has mixed, mix double for her. 7 In the measure that she glorified herself and lived luxuriously, in the same measure give her torment and sorrow; for she says in her heart, I sit as queen, and am no widow, and will not see sorrow. 8 Therefore her plagues will come in one day - death and mourning and famine. And she will be utterly burned with fire, for strong is YHWH Elohim who judges her. 9 The kings of the earth who committed fornication and lived luxuriously with her will weep and lament for her, when they see the smoke of her burning, 10 standing at a distance for fear of her torment, saying, Alas, alas, that great city Babylon, that mighty city! For in one hour your judgment has come.*" Revelation 18:5-10

The statement of this harlot is reminiscent of Semiramis of Babylon, also known as Ishtar and Easter. Remember that after the death of Nimrod, she claimed that she was impregnated by the ascended Nimrod. This resulted in the birth of her son Tammuz, currently worshipped as Jesus through the Babylonian system of the Roman Catholic Church and her offspring the Protestant Christians.

The language used in the text is the same as we read about the "daughter of Babylon" in Isaiah 47. The punishment would come "suddenly" so we can see that these texts are linked. In fact, in Isaiah 48 we read about the Creator and the Redeemer declaring: "*I am the first and the last,*" and instructing His people to "flee" from Babylon and the Chaldeans.

"*20 Go forth from Babylon! Flee from the Chaldeans! With a voice of singing, Declare, proclaim this, utter it to the end of the earth; Say, YHWH has redeemed His servant Yaakob! 21 And they did not thirst when He led them through the deserts; He caused the waters to flow from the rock for them; He also split the rock, and the waters gushed out. 22 There is no peace, says YHWH, for the wicked.*" Isaiah 48:20-22

Again, the punishment rendered upon "mystery Babylon" is directly connected with the release of bondage and regathering of Yaakob. Notice also the direct reference to the exodus from Egypt, when YHWH provided water from the Rock – the Aben stone. During this time of provision for the regathered – there is no peace for the wicked. The righteous will be redeemed and the wicked will be judged. So here we can see how prophecies of old must be carefully examined and distinguished between past fulfillments and future fulfillments.

After the judgment of the harlot we hear about the wedding of the true Bride. *"⁹ Then he said to me, Write: <u>Blessed are those who are called to the marriage supper of the Lamb!</u> And he said to me, These are the true sayings of Elohim. ¹⁰ And I fell at his feet to worship him. But he said to me, "See that you do not do that! I am your fellow servant, and of your brethren who have the testimony of Yahushua. Worship Elohim! For the testimony of Yahushua is the spirit of prophecy."* Revelation 19:9-10

Remember that a traditional wedding involves a 7 day feast. That would be Succot, also known as the Feast of Tabernacles. This is a Feast focused on dwelling with YHWH, which is the goal of restoration. Succot is connected with leaving Egypt (Shemot 12:37), and returning to the Land. (Beresheet 33:17) It is the conclusion of the exodus.

It is the completion of all the harvests. The new wine is flowing and it is a time of great rejoicing. This is the great multitude gathered in heaven to attend the wedding. (Revelation 19:1-8)

Once the wedding is over and the King has married His Bride, He is ready to claim His Kingdom. The beast, the kings of the earth and the armies gathered together to make war against Him. He is on a white horse. The beast and the false prophet are cast alive into the lake of fire. All others are killed with the "sword" that proceeded out of the mouth of Yahushua.

"¹¹ Now I saw heaven opened, and behold, a white horse. And He who sat on him was called Faithful and True, and in righteousness He judges and makes war. ¹² His eyes were like a flame of fire, and on His head were many crowns. He had a name written that no one knew except Himself. ¹³ He was clothed with a robe dipped in blood, and His Name is called The Word of Elohim. ¹⁴ And the armies in heaven, clothed in fine linen, white and clean, followed Him on white horses. ¹⁵ Now out of His mouth goes a sharp sword, that with it He should strike the nations. <u>And He</u>

Himself will rule them with a rod of iron. He Himself treads the
winepress of the fierceness and wrath of Almighty Elohim. [16] *And
He has on His robe and on His thigh a name written: KING OF
KINGS AND MASTER OF MASTERS.* [17] Then I saw an angel
standing in the sun; and he cried with a loud voice, saying to all the
birds that fly in the midst of heaven, Come and gather together for
the supper of the great Elohim, [18] *that you may eat the flesh of kings,
the flesh of captains, the flesh of mighty men, the flesh of horses and
of those who sit on them, and the flesh of all people, free and slave,
both small and great.* [19] And I saw the beast, the kings of the earth,
and their armies, gathered together to make war against Him who
sat on the horse and against His army.* [20] *Then the beast was
captured, and with him the false prophet who worked signs in his
presence, by which he deceived those who received the mark of the
beast and those who worshiped his image. These two were cast alive
into the lake of fire burning with brimstone.* [21] *And the rest were
killed with the sword which proceeded from the mouth of Him who
sat on the horse. And all the birds were filled with their flesh.*"
Revelation 19:11-21

The description in Revelation of the great massacre of
the beast and the kings provides the answer to Yahushua's
riddle when He answered: "*Wherever the body is, there the
eagles will be gathered together.*" Luke 17:37 A messenger
actually calls the birds for this feast.

The method of slaughter is quite interesting. The
word used to describe the "sword" coming from the mouth of
Yahushua is "rhomphaia" (ῥομφαία). The typical word for
"sword" in the New Testament is "machaira" (μαχαίρα).
Another common Greek word for "sword" is "kopis" (κοπίς).
Here, the sword emitting from the mouth of Yahushua is not
just any normal sword. It is specially referred to as a "two
edged sword." (Revelation 1:16, 2:12). This appears to be in
direct contrast to the single curved bladed scimitar, that
currently represents the sword of submission in Islam.

This "sword" represents the "word." (Hebrews 4:12) It is not a metallic weapon, but rather a weapon of sound. Here we see the voice of Elohim rendering judgment upon the wicked.

Just as shown in Daniel, the Rock (the Messiah) destroys the beast – the final Kingdom. The dragon, representing satan, is bound and chained and thrown into the abyss for 1,000 years. This is the same place that the destroyer was held pending a future release. The same would occur with the dragon. After the 1,000 years he will be released to once again to deceive the nations. Notice that this is the same "pit" or "abyss" where the locust came from.

While the dragon awaits his future release, the ones killed by the beast are resurrected in what is known as "the first resurrection." These will be priests and will reign with the Messiah for 1,000 years.

"*4 And I saw thrones, and they sat on them, and judgment was committed to them. Then I saw the souls of those who had been beheaded for their witness to Yahushua and for the word of Elohim, who had not worshiped the beast or his image, and had not received his mark on their foreheads or on their hands. And they lived and reigned with Messiah for a thousand years. 5 But the rest of the dead did not live again until the thousand years were finished. This is the first resurrection. 6 Blessed and set apart is he who has part in the first resurrection. Over such the second death has no power, but they shall be priests of Elohim and of Messiah, and shall reign with Him a thousand years.*" Revelation 20:4-6

It is interesting that the martyrs are "beheaded" which tends to lend credence to the fact that Islam will be a major tool of the beast to persecute the set apart ones. If that is the case, then the mark would also be directly connected to moon worship.

This point will mark a resurrection of the dead as described in Daniel. "*1 At that time Michael shall stand up, the* great prince who stands watch over the sons of your people; and there shall be a time of trouble, *auch* as never was since there was a nation, *aven* to that time. *And at that time your people shall be delivered, every one who is found written in the Scroll.* ² *And many of those who sleep in the dust of the earth shall awake, some to everlasting life, some to shame and everlasting contempt.* ³ *Those who are wise shall shine like the brightness of the firmament, and those who turn many to righteousness like the stars forever and ever."* Daniel 12:1-3

Again, the stars are likened to the "sons of Elohim" so we see these in the first resurrection are essentially re-populating the Kingdom of YHWH. Those who are redeemed by the Messiah are adopted into the Kingdom and become "sons of the living El." (Hosea 1:10)

Very little is said in this text about the 1,000 year reign, probably because there is really no need for us to know specific details at this time. We need to focus on getting there. Then we will have much to learn.

We do know from the prophets that this will be the Sabbath Millenium – the Covenant of Peace. This Millennial Kingdom is a fulfillment of the Covenant made with David. Remember the unconditional Covenant made with David because of his heart to build a House for YHWH.

"*¹⁰ Moreover I will appoint a place for My people Yisrael, and will plant them, that they may dwell in a place of their own and move no more; nor shall the sons of wickedness oppress them anymore, as previously,* ¹¹ *since the time that I commanded judges to be over My people Yisrael, and have caused you to rest from all your enemies. Also YHWH tells you that He will make you a house.* ¹² *When your days are fulfilled and you rest with your fathers, I will set up your seed after you, who will come from your body, and I will establish his kingdom.* ¹³ *He shall build a house for My Name, and I will establish the throne of his kingdom forever.* ¹⁴ *I will be his Father, and he shall be My son. If he commits iniquity,*

I will chasten him with the rod of men and with the blows of the sons of men. *15* But My mercy shall not depart from him, as I took it from Saul, whom I removed from before you. *16* And your house and your kingdom shall be established forever before you. Your throne shall be established forever." 2 Shemuel 7:10-16

So the Messiah will establish the throne of David Forever, which means: "through the ages." It is a pattern to fulfill until the earth and all of creation is renewed. This was specifically prophesied by Isaiah: "*6* For unto us a Child is born, unto us a Son is given; and the government will be upon His shoulder. And His name will be called Wonderful, Counselor, Mighty God, Everlasting Father, Prince of Peace. *7* Of the increase of His government and peace there will be no end, Upon the throne of David and over His kingdom, to order it and establish it with judgment and justice from that time forward, even forever. The zeal of the Lord of hosts will perform this." Isaiah 9:6-7

This was also specifically provided by Gabriel: "*30* Then the angel said to her, Do not be afraid, Mary, for you have found favor with Elohim. *31* And behold, you will conceive in your womb and bring forth a Son, and shall call His name Yahushua. *32* He will be great, and will be called the Son of the Highest; and the Master YHWH will give Him the throne of His father David. *33* And He will reign over the House of Yaakob forever, and of His kingdom there will be no end." Luke 1:30-33

The time of Yahushua ruling over the earth will be on the Throne of David. The Throne of David was typified through the union of the Two Houses of Yaakob – the House of Yisrael and the House of Yahudah.

He will rule over the earth, likely above earth on Mount Zion. This may be the time when the Temple prophesied in Ezekiel is on the earth, sending forth water toward the east and the west.

This will be an incredible time. Healing waters will flow from the House and will actually make the Dead Sea come alive. Everywhere the river flows will grow trees for food and the water will contain an abundance of fish.

The House of YHWH will be restablished. "The Prince" will oversee the House, and the sons of Zadok will be restored to the Priesthood. All of the other Levites will be relegated to lower duties in the House as punishment for allowing Yisrael to fall away from YHWH in the past. The Prince will also provide the offerings for the Appointed Times, including Sabbaths and New Moons. (see Ezekiel 40-48) Interestingly, this revelation was given to Ezekiel at the start of a Jubilee. (see Ezekiel 40:1)

The weekly Sabbath has always been related to peace. Thus the greeting "Shabbat Shalom" – Sabbath Peace. This Sabbath Millenium is described as the time of the Covenant of Peace, although it will come about through the Day of YHWH. This peace will be preceded by judgment.

Through that process the fire that kills the wicked will refine the righteous. This is the salvation that we should be looking for. Interestingly, when most Christians consider the notion of salvation they look to the writings of Paul, as if Paul alone provides the "formula" for eternal life.

Let us take a moment and look at salvation. Here is an often quoted "formula" from the Letter to the Romans: "*that if you confess with your mouth the Lord Jesus and believe in your heart that God has raised Him from the dead, you will be saved.*" Romans 10:9

Interestingly, Paul is actually referencing Mosheh for this synopsis of salvation. Here is the quote in full context. "*[5] For Mosheh writes about the righteousness which is of the Torah, The man who does those things shall live by them. [6] But the righteousness of faith speaks in this way, Do not say in your heart, Who will ascend into heaven? (that is, to bring Messiah down from above) [7] or, Who will descend into the abyss? (that is, to bring Messiah up from the dead). [8] But what does it say? The word is*

*near you, in your mouth and in your heart (that is, the word of faith
which we preach):* ⁹ *that if you confess with your mouth the Master
Yahushua and believe in your heart that Elohim has raised Him
from the dead, you will be saved.* ¹⁰ *For with the heart one believes
unto righteousness, and with the mouth confession is made unto
salvation.* ¹¹ *For the Scripture says, Whoever believes on Him will
not be put to shame.* ¹² *For there is no distinction between Yahudim
and Greek, for the same Master over all is rich to all who call upon
Him.* ¹³ *For whoever calls on the Name of YHWH shall be saved."*
Romans 10:5-13

Many fail to make the connection that Paul was
simply teaching the Torah. He was writing about what the
Torah of Mosheh says. He was not providing a new formula
for salvation for Christians. He was elaborating upon the
words spoken by Mosheh in the text of Debarim.

Here is what Mosheh said to the Children of Yisrael
if they repented after straying away from YHWH: *"⁹ . . . For
YHWH will again rejoice over you for good as He rejoiced over
your fathers,* ¹⁰ *if you obey the voice of YHWH your Elohim, to
keep His commandments and His statutes which are written in this
Scroll of the Torah, and if you turn to YHWH your Elohim with
all your heart and with all your soul.* ¹¹ *For this commandment
which I command you today is not too difficult (mysterious) for
you, nor is it far off.* ¹² *It is not in heaven, that you should say, Who
will ascend into heaven for us and bring it to us, that we may hear it
and do it?* ¹³ *Nor is it beyond the sea, that you should say, Who will
go over the sea for us and bring it to us, that we may hear it and do
it?* ¹⁴ *But the word is very near you, in your mouth and in your
heart, that you may do it.* ¹⁵ *See, I have set before you today life and
good, death and evil,* ¹⁶ *in that I command you today to love
YHWH your Elohim, to walk in His ways, and to keep His
commandments, His statutes, and His judgments, that you may live
and multiply; and YHWH your Elohim will bless you in the land
which you go to possess." Debarim 30:9b-16*

Paul was simply showing that salvation was provided in the Torah, through the Messiah, and blessings came from obedience. This makes more sense since the Torah is the righteous instructions and Yahushua clearly indicated that He was teaching Mosheh.

In fact, Yahushua went so far as to state that Mosheh wrote about Him. *"⁴⁵ Do not think that I shall accuse you to the Father; there is one who accuses you - Mosheh, in whom you trust. ⁴⁶ For if you believed Mosheh, you would believe Me; for he wrote about Me."* John 5:45-46

In other words, the Torah was about Yahushua the Messiah coming for His Bride and establishing the Kingdom. The Commandments are essentially the rules of that Kingdom. That is why Yahushua specifically stated: *"Do not think that I came to destroy the Torah or the Prophets. I did not come to destroy but to fulfill."* Matthew 5:17

So salvation was provided through the Covenant. It was revealed through the life of Abraham, spoken by Mosheh and fulfilled by Yahushua. That Covenant path is the righteous path, and it is those on the path who will be the Redeemed. In fact, the fine linen that clothes the Bride are the righteous acts of the set apart ones. Righteous acts are defined by the Torah. In fact, the Torah is righteousness. (Psalm 119:172)

Remember the 1/3 of the "sons of Elohim" who were spared by Elijah? 153 went to Elijah. 102 (2/3) were burned by fire, and 51 (1/3) were spared. The gematria equivalent of the number 153 is "the sons of Elohim." So the 1/3 who were not burned by fire represent the 1/3 sons of Elohim who will pass through the fire.

"¹ In that day a fountain shall be opened for the house of David and for the inhabitants of Jerusalem, for sin and for uncleanness. ² It shall be in that day, says YHWH of hosts, that I will cut off the names of the idols from the land, and they shall no

longer be remembered. I will also cause the prophets and the unclean spirit to depart from the land. *3 It shall come to pass that if anyone still prophesies, then his father and mother who begot him will say to him, You shall not live, because you have spoken lies in the name of YHWH.' And his father and mother who begot him shall thrust him through when he prophesies. *4 And it shall be in that day that every prophet will be ashamed of his vision when he prophesies; they will not wear a robe of coarse hair to deceive. *5 But he will say, I am no prophet, I am a farmer; for a man taught me to keep cattle from my youth. *6 And one will say to him, What are these wounds between your arms? Then he will answer, Those with which I was wounded in the house of my friends. *7 Awake, O sword, against My Shepherd, against the Man who is My Companion, Says YHWH of hosts. Strike the Shepherd, and the sheep will be scattered; Then I will turn My hand against the little ones. *8 And it shall come to pass in all the land, says YHWH, That two-thirds in it shall be cut off and die, But one-third shall be left in it: *9 I will bring the one-third through the fire, will refine them as silver is refined, and test them as gold is tested. They will call on My Name, and I will answer them. I will say, This is My people and each one will say, YHWH is my Elohim." Zechariah 13:4-9

Here we see the 1/3 passing through the fire so that they can be refined. When we think of salvation, it is in the context of being saved from judgment. Recognize that this is the language of a restored Covenant relationship – "This is My People and YHWH is my Elohim." So in order to be "saved," we need to be in Covenant relationship with the Elohim of Yisrael.

Those who are refined will dwell in His Kingdom. Here is a description of that Kingdom. "*1 Oh, clap your hands, all you peoples! Shout to Elohim with the voice of triumph! *2 For YHWH Most High is awesome; He is a great King over all the earth. *3 He will subdue the peoples under us, and the nations under our feet. *4 He will choose our inheritance for us, the excellence of

Yaakob whom He loves. Selah ⁵ Elohim has gone up with a shout, YHWH with the sound of a shofar. ⁶ Sing praises to Elohim, sing praises! Sing praises to our King, sing praises! ⁷ For Elohim is the King of all the earth; sing praises with understanding. ⁸ Elohim reigns over the nations; Elohim sits on His holy throne. ⁹ The princes of the people have gathered together, the people of the Elohim of Abraham. For the shields of the earth belong to Elohim; He is greatly exalted." Psalm 47:1-9

Notice the sound of the shofar associated with the establishment of YHWH's Kingdom on Earth. YHWH is a great King <u>above</u> all the earth. Again we have the allusion to Him being over the earth, in the Heavens. He will be above, ruling <u>over</u> the earth. He reigns over the nations so there were still be divisions of different people around the earth.

When He establishes the Kingdom He will reign from Mount Zion. "¹ Great is YHWH, and greatly to be praised in the city of our Elohim, <u>in His set apart mountain</u>. ² <u>Beautiful in elevation</u>, the delight of the whole earth, is Mount Zion on the sides of the north, the city of the great King. ³ Elohim is in her palaces; He is known as her refuge. ⁴ For behold, the kings assembled, they passed by together. ⁵ They saw it, and so they marveled; they were troubled, they hastened away. ⁶ Fear took hold of them there, and pain, as of a woman in birth pangs, ⁷ As when You break the ships of Tarshish with an east wind. ⁸ As we have heard, so we have seen in the city of YHWH of hosts, in the city of our Elohim: Elohim will establish it forever. Selah ⁹ We have thought, O Elohim, on Your lovingkindness, in the midst of Your temple.10 According to Your Name, O Elohim, So is Your praise to the ends of the earth; your right hand is full of righteousness. ¹¹ Let Mount Zion rejoice, let the daughters of Yahudah be glad, because of Your judgments. ¹² Walk about Zion, and go all around her. Count her towers; ¹³ Mark well her bulwarks; consider her palaces; that you may tell it to the generation following. ¹⁴ For this is Elohim, our Elohim forever and ever; He will be our guide even to death." Psalm 48:1-14

It is important to understand all these descriptions of Mount Zion, and the establishment of the Kingdom, are within the context of a wedding. The culmination of everything revolves around YHWH providing a Bride for His Son Yahushua the Messiah.

Yahushua made this abundantly clear in one of His parables. *"² The kingdom of heaven is like a certain king who arranged a marriage for his son, ³ and sent out his servants to call those who were invited to the wedding; and they were not willing to come. ⁴ Again, he sent out other servants, saying, Tell those who are invited, See, I have prepared my dinner; my oxen and fatted cattle are killed, and all things are ready. Come to the wedding. ⁵ But they made light of it and went their ways, one to his own farm, another to his business. ⁶ And the rest seized his servants, treated them spitefully, and killed them. ⁷ But when the king heard about it, he was furious. And he sent out his armies, destroyed those murderers, and burned up their city. ⁸ Then he said to his servants, The wedding is ready, but those who were invited were not worthy. ⁹ Therefore go into the highways, and as many as you find, invite to the wedding. ¹⁰ So those servants went out into the highways and gathered together all whom they found, both bad and good. And the wedding hall was filled with guests. ¹¹ But when the king came in to see the guests, he saw a man there who did not have on a wedding garment. ¹² So he said to him, Friend, how did you come in here without a wedding garment? And he was speechless. ¹³ Then the king said to the servants, Bind him hand and foot, take him away, and cast him into outer darkness; there will be weeping and gnashing of teeth. ¹⁴ For many are called, but few are chosen."* Matthew 22:2-14

This Bride will live in the House of YHWH. The House now represented by the City of Jerusalem during the Millenial Reign. It is not on the earth during the Millenial Reign. It is in the heavens, likely "in the clouds" where Yahushua met with His gathered elect. It may be that Mount

Zion, the Renewed Jerusalem, is connected with the earthly Temple at Beth El – the gate to the heavens that leads up to the House of Elohim.

As stated previously, this may be the actual fulfillment of Isaiah 2:3. *"Many people shall come and say, Come, and let us go up to the mountain of YHWH, to the House of the Elohim of Yaakob; He will teach us His ways, and we shall walk in His paths. For out of Zion shall go forth the Torah, and the word of YHWH from Jerusalem."* So during the Millenial reign people may go up "Jacob's Ladder" at Beth El to see the Elohim of Yaakob. It will later come down from the Heavens as the New Jerusalem at the end of the ages.

Remember that the guests and the bride are not the same. Just because you are a guest, does not mean that you are the bride. In order to understand the identity of the individuals in the end it is important to understand when they are harvested. According to the parble of Yahushua, the timing of the wedding feast is important. It occurs <u>after</u> the king becomes furious and destroys those who killed His messengers.

That destruction is the Day of YHWH, so the Wedding occurs after the Day of YHWH – after the wrath of YHWH is poured out. This wedding feast ushers in the millennial kingdom. The millennial kingdom involves the Bride and the Bridegroom joined together as One, living together in the House ruling over the earth.

This was never the case with Yisrael, they were not permitted in the House due to the sin of the golden calf at Sinai. In the future this breach will be repaired and the relationship restored.

"¹ For Zion's sake I will not hold My peace, and for Jerusalem's sake I will not rest, until her righteousness goes forth as brightness, and her salvation as a lamp that burns. ² The Gentiles shall see your righteousness,

and all kings your glory. You shall be called by a new name, which the mouth of YHWH will name. ³ You shall also be a crown of glory in the hand of YHWH, and a royal diadem in the hand of your Elohim. ⁴ <u>You shall no longer be termed Forsaken, nor shall your land any more be termed Desolate; but you shall be called Hephzibah, and your land Beulah; For YHWH delights in you, and your land shall be married.</u> ⁵ For as a young man marries a virgin, so shall your sons marry you; and as the bridegroom rejoices over the bride, so shall your Elohim rejoice over you. ⁶ I have set watchmen on your walls, O Jerusalem; they shall never hold their peace day or night. You who make mention of YHWH, do not keep silent, ⁷ And give Him no rest till He establishes and till He makes Jerusalem a praise in the earth. ⁸ YHWH has sworn by His right hand and by the arm of His strength: Surely I will no longer give your grain as food for your enemies; and the sons of the foreigner shall not drink your new wine, for which you have labored. ⁹ But those who have gathered it shall eat it, and praise YHWH; those who have brought it together shall drink it in My holy courts. ¹⁰ Go through, go through the gates! Prepare the way for the people; Build up, Build up the highway! Take out the stones, lift up a banner for the peoples! ¹¹ Indeed YHWH has proclaimed to the end of the world: Say to the daughter of Zion, Surely your salvation is coming; Behold, His reward is with Him, and His work before Him. ¹² And they shall call them The Holy People, The Redeemed of YHWH; and you shall be called Sought Out, A City Not Forsaken." Isaiah 62:1-12

Here we can see the fulfillment of the Covenant of Marriage with the people and the Land. It is through this Convenant of Peace that we see the Bride restored to her

Husband.

"*¹ Sing, O barren, you who have not borne! Break forth into singing, and cry aloud, You who have not labored with child! For more are the children of the desolate than the children of the married woman,*" *says YHWH.* *² Enlarge the place of your tent, and let them stretch out the curtains of your dwellings; Do not spare; lengthen your cords, and strengthen your stakes.* *³ For you shall expand to the right and to the left, and your descendants will inherit the nations, and make the desolate cities inhabited.* *⁴ Do not fear, for you will not be ashamed; neither be disgraced, for you will not be put to shame; for you will forget the shame of your youth, and will not remember the reproach of your widowhood anymore.* *⁵ For your Maker is your Husband, YHWH of hosts is His name; and your Redeemer is the Holy One of Yisrael; He is called the Elohim of the whole earth.* *⁶ For YHWH has called you like a woman forsaken and grieved in spirit, like a youthful wife when you were refused, says your Elohim.* *⁷ For a mere moment I have forsaken you, but with great mercies I will gather you.* *⁸ With a little wrath I hid My face from you for a moment; but with everlasting kindness I will have mercy on you,*" *says YHWH, your Redeemer.* *⁹ For this is like the waters of Noah to Me; for as I have sworn that the waters of Noah would no longer cover the earth, so have I sworn that I would not be angry with you, nor rebuke you.* *¹⁰ <u>For the mountains shall depart and the hills be removed, but My kindness shall not depart from you, nor shall My Covenant of peace be removed, says YHWH, who has mercy on you.</u>* *¹¹ O you afflicted one, tossed with tempest, and not comforted, Behold, <u>I will lay your stones with colorful gems, and lay your foundations with sapphires.</u>* *¹² <u>I will make your pinnacles of rubies, your gates of crystal, and all your walls of precious stones.</u>* *¹³ All your children shall be taught by YHWH, And great shall be the peace of your children.* *¹⁴ In righteousness you shall be established; You shall be far from oppression, for you shall not fear; and from terror, for it shall not come near you.* *¹⁵ Indeed they shall surely assemble, but not because* *of Me. Whoever assembles against you shall fall for your sake. [16] Behold, I have created the blacksmith Who blows the coals in the fire, Who brings forth an instrument for his work; And I have created the spoiler to destroy. [17] No weapon formed against you shall prosper, and every tongue which rises against you in judgment you shall condemn. This is the heritage of the servants of YHWH, and their righteousness is from Me, Says YHWH."* Isaiah 54:1-17

After the Millenial Kingdom, at the end of year 7,000, YHWH will be finished with this cycle - the cycle of 7. Satan, the dragon that was bound and held in the Abyss, is unleashed for a short time.

He will go about to the 4 corners of the Earth and gather those opposed to YHWH against the City of Jerusalem. The Book of Revelation specifically references Gog-Magog, which was previously found in Ezekiel 38-39. As stated, this appears to be the same Gog who attacked the Mountains of Yisrael, but it is a different attack. The numbers gathered against YHWH will be like the sand of the sea. (Revelation 20:8)

It seems incredible that this many people would come against YHWH after the Millenial Kingdom period. It may be that they do not have access to Mount Zion and remain separated from Yahushua. Could it be that Yahushua is ruling by proxy through His resurrected servants?

Is it possible that they can actually look up at Mount Zion in the clouds. In other words, is it hovering in the realm and domain of the clouds? Maybe the ones who remain on earth become jealous of the ones who reside in the crystalline city above. Are they trying to storm the gates of Jerusalem so that they can take over the Kingdom and force their way into the House? This is not unlike what the serpent and the sons of Elohim had previously attempted. This is also what Nimrod was attempting with the Tower of Babel. Again, it appears that history repeats itself and the serpent dragon is

again able to deceive mankind.

"*7 Now when the thousand years have expired, Satan will be released from his prison *8 and will go out to deceive the nations which are in the four corners of the earth, Gog and Magog, to gather them together to battle, whose number is as the sand of the sea. *9 They went up on the breadth of the earth and surrounded the* camp of the set apart ones and the beloved city. And fire came down from Elohim out of heaven and devoured them. *10 The devil, who deceived them, was cast into the lake of fire and brimstone where the beast and the false prophet are. And they will be tormented day and night forever and ever. *11 Then I saw a great white throne and Him who sat on it, from whose face the earth and the heaven fled away. And there was found no place for them. *12 And I saw the dead, small and great, standing before Elohim, and books were opened. And another book was opened, which is the Scroll of Life. And the dead were judged according to their works, by the things which were written in the scrolls. *13 The sea gave up the dead who were in it, and Death and Hades delivered up the dead who were in them. And they were judged, each one according to his works. *14 Then Death and Hades were cast into the lake of fire. This is the second death. *15 And anyone not found written in the Book of Life was cast into the lake of fire.*" Revelation 20:7-15

One thousand years amounts to 20 Jubilee Cycles. After the 1,000 year Sabbath Millenial reign, the end will come quickly. Satan will have one final opportunity to deceive mankind, and it appears that he will once again succeed. The earth is obviously fully populated since he goes to the 4 corners of the earth. There is likely modern communication and transportation, and we see a familiar ensemble – Gog and Magog.

So there are nations and peoples once again, and a great multitude numbered as the sand of the seas comes against Jerusalem – the camp of the set apart ones and thecapital of the Kingdom. They are quickly disposed of, which then leads to the second resurrection and the "Great White Throne."

The Great White Throne is when all of the dead are judged. Those who are not found in the Scroll of Life are cast into the Lake of Fire. Most sources describe this "lake of fire" in the bowels of the earth.[254] It is definitely a different location from the "bottomless pit" or the "abyss," which is a type of interdimensional holding place.

The important thing to understand is that hell was not made for man. This was confirmed by Yahushua when He stated: *"Then He will also say to those on the left hand, depart from Me, you cursed, into the everlasting fire prepared for the devil and his angels."* Matthews 25:41 Man was supposed to live in paradise with YHWH.

So hell was not created for man, but for the serpent dragon and the fallen sons of Elohim who followed him when he rebelled against Elohim and tried to exalt his throne above the throne of the Most High (Ezekiel 28:13-17 and Isaiah 14:12-15). Yahushua revealed that He now holds the keys to "Hades and Death." *"I am He who lives, and was dead, and behold, I am alive forevermore. Amen. And I have the keys of Hades and of Death."* Revelation 1:18

The Scroll of Life is interesting because it appears that everyone's name is in this Scroll when they are born. Your name is removed from the Scroll of Life when it is "blotted out." It is therefore your decision, followed by your actions that result in your being blotted out.

The end will come quickly as YHWH will send fire, and the final judgment will be rendered. This final judgment will result in a creation reset, likely as was done in the past – before the beginning described in Beresheet 1:1.

Here is a description of that renewal of Creation.

"¹ Behold, YHWH makes the earth empty and makes it waste, distorts its surface and scatters abroad its

inhabitants. ² *And it shall be: As with the people, so with the priest; As with the servant, so with his master; As with the maid, so with her mistress; As with the buyer, so with the seller; As with the lender, so with the borrower; As with the creditor, so with the debtor.* ³ *The land shall be entirely emptied and utterly plundered, for YHWH has spoken this word.* ⁴ *The earth mourns and fades away, the world languishes and fades away; The haughty people of the earth languish.* ⁵ *The earth is also defiled under its inhabitants, because they have transgressed the torote (Torah), changed the ordinance, broken the everlasting Covenant.* ⁶ *Therefore the curse has devoured the earth, and those who dwell in it are desolate. Therefore the inhabitants of the earth are burned, and few men are left.* ⁷ *The new wine fails, the vine languishes, all the merry-hearted sigh.* ⁸ *The mirth of the tambourine ceases, the noise of the jubilant ends, the joy of the harp ceases.* ⁹ *They shall not drink wine with a song; strong drink is bitter to those who drink it.* ¹⁰ *The city of confusion is broken down; every house is shut up, so that none may go in.* ¹¹ *There is a cry for wine in the streets, all joy is darkened, the mirth of the land is gone.* ¹² *In the city desolation is left, and the gate is stricken with destruction.* ¹³ *When it shall be thus in the midst of the land among the people, It shall be like the shaking of an olive tree, like the gleaning of grapes when the vintage is done.* ¹⁴ *They shall lift up their voice, they shall sing; For the majesty of YHWH they shall cry aloud from the sea.* ¹⁵ *Therefore glorify* <u>YHWH in the dawning light, the Name of YHWH Elohim of Yisrael in the coastlands of the sea.</u> ¹⁶ *From the ends of the earth we have heard songs: Glory to the righteous! But I said, I am ruined, ruined! Woe to me! The treacherous dealers have dealt treacherously,* indeed, the treacherous dealers have dealt very treacherously. [17] *Fear and the pit and the snare are upon you, O inhabitant of the earth. [18] And it shall be that he who flees from the noise of the fear shall fall into the pit, and he who comes up from the midst of the pit shall be caught in the snare; for the windows from on high are open, and the foundations of the earth are shaken. [19] The earth is violently broken, the earth is split open, the earth is shaken exceedingly. [20] The earth shall reel to and fro like a drunkard, and shall totter like a hut; its transgression shall be heavy upon it, and it will fall, and not rise again. [21] It shall come to pass in that day that YHWH will punish on high the host of exalted ones, and on the earth the kings of the earth. [22] They will be gathered together, as prisoners are gathered in the pit, and will be shut up in the prison; after many days they will be punished. [23] Then the moon will be disgraced and the sun ashamed; for YHWH of hosts will reign on Mount Zion and in Jerusalem and before His elders, gloriously.*" Isaiah 24:1-23

Notice His elders. These are the elders who sit on thrones before the Throne of YHWH. This reveals the distinction between Mount Zion and Jerusalem. These are not the same place. Mount Zion is in the Heavens – "on high." Jerusalem is on the earth. Mount Zion is the Throne Room in the Heavens, the Capital of the Kingdom of YHWH. Jerusalem is the earthly throne where the Prince rules from. Once the earth is purified by the fires of judgment, Yahushua can then bring His Bride, the New Jerusalem down to their new marital residence.

"*[1] Now I saw a new heaven and a new earth, for the first heaven and the first earth had passed away. Also there was no more sea. [2] <u>Then I, John, saw the set apart city, New Jerusalem, coming down out of heaven from</u>*

Elohim, prepared as a bride adorned for her husband. [3] And I heard a loud voice from heaven saying, Behold, the tabernacle of Elohim is with men, and He will dwell with them, and they shall be His people. Elohim Himself will be with them and be their Elohim. [4] And Elohim will wipe away every tear from their eyes; there shall be no more death, nor sorrow, nor crying. There shall be no more pain, for the former things have passed away. [5] Then He who sat on the throne said, Behold, I make all things new. And He said to me, Write, for these words are true and faithful. [6] And He said to me, It is done! I am the Aleph ($\mathbf{K}$) and the Taw ($\mathbf{X}$), the Beginning and the End. I will give of the fountain of the water of life freely to him who thirsts. [7] He who overcomes shall inherit all things, and I will be his Elohim and he shall be My son. [8] But the cowardly, unbelieving, abominable, murderers, sexually immoral, sorcerers, idolaters, and all liars shall have their part in the lake which burns with fire and brimstone, which is the second death. [9] Then one of the seven angels who had the seven bowls filled with the seven last plagues came to me and talked with me, saying, Come, I will show you the bride, the Lamb's wife. [10] And he carried me away in the Spirit to a great and high mountain, and showed me the great city, the holy Jerusalem, descending out of heaven from Elohim, [11] having the glory of Elohim. Her light was like a most precious stone, like a jasper stone, clear as crystal. [12] Also she had a great and high wall with twelve gates, and twelve angels at the gates, and names written on them, which are the names of the twelve tribes of the children of Yisrael: [13] three gates on the east, three gates on the north, three gates on the south, and three gates on the west. [14] Now the wall of the city had twelve foundations, and on them were the names of the twelve apostles of the Lamb. [15] And he who talked with me had a gold reed to measure the city, its gates, and its wall. [16] The city is laid out as a square; its length is as great as its breadth. And he measured the city with the reed: twelve thousand furlongs. Its length, breadth, and height are equal. [17] Then he measured its wall: one hundred and forty-four cubits, according to the measure of a man, that is, of an angel. [18] The construction of its wall was of jasper; and the city was pure gold, like clear glass. [19] The foundations of the wall of the city were adorned with all kinds of precious stones: the first foundation was jasper, the second sapphire, the third chalcedony, the fourth emerald, [20] the fifth sardonyx, the sixth sardius, the seventh chrysolite, the eighth beryl, the ninth topaz, the tenth chrysoprase, the eleventh jacinth, and the twelfth amethyst. [21] The twelve gates were twelve pearls: each individual gate was of one pearl. And the street of the city was pure gold, like transparent glass. [22] But I saw no temple in it, for YHWH El Shaddai and the Lamb are its Temple. [23] The city had no need of the sun or of the moon to shine in it, for the glory of Elohim illuminated it. The Lamb is its light. [24] And the nations of those who are saved shall walk in its light, and the kings of the earth bring their glory and honor into it. [25] Its gates shall not be shut at all by day (there shall be no night there). [26] And they shall bring the glory and the honor of the nations into it. [27] But there shall by no means enter it anything that defiles, or causes an abomination or a lie, but only those who are written in the Lamb's Book of Life." Revelation 21:1-27

It is the fulfillment of the promise made by Yahsuhua. "*In My Father's house are many mansions; if it were not so, I would have told you. I go to prepare a place for you.*" John

14:2 In this Kingdom of YHWH there are many mansions, or palaces, if you will. This reality that we observe on planet earth, and find recorded throughout time, is the process of filling the Kingdom of YHWH, His heavenly Kingdom.

Notice that this city, the Bride, is likened to the encampment of the tribes of Yisrael. This is because the Bride is Yisrael, not the Church. The Church is a bride, but more likely associated with Mystery Babylon. That is why YHWH warns "come out of her My people." There are those in Babylon who need to come out of the Babylonian religious system and join in the Covenant if they want to be part of the Bride. The patterns provided in the Torah will be fulfilled in the end – all within the context of the Covenant.

Also notice that the City is prepared as a Bride adorned for her Husband. The description seems to be a wedding. Notice also the allusion to the Feast of Tabernacles. This is the 7 day Feast that leads into the Feast of the 8th Day – Shemini Atzeret. Therefore, it seems highly likely that Succot, the Feast of Tabernacles, is when the Husband marries the Bride. This is likely why the nations who do not observe this significant Feast are punished in the millennial kingdom. The 8th Day following Succot is a sort of "honeymoon" that leads into the eternal dimension.

The city is described as a great mountain. The city is layed out as a square footprint, but that does not mean it is a cube. Since it is described as consisting of precious stones and emitting light that puts the sun and the moon to shame, it may have a crystalline shape or pyramid type shape with Yahushua, the light of the world as the Rosh Pina.[255] "Rosh" means: "head" and it is literally on top. The "Rosh Pina" is the "head cornerstone," or rather "Chief Capstone." This City is from Mount Zion that has been over the earth. When it descends to earth it is the renewed Jerusalem.

Now we can see balance restored to the heavens and

fulfillments of the previous patterns. Remember how the serpent was described similar to this Bride. He was adorned with precious stones – perfect and beautiful. He was anointed and made to worship at the Throne. He was also originally attached to the Aleph Taw (✗✗). He was a pattern that eventually pointed to a fulfillment through the Bride.

This is what the serpent desired through the New World Order. We saw this on the Seal of the United States of America as the serpent, represented as the eye of Horus, desired to be enthroned upon the Holy Mountain and shine as the light of the world. That was the destiny of mankind – those who are overcomers. Incredibly, through his attempt to establish his own kingdom, he helped to refine and perfect the true Bride.

With the adversary thrown into the Lake of Fire, and the earth cleansed of all of the filth, this renewed earth will be paradise. It is the renewed Garden of Eden. The occupants are sealed with the Name of YHWH. *"¹ And he showed me a pure river of water of life, clear as crystal, proceeding from the throne of Elohim and of the Lamb. ² In the middle of its street, and on either side of the river, was the tree of life, which bore twelve fruits, each tree yielding its fruit every month. The leaves of the tree were for the healing of the nations. ³ And there shall be no more curse, but the throne of Elohim and of the Lamb shall be in it, and His servants shall serve Him. ⁴ They shall see His face, and His Name shall be on their foreheads. ⁵ There shall be no night there: They need no lamp nor light of the sun, for YHWH Elohim gives them light. And they shall reign forever and ever. ⁶ Then he said to me, These words are faithful and true. And YHWH Elohim of the set apart prophets sent His angel to show His servants the things which must shortly take place. ⁷ Behold, I am coming quickly! Blessed is he who keeps the words of the prophecy of this scroll. ⁸ Now I, John, saw and heard these things. And when I heard and saw, I fell down to worship before the feet of the angel who showed*

me these things. ⁹ Then he said to me, See that you do not do that. For I am your fellow servant, and of your brethren the prophets, and of those who keep the words of this scroll. Worship Elohim. ¹⁰ And he said to me, Do not seal the words of the prophecy of this book, for the time is at hand. ¹¹ He who is unjust, let him be unjust still; he who is filthy, let him be filthy still; he who is righteous, let him be righteous still; he who is holy, let him be holy still. ¹² And behold, I am coming quickly, and My reward is with Me, to give to every one according to his work. ¹³ I am the Aleph and the Taw (✗✦), the Beginning and the End, the First and the Last. ¹⁴ *Blessed are those who do His commandments, that they may have the right to the Tree of Life, and may enter through the gates into the city.* ¹⁵ But outside are dogs and sorcerers and sexually immoral and murderers and idolaters, and whoever loves and practices a lie. ¹⁶ I, Yahushua, have sent My angel to testify to you these things in the churches. I am the Root and the Offspring of David, the Bright and Morning Star. ¹⁷ And the Spirit and the bride say, Come! And let him who hears say, Come! And let him who thirsts come. Whoever desires, let him take the water of life freely. ¹⁸ For I testify to everyone who hears the words of the prophecy of this scroll: If anyone adds to these things, Elohim will add to him the plagues that are written in this scroll; ¹⁹ and if anyone takes away from the words of the scroll of this prophecy, Elohim shall take away his part from the Scroll of Life, from the set apart city, and from the things which are written in this book. ²⁰ He who testifies to these things says, "Surely I am coming quickly. Amen. Even so, come, Master Yahushua! ²¹ The grace of our Master Messiah Yahushua be with you all. Amen."
Revelation 22:1-21

What an amazing ending to an incredible text. There is no mistaking the symbolism of the Aleph Taw (✗✦) in this closing chapter and the Aleph Taw (✗✦) in the first chapter. While there were no numbered chapters in the original scroll one cannot ignore the fact that there are 22 Chapters in the text, equal to the number of characters in the Hebrew alphabet (alephbet.) The "aleph" ($\mathbf{\mathcal{K}}$) is the 1st letter in the Hebrew alephbet, and the "taw" ($\mathbf{X}$) is the 22nd letter in the Hebrew alephbet. Chapter 1 and Chapter 22 both describe the Aleph Taw ($\mathbf{X}\mathbf{\mathcal{K}}$) – both the beginning and the end. This is like the seal of the Spirit on this text.

As we saw in the pattern of the first week, the time of this present existence on earth is encompassed within seven millennium. The Kingdom is the fulfillment of the Covenant made with Abram. He was an uncircumcised man coming out of Babylon, which was the bride of the beast. He was cleansed and covered by the blood of the Covenant. He was allowed to enter into a relationship with the Creator of the Universe. He was promised a multitude of descendants who would be kings. He was also promised a large piece of land. Notice the dimensions of this great City, and we can see the dimensions of the Promised Land. (Revelation 21:16)

All of these promises were made before the Covenant of Circumcision. The point was clear, YHWH first desires for us to walk in faith. Abraham was circumcised 24 years after he finally departed from Haran, and crossed over the Euphrates River. That circumcision ultimately pointed to the circumcision of the heart.

Through this Covenant made with an uncircumcised man called out of Babylon, YHWH has established a perpetual Kingdom. Those who believed and obeyed would receive the circumcision of the heart so that they can share an intimate relationship with YHWH. From the union of His Son and the fertile Bride, they will expand and populate the Kingdom of YHWH throughout all of creation.

This is the restoration of the Garden, which was the purpose of establishing the Promised Land. It was intended to be Paradise on Earth. Yahushua, the Last Adam has finally restored that which was lost by the First Adam. He has also found a new Bride and her name is Yisrael.

The end of the age is an exciting fulfillment of the Covenant, and it is only something to be feared if you belong to the bride of the serpent. If you are part of the Bride of Messiah, you can look forward to the end with anxious anticipation. The Scriptures are really the love story of the ages. We must remember that when we consider the end of the age. Here are the words from the Prophet Hoshea that express the heart of YHWH as He sums things up.

"*¹ When Yisrael was a child, I loved him, and out of Egypt I called My son. ² As they called them, so they went from them; they sacrificed to the Baals, and burned incense to carved images. ³ I taught Ephraim to walk, taking them by their arms; but they did not know that I healed them. ⁴ I drew them with gentle cords, with bands of love, and I was to them as those who take the yoke from their neck. I stooped and fed them. ⁵ He shall not return to the land of Egypt; but the Assyrian shall be his king, because they refused to repent. ⁶ And the sword shall slash in his cities, devour his districts, and consume them, because of their own counsels. ⁷ My people are bent on backsliding from Me. Though they call to the Most High, none at all exalt Him. ⁸ How can I give you up, Ephraim? How can I hand you over, Yisrael? How can I make you like Admah? How can I set you like Zeboiim? My heart churns within Me; My sympathy is stirred. ⁹ I will not execute the fierceness of My anger; I will not again destroy Ephraim. For I am Elohim, and not man, the Holy One in your midst; and I will not come with terror. ¹⁰ They shall walk after YHWH. He will roar like a lion. When He roars, then His sons shall come trembling from the west; ¹¹ They shall come trembling like a bird from Egypt, Like a dove from the land of Assyria. And I will let them dwell in their houses, Says YHWH. ¹² Ephraim has encircled Me with lies, and the House of Yisrael with deceit; But Yahudah still walks with Elohim, even with the Holy One who is faithful.*" Hosea 11:1-12

YHWH loves His people and He will not destroy Ephraim. He will not come with terror for His people. So we have some incredible expectations for the end, but it is not meant to terrorize Ephraim.

These are the words of a loving carrying Father. Did you notice the language of teaching His child to walk. If you are a parent having shared that experience you can feel the tug at your heart. This is a kind, gentle, patient, loving Father Who cares for His children - So much so that He keeps His Word. He punishes His children, but He does it for their own good. Because He is a just Elohim, He also punishes all sin. That is the context of the end times.

When I grew up in the Christian Church I was placed in fear by certain pastors who failed to understand the Covenant plan of YHWH, and taught errors concerning the end. I was lead to believe that the people of YHWH would be running and hiding in fear for their lives from the antichrist and his minions.

No doubt the description of future events provided in the Book of Revelation and Daniel are hard to imagine. That is why many do not interpret the texts literally. They fail to recognize the true history of Creation, and are likely to be in a state of disbelief when angelic beings begin to manifest in this physical realm. While certain descriptions of kingdoms and beasts in the Book of Daniel and Revelation are symbolic, that is not true for all.

We must rightfully divide the word and prayerfully consider the events foretold to occur in order to prepare ourselves for the exciting and incredible days ahead. We are not to fear, but rather prepare. As we walk the straight path in the light of YHWH, darkness cannot prevail against us. Remember that within the cycles of righteousness, the physical death of the righteous to eternal life.

The great King and Psalmist David wrote comforting words for those experiencing great tribulation. In fact, it appears to be specifically written for those at the end of the age. "[1] Elohim is our refuge and strength, a very present help in trouble. [2] Therefore we will not fear, even though the earth be removed, and though the mountains be carried into the midst of the sea; [3] Though its waters roar and be troubled, though the mountains shake with its swelling. Selah [4] There is a river whose streams shall make glad the City of Elohim, the set apart place of the Tabernacle of the Most High. [5] Elohim is in the midst of her, she shall not be moved; _Elohim shall help her, just at the break of dawn._ [6] The nations raged, the kingdoms were moved; He uttered His voice, the earth melted. [7] YHWH of hosts is with us; The Elohim of Yaakob is our refuge. Selah [8] Come, behold the works of YHWH, Who has made desolations in the earth. [9] He makes wars cease to the end of the earth; He breaks the bow and cuts the spear in two; He burns the chariot in the fire. [10] Be still, and know that I am Elohim; I will be exalted among the nations, I will be exalted in the earth! [11] YHWH of hosts is with us; The Elohim of Yaakob is our refuge." Psalm 46:1-11

There is no need to dread the future. YHWH is our refuge. Notice the following: "_Elohim is in the midst of her, she shall not be moved; Elohim shall help her, just at the break of dawn._" He saves His people at "the dawning of the day." Remember the tradition discussed in the previous chapter involving the last day of Succot. There is a saying that it is always darkest just before the dawn. So His help comes when the darkness begins to recede. This is after light has begun to shine forth and overcome the darkness of "ben-shakar" – the son of darkness.

There are those who teach a "pre-tribulation rapture" theory. They essentially teach that "the Church" will avoid all difficulty and simply disappear at any given time while the remaining inhabitants of the earth experience the above-described tribulations. There is no Scriptural basis for this belief. While there is a point when Yahushua will send out His messengers to gather His elect, and His elect will not experience His wrath, the Scriptural patterns repeatedly reveal those in the Covenant being set apart and protected in the midst of judgment. In fact, Yahushua specifically prayed: *"I do not pray that You should take them out of the world, but that You should keep them from the evil one."* John 17:15

Still others believe that all prophecy was fulfilled thousands of years ago, including the second coming of the Messiah. While many prophecies in the Scripture have been fulfilled in the past, many have not, and we must always be open to the possibility of multiple fulfillments.

Amidst all of this confusion, Bible prophecy has proven to be a daunting subject for most people. To properly understand eschatology and the end of the age we must be prepared to place Scriptures and prophecies within their proper historical context.

While some prophecies may have multiple layers of fulfillment, we should be ready to recognize the fulfillment of certain prophecies when history supports such a position. This will avoid the mistake of expecting a fulfillment that has already occurred in the past and will likely not be repeated in the future.

It appears that many will fall asleep and be unprepared for future events, erroneously expecting things to occur that already occurred almost 2,000 years ago. We must set aside the paradigms and traditional beliefs that we have been taught, and examine all prophecy in the light of history.

When we do this we come away with a very balanced understanding of prophecy, and are better prepared to face the challenges of the end of the age. After all, everything that Yisrael experienced in the past was for future generations to learn from.

"¹ Moreover, brethren, I do not want you to be unaware that all our fathers were under the cloud, all passed through the sea, ² all were immersed into Mosheh in the cloud and in the sea, ³ all ate the

same spiritual food, *⁴ and all drank the same spiritual drink. For they drank of that spiritual Rock that followed them, and that Rock was Messiah. ⁵ But with most of them Elohim was not well pleased, for their bodies were scattered in the wilderness. ⁶ Now these things became our examples (τύποι), to the intent that we should not lust after evil things as they also lusted. ⁷ And do not become idolaters as were some of them. As it is written, The people sat down to eat and drink, and rose up to play. ⁸ Nor let us commit sexual immorality, as some of them did, and in one day twenty-three thousand fell; ⁹ nor let us tempt Messiah, as some of them also tempted, and were destroyed by serpents; ¹⁰ nor complain, as some of them also complained, and were destroyed by the destroyer. ¹¹ <u>Now all these things happened to them as examples (τυπικῶς), and they were written for our admonition, upon whom the ends of the ages have come</u>.*" 1 Corinthians 10:1-10*

If these were all examples for those in the end of the age, then there will come a day when YHWH will, once again, gather His people. They will also likely experience some of the trials and tests of their predecessors. The key is to be an overcomer, and not die in the wilderness. You must not fear the giants – you must trust YHWH.

That is why Yahushua specifically instructed the Assemblies to be overcomers. After the millennial reign, YHWH will renew the heavens and the earth. The New Jerusalem will finally touch down upon the earth.

This will begin a new age, an eighth millennium, if you will. This is the fulfillment of the Feast of the 8th Day – Shemini Atzeret. Interestingly, this Feast occurs on Day 22 of Month 7. The numerical significance is quite profound. The number 7 is often associated with "completion." The number 22 is the number of letters in the alephbet. It represents the Aleph Taw (𐤗𐤖).

The eighth day represents new beginnings and as we discussed, it represents the blood and the DNA of the

Covenant. This is the day when the flesh of the male is circumcised, which foreshadows the circumcision of the heart. Of course, the fact that the circumcised male organ is the sign of the Covenant reveals the nature of the relationship. This is an intimate, loving relationship that involves the participants of the Covenant becoming one – echad.

Everything in the Covenant plan points to the promise of an eighth day. From the entry point into the Covenant when every child is circumcised on the eighth day until the final Feast in the Appointed Times – Shemini Atzeret – the eighth day.

The seven day cycle established in the beginning will come to an end, and the earth will be renewed. This is likely similar to what occurred before "the beginning" described in Beresheet. In other words, these heavens and this earth will be completing and restarting another cycle in the eternal plan of YHWH.

Isaiah clearly describes this renewal. "*22 For as the new heavens and the new earth which I will make shall remain before Me, says YHWH, So shall your descendants and your name remain. 23 And it shall come to pass that from one New Moon to another, and from one Sabbath to another, all flesh shall come to worship before Me, says YHWH. 24 And they shall go forth and look upon the corpses of the men who have transgressed against Me. For their worm does not die, and their fire is not quenched. They shall be an abhorrence to all flesh.*" Isaiah 66:22-24

This is a great and wonderful promise and a grave warning. As we anticipate the end of the age we must be sober and vigilant and anticipate, rather than fear, the fulfillment of the Covenant promises.

Just exactly how all will be accomplished remains to be seen, but YHWH will surely make known His plan when His servants need to know. YHWH will always send a messenger to His people. (Amos 3:7). Remember, when it was finally time for YHWH to deliver the Children of Yisrael from Egypt He sent Mosheh, and things transpired quite rapidly. In fact, we know that from the appearance of Mosheh, the entire redemption took place within the span of a year.[256]

Tradition holds that the plagues lasted for only six months. According to Seder Olam, the plagues began on Day 1 of Month 7 – Yom Teruah. We know that Yisrael departed Egypt on the First Day of Unleavened Bread, under the light of the full moon when the shofar is sounded at the Feast. (Psalm 81:3)

Knowledge and revelation are often withheld until the last minute, and we should not be disturbed by this. We need to be obeying the commandments and thus participating in the "rehearsals" – the Appointed Times. If we are rehearsing at the proper time then we will be prepared. When we see the signs we need to patiently pray concerning timing and information as Daniel did.

There are currently many people with differing opinions on the issues concerning the end of the age. We would do well to take a lesson from the appearance of the Messiah over 2,000 years ago. Daniel gave precise timing concerning the appearance of the Messiah, and many were certainly anticipating a Messiah. The people also had a variety of preconceived notions and expectations concerning the Messiah. When those expectations were not met, many rejected Yahushua as the Messiah. Despite their education, training and knowledge of the Scriptures, they refused to accept Him as He came.

I believe the same will hold true in the future. Many people have expectations regarding the end of the age, and most will likely be wrong. In fact, the Scriptures speak of a great falling away toward the end. (2 Thessalonians 2:3) This

may be the result of disappointment, discouragement, unmet expectations, fear or outright panic. When people discover they have been taught or believed lies they may, in fact, rebel against YHWH.

While we have discussed possible fulfillments of future prophecies through organizations such as the European Union, the United Nations, the Roman Catholic Church and the Religion of Islam, there are still others too numerous to discuss in this book. Certainly the United States of America contains many of the signs and symbols of the New World Order, and has been used throughout the world, particularly the Middle East, to prepare the way for the final kingdom.

We have only briefly touched upon the Nephilim and their hybrid offspring that are sure to play a role in the events at the end of the age. In fact, many believe that they have been working throughout the ages to continue the pre-flood disruption of Creation. As science clones both man and beast in the quest for transhumanistic superbeings, those who are asleep will likely be horrified by the results when their senses are contradicting rational man's concensus of reality. Those who rely solely upon reason may be in for a big surprise.

The reason why the Scriptures describe the new world order, promulgated by the successive kingdoms of man, as a beast is because it is a hybrid, mixed entity. The world systems are currently controlled by spiritual entities promoting men and women who will do their bidding. These individuals have essentially "sold their souls" to satisfy their lust for power and prestige, and what they believe will be eternal life. Sadly, they may be the most deceived of all, as they sell out their fellow man for their own selfish ambitions.

The Nephilim were once "Sons of Elohim," but they left their habitation. Through their rebellion they lost their position, and YHWH through His Son Yahushua has been in the process of re-populating His Kingdom through the

Covenant. The promise given through Hosea was that the Children of Yisrael would be called "sons of the living El." (Hosea 1:10)

When asked about a woman's marital status in the Age to Come, Yahushua made the following statement: *"³⁴ . . . The sons of this age marry and are given in marriage. ³⁵ But those who are counted worthy to attain that age, and the resurrection from the dead, neither marry nor are given in marriage; ³⁶ nor can they die anymore, for they are equal to the angels and are sons of Elohim, being sons of the resurrection."* Luke 20:34-36

The Nephilim were "fallen," and destined judgment and death. They were being replaced by other sons, "sons of the living El" – sons of the resurrection. These resurrected sons of Elohim are being transformed from their fallen condition through Yahushua. *"For you are all sons of Elohim through faith in Messiah Yahushua."* Galatians 3:26 This is the mystery of Elohim and the culmination of the ages. *"For the earnest expectation of the creation eagerly waits for the revealing of the sons of Elohim."* Romans 8:19

This is why those in the Covenant must be "born again." We were all born in the image of Adam. In order to be transformed into a "son of Elohim" from a "son of Adam" we must be born again. This is the message seen from Enoch, the seventh generation from Seth – the Sabbath Generation. So many use this term without really understanding the deep and transformative meaning.

So this is a very personal struggle that is taking place as the Nephilim, the fallen ones, try to build their own kingdom, and destroy their replacements.

Until now, the masses have been allowed to remain in their perpetual state of apathy. Like cattle being fattened for the slaughter, most are completely unaware of what the future holds as they daily set out to pasture, grazing on the pleasures of life. When they are eventually led to the slaughterhouse many will find themselves in a state of shock as their normalcy bias and paradigms are completely disrupted by the revelation that they have been deceived. Sadly, many may never comprehend the depth of the deception before it is too late.

Imagine the reaction of many Christians if one or more humanoid beings descended in a spacecraft claiming to be the Savior or the originator of our species. What if one of them actually claims to be Jesus and explains that he was one of many ascended masters, like Buddha and Mohammed, sent to lead mankind to a higher state of consciousness and singularity. Has their religion equipped them to deal with such a situation?

Sadly, most are not prepared because their religion has removed them far away from the Covenant and the Torah. As a result, they do not understand the terms of the Covenant. Many are busy being entertained in exciting services, seminars and conferences searching for a "fresh" move of the spirit and "new" revelation. They have been so deceived by the false teachings regarding "grace" that there is no longer a righteous standard being raised in Christianity.

During the writing of this book, Pope Francis essentially threw out the Commandmnets of Elohim in lieu of his misunderstanding of grace. So this Jesus would not have to follow the Scriptures to be accepted by people. He could simply promote love and peace and most Christians would likely readily receive him.

Muslims actually believe that Jesus will return in the future in Damascus. They believe when he returns he will perform all of the prayers of a faithful Muslim. He will institute Islamic Law according to the Qur'an, and he will abolish all other religions and tell Christians to convert to Islam. He will deny that he was Elohim, or the Son of Elohim. He will simply be Allah's slave and messenger. He

will kill the Muslim antichrist then get married, have children and die. He will then be buried next to the Prophet Muhammad.[257]

So while Muslims believe in Jesus and his return to Earth, they do not see him as the Messiah. In fact they believe that he will submit to Imam Mahdi, the Muslim messiah. Interestingly, both Christians and Muslims believe in an "anti-christ" and they both expect a messiah, along with the Jews.

Al-Mahdi is anticipated by Muslims to rule a Caliphate that has been established before his coming. This Islamic Caliphate will essentially be a unified kingdom submitted to Allah. This kingdom will be ruled by Shariah Law, and those who refuse to submit will be beheaded by the sword of Allah. We can see how things are closer than ever to a fulfillment.

With the American action and inaction in certain Middle Eastern countries, many regimes that stood in the way of such a Caliphate have been toppled. The so-called "Arab Spring" was a contrived event to prepare the way for the Caliphate and it appears that America is responsible for funding various Jihadist groups responsible for the current instability in the region. The entire Middle East is a powder keg ready to explode as Russia, Turkey, China, Iran, the Eurpoean Union and the United States all assert their own intersts and play out their individual proxy wars in Syria.

It appears that the stage is being set for the fulfillment of the prophecy given by Isaiah. "*The burden against Damascus.* "*Behold, Damascus will cease from being a city, and it will be a ruinous heap.*" Isaiah 17:1

When considering the end of the age, we need to expect the unexpected, and be prepared for just about anything. If you are still reading this book then you surely recognize that you have been lied to your entire life. You were provided with a paradigm of reality from your youth, and expected to view the world through a certain lens that hid the serpent kingdom from plain sight. We are daily being fed lies through all of the corporate owned and manipulated news sources that support the illusion. In fact, the propaganda they espouse is better described as "disinformation" than "news."

What if advanced being appears that can merge the three major religions of Christianity, Islam and Judaism, including the other religions of the world. This would certainly bring the appearance of peace to the planet. And what if a being named Jesus appears, demonstrating power and directs all people to the Imam Mahdi? What if the Pope endorses the Imam Mahdi as the messiah? Under this scenario, or something similar, would people lose their faith in the Elohim of the Scriptures or would they recognize the deception?

We do not know exactly how things will play out. In fact, the possible scenarios are endless. The point is that we remain ready and watchful. We do know that many will be deceived, because they will fall asleep – they will forget the Commandments and they will not have the oil of the Spirit.

As a result, we should expect to see a lie that would embrace as many people and religions as possible, and redirect them all into a newly evolved one world religion. A religion that would require worship in opposition to the Commandments of YHWH and Yahushua the Messiah. A religion that would also include a political and economic system.

Those who stand firm in the Covenant of YHWH would be considered intolerant, non-compliant hatemongers. They would likely become enemies of the state. Actually, this has already occurred in America as those who believe the Torah are being targeted by progressives in society.

Sadly, individuals have become apathetic and mankind has descended into a veritable mass stupor. This is the result of many factors, from the effects of Genetically Modified Organisms (GMOs), that are mutating food and attacking our own genetic makeup, to the mass drugging of society through vaccines, prescription and non-prescription drugs (pharmacia). (Revelation 22:15)

There are also numerous envirommental causes. Enormous geoengineering projects are inundating the atmosphere with barium and aluminum causing people to experience debilitating mental and physical effects.[258]

The environmental impact of plastics and chemicals is causing hormonal disruption and illness. The effects of xenoestrogens are destroying the testosterone levels in men and society is essentially being demasculated and in a state of hormonal flux. We can see the effects of this through the rise in the transgender movement and the increase in gender confusion.

Also, people in technologically developed areas are experiencing the effects of "electro-smog" reducing their energy, placing their minds in a fog and possibly even damaging their DNA.[259] Our bodies are electrical, and we live in a charged atmosphere. The earth resonates at measurable frequencies and our bodies should be "gounded" and synchronized with those frequencies. We were, after all, made from the ground (adamah).

These are just a sampling of the environmental and physical attacks on mankind. As we discussed, there is a battle raging in the spirit realm as well. Man is a unique being connected to both the physical and the spirit realm. We are witnessing the moral decline of society as families are disintegrating. People are completely distracted by sports, entertainment, careers, jobs, bills and the various troubles of life.

As we become more and more dependent upon technology, individuals become less able to provide for themselves. Most are forced to make money in order to survive. Few can live a completely self-sufficient life "off the grid," disconnected from the goods and services provided by modern society. As a result, most spend their entire existence obsessed with earning and consuming. Children are often more influenced by music and Hollywod "idols" and television shows, than they are their parents.

While all of these attacks are occurring on mankind, the earth is undergoing extraordinary disasters.[260] Earthquake and volcanic activity is increasing in frequency. Tsunamis, hurricanes, cyclones, tornadoes, forest fires and other disaters are wreaking havoc as the earth undergoes the prophesied "birth pangs." (Romans 8:22) As this book was written the core melt-downs at the Fukashima Daiichi Nuclear Plant in Japan continue to flood the Pacific Ocean with radioactive poison while most remain unaware of the looming disaster and the environmental impact.

Amazingly, most people barely express any awareness or concern, too consumed and distracted by the great delusion of daily stresses, sports, entertainment and materialism that are spiritually blinding and debilitating mankind. The inhabitants of the planet are fed a fairly controlled diet of information that is more of a distraction from the truth than anything else. It is intentionally controlled and censored in order to keep the masses in lethargic submission.

As a result, most are oblivious to the events leading up to the end of the age. Likely, there will be a culmination of these events involving a mixing and merging of the governments and institutions of the world that will supposedly provide a solution to all of the "problems" plaguing mankind. This is likely a large part of the delusion. The result may be shocking to many, yet it may be welcomed by others. In fact, it may be that Christians still believe they can be Christians, and Muslims still believe they can be Muslims – all while they participate in the beast system. On the other hand, all religion may simply be disgarded after some purported alien entity appears and destroys the religious paradigms of those who inhabit the planet.

No matter what form the final beast system assumes, it all distills down into a very simple conflict – the Kingdom of Light against the Kingdom of Darkness. The end of the age is the culmination of an ancient struggle between 2 seeds, 2 families, 2 brides, 2 cities – 2 kingdoms.

As we approach the end of the age it is imperative to know the truth and then walk in it. While a perfect and precise timeline would be desirous, in the end it makes no difference if you know when things will happen if you are not in a Covenant relationship with YHWH.

For those in the Covenant, the Torah is the roadmap. As the set apart people walk in the Light, they will be led down the proper path. The prophecies contained in the Scriptures will unfold exactly as foretold, and those with eyes to see and ears to hear will discern them in their proper time. Of course, Yahushua stated that He will send messengers.

This book is filled with a lot of valuable information. It is intended to open your mind, expand your understanding and possibly challenge your inherited traditions. The question is what are you going to do with this information. Knowledge is just the beginning. The Scriptures declare that: *"My people are destroyed for lack of knowledge. Because you have rejected knowledge, I also will reject you from being priest for Me; Because you have forgotten the Torah of your Elohim, I also will forget your children."* Hosea 4:6

Remember that Hoshea was speaking to the House of Yisrael. He later exhorted: *"Let us know, Let us pursue the*

knowledge of YHWH. His going forth is established as the morning; He will come to us like the rain, like the latter and former rain to the earth." Hoshea 6:3

YHWH also proclaimed: *"For I desire mercy and not sacrifice, and the knowledge of Elohim more than burnt offerings."* Hoshea 6:6 The root of the word described as "knowledge" is "yada" (**⊙◁ረ**). It is the same word used to express the relationship when a man "knows" a woman. This act of "knowing" is not only a physical union, it is a spiritual union. So the knowledge of Elohim is not about simply memorizing facts or Scripture verses. It involves an intimate relationship. The forgotten knowledge is the Torah, which contains the instructions for righteousness. As we walk in the way of the Torah we are expressing our love to YHWH.

Yahushua came as the representative of the Father. He specifically stated: *"⁶ I am the way, the truth, and the life. No one comes to the Father except through Me. ⁷ If you had known Me, you would have known My Father also; and from now on you know Him and have seen Him."* John 14:6-7

Yahushua made it very clear that He and the Father were One – Echad. He also identified Himself with the Torah, which has always been described as "the way," "the truth" and "life."²⁶¹

Notice His emphasis on knowing Him. Knowledge from YHWH points us to His Torah and to His Son. *"He shall see the labor of His soul, and be satisfied. By His knowledge My righteous Servant shall justify many, for He shall bear their iniquities."* Isaiah 53:11

It is through this knowing relationship with Yahushua that we are justified, and may then approach and know the Father. This is why the Children of Yisrael were instructed to select a lamb and treat is like a "son" in their house 4 days before the Passover. (Shemot 12:5). It became part of the family before it was then killed and the blood of

the lamb placed on the doorpost as a sign.

Yahushua, as the Lamb of Elohim was the Sun of Righteousness. The sun was created on the 4th day. Yahushua came died on the 4th day, the 4th millennium, just as the Yisraelites killed the Lamb on the 4th day – the Passover.[262]

In the end it is not what you know, but Who you know and Who knows you. There are many who believe that they are in the Kingdom based upon their works, but they are deceived. There are many who believe that they are the Bride, and claim their "liberty" in Christ by showing disdain for His Torah. The true Messiah has benn is clear that He does not know these people. They have chosen to follow their own path, or the traditions of men established through some religious system. Yahushua does not know these people, despite their self-proclaimed "mighty" works.

"*13 Enter by the narrow gate; for wide is the gate and broad is the way that leads to destruction, and there are many who go in by it. 14 Because narrow is the gate and difficult is the way which leads to life, and there are few who find it. 15 Beware of false prophets, who come to you in sheep's clothing, but inwardly they are ravenous wolves. 16 You will know them by their fruits. Do men gather grapes from thorn bushes or figs from thistles? 17 Even so, every good tree bears good fruit, but a bad tree bears bad fruit. 18 A good tree cannot bear bad fruit, nor can a bad tree bear good fruit. 19 Every tree that does not bear good fruit is cut down and thrown into the fire. 20 Therefore by their fruits you will know them. 21 Not everyone who says to Me, 'Lord, Lord,' shall enter the kingdom of heaven, but he who does the will of My Father in heaven. 22 Many will say to Me in that day, Lord, Lord, have we not prophesied in Your name, cast out demons in Your name, and done many wonders in Your name?' 23 And then I will declare to them, I never knew you; depart from Me, you who practice lawlessness! 24 Therefore whoever hears these sayings of Mine, and does them, I will liken him to a wise man who built his house on the rock: 25 and the rain* descended, the floods came, and the winds blew and beat on that house; and it did not fall, for it was founded on the rock. ²⁶ But everyone who hears these sayings of Mine, and does not do them, will be like a foolish man who built his house on the sand: ²⁷ and the rain descended, the floods came, and the winds blew and beat on that house; and it fell. And great was its fall." Matthew 7:13-27

Notice that none of the examples cited by these "many" individuals involve the commandments in the Torah. They are signs and wonders, but they are not commandments. So it appears that the deceived will be chasing after signs and will be neglecting the Torah. In fact, "lawlessness" specifically means "without Torah."

You will "know" them "by their fruits." Their fruits are the results of their actions. You can only bear good fruits if you are planted in good ground, and your roots draw from the source of Life. This is how we become one with YHWH, through the Son. Our roots must draw upon Him for our life.

These are the words of the Messiah concerning His Kingdom, and those who belong in His Kingdom. You must know Him and He must know you. This is about a relationship. Yahushua specifically stated: "¹⁵ *If you love Me, keep My commandments.* ¹⁶ And I will pray the Father, and He will give you another Helper, that He may abide with you forever ¹⁷ the Spirit of truth, whom the world cannot receive, because it neither sees Him nor knows Him; but you know Him, for He dwells with you and will be in you. ¹⁸ I will not leave you orphans; I will come to you." John 14:15-18

These are comforting words, and they are all about being in a family relationship. At the heart of this relationship is love, and we express our love for Yahushua if we "keep" (shamar) His commandments. This is how we bear good fruit.

Adam was placed in the Garden, and was literally supposed to bear good fruit. He was to "keep" the commandments by guarding, watching and tending the garden. He disobeyed and brought sin into the Kingdom. This allowed the serpent to step in and steal, kill and destroy. The serpent has been waging war ever since, and it is within the context of this battle that Yahushua came to restore creation.

Yahushua was doing battle in a garden immediately prior to His execution, inorder to restore what Adam had lost in the Garden. Through His obedience, death and resurrection many will be made righteous. Once cleansed and made righteous by His blood, we are then supposed to guard the commandments. Our obedience is our expression of love.

Sadly, most in Christianity have been taught that obedience is somehow bad. They equate obedience with legalism, and that is an incredible mistake. They intimately tie the sacrificial system with obedience, as if the Temple service was the ultimate goal of the plan of YHWH. That was clearly not the case.

"... Does YHWH delight in burnt offerings and sacrifices, as in obeying the voice of YHWH? Behold, to obey (shema) is better than sacrifice, and to heed (qashab) than the fat of rams." 1 Samuel 15:22 The Temple Service was intended to point us to the need for an atoning sacrifice and the Messiah. YHWH does not delight in the system of sacrifices. He was teaching the importance of obedience. Notice "shema" (ⵁⵁW) and "qashab" (ⵁWⵁ). They both refer to "hearing" and "obeying."

It is through our obedience that we meet with Him and learn His ways – ways that are pleasing to him. It is through obedience that we walk the "narrow" Covenant path. This is the way of restoration. Remember when Nehemiah was praying for a restoration and return he quoted the promise spoken through Mosheh: "but if you return to Me, and keep (shamar) My commandments and do them, though some of you *were cast out to the farthest part of the heavens, yet I will gather them from there, and bring them to the place which I have chosen as a dwelling for My Name.*" Nehemiah 1:9

This is the promise given to those in the Covenant who are exiled and scattered throughout the world. This is a promise and a solution for our time. Our actions define our relationship, and only those "keep" (ꓷꓬꟿ) and "do" (ꓯꟿꙩ) the commandments will escape the judgment that awaits this planet and the kingdoms therein. Of course, these were the same instructions given to Adam. Our sojourn on this earth is to prepare us to return to the Garden. Yahushua, the Last Adam, through obedience repaired the breach caused by Adam.

Remember it was through obedience that Noah was delivered from the judgment on the entire planet. It was through obedience that Lot and his daughters were spared the judgment rendered on Sodom, Gomorrah, Admah and Zeboiim. It was through obedience that the children of Yisrael were protected from the plagues, redeemed and delivered from slavery. It was through obedience that the Children of Yisrael eventually entered into the Promised Land.

These were patterns for the future redemption and deliverance under the Covenant. It is provided for those who are covered by the Blood of the Lamb, and obey the Commandments of Elohim. Yahushua is the door to life, but we must be obedient and walk the Covenant path through the door that leads to life. If you are known by Yahushua, He will make you into a jewel. He will join with you as His Bride. You can contain His Light and dwell in His Kindgom of Light.

Adam was a creature of light. That light of life was in him as long as he partook of the Tree of Life. The serpent revealed himself as a "messenger of light." (2 Corinthians

11:14) He deceived man and as a result, man lost that light. From Adam to Yahushua, the serpent has desired to destroy the blood of man. Yahushua came to restore that light in man. After Yahushua, the serpent has been trying to destroy mankind, the containers of that light. He has attempted to suppress, distort and alter the message and identity of Yahushua – the Light of the World.

Once we see the Light and have the Light within us, we must then walk in the Light, and become "sons of light." (John 12:36) There is a spiritual battle occurring that most of the world is oblivious to. At the center of this battle are the souls of men. Yahushua won the battle in a garden that Adam lost in the Garden. Everything that occurs in the physical realm is a mirror of the spiritual realm. The events that we read about in the prophecies are both spiritual and physical.

When the spiritual and the physical intersect at the end of the age those who are not ready will be overwhelmed. The Scriptures are clear that the Nephilim were before and after the flood. These fallen angels and their wicked offspring did not disappear after the flood. They are found throughout the Tanak. They physically littered the Promised Land, and history recounts their presence throughout the world.

I believe there will come a day when the world will experience the reappearance of these hideous creatures that have remained behind the scenes, although it would be error to assume that the entire world will see every manifestation described in the prophecies. Those texts are revealing the powers controlling the beast kingdom, but that does not necessarily mean that the people of the world will see the underlying powers of those beast systems. Indeed, it is evident that unseen forces have been controlling these empires for centuries, and there is nothing to indicate that this will change in the future.

We must understand that the kingdoms of this world are currently controlled by the serpent, the Nephilim, their offspring and their minions. We do not see these entities, and therefore we may not see many of the manifestations in the end. That may be the mystery of these prophecies. We see the physical, but we need to discern the spiritual dimension. The prophecies are giving us the spiritual explanation of what is happening in the physical realm.

As we approach the end of the age, and await the return of the Messiah, we should expect to see things as they were in the days of Noah. As Messiah comes in wrath to judge the world we must be ready to take instruction from His 2 messengers as did Lot. Lot was considered righteous, but he was mixed with in a pagan culture. As a result, he was *"oppressed by the filthy conduct of the wicked."* 2 Peter 2:7

This is a condition that many find themselves today. While Abraham was set apart, he was able to meet and eat with YHWH and His 2 messengers. Lot, on the other hand, was not set apart. He was dwelling in the place of judgment and needed to be physically removed. Lot barely escaped with his life while Abraham remained set apart, and was not within the scope of judgment.

There is an important lesson to be learned that YHWH will not judge the righteous with the wicked. We also saw from Daniel that when we refuse to serve other gods, YHWH will protect us when thrown into the den of lions or the fiery furnace

Judgment may be sudden. If not prepared, many will be caught off guard and end up dead, and even worse yet, shut out of the Feast. Therefore, how and where we walk may make the difference between life and death. If we stay close to the Shepherd, and feed in His pastures, He will protect us. If we disobey and stray from the Shepherd we may end up dead.

In the future, as we approach the end of the age, there will be many incredible, supernatural events that will likely send some unprepared into "disaster shock" as they experience traumatic distress.

Yahushua specifically stated that after the times of the Gentiles are fulfilled "²⁵ . . . *there will be signs in the sun, in the moon, and in the stars; and on the earth distress of nations, with perplexity, the sea and the waves roaring;* ²⁶ <u>*men's hearts failing them from fear and the expectation of those things which are coming on the earth, for the powers of the heavens will be shaken.*</u> ²⁷ *Then they will see the Son of Man coming in a cloud with power and great glory.* ²⁸ *Now when these things begin to happen, look up and lift up your heads, because your redemption draws near.*" Luke 21:25-28

So there will come a time when there will be signs in the sun, the moon and the stars. We are currently seeing some of those signs, and expect more incredible signs in the future. We are also seeing and hearing strange and ominous phenomena, and witnessing incredible natural disasters. These are all pointing to things becoming increasingly worse. Specifically, men's hearts will fail them from fear and expectation from the things that are <u>coming on the earth</u>.

Some day in the future, people will know and fear the things coming to the earth. This will be directly related to the "powers of the heavens being shaken." The Greek word for "powers" is "dunamis" (δυνάμεις). That word often deals with "spiritual" powers - angelic and otherwise.²⁶³ So before the Son of Elohim returns, the powers of the heavens will be unleashed upon the earth. While the inhabitants of the earth are in fear, those in Covenant with YHWH are to lift their heads. Your response is directly related to your relationship.

Most will remain under the strong delusion currently engulfing the planet until the very end. They will fail to see the signs and discern the times until it is too late. Even some elect may possibly be deceived, and some will perish because they lack knowledge and fail to understand what is happening. (Matthew 24:24, Mark 13:22; Hosea 4:6)

As SETI, the Vatican and many others are poised to welcome the Nephilim, allegedly guised as benevolent extraterrestrials, those with discernment will understand that *"there is nothing new under the sun"* (Ecclesiastes 1:9) These old deceptions will be repackaged with "modern" trappings as the world returns to the days of Noah awaiting imminent judgment.

This book may not have answered all of your questions about the end times. That was neither possible, nor was it even the purpose. Rather, this book was meant to provide focus and clarity to the signs of the times, so that the mystery of Elohim can be seen as it unfolds – for those who have eyes to see.

In the end, it goes beyond what we know or think that you know. There are many who are busy seeking the latest "intel," and prepping for the end of days. While it is good that people are recognizing the deception and preparing for the future - that is only the beginning. In the end it is not what you think you know or what you think you have, but how you live. Many have faith in what they believe to be true, but if their faith is not based upon truth it is of no use. Therefore, it is critical to obtain truth, and then live that truth.

After speaking the parable of the 10 virgins, Yahushua then gave the parable of the talents. He holds His servants responsible for what has been given to them. He stated that He will *"cast the unprofitable servant into the outer darkness. There will be weeping and gnashing of teeth."* (Matthew 25:30)

Yahushua then went on to provide His final Parable before He attended the Passover, renewed the Covenant and presented Himself as the Lamb of Elohim. Here is what He

taught. "*³¹ When the Son of Man comes in His glory, and all the set apart angels with Him, then He will sit on the throne of His glory. ³² All the nations will be gathered before Him, and He will separate them one from another, as a shepherd divides his sheep from the goats. ³³ And He will set the sheep on His right hand, but the goats on the left. ³⁴ Then the King will say to those on His right hand, Come, you blessed of My Father, inherit the kingdom prepared for you from the foundation of the world (katabole): ³⁵ for I was hungry and you gave Me food; I was thirsty and you gave Me drink; I was a stranger and you took Me in; ³⁶ I was naked and you clothed Me; I was sick and you visited Me; I was in prison and you came to Me. ³⁷ Then the righteous will answer Him, saying, Master, when did we see You hungry and feed You, or thirsty and give You drink? ³⁸ When did we see You a stranger and take You in, or naked and clothe You? ³⁹ Or when did we see You sick, or in prison, and come to You? ⁴⁰ And the King will answer and say to them, Assuredly, I say to you, inasmuch as you did it to one of the least of these My brethren, you did it to Me. ⁴¹ Then He will also say to those on the left hand, Depart from Me, you cursed, into the everlasting fire prepared for the devil and his angels: ⁴² for I was hungry and you gave Me no food; I was thirsty and you gave Me no drink; ⁴³ I was a stranger and you did not take Me in, naked and you did not clothe Me, sick and in prison and you did not visit Me. ⁴⁴ Then they also will answer Him, saying, Master, when did we see You hungry or thirsty or a stranger or naked or sick or in prison, and did not minister to You? ⁴⁵ Then He will answer them, saying, Assuredly, I say to you, inasmuch as you did not do it to one of the least of these, you did not do it to Me. ⁴⁶ And these will go away into everlasting punishment, but the righteous into eternal life."
Matthew 25:31-46

This final book in the Walk in the Light series was meant to prepare His servants for the final shofar. It is an attempt to reveal the heart of the Master, and what He expects from His servants. In fact, it is intended to be a

shofar blast – for those who have ears to hear. It is a warning cry for the Covenant Assembly to get ready for the end of the age.

It provides much information, but that information is useless unless it leads a person to righteousness and eternal life – to the path of the overcomer that has been revealed through the Covenant. Once we recognize that ancient path we must walk in the way that leads us back to the beginning – a new beginning.

The end, after all, is about a new beginning. It concerns the *Restoration* of creation and mankind. It will be a culmination of the patterns provided through creation and described in the *Scriptures* as the *Messiah* ushers in the *Sabbath* millennium of peace. For those in the *Covenant* it will be a fulfillment of the promise as YHWH establishes His Kingdom on earth. In the end, many will experience difficulties, but *The Redeemed* will call upon the *Name* of YHWH and be saved. They will be refined as they are guided by the *Appointed Times*. They must heed the warning to "come out of Babylon," and be separated from those who participate in the *Pagan Holidays* and practices of Babylon. They must walk in the *Law and Grace*, the Torah and the mercy, of YHWH and prepare themselves for the *Kosher* Wedding Feast He has prepared for the ones *"who keep the commandments of Elohim and the faith of Yahushua."* Revelation 14:12 While the nations look upon the future with dread, this is the hope that we have as we await the sounding of *the Final Shofar*.

Endnotes

[1] See the works of Caltech astrophysicist Dr. Hugh Ross who argues that the probability of finding just one planet capable of supporting life within the observable universe is less than 1 chance in 10^{174}. *Lights in the Sky & Little Green Men: A Rational Christian Look at UFOs and Extraterrestrials* by Hugh Ross, Kenneth Samples and Mark Clark (Colorado Springs, CO: NavPress, 2002) p. 39. This number is incomprehensible and defies all probability. In fact, in mathematics it is commonly held that if something is beyond 10^{50} to 1 it is impossible. "Scientists have made many discoveries over the past century which demonstrate that the size, structure, and content of our universe all depend in very sensitive ways to a number of finely-tuned constants such as the speed of light, the electron charge, etc. Mathematical physicist Roger Penrose, in *The Emperor's New Mind* has calculated that the overall accuracy in choosing all of these constants had to be on the order of one part in $10^{\wedge}10^{\wedge}123$ (ten raised to the power of ten raised to the power of 123). This number is so large that if you were to write it out, with each zero the size of a proton, it could not fit within the known universe." (Quoting from On Universes and Firing Squads or "How I Learned To Stop Worrying About the Origin of the Cosmos" written by Michael J. Hurben. Regardless, the proponents of extraterrestrial life, particularly those belonging to the SETI (Search for Extraterrestrial Intelligence) faith, fondly quote "the Drake Equation" ($N = R^{*} \cdot f_p \cdot n_e \cdot f_1 \cdot f_i \cdot f_c \cdot L$) to justify the notion that Earth is a mediocre planet and that there are millions of other habitable planets in the cosmos. Added with their belief in evolution, the SETI faithful then propose that there must be many more civilizations in existence, some of which are more advanced than earth. These are all grand leaps of faith that when properly scrutinized defy all statistical possibility. It is essentially a desperate attempt by those opposed to the concept that a Creator is responsible for our existence, and that the Scriptures provide an accurate account of our existence and our

purpose. It has been held that "the Drake equation is literally meaningless, and has nothing to do with science . . . science involves the creation of testable hypothesis. The Drake equation cannot be tested and therefore SETI is not science. SETI is unquestionably a religion." *Exo-Vaticana* by Chris Putnam and Thomas Horn, Defender, Crane, MO (2013) quoting Michael Crichton, *Aliens Cause Global Warming*, Caltech Michelin Lecture, January 17, 2003. *Exo-Vaticana* also the source for the Ross quote.

[2] See www.collective-evolution.com/2011/09/02/scientist-prove-dna-can-be-reprogrammed-by-words-and-frequencies/#sthash.P1niUBcJ.dpuf

[3] There is no doubt that we live in a finite "digital" universe. Our physical universe is controlled by mathematical laws. That is why the language of creation, Hebrew, is a mathematical language. For a purely scientific examination of this subject see *Cosmic Numbers* by James D. Stein and *The Mathematics of Life* by Ian Stewart. Therefore, this present physical universe is essentially a digital simulation in a finite universe. See also teachings of Chuck Missler on Genesis 1. There are many who have demonstrated through mathematics, the statistical impossibility of evolution. It does not take a mathematical genius to imagine the difficulty of such incredible complexity occurring from a random explosion. When provided with these statistics there are those who will doggedly attempt to dispel them, but the bottom line is that those who honestly and objectively examine this issue in light of the continual advances in science must surely acknowledge that the hypothesis called evolution has crumbled. See *Evolution: A Theory in Crisis* by Michael Denton, Burnett Books 1985. For interesting video presentations on evolution see *Unlocking the Mystery of Life* and *Darwin's Dilemma*, Illustra Media 2009. When dealing with the complexity of cells and organisms the reader is referred to Michael Behe and his argument of Irreducible Complexity. "Irreducible complexity (IC) is an argument by proponents of intelligent design that certain biological systems are too complex to have evolved from simpler, or "less complete" predecessors, through natural selection acting upon a series of advantageous naturally occurring, chance mutations. The argument is central to intelligent design, and is rejected by the scientific community at large, which overwhelmingly regards intelligent design as

pseudoscience. Irreducible complexity is one of two main arguments used by intelligent design proponents, the other being specified complexity." See en.wikipedia.org/wiki/ and the subject of irreducible complexity. Of course, science utterly rejects this argument, and has done everything possible to discredit that position.

4   The word "Bible" possibly carries with is various pagan connotations. As a result, we will use the word Scriptures to reference the texts selected as "inspired" and contained within the book commonly called "The Bible." This subject is discussed further in the Walk in the Light series book entitled *The Scriptures.*

5   *"By faith we understand that the worlds were framed by the word of God, so that the things which are seen were not made of things which are visible."* Hebrews 11:3. While the notion that the Hebrew Language is the "mother tongue" of the planet is not a popular notion with secular scholars, there is evidence pointing to that fact. See *The Origin of Speeches Intelligent Design in Language*, Isaac E. Mozeson, Lightcatcher Books, 2006. While this author disagrees with the calendar concepts in the text there is useful information that can be gleaned from the Book of Jubilees. Here is a quote referencing the Hebrew tongue as the language of Creation. *"[25] And YHWH Almighty said: 'Open his mouth and his ears, that he may hear and speak with his mouth, with the language which has been revealed' for it had ceased from the mouths of all the children of men from the day of the overthrow (of Babel). [26] And I opened his mouth, and his ears and his lips, and I began to speak with him in Hebrew in the tongue of the creation. [27] And he took the books of his fathers, and these were written in Hebrew, and he transcribed them, and he began from henceforth to study them, and I made known to him that which he could not (understand), and he studied them during the six rainy months."* The Book of Jubilees Chapter 12:25-27. It is clear that the universe was designed by a mathematician. (see Hugo de Garis, *From Cosmism to Deism*, Kurzweil Accelerating Intelligence). Our physical universe is controlled by mathematical laws. That is why the language of creation, Hebrew, is a mathematical language. For a purely scientific examination of this subject see *Cosmic Numbers* by James D. Stein and *The Mathematics of Life* by Ian Stewart. Numbers and letters are actually the same in Hebrew, they simply describe creation in a different way For instance the word for "water" is

"mayim" (**ᵞ𐤆ᵞ**). Now the letter "mem" (**ᵞ**) actually means: "water" and we can see it in the pictograph. The word "mayim" also clearly represents the motion as two "mems" (**ᵞ**) surrounding a "yud" (**𐤆**). Interestingly, modern science also attributes this same ration to water - H_2O. The scientific formula of water consists of 2 Hydrogen atoms and 1 oxygen atom. So the essential elements are the same, just described differently. For a further discussion of this subject see *Letters of Fire*, Mattityahu Glazerson, The Kest-Lebovits JHRL, Jerusalem 1991 (English).

The current modern Hebrew character set is sometimes referred to as Chaldean flame letters. This language was brought with the Yahudim (exiles from the House of Judah) after their Babylonian exile. It is important to understand a bit of history involving the Kingdom of Israel (Yisrael). After the death of King Shlomo (Solomon), the Kingdom was divided in two. The Northern Tribes were referred to as the House of Yisrael and the Southern Tribes were referred to as the House of Judah. The House of Yisrael was conquered and exiled by the Assyrians in the North. The House of Judah was conquered and exiled by the Babylonians in the South. There is a great deal of mystery associated with this language which is really a not a modern language, although comparatively newer than ancient Hebrew. One thing is certain, it is not the original language of Yisrael. In fact, it is really a language that exclusively belongs to the Judaism. Those from the House of Yisrael who desire to truly learn about their Hebrew Roots should be looking at the original Hebrew Language often referred to as Ancient Hebrew or Paleo Hebrew. This would have been the language used by Abraham, Yitshaq, Yaakob, Mosheh and the Assembly of Yisrael.

The term "god" is a generic term which can be attached to any number of powerful beings described in mythology and worshipped in pagan religions. Some use a capital "G" to refer to "the God of the Bible" but I find it a disservice to apply this label to the Creator of the Universe when the Hebrew Scriptures clearly refer to Him as Elohim. The pagan origins of the word "god" are discussed in the Walk in the Light series book entitled "Names." Elohim (**ᵞ𐤆ᵃ𐤊ᛕ**) is technically plural, but that does not designate more than one Creator. The singular form is El (**𐤊ᛕ**) and could refer to any "mighty one," but because the plural is used to describe the Creator, it means that Elohim is qualitatively stronger or more powerful than any singular El (𝑙𝑋). In Hebrew, the plural form can mean that something or someone is qualitatively greater not just quantitatively greater. We see in the first sentence of the Scriptures that "In the Beginning Elohim created" the Hebrew for "created" is "bara" (𝑋𝟵𝒴) which literally is "He created." It is masculine singular showing that while Elohim is plural He is masculine singular. For an excellent discussion of the Hebrew Etymology of the Name of Elohim I recommend *His Name is One* written by Jeff A. Benner, Virtualbookworm.com Publishing 2002. The Hebrew language currently in use, often called modern Hebrew, is not the language used when the Scriptures were first spoken and written. The original Hebrew language is often called "ancient" or "paleo" Hebrew.

8 Indeed since Elohim is plural, it could be argued that there were two witnesses to Creation – the Father and the Son. The Son was actually the One Who Created and the purpose of this Creation is to expand the Kingdom of the Father through His Son. That concept will be examined further throughout this text as we look to the culmination of the end of the age and the final purpose of this existence.

9 The notion that we are only around 6,000 years in this cycle of time appears to fly in the face of modern science, which places the age of the universe at over 13 billion years. The issue in Genesis is not necessarily the age of the universe, but rather the beginning of this present Age, or physical existence. One problem with science is that it primarily rejects the notion of a Creator, and the creation of man. As a result, science needs a lot of time to explain and justify the notion of evolution. The simple fact is that if we calculate time from the Hebrew texts we are approximately 6,000 years in the cycles of the ages since mankind was created. Just exactly what occurred before Genesis 1:1 and 1:2 is a mystery, but we are able to calculate time from Creation Day 1, which was Day 1 of Month 7 3,986 BCE or October 7, 3986 BCE. (see www.torahcalendar.com). This book is written in English, which is a western language. Western languages are very different from eastern languages. These language distinctions (east v. west) are important because they determine the way people communicate, and how they think. Believe it or not, people in the East actually think differently from people in the West. Eastern thought tends to be cyclical,

while Western thought is linear. Western languages tend to be very abstract, while Eastern Languages tend to be very concrete. Western languages tend to be static while Eastern languages are active. In fact, an example of how opposite they are is demonstrated by the fact that Eastern languages typically flow from right to left, while Western languages tend to flow from the left to the right. This is significant and explains why there are often so many differences between Eastern and Western religions. Language actually influences the way we think and the way we perceive the world that we live in. This is the source of many of the tensions that exist in the world today – the disconnect between Eastern and Western cultures. This is what occurred when Christianity and Judaism originally both strayed from the Covenant made with Israel (Yisrael), and developed into two religions. Christianity became heavily influenced by the west, and Judaism remained an eastern religion. Now both have a mixture of Eastern and Western influences, but the original separation remains.

10 In order to understand the development of the modern Hebrew language it is important to understand the history of the Kingdom of Yisrael as briefly summarized in Footnote number 6. Because the House of Yisrael has been lost, the original language of Yisrael has also been lost. It is commonly believed that the House of Yahudah brought the Modern Hebrew language out of their Babylonian exile, thus the reference to Chaldean flame letters. In fact, it is really a language that exclusively belongs to the Yahudim. Those from the House of Yisrael who desire to truly learn about their Hebrew Roots should be looking at the original Hebrew Language often referred to as Ancient Hebrew or Paleo Hebrew. This would have been the language used by Abraham, Yitshaq, Yaakob, Mosheh and the Assembly of Yisrael. Essentially, Yahudah is one tribe of Yisrael and the House of Yahudah originally represented 3 Tribes, namely Yahudah, Benjamin and Levi. After the split in the Kingdom, which is discussed in detail in this book, many from the other tribes mixed with Yahudah. So these Yisraelites consisting of the House of Yahudah were a mixture of all Israelites but became known as an exclusive people group known as Yahudim or "Jews." Over time, they separated from their ancient Yisraelite roots by creating a unique language and a unique religion called "Judaism." This division and separation is described in greater

detail in the Walk in the Light series book entitled *The Redeemed*. While the notion that the Hebrew Language is the "mother tongue" of the planet is not a popular notion with secular scholars, there is evidence pointing to that fact. See *The Origin of Speeches Intelligent Design in Language*, Isaac E. Mozeson, Lightcatcher Books, 2006. The ancient Hebrew language actually tells a story that begins with the Aleph (𐤀) – "the strong one" and ends with the Taw (𐤕) – "the covenant."

There are many different Ancient Hebrew scripts discovered through archaeology. Since they were all written by different individuals there are stylistic variances between them. The modern Hebrew used today is not the same language as the Ancient or Paleo Hebrew used by Ancient Yisrael. Therefore, throughout this text we will attempt to provide examples of words and phrases in their Ancient Script in order to glean the depth of their meaning. The Paleo Hebrew font primarily used in this book is an adaptation and interpretation of the various examples of Paleo Hebrew found throughout archaeology. Since there are a variety of scripts found in academia, this one script font developed by the author is being used for consistency and clarity in an attempt to represent the Creator's meaning in the "original" language. The author has developed a Font intended to represent the ancient language as might have been written by an individual person thousands of years ago.

It is important to recognize that there was a spiritual universe before "the beginning" of the physical universe. "The *time* between the *foundation of the world* in the *spiritual universe*, and Day One of the *physical universe* is referred to as Olam She'avar or The World that Was in Hebraic thought . . . Everything in the *spiritual universe*, including the angels and the *souls* of all people, were created *before the time of the ages* according to 2 Timothy 1:8-11, Titus 1:1-3 and Jude 1:6. This time in history is referred to as Olam She'avar or The World that Was in Hebraic thought. This was when the *foundation* of the earth was laid according to Job 38:4, Psalms 102:25, Isaiah 48:13, Zechariah 12:1 and Hebrews 1:10. Olam She'avar is referred to as the time *before the disruption of the world* in John 17:24 and 1 Peter 1:17-21. The children of Elohim were chosen during Olam She'avar *before the disruption of the world* according to Ephesians 1:3-6." *The 7000 Year Plan*, www.torahcalendar.com.

The Hebrew Scriptures contain numerous instances of what are commonly called jots and tittles. These typically include enlarged, diminished or reversed characters intended to draw the readers attention to something. No one knows exactly how they came into existence, although the popular opinion is that Mosheh included them in the original Torah. One thing is certain, they are not considered to be scribal errors and they have been maintained in all copies of the Hebrew texts, although you will not see them in a translation.

The word "shi" (𝐙𝐖) is used only three times in the Scriptures - Isaiah 18:7 and Psalms 68:29 and 76:11. In each case it has profound prophetic significance.

It is important to recognize that there is no such thing as a Hebrew numeral set, separate and apart from the Hebrew letters. As a result, each Hebrew character has a corresponding numeric value. This adds an interesting dimension to the study of Scriptures. Commonly called gematria, the study of the numeric values of characters and words can be quite revealing. There are various ways to count and study the numbers and the Chart in the Appendix merely provides the ordinal numbering and the primary gematria.

The numerical value of "beresheet" (𝐗𝐙𝐖𝐊𝟒𝟗) is 913, calculated as follows: 𝟗 = 2, 𝟒 = 200, 𝐊 = 1, 𝐖 = 300, 𝐙 = 10, 𝐗 = 400. The numerical value of "beit" (𝐗𝐙𝟗) is and has a 412, calculated as follows: 𝟗 = 2, 𝐙 = 10, 𝐗 = 400. The numerical value of "rosh" (𝐖𝐊𝟒) is 501, calculated as follows: 𝟒 = 200, 𝐊 = 1, 𝐖 = 300.

While the most common form of son is "ben" (𝐘𝟗) in the Hebrew Script, the word "bar" (𝟒𝟗) can also mean son. While there are some who advocate that bar is strictly Aramaic, there is evidence that bar was used in the Hebrew. (see Psalm 2:12).

The Hebrew word "et" (𝐗𝐊), otherwise known as the Aleph Taw, consists of two" Hebrew characters - the aleph (𝐊) which is the first character in the Hebrew alphabet, and the taw (𝐗) which is the last letter in the Hebrew alphabet. "This word 𝐗𝐊 is used over 11,000 times (and never translated into English as there is no equivalent) to point to the direct object of the verb." (from Benner, Jeff A., *Learn to Read Biblical Hebrew*, Virtualbookworm.com 2004 Page 41.). It is embedded throughout the Hebrew Scriptures and while it has a known grammatical function, the Sages have long understood that it has a much deeper and mysterious function – many believe that it is a direct reference to the Messiah. As such, it plays an important part in understanding the Scriptural Covenants so we will, at times, examine its existence and relevance throughout this text.

20 Nahum of Gimzo was one individual who studied the Aleph Taw (𐤗𐤀). He was the teacher of Akiba and used to explain the accusative particle "et" by saying that it implied the inclusion in the object of something besides that which is explicitly mentioned. See Jewish Encyclopedia.

21 Memra actually means "word" in Aramaic. The notion of the Memra comes from the root mem resh (𐤓𐤌) which was the root used through Creation when Elohim "said" (𐤓𐤌𐤀𐤉), and the material world came into existence. The Memra became known as the Divine Mediator in Ancient thought. The Memra would mediate between the unapproachable Creator Elohim and created man. The Memra appears hundreds of times in the Aramaic Targums. Targum means: "translation" or "explanation." In the Aramaic Peshitta John 1:1 refers to that "Word" as the "Miltha."

22 Since the Aleph Taw (𐤗𐤀) represents the entire Aleph Bet, all of the characters contained between the aleph (𐤀) and the taw (𐤗), this is why the Messiah would be called the Word, or the Memra. Messiah is the utterance of the Creation within the physical universe. The Word, which came from and through the Creator in the spiritual realm then manifested in the physical.

23 Time is often described as a physical dimension. Just as height, length and width constitute the dimensions of our three dimensional physical world, so time is another dimension in the world as we know it. Despite the fact that we can measure time, it appears that there are still mysteries associated with this fourth dimension that we do not fully understand.

24 There are many who have demonstrated through mathematics, the statistical impossibility of evolution. It does not take a mathematical genius to imagine the difficulty of such incredible complexity occurring from a random explosion. When we look at all of the marvelously complex systems that all must have been put in place at the same time to make a functioning mammal for example, it really must have resulted from intelligent design. For instance, you would need blood, a fully functioning circulatory system with a heart that beats on its own and a fully integrated respiratory system that also operates on "autopilot" otherwise the mammal could never sleep. The respiratory system must immediately integrate with the

circulatory system, feeding oxygen throughout the body which also must contain a skeletal and muscular system, as well as a reproductive system with both male and female species all appearing at the same time and same location. This is just scratching the surface regarding the systems that all must be in place at the same time in order for the being to exist. There is no time for evolution, and the idea that all of these necessary systems occurred by chance at just the right time, for each species, is simply absurd. Instead of billions of years of progressive evolution, you need complex systems to occur at the same moment in time – this is the opposite of evolution and supports creation. Indeed, the Cambrian explosion clearly reveals that complex life came into existence suddenly, and the fossil record does not support the gradual progression espoused by evolution. Charles Darwin even admitted that without the support from the fossil record of the lengthy and gradual evolution his notions would fall flat, and they have. It is time for people to actually use their common sense and consider this complex universe rather than simply swallowing the ignorance of so-called "scientists" whose primary agenda is to disprove the existence of a creator. When provided with these statistics there are those who will doggedly attempt to dispel them, but the bottom line is that those who honestly and objectively examine this issue in light of the continual advances in science must surely acknowledge that the hypothesis called evolution has crumbled. See *Evolution: A Theory in Crisis* by Michael Denton, Burnett Books 1985. For interesting video presentations on evolution see *Unlocking the Mystery of Life* and *Darwin's Dilemma*, Illustra Media 2009.

²⁵ This physical existence has experienced an incredible history, much of which is not specifically addressed in and through the Scriptures, although there is enough information to ascertain what happened. We know that spiritual beings, known as fallen angels and watchers, mixed with mankind resulting in a hybrid species of beings known as Nephilim. These Nephilim and their action were likely the reason for the flood. They resulted in giants and many hybrid species that likely built some of the incredible ancient structures that continue to baffle scientists and archaeologists who, espousing evolutionist ideas, believe that mankind was not advanced enough to build such structures. As a result, many try to attribute those past advances to the

intervention of extraterrestrials. This then sets the stage for a future "return" of those extraterrestrials and we will likely see such a deception occur in the future. For an interesting discussion of this scenario and the groundwork being laid by both science and religions see the book *Exo-Vaticana* by Tom Horn.

26 There is no doubt that we live in a finite "digital" universe. Our physical universe is controlled by mathematical laws. That is why the language of creation, Hebrew, is a mathematical language. For a purely scientific examination of this subject see *Cosmic Numbers* by James D. Stein and *The Mathematics of Life* by Ian Stewart.

27 Numbers and letters are actually the same in Hebrew, they simply describe creation in a different way. For instance the word for "water" is "mayim" (messages). Now the letter mem () actually means: "water" and we can see it in the pictograph. The word "mayim" also clearly represents the motion as two mems () surround a yud (). Interestingly, modern science also attributes this same ration to water - H_2O. The scientific formula of water consists of 2 Hydrogen atoms and 1 oxygen atom. So the essential elements are the same, just described differently. For a further discussion of this subject see *Letters of Fire*, Mattityahu Glazerson, The Kest-Lebovits JHRL, Jerusalem 1991 (English).

28 It is important to recognize that because Hebrew is an eastern language, which tends to be more concrete than the abstract western languages, a direct translation would be quite choppy. One of the tasks of a translator is to smooth out that choppiness. In doing so they may actually change a concept or miss something important. Sometimes it is helpful to examine the rough "mechanical translation" to discern the original meaning of the text. Jeff Benner has developed some wonderful tools through examining the Ancient Language and providing mechanical translations of the Hebrew texts. The portion of text in the main body of the book was taken from Jeff Benner's, *Mechanical Translation of Genesis*.

29 *The American Heritage Dictionary of the English Language*, Fourth Edition, Houghton Mifflin Company, 2000, archived from the original on June 25, 2008, retrieved May 20, 2010 quoted from Wikipedia.

30 http://www.livescience.com/5045-scientists-sound.html.

31 The description of Creation is not what many would expect if it

were describing perfection at the very beginning. We read: *"The earth was without form, and void; and darkness was on the face of the deep. And the Spirit of Elohim was hovering over the face of the waters."* Beresheet 1:2. It appears to be a dark and ominous event, and many speculate why creation was in such a state. When we read about the time "before the foundation of the world" – "katabole" (καταβολῆς), we see something very interesting. The Greek word "katabole" (καταβολῆς) actually means: "destruction, a casting down, break down or disintegration." So it appears that there was a spiritual existence that occurred before the "casting down or destruction." This explains the New Testament text of 1 Peter 1:20 which indicates that the Messiah *"was foreordained before the 'foundation of the world'* (καταβολῆς), *but was manifest in these last times for you."* It also explains the idea of predestination as described in the text of Ephesians 1:4. *"Just as He chose us in Him before the 'foundation of the world'* (καταβολῆς), *that we should be set apart and without blame before Him in love."* So things happened, decisions were made, and destinies were determined before the destruction which leads us to understand that there was a destruction prior to the creation that we read about in Beresheet, which means that there was a creation before the destruction. For a more detailed discussion of the Greek word "katabole" see *Did God Know? A Study of the Nature of God* by Howard R. Elseth, Chapter 16, Calvary United Church, Inc. (1977). See also Endnote 7. This word is found ten times in the New Testament texts and is translated as "foundation." (see Matthew 13:35, Matthew 25:34, Luke 11:50, John 17:24, Ephesians 1:4, Hebrews 4:3, Hebrews 9:26, 1 Peter 1:20, Revelation 13:8 & Revelation 17:8). Interestingly, there is one verse where it is translated as "conceive." In Hebrews 11:11 we read: *"Through faith also Sara herself received strength to 'conceive'* (καταβολῆς) *seed, and was delivered of a child when she was past age, because she judged him faithful who had promised."* KJV. How amazing that the birth of the promised son, the son of the Covenant, is connected with the word "katabole" (καταβολῆς).

YHWH is an English representation of יהוה in Modern Hebrew and 𐤉𐤄𐤅𐤄 in Paleo Hebrew. It is the four letter Name of the Elohim described in the Scriptures. This four letter Name has commonly been called the "Tetragrammaton" and traditionally has been considered to be ineffable or unpronounceable. As a result, despite the fact that it is found nearly 7,000 times in the

Hebrew Scriptures, it has been replaced with such titles as "The Lord," "Adonai" and "HaShem." I believe that this practice is in direct violation of the First and Third Commandments.

33 Some commonly accepted pronunciations are: Yahweh, Yahuwah and Yahowah. Since there is debate over which pronunciation is correct, I simply use the Name as it is found in the Scriptures, although I spell it in English from left to right, rather than in Hebrew from right to left. For the person who truly desires to know the nature of the Elohim described in the Scriptures, a good place to start is the Name by which He revealed Himself to all mankind. A more detailed discussion of this very important issue can be found in the Walk in the Light series book entitled *Names*.

34 The ancient alephbet is the code from which all of existence was made and exists. As we examine the combinations of these characters on multiple dimensions and examine the numerical relationships with words we can gain amazing insight into the Creator and Creation. Of course this examination must be conducted in the Ancient Language.

35 *Letters of Fire, Mystical Insights into the Hebrew Language*, Matityahu Glazerson, The Kest-Lebovits Jewish Heritage and Roots Library, 1984 quoting Sefer Ha-Yetzirah.

36 It is well established that YHWH has a 7,000 year plan for creation patterned upon the first seven words of the Hebrew Scriptures and the seven day weekly cycle. There are six days for man, or flesh, and the seventh is the Sabbath of YHWH. This time is divided into 50 year Jubilee cycles so the time allotted to man is 120 Jubilee Cycles, which is 6,000 years. (see Beresheet 6:3). For a detailed discussion of the Sabbath see the Walk in the Light series book entitled *The Sabbath*.

37 Exodus (Shemot) 23:22 provides: "*But if you indeed obey His voice and do all that I speak (אׁשׁדׁאׁ), then I will be an enemy to your enemies and an adversary to your adversaries.*" The word for speak (אׁשׁדׁאׁ) is essentially aleph (אׁ) preceding "word" (אׁשׁדׁ). The Gematria for "speak" is 207. It is the same as "light" and "see" so it appears that the Word of YHWH is something that we are supposed to see, not just hear.

38 The Appointed Times of YHWH are described in greater detail in the Walk in the Light series entitled *Appointed Times*.

39 Beresheet 28:10-22. See also Beresheet 35:14.

40 As discussed, time was a dimension created at the beginning of

the physical universe. As such, it can be measured. The Creator set the sun and the moon for markers and we can measure days, weeks, months and years using these markers. Just as the Creator established the seven count of days from the beginning, He does the same for years. Years are counted in sevens, often referred to as Shemitah cycles. After seven Shemitah cycles (49 years) the 50th year is known as a Jubilee year. The Jubilee is when a restoration occurs. (Vayiqra 25) Many believe that the Messiah will restore all things in a Jubilee year.

41 The Creator is definitely concerned about what we put into our bodies. Since we were made in His Image it is important that we function with His Creation as intended. There are things in Creation that He made for food and things which were prohibited to be eaten. This began in the Garden and continues to this day. There is a reason for these instructions, but men continue to be "hell bent" to do as they please and make every excuse to profane themselves and disobey the commands. For a more detailed discussion regarding the dietary commandments see the Walk in the Light series book entitled *Kosher*. Interestingly, the first time that green foods are mentioned in Beresheet 1:30 the Aleph Taw (X𐤊) is affixed to "every green" (𐤐𐤒𐤆-𐤋𐤏-X𐤊).

42 Beresheet 1:27; 2:7; 2:8; 2:15.

43 The events in the Scriptures often provide us with patterns that reveal mysteries. As was seen with Adam, we also saw Abram being placed in a "deep sleep." This was essentially connecting these two events, which were both an important part of the Covenant process. For a more detailed description of these events and their connection see the Walk in the Light series book entitled *Covenants*.

44 See Appendix A for the ordinal and gematria values of the Hebrew alephbet.

45 If you have even a minimal understanding of the Scriptures, you will discern the connection that all of these share with "cleansing" including the Passover and the Red Heifer. (see Shemot 12; Vayiqra 14; Bemidbar 19). The notion of cleansing therefore ultimately involves our DNA. All of the sacrifices involve blood and they are all intimately connected with the Messiah. The Passover is interesting because the first instance occurred in Egypt and the blood was placed on the doorposts of the peoples homes. Thereafter, the sacrifice occurred at the

House of YHWH and the sacrifice was thereafter eaten in the homes of those offering the lamb. The Red Heifer sacrifice is very unique and special as it is the one sacrifice always made outside the camp. This is significant because it relates to the first Passover and was necessary to transition a person from an unclean state to a clean state. There is a great mystery associated with this "red heifer" which is described as "para adamah" (𐤄𐤌𐤃𐤀 𐤄𐤓𐤐) in Hebrew. It literally means: "fruitful ground." Notice the word "adamah" which contains "adam" (man) and "dam" (blood). This subject is described in further detail in an article entitled *The Mystery of the Red Heifer* located at www.shemayisrael.net.

46 For an interesting discussion that focuses on the modern Hebrew language see video presentation entitled The Hebrew Language the DNA of Creation, Rabbi Mordechai Kraft www.youtube.com/watch?v=6_aFvmY8ZbI. While this video focuses on the modern Hebrew language it provides interesting insight and comments, some of which can be applied to the Ancient Hebrew Language.

47 See the text in Deuteronomy (Debarim) 6:4. Undoubtedly, the most significant prayer in the Torah is known as The Shema found at Debarim 6:4. In fact, it was declared to be the first (resheet) of all the commandments by Yahushua. (see Mark 12:29). The Shema proclaims: "[4] *Hear, O Yisrael: YHWH our Elohim, YHWH is one. (echad)* [5] *Love YHWH your Elohim with all your heart and with all your soul and with all your strength.* [6] *These commandments that I give you today are to be upon your hearts.* [7] *Impress them on your children. Talk about them when you sit at home and when you walk along the road, when you lie down and when you get up.* [8] *Tie them as symbols on your hands and bind them on your foreheads.* [9] *Write them on the doorframes of your houses and on your gates."* Debarim 6:4-9. The Command to write the commands on our doorposts and our gates means that YHWH is in control of that space. His Commandments are the rule of that property, which represents His Kingdom on the Earth. So we are instructed to essentially establish the Kingdom of YHWH in every area of our lives. The text of the Shema in Hebrew is quite profound and contains an enlarged ayin (𐤏) at the end of the word "shema" and an enlarged dalet (𐤃) at the end of the word "echad." The ayin dalet (𐤃𐤏) is essentially announcing that we should "see" the "door." The Shema text is provided in

⁴⁸
Appendix D.

The life of a creature is in its' blood. As a result, we are not to consume the blood. See Vayiqra 17:14; Debarim 12:16 and 15:23. Indeed, the texts actually state "the nephesh" is in the blood. Nephesh (ﬨﬧﬔﬖ) is often translated as "soul," but it really means: "breath." So the life of a being is the breath of YHWH Elohim that was breathed into man. Man was initially formed from "dust" - aphar (ﬠﬗﬖ) in Hebrew. *"And YHWH Elohim formed man of the dust of the ground, and breathed into his nostrils the breath of life; and man became a living being."* Beresheet 2:7. We must therefore recognize that our bodies are not just dust, or flesh. We actually contain the "breath of life" and only when Adam received that breath of life did he become a living being. We are actually the merging of the spirit and the physical, we are the image of YHWH - the representation of the Spiritual Creator in the physical realm. Man is in a fallen state and deserves to die because of the sin that infects our bodies. We are all worthy of death because of that sin, and that is why YHWH established the concept of atonement. The blood of another can atone for our sins. The blood represents the life of a being, and this is why the blood is sprinkled on the altar. As we recognize that we should be placed on the altar, yet the blood of another will be sprinkled in our place, we see the Plan of Redemption orchestrated by and through YHWH.

⁴⁹
Some believe that blood is actually congealed light. We know that the life is in the blood. (Debarim 12:23). That life was the "breath of YHWH." It is important to understand that the life of YHWH was the first words spoken "exist light." (Beresheet 1:3). So that "light" was "life." As the dust of the ground was formed into flesh, the blood within coursed through his veins carrying that light of life. When that blood stops flowing, the light goes out and the "nephesh" departs from the flesh. The flesh then returns to the dust of the ground from which it came. Now some claim that this is a cultic doctrine originating from *Love, The Law of the Angels* by Gwen Shaw (Engeltal Press, 1979), but the concept traces right back from the beginning. Just how exactly the light of life is in the blood is a mystery, but it is clearly a spiritual truth that science has yet to explain.

⁵⁰
The light of life is the Messiah, and when we express belief in the Light we become Children of the Light. (John 12:36). See also Ephesians 5:8: *"For you were once darkness, but now you are light in*

YHWH. *Walk as children of light.*" See also 1 Thessalonians 5:5. Many of the Dead Sea Scrolls attributed to the Essenes describe the struggle between the children of the light and the children of the dark.

51 *The Persecution and Trial of Gaston Naessens* by Christopher Bird at http://customers.hbci.com.

52 According to Beresheet 3:15 "*And I will put enmity between you and the woman, and between your seed and her Seed; He shall bruise your head, and you shall bruise His heel.*" This has long been held to be a prophecy concerning the Messiah. In between the phrase "He shall bruise your head" and "you shall bruise His heel" is the word "etah" (ᴀXᴌ). Essentially it is the Aleph Taw (Xᴌ) with a hey (ᴀ) at the end. The hey (ᴀ) represents a man with upstretched arms and means: "behold." So it appears that there is something very significant occurring in this passage and an examination in the Hebrew language reveals very important information that is not seen in the English.

53 "*Elohim called the light Day, and the darkness He called Night. So the evening and the morning were the first day.*" Beresheet 1:5. So the darkness preceded the light. This was the pattern of creation as light was introduced into creation. The day pattern of dark preceding light is a pattern that we are supposed to learn from.

54 See Psalm 136:9 and Psalm 89:37.

55 See Psalm 90:4: "*For a **thousand years** in Your sight are like yesterday when it is past, and like a watch in the night.*" Also, 2 Peter 3:8: "*But, beloved, do not forget this one thing, that with YHWH one day is as a thousand years, and a thousand years as one day.*" This passage from Peter is prefaced by the statement that the world was judged by a flood in the past and will be judged by fire in the future.

56 The first woman, often called Eve, was actually named Hawah (ᴀYᴴ) in Hebrew.

57 The names of the first sons of Adam and Hawah, often called, Cain and Abel. Their actual names in Hebrew are: Qayin (ʏᴢᴘ) and Hebel (ʟᴎᴀ).

58 The instructions of YHWH are known as the Torah. In a very general sense, the word Torah is used to refer to the first five books of the Scriptures which some call the Pentateuch, or the five books of Moses. Torah may sound like a strange word to anyone who reads an English translation of the Scriptures, but it is found throughout the Hebrew text. The reason is because it is

a Hebrew word which translators have chosen to replace with "the Law." Whenever the word "Torah" is found in the Hebrew, it has been translated as "the Law" in English Bibles. Therefore, if you grew up reading an English Bible then you would never have come across this word. On the other hand, if you read the Hebrew Scriptures the word Torah is found throughout the text. The word Torah (ᛏᛦᛏX) in Hebrew means: *"utterance, teaching, instruction or revelation from Elohim."* It comes from horah (ᛏᛦᛏᛏ) which means: *"to direct, to teach,"* and derives from the stem yara (ᛏᛦᛏ) which means: *"to shoot or throw."* Therefore there are two aspects to the word Torah: 1) aiming or pointing in the right direction, and 2) movement in that direction. The Torah (ᛏᛦᛏX) is the first five books of the Hebrew and Christian Scriptures. The Torah is more accurately defined as the "instruction" of YHWH for His set apart people. The Torah contains instruction for those who desire to live righteous, set apart lives in accordance with the will of YHWH. Contrary to popular belief, people can obey the Torah. (Deuteronomy (Debarim) 30:11-14). It is the myriads of regulations, customs and traditions which men attach to the Torah that make it impossible and burdensome for people to obey. The Torah has been in existence as long as Creation and arguably forever because the instructions of YHWH are the ways of YHWH. The names of the five different "books" are transliterated from their proper Hebrew names as follows: Genesis – Beresheet, Exodus – Shemot, Leviticus – Vayiqra, Numbers – Bemidbar, Deuteronomy – Debarim. While it is generally considered that the Torah is contained exclusively within the 5 Books of Moses, in a broader sense one might argue that they are included in the The Torah, The Nebiim (The Prophets) and the Ketubim (The Writings).

59 http://en.wikipedia.org/wiki/Antikythera_mechanism
60 See *Technology of the Gods – The Incredible Sciences of the Ancients*, David Hatcher Childress, Adventures Unlimited Press, 2000. For an interesting review of how the history and advancements of ancient civilizations in North America have been intentionally suppressed see the DVD entitled *The Lost Civilizations of North America*, NA Discoveries, 2010.
61 *Panorama of Creation*, Carl E. Baugh, Hearthstone Publishing, 2002.
62 Television shows such as the History Channels *Ancient Aliens*

and related books attribute many mysteries from ancient time to aliens. Incredibly, when viewed within the context of Scriptural records and related texts the information clearly supports the Scriptural account of history. The many acts that these books and television programs attribute to ancient aliens were actually the result of the Nephilim and their progeny.

63   English translations of the Scriptures describe a "serpent" in the Garden. In Hebrew, the word is "nachash" (𐤅𐤇𐤔) clearly the meaning of "serpent" but it also refers to "divination" or "casting spells." It can also mean "shining one." So the "serpent" in the Garden was likely an enchanting deceiver appearing "as an "angel of light." 2 Corinthians 11:14.

64   𐤅𐤆𐤀𐤋𐤊𐤄𐤆𐤉𐤔 equals 153 as follows: "𐤔" = 2, "𐤉" = 50, "𐤆" = 10, "𐤄" = 5, "𐤊" = 1, "𐤋" = 30, "𐤀" = 5, "𐤆" = 10, "𐤉" = 40.

65   The Hebrew word "nephilim" (𐤉𐤆𐤋𐤉𐤍) is typically translated as "giant" in English translations of the Scriptures. This is partly because of the Greek Septuigant. There are other Hebrew words that can "giant" such as "anaq" (𐤒𐤍𐤏). The word "nephilim" should not exclusively and strictly be limited to mean: "giant." It can also mean: "fallen ones" or "apostates."

66   Beresheet 1:12

67   Vayiqra 18, Debarim 23:2-3 and Debarim 27

68   Beresheet 5:3

69   The reference to Watchers can be seen in the Book of Daniel 4:13, 17, 23; Books of Enoch; and Jubilees 4:15, 5:1. A reference to the "fall of the watchers from heaven" is found in Hebrew in the Damascus Document 2:18 which seems to be quoting 1 Enoch 13:10.)

70   See *The Nephilim and the Pyramid of the Apocalypse,* Patrick Heron, Xulon Press 2005. See also *Genesis 6 Giants Master Builders of Prehistoric and Ancient Civilizations* written by Stephen Quayle, End Time Thunder Publishers, 2010.

71   *The First Fossil Hunters: Paleontology in Greek and Roman Times,* written by Adrienne Mayor Princeton University Press 2000.

72   Beresheet 4:19-22

73   The use and value of extra Scriptural texts is discussed in greater detail in the Walk in the Light series book entitled *The Scriptures.*

74   Ginzberg, *Legends of the Jews* 1:137

75   The proper Hebrew Name of the Messiah of Yisrael is transliterated as Yahushua. It is the same name as the Patriarch known as Joshua. It surely was not Jesus, which has not Hebrew

meaning and was not even a name until the development of the English language around 500 years ago. For a more detailed discussion of the Name of Yahushua see the Walk in the Light series entitled *Names*.

76 Brown-Driver-Briggs Hebrew Lexicon

77 *Genesis 6 Giants Master Builders of Prehistoric and Ancient Civilizations, ibid.*

78 See Shemot 12:5 and 1 Peter 1:19. Clearly the Passover Lamb represented the Messiah as the Lamb of Elohim. A "clean" sacrifice with the same DNA as Adam was needed in order to cover the sins of man. The blood of animals could never suffice since their DNA did not contain the coding of the Image of YHWH. Only the blood of Messiah can make people "clean" and it is by His blood that His Bride will be purified.

79 From the teachings of Stephen P. Quayle, see www.stevequayle.com.

80 *The Dead Sea Scrolls - A New Translation*, Michael Wise, Martin Abegg Jr., and Edward Cook, Harper Collins, 2005, p. 94.

81 According to Beresheet 7:11 the flood began on Day 17 of Month 2. According to www.torahcalendar.com the flood began in year 2,328. It is significant since the flood actually occurred in the eighth year of the Jubilee Cycle. It was also on Yom Rishon, which is the first day of the week. In a sense it is also the "eighth day." The flood started on Day 31 of the Omer count between Passover and the Feast of Shabuot. This was in the middle of the grain harvest leading up to the First Fruits (Bikkurim) offering. It was a 50 day count that was a yearly rehearsal of the Jubilee Count.

82 For further discussions concerning this issue, reference is made to the Walk in the Light series books entitled *The Messiah* and *The Appointed Times*.

83 *Serpent Secrets Revealed*, Michael Tsarion,www.astradome.com. This author does not agree with many of the doctrinal theories espoused, the citation is simply made in support of the facts therein.

84 It is important to understand that YHWH has segmented time into Ages. Just as the Jubilee was previously mentioned as a segment of time, those Jubilees are also combined into Ages.

85 Yeshayahu (𐤉𐤔𐤏𐤉𐤄𐤅) is the proper transliteration for the Prophet commonly called Isaiah. His name in Hebrew means "YHWH saves."

86 See Revelation 4:3 and Revelation 10:1

87 *Who was Nimrod?* Dr. David Livingston, davelivingston.com/nimrod.htm

88 Where in the World is the Tower of Babel by Anne Habermehl, March 23, 2011 found in *Answers Research Journal* 4 (2011): 25-53. See www.answersingenesis.org.

89 Pes. 94b; comp. Targ. of pseudo-Jonathan and Targ. Yer. to Gen. x. 9

90 Keil and Delitzsch 1975: 165

91 Wikipedia citing Dietz Otto Edzard: *Geschichte Mesopotamiens. Von den Sumerern bis zu Alexander dem Großen*, Beck, München 2004, p. 121.

92 See Beresheet 14:18. Melchizedek is often seen as a great mystery in the Scriptures. It is important to understand that this is a title combining two words: 1) king (melech), and 2) tzedek (righteous). The Melchizedek is both king and priest. These are the two "anointed" (moshiach) postitions in the Kingdom of YHWH. They were separated in man's kingdom, but united in the Messiah.

93 Jewish Encyclopedia citing Pirḳe R. El. xxiv.; "Sefer ha-Yashar," *l.c.*; comp. Gen. R. lxv. 12

94 We do not know exactly what animals were used to clothe Adam and Hawah, although one could safely assume that it was a Lamb, a sheep or a goat, since the Lamb of Elohim was later shown through Abraham and Yisrael to be the required sacrifice of the Covenant.

95 http://www.jewishencyclopedia.com/articles/11548-nimrod

96 *Epic of Gilgamesh*, Tablet IX

97 The Bavarian Department of Historical Monuments in Munich.

98 http://news.bbc.co.uk/2/hi/science/nature/2982891.stm

99 The Easter celebration is an ancient fertility rit founded in sun worship and deriving from Babylon. It occurs at the time of the Vernal Equinox. For more information concerning this issue see the Walk in the Light series books entitled *Restoration* and *Pagan Holidays*. Christmas originated as a celebration of the rebirth of the sun god at the time of the winter solstice. The winter solstice is the shortest day of the year, and from that point forward days become longer until the time of the summer solstice. From that point the days begin to grow shorter until the time of the winter solstice. Christmas derives from Babylon and is rooted in sun worship. For more information concerning this issue see the

Walk in the Light series books entitled *Restoration* and *Pagan Holidays*.

100   There are numerous writings on this subject. For a brief article on the history of the Yisraelite Divine Council verses neighboring peoples see *The Divine Council* by Michael S. Heiser. www.divinecouncil.com.

101   See *New World Order: The Ancient Plan of Secret Societies* by William T. Still cited by www.humansarefree.com in article entitled *America's Name Derived From The Peruvian AMARUCA - Solid Evidence.*

102   For extensive information concerning the existence of giants, the myths associated with them and the truth of those myths see the books written by Stephen Quayle entitled *Genesis 6 Giants, Master Builders of Prehsitoric and Ancient Civilizations* as well as *True Legends*, End Time Thunder Publications, Bozeman Montana. Also for ancient history in America see *Before Columbus: Links Between the Old World and Ancient America*, Cyrus H. Gordon, Crown Publishers, 1971.

103   Some believe a great planetary event may have occurred resulting in the breakup of the continents. This would have created diversity among the population on the planet. See *Worlds in Collision*, Immanuel Velikovsky, Paradigma Ltd. 2009. Seder Olam I says that Abram was 48 at the time of the dispersion. Midrash Yalkut Divrie HaYamim I states that construction on the Tower of Babel ended when Abram was 48.

104   Jewish Encyclopedia i. 86a, *s.v. Abraham in Rabbinical Literature.* Also, the Book of Yasher is an ancient text that provides significant "background" information relative to the Scriptures. It is not a "canonized" text, but it is actually referenced twice in the Scriptures. See Joshua 10:13 and 2 Samuel 1:18.

105   There are two words that are repeatedly related to the Gematria value of 318 in the Torah namely: "dwell" (𐤏𐤅𐤔𐤉) and "return" (𐤉𐤅𐤔𐤅) Both of these words are intimately connected with the Covenant.

106   See *The Gospel in the Stars*, Joseph A. Seiss, Kregel Publications. Also *Witness in the Stars* by E. W. Bullinger 1893.

107   See Isaiah 19

108   There are many who believe that all they need is faith to be part of the Covenant, but that is not a complete understanding. While faith is the entrance point to the Covenant, that faith is always demonstrated by conduct. In other words, you do not simply

think your way into the Covenant, you walk the Covenant walk. James (Yaakob) said it best when he stated: "¹⁴ *What does it profit, my brethren, if someone says he has faith but does not have works? Can faith save him?* ¹⁵ *If a brother or sister is naked and destitute of daily food,* ¹⁶ *and one of you says to them, Depart in peace, be warmed and filled, but you do not give them the things which are needed for the body, what does it profit?* ¹⁷ *Thus also faith by itself, if it does not have works, is dead.* ¹⁸ *But someone will say, You have faith, and I have works."* *Show me your faith without your works, and I will show you my faith by my works.* ¹⁹ *You believe that there is one Elohim. You do well. Even the demons believe and tremble!* ²⁰ *But do you want to know, O foolish man, that faith without works is dead?* ²¹ *Was not Abraham our father justified by works when he offered Isaac his son on the altar?* ²² *Do you see that faith was working together with his works, and by works faith was made perfect?* ²³ *And the Scripture was fulfilled which says,* *"Abraham believed Elohim, and it was accounted to him for righteousness. And he was called the friend of Elohim.* ²⁴ *You see then that a man is justified by works, and not by faith only.* ²⁵ *Likewise, was not Rahab the harlot also justified by works when she received the messengers and sent them out another way?* ²⁶ *For as the body without the spirit is dead, so faith without works is dead also."* James 2:14-26.

Our actions are the very expression of our faith. If we believe YHWH we express that belief by our obedience. For instance, He instructs those in His Covenant to keep the Sabbath as a sign of the Covenant. (Shemot 31:13-17). Therefore, if you are in Covenant, you keep the Sabbath. It is that simple. Your actions are a sign of your beliefs. This is different from popular Christian teachings concerning "grace." While it is true that we are "saved" by the unmerited favor of YHWH, we are expected to obey Him as an expression of our faith. For a more detailed discussion of this subject see the Walk in the Light series book entitled *The Law and Grace.*

¹⁰⁹ For an interesting description of the specific sacrifices involved in the Covenant with Abram and the path of the Covenant see the *Mystery of the Red Heifer* article located at www.shemayisrael.net.

¹¹⁰ For a more detailed description of the Appointed Time of the 8th Day, also known as Shemini Atzeret see the Walk in the Light series book entitled *The Appointed Times.*

¹¹¹ Passover is an important Appointed Time. It is a meal with a related sacrifice and it is intended to point out the redemptive

work through the shed blood of the Lamb of Elohim. The Passover is repeatedly commanded to be kept at "twilight" of Day 14 of Month 1. (see Shemot 12:6, Vayiqra 23:5, Bemidbar 9:3-5, Debarim 16:4-6, Joshua 5:10). The Hebrew phrase for "twilight" is "bein ha'erabim" (ביןהערבים יבם) – literally "between the evenings." Essentially, there are two demarcation points at the end of a day – sunset and complete darkness. This is the transition from day to night – from one day to another. So the Passover was to be sacrificed after sunset following Day 13, at twilight beginning Day 14.

112 It may be that Abram saw the fate of those outside the Covenant or the fate destined for the One Who would suffer the punishment for breaking the Covenant.

113 According to the Torah, Shemini Atzeret occurs on Day 22 of Month 7. It is not the eighth day of the the month, but rather the eighth day from the beginning of Succot. (Vayiqra 23:36). Interestingly, "the eighth day" is the day when the firstborn are offered to YHWH. (Shemot 22:29-30). The shedding of blood during the circumcision is actually symbolic of sacrificing the child to YHWH. At that point the male receives the "mark" of the Covenant. The individual then relies upon the shed blood of the Lamb of Elohim for redemption. This is why only those who are circumcised may participate in the Passover. (Shemot 12:48). Interestingly, "the eighth day" is also the day established for the cleansing of the leper. (see Vayiqra 14).

114 See Endnote 49

115 Yirmeyahu (ירמיהו) is the proper transliteration for the Hebrew name of the prophet commonly called Jeremiah.

116 The Appointed Times are primarily detailed in Shemot 23 and 34; Vayiqra 16 and 23 Bemidbar 9, 28 and 29 and Debarim 16.

117 It is impossible to understand the prophetic implications of this event without a basic understanding of the history of Yisrael. The Kingdom of Yisrael was the Bride of YHWH. She was divided after the death of Solomon (Shlomo). There were 10 Northern Tribes called the House of Yisrael and the Southern Kingdom, called the House of Yahudah, consisting of the tribes of Yahudah, Benjamin and Levi. The House of Yisrael set up abominations and a Babylonian/Egyptian system of worship. She was ultimately divorced and ejected from the house, the Promised Land, and exiled to the north. The Covenant promised a return, so somehow those northern tribes needed to be restored

to the Covenant, return to the Land and marry. This would occur through the Messiah who would come from the South, the Tribe of Yahudah. This is the culmination of the end of the age that we will read about in this book. It is also discussed in several book in the Walk in the Light series.

[118] Smith's Bible Dictionary 1884.

[119] See *The Rod of an Almond Tree in God's Master Plan*, Peter A. Michas, Wine Press Publications, 1997.

[120] Succot is a seven day Feast that occurs in month 7. It is also called the Feast of Tabernacles and requires those in the Covenant to meet with YHWH at His House and dwell in temporary dwellings. It is discussed in greater detail in the Walk in the Light series entitled *Appointed Times*.

[121] There are two basic understandings regarding the work of the Messiah provided through the Scriptures. One is the Messiah, son of Joseph – the suffering servant. The second is the Messiah, son of David – the conquering King. The eventual division of the Kingdom of Yisrael into 10 northern tribes called the House of Yisrael and the remaining southern tribes known as the House of Yahudah. These two roles are discussed in detail in the Walk in the Light series book entitled *The Messiah*. The division of the Kingdom of Yisrael is discussed in the Walk in the Light series book entitled *The Redeemed*.

[122] This entire event sheds light on the mysterious ritual that takes place on Yom Kippur – the Day of Atonement. See Vayiqra 16. In fact, there is a tradition that the blood soaked robe was presented to the father (Yaakob) on Yom Kippur.

[123] See Endnote 18

[124] The significance of this event cannot be ignored as we examine the end of the age. There will be a future gathering of "sons" and the connection with grain leads us to the Appointed Times of YHWH involving the grain harvest. The harvest begins with the first (resheet) offering of barley during the Feast of Unleavened Bread. From that point, the grain harvest begins and flows into the wheat harvest. The grain harvest culminates with people gathering from wherever they live to the House of YHWH during Shabuot. Shabuot occurs after a 50 day count from the resheet barley offering. The entirely of the grain harvest occurs within that 50 day period. One cannot ignore the connection with the Yobel and the 50 year count. During Shabuo, the people offer up their firstfruits (bikkurim) to YHWH. As a

result, we can expect to see a great regathering of the "sons" of the Covenant at Shabuot, possibly during a Jubilee year.

The life of Joseph is filled with patterns, as is the life of Abram, later renamed Abraham. There are traditions that Joseph was born on Day 1 of Month 7 and made Vice Regent of Egypt on that same day. There is also tradition that the seven years of plenty and famine began and ended on that day. Day 1 of Month 7 is the Appointed Time of YHWH known as Yom Teruah - the Feast of Blasting, also known as the Feast of Trumpets. It is a day of blowing shofars. There is an interesting passage found in Psalm 81 that provides the following: "*¹ Sing aloud to Elohim our strength; make a joyful shout to the Elohim of Yaakob. ² Raise a song and strike the timbrel, the pleasant harp with the lute. ³ Blow the shofar at the time of the New Moon, at the full moon, on our solemn feast day. ⁴ For this is a statute for Yisrael, a law of the Elohim of Yaakob. ⁵ This He established in Joseph (ﬧﬤ﬩ﬤﬨ) as a testimony, when He went throughout the land of Egypt, where I heard a language I did not understand.*" Psalm 81:1-5. Notice the spelling of the name of Joseph. It is the only place in the Scriptures where the name of Joseph contains the Name of YHWH (ﬤ﬩ﬤﬨ). Typically it is spelled as follows: " ﬧﬤ﬩ﬨ ". Some state that the spelling is an intentional scribal insertion, but it is very likely a Messianic hint to Joseph in Egypt. This alludes to the Messianic pattern established in Joseph as well as a future time when Yisrael will be drawn to YHWH through Joseph. Interestingly, there is significant proof that Yahushua the Messiah was actually born on Yom Teruah. So this special Appointed Time associated with Joseph was also the Day that the Messiah was revealed to the world. As with the Messiah, it was likely the day that Joseph was revealed to his brothers in Egypt. It was Joseph providing "salvation" to the world all along, his brothers simply did not understand who he was. The same holds true with Yahushua the Messiah. He has been cloaked by pagan religions and tradtions and He true identity has been hidden. In the end, it also seems clear that the House of Yisrael (Joseph), is currently hidden in plain sight. Having been exiled and divorces from YHWH - seemingly dead – some day soon Joseph will once again appear and be recognized.

Yahudah is the proper transliteration of the name traditionally pronounced as Judah. It means "Yah be praised." (Beresheet 29:35). There is no "J" in the Hebrew language and Judah loses the Name of Yah that is intended to be a central part of the name. The name was first attributed to a child of Yaakob. Yahudah later became a Tribe and then it represented the Kingdom of the South after Yisrael was divided. The term also became known as the region the Tribe and Kingdom of Yahudah occupied. Ultimately, the word has transitioned into the word "Jew." The term originally referred to a member of the Tribe of Yahudah or a person that lived in the region of Yudea (Judea). After the different exiles of the House of Yisrael and the House of Yahudah, it was the Yahudim that returned to the Land while the Northern Tribes, known as the House of Yisrael, were scattered to the ends of the earth (Yirmeyahu 9:16). The Yahudim retained their identity to their culture and the Land and thus came to represent all of Yisrael, despite the fact that the majority of Yisrael, the 10 tribes of the Northern Kingdom, remained "lost." As a result, the word "Jew" is erroneously used to describe a Yisraelite. While this label became common and customary, it is not accurate and is the cause of tremendous confusion. This subject is described in greater detail in The Walk in the Light Series book entitled *The Redeemed*.

127 The name of the Scriptural text often called "Exodus" is "Shemot" (ΧΥ𐤲W) in Hebrew. It literally means: "names." This confirms that the main thrust of the text is not about Yisrael leaving Egypt, but rather the process by which YHWH would reveal His Name.

128 The religion of Judaism is largely responsible for distinguishing between Jews and Gentiles. Their definition of a Jew is clouded between genetics and religious affiliation. While ancient Yisrael was defined as a people in Covenant with YHWH and included all 12 Tribes of Yisrael, the religion of Judaism is focused primarily on the House of Yahudah and the new religion that they developed after the destruction of Jerusalem in 70 AD. Jews generally define a Gentile as a non-Jew, but that is not correct. The Scriptural distinction would be between Yisrael and the Gentiles. As we already saw in Endnote 126, Jews essentially derive from the House of Yahudah. Judaism is a separate religion from the faith of Yisrael, so it is not correct to define a Gentile and a non-Jew. Gentiles, or rather "The Nations" are those outside the Covenant Assembly of Yisrael. The religious system commonly called Messianic Judaism tends to perpetuate this division. Even though they teach Yahushua as the Messiah, they

still continue to perpetuate the divisions of associated with the labels.

129 See Beresheet 15:13-15

130 The number 70 has great significance in the Scriptures. One thing that it represents is all of the nations or people on the Earth. This derives from the fact that there were seventy nations who repopulated the earth after the flood. (Beresheet 10). 70 was also the number of beings, or souls, who went into Egypt with Yisrael. (Beresheet 46).

131 The mixing and deliverance from Egypt was a precursor for another greater fulfillment of this Covenant that will occur through another cycle in the end. The Covenant people are currently mixed within the nations, and will some day be delivered from the Nations as Yisrael was once delivered from Egypt.

132 *Genetically Modified Prophecies*, Victor Schlatter, Evergreen Press, 2012 p. 32.

133 Shemot 21:2 and Debarim 15:12

134 see Vayiqra 25:9

135 According to Vayiqra 23:17: "*You shall bring from your dwellings two wave loaves of two-tenths of an ephah. They shall be of fine flour; they shall be baked with leaven. They are the firstfruits to YHWH.*" So the two leavened loaves represent the "firstfruits" (bikkurim).

136 Interestingly, the marriage Covenant is the only time when blood can be involved in the union between the husband and the wife. After the marriage ceremony, when the woman is in her monthly period where blood is flowing, she is considered ritually "unclean." The flow of blood creates a condition of menstrual impurity known as "niddah" (ה ד נ). The flow of blood makes her unclean for seven days. (see Vayiqra 15). During this period her husband is to refrain from having relations with her, otherwise he becomes unclean also. The implications are profound when you consider YHWH as the Husband of Yisrael.

137 When one understands the connection between the Covenant process and the Appointed Times, the Plan of YHWH becomes clear. He sent His Son to shed the blood necessary to Redeem the Bride. The future gathering of the Bride and the wedding of the Lamb will all occur within the pattern of the Appointed Times. Succot is the last harvest gathering of the yearly cycle. It occurs in Month 7 and is called the Feast of Ingathering. (Shemot 23:16, 34:22). It is a time of joy and clearly symbolizes a wedding feast.

In fact it is a time when the people are specifically commanded to rejoice for seven days. (Vayiqra 23:40). For more information on the Appointed Times see the Walk in the Light series book entitled *Appointed Times*.

138 The timing of the wedding ceremony is very specific. It was "the third day" which means our Tuesday. It was the same day that the Children of Yisrael left Egypt, which would have been the last day of the Feast of Unleavened Bread. (See Shemot 19:1-2). So we know that the wedding ceremony occurred on a Tuesday in the Third month which turns out to be Shabuot – an Appointed Time marking the end of the grain harvest. This is an important time in the gathering of the bride. For more specific information concerning the timing of the wedding ceremony on Shabuot see the Walk in the Light series book entitled *Appointed Times*.

139 Revelation 10:3

140 The event at Sinai is literally shrouded in mystery. It may actually provide some insight into a future event when the Bride of YHWH will actually descend upon the earth. It is possible that the Throne Room of YHWH, the Mountain of Elohim, known as Mount Zion had come down upon Sinai and was covered with this clouds to shroud it. When the Elders went up on Sinai the could see up

141 See Ezekiel 1:26 and 10:1

142 The name often shown as Joshua was actually Yahushua (ⵔWY⮑ᒪ) in Hebrew. According to David Talshir, Galileans tended to keep the traditional spelling of Yahushua (ⵔYWY⮑ᒪ) with the letter "vav" (Y) inserted between the "shin" (W) and the "ayin" (ⵔ). David Talmshir, "Rabbinic Hebrew as Reflected in Personal Names" in *Scripta Hierosolymitana: Publications of the Hebrew University of Jerusalem*, vol. 37 (Jerusalem: Magnes Press: Hebrew University of Jerusalem 1998). The Messiah came in the Name of Yahushua revealing the patterns that He would fulfill, including the High Priest according to the Order of Melchizedek. For a further discussion of the Patterns that Yahushua fulfilled see the Walk in the Light series entitled *The Messiah*.

143 We know that aperson cannot survive without water for more than a few days. When Mosheh was away for 40 days and 40 nights he did not eat bread or drink water. (Shemot 34:28 and Debarim 9:9). It is possible that he went through a sort of time

warp. Since YHWH is not subject to physical time, Mosheh could have been translated out of time and into the presence of YHWH where YHWH spoke the words to him.

[144] When one considers that the original Tablets came directly from the Mountain of YHWH, there is a strong possibility that they were a unique stone from the heavens. In fact, tradition holds that the tablets were made of sapphire. They were made from the very Throne of YHWH and were likely blue crystals. Once broken, it is possible that they were used for the Urim and Thummim. Even though the Urim and Thummim were mentioned before the tablets were broken we are not given any information comcerning where they came from. One thing is certain, they are directly connected with the Aleph Taw (𐤕𐤀). In he two instances where they are mentions in this order we read "𐤕𐤀-the Urim and 𐤕𐤀-the Thummim" (𐤅𐤆𐤅𐤗𐤀-𐤕𐤀 𐤅𐤒𐤉𐤗𐤀-𐤕𐤀). (Shemot 28:30, Vayiqra 8:8). Amazingly, Urim (𐤅𐤒𐤉𐤀) starts with Aleph (𐤀) and Thummin (𐤅𐤆𐤅𐤗) starts with Taw (𐤗). So the Urim and the Thummim represent the Aleph Taw (𐤕𐤀) as the High Priest.

[145] See Rashi's commentary to Exodus 32:1 and 33:11.

[146] See www.torahcalendar.com

[147] In Shemot 16:3 we read that "the whole assembly" of Yisrael was refered to as "et-kol-ha'gahal" (𐤋𐤒𐤔𐤒-𐤋𐤉-𐤕𐤀) Notice the Aleph Taw (𐤕𐤀) associated with "the whole assembly" of Yisrael. Christianity makes the grevious mistake of believing that "The Church" is an assembly of Christians that have somehow taken the place of the Assembly of Yisrael. There is no place in the Covenant for a new or different Assembly separate from Yisrael. They perpetuate this mistake translating the Greek word "ekklesia" (ἐκκλησίαν) as "church." As a result, most English New Testament texts mention "the church" instead of Yisrael, leaving the reader with the impression the assembly of Christians called the Church has replaced the Assembly of Yisrael. Nothing could be further from the truth. The only Covenant Assembly is Yisrael. This is evident when we recognize that the Septuagint, which is a Greek translation of the Tanak, translated "qahal" (𐤋𐤒𐤔) as "ekklesia" (ἐκκλησίαν). In other words, the word used for Yisrael was "qahal" (𐤋𐤒𐤔) in Hebrew and "ekklesia" (ἐκκλησίαν) in Greek. Therefore, Christians should not be translating the New Testament texts to refer to a "church" when they clearly refer to the Covenant

Assembly of Yisrael.

¹⁴⁸ Judaism, in an attempt to strengthen Rabbinic authority teaches to "incline after the majority." According to the Babylonian Talmud, Baba Mezia 59a-59b, "Rabbi Eliezer then said to the Sages: `If the Halakhah is in accordance with me let it be proved directly from Heaven.' Suddenly a heavenly voice went forth and said to the Sages, `Why are you disputing with Rabbi Eliezer? The Halakhah is in accordance with him in all circumstances!' Rabbi Yehoshua rose to his feet and quoted a portion of a verse (Deuteronomy 30:12), saying, The Torah is not in heaven!" The Gemara interrupts the Baraita and asks for a clarification: "What did Rabbi Yehoshua mean when he quoted the Scriptural verse that the Torah is not in heaven? Rabbi Yirmeyah said in reply: Since God already gave the Torah to the Jewish people on Mount Sinai, we no longer pay attention to heavenly voices that attempt to intervene in matters of Halakhah. For You, God, already wrote in the Torah at Mount Sinai, after the majority to incline." This is actually a misrepresentation of Shemot 23:2 and in complete contradiction to the text that provides: "*You shall not follow a crowd to do evil; nor shall you testify in a dispute so as to turn aside after many to pervert justice.*"

¹⁴⁹ Circumcision is a very controversial issue, but the Torah is clear. No one is to partake of the Covenant meal of Passover unless they are circumcised. (Shemot 12). It is a sign of the Covenant. (Beresheet 17:11). It is an important part of the Covenant, but as we saw with the generation that entered the Promised Land, it was not a prerequisite to their salvation. Indeed, no one was circumcised in the wilderness, yet they were still allowed to dwell in the Camp and YHWH provided them with food and water. Ultimately though, if we want to live with Him in a Covenant relationship, we must bear the sign of His Covenant.

¹⁵⁰ For a more detailed discussion of Shabbat see the Walk in the Light series book entitled *The Sabbath*.

¹⁵¹ Despite the variant teachings of Judaism and Christianity, there is only one path back to the Garden. It is the ancient path, revealed through the Covenant life of Abraham. While Yisrael was chosen to reveal the Covenant, it was not something exclusively for physical decendents of the Tribes of Yisrael. The Covenant is available for everyone. (Shemot 12:49; Bemidbar 15:16,29).

¹⁵² The time selected by YHWH to punish His people is a year for a

day. See Bemidbar 14:34. He would show them how it feels to be rejected. This pattern would not only occur before they entered the Promised Land. It would apply for periods of exile afterward. Gilgal was the name of the first camp of Yisrael in the Land. It was the place where the Ark initially rested. The Hebrew word "gilgal" (ל ג ל ג) is often described as "rolling" and thought to refer to the rolling away of the foreskins during the circumcisions of the Yisraelites. It also refers to the shame of Yisrael being rolled away. It actually derives from the word "gilah" (ה ל ג) which means" "uncover nakedness, to lay bare." This place is where the 12 stones were taken from the Jordan and placed (Joshua 4:20), just as was done at Sinai. (Shemot 24:4). Interestingly, there are various references in the Scriptures to The Gilgal – ha'gilgal (ל ג ל ג ה). This reveals that "the gilgal" was not simply the name of one place, but rather a "meeting place." Some believe that ha'gilgal actually refers to a circle of standing stones. Recent archeological discoveries seem to have confirmed the notion that gilgals were circular meeting places, not unlike the Neolithic circles observed all throughout the world in places like Stonehenge. For an interesting article on the various gilgals found in Israel see http://www.israelhayom.com/site/newsletter_article.php?id=120 89.

Interestingly, the period of time described in the text known as the Judges involves Yisrael with no King. After the death of Joshua the leadership of Yisrael would have beed divided between the princes and elders of the Tribes. The one common leader would have been the High Priest. All tribes shold have gathered at the House of YHWH, but under this scenario we see Yisrael fragmented and divided. Interestingly, it was during this time that the Ark of the Covenant and the House of YHWH, known as the Mishkan, were located in the Land of Ephraim - Joseph.

Notice that the locations and the fleece all have symbolic meaning. The wine press was a place for grapes, yet it was filled with grain. The threshing floor was the place for grain, yet Gideon was placing the skin of an animal on the threshing floor. The altar was the place for animals. All of these elements are found at the House of YHWH that would later be built on a threshing floor. They all involve the firstfruits that belonged to the priest. (Debarim 18:4).

157 See Amos 9:11. This prophecy specifically connects the Aleph Taw (X𐤊) with the succa set up by the Covenant King. The prophecy in Amos reveals that the Aleph Taw () will rebuild the fallen succa of David when the House of Yisrael is regathered.

158 There are many important concepts associated with the number 73, including the tree of "life" (Beresheet 2:9), the "garden" of YHWH (Beresheet 13:10). There are also connections when Abraham prepared a meal and YHWH "ate" it. (Beresheet 18:8). Clearly, the unity associated with the Kingdom of Yisrael equates with YHWH dwelling with His people.

159 This is all that YHWH asks of His people and they continually refuse to do what He says. Adam was permitted to live in paradise if he would only "guard" (shamar) the commandments. There are rich blessings for those who obey – like David. There are also curses for those who disobey – like Shlomo.

160 See Beresheet 49.

161 For more information regarding the Scriptural Appointed Times see the Walk in the Light series book entitled *Appointed Times*.

162 Calculated exile dates for the House of Yisrael derived from the research of Eliyahu David ben Yissachar of Jerusalem, Yisrael. See www.torahcalendar.com.

163 During the vision of Ezekiel an amazing being, like fire and amber appeared before him. It stretched out the form of a hand and took him by the "tzitzit roshi" (𐤆W𐤊𐤒 X𐤥𐤆𐤚𐤥). While most translations provide that this was a "lock of hair" one cannot ignore the significance of the word "tzitzit" which refers to a tassel worn in remembrance of the commandments. (Bemidbar 15:39, Debarim 22:12).

164 See Endnote 31 for a discussion of the prior judgment rendered upon the planet.

165 Calculated exile dates for the House of Yahudah derived from the research of Eliyahu David ben Yissachar of Jerusalem, Yisrael. See www.torahcalendar.com.

166 See Shemot 9:16. It is imperative to understand that YHWH does things for the sake of His Name. He entered into Covenant and gave certain promises. He gave His Word and therefore His Name must be protected and esteemed. He must keep His word

and He desires that the entire worlds knows His Name. As if there is any question about this fact, the entire exodus event was prefaced by YHWH revealing His Name to Mosheh. So the Name of YHWH was intimately involved in the past redemption and deliverance of Yisrael. Likewise, it will be at the center of future events as He fulfills His Word.

167 Brown Driver Briggs Hebrew Lexicon.

168 It is important not to be confused by the name of the Modern State of Israel. The founders of this nation are likely the descendants of the House of Yahudah. So the nation should more accurately be called the Nation of Yahudah. By calling themselves Israel, they give the impression that they represent the return and regathering of all the tribes of Yisrael, an event that has yet to occur. It is also important to recognize that to be in the Community of Yisrael, you must be in Covenant with YHWH. At present, the majority of the inhabitants of the Modern State of Yisrael are secular. Those who are classified as "religious" are either part of the hybrid religion known as Rabbinic Judaism, Orthodox Christianity or Islam. Only a small fraction of the inhabitants would be considered Protestant or Messianic. So the current Modern State of Yisrael is following YHWH and living according to His Torah.

169 153 occurences of this word is significant. Strongs 6828 http://www.blueletterbible.org/lang/lexicon/lexicon.cfm?Stron gs=H6828&t=KJV

170 Victor Schlatter, *Genetically Modified Prophecies*, Evergreen Press, Mobile Alabama 2012.

171 While there is compelling evidence that the actual crossing site occurred at the location of Nuweba Beach in Egypt, one cannot ignore other compelling positions that meet Scriptural descriptions. For an excellent argument in support of the Nuweba site see *The Exodus Case New Discoveries Confirm the Historical Exodus* by Dr. Lennart Möller, Scandinavia Publishing House 2002. This text relies largely upon geography for the location, which is quite compelling. It cannot explain the location of Baal Tsephon though, which seems to miss an important detail. (see Page 177). I found an interesting article on an alternative site that uses the mention of Baal Tsephon as a key reference point. This location also appears to have merit, although to my knowledge there has bee no physical underwater exploration to find debris or archaeological evidence to support

the theory. See http://www.bible.ca/archeology/bible-archeology-exodus-route-goshen-red-sea.htm.

[172] Brown Driver Briggs Hebrew Lexicon

[173] For a detailed discussion on the timing of the appearance of Messiah Yahushua see the Walk in the Light series book entitled *The Messiah*.

[174] The Christian tradition of separating the Bible into two parts, namely 1) The Old Testament, and 2) The New Testament is confusing and misrepresents the texts. All of the texts in the Bible are old. To separate them as "Old" and "New" gives the impression that those considered "old" are not as relevant as those considered "new."

[175] The Book of Daniel has often been attacked because of the incredible accuracy and detail contained therein. As a result, some attempt to give it a late date – to the time of the Maccabees. For a discussion on the arguments and defenses of Daniel see www.tektonics.org/af/danieldefense.html.

[176] This is an important point o recognize as those from the House of Yisrael rediscover their "Hebrew Roots." Many tend to try to adopt Jewish traditions and culture, including their language. If one truly desired to get back to their Hebrew roots then they should be examining the original language of Yisrael.

[177] Eliyahu David Ben Yissachar, Jerusalem, Israel.

[178] See Debarim 25:4. Remember that the Aleph (𐤀) represents an "ox." We have seen that the Aleph (𐤀), in the beginning was associated with YHWH. Also the banner of Joseph/Ephraim is the ox.

[179] For a detailed summary of the Holy Roman Empire see http://en.wikipedia.org/wiki/Holy_Roman_Empire

[180] From a Christian perspective see the writings of Steven M. Collins (stevenmcollins.com). From a Jewish perspective see the writings of Yair Davidy (www.britam.org).

[181] See Endnote 180

[182] Depuydt, L. *The Time of Death of Alexander the Great: 11 June 323 BC, ca. 4:00–5:00 pm, Die Welt des Orients* 28: 117-35.

[183] Through the number 70 we can see incredible connections concerning the Plan of YHWH. The fact that it is a number associated with the punishment of Babylon and the completion of the punishment of the people of YHWH is incredibly significant, especially as we approach the end of the age. So we see a punishment upon the world system connected with a return

to the Land of Elohim's Covenant people. The number 70 is also associated with the word for "wine" which is "yayin" (ין‎‎‎). Grapes are harvested and made into wine before the Fall Feast of Succot. This is a very joyful Feast because of the presence of the new wine. It is also associated with "the mezuzah" (המזוזה‎), which is a command to place the Word of YHWH of our doorposts. The doorpost is the place where the ear of the servant is pierced when he joins the household of his master. (see Shemot 21:6; Debarim 15:17). When a Hebrew servant serves for six years he has the option of going free in the seventh year or remaining in the household of his master. The text describes that if the servant "loves" his master then he goes to the door (dalet) or the doorpost (ha'mezuzah) and his master will pierce his ear and he will serve his master through the ages (olam). This is a prophetic pattern symbolizing that when we appear at the House of our Master, after being purchased by His blood, because of our love we willingly take His mark and dwell in His House forever. This is the pattern of the Redemption in the first month leading up the the Feasts of the Seventh month, when we dwell with the Master.

¹⁸⁴ Very interestingly, if you perform a search in the Scriptures for words valued at 9 you find in this order: "come" (בא‎), "brethren" (אח‎), "come" (בא‎), "troop" (גד‎), "triumph" (הך‎). This is providing the pattern of a return from exile back – to Jerusalem.

¹⁸⁵ *The Coming Prince* by Sir Robert Anderson, page 64 and Appendix 2, quoting Clinton, Fasti Hellenici, vol. 2, page 380. The Elephantine Letters are a collection of more that twenty ancient documents written primarily in Aramaic between priests and family members who were exiles of Yahudah. They were found on an Island in the Nile in Egypt where a community of Yahudim resided. The documents provide corresponding dates between the Persian lunar calendar, and the Egyptian calendar that can be helpful in synchronizing various events that occurred during the period of time that they were written.

¹⁸⁶ *The Coming Prince* by Sir Robert Anderson, page 67, Footnote 10. Shemitah years and Jubilee years can be viewed using the data contained in www.torahcalendar.com.

¹⁸⁷ The date of the crucifixion of the Messiah is detailed in the Walk in the Light series book entitled *The Messiah*.

¹⁸⁸ Special thanks to Elijah David ben Issachar, Jerusalem, Israel for

189   his dating assistance relative to the 70 weeks.

The Seventy Weeks and the Great Tribulation, Philip Mauro, Old Paths Gospel Press, pp 92-93.

190   en.wikipedia.org/wiki/Aelia_Capitolina

191   *The Seventy Weeks and the Great Tribulation*, Philip Mauro p. 104.

192   E.B. Elliott, *Horae Apocalypticae*

193   Rabbi Professor David Golinkin, *Prayers for the Government and the State of Israel*, http://judaism.about.com/od/conservativegolinkin/a/israel_prayers.htm

194   The historical information regarding Daniel 11 was gleaned from the very detailed article by Bryan T. Huie entitled *Daniel 11 – Prophecy Fulfilled!* December 30, 2005. For a copy of the article see www.herealittletherealittle.net.

195   As with the Tanak, the Messianic writings are divided into various groups. The first is referred to as The Gospels. The word "gospel" derives from the Old English word "god spell," and is intended to mean: "good news." From these texts we can know that Yahushua was indeed the promised Messiah Who was sent to renew the Covenant. These consist of four writings known as Matthew, Mark, Luke and John. Named after their purported authors, these texts describe a portion of the life and teachings of Yahushua son of Joseph and Miryam - not a man named Jesus. The name Jesus will be discussed in the following chapter. These four texts were not just a haphazard compilation of information. Rather, they were each written to highlight a specifc aspect of Yahushua as the Messiah of Yisrael. For instance, Matthew was written to reveal Messiah the King, the Branch of David (Yirmeyahu 23:5-6; Yeshayahu 11:1). Mark was written to reveal Messiah the Servant, "My servant the Branch" (Zekaryah 3:8). Luke was written to reveal Messiah as the Son of Man, The Man called the Branch (Zekaryah 6:12). John (Yahanan) was written to reveal the Messiah as the Son of Elohim, The Branch of YHWH (Yeshayahu 4:2).

196   From *Chronological Study of the Life of Christ* by Dennis McCallum, www.xenos.org/classes/chronc.htm.

197   The differences between the Scriptural Calendanr and different man-made calendars are discussed in the Walk in the Light series book entitled The Ammointed Times. The Scriptures clearly reveal that the sun and the moon were created for Appointed Times. (Beresheet 1:14).

198   The current calendar that dominates most of the modern world is called the Gregorian Calendar. It was developed in 1582 and named after the Roman Pope Gregory XIII by papal bull "Inter gravissimas" dated 24 February 1582. It is a solar calendar. This stands in stark contrast to the Scriptural Calendar, which is a luni-solar calendar. It was developed to reform the Julian Calendar, named after the Roman Emperor Julius Ceasar. Interestingly, the primary purpose of the reform was to calculate the date of the pagan fertility celebration of Easter. It was supposed coordinate the celebration to the time of the year in which the First Council of Nicaea had agreed upon in 325 CE. See http://en.wikipedia.org/wiki/Gregorian_calendar.

199   *Handbook of Biblical Chronology*, Jack Finegan, Hendrickson Publishers, 1998 p. 583 and Table 169.

200   *In the Fullness of Time*, Paul L. Maier, (New York: HarperCollins Publishers, 1991.

201   *The Star That Astonished the World*, Ernest L. Martin, ASK Publications 1998.

202   *Ibid*, Martin quoting Thiel, *The Mysterious Numbers of the Hebrew Kings*.

203   Eliyahu David ben Yissachar, Jerusalem, www.torahcalendar.com

204   *The "Lost" Ten Tribes of Israel . . . Found!* Steven M. Collins, CPA Book Publisher 1995 4th Printing p.268.

205   *Antiquities of the Jews*, 11.5.2, from The Works of Josephus, translated by Whiston, W., Hendrickson Publishers 1987 13th Printing. p 294.

206   *Ibid*, Martin at p. 66.

207   For more information concerning the messages communicated through the signs in the sky see the Wall in the Light series entitled *The Scriptures*.

208   Above information gleaned from various sources including Ernest L. Martin, *The Star That Astonished the World*.

209   Remember the stones that Yahushua was commanded to place in the Jordan. They marked the spot of the crossing and it is likely that John the Immerser immersed people at that same spot. In fact, when rebuking the Pharisees and Sadducees at the Jordan he specifically stated: " . . . and do not think to say to yourselves, 'We have Abraham as our father.' For I say to you that Elohim is able to raise up children to Abraham from these stones." Matthew 3:9. See the teachings of Chuck Missler.

210 For additional information discussing the Hebrew and Aramaic origins of the text of Matthew see the Walk in the Light series entitled *The Scriptures*.

211 Zion is associated with the City of David. (See 2 Samuel 5:7; 1 Kings 8:1; 1 Chronicles 11:5, 2 Chronicles 5:2). It is named this because it is an earthly pattern of the Mountain of YHWH that will descend upon the Earth in the future. YHWH lives in Mount Zion and from this Mountain the Kingdom of YHWH is ruled. See Isaiah 8:18.

212 See Nachmanides, Sifre on Bemidbar, par. 80-81. See also Mishnah Tractate Ma'aser Sheni 5.14; Bikkurim 1.4; Sifre on Debarim par. 299, 301. Some of these discussions focus on whether Yithro's descendents returned to the Land and it is extended to the goyim.

213 E.W. Bullinger, *Companion Bible*, Appendix 153.

214 See Wikipedia subject Eliezar ben Hanania. This rendition of history is also confirmed by the audio commentary at Masada, Israel.

215 **Josephus**, *The* Wars of the Jews, VII. 1,1

216 See Josephus, *The Wars of the Jews*

217 See Matthew 21:18-22; Mark 11:12-14, 20-24.

218 The absence of the Ark in the House of YHWH is quite significant. It symbolized His Throne. YHWH sat on a sapphire throne in the heavens. The Ark was His throne on earth. The Ark was the very symbol of YHWH reigning over Yisrael. When they would bring the Ark out to battle it signified YHWH as their King fighting for them. After the Kingdom was divided and both Houses were exiled, there was never an Ark in the Temple. Only when the Kingdom is reunited will YHWH sit on the Throne of a united Kingdom.

219 See *Hebrew Gospel of Matthew*, George Howard. The Hebrew texts specifically details a shofar being sounded.

220 "*34 The word of YHWH that came to Jeremiah the prophet against Elam, in the beginning of the reign of Zedekiah king of Judah, saying, 35 Thus says YHWH of hosts: Behold, I will break the bow of Elam, The foremost of their might. 36 . . . Against Elam I will bring the four winds from the four quarters of heaven, and scatter them toward all those winds; There shall be no nations where the outcasts of Elam will not go . . . 39 But it shall come to pass in the latter days: I will bring back the captives of Elam, says YHWH.*" Jeremiah 49:34-36, 39.

221 There are different levels of knowledge. Some knowledge is

intuitive while other knowledge must be acquired. While we do not intuitively know all things, were are able to acquire knowledge of certain mysteries through revelation. See Matthew 13:11. The ultimate "knowledge" comes through the union with Elohim. See Mathew 11:27.

222   See Matthew 4:23, 6:10, 7:21, Mark 1:15, 4:11, 14:25 and Luke 4:43, 8:10, 9:2,11,62 to name some.

223   Matthew 26:1-7. See also Acts 4:27

224   The fact that His feet were anointed before His head is quite significant. The fact that after He was anointed He washed the feet of His disciples revealed that He was the prophesied Servant of YHWH.

225   It is important to understand that a day begins at sundown, and the Passover meal begins at sundown. Yahushua was crucified on the following day which was Passover Day.

226   *Handbook of Biblical Chronology*, Jack Finegan, Hendrickson Publishers, 1998 p. 583 and Table 169. See also the Walk in the Light series book entitled *The Messiah*.

227   See *Stone Vessels of the Early Roman Period from Jerusalem and Palestine. A Reassessment*, Shimon Gibson, Offprint of One Land – Many Cultures, Archaeological Studies in Honour of S. Loffreda edited by G. C. Bottini, L. Di Degni and L. D. Chrupcala (Studium Biblicum Franciscanum Collectio Maior 41) Jerusalem 2003. A good example of one of these stone jars can be seen at the entrance of Tel Megiddo in northern Israel.

228   Thayer's Greek-English Lexicon of the New Testament

229   Affirmed by Irenaeus in *Contra Haeres*, v. 20; Victorinus in *Works*, p. 90, Eusebius in *Ecc. Hist. Lib.* 3, *cap.* 18; Jerome in *Works*, vol. vi. p. 446; Sulpicius Severus in *Works*, vol. iv. chap. 120.

230   While the modern State of Israel is certainly a part of the plan of YHWH, it is certainly not the complete fulfillment of the prophesied restoration of the House of Yisrael and the House of Yahudah.

231   There was a pattern provided by Yahudah according to the Book of Yasher. Yahudah called out in the midst of Battle "YHWH Save us." It occurred on Day 5 (Thursday) that happened to be the Last Day of Succot. This may be a clue to YHWH saving His people in the future - In the future at sunrise during a Succot with the 7th day landing on Day 5. This insight was provided by Eliyahu David ben Yissachar, Jerusalem, Israel.

232   *The Temple, Its Ministry and Services*, Alfred Edersheim, Hendrickson Publishers, Inc., 1994.

233   *Nephilim Stargates: The Year 2012 and the Return of the Watchers*, Thomas Horn, Crane, MO, Anomalos Publishing, 2007, pp. 60-61.

234   See article Top Physicist at CERN Stargate says Something May Come Through Dimensional 'Doors' At Large Hadron Collider, January 14, 2013, jedicommander.wordpress.com. See also *CERN: THE MAYAN DOPPELGÄNGER!* by Clyde Lewis, www.groundzeromedia.org

235   The Book of Giants is an ancient text found along with the Dead Sea Scrolls. Only fragments were found, but there is plenty of interesting information that can be discerned from the text when read along with other writings such as the Books of Enoch. See *The Dead Sea Scrolls Translated, The Qumran Texts in English*, Florentino Garcia Martinez, E.J. Brill (1996). Concerning "locust" definition see *Jewish New Testament Commentary*, David H. Stern, p. 816.

236   Hebrew Gospel of Matthew, George Howard, Mercer University Press 1995. See Shem Tob translation of Matthew 17:3.

237   Eusebius, *hist. Eccl*. iii.5; cf. Mark in Revelation 13:14—Robert H. Mounce, *The Book of Revelation* (Grand Rapids, MI: William B. Eerdmans Publishing Co., 1977), Rev. 12:6.)

238   Wikipedia

239   See the Walk in the Light series book entitled *Restoration*.

240   See www.un.org and reference "Millennium Development Goals Report."

241   Art. 10, Creed of Pope Pius IV. Double Bull of Pope Pius IV, Nov. 13 and Dec. 9, 1564, trans. in Philip Schaff, The Creeds of Christendom, New York: Harper, 1919, Vol. 1, p. 99.

242   *Who or What Is the Beast of Revelation?* by David C. Pack

243   www.pacinst.com quoting W. E. H. Lecky, History of the Rise and influence of the Spirit of Rationalism in Europe, (reprint: New York: Braziller, 1955), Vol. 2, pp. 40-45.

244   *Rulers of Evil*, F. Tupper Saussy, Ospray Bookmakers, 1999.

245   "In a letter from John Adams to then President Thomas Jefferson about the Jesuits, we read: "Shall we not have regular swarms of them here, in as many disguises as only a king of the gypsies can assume, dressed as painters, publishers, writers, and schoolmasters? If ever there was a body of men who merited eternal damnation on earth and in hell it is this Society of

Loyola's. - George Reimer, *The New Jesuits*, Little, Brown, and Col. 1971, p. 14." From amazingdiscoveries.org.

246 Charles Chiniquy, *Fifty Years in the Church of Rome*, The Wickliffe Press, Protestant Truth Society, Wickliffe Avenue, 104 Hendon Lane, Finchley, London, N3., 1885, p. 388.

247 See the Walk in the Light series books entitled *Restoration* and *Pagan Holidays*.

248 See claims of Alberto Rivera among others.

249 See the Walk in the Light series book entitled *The Sabbath*.

250 The Jubilee Year has been talked about more and more throughout recent years and it seems that every year is being declared a Jubilee by someone. As with Yisrael coming out of Egypt the redemption process could begin in Year 49.

251 See Chuck Missler Commentary on Ezekiel. While Chuck Missler has many very interesting teachings, this author does not subscribe to all of his teachings, particularly those concerning the rapture.

252 *The Antichrist and a Cup of Tea*, Tim Cohen, Prophecy House, Inc, 1998.

253 *World War III Unmasking the End-Times Beast (Volume II)*, Simon Atlaf, Abrahamic Faith 2011.

254 Debarim 32:22, Proverbs 5:5, 7:27, 9:18, 15:11, 15:24, Isaiah 14:9, Ezekiel 31:15.

255 *Better than Nostradamus*, Barry R. Smith, International Support Ministries, 1996.

256 We know that the redemption from Egypt had to occur within a year or less because Mosheh was 80 years old when he first went in to see Pharaoh with Aaron. (Shemot 7:7). The children of Yisrael wandered in the wilderness for 40 years. (Bemidbar 14:33). They began eating manna one month after departing from Egypt. (Shemot 16:1-4). They ate manna for 40 years (Shemot 16:35). The manna ceased after they entered into the Promised Land, ate the Passover and then ate the produce of the Land – Day 16 of Month 1. (Joshua 5:11-12) Mosheh was 120 years old when he died. Tradition holds that his birthday was on the 7th of Adar – month 12. So he turned 120 immediately prior to the Children of Yisrael entering into the Promised Land in Month 1. This would mean that he did not spend more than a full year in Egypt from the time that he first met Pharaoh until the plagues were over, they left Egypt and began eating manna.

257 *The Islamic AntiChrist*, Joel Richardson WND Books (2009).

258 See www.geoengineering.org and the work of Dane Wigington.

259 For more information concerning our toxic environment see the article entitled *Our Chemical Culture* at www.shemayisrael.net. It is also important to recognize that the environment is not only being polluted by chemical and plastics, but also such things as electromagnetic frequency radiation. Interestingly, it was discovered that the earth actually resonates what are known as Schumann resonance that occur at a frequency of approximately 7.83 Hz. Mankind should be receiving that same resonance since this planet was made for man and man was actually taken out of the ground (adamah). Instead, modern technological civilizations are being bombarded by a variety of frequencies that are disturbing and interrupting the ability to receive the Schuman resonances from the earth. This is multiplied by the fact that the modern man is not connected to the earth, and most rarely touch their flesh to the ground. We are insulated and separated by asphalt and shoes. The first man was commissioned to be a gardener, and I believe there is much to be derived from connecting with the ground (adamah).

260 At the time that this book was published the Fukushima Daiichi nuclear plant in Japan had been in meltdown for over two years spewing radiation daily into the Pacific Ocean in what will likely be the greatest ecological disaster in recorded history. There is no real solution is sight, yet the majority of the world is essentially disinterested in this subject. It is a symptom of the epidemic level of apathy that exists throughout the world.

261 The Torah and the commandments are repeatedly referred to as The Way, The Truth and the Life. See Proverbs 2, Proverbs 6:3 and Psalm 119 as examples.

262 The Passover Lamb was killed "between the evenings" on Day 14 of Month 1. They were instructed to choose a lamb on Day 10 of Month 1. The text in Shemot 12:5 literally describes the unblemished lamb as "zakar ben-shanah." The Hebrew word "ben" (ﬧﬨ) means: "son." So this "son" remained in the house for 4 days until it was slaughtered to protect the family. This was a prophetic fulfillment of the Aleph Taw (Ⅹ𐤕), the 4th word in the Scriptures coming at a precise time in history to fulfill a specific purpose.

263 See Thayer's Greek-English Lexicon of the New Testament 2 Timothy 1:7; *dunamis* is used of the power of angels: Eph. 1:21 (cf. Meyer at the passage) 2 Peter 2:11; of the power of the devil and

evil spirits, 1 Corinthians 15:24; *tou echthrou*, i.e. of the devil, Luke 10:19; *tou drakontos*, Revelation 13:2; angels, as excelling in power, are called *dunameis* (cf. (Philo de mutat. nora. sec. 8 *dunameis asœmatoi*) Meyer as above; Lightfoot on Col. 1:16; see *angelos*): Romans 8:38; 1 Peter 3:22.

A Note on Dates

Historical dating has long been a subject of controversy and debate in the academic community. While certain dates involving particular aspects of a civilization may be agreed upon others are not. This sometimes leads to problems creating a complete timeline of history. Very recently some intensive and compelling work has been completed by using astronomical data, particularly eclipse data, which can then be used to lock together histories of various cultures thereby providing an accurate look at history. The dates used in this book may not always be the same as academia purports but they are believed to be the most accurate available. Dates provided by Eliyahu David Ben Yissachar have been denoted by placing an asterisk (*) next to them.

Author's Note

As I sit in my apartment overlooking the Old City of Jerusalem writing this final book in the Walk in the Light series I cannot help but feel the enormity of the task. Many of the books in this series have been written out of numerical order as the inspiration came to me. This book always loomed heavily in the backdrop, and I knew it would be the last to be written. I intentionally avoided any work on it until the time came, and while I have not been an avid student of eschatology I realized why YHWH chose me to write this book. While I certainly have significant experience with prophetic doctrines and teachings, I understood the need to let the patterns of the past provide the path to the future. While placing the final contents into the text on Shemini Atzeret, the Eighth Day, it is my hope and prayer that the reader can gain a better understanding of the meaning and purpose of future events. With that knowledge may you be able to walk the Covenant path and love YHWH with all your heart and all your being and all your strength so that you will overcome in the end.

Appendix A

Tanak Hebrew Names

Torah (Instruction)

English Name	Modern Hebrew	Transliteration
Genesis	בראשית	Beresheet
Exodus	שמות	Shemot
Leviticus	ויקרא	Vayiqra
Numbers	במדבר	Bemidbar
Deuteronomy	דברים	Debarim

Nebi'im (Prophets)

Joshua	יהושע	Yahushua
Judges	שופטים	Shoftim
Samuel	שמואל	Shemu'el
Kings	מלכים	Melakhim
Isaiah	ישעיהו	Yeshayahu
Jeremiah	ירמיהו	Yirmeyahu
Ezekiel	יחזקאל	Yehezqel
Daniel	דניאל	Daniel
Hosea	השוע	Hoshea
Joel	יואל	Yoel
Amos	עמוס	Amos
Obadiah	עבדיה	Obadyah

Jonah	יונה	Yonah
Micah	מיכה	Mikhah
Nahum	נחום	Nachum
Habakkuk	חבקוק	Habaquq
Zephaniah	צפניה	Zephaniyah
Haggai	חגי	Chaggai
Zechariah	זכריה	Zekaryah
Malachi	מלאכי	Malachi

Kethubim (Writings)

Psalms	תהלים	Tehillim
Proverbs	משלי	Mishle
Job	איוב	Iyov
Song of Songs	שיר השירים	Shir ha-Shirim
Ruth	רות	Ruth
Lamentations	איכה	Eikhah
Ecclesiastes	קהלת	Qohelet
Esther	אסתר	Ester
Ezra	עזרא	Ezra
Nehemiah	נחמיה	Nehemyah
Chronicles	דברי הימים	Dibri ha-Yamim

Appendix B

Hebrew Language Study Chart

Gematria	Letter	Ancient	Modern	English	Picture/Meaning
1	Aleph	𐤀	א	A	ox head
2	Bet	𐤁	ב	B, Bh	tent floor plan
3	Gimel	𐤂	ג	G	foot, camel
4	Dalet	𐤃	ד	D	door
5	Hey	𐤄	ה	H	man raised arms
6	Waw	𐤅	ו	W, O, U	tent peg, hook
7	Zayin	𐤆	ז	Z	weapon
8	Het	𐤇	ח	Hh	fence, wall
9	Tet	𐤈	ט	T, Th	basket, container
10	Yud	𐤉	י	Y	closed hand
20	Kaph	𐤊	כ	K, Kh	palm, open hand
30	Lamed	𐤋	ל	L	shepherd staff
40	Mem	𐤌	מ	M	water
50	Nun	𐤍	נ	N	sprout, seed
60	Samech	𐤎	ס	S	prop, support
70	Ayin	𐤏	ע	A	eye
80	Pey	𐤐	פ	P, Ph	open mouth
90	Tsade	𐤑	צ	Ts	hook
100	Quph	𐤒	ק	Q	back of the head
200	Resh	𐤓	ר	R	head of a man
300	Shin	𐤔	שׁ	Sh, S	teeth
400	Taw	𐤕	ת	T	mark, covenant

Note: Gematria in a very simple sense is the study of the various numerical values of the Hebrew letters and words. Since there is no separate numerical system in the Hebrew language, all Hebrew letters have a numerical value so it is a very legitimate and valuable form of study. There are many different forms of Gematria. The Gematria system used in this chart is "mispar hechrachi," also known as Normative value. The Ancient font used is an attempt to blend the ancient variants into a uniform and recognizable font set that accurately depicts the original meaning of each character.

Appendix C

The Walk in the Light Series

Book 1   Restoration – A discussion of the pagan influences that have mixed with the true faith through the ages which has resulted in the need for restoration. This book also examines true Scriptural restoration.

Book 2   Names – Discusses the True Name of the Creator and the Messiah as well as the significance of names in the Scriptures.

Book 3   The Scriptures – Discusses the ways that the Creator has communicated with Creation. It also examines the origin of the written Scriptures as well as the various types of translation errors in Bibles that have led to false doctrines in some mainline religions.

Book 4   Covenants – Discusses the progressive covenants between the Creator and His Creation as described in the Scriptures which reveals His plan for mankind.

Book 5   The Messiah – Discusses the prophetic promises and fulfillments of the Messiah and the True identity of the Redeemer of Yisrael.

Book 6   The Redeemed – Discusses the relationship between Christianity and Judaism and reveals how the Scriptures identify True Believers. It reveals how the Christian doctrine of Replacement Theology has caused confusion as to how the Creator views the Children of Yisrael.

Book 7   The Law and Grace – Discusses in depth the false doctrine that Grace has done away with the Law and demonstrates the vital importance of obeying the commandments.

Book 8   The Sabbath – Discusses the importance of the Seventh Day Sabbath as well as the origins of the tradition concerning Sunday worship.

Book 9	Kosher – Discusses the importance of eating food prescribed by the Scriptures as an aspect of righteous living.
Book 10	Appointed Times – Discusses the appointed times established by the Creator, often erroneously considered to be "Jewish" holidays, and critical to the understanding of prophetic fulfillment of the Scriptural promises.
Book 11	Pagan Holidays – Discusses the pagan origins of some popular Christian holidays which have replaced the Appointed Times.
Book 12	The Final Shofar – Examines the ancient history of the earth and prepares the Believer for the deceptions coming in the end of the age. Also discusses the walk required by the Scriptures to be an overcomer and endure to the end.

The series began as a simple Power point presentation which was intended to develop into a book with twelve different chapters but ended up being twelve different books. Each book is intended to stand alone although the series was originally intended to build from one section to another. Due to the urgency of certain topics, the books have not been published in sequential order.

For anticipated release dates, announcements and additional teachings go to:
www.shemayisrael.net

Appendix D

The Shema
Deuteronomy (Debarim) 6:4-5

Traditional English Translation

Hear, O Israel: The LORD our God, the LORD is one!
You shall love the LORD your God with all your heart, with all
your soul, and with all your strength.

Corrected English Translation

Hear, O Yisrael: YHWH our Elohim, YHWH is one (unified)!
You shall love YHWH your Elohim with all your heart, with all
all your soul, and with all your strength.

Modern Hebrew Text

שמע ישראל יהוה אלהינו יהוה אחד
ואהבת את יהוה אלהיך בכל־ לבבך ובכל־ נפשך ובכל־ מאדך

Ancient Hebrew Text

𐤔𐤌𐤏 𐤉𐤔𐤓𐤀𐤋 𐤉𐤄𐤅𐤄 𐤀𐤋𐤄𐤉𐤍𐤅 𐤉𐤄𐤅𐤄 𐤀𐤇𐤃
𐤅𐤀𐤄𐤁𐤕 𐤀𐤕 𐤉𐤄𐤅𐤄 𐤀𐤋𐤄𐤉𐤊 𐤁𐤊𐤋 𐤋𐤁𐤁𐤊 𐤅𐤁𐤊𐤋
𐤍𐤐𐤔𐤊 𐤅𐤁𐤊𐤋

Hebrew Text Transliterated

Shema, Yisra'el: YHWH Elohenu, YHWH echad!
V-ahavta et YHWH Elohecha b-chol l'bacha u-b-chol naf'sh'cha
u-b-chol m'odecha.

The Shema has traditionally been one of the most important prayers in
Judaism and has been declared the first (resheet) of all the Commandments.
(Mark 12:29-30).

Appendix E

Shema Yisrael

Shema Yisrael was originally established with two primary goals: 1) The production and distribution of sound, Scripturally based educational materials which would assist individuals to see the light of Truth and "Walk in the Light" of that Truth. This first objective was, and is, accomplished through Shema Yisrael Publications; and 2) The free distribution of those materials to the spiritually hungry throughout the world, along with Scriptures, food, clothing and money to the poor, the needy, the sick, the dying and those in prison. This second objective was accomplished through the Shema Yisrael Foundation and through the Foundation people were able to receive a tax deduction for their contributions.

Sadly, through the passage of the Pension Reform Act of 2006, the US Congress severely restricted the operation of donor advised funds which in essence, crippled the Shema Yisrael Foundation by requiring that funds either be channeled through another Foundation or to a 501(c)(3) organization approved by the Internal Revenue Service. Since the Shema Yisrael Foundation was relatively small and operated very "hands on" by placing the funds and materials directly into the hands of the needy in Third World Countries, it was unable to effectively continue operating as a Foundation with the tax advantages associated therewith.

As a result, Shema Yisrael Publications has essentially functioned in a dual capacity to insure that both objectives continue to be promoted, although contributions are no longer tax deductible. To review some of the work being accomplished you can visit www.shemayisrael.net and go to the "Missions" section.

We gladly accept donations, although they will not be tax deductible. To donate, please make checks payable to "Shema Yisrael Publications" and mail to:

Shema Yisrael
123 Court Street • Herkimer, New York 13350

You may also visit our website or call (315) 939-7940 to make a donation or receive more information.